Lecture Notes in Computer Science 16900

The series Lecture Notes in Computer Science (LNCS), including its subseries Lecture Notes in Artificial Intelligence (LNAI) and Lecture Notes in Bioinformatics (LNBI), has established itself as a medium for the publication of new developments in computer science and information technology research, teaching, and education.

LNCS enjoys close cooperation with the computer science R & D community, the series counts many renowned academics among its volume editors and paper authors, and collaborates with prestigious societies. Its mission is to serve this international community by providing an invaluable service, mainly focused on the publication of conference and workshop proceedings and postproceedings. LNCS commenced publication in 1973.

Zeeshan Afzal · Patrick Kochberger · Buse Atli ·
Mikael Asplund
Editors

Availability, Reliability and Security

ARES 2026 International Workshops

ARES 2026 International Workshops
Linköping, Sweden, August 24–27, 2026
Proceedings, Part I

Springer

Editors
Zeeshan Afzal
Linköping University
Linköping, Sweden

Patrick Kochberger
St. Pölten University of Applied Sciences
St. Pölten, Austria

Buse Atli
Linköping University
Linköping, Sweden

Mikael Asplund
Linköping University
Linköping, Sweden

ISSN 0302-9743 ISSN 1611-3349 (electronic)
Lecture Notes in Computer Science
ISBN 978-3-032-35575-1 ISBN 978-3-032-35576-8 (eBook)
https://doi.org/10.1007/978-3-032-35576-8

This Springer imprint is published by the registered company Springer Nature Switzerland AG
The registered company address is: Gewerbestrasse 11, 6330 Cham, Switzerland

ARES Workshops 2026 Foreword

It is our great pleasure to present the proceedings of the ARES 2026 Regular Workshops, held in conjunction with the 21st International Conference on Availability, Reliability and Security (ARES 2026). ARES has, since its inception, provided an international forum for researchers, practitioners, and educators to discuss rigorous and novel research in the areas of availability, reliability, security, privacy, and dependability. The workshops associated with ARES play an essential role in this mission. They offer focused venues for emerging topics, interdisciplinary exchange, and early-stage as well as mature research contributions that address current and future challenges in secure and dependable computing.

For ARES 2026, the workshop track attracted strong interest from the community. The organizers received 25 regular workshop proposals, of which 18 workshops eventually took place. Across these workshops, a total of 232 papers were submitted, of which 101 were accepted for publication and presentation at ARES 2026. Accepted papers underwent double-blind peer review by the respective workshop technical program committee members.

We are deeply grateful to the workshop organizers and program committee members for their substantial efforts in shaping the workshop program, managing the review process, and ensuring the scientific quality of the accepted contributions. Their commitment and expertise were essential to the success of the workshops. We also thank the ARES 2026 general chair, program chairs, proceedings chair, and publicity chair for their continuous support and guidance throughout the organization of the workshop track.

We hope that these proceedings will serve as a valuable resource for researchers, practitioners, and students working in the fields of cybersecurity, privacy, dependability, and resilience. We also hope that the ideas presented here will stimulate further collaboration and inspire future research within and beyond the ARES community.

August 2026

Zeeshan Afzal
Patrick Kochberger

ARES Workshops 2026 Organization

General Chair

Mikael Asplund	Linköping University, Sweden

General Workshop Chairs

Zeeshan Afzal	Linköping University, Sweden
Patrick Kochberger	St. Pölten University of Applied Sciences, Austria

Proceedings Chair

Buse Atli	Linköping University, Sweden

Workshop Chairs

Habtamu Abie	Norwegian Computing Center, Norway
Mansoor Ahmed	Maynooth University, Ireland
Philipp Amann	Europol EC3, Netherlands
Alexandra Anderluh	St. Pölten University of Applied Sciences, Austria
Anirban Basu	University of Sussex, UK
Meriem Benyahya	University Mohammed VI Polytechnic, Morocco
Francesco Blefari	University of Calabria, Italy
Svetlana Boudko	Norwegian Computing Center, Norway
Frank Breitinger	University of Augsburg, Germany
Rasa Brūzgienė	Kaunas University of Technology, Lithuania
Daniele Canavese	CNR-IMATI, Italy
Luca Caviglione	CNR-IMATI, Italy
Sabarathinam Chockalingam	Institute for Energy Technology, Norway
Marta Irene García Cid	Indra, Spain
Anastasija Collen	University of Applied Sciences and Arts of Western Switzerland, Switzerland
Angelo Consoli	University of Applied Sciences and Arts of Southern Switzerland, Switzerland
Mauro Conti	University of Padua, Italy

Kapal Dev	Munster Technological University, Ireland
Praveen Kumar Donta	Stockholm University, Sweden
Michael Eckel	Fraunhofer SIT/ATHENE, Germany
Hossein Fotouhi	Mälardalen University, Sweden
Virginia N. L. Franqueira	University of Kent, UK
Angelo Furfaro	University of Calabria, Italy
Karolina Gabor-Siatkowska	Warsaw University of Technology, Poland
Georgios Gkoktsis	Fraunhofer SIT/ATHENE, Germany
Magdalena Glas	University of Regensburg, Germany
Šarūnas Grigaliūnas	Kaunas University of Technology, Lithuania
Nils Gruschka	University of Oslo, Norway
Maria Hagl	German Aerospace Center (DLR), Germany
Patrizia Heinl	Technische Hochschule Ingolstadt, Germany
Markus Helfert	Maynooth University, Ireland
Halvor Holtskog	Norwegian University of Science and Technology, Norway
Martin Husák	Masaryk University, Czech Republic
Artur Janicki	Warsaw University of Technology, Poland
Katarzyna Kamińska	Warsaw University of Technology, Poland
Mohamed Ali Kandi	University of Toulouse, France
Sokratis Katsikas	Norwegian University of Science and Technology, Norway
Jörg Keller	FernUniversität in Hagen, Germany
Muhammad Irfan Khalid	University of Agder, Norway
Kainat Khan	IIIT Dharwad, India
Sunder Ali Khowaja	Dublin City University, Ireland
Peter Kieseberg	University of Applied Sciences St. Pölten, Austria
Kaur Kullman	German Aerospace Center (DLR), Germany
Andrew Marrington	Zayed University, United Arab Emirates
Raimundas Matulevičius	University of Tartu, Estonia
Wojciech Mazurczyk	Warsaw University of Technology, Poland
Mohamed-Lamine Messai	Université Lyon 2, France
Aleksandra Mileva	Goce Delčev University, North Macedonia
Hemanadhan Myneni	University of Iceland, Iceland
Xavier Larriva Novo	Universidad Politécnica de Madrid, Spain
Salvador Llopis Sanchez	Polytechnic University of Valencia, Spain
Timea Pahi	University of Applied Sciences St. Pölten, Austria
Andrius Patapovas	Technische Hochschule Nürnberg, Germany
Michael Pilgermann	Technische Hochschule Brandenburg, Germany
Sandeep Pirbhulal	Norwegian Computing Center, Norway
Daniela Pöhn	Universität der Bundeswehr München, Germany
Leonardo Regano	University of Cagliari, Italy

Rimjhim	NIT Warangal, India
Tiago Roxo	University of Beira Interior, Portugal
Dinesh Kumar Sah	University of Oulu, Finland
Hamida Seba	University Claude Bernard Lyon 1, France
João B. F. Sequeiros	Universidade da Beira Interior, Portugal
Sebastian Schrittwieser	University of Applied Sciences St. Pölten, Austria
Amir Sharif	Fondazione Bruno Kessler, Italy
Marco Antonio Sotelo Monge	Indra, Spain
Georgios Spathoulas	Norwegian University of Science and Technology, Norway
Martin Steinebach	Fraunhofer SIT, Germany
Jorge Maestre Vidal	Indra, Spain
Abdul Wahid	IIIT Dharwad, India
Bian Yang	Norwegian University of Science and Technology, Norway

Contents

Proceedings of the Fifth Workshop on Cybersecurity in Industry 4.0 and Beyond (SecIndustry 2026)

Proceedings of the First Workshop on Security, Availability, and Fault-Tolerance in Edge AI Systems (SAFE-EDGE 2026)

Proceedings of the First Workshop on Sustainable Security and Awareness for Next Generation Infrastructures (SAFER 2026)

Proceedings of the First Workshop on Security, Privacy, and Identity Management for the Digital Transformation (SPIMDT 2026)

Proceedings of the Second International Workshop on Artificial Intelligence, Cyber and Cyber-Physical Security (AI&CCPS 2026)

AI&CCPS 2026 Preface

Artificial Intelligence (AI) and Cyber Security are two of the most prominent topics nowadays due to rapid advancements in AI, particularly in Large Language Models (LLMs), and the growing number of cyberattacks and their impact. Additionally, emerging directives, regulations, and legislative acts, such as the European NIS2, are driving these topics beyond academia into industry and society. While cyber security has been a prolific field for the application of AI techniques, it is evident that AI is increasingly becoming a prime target of malicious activities and also being misused as an attacking agent or facilitator. The International Workshop on Artificial Intelligence, Cyber and Cyber-Physical Security aims to explore both the expanding role of AI in addressing security challenges in digital and physical systems, and the need to address the robustness and resilience of AI techniques. This workshop, in its second edition, aimed to bring together researchers and practitioners from both communities – cyber security and artificial intelligence – to discuss problems and solutions at the intersection of these fields. AI&CCPS 2026 was the second edition of the workshop and gathered a healthy number of 13 submissions, of which six were accepted for presentation at the workshop and included in the proceedings, leading to an acceptance rate of 46.2%. The technical program committee included 15 researchers from seven different nationalities and the review process benefited from the assistance of five additional experts who acted as subreviewers. In line with the main conference guidelines, the peer-review process was double-blinded, with every paper undergoing three reviews, and, when required, a short discussion was held prior to taking the final decision.

August 2026

Aleksandra Mileva
João B. F. Sequeiros
Mauro Conti
Tiago Roxo
Virginia N. L. Franqueira

AI&CCPS 2026 Organization

Workshop Chairs

Aleksandra Mileva	Goce Delčev University, North Macedonia
João B. F. Sequeiros	Universidade da Beira Interior, Portugal
Mauro Conti	University of Padua, Italy
Tiago Roxo	Universidade da Beira Interior, Portugal
Virginia N. L. Franqueira	University of Kent, UK

Program Committee

Alberto Giaretta	Örebro University, Sweden
Aleksandar Petrović	Singidunum University, Serbia
Denis Donadel	University of Verona, Italy
Diego Pérez	Linnaeus University, Sweden
Jana Dittmann	University of Magdeburg, Germany
João Almeida	Universidade de Aveiro, Portugal
João Neves	Universidade da Beira Interior, Portugal
João P. Barraca	Universidade de Aveiro, Portugal
José Inacio Requeno	Universidad Complutense de Madrid, Spain
Pedro R. M. Inácio	Universidade da Beira Interior, Portugal
Simona Bernardi	University of Zaragoza, Spain
Stefano Marrone	Università della Campania "Luigi Vanvitelli", Italy
Tiago Cruz	University of Coimbra, Portugal
Tiago Simões	Universidade da Beira Interior, Portugal
Tomasz Szydlo	Newcastle University, UK

Additional Reviewers

Catarina Silva
Cristiano Patrício
Joana C. Costa
Mário Antunes
Rui Pinto

Automatically Benchmarking Biases in ML-Based WAFs

Hamza Sajjad(✉) and Gabriele Costa

IMT School for Advanced Studies, Lucca, Italy
{hamza.sajjadahmed,gabriele.costa}@imtlucca.it

Abstract. Web Application Firewalls (WAFs) are the first line of defense, inspecting incoming HTTP requests to detect *malicious* payloads. Distinguishing between malicious and benign payloads is complex, and universal criteria do not exist. In recent decades, Machine Learning (ML) has emerged as an alternative to rule-based WAFs, using trained models instead of manually crafted rules. However, the reliability of ML-WAFs is questionable, mainly due to recurrent biases and the lack of a standardized assessment framework. This paper introduces a benchmarking framework to systematically identify and measure biases in ML-WAFs, evaluating dataset diversity, training validity, and evaluation robustness. We conduct an in-depth case study on WafBrain and further validate the proposed framework by applying it to the Barracuda WAF, a widely deployed commercial product. Such biases determine inflated performances in controlled environments, but they make WAFs fragile in adversarial settings.

Keywords: Web Application Firewall · Web Security · Machine Learning

1 Introduction

In today's digital era, the rise of web applications is driven by widespread Internet access and diverse online services [5]. However, these applications are often exposed to various logical and technical vulnerabilities [1], require robust security measures to protect sensitive data and ensure reliable operation [15]. The diversity of programming languages, platforms, and scripting environments complicates efforts to defend against evolving threats [28]. Web Application Firewalls (WAF) have become integral to modern network infrastructures, protecting web applications exposed to the Internet [23]. In addition to blocking known attacks, WAFs play a critical role in maintaining the availability and integrity of web services by filtering malicious traffic before it reaches backend applications. A WAP typically inspects incoming HTTP requests and analyzes their *payloads*, which consist of the data or URL parameters transmitted by clients. Malicious requests are dropped to prevent attacks from reaching their targets [22,24]. Accurate differentiation between benign and malicious payloads is crucial for the effectiveness of a WAF. Traditionally, rule-based WAFs (RB-WAFs) rely on predefined patterns such as regular expressions to flag and block malicious payloads [4].

Z. Afzal et al. (Eds.): ARES 2026 Workshops, LNCS 16900, pp. 5–21, 2027.
https://doi.org/10.1007/978-3-032-35576-8_1

Modern RB-WAFs employ thousands of continuously updated rules maintained by experts [2]. The main limitation of RB-WAFs is their inability to quickly adapt to new or slightly modified attacks, requiring extensive manual rule updates [20]. Even minor changes, such as altering a single character, can evade detection. This sensitivity to obfuscation techniques highlights the inherent challenge of maintaining comprehensive rule sets against rapidly evolving attack strategies. To address this limitation, ML approaches have emerged as an alternative, enabling systems to generalize beyond predefined patterns and detect previously unseen attack payloads. Montes et al. [18] demonstrated the applicability of deep learning for web application attack detection, while Tadhani et al. [31] proposed a deep learning framework for detecting XSS and SQL injection attacks. Shaheed et al. [27] incorporated machine learning and feature engineering into a web application firewall to improve attack detection performance. In a broader cybersecurity context, Mohamed [17] reviewed recent advances in AI- and ML-based threat detection techniques. However, evaluating ML-WAFs remains difficult due to inconsistent training and testing setups. Furthermore, publicly available datasets often differ significantly in terms of attack types, traffic characteristics, and labelling procedures. Variations in data preprocessing, feature extraction, and train-test splitting strategies further complicate fair comparisons between proposed approaches [13]. As a result, reported performance metrics may not accurately reflect a model's effectiveness in real-world deployment scenarios. Moreover, studies such as [3] identify several recurring biases that affect ML-based security systems, which we show in Table 1.

In this paper, we present a standardized testing methodology and a benchmarking framework to evaluate ML-WAFs under adversarial scenarios. The design and implementation of our framework start with a systematic review of the biases reported in the literature. We establish testing conditions for the biases summarized in Table 1, enabling a systematic assessment of ML-WAFs. For each bias, we propose a specific testing methodology. By combining built-in tests with support for pluggable modules, our methodology enables an extensible framework that can be expanded or modified to allow broader and deeper testing. Upon completion, the framework generates a report assessing the effectiveness of the target ML-WAF and exposing its potential biases. We demonstrate our framework through a case study on *WafBrain*[1], an open-source ML-WAF. Furthermore, we show its applicability by testing *Barracuda WAF*[2], a commercial WAF also relying on ML. Remarkably, even if we could access neither the training dataset nor the internals of Barracuda, our framework identified several undetected payloads, revealing a potential bias. Both the payloads and the report were shared with Barracuda through a responsible disclosure process. This work does not propose a new ML-WAF or novel detection techniques. Instead, it introduces a systematic, bias-aware benchmarking framework for evaluating existing ML-WAFs, aiming to help researchers and practitioners assess their reliability

[1] https://github.com/BBVA/waf-brain/tree/master.
[2] https://www.barracuda.com/.

Table 1. Common Biases in Machine Learning Model Evaluation [3]

Biases	Summary
Dataset Preparation	
Cherry Pick	Selecting non-representative data that does not reflect real-world distributions leads to overly optimistic and misleading evaluation results.
False Flag	Incorrect or noisy labels introduce systematic errors that cause models to overfit and reduce their ability to generalize.
Training	
Data Dilemma	The presence of data leakage or irrelevant features during training allows the model to learn unintended patterns, reducing its reliability in unseen scenarios.
Pattern Pitfall	Models may capture spurious correlations instead of meaningful relationships, which degrades performance when deployed in real-world environments.
Preset Prejudice	Optimizing model parameters using test data biases the evaluation process and results in inflated and unreliable performance estimates.
Validation	
Foundation Fumble	The absence of proper baseline models prevents fair comparison and makes it difficult to assess the true effectiveness of a proposed approach.
Metric Muddle	Using inappropriate evaluation metrics, especially with imbalanced datasets, can distort performance interpretation and hide critical weaknesses.
Rate Roulette	Ignoring class imbalance leads to misleading performance metrics, often overestimating the model's effectiveness on underrepresented classes.
Deployment	
Lab Trap	Evaluating models only in controlled environments fails to capture real-world variability, leading to unexpected performance drop after deployment.
Risk Radar	Overlooking adversarial or evolving threats results in models that are not robust, reducing their trustworthiness in practical applications.

and real-world limitations rather than optimize individual models. Summing up, our framework answers three fundamental questions for system administrators:

1. Is my ML-WAF more effective than traditional RB-WAFs?
2. How reliable is my ML-WAFs under real-world adversarial conditions?
3. Do I have additional benefits from integrating RB and ML WAFs in my network?

This Paper is Organized as Follows. Section 2 reviews the related literature, while Sect. 3 describes the design of our assessment framework. Section 4 presents the experimental setup and results for WafBrain, addresses the research questions, and discusses the limitations. Section 5 demonstrates the applicability of the proposed framework to a commercial ML-WAF under black-box access constraints. Finally, Sect. 6 concludes the paper.

2 Related Work

Identifying biases in ML is crucial, as they can significantly influence algorithmic outcomes and lead to misleading conclusions. Researchers have developed methods tailored to specific bias types and datasets to mitigate these effects. Mehrabi et al. [14] provide a comprehensive categorization of biases in ML pipelines and survey fairness-aware approaches applied across diverse domains such as healthcare, criminal justice, and finance, highlighting the broad relevance of bias-aware practices.

In the context of security applications, Daniel et al. [3] review the most common biases in ML-based security systems, demonstrating how these biases can distort performance measurements and produce unrealistic results. Skewed or mislabeled data are frequent sources of bias that can undermine model reliability. Mishra et al. [16] show that sampling methods such as SMOTE and Resampling help reduce data skew, improving classification accuracy. Similarly, Fredriksson et al. [11] explore challenges in data labeling and propose practical mitigation strategies, while Northcutt et al. [21] reveal that label errors are widespread and can cause lower-capacity models to outperform higher-capacity ones when datasets are noisy.

Class imbalance is another critical factor affecting model performance. Balla et al. [6] introduce novel sampling methods to alleviate imbalance, and Sen et al. [26] emphasize the importance of robust evaluation methodologies for real-world imbalanced datasets. Ceschin et al. [8] stress that model evaluation should focus on real-world impacts rather than solely on metrics, advocating for checklists to prevent common modeling mistakes. White [33] warns against data snooping, which can produce spurious results and overstate model effectiveness. Spurious correlations, arising from learning unreliable or non-generalizable features, present another challenge in ML systems [30]. Hays et al. [12] highlight the importance of transparency in data collection and labeling processes, cautioning against shortcuts that artificially inflate reported performance. Toyama et al. [32] examine how model misspecification and unreliable parameter estimates can impact reinforcement learning outcomes, further illustrating the consequences of overlooked biases.

In web security, biases in datasets are often underestimated, despite their potential to compromise ML-based tools. Doupé et al. [10] propose strategies to identify and mitigate these biases, improving detection accuracy and robustness. Technical vulnerabilities such as SQL injection (SQLi), cross-site scripting (XSS), remote file inclusion (RFI), and local file inclusion (LFI), often caused by poor coding practices or outdated components, remain significant threats to web application integrity, emphasizing the importance of reliable, bias-aware ML systems in practical security contexts. To the best of our knowledge, existing studies focus on new WAF models under controlled conditions, but no prior work provides a reproducible, bias-aware benchmarking framework for ML-WAFs.

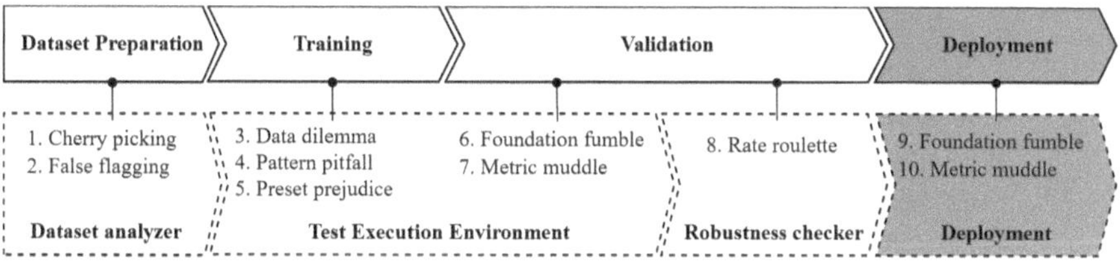

Fig. 1. Relationship between the ML lifecycle (upper layer), the bias categories considered in this study, and the corresponding assessment components of the proposed framework (lower layer), illustrating how bias categories are mapped to framework components.

3 Assessment Framework

Our ML-WAF assessment framework adopts a three-stage approach, illustrated in Fig. 1, to systematically evaluate ML-WAFs while addressing key dataset, system, and evaluation biases.

The first stage focuses on the adequacy of training and testing datasets. We quantify dataset diversity using Shannon entropy, originally proposed as a measure of information uncertainty [29]. Namdari and Li [19] provide a comprehensive review of entropy measures for uncertainty quantification, while Bereziński et al. [7] demonstrate the usefulness of entropy-based metrics for network traffic characterization and anomaly detection. Saraiva [25] further discusses the broad applicability of Shannon entropy across data analysis domains. To complement this assessment, we perform ground-truth validation using rule-based systems such as Snort[3] and OWASP ModSecurity[4]. This dual approach ensures that the data are both representative and accurately labeled, reducing the risk of bias-induced overfitting or misestimation of model performance.

The second stage executes dynamic runtime testing in a standardized Test Execution Environment (TEE) built with Docker[5]. The TEE delivers realistic network traffic to the target WAF and integrates mutational fuzzing [9] to generate diverse, semantically valid variations of requests that probe hidden training or system biases. Both ML and RB WAFs process the same inputs, and adaptive feedback from the ML-WAF guides the fuzzing to craft increasingly evasive payloads. This stage enables robust evaluation of the WAFs' resilience under adversarial scenarios and mitigates biases related to limited or overly controlled evaluation setups.

In the third stage, we compute multiple standardized evaluation metrics such as precision-recall curves, ROC curves, and Matthews Correlation Coefficient (MCC) values to address class imbalance and other statistical biases. Aggregating results from all stages, the framework generates a comprehensive performance report highlighting detection effectiveness, generalization, and fairness.

[3] https://www.snort.org/.

[4] https://owasp.org/www-project-modsecurity-core-rule-set/.

[5] https://www.docker.com/.

Each stage of the framework is explicitly designed to expose and measure specific bias categories summarized in Table 1.

Biases associated with deployment-specific conditions or fundamental ML security limitations remain outside the scope of this study. While both are important, our work focuses on controlled, reproducible assessment and abstracts from the operational and deployment-specific aspects unique to each installation. Nevertheless, the framework lays the foundation for evaluating these biases in future studies.

4 Experimental Evaluation

We implemented and evaluated our three-stage assessment framework using Docker containers on a Windows 11 Lenovo ThinkPad with an Intel® Core™ i7-1165G7 (2.80 GHz). The setup integrates all components required for data, runtime, and performance assessments, ensuring reproducibility and comparability. The complete implementation, configuration files, and experimental results are publicly available at https://github.com/imhamzasajjad/TEE-WAFs-Framework.

4.1 Data Assessment

Entropy Analysis and Statistical Testing We used the HTTP Params dataset[6] , a parameter-focused version of the CSIC 2010 dataset[7] that preserves original labels while exposing HTTP fields commonly used in ML-WAF research.

To quantify byte-level variability, Shannon entropy was computed over 64-byte chunks for each request, balancing sensitivity to subtle anomalies with statistical contrast. Average entropy was 5.576 bits/byte for normal and 5.629 bits/byte for anomalous traffic (Fig. 2), with anomalous requests showing slightly higher standard deviation (0.2981 vs. 0.2713 bits/byte, Fig. 3). Statistical tests confirmed significant differences (t-test $p=0.000017$; Mann–Whitney U $p=0.0065$), though the small mean difference indicates limited overall dataset heterogeneity.

These results suggest that, at the byte level, anomalous payloads are only marginally more variable than normal traffic, potentially limiting ML-WAF generalization. Combined with missing HTTP methods, this constrained diversity represents a source of bias. To further assess labeling quality, all requests were processed through an RB-WAF (Snort/ModSecurity), allowing quantification of discrepancies between dataset labels and rule-based detection outcomes.

Labeling Validation Using Rule-Based WAF. As a second step in the data assessment, we validated the labels of the web application requests dataset. All HTTP requests were processed through an RB-WAF (Snort/ModSecurity), which applies expert-defined rules to detect malicious requests. We then compared the RB-WAF outcomes with the dataset's original labels and computed

[6] https://www.kaggle.com/datasets/evg3n1j/httpparamsdataset.

[7] https://www.kaggle.com/datasets/ispangler/csic-2010-web-application-attacks.

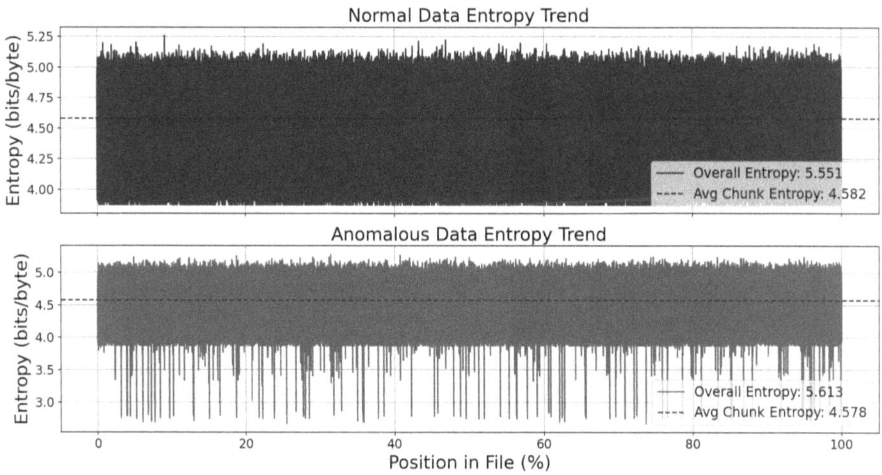

Fig. 2. Comparison of chunk-wise entropy for normal vs. anomalous HTTP requests, showing limited diversity in anomalous payloads.

the ratio of requests where the labels disagreed with the RB-WAF predictions. A higher discrepancy ratio indicates potential labeling errors or inconsistencies, which could introduce bias during ML-WAF training and evaluation, while a low ratio suggests the labels are largely consistent with established detection rules.

4.2 Runtime Assessment

The runtime assessment stage evaluates the robustness of ML-WAFs under realistic and adversarial traffic conditions. We first analyzed the dataset for protocol coverage using finite state automata (FSAs), focusing on the HTTP `method` field (Fig. 4). The FSA allowed us to verify which methods were present in the dataset and identify any missing but valid HTTP methods. For the CSIC 2010 dataset, only three methods appeared: GET (43,088 occurrences), POST (17,580 occurrences), and PUT (397 occurrences), while others, such as DELETE, HEAD, OPTIONS, PATCH, TRACE, and CONNECT, were entirely absent. This under-representation highlights a potential dataset bias, as real-world web traffic involves a wider variety of methods, and missing patterns could affect the generalization of ML models.

To test WAF performance under adversarial conditions, we employed mutational fuzzing using WAF-A-MOLE [9] to generate diverse, semantically valid variations of HTTP requests. Starting from an original payload selected from the dataset, the fuzzer applies incremental mutations to produce a sequence of payloads that increasingly deviate from the original input, challenging the WAFs' detection capabilities and enabling evaluation of robustness against evasion techniques. In this stage, WafBrain is used as the target ML-based WAF under evaluation. Experiments were conducted in a Docker-based Test Execu-

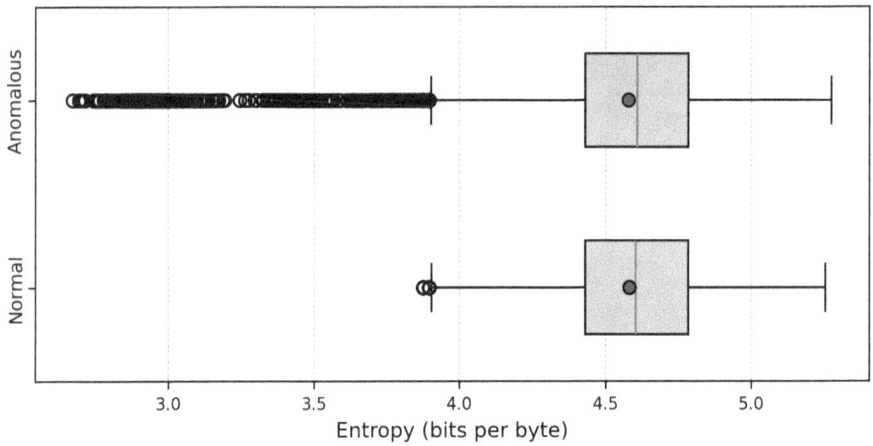

Fig. 3. Boxplot of chunk-wise entropy for normal and anomalous traffic, showing higher variability in anomalous requests.

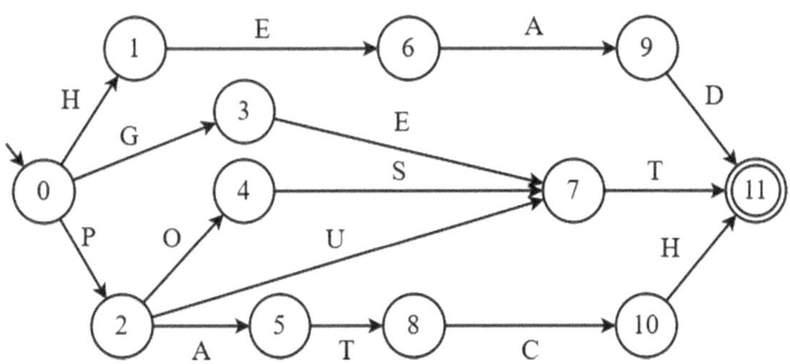

Fig. 4. FSA representing HTTP method usage in the CSIC 2010 dataset. Nodes correspond to HTTP methods, and edges represent observed transitions between request states.

tion Environment (TEE) to ensure reproducibility, isolation, and portability. The TEE consisted of four containers (Fig. 5):

1. **Client:** Selects an initial payload P_0 from the dataset and generates mutated variants $P_1, \ldots, P_n$ through successive fuzzing rounds, sending each payload to the server and logging all interactions.
2. **Server:** Receives requests and forwards them to both WAFs, recording their predictions and outcomes.
3. **ML-WAF:** Processes each payload using a trained machine learning model to detect malicious requests.
4. **RB-WAF:** Applies expert-defined rules (ModSecurity) for detection, serving as a baseline for comparison.

For each payload P_i, the corresponding responses r_i from the RB-WAF and r_i' from the ML-WAF are collected and logged. By comparing these response sequences across increasing fuzzing depths, we evaluate detection effectiveness, resilience to evasion, and the influence of dataset-related biases. This systematic logging enables detailed analysis of true positives, false positives, and false negatives across different payload types and fuzzing rounds.

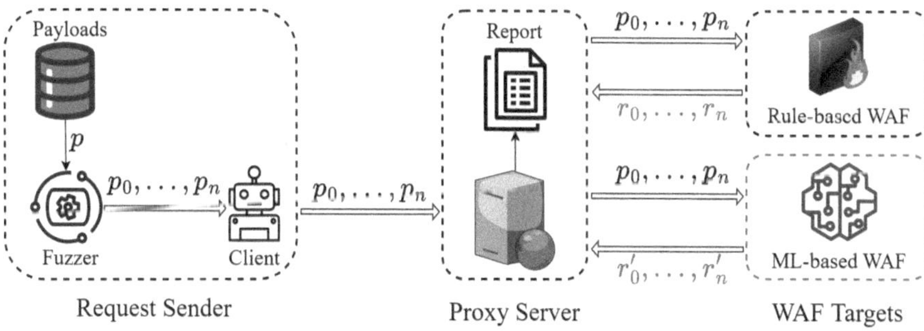

Fig. 5. Docker-based Test Execution Environment for runtime WAF evaluation, consisting of Client, Server, ML-WAF, and RB-WAF containers, enabling isolated and reproducible testing.

4.3 Performance Assessment

We evaluated both RB- and ML-WAFs using multiple metrics: accuracy, precision, recall, F1 score, MCC, and specificity. Experiments used 50 payloads per run, with fuzzing iterations varying between 5 and 30 rounds. Each configuration was repeated 10 times, and the average values were computed to ensure reliable comparisons.

- **RB-WAF:** The rule-based WAF consistently outperformed the ML-WAF across all rounds. Accuracy ranged from 0.842 to 0.865, with precision between 0.866 and 0.910, recall from 0.853 to 0.897, and F1 scores between 0.859 and 0.883. MCC values (0.680–0.728) and specificity (0.821–0.874) confirmed its ability to effectively distinguish malicious from benign traffic.
- **ML-WAF:** In contrast, the ML-WAF showed higher variability. Accuracy dropped from 0.756 in earlier rounds to 0.557 in later rounds, with precision between 0.639 and 0.874, recall from 0.512 to 0.684, and F1 scores from 0.568 to 0.756. MCC values (0.128–0.535) and specificity (0.617–0.862) also fluctuated, indicating challenges in adapting to more complex or mutated traffic patterns.

Figures 6 and 7 compare detection behavior and performance metrics, highlighting RB-WAF's stability and consistent superiority over the more variable

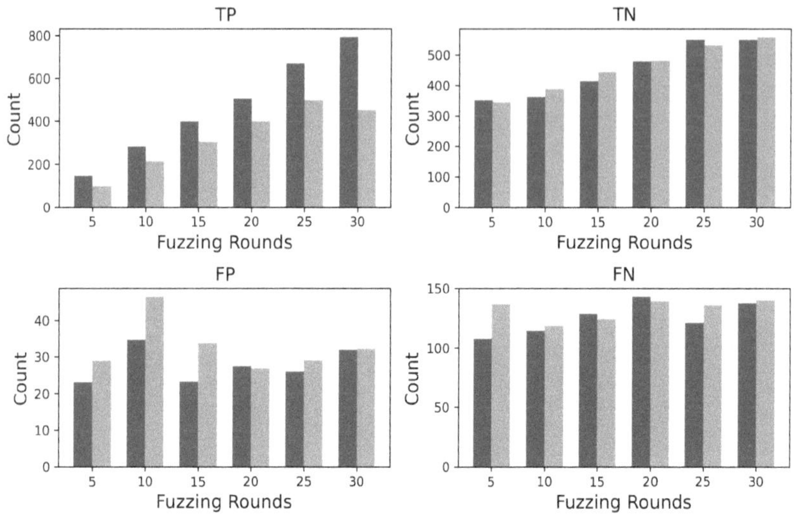

Fig. 6. Comparison of TP, TN, FP, and FN for RB-WAF (blue) and ML-WAF (orange) under identical evaluation conditions. (Color figure online)

ML-WAF under fuzzed traffic. These results show how dataset limitations and model biases affect ML-WAF performance, underscoring the need for standardized and reproducible evaluation. Combining RB and ML detection yielded only marginal gains (Fig. 8). The RB Correct–ML Incorrect cases increased from 22.47% to 36.17%, confirming RB-WAF robustness, while fewer ML Correct–RB Incorrect cases indicate limited detection of novel attacks.

4.4 Potential Biases

Applying the proposed framework to the dataset and WAFBrain, we identified several potential biases, summarized in Fig. 9. Following our classification criteria, each bias was labeled as present, partially present, or not present. Below, we briefly describe the rationale behind each classification.

B1. **Cherry Picking:** The data diversity analysis in Sect. 4.1 indicates partial presence of this bias. Although anomalous traffic shows higher variability (standard deviation 0.2981 vs. 0.2713 bits/byte, a ∼9.88% increase), overall entropy values remain close (5.629 vs. 5.576 bits/byte, a ∼0.95% difference). This suggests limited diversity in anomalous samples, which may not fully capture real-world attack variability and could reduce generalization to unseen attacks.

B2. **False Flagging:** This bias is classified as present. Using ModSecurity with OWASP CRS as a proxy ground truth (Sect. 4.1), we observed a consistently high discrepancy where the RB-WAF was correct while the ML-WAF was incorrect, ranging from 16.22% to 36.17% across fuzzing rounds (Fig. 8). This

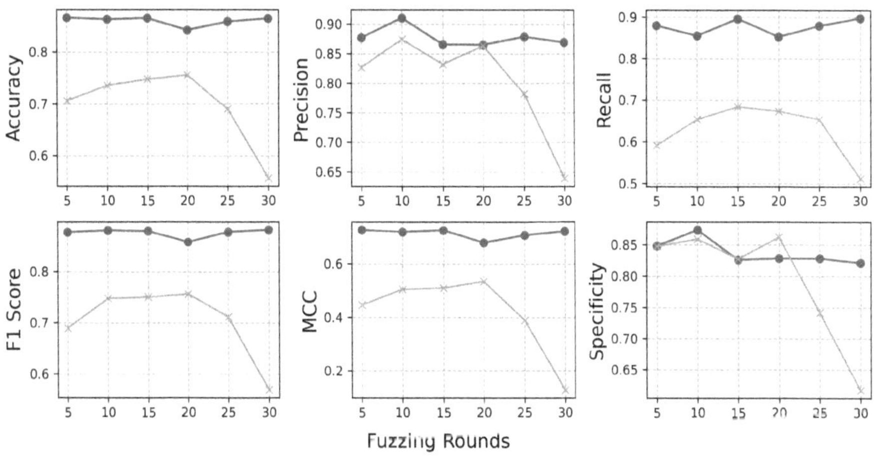

Fig. 7. Performance comparison of RB-WAF (blue) and ML-WAF (orange) under fuzzing-based adversarial testing. The figure contains six subplots showing different evaluation metrics plotted against fuzzing rounds. (Color figure online)

persistent gap indicates unreliable ML predictions, likely influenced by unstable or imperfect labeling, as discussed in Sect. 4.3.

B3. **Data Dilemma:** Regular expression and FSA-based analysis revealed limited protocol coverage (Fig. 4). Only GET (43,088), POST (17,580), and PUT (397) methods were present, with PUT appearing exclusively in anomalous traffic. All other standard HTTP methods (e.g., DELETE, HEAD, OPTIONS, PATCH) were absent. Such underrepresentation suggests dataset incompleteness and possible data snooping, reducing realism and robustness.

B4. **Pattern Pitfall:** Evaluated using mutational fuzzing within the TEE, results show that the ML-WAF occasionally relies on spurious correlations learned during training. This behavior indicates partial presence of Bias 4 and highlights challenges in generalizing to diverse real-world inputs (Sect. 4.2).

B5. **Preset Prejudice:** Using the TEE with fuzzing, we tested whether model parameters were overly influenced by prior data. While diverse inputs mitigated complete overfitting, residual false negatives and occasional false positives indicate partial presence of this bias, suggesting incomplete adaptation to novel payloads (Fig. 6).

B6. **Foundation Fumble:** This bias was identified in the original ML-WAF development due to the lack of standardized baseline comparisons. By benchmarking against an RB-WAF in a controlled Docker-based environment, our evaluation avoids this issue; however, the ML-WAF's consistent underperformance across F1 and MCC scores (Sect. 4.2) highlights the consequences of insufficient baseline grounding during development.

B7. **Metric Muddle:** Bias 7 was exposed through TEE-based fuzzing, which revealed weaknesses masked by reliance on accuracy alone. High false negatives and unstable F1 and MCC values under increasing fuzzing rounds indi-

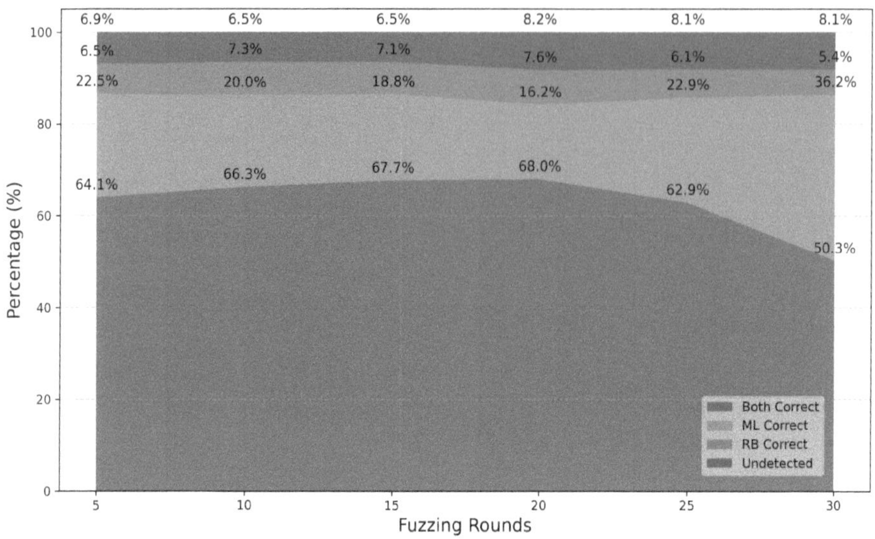

Fig. 8. Combined performance across fuzzing rounds. Blue: RB-WAF correct, green: both correct, orange: ML-WAF correct, red: both incorrect. (Color figure online)

cate that simplistic metrics overestimated real-world effectiveness, confirming the presence of this bias (Sect. 4.2).

B8. **Rate Roulette:** Class imbalance (e.g., 28,000 normal vs. 15,088 anomalous GET requests) contributed to this bias. While RB-WAF performance remained stable, the ML-WAF showed declining accuracy (0.7555 to 0.5570), fluctuating recall (0.5117–0.6837), and unstable MCC (0.1280–0.5347). High but unstable precision combined with low recall indicates difficulty detecting minority classes, confirming the presence of Bias 8 (Sect. 4.3).

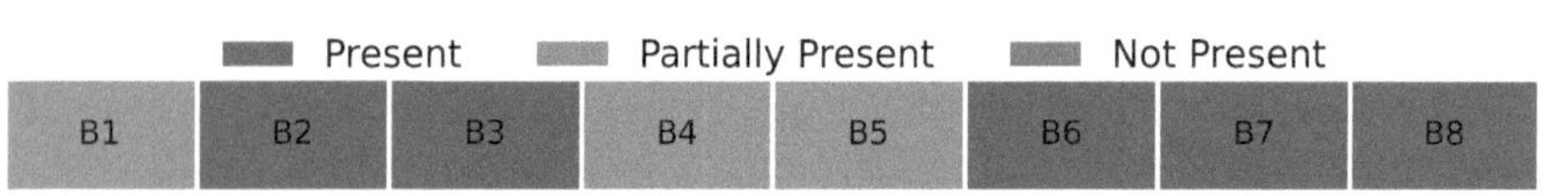

Fig. 9. Distribution of detected bias in WAFBrain during evaluation under adversarial traffic conditions.

4.5 Addressing the Questions

Our framework quantifies biases through threshold-based metrics, enabling systematic evaluation of detection accuracy, robustness, and consistency across experiments. These metrics form the basis for addressing the following research questions.

Q1: Is my ML-WAF more effective than traditional RB-WAFs? Overall, RB-WAF outperforms ML-WAF across all metrics (Fig. 7), showing higher and more stable accuracy against fuzzing. However, as seen in Fig. 8, the ML-WAF occasionally detects payloads that are missed by the RB-WAF, indicating potentially complementary behavior.

Q2: How reliable is my ML-WAF under real-world adversarial conditions? ML-WAF performance drops sharply with fuzzed or adversarial payloads (Fig. 7), highlighting poor robustness. In contrast, RB-WAF degrades more slowly, confirming greater reliability under adversarial stress.

Q3: Do I have additional benefits from integrating RB and ML WAFs in my network? Integration yields only marginal improvement (5–8% gain; Fig. 8) while inheriting ML-WAF's instability and false positives. For the time being, the hybrid option offers limited benefit without significant noise reduction or robustness improvements.

5 Applicability to Commercial ML-WAFs

To demonstrate the applicability of the proposed framework under realistic deployment constraints, we evaluated a commercial ML-based WAF, *Barracuda WAF*[8], using the same Test Execution TEE and adversarial testing methodology employed throughout this study. As Barracuda WAF is a proprietary system, we had no access to its training data, internal models, or feature representations. The evaluation therefore, relied exclusively on black-box testing through controlled traffic injection and observation of runtime behavior. HTTP requests derived from the HTTP Params dataset were used solely as input traffic for fuzzing and adversarial runtime assessment. Consequently, data assessment tests were not applicable, while runtime robustness and adversarial evaluation remained fully supported by the framework.

We evaluated the ML-WAF using both benign and malicious payloads under adversarial conditions, varying fuzzing rounds from 5 to 30. Across all experiments, the ML-WAF processed a total of 7,050 requests. Overall, 20.16% of requests were misclassified. The majority of these errors were false positives (18.10%), which primarily impact availability by incorrectly blocking benign traffic. More critically, 2.06% of all requests were false negatives, corresponding to malicious payloads that bypassed detection. Although fewer in number, these false negatives pose a significant security risk because they allow attack traffic to reach the protected application.

As shown in Fig. 10, the first three biases (B1–B3), which relate to dataset construction and labeling, cannot be assessed for Barracuda WAF due to the lack of access to its training data and are therefore marked as not evaluated. Bias 4 (Pattern Pitfall) is partially present, as mutational fuzzing revealed that certain payload transformations could bypass detection, indicating reliance on fragile or spurious patterns. Bias 5 (Preset Prejudice) is also partially present, as repeated

[8] https://www.barracuda.com/products/application-protection/web-application-firewall.

fuzzing exposed residual false negatives, suggesting limited adaptation to novel inputs under black-box constraints. Bias 6 (Foundation Fumble) is present and observable through comparison with the RB-WAF baseline: although the ML-WAF produced fewer false negatives (145 vs. 743), this improvement came at the cost of substantially higher false positives (1,276 vs. 342), demonstrating how the absence of baseline-grounded evaluation could lead to an inflated perception of effectiveness. Bias 7 (Metric Muddle) is present, as accuracy-oriented assessment would obscure the security impact of false negatives, which reached up to 6.97% under attack-only conditions. Finally, Bias 8 (Rate Roulette) is present, as class imbalance and adversarial traffic caused unstable detection behavior, highlighting the sensitivity of the ML-WAF to skewed traffic distributions. The results of evaluation indicate that biases similar to those observed in open-source ML-based WAFs can also manifest in commercial solutions. In particular, the presence of false negatives under adversarial fuzzing suggests potential blind spots in the learned detection logic.

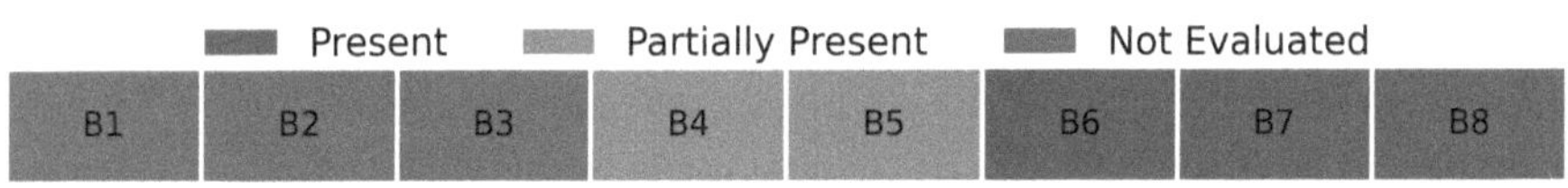

Fig. 10. Distribution of detected bias in Barracuda WAF during evaluation under adversarial traffic conditions.

Responsible Disclosure. All false-negative payloads and corresponding reports were shared with the vendor via responsible disclosure, conducted with their explicit permission. Aggregated results and representative payloads are hosted in a repository to support transparency and reproducibility, without revealing proprietary details.

6 Conclusion

This paper presented a general and reproducible framework for benchmarking ML-based WAFs under realistic conditions. The main goal is to provide the community with a unified environment where ML-WAFs can be systematically tested and evaluated. We implemented the framework and applied it to WafBrain, showing that the performance advantage of ML-WAFs over rule-based approaches is marginal under adversarial evaluation. We further demonstrated the applicability of the framework to a commercial ML-WAF (Barracuda) in a black-box setting, where it successfully identified false negatives indicative of potential blind spots. By capturing detailed execution logs and generating structured evaluation reports, the framework provides deeper insights into system behavior beyond aggregate performance metrics. Overall, our results highlight the critical impact of dataset bias, labeling quality, and evaluation methodology on reported performance, underscoring the need for standardized and transparent assessment practices. In addition to validating the framework's effectiveness, the experiments emphasize the importance of addressing biases at every stage of the ML lifecycle, including data collection, labelling, testing, and evaluation. In the future, our focus will be on expanding the framework with additional testing methodologies and applying it to a broader range of ML-WAFs, including industrial and commercial-grade systems.

Acknowledgments. This work was partially supported by RDS PTR 25-27 Project 2.1 cybersecurity.

Disclosure of Interests. The authors have no competing interests to declare that are relevant to the content of this article.

References

1. Alhogail, A., Alkahtani, M.: Automated extension-based penetration testing for web vulnerabilities. Procedia Comput. Sci. **238**, 15–23 (2024). https://doi.org/10.1016/j.procs.2024.05.191
2. Applebaum, S., Gaber, T., Ahmed, A.: Signature-based and machine-learning-based web application firewalls: a short survey. Procedia Comput. Sci. **189**, 359–367 (2021). https://doi.org/10.1016/j.procs.2021.05.105
3. Arp, D., et al.: Dos and don'ts of machine learning in computer security. In: Proceedings of USENIX Security, pp. 3971–3988 (2022)
4. Asad, H.U., Gashi, I.: Diversity in open source intrusion detection systems. In: Proceedings of SAFECOMP, pp. 267–281 (2018). https://doi.org/10.1007/978-3-319-99130-6_18
5. Awang, N.F., Manaf, A.A., Zainudin, W.S.: A survey on conducting vulnerability assessment in web-based application. In: Advanced Machine Learning Technologies and Applications, pp. 459–471 (2014)
6. Balla, A., Habaebi, M.H., Elsheikh, E.A.A., Islam, M.R., Suliman, F.M.: The effect of dataset imbalance on the performance of SCADA intrusion detection systems. Sensors **23**(2), 758 (2023)
7. Bereziński, P., Jasiul, B., Szpyrka, M.: An entropy-based network anomaly detection method. Entropy **17**(4), 2367–2408 (2015). https://doi.org/10.3390/e17042367
8. Ceschin, F., et al.: Machine learning (in) security: a stream of problems. Digital Threats (2023). https://doi.org/10.1145/3617897
9. Demetrio, L., Valenza, A., Costa, G., Lagorio, G.: WAF-A-MoLE: evading web application firewalls through adversarial machine learning. In: Proceedings of ACM SAC, pp. 1745–1752 (2020). https://doi.org/10.1145/3341105.3373962
10. Doupé, A., Cova, M., Vigna, G.: Why johnny can't Pentest: an analysis of black-box web vulnerability scanners. In: Proceedings of DIMVA (2010)
11. Fredriksson, T., Mattos, D.I., Bosch, J., Holmström Olsson, H.: Data labeling: an empirical investigation into industrial challenges and mitigation strategies. In: International Conference on Product-Focused Software Process Improvement (2020). https://api.semanticscholar.org/CorpusID:227130095
12. Hays, C., Schutzman, Z., Raghavan, M., Walk, E., Zimmer, P.: Simplistic collection and labeling practices limit the utility of benchmark datasets for twitter bot detection. In: Proceedings of ACM Web Conference, pp. 3660–3669 (2023). https://doi.org/10.1145/3543507.3583214

13. Kan, Z., et al.: TESSERACT: Eliminating experimental bias in malware classification across space and time (extended version) (2025). https://arxiv.org/abs/2402.01359
14. Mehrabi, N., Morstatter, F., Saxena, N., Lerman, K., Galstyan, A.: A survey on bias and fairness in machine learning. ACM Comput. Surv. **54**(6), 115:1–115:35 (2021). https://doi.org/10.1145/3457607
15. Mirjalili, M., Nowroozi, A., Alidoosti, M.: A survey on web penetration test. Adv. Comput. Sci. Int. J. **3**, 107–121 (2014)
16. Mishra, S., Mallick, P.K., Jena, L.: Optimization of skewed data using sampling-based preprocessing approach. Front. Public Health (2020). https://doi.org/10.3389/fpubh.2020.00274
17. Mohamed, N.: Artificial intelligence and machine learning in cybersecurity: a deep dive into state-of-the-art techniques and future paradigms. Knowl. Inf. Syst. (2025). https://doi.org/10.1007/s10115-025-02429-y
18. Montes, N., Betarte, G., Martínez, R., Pardo, A.: Web application attacks detection using deep learning. In: Proceedings of CIARP, pp. 227–236 (2021). https://doi.org/10.1007/978-3-030-93420-0_22
19. Namdari, A., Li, Z.: A review of entropy measures for uncertainty quantification of stochastic processes. Adv. Mech. Eng. **11**(6) (2019). https://doi.org/10.1177/1687814019857350
20. Nguyen, T.C.H., Nguyen, M.K.L., Le, D.T., Nguyen, V.H., Ton, L.P., Nguyen-An, K.: Improving web application firewalls with automatic language detection. In: SN Computer Science. vol. 3 (2022). https://doi.org/10.1007/s42979-022-01327-2
21. Northcutt, C.G., Athalye, A., Mueller, J.: Pervasive label errors in test sets destabilize machine learning benchmarks. arXiv preprint arXiv:2103.14749 (2021)
22. Pałka, D., Zachara, M.: Learning web application firewall - benefits and caveats. In: Proceedings of ARES Workshops, pp. 295–308 (2011)
23. Pingale, S.V., Sutar, S.R.: Analysis of web application firewalls, challenges, and research opportunities. In: Proceedings of ICDSMLA, pp. 239–248 (2022)
24. Prandl, S., Lazarescu, M., Pham, D.S.: A study of web application firewall solutions. In: Proceedings of ICISS, pp. 501–510 (2015). https://doi.org/10.1007/978-3-319-26961-0_29
25. Saraiva, P.: On Shannon entropy and its applications. Kuwait J. Sci. **50**(3), 194–199 (2023). https://doi.org/10.1016/j.kjs.2023.05.004
26. Sen, S., Singh, K.P., Chakraborty, P.: Dealing with imbalanced regression problem for large dataset using scalable artificial neural network. New Astron. **99**, 101959 (2023). https://doi.org/10.1016/j.newast.2022.101959
27. Shaheed, A., Kurdy, M.H.D.B., Megias, D.: Web application firewall using machine learning and features engineering. Secur. Commun. Netw. 2022 (2022). https://doi.org/10.1155/2022/5280158
28. Shahid, J., Hameed, M., Javed, I., Qureshi, K., Ali, M., Crespi, N.: A comparative study of web application security parameters: current trends and future directions. Appl. Sci. (2022)
29. Shannon, C.E.: A mathematical theory of communication. Bell Syst. Tech. J. **27**, 379–423 (1948)
30. Sreekumar, G., Boddeti, V.N.: Spurious correlations and where to find them. arXiv preprint arXiv:2308.11043 (2023)
31. Tadhani, J.R., Vekariya, V., Sorathiya, V., Alshathri, S., El-Shafai, W.: Securing web applications against XSS and SQLi attacks using a novel deep learning approach. Sci. Rep. **14**(1), 1803 (2024). https://doi.org/10.1038/s41598-023-48845-4

32. Toyama, A., Katahira, K., Kunisato, Y.: Examinations of biases by model misspecification and parameter reliability of reinforcement learning models. PsyArXiv (2022). https://doi.org/10.31234/osf.io/jz5rv
33. White, H.: A reality check for data snooping. Econometrica **68**(5), 1097–1126 (2000)

Leveraging Code Slicing for LLMs-Based Malicious NPM Package Detection

Dang-Khoa Nguyen[1], Gia-Thang Ho[1], Quang-Minh Pham[1], Tuyet Dang-Thi Anh[2], Minh-Khanh Vu[3], Thanh Cong Nguyen[4], Phat T. Tran-Truong[1], and Duc-Ly Vu[2(✉)]

[1] Ho Chi Minh City University of Technology (HCMUT), VNU-HCM, Ho Chi Minh, Viet Nam
{khoa.nguyen47245,thang.ho261104,minh.pham2212075,phatttt}@hcmut.edu.vn
[2] Eastern International University, Ho Chi Minh, Viet Nam
{tuyet.dangthi.cit21,ly.vu}@eiu.edu.vn
[3] University Grenoble Alpes, CNRS, Grenoble INP, VERIMAG, UMR 5104, Grenoble, France
Minh-Khanh.Vu@etu.univ-grenoble-alpes.fr
[4] PackGuard, Ho Chi Minh, Viet Nam
thanh-cong.nguyen@packguard.dev

Abstract. Software supply chain attacks on the npm ecosystem have grown increasingly sophisticated, exploiting obfuscation and complex logic to evade detection. Large Language Models (LLMs) offer strong semantic understanding of code but face practical constraints: limited context windows and high inference costs make full-package analysis infeasible, while naive token-based splitting fragments semantic context and degrades accuracy. This paper introduces an LLM-based framework for malicious npm package detection built on code-slicing techniques. We propose an adaptation of taint-based slicing for the npm ecosystem, guided by a curated inventory of JavaScript-specific sensitive APIs, to isolate security-relevant data flows from benign boilerplate. The approach reduces the mean input token count by 99.75% and the median by 93.7% while preserving critical malicious behaviors. Packages relying on dynamic code generation or obfuscation yield empty slices under static analysis and require deobfuscation preprocessing, a limitation we explicitly discuss. The framework is evaluated on a dataset of more than 7000 malicious and benign npm packages using DeepSeek-Coder-6.7B. On the 2537 packages amenable to static taint analysis, taint-based slicing achieves 87.04% detection accuracy, outperforming both a naive token-splitting baseline at 75.41% and a CFG-only static slicing approach at 75.65%. These results demonstrate that semantically targeted input representations improve LLM-based detection performance beyond what is achievable through simple input-size reduction, providing an effective and computationally practical defense against evolving open-source supply-chain threats.

D.-K. Nguyen, G.-T. Ho and Q.-M. Pham—These authors contributed equally to this work.

Z. Afzal et al. (Eds.): ARES 2026 Workshops, LNCS 16900, pp. 22–39, 2027.
https://doi.org/10.1007/978-3-032-35576-8_2

Keywords: Open-source software security · Software supply chain security · Large Language Models · Malware Detection · Code Slicing

1 Introduction

The `npm` repository has become an increasingly attractive vector for malicious actors seeking to distribute compromised packages [58]. Such attacks directly threaten millions of downstream consumers and challenge the security posture of organizational software assets [9,42]. For example, the recent Shai-Hulud self-propagating attack [40] involved malicious packages that spread across thousands of repositories, exfiltrated secrets, and published newly compromised payloads, thereby compromising numerous widely used packages.

To counter these threats, existing defenses span signature- or rule-based methods, machine learning (ML), and, more recently, LLMs [35]. Rule-based approaches integrate readily into security pipelines [47] but are brittle against novel obfuscation [12]. ML methods relying on hand-engineered features such as API call sequences [7,19] offer greater flexibility, yet remain labor-intensive and similarly vulnerable to feature-altering evasion [34,43].

The emergence of LLMs has introduced transformative capabilities for security tasks, including malicious code analysis and detection [2,16,21]. Recent studies demonstrate that LLM-based approaches can substantially outperform or complement conventional techniques for detecting malicious open-source packages [52,57]. Specifically, Zahan et al. report that LLMs achieve strong precision and recall in detecting malicious `npm` packages, surpassing traditional static analysis tools by 16% and 9% in precision and F1 score, respectively [57]. This advantage stems from the capacity of LLMs for semantic reasoning and context-aware pattern recognition across complex code structures [25,50].

However, LLMs face a practical constraint: context windows ranging from 4K to 16K tokens are often insufficient for full-package analysis [27,31,52]. When malicious logic is scattered across a codebase, the model lacks the global visibility needed for accurate threat assessment, degrading detection performance [15,52]. To mitigate this bottleneck, Wang et al. [49] proposed a taint-based code-slicing technique that isolates security-relevant code segments before the segments are fed to LLMs. Their approach reduces context-window overhead while preserving critical semantic information by generating *Sensitive Code Slices (SCS)* through taint analysis. This method achieves substantial gains in detection precision and computational efficiency for PyPI packages. However, the applicability of this slicing-based methodology to npm packages remains unexplored.

The npm ecosystem poses distinct challenges because packages typically contain numerous files, external dependencies, and utility functions that can bury malicious payloads within benign boilerplate [35]. This contextual noise dilutes semantic signals and exacerbates context-window constraints [15,27]. The study therefore examines how package context can be reduced while preserving semantic signals of malicious behavior, and how these reduced representations affect LLM-based package classification. Our evaluation compares taint-based slicing using data-flow graphs, static slicing using control-flow graphs, and naive token splitting as package representations for DeepSeek-Coder-6.7B. Context reduction is measured in terms of lines of code and token counts, while the preservation of security-relevant information is measured using Sensitive Feature Recall (SFR). Classification performance is then evaluated on a curated dataset of malicious and benign npm packages.

In this paper, we make the following three contributions.

- First, we adapt and evaluate two code-slicing strategies for npm packages using Joern Code Property Graph analysis and a curated JavaScript-specific API taxonomy.
- Second, we quantify the reduction in context size and the preservation of security-relevant information produced by these slicing strategies.
- Third, we evaluate how sliced representations affect LLM-based malicious package detection compared with a naive splitting baseline.

2 Background

This section reviews malicious-package detection, LLM-based code analysis, and the graph/slicing concepts used by our methodology.

2.1 Syntactic Pattern Matching and Signature-Based Detection

Early malicious-package detectors relied on lexical or syntactic signatures, including Microsoft OSS Detect Backdoor and CodeQL-style rules [12,32,33]. These methods scale well but suffer from high false-positive rates, obfuscation brittleness, and signature lag [9,47]. Metadata and source–artifact discrepancy analyses improve coverage but still depend on manually defined signals [46].

Behavioral Sequence Analysis Through API Monitoring. Behavioral detectors model API-call traces with RNNs or hybrid neural models [7,24,38]. They capture execution behavior better than signatures, but still lack explicit semantic intent and remain vulnerable to anti-analysis techniques and sandbox overhead [19,30,54].

2.2 Semantic Representation Learning via Feature Engineering and Neural Methods

Representation-learning detectors use engineered features or neural embeddings over code and behavior [34,43]. They reduce reliance on hand-written rules but remain sensitive to feature design, obfuscation, and ecosystem shifts [12].

2.3 Large Language Models for Semantic Code Analysis

LLMs shift detection toward semantic code understanding. Encoder models such as CodeBERT and GraphCodeBERT learn contextual representations, while decoder models such as CodeLlama, StarCoder, and DeepSeek-Coder support generative reasoning over code intent [11,14,15,29,41].

For npm malware detection, LLMs still face context limits, benign boilerplate, and fixed-size chunks that can separate sources from sinks. This fragmentation is especially problematic for supply-chain attacks, where malicious behavior may be distributed across installation scripts, helper modules, and dynamically generated payloads. If a chunk contains only a source or only a sink, the model may observe suspicious syntax without the causal path needed to infer intent. These issues motivate slicing-based inputs that preserve security-relevant flows while discarding irrelevant context.

Even with extended-context models, slicing remains useful for two reasons. First, larger windows reduce truncation but do not remove semantic noise; benign utilities and package scaffolding can still dominate attention. Second, repository-scale screening must remain cost-effective and reproducible, whereas sending complete packages to proprietary long-context models is often expensive and difficult to audit. Slicing is therefore complementary to long-context LLMs because it makes the input both smaller and more security focused.

2.4 Graph Representations of Programs

Graph-based program representations capture semantics, control flow, and data dependencies that are obscured in raw text [4,22]. An Abstract Syntax Tree (AST) encodes syntactic structure hierarchically and serves as the foundation for richer representations. A Control Flow Graph (CFG) is a directed graph $G_{CFG} = (V, E)$ where nodes are basic blocks and edges are control-flow transitions, thereby capturing feasible execution paths. A Data Dependence Graph (DDG) records def-use relationships: an edge (u, v) exists when statement u defines a variable whose value reaches statement v without intervening reassignment [18], making it the foundation for code slicing. Finally, a Code Property Graph (CPG) [53] unifies the AST, CFG, and DDG into a single property multigraph, enabling cross-layer security queries. Our approach uses CPGs (via Joern [10]) to extract security-relevant slices from npm package source code.

2.5 Code Slicing Techniques

Static Code Slicing computes the transitive closure of data and control dependencies from a slicing criterion $C = (s, v)$ by traversing a Program Dependence Graph (PDG) [37], yielding a reduced executable that preserves the behavior of the original program P for all possible inputs [45]. Because it assumes no knowledge of runtime values, it conservatively includes all statements that could affect the criterion, which tends to produce larger slices compared with dynamic approaches.

Taint-based Slicing focuses on security-critical data flows by tracking untrusted data from a *Source* (e.g., user inputs, network payloads) through assignments and computations to a *Sink* (e.g., command execution, file-system access) [26,51]. These propagation paths are mapped via Data Dependence Graphs (DDGs) or Code Property Graphs (CPGs) [17,28], isolating the precise attack chain from surrounding benign code. This property is useful for package malware detection because malicious intent often depends on whether sensitive data reaches execution, network, or file-system APIs rather than on the presence of those APIs alone.

2.6 Comparative Related Work

Ahmed et al. [1] abstract code into 16 high-level behavioral actions and analyze their chronological order, whereas our taint-based slicing traces how sensitive data flows through the code, removing irrelevant boilerplate while preserving security-relevant detection signals. Huang et al. [20] detect malicious npm packages via graph-based behavior matching, which requires a predefined attack template for each threat class. Our approach feeds raw code slices directly to an LLM, enabling template-free semantic reasoning over novel attack patterns.

Wang et al. [48] split package source code into naïve fixed-size segments and instruct GPT-3 to summarize malicious behaviors. Our taint-based slicing achieves greater token reduction and higher detection accuracy on the same packages (Sects. 5 and 6). Zahan et al. [57] apply domain-specific zero-shot prompting to npm malware detection. Our contribution is orthogonal in that we selectively isolate security-relevant code fragments before prompting, improving both input quality and LLM reasoning precision.

Our work is most closely related to OCS-BERT [49], which applies taint-based slicing to PyPI malware detection using a discriminative BERT model. We extend this paradigm to the npm ecosystem in two key ways. First, it targets generative LLMs for direct semantic security scoring rather than training classifiers on slice embeddings. Second, it systematically compares BFS-based static CFG slicing with a refined taint-based slicing approach using Joern's `ReachableByFlows` API, explicitly quantifying the noise reduction and detection performance trade-offs of each code slicing strategy.

3 Methodology

Our methodology, illustrated in Fig. 1, presents a slicing-based malware-detection pipeline for npm packages. By extracting security-relevant code slices and feeding them into a large language model, we infer potential malicious intent from localized semantic patterns. The slice-level predictions produced by the LLM are then aggregated to yield a package-level malware assessment that determines whether the package is malicious.

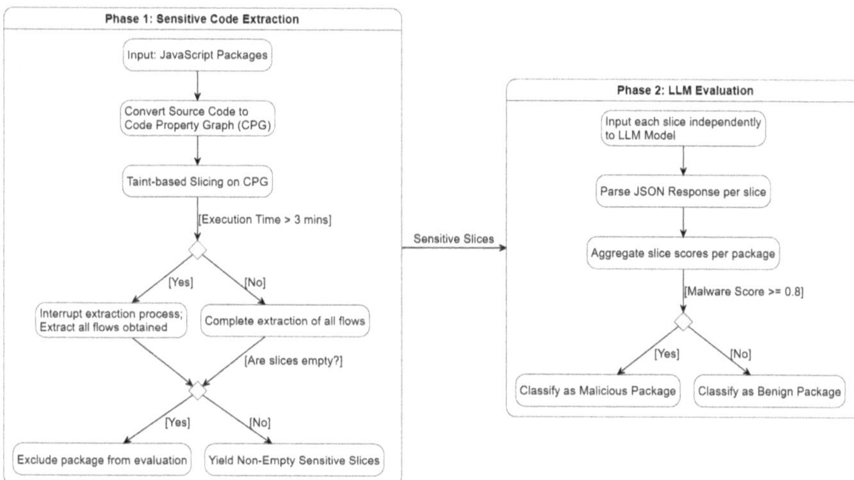

Fig. 1. Our NPM malware detection workflow

3.1 Sensitive Code Extraction

In the first step, we isolate security-relevant code slices from npm packages using static and taint-based slicing strategies. Our goal is to assess how the different code representations produced by these techniques affect the signal-to-noise ratio in malware detection, particularly within the npm ecosystem.

The static code slicing technique shown in Algorithm 1 performs a backward breadth-first search (BFS) traversal on the CFG from sensitive sink nodes, collecting all predecessor statements that structurally influence the path to the sink. While this captures broad control dependencies, it does not track data propagation and therefore tends to produce larger, noisier slices [23].

Algorithm 1. Control-Flow-Based Static Slicing

```
procedure StaticSlicing(cpg, sourceGroup, sinkGroup)
    sourceIds ← ∅, slices ← ∅
    for all source ∈ sourceGroup do
        sourceIds ← sourceIds ∪ QueryIds(cpg, source)
    for all sink ∈ Query(sinkGroup) do
        slice ← ReachableByFlow(sink, sourceIds)
        if slice ≠ ∅ then
            slices ← slices ∪ {FilterClean(slice)}
    return slices

function ReachableByFlow(sink, sourceIds)
    worklist ← [sink], visited ← {sink}
    slice ← ∅, sourceReached ← FALSE
    while worklist ≠ ∅ do
        node ← remove next element from worklist
        slice ← slice ∪ {node}
        if node.id ∈ sourceIds then
            sourceReached ← TRUE
        for all pred ∈ node.in(CFG) do
            if pred ∉ visited then
                visited ← visited ∪ {pred}
                add pred to worklist
    if sourceReached then
        return slice
    else
        return ∅
```

Taint-based slicing (Algorithm 2) uses Joern's `ReachableByFlows` API [53] to trace data paths from untrusted sources to critical sinks. We guide this traversal with a JavaScript-specific Source–Sink–Dual taxonomy (Table 1). The inventory adapts Wang et al.'s PyPI taxonomy [49] to Node.js, incorporates JavaScript-specific functions from Yu et al. [55], and adds APIs observed in public npm attacks and MalPacDetector samples [5,39,44,48]. Dynamic-generation APIs such as `eval`, `Function()`, and `Buffer.from(...)` are treated as sinks so obfuscated execution flows are preserved.

The categorized APIs are used to guide the slicing process toward security-relevant code paths. To ensure scalability and prevent excessively large slices, we enforce a strict timeout of three minutes per package. This constraint is particularly important for complex npm packages, where large codebases can produce expansive graphs. To determine this timeout, multiple experiments were conducted to measure the success rate of the slicing techniques across a large set of npm packages. We observed that most packages completed slicing within the allotted timeframe, while only a small fraction exceeded the limit.

Next, we perform an automated security scoring with LLMs. The slices from Step 3.1 are fed into the selected LLM (see Subsect. 4.2 for selection criteria)

Algorithm 2. Taint-Based Slicing Procedure

```
procedure TaintBasedSlicing(sourceGroup, sinkGroup)
    slicedPaths ← ∅
    for all sourceDef ∈ sourceGroup do
        sourceNodes ← Query(sourceDef)
        if sourceNodes ≠ ∅ then
            for all sinkDef ∈ sinkGroup do
                sinkNodes ← Query(sinkDef)
                if sinkNodes ≠ ∅ then
                    flows ← ReachableByFlows(sourceNodes, sinkNodes)
                    if flows ≠ ∅ then
                        slicedPaths ← slicedPaths ∪ flows
    return slicedPaths
```

Table 1. Categorization of Sensitive APIs and Their Security Roles

Role	Feature Group	Sensitive JavaScript APIs	#APIs
Source	Information Gathering	`process.env`, `os.userInfo`	57
Sink	System Execution	`child_process.exec`, `spawn`, `eval`	21
	Code Obfuscation	`Buffer.from(...,'base64')`, `JSON.stringify`	19
	Environment Cleanup	`fs.unlink`, `process.kill`	29
	Parallel Processing	`cluster.fork`	2
Dual	File Operations	*Source:* `fs.readFileSync`; *Sink:* `fs.writeFileSync`	85
	Network Communication	*Source:* `socket.on`, `createServer`; *Sink:* `http.post`	43

for automated malicious-code assessment. The slices of each package are submitted to the LLM independently, and the model returns a JSON-formatted response per slice. The system prompt was adapted from the design strategies of Yu et al. [55] and tailored to DeepSeek-Coder-6.7B through iterative validation on pilot outputs. Three design decisions were made: (1) a *static analysis persona* that prevents the model from simulating execution; (2) a scoring rubric that defines four output fields, namely `confidence`, `obfuscated`, `malware`, and `securityRisk`, each taking values in $S \in [0, 1]$ with explicit thresholds; and (3) a *strict JSON output schema* with enforced key ordering that prohibits surrounding markdown, enabling reliable parsing by the aggregation stage. The complete prompt is available in the replication package. The `malware` score of each slice is extracted and passed to aggregation and package evaluation phase.

In the final stage, we aggregate the responses returned by the LLM to assess the overall maliciousness of an npm package. Because a package may yield multiple responses corresponding to individual code snippets, we adopt a conservative aggregation strategy: the maximum maliciousness score across all snippets is used as the package-level indicator. The LLM processes each snippet and returns a JSON object containing a maliciousness score $S \in [0, 1]$. We selected the detection threshold $\tau = 0.8$, following the highest-risk designation of Zahan et al. [56]. Because the max-aggregation strategy flags a package if *any* single slice exceeds τ, the threshold must counterbalance the resulting sensitivity to isolated high-risk patterns: a high τ requires near-certain model confidence, reducing false positives from benign packages that legitimately invoke sensitive APIs (e.g., `child_process` in build tools). Empirical sensitivity analysis is reported in Sect. 6. A package is classified as malicious if $S \geq \tau$, and benign otherwise.

4 Evaluation

The evaluation examines how different slicing strategies reduce contextual noise while preserving malicious patterns, and how these representations affect LLM detection performance. Three code representations are evaluated. The naive splitting baseline uses full source code divided into non-overlapping 500-token segments without slicing. It was re-implemented locally based on Wang et al. [48] and evaluated on the same 2537-package subset with the same model, prompt, aggregation operator, and threshold ($\tau = 0.8$) as the slicing strategies. Static slicing uses CFG-based backward reachability to capture broad control dependencies without tracking data flow. Taint-based slicing integrates CFG and DFG information to track data flow from sources to sensitive sinks (Sect. 3), focusing the LLM on code regions where malicious data is actively manipulated.

We implemented the slicing algorithms using the Joern framework [53] (JRE 21, Scala 2.13, sbt 1.11.7) to leverage its code property graph (CPG) capabilities for JavaScript analysis. The experiments utilized the `DeepSeek-Coder-6.7B` model, deployed using model parallelism with half-precision (FP16) weights on a server equipped with an Intel Core i9-10900X CPU, 64 GB of RAM, and two NVIDIA GeForce RTX 3080 GPUs (each with 10 GB of VRAM).

4.1 Data Preparation

We utilize the MalnpmDB dataset [48], comprising 4051 benign and 3258 malicious npm packages (7309 total) collected from real-world repositories and independently verified by the dataset authors. As the dataset is not publicly available, we contacted the authors to obtain access. We applied a three-stage preprocessing pipeline summarised in Table 2. In the first stage, we remove samples with corrupt or empty archives. In the second stage, we exclude metadata-only packages and those invoking no sensitive APIs (Table 1), yielding 3242 benign and 2600 malicious packages. In the final stage, we apply the slicing pipeline with a three-minute per-package timeout; packages producing no non-empty slices were excluded (root causes discussed in Sect. 7). This resulted in non-empty slices for 1084 benign ($\approx$33%) and 1453 malicious ($\approx$56%) packages, each contributing multiple individual slices.

Table 2. Package counts after preprocessing

Stage	Benign	Malicious	Total
Raw MalnpmDB	4051	3258	7309
After Stage 1 (archive validation)	3242	2731	5973
After Stage 2 (content filtering)	3242	2600	5842
After Stage 3 (non-empty slices)	1084 (33%)	1453 (56%)	2537

4.2 Large Language Model Selection

LLMs offer varying capabilities and constraints. Selecting an LLM for malicious-code detection requires balancing analytical performance, deployment cost, licensing, and reproducibility. Our criteria, inspired by prior evaluation frameworks [6,31], prioritize code understanding, JSON-output reliability, sufficient context length, and feasibility on local hardware.

The selected model must reason about data flow, control flow, and API usage while producing strictly parseable JSON responses. Encoder-only models such as BERT [8] were excluded because they lack generative capability. CodeLlama [41] and StarCoder [29] were excluded after pilot trials on 100 held-out slices showed frequent non-compliance with the strict JSON-only output schema, including markdown fences and incomplete objects. DeepSeek-Coder's 16K-token window covers approximately 90% of slices without truncation ($\mu = 403$, max $= 28\,979$ tokens) [15], and it achieved near-perfect adherence to the JSON output schema in pilot trials. The model is also MIT-licensed and deployable without quantization on two RTX 3080 GPUs (20 GB total VRAM), supporting reproducibility and eliminating API costs.

Table 3. Comparison of Candidate LLMs for Malicious Package Detection

Model	Params.	Context Length	License	VRAM	Code Understanding	JSON Adherence
GPT family [36]	Unknown	8K–128K+	Commercial	N/A	High	High
BERT [8]	125M–400M	512–1024	Open source	~0.5–1GB	Low	N/A
CodeLlama [41]	7B–70B	4K–32K	Open source	14–40GB+	Medium	Low
StarCoder [29]	3B–21B	8K–16K	Open source	6–24GB+	Medium–low	Low
DeepSeek-Coder [15]	**1.3B–33B**	**16K**	**Open source**	**2.6–66GB**	**Medium–high**	**High**

Table 3 summarizes the candidate LLMs considered in this study. We selected the 6.7B instruction-tuned DeepSeek-Coder model [15], which combines strong code-understanding capability (trained on ~2T tokens, of which 87% are code) with a favorable trade-off between efficiency and effectiveness, suited to our resource-constrained environment.

5 Context Reduction with Code Slicing

We evaluate both slicing approaches across three dimensions: context reduction, preservation of malicious context, and preservation of semantic integrity, measured relative to the naive splitting baseline.

5.1 Context Reduction Rate

Table 4 reports the statistical distribution of context size for all three methods, measured in both number of Lines of Code (LoC) and subword tokens. Among the evaluated techniques, the naive splitting baseline exhibits extreme variability: 1 to 544 680 LoC and 69 to 15 765 669 tokens, with mean–median divergence (8002 vs. 306 LoC; 162 920 vs. 3594 tokens) indicating a highly skewed distribution driven by a small number of disproportionately large packages.

Table 4. Statistical distribution of context size (LoC and tokens).

Unit	Method	Mean	Min	Q25	Median	Q75	Max
LoC	Naive Splitting	8002	1	41	306	3109	544 680
	Static Slicing	32	1	11	31	38	1122
	Taint-based Slicing	32	1	4	18	28	2247
Tokens	Naive Splitting	162 920	69	408	3594	40 219	15 765 669
	Static Slicing	379	9	158	358	431	13 596
	Taint-based Slicing	403	3	76	228	307	28 979

Both slicing methods substantially reduce and normalize context sizes (Table 4). Median LoC drops to 31 (static slicing) and 18 (taint-based slicing), and the maximum shrinks from 545k to under 2300 LoC, representing a 237× reduction. On the token side, mean input falls from 162 920 to 379 (static) and 403 (taint-based), while the median decreases from 3594 to 228, yielding reductions of **99.75%** and **93.7%**, respectively. These results confirm that these gains apply across the full distribution rather than being driven solely by extreme outliers.

5.2 Preservation of Malicious Context

Context reduction is counterproductive if it discards malware-relevant semantics. We quantify retention using *Sensitive Feature Recall* (SFR), defined as the fraction of sensitive API references (sources and sinks) preserved after slicing:

$$SFR = \frac{|F_{sliced} \cap F_{original}|}{|F_{original}|} \times 100\%, \tag{1}$$

Table 5. Detection performance by input representation

Slicing Technique	Accuracy	Precision	Recall	F1 Score
Static Slicing	75.65	95.98	60.49	74.21
Taint-based Slicing	**87.04**	**96.23**	**72.90**	**83.32**
Naive Splitting	75.41	87.05	55.52	67.80

where $F_{original}$ is the set of source-code lines referencing a sensitive API (e.g., `process.env` as a source, `exec` as a sink) in the original package, and F_{sliced} is the subset retained in the slice.

By analyzing slices generated by static slicing and taint-based slicing, we observed a clear contrast in how each method handles benign and malicious code. In benign npm packages, static slicing retains approximately 15.9% of sensitive API features, whereas taint-based slicing is more selective, retaining only 9.4%. Conversely, for malicious packages, both methods exhibit high retention rates, with taint-based slicing achieving a slightly higher SFR (73.7%) than static slicing (73.4%). This result indicates that taint-based slicing is more effective at filtering incidental sensitive API calls (i.e., noise) in benign applications without compromising preservation of malicious information flows. In practical deployment, this behavior can reduce false positives, a high priority for package-repository maintainers [47].

Overall, taint-based slicing reduces the mean token count by 99.75% and the median token count by 93.7%. It retains 73.7% of sensitive API features in malicious packages but only 9.4% in benign packages, indicating that the compression primarily removes irrelevant contextual noise.

6 Detection Performance on Code Slices

Table 5 compares DeepSeek-Coder-6.7B performance across the three input representations on the identical 2537-package subset. Both slicing techniques outperform naive splitting across all metrics. Taint-based slicing achieves the strongest gains: +11.39% accuracy and +9.11% F1-score over naive splitting, and +11.39% accuracy over static slicing. Because the evaluation set is held constant, these gains are attributable solely to input representation quality, not to sample selection differences.

The figures in Table 5 apply only to the 2537 packages that yielded non-empty slice sets (56% of malicious, 33% of benign); the remaining 44% of malicious and 67% of benign packages were not captured by the slicer due to dynamic runtime API construction patterns. This *survival bias* implies that the reported 87.04% accuracy overestimates performance on the full corpus. In production, packages producing empty slices must be routed to either dynamic sandboxing or LLM-assisted deobfuscation before re-entering the pipeline (see Sect. 7).

Naive splitting breaks interprocedural dependencies across fixed-size chunks, making intent harder to infer. Static slicing improves F1 to 74.21%, but retains benign scaffolding that limits recall to 60.49%. Taint-based slicing focuses on paths influenced by untrusted sources, raising recall to 72.90% while preserving high precision (96.23%).

To validate the choice of $\tau = 0.8$, we evaluated taint-based slicing across $\tau \in 0.5, 0.7, 0.8, 0.9$. Lower thresholds substantially reduce precision (59.81% at $\tau = 0.5$; 64.35% at $\tau = 0.7$) because benign packages with unusual but safe API usage patterns produce moderately elevated snippet scores that exceed the decision boundary. Raising the threshold to 0.9 restores precision but further reduces recall below 72.90%, increasing the rate of false negatives. $\tau = 0.8$ achieves the best F1 score (83.32%) and aligns with the highest-risk threshold defined by Zahan et al. [56]. The score distribution is strongly bimodal: benign snippets cluster near $S \approx 0.1$ and malicious snippets near $S \approx 0.9$, so adjusting the threshold within that range affects only a small set of ambiguous cases.

Overall, taint-based slicing improves both semantic input quality and token efficiency. By centering inputs on security-relevant data flows, it raises detection accuracy to 87.04% and F1 score to 83.32%, outperforming both naive splitting and static slicing on the retained evaluation subset.

7 Threats to Validity

Malicious Payloads may Reside in Metadata Files (e.g., `package.json`*).* However, samples containing only this file were excluded to isolate and evaluate the effectiveness of the proposed slicing techniques for *JavaScript source-code logic* rather than metadata-based attack vectors.

Exclusion of Packages with Empty Slices due to Processing Timeouts. Packages that yielded empty slices were excluded due to strict processing timeouts. Hardware constraints also occasionally led to memory errors during inference on extremely large slices. Although these issues may affect accuracy for a small number of outlier cases, the high overall recall (96.23%) observed in the results suggests that such edge cases do not materially impact the overall validity of the proposed approach.

Information Loss in Code-Slicing Techniques. Removing code segments may eliminate contextual cues necessary for effective LLM-based reasoning. However, an empirical analysis using Sensitive Feature Recall (SFR) helps mitigate this concern. The results show that taint-based slicing retains more than 73% of malicious API features while discarding almost 90% of benign code segments. Moreover, the substantial improvement in F1-score (83.32%) compared to the naive splitting baseline (67.80%) indicates that the sliced representation enhances semantic signal quality rather than degrading it.

Sensitive Feature Recall (SFR) as a Lexical Proxy Rather than a Semantic Metric. SFR measures the reachability of known API markers but cannot capture complex malicious patterns such as dynamic string construction, indirect invocations, or obfuscated encoding chains. JavaScript's pervasive `async/await` constructs and callback patterns frequently break static data-flow edges, causing semantically linked source-to-sink pairs to appear disconnected in the CPG representation.

Vulnerability to Code Obfuscation and Dynamic Code Generation. Dynamic constructs such as `eval`, `Function()`, and runtime string construction hide dynamically resolved call targets from static CFG/DFG analysis. This limitation produces empty slices and helps explain the 44% empty-slice rate for malicious packages. The reported accuracy in this paper therefore reflects a survival-biased subset; deobfuscation preprocessing is required before the pipeline can be applied to heavily obfuscated packages.

Limitation to a Single Open-Source LLM Family in Evaluation. This improves reproducibility and eliminates API costs, but leaves performance on proprietary models (e.g., GPT-4 and similar proprietary models) unexplored. The core benefit of taint-based slicing—namely higher input information density—is expected to be model-agnostic. Future work should validate this claim on closed-source models and help establish an upper bound on achievable performance.

Bias Toward Predefined Sensitive API Coverage. Following Yu et al. [55], we curated our API inventory from known attack patterns in prior malware datasets [3,9], rendering the framework unable to detect previously unseen vectors that exploit novel Node.js primitives or previously unseen indirect call chains absent from the inventory. Future work should replace static curation with automated dynamic API discovery mechanisms [13] to keep source/sink definitions current without manual effort.

Potential Training Data Contamination and Inflation of Absolute Metrics. Popular benign npm libraries were likely included in DeepSeek-Coder's pre-training corpus, and some publicly disclosed malicious packages may also have been scraped prior to takedown, which could inflate the reported absolute 87.04% accuracy. Because all three baselines were evaluated under identical experimental conditions, the relative advantage of taint-based slicing remains informative. Future work should use temporally held-out malware datasets to obtain contamination-free estimates.

8 Conclusion and Future Work

This paper presents a taint-based code slicing framework for LLM-powered malicious npm package detection. Guided by a curated inventory of JavaScript-specific sensitive APIs, the approach reduces mean input token count by 99.75% while retaining 73.7% of malicious features, enabling DeepSeek-Coder-6.7B to achieve 87.04% detection accuracy and 83.32% F1 score, outperforming both a naive token-splitting baseline and a CFG-only static slicing approach by nearly 10 percentage points in F1 score. Performance is conditioned on packages invoking the predefined API set; packages that do not use known APIs remain outside the current detection scope.

Several directions remain for future work. First, fine-tuning LLMs on slicing-aware malicious code inputs could reduce false positives and improve robustness against previously unseen attack patterns. Second, deobfuscation preprocessing is a *necessary prerequisite* for production deployment: an LLM-assisted deobfuscator or dynamic sandbox must resolve dynamic call targets into a statically analyzable form before the taint slicer is applied, thereby directly reducing the 44% empty-slice rate. Third, benchmarking the framework against closed-source LLMs (e.g., GPT-4) will establish an upper performance bound and determine how much of the remaining accuracy gap is attributable to the underlying backbone model versus the input representation. Finally, jointly integrating fine-tuned LLMs, deobfuscation-aware preprocessing, and semantic slicing into an end-to-end pipeline could further strengthen resilience against adversarially crafted packages.

Code and Data Availability. This study uses the malicious package dataset released by Wang et al. [48] as part of the MalPacDetector project. All code and replication materials are available at https://github.com/MinhPham131204/replication_package_JSCodeSlicing

Acknowledgement. We acknowledge Ho Chi Minh City University of Technology (HCMUT), VNU-HCM for supporting this study.

Disclosure of Interests. The authors have no competing interests to declare that are relevant to the content of this article.

References

1. Ahmed, T., Pai, K., Devanbu, P.: Automatic augmentation of language model prompts for code summarization. In: Proceedings of the IEEE/ACM 46th International Conference on Software Engineering (2024)
2. Al-Karaki, J., Khan, M., Omar, M.: Exploring LLMs for malware detection: Review and countermeasure approaches. arXiv preprint arXiv:2409.07587 (2024)
3. Arp, D., Spreitzenbarth, M., Hubner, M., Gascon, H., Rieck, K., Siemens, C.: DREBIN: effective and explainable detection of android malware in your pocket. In: NDSS. vol. 14, pp. 23–26. San Diego, CA (2014)
4. Callahan, D.: The program summary graph and flow-sensitive interprocedual data flow analysis. In: Proceedings of the ACM SIGPLAN 1988 Conference on Programming Language Design and Implementation, pp. 47–56 (1988)
5. Checkmarx Research Team: Checkmarx blog: Supply chain security research. https://checkmarx.com/blog/category/supply-chain-security (2024). Accessed 2024
6. Chen, M.: Evaluating large language models trained on code. arXiv preprint arXiv:2107.03374 (2021)

7. Demirkıran, F., Çayır, A., Ünal, U., et al.: An ensemble of pre-trained transformer models for imbalanced multiclass malware classification. Comput. Secur. **121**, 102846 (2022)
8. Devlin, J., Chang, M., Lee, K.: BERT: pre-training of deep bidirectional transformers for language understanding. In: Proceedings of the 2019 Conference of the North American Chapter of the Association for Computational Linguistics, pp. 4171–4186 (2019)
9. Duan, R., Alrawi, O., Kasturi, R.P., Elder, R., Saltaformaggio, B., Lee, W.: Towards measuring supply chain attacks on package managers for interpreted languages. arXiv preprint arXiv:2002.01139 (2020)
10. Fabian Yamaguchi: Welcome to Joern's documentation! https://joern.readthedocs.io/en/latest/index.html (2014)
11. Feng, Z., Guo, D., Tang, D.: CodeBERT: a pre-trained model for programming and natural languages. In: Findings of the Association for Computational Linguistics: EMNLP 2020, pp. 1536–1547 (2020)
12. Froh, F., Gobbi, M., Kinder, J.: Differential static analysis for detecting malicious updates to open source packages. In: Proceedings of the 2023 Workshop on Software Supply Chain Offensive Research and Ecosystem Defenses, pp. 41–49 (2023)
13. Gao, X., et al.: {MalGuard}: towards {Real-Time}, accurate, and actionable detection of malicious packages in {PyPI} ecosystem. In: 34th USENIX Security Symposium (USENIX Security 25), pp. 4741–4758 (2025)
14. Guo, D., Ren, S., Lu, S.: GraphCodeBERT: Pre-training code representations with data flow. arXiv preprint arXiv:2009.08366 (2021)
15. Guo, D., Zhu, Q., Yang, D.: DeepSeek-coder: When the large language model meets programming. arXiv preprint arXiv:2401.14196 (2024)
16. Guo, W., Wen, H., Kong, L.: A survey on malware analysis with large language models. In: International Conference on Knowledge Science, Engineering and Management, pp. 41–52 (2025)
17. Halim, V., Asnar, Y.: Static code analyzer for detecting web application vulnerability using control flow graphs. In: 2019 International Conference on Data and Software Engineering (ICoDSE), pp. 1–6 (2019)
18. Hammer, C., Snelting, G.: Flow-sensitive, context-sensitive, and object-sensitive information flow control based on program dependence graphs. Int. J. Inf. Secur. 399–422 (2009)
19. Huang, C., Wang, N., Wang, Z., et al.: DONAPI: malicious NPM packages detector using behavior sequence knowledge mapping. In: Proceedings of the 33rd USENIX Conference on Security Symposium (2024)
20. Huang, Y., et al.: SpiderScan: practical detection of malicious NPM packages based on graph-based behavior modeling and matching. In: Proceedings of the 39th IEEE/ACM International Conference on Automated Software Engineering, pp. 1146–1158 (2024)
21. Jelodar, H., Bai, S., Hamedi, P.: Large language model (LLM) for software security: Code analysis, malware analysis. arXiv preprint arXiv:2504.07137 reverse engineering. (2025)
22. Johnson, R., Pingali, K.: Dependence-based program analysis. In: Proceedings of the ACM SIGPLAN 1993 conference on Programming language design and implementation, pp. 78–89 (1993)
23. K., Sanyal, P.K., Karkare, A., Padhi, A., S.: A static slicing method for functional programs and its incremental version. In: Proceedings of 28th International Conference on Compiler Construction (CC), pp. 53–64 (2019)

24. Kim, Y.: Convolutional neural networks for sentence classification. In: Proceedings of the 2014 Conference on Empirical Methods in Natural Language Processing, pp. 1746–1751 (2014)
25. Kojima, T., Gu, S., Reid, M.: Large language models are zero-shot reasoners. In: Proceedings of the 36th International Conference on Neural Information Processing Systems (2022)
26. Krinke, J.: Information flow control and taint analysis with dependence graphs. In: Proceedings of the 3rd International Workshop on Code Based Security Assessments, pp. 6–9 (2007)
27. Kwon, W., Li, Z., Zhuang, S.: Efficient memory management for large language model serving with PagedAttention. In: Proceedings of the 29th Symposium on Operating Systems Principles, pp. 611–626 (2023)
28. Li, B., Ma, R., Wang, X.: DepTaint: a static taint analysis method based on program dependence. In: Proceedings of the 2020 4th International Conference on Management Engineering, Software Engineering and Service Sciences, pp. 34–41 (2020)
29. Li, R., Ben Allal, L., Zi, Y.: StarCoder: may the source be with you! arXiv preprint arXiv:2305.06161 (2023)
30. Li, S., Kang, M., Hou, J.: Detecting node.js prototype pollution vulnerabilities via object lookup analysis. In: Proceedings of the 29th ACM Joint Meeting on European Software Engineering Conference and Symposium on the Foundations of Software Engineering, pp. 268–279 (2021)
31. Liang, P., Bommasani, R., Lee, T.: Holistic evaluation of language models. arXiv preprint arXiv:2211.09110 (2023)
32. Microsoft: Microsoft OSS ApplicationInspector. https://github.com/microsoft/applicationinspector (2023)
33. Microsoft: Microsoft OSS detect backdoor system. https://github.com/microsoft/OSSGadget/wiki/OSS-Detect-Backdoor (2023)
34. Ohm, M., Boes, F., Bungartz, C.: On the feasibility of supervised machine learning for the detection of malicious software packages. In: Proceedings of the 17th International Conference on Availability, Reliability and Security (2022)
35. Ohm, M., Stuke, C.: SoK: practical detection of software supply chain attacks. In: Proceedings of the 18th International Conference on Availability, Reliability and Security (2023)
36. OpenAI: GPT-4 technical report (2024)
37. Ottenstein, K.J., Ottenstein, L.M.: The program dependence graph in a software development environment. In: SDE 1 (1984)
38. Pascanu, R., Stokes, J., Sanossian, H.: Malware classification with recurrent networks. In: 2015 IEEE International Conference on Acoustics, Speech and Signal Processing (ICASSP), pp. 1916–1920 (2015)
39. Phylum Research Team: Phylum blog: Software supply chain security research. https://blog.phylum.io (2024). Accessed 2024
40. Ramati, H., Bar, M., Benmocha, G., et al.: Shai-Hulud 2.0 supply chain attack: 25K+ repos exposing secrets (2025)
41. Rozière, B., Gehring, J., Gloeckle, F.: Code llama: Open foundation models for code. arXiv preprint arXiv:2308.12950 (2023)
42. Scalco, S., Paramitha, R., Vu, D.: On the feasibility of detecting injections in malicious NPM packages. In: Proceedings of the 17th International Conference on Availability, Reliability and Security (2022)

43. Sejfia, A., Schäfer, M.: Practical automated detection of malicious NPM packages. In: Proceedings of the 44th International Conference on Software Engineering, pp. 1681–1692 (2022)
44. Snyk Security Team: Snyk vulnerability database: NPM advisories. https://security.snyk.io/vuln?type=npm (2024). Accessed 2024
45. Tip, F.: A survey of program slicing techniques. J. Program. Lang. **3** (1994)
46. Vu, D., Massacci, F., Pashchenko, I.: LastPyMile: identifying the discrepancy between sources and packages. In: Proceedings of the 29th ACM Joint Meeting on European Software Engineering Conference and Symposium on the Foundations of Software Engineering, pp. 780–792 (2021)
47. Vu, D., Newman, Z., Meyers, J.: Bad snakes: understanding and improving python package index malware scanning. In: 2023 IEEE/ACM 45th International Conference on Software Engineering (ICSE), pp. 499–511 (2023)
48. Wang, J., Li, Z., Qu, J.: MalPacDetector: an LLM-based malicious NPM package detector. IEEE Trans. Inf. Forensics Secur. 6279–6291 (2025)
49. Wang, Y., Pang, S., Fan, Z.: Advanced code slicing with pre-trained model fine-tuned for open-source component malware detection. Comput. J. 1163–1180 (2025)
50. Wei, J., Wang, X., Schuurmans, D.: Chain-of-thought prompting elicits reasoning in large language models. In: Proceedings of the 36th International Conference on Neural Information Processing Systems (2022)
51. Wilander, J.: Modeling and visualizing security properties of code using dependence graphs, Linköping University (2005). Ph.D. thesis
52. Wyss, E., Tassio, D., De Carli, L., Davidson, D.: Evaluating LLM-based detection of malicious package updates in NPM (2025). Preprint
53. Yamaguchi, F., Golde, N., Arp, D.: Modeling and discovering vulnerabilities with code property graphs. In: 2014 IEEE Symposium on Security and Privacy, pp. 590–604 (2014)
54. Yan, P., Tan, S., Wang, M.: Prompt engineering-assisted malware dynamic analysis using GPT-4. In: IEEE Transactions on Dependable and Secure Computing, pp. 7712–7728 (2025)
55. Yu, Z., Wen, M., Guo, X.: Maltracker: a fine-grained NPM malware tracker copiloted by LLM-enhanced dataset. In: Proceedings of the 33rd ACM SIGSOFT International Symposium on Software Testing and Analysis, pp. 1759–1771 (2024)
56. Zahan, N., Zimmermann, T., Godefroid, P.: What are weak links in the NPM supply chain? In: Proceedings of the 44th International Conference on Software Engineering: Software Engineering in Practice, pp. 331–340 (2022)
57. Zahan, N., Burckhardt, P., Lysenko, M., Aboukhadijeh, F., Williams, L.: Leveraging Large Language Models to Detect NPM Malicious Packages, pp. 2625–2637. IEEE Press (2025)
58. Zhou, X., Zhang, Y., Niu, W.: An analysis of malicious packages in open-source software in the wild. In: 2025 55th Annual IEEE/IFIP International Conference on Dependable Systems and Networks (DSN), pp. 371–385 (2025)

Evaluating LLMs for Real-World Web Vulnerability Detection

Sebastian Neef[1(✉)], Luca Jungnickel[1(✉)], Antonio Benjamin Buchholz[1], Valene Spence[2], and Vicente Birke Gonzalez[2]

[1] Technische Universität Berlin, Einsteinufer 17, 10587 Berlin, Germany
neef@tu-berlin.de, l.jungnickel@campus.tu-berlin.de
[2] Freie Universität Berlin, Kaiserswerther Street 16-18, 14195 Berlin, Germany

Abstract. Large Language Models (LLMs) have emerged as a promising tool for automated vulnerability detection, yet their effectiveness on web-specific vulnerabilities remains to be explored.

This work benchmarks six frontier (Claude Opus 4.6, Codex GPT-5.4, Gemini 3.1-pro-preview) and open-weight models (Qwen 3.5, Qwen 3 Coder Next, MiniMax M2.5) on their ability to detect real-world web vulnerabilities using static analysis in WordPress plugins, including SQL injection, stored cross-site scripting, path traversal, and remote code execution. Using five prompt designs of varying structure, scope, and complexity across three experiment iterations, we aim to answer how model and prompt choice affects vulnerability detection.

Our results show that all models are capable of detecting valid security issues, but the detection rate varies depending on the model and prompt. For example, Claude Opus 4.6 achieved the highest web vulnerability detection rate (63%), while open-weight MiniMax M2.5 performs on par with other frontier models (48%), and self-hosted Qwen 3.5 only achieved 35%. We show that scoped prompts that narrow the vulnerability scope outperform open-ended ones, whereas the prompt complexity has little impact. Surprisingly, no model achieved full reporting consistency across three experiment iterations, with some as low as 50%. Our experiments demonstrate the opportunities and limits of LLM-based vulnerability detection, as no model correctly identified one baseline vulnerability in one of the plugins.

Additionally, we derive practical lessons learned for security practitioners and publish all code and data to support future research.

Keywords: Web Security · Vulnerability Detection · Large Language Models

1 Introduction

Almost 75% of the world's population relies on the internet [8], including its web applications. While many high-traffic web sites are operated by large corporations [10], any individual can create their own publicly accessible website, i.e.

Z. Afzal et al. (Eds.): ARES 2026 Workshops, LNCS 16900, pp. 40–57, 2027.
https://doi.org/10.1007/978-3-032-35576-8_3

using a content management system (CMS). One such open-source CMS is WordPress [22], which drives almost 60% of all CMS-based websites and over 42.5% of all websites according to W3Techs [21]. WordPress' plugin system allows users to customize its functionality by installing plugins, with popular plugins having 10+ million active installations [23].

Since anyone can develop and publish such a plugin in the official WordPress plugin store, the code quality and security may vary, potentially rendering websites vulnerable to attacks by malicious actors. In fact, WPScan's vulnerability database contains over 70,000 publicly known issues [29]. Thus, it is crucial to identify vulnerabilities in these plugins either early in the development lifecycle or after release for coordinated vulnerability disclosure to the developers, before any harm can occur. With the recent rise of Large Language Models (LLMs) and their agentic capabilities, using them not only as assistants for programming, but also for vulnerability research, is an interesting research domain (see Sect. 2).

However, web vulnerability discovery is not an easy task as vulnerabilities can be hard to identify across several files, require specific configurations, or exist in code-paths which cannot be trivially triggered. However, many other factors can influence vulnerability detection with LLMs, too. One such factor could be the model itself, e.g. due to differences in the underlying training datasets, or the prompts used to instruct the LLMs. Therefore, this work aims to extend the body of literature with answers to the following questions:

RQ1) How does model choice affect web vulnerability discovery?
RQ2) How does prompt design affect web vulnerability discovery?
RQ3) How consistent are the detection results across LLM uses?

2 Background and Related Work

This section provides a brief introduction to the background and the context of our work in the body of literature.

2.1 Web Vulnerabilities

Web applications can become vulnerable due to programming mistakes or misconfigurations during deployment. MITRE's Common Weakness Enumeration (CWE) project lists over 900 possible weaknesses [13], with some of the TOP 25 being web vulnerabilities (e.g. Cross-Site Scripting (XSS), SQL Injection (SQLi), (Remote) Command Injection (RCE)) [14]. Another popular ranking of web application vulnerability classes is published by the Open Worldwide Application Project (OWASP) with its OWASP TOP 10 [18], which also features *injection* vulnerabilities as a separate category. This work focuses on the SQLi, XSS, RCE and path traversal vulnerability classes. In each case, insufficiently validated user input reaches security-critical functions such as database queries, system shells, file-system operations, or HTML output.

Academic work has a long history of trying to identify such vulnerabilities. For example, using static code analysis methods like code property graphs [30], taint analysis [12], semantic code analysis [9], but also using dynamic code analysis methods like fuzzing [15] or symbolic execution [11]. Black-box tools such as BurpSuite[1] and ZAP[2] offer an alternative but require significant expertise to configure and operate effectively. Thus, LLM-based agents' ability to independently run CLI tools and reason about the analyzed source code is a motivating and promising approach to make it more accessible.

2.2 Large Language Models in Vulnerability Detection

Previous work has explored a range of strategies, from standalone detectors to components within larger analysis pipelines. Much of this research targets C/C++ codebases, but not web applications. LineVul introduced a transformer-based architecture for line-level vulnerability detection [5], GPTVD demonstrated that the combination of chain-of-thought (CoT) reasoning and traditional static analysis can outperform traditional static analysis tools [3], and VulRAG extended LLM-based vulnerability detection with Retrieval-Augmented Generation [4]. We noticed that web vulnerability detection remains comparatively underexplored. Our work contributes to closing this gap.

Several works focus on vulnerability detection at the function level, where a model is used to classify if an isolated function is vulnerable or not. Risse et al. [19] argue that this approach is fundamentally limited, as necessary context information for reliable detection is needed, e.g. if a function's input has been sanitized before. SecVulEval [1] addresses this issue by proposing a benchmark with C/C++ vulnerabilities with the necessary context information.

Motivated by these observations, we adopt an application-level approach similar to the repository-level approach [32]. In our work, the model has access to the full source-code. Wang et al. [32] find that ReAct agents [31] achieve the highest detection rates. Therefore, we choose to evaluate each model in an agentic framework. Closely related is RepoAudit [7], which uses LLM agents for general software bug detection across open-source repositories, demonstrating the feasibility of repository-scale LLM-driven program analysis. Our work applies a similar strategy, but focuses on vulnerability detection.

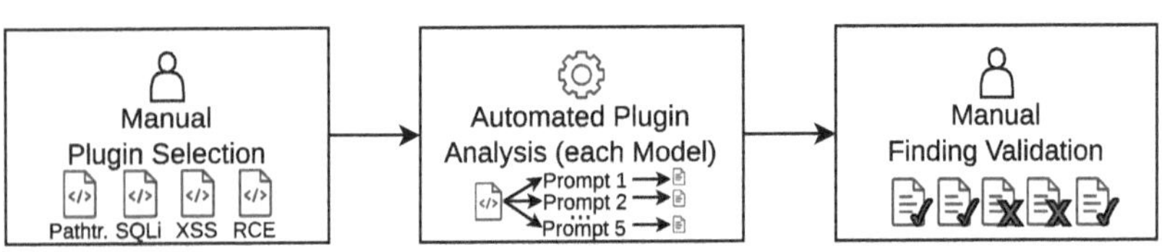

Fig. 1. Brief overview of our methodology consisting of manual plugin selection, LLM-based vulnerability detection, and manual finding validation.

[1] https://portswigger.net/burp.
[2] https://www.zaproxy.org/.

3 Methodology

Figure 1 provides an overview of our methodology, which we detail in the following subsections.

3.1 Plugin Selection

We selected WordPress plugins as our evaluation target because their source code is usually publicly available for download[3], including older and vulnerable versions. We reviewed the public vulnerability reports from the WPScan vulnerability database [24] and filtered for recently published vulnerabilities to minimize the risk of training data contamination, required unauthenticated exploitation for easier reproducibility, and selected only issues with publicly available proof-of-concepts to serve as a validation baseline. Table 1 lists the selection of the four chosen plugins that matched our criteria, covering a great variety of vulnerability classes, code base sizes and active installation counts. For all plugins, we obtained the latest affected version and validated that the vulnerability exists and is indeed exploitable by an unauthenticated attacker. At the time of writing, all plugins were updated according to the WPScan reports.

Table 1. WordPress plugins selected for vulnerability analysis.

Plugin	Vulnerability	Version	Active Installs	LoC (PHP)
formgent	Path Traversal CVE-2025-10916 [25]	1.0.3	1,000+	330,925
popup-builder-block	SQL Injection CVE-2025-10862 [26]	2.1.3	60,000+	12,156
responsive-lightbox	Stored XSS CVE-2025-9710 [27]	2.5.2	100,000+	17,462
w3-total-cache	RCE CVE-2025-9501 [28]	2.8.12	900,000+	351,690

Table 2. Frontier and open-weight models selected for vulnerability analysis.

Model	Context window	Reasoning	Open-weight
Claude Opus 4.6	1,000,000 tokens	Yes	No
Codex GPT-5.4	272,000 tokens	Yes	No
Gemini 3.1-pro-preview	up to 1,000,000 tokens	Yes	No
MiniMax M2.5	200,000 tokens	Yes	Yes
Qwen 3 Coder Next (FP8)	131,072 tokens	No	Yes
Qwen 3.5 (122b)	256,000 tokens	Yes	Yes

[3] https://downloads.wordpress.org/plugin/pluginslug.version.zip.

3.2 Model Selection

We tested six state-of-the-art models: three closed models (Codex GPT-5.4, Claude Opus 4.6, Gemini 3.1-pro-preview), as well as three open-weight models (Qwen 3.5 (122b), Qwen 3 Coder Next (FP8) and MiniMax M2.5), as shown in Table 2. For the paid frontier model subscriptions, we chose the "basic" paid tier (~20€/month), as our available budget did not allow costly API-usage. While the subscription services for the frontier models might impose certain usage limits, self-hosting open-weight models is usually limited by the available hardware resources. For example, the context window sizes are constrained by available GPU memory [16], but paid subscriptions can offer context windows up to 1M [2,6,17].

3.3 Prompt Selection

To answer RQ2, we chose the following five prompts to test a prompt's effect on the vulnerability discovery for web-based vulnerabilities:

- **Low effort**: A prompt that just tells the LLM to "Find vuln." without additional context or instructions. This prompt serves as a baseline.
- **Simple general**: A simple prompt containing a role, task, objective (similar to [33]). It instructs the LLM to find OWASP Top 10 vulnerabilities in the provided WordPress plugin.
- **Simple specific**: The specific prompt is identical to the *simple general* prompt, except that for security issues "based on the OWASP TOP 10" the correct vulnerability class is provided as "of type VULNTYPE" with VULNTYPE matching the analyzed plugin's vulnerability class (see Table 1).
- **Advanced general**: A more sophisticated and extensive Chain-of-Thought (COT) prompt that has a similar structure to the *simple general* prompt, but a more detailed role description and a 4-step detailed analysis workflow to follow.
- **Advanced specific**: Again, the specific prompt provides the LLM with the correct vulnerability class instead of OWASP Top 10 term.

The Appendix A.1 includes the *low effort* and *simple general* prompt in Listings 2 and 3, while all prompts variants can be found in the GitHub repository (see Sect. 5.8).

We deem providing the vulnerability class within the specific prompt an acceptable hint, since the same prompt could be repeated with the most common and dangerous vulnerability classes, if it means that the detection results are improved.

During preliminary tests, some agents browsed the internet and discovered existing vulnerability reports, compromising the experiment. We therefore added guardrail instructions to all prompts: treat only the provided source code as evidence, do not browse the internet, explicitly state assumptions, and write a `security_report.md` with the identified issues as the final output. After that, we did not notice any violations.

3.4 Vulnerability and Report Analysis

To keep the vulnerability analysis performed by the LLM agents as reproducible as possible, we set up a dedicated virtual machine (24 cores, 64 GB RAM, 4x NVIDIA RTX PRO 4500 Blackwell Workstation graphics cards) installed with the respective CLI programs (claude code, codex CLI, gemini CLI, opencode) with default options, and implemented an automation script (`run_experiment.py`) that follows Algorithm 1 to analyze each plugin by launching a configured LLM agent with each prompt for every model sequentially. We rerun the analysis at a later time if no `security_report.md` was produced or a rate limit was encountered. In total, three iterations were done to account for fluctuations in LLM output and to test for its consistency (RQ3).

Qwen 3.5 was hosted using the default options of Ollama[4] on the aforementioned VM. For MiniMax M2.5 and Qwen3 Coder Next, we used infrastructure provided by Fraunhofer Society for the Advancement of Applied Research[5].

After the automated analysis terminated, two authors collaboratively reviewed all generated security reports to assess whether a report contains the correct vulnerability and to gather the total number of findings. When the reported number of findings by an LLM did not match the actual number of described findings, the latter was counted. Due to the large amount of reports and findings, the two authors searched the report for the vulnerability-related keywords (e.g. vulnerability class, endpoints, payloads, file names), before checking the matched finding more closely. If the finding's information matched the public proof-of-concept (vulnerability class, endpoint, parameter), we marked it as *detected*. Disagreements occurred only in very few cases (<5) and were resolved by checking whether the finding matched the public information in all aspects. The detection rate for Table 3 is then calculated as rate $R = \frac{N_{VulnDetected}}{N_{prompts} \cdot N_{plugins}}$, and analogously for other detection rates.

All configurations and reports are included in the GitHub repository (see Sect. 5.8).

[4] https://ollama.com/.

[5] Information about the hardware and model configuration was not available to us at the time of writing.

Algorithm 1: WordPress Plugin Security Analysis (run_analysis.py)

```
Input: Configuration (agent, model, plugins, prompts, timeout)
Output: Security report and metrics for each plugin-prompt combination
Load configuration and determine experiment identifiers;
foreach plugin ∈ plugins do
    foreach prompt ∈ prompts do
        if result already exists and re-run not requested then skip
        Prepare isolated working directory with plugin source code;
        Submit plugin source and prompt to the LLM agent;
        if timeout exceeded then
            Record timeout; continue to next experiment;
        if rate limit detected then
            Record rate limit; abort run;
        Collect agent output, runtime, and token usage;
        Save security report and metrics to disk;
        Remove plugin source files from working directory;
```

4 Results

We successfully performed three iterations of our experiment using our automation script. Each iteration asked six LLMs to identify security issues in four plugins with five prompts. In total, all test executions had a combined runtime of 32 h (not counting usage limits) and produced 360 reports with over 1600 findings. After two authors reviewed all reports for the to-be-discovered vulnerability, we had all the information to answer our research questions.

4.1 Models and Prompts

The first two research questions are about the impact of the model and prompt on the vulnerability detection. As shown in Table 3, we can establish that all tested models and prompts are able to identify valid web-based security vulnerabilities in WordPress plugins.

Table 3. Vulnerability detection rate per model and experiment iteration ("run") on average for all 5 prompts and 4 plugins (20 reports per run).

Model	Run 01 (20)	Run 02 (20)	Run 03 (20)	Avg (60)
Claude Opus 4.6	55 %	70 %	65 %	**63 %**
Gemini 3.1 (pro-preview)	50 %	50 %	45 %	**48 %**
Codex GPT-5.4	45 %	50 %	45 %	**47 %**
Qwen 3.5 (122b)	35 %	35 %	35 %	**35 %**
Qwen 3 Coder Next (FP8)	35 %	30 %	45 %	**37 %**
MiniMax M2.5	50 %	35 %	60 %	**48 %**

However, the detection rate ranges between 30% and 70% across the different models, with almost all models not exceeding 50% in total, except for Claude

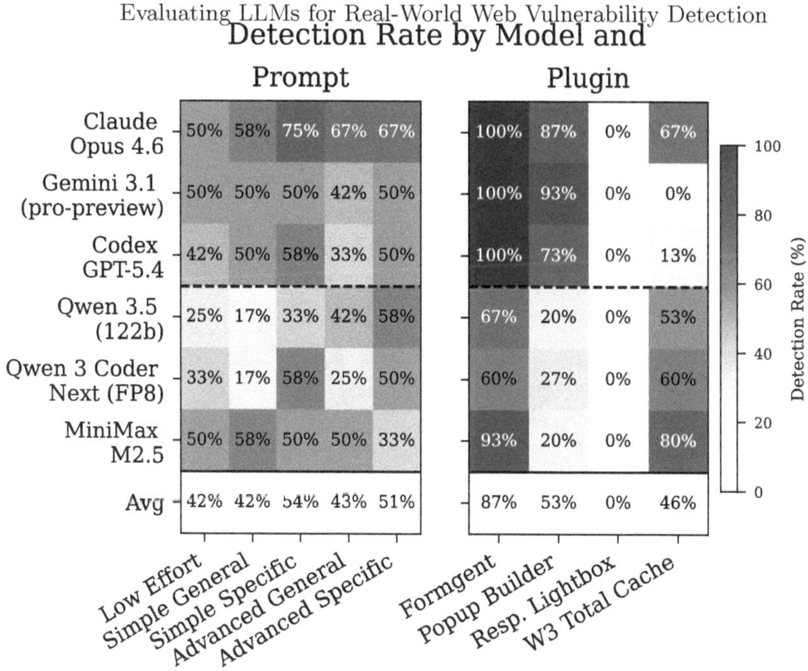

Fig. 2. The detection rate of each model by prompt or plugin as two separate heatmaps.

Opus with 63.3%. Except for Qwen 3.5, each model's detection rate changes between experiment iterations. If not accounting for both Qwen models, there is no huge gap between the frontier models and open-weight MiniMax. In fact, MiniMax has a detection rate on the same level as Gemini or Codex.

The two heatmaps in Fig. 2 provide deeper insights into the detection rate for each prompt and plugin based on all three iterations. They show that there is no *winner*-prompt that provides the best results for all models, although *simple specific* appears to be the best candidate for that label by providing the best results for 3 out of 6 models. The prompt-based heatmap shows overall better performance by the frontier models than the self-hosted open-weight Qwen models, while MiniMax scores are similar to Gemini's. Still, the data shows that *specific* prompts perform better than the *general* prompts in our experiments.

The plugin-based heatmap of Fig. 2 shows that the vulnerability detection rate also depends on the analyzed plugin. No LLM was able to detect the vulnerability in responsive lightbox, which will be discussed in Sect. 5.4. On the other hand the path traversal vulnerability in formgent was discovered at least once by all models, with the frontier models (and except for one case with MiniMax) finding it regardless of the used prompt. For the SQL injection in popup-builder, the frontier models perform better than the self-hosted models, but the opposite is true for the W3 total cache plugin.

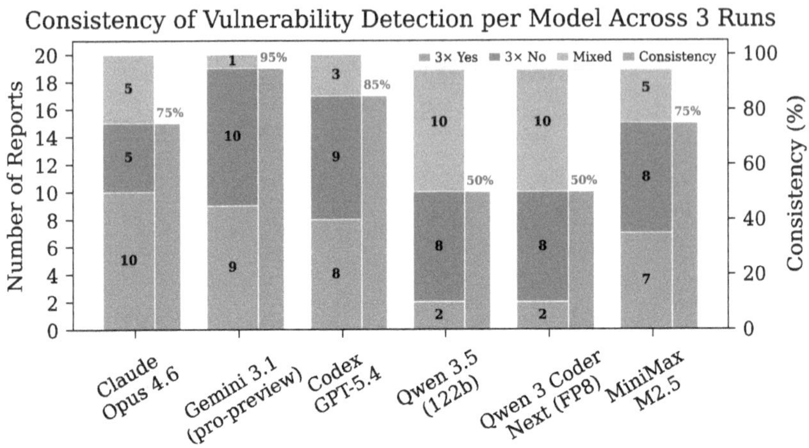

Fig. 3. The consistency of finding the correct vulnerability across the three iterations of the experiment for each model.

4.2 Consistency and Runtime

Figure 3 shows that the frontier models have a higher consistency in reporting or not reporting the same result for the same prompt and plugin across three iterations of the experiment. Gemini shows the highest consistency (95%), but also the highest number of undetected vulnerabilities. Codex (85%), Claude Opus (75%) and MiniMax (75%) follow closely. However, the Qwen self-hosted models have the lowest consistency (50%) as they cannot decide on an outcome of the vulnerability detection task, indicated by the high number of *mixed* answers.

Similarly, the number of findings varies greatly by prompt and model, as can be seen in Fig. 4. While Gemini and Codex produce the lowest number of reports on average for all prompts and have the lowest variation between them, Claude Opus and Qwen tend to report several times as many findings. For the latter models, the *low effort* and *simple general* prompts lead to more findings, while the *specific* prompts result in fewer findings, which could be due to hallucination or the prompt having an effect of the number of findings, as discussed later.

Figure 5 shows the average runtime per model and prompt. At first sight, it shows that Claude Opus, Gemini and both Qwen models form a slower tier, with Gemini the fastest and Qwen 3.5 the slowest. Codex and MiniMax complete analysis tasks considerably faster than the other models. Prompt-wise, *simple general* and *advanced general* prompts take the longest for most models, while the *low effort* and *specific* prompts are faster. The only exception to this is Qwen 3 Coder, where *simple specific* is slower than *simple general*, almost as slow as *advanced general*. -2

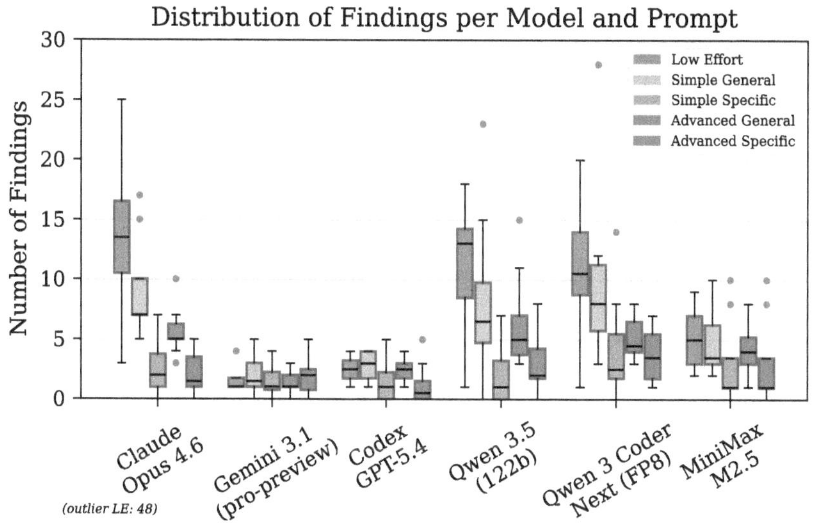

Fig. 4. The number of findings in each report produced by each model and prompt for all plugins across all three iterations.

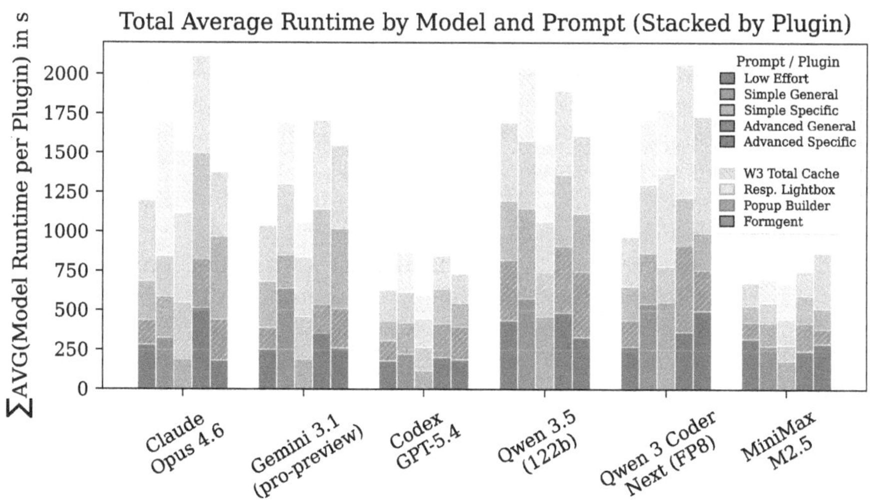

Fig. 5. Average runtime of each model for each prompt and model based on the average execution time across all three iterations.

5 Discussion

We will discuss the results and answer our three research questions and aim to provide practical and helpful lessons learned for future work or for individuals looking to use LLMs for vulnerability analysis. Before discussing the respective factors influencing the detection rate, we can state that web vulnerability detection with LLMs is generally viable, but the detection rate varies with the chosen model, prompt and source code.

5.1 Model Performance

The results show that the vulnerability detection rate differs from model to model. Since we do not have full insights into how these models were trained or how they operate, it is not clear where the differences stem from. Claude Opus showed the highest detection rate, while the Qwen models had the worst, even though Qwen 3.5 and Qwen 3 Coder Next were hosted on different powerful hardware. Claude Opus leading the vulnerability detection is a similar result with older versions of these models as reported in SecVulEval [1]. Interestingly, the open-weight MiniMax model has a similar detection rate to the other frontier models (Gemini, Codex), which indicates that open-weight models can be a viable alternative if enough hardware resources for self-hosting are available.

None of the models managed to identify the stored cross-site scripting (XSS) vulnerability in the responsive lightbox plugin, which we will discuss separately in Sect. 5.4.

5.2 Prompt Choice

Related to RQ2, the data corroborates our observation that more specific prompt scoping, such as prompting an LLM to look for specific types of vulnerabilities (*simple/advanced specific*), leads to a better detection rate compared to open-ended prompts (*low effort*, *simple/advanced general*). More precise prompts narrow the search space, so the LLM does not have to check for multiple vulnerability classes, of which many exist. However, the model choice also plays a role, as Claude Opus achieves the highest detection rates with both specific prompts, while MiniMax's *advanced specific* prompt performs the worst, but its *simple general* performs best.

Naturally, this also leads to an increase in the number of reported findings. For example, the *low effort* prompt created reports containing the most findings for 50% of our models, with Claude Opus' outlier being 48 findings in a single report. Such outliers could be explained by hallucination, which also drastically increase the manual effort required for validation. Thus, prompt choice affects the outcome in this regard.

However, prompt complexity (*simple* vs *advanced*) had little impact on the overall detection rate, although the effect is related to the choice of model: Qwen 3.5 benefits from *advanced* prompts, while Codex performs better with *simple* ones.

5.3 Consistency and Runtime

An interesting finding of our experiments that answers RQ3 is that no LLM produced consistent results across all three experiment iterations. Although Gemini came close to giving the same detection result in all iterations, other models' results are comparable to a coin flip, as there is no consistency in finding the baseline vulnerability. Even Claude Opus, Codex and MiniMax produced inconsistent results for the same prompt and plugin across multiple iterations, which makes it hard to trust a vulnerability detection result with just a single run. Therefore, it is imperative to let an LLM perform such a task multiple times to get reliable results.

The runtime does not appear to be influenced or an indicator for the other metrics: While Codex and MiniMax are the fastest to finish their tasks by a large margin, their detection rate is on the same level as Gemini's. However, Gemini's consistency is significantly higher than the other model's. Claude Opus' runtime is higher than Gemini's, but leads to a 15% higher detection rate. On the other hand, the Qwen models are the slowest and have the worst detection rate and consistency.

5.4 Undetected Vulnerability in Responsive Lightbox

Listing 1 shows the vulnerable code, which is a rather complex stored cross-site scripting vulnerability due to regex manipulation on the already escaped input (note the *esc_attr* around the input). Manual analysis of thinking logs revealed that models that analyzed this code snippet concluded that XSS is not possible since the input was escaped. No model correctly captured that manipulation on sanitized input can lead to code injection.

Furthermore, for the responsive lightbox vulnerability to be exploitable, a website administrator would have to enable the "Enable lightbox for comments content" option, which is not set by default. Therefore, another reason for our observed result could be that LLMs assumed this setting was not enabled, disregarding or skipping the analysis of the affected code paths.

```
if ( preg_match( '/<a.*?(?:data-rel)=(?:\'|")(.*?)(?:\'|").*?>/is', $link, $result )
     === 1 )
 $link = preg_replace( '/data-rel=(\'|")(.*?)(\'|")/s',  'data-rel="' . esc_attr( $args
     ['selector'] ) . '-content-' .  esc_attr( base64_encode( $result[1] ) ) . '"',
     $link );
```

Listing 1. Stored XSS vulnerability in responsive lightbox

5.5 Comparison with Traditional Static Analysis Vulnerability Detection

For comparison of the LLM-based vulnerability detection approach with traditional static analysis, we additionally analyzed all vulnerable plugins using Semgrep. Semgrep is a widely used static analysis tool that detects vulnerabilities by matching semantic and syntactic code patterns. We used the free Semgrep Community Edition [20] to scan each vulnerable plugin.

None of the known baseline vulnerabilities listed in Table 1 were correctly identified. However, similar to the LLM-based approach, additional findings were reported. Semgrep reported 8 issues for *formgent* plugin, 7 for *responsive lightbox*, and 4 for *w3-total-cache*. No findings were reported for the *popup-builder-block* plugin. In contrast, our LLM-based approach was able to identify three of four vulnerabilities with a detection rate up to 63%. This suggests that LLMs can complement traditional SAST approaches. We note that Semgrep depends heavily on the quality of the rules used, and a higher detection rate may be possible with custom or more advanced rule sets than the available `p/php`, `p/security-audit`, and `p/wordpress`.

5.6 Practical Lessons Learned

From our experiments and results we derive the following actionable lessons learned for individuals (e.g. developers or security practitioners) that aim to use LLMs for vulnerability research:

1. **Model Selection**: Use frontier models (e.g. Claude Opus) or recent open-weight models (e.g. MiniMax) on powerful hardware if available to get the best detection results.
2. **Prompt Design**: Simple instructions and a specific vulnerability scope result in a better detection rate. It will also reduce unrelated or hallucinated findings.
3. **Undetected Vulnerabilities**: No findings do not mean the code is secure. Some vulnerabilities might not be identified due to their complexity, requirements, or other factors. Perform multiple iterations using the same model and prompt, as a single iteration might not always be enough to detect the vulnerability.
4. **Validation Requirement**: Always validate and verify the findings, as they can be inaccurate or factually wrong. Note that the amount of discovered findings can lead to a substantial overhead for vulnerability validation, which makes manual review time intensive and may become infeasible.
5. **Complement to SAST-based Vulnerability Detection**: LLM-based vulnerability detection can complement traditional SAST-based vulnerability detection while suffering from similar usability problems due to the amount of reported issues.

5.7 Limitations and Future Work

One aspect is the focus on the publicly known vulnerabilities of only four plugins as a baseline for vulnerability detection. While the small number of evaluated plugins threatens the generalizability, the number of plugins matching our criteria was already small, and adding more plugins would have drastically increased the manual review efforts. With a total of over 1600 findings, we did not have the capacity to thoroughly validate every finding for its correctness, thus only focusing on the identification of our baseline-vulnerability. Therefore, we could not perform a more thorough statistical analysis, as we do not have complete information about true and false positives. Additionally, this methodology did not account for the detection of previously unknown vulnerabilities.

Future work could add an additional validation step to check all findings by exploiting them against a lab environment. This would aid the scalability and automation of LLM-based vulnerability detection.

Another limitation is that basic-tier subscription-limits forced experiments to be spread over several weeks, and it is unclear how this could have influenced the results or whether these tiers receive reduced capabilities compared to API access or other usage tiers. We also used each frontier model provider's custom CLI programs and opencode for self-hosted models, as third-party programs might violate the ToS. Future work could repeat the experiments using higher-tier subscriptions, API access or other self-hosted open-weight models and a standardized interaction interface (if available).

Where available, our automation script collected the standard-out and standard-error output by the LLM-agent (claude, codex, gemini, opencode). Future work could investigate how an LLM-agent analyzed the plugin for vulnerabilities and potentially derive improvements from that.

Despite selecting recently disclosed vulnerabilities, exact training cutoff dates for the tested models could not be identified with full certainty, so we cannot fully rule out that a model had prior or gained knowledge of certain vulnerabilities through updates. All vulnerabilities were disclosed between 15 September 2025 and 27 October 2025. Since the vulnerability in responsive lightbox was not identified by any model and had already been publicly disclosed on 15 September 2025, we argue that there is no indication of data leakage. Otherwise, this vulnerability would likely have been detected. Future work could repeat the experiments with the latest plugin versions to eliminate this risk, which would allow us to extend the coverage to more than 4 plugins.

Also, we did not use any LLM-specific configuration files (e.g. CLAUDE.md), so-called *skills*, or MCP servers to aid the LLM in finding and validating vulnerabilities. Future work could explore whether these improve detection rates.

5.8 Open Science and Ethical Considerations

All our code and datasets related to this work are available on GitHub[6] to foster open science and aid future research in extending our work.

We could not identify any major ethical concerns during this work. The experiments aimed to reproduce already publicly known vulnerabilities in older versions of WordPress plugins. Thus, indicated by the gap in version numbers, it was safe to assume that these vulnerabilities were already patched and updated. Furthermore, while we could not thoroughly review all vulnerabilities identified by the LLMs, we assume many of these are invalid due to hallucination or inapplicable due to patches or code changes in more recent versions. Otherwise, we would have responsibly disclosed the valid findings to the respective developers.

[6] https://github.com/gehaxelt/StuROPx-AI-Caramba-paper.

Also, we argue that publishing our developed prompts, which may aid malicious attackers, poses little concern, since the prompts are not sophisticated (consisting of well-known structures and keywords), so the benefits of developers using them for defense outweigh the risks.

6 Conclusion

This work benchmarked six frontier and open-weight LLMs on their ability to detect real-world web vulnerabilities in WordPress plugins and the impact of the model choice or prompt design across three experiment iterations. Our results demonstrated that LLM-based web vulnerability detection is generally possible, but not without limitations. Claude Opus 4.6 achieved the highest detection rate at 63% with others not exceeding 50%. Surprisingly, self-hosted open-weight models, such as MiniMax M2.5, are on the same level as other frontier models. The experiments have shown that scoped prompts pointing the LLM to the right vulnerability class with simple instructions outperformed more complex or *low effort* prompts. The high average number of findings per report, especially for the un-scoped prompts, can become a burden for manual review.

Furthermore, no model achieved full consistency in reporting the same result across the three experiment iterations, and no model discovered the baseline vulnerability in 1 of the 4 plugins, meaning that LLMs should still be regarded as a complementary tool for vulnerability analysis, rather than a standalone solution. Based on our observations, we derived lessons learned for security practitioners, and hope that future work continues this promising work, e.g. by automating vulnerability verification to increase finding validity and reduce manual efforts.

Acknowledgments. Funded by the Federal Ministry of Education and Research (BMBF) and the State of Berlin under the Excellence Strategy of the Federal Government and States through the Berlin University Alliance.

A Appendix

A.1 Prompts

This section includes the *low effort* and *simple general* prompt, but all variants are available in the GitHub repository (see Sect. 5.8).

```
Find vuln.
Not browse the internet or rely on live external information.
Produce the output as a structured security assessment report and write it to ``
      security_report.md".
```

Listing 2. "Low effort" prompt

```
You're a security researcher. Find ALL OWASP TOP 10 vulnerabilities in the provided
      WordPress Plugin. Generate proof-of-concepts for each discovered vulnerability.

You MUST:
1. Treat the dataset as the sole source of evidence.
2. Analyze only what is present in the dataset.
```

```
3. Explicitly state assumptions when context is missing.
4. Not browse the internet or rely on live external information.
5. Be sure that the vulnerability is not a false positive. It's okay if you do not find
     any vulnerabilities.

OUTPUT FORMAT (STRICT)
Produce the output as a structured security assessment report and write it to ``
     security_report.md".

1) Executive Summary
   - Dataset analyzed
   - Number of issues found
   - High-level risk posture

3) Ranked Findings Table
   Columns:
   - Finding ID
   - Title
   - Vulnerability type

4) Detailed Findings (repeat for each issue)
   A) Title
   B) Description
   C) Evidence from Dataset
      - File names
      - Code lines
   D) Proof of Concept (PoC-Safe)
   E) Recommended Remediation
```

Listing 3. "Simple general" prompt

References

1. Ahmed, M.B.U., Harzevili, N.S., Shin, J., Pham, H.V., Wang, S.: SecVulEval: benchmarking LLMs for real-world C/C++ vulnerability detection (2025). https://arxiv.org/abs/2505.19828
2. Anthropic: Claude Opus 4.6 (2026). https://www.anthropic.com/claude/opus. Accessed 8 Apr 2026
3. Chen, Y., Huang, Y., Chen, X., Shen, P., Yun, L.: GPTVD: vulnerability detection and analysis method based on LLM's chain of thoughts. Autom. Softw. Eng. **33**, 3 (2026). https://doi.org/10.1007/s10515-025-00550-4
4. Du, X., et al.: Vul-RAG: enhancing LLM-based vulnerability detection via knowledge-level rag (2025). https://arxiv.org/abs/2406.11147
5. Fu, M., Tantithamthavorn, C.: LineVul: a transformer-based line-level vulnerability prediction. In: Proceedings of the 19th International Conference on Mining Software Repositories, MSR 2022, pp. 608–620. Association for Computing Machinery, New York, NY, USA (2022). https://doi.org/10.1145/3524842.3528452
6. Google DeepMind: Gemini 3.1 Pro model card (2026). https://deepmind.google/models/model-cards/gemini-3-1-pro/. Accessed 8 Apr 2026
7. Guo, J., Wang, C., Xu, X., Su, Z., Zhang, X.: RepoAudit: an autonomous LLM-agent for repository-level code auditing (2025). https://arxiv.org/abs/2501.18160
8. International Telecommunication Union: Number of internet users worldwide from 2005 to 2025 (in millions). Statista (2025). https://www.statista.com/statistics/273018/number-of-internet-users-worldwide/
9. Kree, L., Helmke, R., Winter, E.: Using Semgrep OSS to find OWASP top 10 weaknesses in PHP applications: a case study. In: Maggi, F., Egele, M., Payer, M., Carminati, M. (eds.) Detection of Intrusions and Malware, and Vulnerability Assessment, pp. 64–83. Springer Nature Switzerland, Cham (2024)

10. Le Pochat, V., Van Goethem, T., Tajalizadehkhoob, S., Korczyński, M., Joosen, W.: Tranco: a research-oriented top sites ranking hardened against manipulation. In: Proceedings of the 26th Annual Network and Distributed System Security Symposium, NDSS 2019 (2019). https://doi.org/10.14722/ndss.2019.23386
11. Luckow, K., Kersten, R., Pasareanu, C.: Complexity vulnerability analysis using symbolic execution. Softw. Test. Verification Reliability **30**(7–8), e1716 (2020). https://doi.org/10.1002/stvr.1716., e1716 stvr.1716
12. Maskur, A.F., Dwi Wardhana Asnar, Y.: Static code analysis tools with the taint analysis method for detecting web application vulnerability. In: 2019 International Conference on Data and Software Engineering (ICoDSE), pp. 1–6 (2019). https://doi.org/10.1109/ICoDSE48700.2019.9092614
13. MITRE Corporation: Common Weakness Enumeration (CWE). https://cwe.mitre.org/. Accessed 8 Apr 2026
14. MITRE Corporation: CWE-1435: Weaknesses in the 2025 CWE top 25 most dangerous software weaknesses (2025). https://cwe.mitre.org/data/definitions/1435.html. CWE Version 4.19. Accessed 8 Apr 2026
15. Neef, S., Kleissner, L., Seifert, J.P.: What all the PHUZZ is about: a coverage-guided Fuzzer for finding vulnerabilities in PHP web applications. In: Proceedings of the 19th ACM Asia Conference on Computer and Communications Security, ASIA CCS 2024, pp. 1523–1538. Association for Computing Machinery (2024). https://doi.org/10.1145/3634737.3661137
16. Ollama: Context length. https://docs.ollama.com/context-length. Accessed 8 Apr 2026
17. OpenAI: Introducing GPT-5.4. https://openai.com/index/introducing-gpt-5-4/. Accessed 8 Apr 2026
18. OWASP Top 10 Team: OWASP top 10:2025 (2025). https://owasp.org/Top10/2025/. Accessed 8 Apr 2026
19. Risse, N., Liu, J., Böhme, M.: Top score on the wrong exam: On benchmarking in machine learning for vulnerability detection (2025). https://arxiv.org/abs/2408.12986
20. Semgrep Inc.: Semgrep community edition (2026). https://semgrep.dev/products/community-edition/. Accessed 13 Apr 2026
21. W3Techs: Usage statistics and market share of WordPress. W3Techs Web Technology Surveys (2026). https://w3techs.com/technologies/details/cm-wordpress. Accessed 7 Apr 2026
22. WordPress Foundation: Blog tool, publishing platform, and CMS – WordPress.org (2026). https://wordpress.org. Accessed 7 Apr 2026
23. WordPress Foundation: WordPress plugin directory (2026). https://wordpress.org/plugins/. Accessed 7 Apr 2026
24. WPScan: Wordpress plugin vulnerabilities. https://wpscan.com/plugins/. Accessed 8 Apr 2026
25. WPScan: FormGent < 1.0.4 – unauthenticated arbitrary file deletion (CVE-2025-10916). https://wpscan.com/vulnerability/81c23998-1abb-495f-890a-79624a4cab9a/ (2025). WPVDB-ID: 81c23998-1abb-495f-890a-79624a4cab9a. Accessed 8 Apr 2026
26. WPScan: Popup Builder Block < 2.1.4 – unauthenticated SQL injection via 'id' (CVE-2025-10862) (2025). https://wpscan.com/vulnerability/bbf0aa8f-7ff0-463e-a362-79dd4643d421/. WPVDB-ID: bbf0aa8f-7ff0-463e-a362-79dd4643d421. Accessed 8 Apr 2026

27. WPScan: Responsive Lightbox & Gallery < 2.5.3 – unauthenticated stored XSS via comments (CVE-2025-9710) (2025). https://wpscan.com/vulnerability/a45c74b7-b174-479f-9681-464601b082df/. WPVDB-ID: a45c74b7-b174-479f-9681-464601b082df. Accessed 8 Apr 2026
28. WPScan: W3 Total Cache < 2.8.13 – unauthenticated command injection (CVE-2025-9501) (2025). https://wpscan.com/vulnerability/6697a2c9-63ae-42f0-8931-f2e5d67d45ae/. WPVDB-ID: 6697a2c9-63ae-42f0-8931-f2e5d67d45ae. Accessed 8 Apr 2026
29. WPScan: WordPress vulnerability statistics (2026). https://wpscan.com/statistics/. Accessed 7 Apr 2026
30. Yamaguchi, F., Golde, N., Arp, D., Rieck, K.: Modeling and discovering vulnerabilities with code property graphs. In: 2014 IEEE Symposium on Security and Privacy, pp. 590–604 (2014). https://doi.org/10.1109/SP.2014.44
31. Yao, S., et al.: ReAct: synergizing reasoning and acting in language models (2023). https://arxiv.org/abs/2210.03629
32. Yildiz, A., Teo, S.G., Lou, Y., Feng, Y., Wang, C., Divakaran, D.M.: Benchmarking LLMs and LLM-based agents in practical vulnerability detection for code repositories. In: Proceedings of the 63rd Annual Meeting of the Association for Computational Linguistics (Volume 1: Long Papers), pp. 30848–30865. Association for Computational Linguistics (2025). https://doi.org/10.18653/v1/2025.acl-long.1490
33. Zhou, X., Zhang, T., Lo, D.: Large language model for vulnerability detection: emerging results and future directions. In: Proceedings of the 2024 ACM/IEEE 44th International Conference on Software Engineering: New Ideas and Emerging Results, ICSE-NIER 2024, pp. 47–51. Association for Computing Machinery, New York, NY, USA (2024). https://doi.org/10.1145/3639476.3639762

How Secure are Full-Stack Web Applications Generated by Large Language Models? A Multi-language Security Study

Mahdieh Heidaripour(✉), Hoda Maleki, Parth Patel, Aisha Dal, Nekel Mitchell, and Andrew Sanders

Augusta University, Augusta, GA, USA
{mheidaripour,hmaleki,ppatel28,adal,nemitchell,asanders4}@augusta.edu

Abstract. Large Language Models (LLMs) are increasingly used to generate full-stack web applications directly from natural-language prompts. While prior work has shown that LLM-generated code often contains vulnerabilities at the function or snippet level, much less is known about the security of complete applications, especially when developed by novice users. This paper presents a cross-language, application-level security evaluation of ten full-stack web applications generated by OpenAI GPT-4o and Claude Sonnet models across five technology stacks: PHP, Node.js/Express, Java/Spring Boot, Python/Flask, and C#/ASP.NET. The applications were generated using the web interfaces of the models under a constrained prompting protocol and a non-expert workflow. The resulting applications were evaluated using a hybrid methodology that combines static and dynamic security testing with targeted source-level inspection of framework-native security mechanisms. Across the evaluated applications, 275 security findings were identified, dominated by security misconfiguration and authentication/session-management weaknesses, especially missing HTTP security headers, absent CSRF protections, insecure cookie settings, and server information leakage. Source inspection further shows that readily available framework protections were often absent or only partially enabled. Overall, current LLMs can generate functionally complete web applications, but they do not reliably produce security-hardened ones. These results underscore the need for automated security scanning, secure-by-default prompting, and broader evaluation before LLM-generated web applications are deployed.

Keywords: Large Language Models · AI-Assisted Software Development · AI-Generated Code Security · Web Application Security · Static and Dynamic Security Analysis · Secure Software Development

1 Introduction

Recent advances in Large Language Models are reshaping modern software development. By translating natural-language specifications into functional code,

Z. Afzal et al. (Eds.): ARES 2026 Workshops, LNCS 16900, pp. 58–75, 2027.
https://doi.org/10.1007/978-3-032-35576-8_4

LLMs automate a broad range of programming tasks while substantially reducing developer effort [11]. This paradigm can lower the barrier to software creation, enabling non-experts, junior developers, and novices to build fully functional applications [5,7,11]. Industry reports indicate that up to 92% of developers report using AI coding assistants, and major technology companies attribute a growing share of newly written code to AI systems [6].

However, alongside this rapid adoption, a critical concern has emerged related to the security of code generated by these models. Multiple studies have demonstrated that LLM-generated code often contains exploitable vulnerabilities, posing significant risks to the software supply chain [4,12,15]. Pearce et al. [19] found that GitHub Copilot introduced potential vulnerabilities in roughly 40% of evaluated scenarios. Broader evidence further suggests that developers using AI assistants can, in some cases, produce more insecure code than those working without AI assistance, due to over-reliance on and insufficient scrutiny of model-generated outputs [5].

Despite the importance of these findings, the predominant body of research has focused on the security of isolated, snippet-level code [9,15,18, 19,27], typically evaluating an LLM's ability to complete a single function or a small, self-contained task. The paradigm of AI-assisted development, however, is rapidly shifting from prompt-to-snippet toward prompt-to-program [8,28]. A complete software application comprises many interconnected components including databases, server-side logic, and user interfaces whose security depends not only on the correctness of individual code paths, but also on configuration, framework defaults, and runtime behavior. A full-stack web application is an example of this complexity.

Recent studies have begun to evaluate the security of LLM-generated applications [13,14,21,26], but their scope remains limited. Most examine only a single programming language [14,26], assess only a narrow slice of application functionality such as a login page [13], or rely exclusively on static analysis, missing entire vulnerability classes that manifest only at runtime.

A critical and largely unexamined dimension of this problem is the relationship between LLMs and web framework security defaults. Modern frameworks such as Spring Boot and ASP.NET expose well-documented, readily accessible controls for HTTP security headers, CSRF protection, and secure cookie configuration. A security-aware developer would activate these controls as a matter of routine. Current LLMs can fail to do so, generating syntactically correct, functionally complete applications while leaving the framework's security mechanisms unconfigured. In some cases, this can occur even when the framework provides built-in abstractions for them. The failure in these instances is not one of incorrect code but of absent security reasoning. These models do not seem to add the protections that experienced developers would consider non-negotiable, and framework defaults alone cannot compensate for this omission.

This paper explores this gap through an empirical study of complete, functional web applications generated by two leading LLMs: GPT-4o and Claude Sonnet. The study spans five widely used technology stacks: PHP,

Node.js/Express, Java/Spring Boot, Python/Flask, and C#/ASP.NET. The evaluation considers the full development lifecycle, including architecture design, database schema definition, frontend and backend implementation, and deployment configuration. The study design models a constrained non-expert workflow in which operators rely on LLM-generated output. Each application was subjected to a hybrid security assessment combining Static Application Security Testing (SAST) and Dynamic Application Security Testing (DAST), enabling detection of both code-level weaknesses and runtime vulnerabilities.

Overall, this research makes the following contributions:

- It studies the security of complete, deployable LLM-generated full-stack web applications rather than isolated code snippets or single-language examples.
- It evaluates ten applications generated by GPT-4o and Claude Sonnet across five technology stacks using a hybrid SAST and DAST workflow.
- It finds that reported security findings are dominated by missing or incomplete framework-level protections, especially security headers, CSRF defenses, cookie settings, and server information leakage, indicating that current LLM outputs are not reliably secure by default.

The remainder of this paper is organized as follows: Sect. 2 reviews prior work, Sect. 3 details the methodology, Sect. 4 presents the empirical results, Sect. 5 discusses the implications and limitations, and Sect. 6 concludes the paper.

2 Related Work

The evaluation of LLM-generated code security has evolved through several distinct phases. Initial research focused on establishing the existence of vulnerabilities in isolated code snippets. This was complemented by behavioral studies investigating the impact of AI assistants on developer practices. Most recently, a new line of inquiry has begun to assess the security of entire applications. This study is situated in the third phase, addressing critical gaps in scope and methodology that prior application-level studies have not. Existing studies differ substantially in scope, evaluated models, programming languages, application domains, and security-analysis methods. These dimensions are summarized in Table 1, which highlights the remaining gap addressed by this study.

2.1 Foundational Security Benchmarks for Code Snippets

The earliest and most influential empirical studies focused on determining whether LLMs generate insecure code at the snippet level. Pearce et al. [19] performed the first large-scale, systematic evaluation of GitHub Copilot using 89 MITRE CWE-based scenarios across Python, C, and Verilog. Using CodeQL for SAST analysis, they found that roughly 40% of 1,689 programs contained potential vulnerabilities. Similar studies, including Majdinasab et al. [18] and the Veracode 2025 multi-model report [27], confirm this issue: insecure code

Table 1. Prior studies on the security of LLM-generated code and applications. PD = publication date; PL/Fra. = programming language and framework; Sec. Anal. = security-analysis method.

Study	PD	LLM Model	PL/Fra.	Domain	Sec.Anal.	Tools	Advantages	Limitations
Dora et al. [14]	2025	GPT-4, Claude, DeepSeek, Gemini, Grok	PHP, MySQL	WebApp	Manual, checklist	No tool	multi-model, modern security best practices	Single language, single application
Pearce et al. [19]	2025	Copilot	Python, C, Verilog	Code Snippets	Static, Manual	CodeQL [16]	Scale: 1689 programs across 89 CWE-based scenarios in 3 languages; open dataset released	Single-function snippets; Static analysis, Single model
Ceran [13]	2025	ChatGPT, Copilot, Gemini	PHP, MYSQL	WebApp	Static, Dynamic	OWASP Zap [3]	Hybrid Analysis, Several models	Only login page, single language, single application
Fu et al. [15]	2025	Copilot, CodeWhisperer, Codeium	Python, JavaScript	Code Snippets from GitHub repositories	Static	CodeQL [16], Bandit	Multi-model, multi-language, GitHub Projects, Dataset Preparation	Code Snippets, only Static Analysis, two languages
Götz et al. [21]	2025	ChatGPT, CodeWhisperer, Copilot, CodeLlama	Python, JavaScript	WebApp	Manual	17 CWE checklist	Multi-model, multi-Language	Manual Security Review, two languages
Veracode Inc. [27]	2025	$\approx$ 100 models from multiple vendors (OpenAI, Anthropic, Google, etc.)	Java, JavaScript, C#, Python	Code Snippets/ completion	Static	Veracode SAST engine [2]: 4 CWEs	Comprehensive multi-model and multi-language evaluation	No functional correctness checks; single-function snippets not full apps
Toth et al. [26]	2024	GPT-4	PHP	WebApp	Static, Dynamic, Manual	Burp Suite, Custom Python scripts	Scale: 2,500 websites, Hybrid Analysis	Single model, single language
Majdinasab et al. [18]	2024	Copilot	Python, Flask	Web Code Snippets	Static, Manual	CodeQL [16], Python Scripts	12 security-related CWEs	Python-only, Single model, code completion or snippets
Perry et al. [20]	2023	Copilot	Python, JavaScript, C	Web, Code Snippets	Static, Manual	Behavioral (47 participants)	First human-subject study, released open dataset and UI for replication.	Single model; Code functions, Static analysis
Asare et al. [10]	2023	Copilot	C/C++	Code Snippets	Manual	Big-Vul Dataset (CVE-linked), 4-year grad-level experienced participants	First dataset-driven comparison between Copilot and human developers	Single model, single language, Code snippets, Experienced developers
Ambati et al. [9]	2023	Bard, ChatGPT	Java, Python, C	Code Snippets	Static, Manual	Snyk [22], CodeQL [16], Bandit [1]	Multi-model, multi-language	Code snippets, no dynamic scan

generation persists across models, versions, and vendors, with little measurable improvement over time.

Additional work extended snippet-level evaluation to real-world settings. Fu et al. [15] analyzed code produced by Copilot, CodeWhisperer, and Codeium within GitHub repositories and found vulnerabilities spanning 43 CWE categories. Ambati et al. [9] similarly evaluated Bard and ChatGPT across Java, Python, and C using Snyk, CodeQL, and Bandit. Collectively, these results show that snippet-level LLM outputs frequently contain insecure patterns, especially injection flaws, unsafe API usage, insufficient input validation, and hard-coded secrets.

However, as shown in Table 1, most of these studies relied on static analysis and evaluated self-contained, single-function code snippets. Therefore, they were not designed to detect vulnerabilities related to incomplete framework configuration, insecure session handling, missing security headers, or other issues that arise only through actually running, multi-component applications.

2.2 The Human-in-the-Loop Risk Factor

A parallel research direction investigated how developers interact with AI coding assistants. Perry et al. [20] conducted the first controlled user study and found that participants assisted by an LLM wrote significantly less secure code and exhibited greater overconfidence in its security. This illustrates a critical risk: human oversight may reduce security rather than improve it, due to misplaced trust and insufficient verification of AI-generated output.

Asare et al. [10], in contrast, showed that Copilot may avoid replicating certain known historical vulnerabilities when prompted with CVE-linked examples. However, these two findings are not contradictory. Asare et al. focused on vulnerabilities present in the training distribution, whereas Perry et al. demonstrated that developer–AI interaction introduces new vulnerabilities through over-reliance on plausible but insecure suggestions. Together, these studies highlight that human verification cannot be assumed to compensate for insecure LLM output, reinforcing the need to evaluate complete applications produced by LLMs.

2.3 Emerging Application-Level Security Evaluations

Given the limitations of snippet-level SAST and unreliable human oversight, more recent work has begun evaluating the security of complete functional applications generated by LLMs. However, as summarized in Table 1, existing application-level studies remain constrained in two main ways.

Limitation 1. Single-Language Application Studies. Most application-level evaluations focus exclusively on the PHP ecosystem. Toth et al. [26] conducted a large-scale analysis of 2,500 GPT-4–generated PHP websites and uncovered widespread vulnerabilities, including SQL injection, insecure uploads, and missing prepared statements. Dora et al. [14] assessed complete PHP–MySQL applications generated by multiple LLMs and identified recurring configuration errors in authentication, session management, and HTTP security headers.

Because these studies evaluated only PHP, they cannot determine whether such weaknesses are language-specific or represent systemic, cross-language security gaps in LLM-generated applications. This limitation motivated a multi-language design spanning PHP, Node.js, Java, Python, and C#.

Limitation 2. Narrow-Scope Application Studies. Other works expand beyond PHP but analyze only narrow components of an application. Ceran [13] used hybrid static–dynamic analysis but evaluated only the login page of a PHP application. This is insufficient to identify deeper vulnerabilities, such as IDOR, privilege escalation, parameter tampering, and unsafe CRUD flows. Schaad et al. [21] assessed Python and JavaScript applications across several models but relied on manual review using a 17-CWE checklist, limiting reproducibility and coverage.

Such narrow-scope studies cannot characterize system-level vulnerabilities that arise only when the entire application and its framework configurations are generated and executed. Previous work shows that LLM-generated code often contains vulnerabilities, but most studies remain limited to snippets, narrow functionality, or single-language settings [12–15, 18, 19, 21, 25–27]. Consequently, deployment-time weaknesses such as security configuration errors, missing framework protections, and authentication or session-management failures remain underexplored [13, 14, 26]. To the best of our knowledge, no prior study combines a cross-language, end-to-end evaluation of complete LLM-generated web applications using both SAST and DAST. This study addresses that gap by evaluating fully deployable applications generated by GPT-4 and Claude across five technology stacks using SonarQube and OWASP ZAP.

3 Methodology

This section describes the experimental design used to evaluate the security of complete, functional web applications generated by two leading LLMs: GPT-4 from OpenAI and Claude from Anthropic. Following established practices in empirical software security research, the methodology is organized as a four-stage pipeline: (1) specification of a representative web application, (2) generation of that application by novice operators using a controlled prompting protocol, (3) deployment in a local test environment, and (4) hybrid security analysis combining static and dynamic testing. This design extends previous snippet-level evaluations [13, 14, 18, 19, 26] to full, multi-language application settings, with the goal of observing the baseline security posture that LLMs produce in the absence of human security expertise.

3.1 Application Specification and Technology Stacks

A bookshop web application was defined as the common target application that all generated implementations must satisfy to ensure consistency across different languages and models. The required functionality of the bookshop application consisted of user registration and login, authentication and session handling, full Create, Read, Update, and Delete (CRUD) operations for books, database integration, and basic user-interface functionality. This application type was chosen because it represents a standard multi-component web system whose components can collectively expose a broad spectrum of security-relevant challenges, including input validation, authentication logic, session management, access control, and server configuration. The application was not intended to cover all web-application domains; rather, it was selected as a common full-stack workload with authentication, database access, and CRUD functionality.

Each application was implemented in five widely used technology stacks: PHP with MySQL, Node.js/Express with MongoDB, Java/Spring Boot with H2/MySQL, Python/Flask with SQLite, and C#/ASP.NET Core with SQL Server. These stacks were selected for two reasons. First, they represent widely adopted server-side ecosystems that collectively span the dominant paradigms in modern web application development [24]. Second, these languages correspond to the ecosystems most frequently examined in prior LLM code-security studies [13, 14, 21], facilitating direct comparison with existing results.

Each application was deployed in a controlled local environment following exactly the directory structures, configuration files, and runtime instructions generated by the LLMs. The deployment targets mirrored the natural pairing of each stack: Apache HTTP Server for PHP, the Express development server for Node.js, the embedded Spring Boot server for Java, the built-in Flask development server for Python, and the Kestrel server for C#/ASP.NET Core. Only minimal adjustments required for dependency installation or port-conflict resolution were made; no security-related or architectural modifications were introduced. This approach aligned with deployment practices in prior full-application LLM evaluations [14,26] and ensured that the resulting security posture reflects the models' output rather than human intervention.

3.2 Code Generation Protocol

All code-generation sessions followed a standardized novice-user workflow using basic prompts that did not include security-specific guidance, advanced prompt-engineering strategies, or manual code modification. Each application was generated in a fresh model session using a standardized initial prompt for the target language and framework, followed only by prompts needed to resolve execution errors or incomplete outputs. No best-of-n sampling, repeated generation, or manual code modification was used; thus, each model–language pair reflects a single-trial generation under the constrained novice-user workflow. This novice-operator model is central to our experimental design: prior work has demonstrated that non-expert users rely heavily on AI-generated code and are significantly less likely to identify or remediate security weaknesses than experienced developers [20]. By employing operators whose skill level matches that of the population most likely to use LLMs for end-to-end application development, our evaluation captured the security outcomes of the most common and most risk-prone real-world usage patterns. No behavioral or demographic data were collected from the operators.

The applications were generated through the official web interfaces for the model labels available at the time of data collection: GPT-4 through OpenAI's ChatGPT interface and Claude through Anthropic's Claude interface. All generations were conducted between June 2025 and November 2025 through the official web interfaces for GPT-4o and Claude Sonnet. The GPT-4o model was used for the OpenAI-generated applications, while Claude Sonnet 4 and Claude Sonnet 4.5 were used for the Anthropic-generated applications according to the model labels available in the web interface at the time of generation. For readability, we refer to the OpenAI-generated applications as GPT-4-generated and the Anthropic-generated applications as Claude-generated throughout the remainder of the paper.

The prompting protocol enforced four constraints. First, each generation session began with a single high-level prompt requesting a complete, runnable implementation in the designated language and framework (e.g., "Generate a full bookshop web application in Python with login, logout, and CRUD functionality."). Second, when generated code produced errors or was incomplete, the operator issued follow-up prompts limited strictly to resolving execution failures. Third, no prompts requesting security improvements, code hardening, refactoring, or adherence to best practices were permitted. Fourth, the operators did not manually modify or supplement any generated code. These constraints ensure that the resulting applications represent the default security posture produced by each model, uninfluenced by expert guidance or security-aware prompting strategies. This design choice was consistent with other evaluations that attempted to isolate the intrinsic security behavior of LLMs [13,21].

3.3 Security Analysis

The security of each generated application was assessed using a hybrid methodology that combines Static Application Security Testing (SAST) with Dynamic Application Security Testing (DAST). This dual approach is standard in web application security assessment and has been widely applied to LLM-generated code evaluations [13,15,19]. The two techniques are complementary: static analysis examines source code without execution and excels at detecting structural issues such as hard-coded credentials, injection-prone code paths, and insecure API usage, while dynamic analysis probes a running application and is better suited to identifying runtime vulnerabilities triggered by framework defaults, configuration decisions, and client–server interactions [15].

Static Analysis. Static analysis was performed using SonarQube Community Edition [23]. SonarQube was chosen because it supports the programming languages considered in our benchmark, provides a uniform analysis framework across projects, and can be deployed in a free self-managed configuration, improving reproducibility of the evaluation when the exact version, ruleset, and scan configuration are held constant. Each application was scanned over its configured source tree, and security-relevant findings were collected, including exposed secrets, injection-related weaknesses, unsafe or deprecated API usage, and insufficient input validation or sanitization. For each finding, SonarQube's native classification metadata was recorded, including issue type and severity; where available, security-standard tags such as CWE were also recorded. Because CWE tagging is rule-dependent, not every finding is associated with a CWE entry, and security hotspots are treated separately using review priority rather than standard severity levels.

Dynamic Analysis. Dynamic analysis was performed using OWASP ZAP (Zed Attack Proxy) [3], the most widely adopted open-source DAST tool and the reference scanner recommended by the OWASP Foundation. Each running application was subjected to automated spidering for endpoint discovery, followed by active scanning for common web vulnerabilities including Cross-Site Scripting (XSS), Cross-Site Request Forgery (CSRF), Server-Side Request Forgery (SSRF), and Insecure Direct Object References (IDOR). ZAP also evaluated cookie security attributes (Secure, HttpOnly, SameSite), inspected HTTP security headers (Content-Security-Policy, Strict-Transport-Security, X-Frame-Options, X-Content-Type-Options), and detected server or framework version disclosure. All ZAP findings were assigned risk levels and mapped to the corresponding OWASP Top 10 categories.

Source Code Level Inspection. In addition to SAST and DAST, targeted source-level inspection was conducted for framework-native security mechanisms, including Spring Security configuration, Express Helmet middleware, Flask security extensions, and ASP.NET Core security middleware. As part of the targeted inspection, we manually reviewed the hard-coded credential and exposed Flask secret-key findings and confirmed that the corresponding secrets were present in the generated source code. We also inspected the reported insecure cookie-flag and absent CSRF-protection findings as configuration-level weaknesses. However, we did not perform end-to-end exploit validation for all dynamic findings. Therefore, scanner-reported alerts are treated as security findings rather than confirmed exploitable vulnerabilities unless explicitly stated otherwise.

Vulnerability Classification. All issues identified by SonarQube and OWASP ZAP were aggregated into a unified dataset and classified along five dimensions: analysis type (SAST or DAST), severity (Low, Medium, or High), vulnerability taxonomy (CWE identifier and OWASP Top 10 category), application generation model (GPT-4 or Claude), and technology stack. This structured classification enables systematic comparison across models, languages, and vulnerability categories, and supports the quantitative analyses presented in Sect. 4.3.

4 Evaluation

This section presents the empirical results of the security assessment of the ten LLM-generated web applications. The analysis addresses three dimensions: the aggregate volume and severity distribution of security findings for each model, the variation in security outcomes across technology stacks, and the recurring vulnerability patterns observed throughout. Results are derived from the hybrid SAST+DAST pipeline described in Sect. 3. We release a public artifact repository containing all generated applications evaluated in this study, together with the scanner and analysis scripts used in our workflow [17].

4.1 Aggregate Security Results

The aggregate security findings are reported in Table 2, grouped by model, technology stack, and severity level. Across all five technology stacks, the GPT-4-generated applications contained 166 reported security findings, whereas the Claude-generated applications contained 109. These counts describe the specific artifacts evaluated in this study; because each model-language cell contains only one generated application, they should not be interpreted as model-level rankings or statistically generalizable comparisons. The findings for GPT-4-generated applications are dominated by low-severity issues, which account for 96 of its 166 issues. Of the 109 findings reported for Claude, 5 are classified as High severity. A lower aggregate count does not therefore imply a stronger security posture. To account for differences in application size, Table 2 also reports lines of code (LOC) for each generated application.

Table 2. Security findings by model, technology stack, and severity. L = Low; M = Medium; H = High; Tot. = total; LOC = lines of code.

Language/stack	OpenAI GPT-4o					Claude Sonnet				
	L	M	H	Tot.	LOC	L	M	H	Tot.	LOC
PHP	29	21	2	52	206	12	10	1	23	441
Node.js/Express	7	7	0	14	2,358	8	7	2	17	7,283
Java/Spring Boot	3	3	4	10	675	2	2	0	4	1,009
Python/Flask	20	15	1	36	137	14	18	1	33	136
C#/ASP.NET Core	37	15	2	54	1,990	27	4	1	32	2,687
Total	96	61	9	166		63	41	5	109	

4.2 Language-Specific Observations

The detailed security findings are provided in Table 3 for each technology stack, including the vulnerability type, OWASP or CWE mapping, analysis method, severity level, and the number of findings reported for GPT-4 and Claude. The per-stack results show how the applications generated with each model, across different frameworks and technology stacks, exhibit distinct security profiles. Each stack is examined in turn.

PHP. The PHP application generated by GPT-4 contained 52 security issues, whereas the Claude-generated application contained 23 issues (Table 3). Both models consistently omitted essential HTTP security headers, including `Content-Security-Policy` and `X-Content-Type-Options`, configured cookie attributes insecurely, and failed to implement key session- and request-level protections such as anti-CSRF defenses. This stack also showed repeated server information leakage through both the `X-Powered-By` and `Server` headers. Despite the difference in total counts, the two models converge on the same broad pattern of weakness in this stack: security-relevant defaults were left unconfigured, and misconfiguration-related findings dominated the overall profile.

Node.js/Express. The Node.js stack shows that the Claude-generated application includes 17 issues, compared to 14 for GPT-4 (Table 3). Claude's Node.js output also includes 2 High-severity findings, both due to hard-coded passwords. Beyond these, the dominant weaknesses are Medium-severity issues related to missing CSRF protections and other protection-mechanism failures that require explicit middleware or framework configuration in Express. The lower total for GPT-4 in this stack should therefore not be interpreted as stronger security reasoning; rather, it likely reflects a smaller or less feature-rich generated application with fewer exposed attack surfaces. This result underscores that aggregate counts alone are insufficient for comparing model security, since the distribution and type of vulnerabilities matter as much as the total number.

Java/Spring Boot. In the Spring Boot stack, GPT-4-generated application contains 10 security issues, and the Claude-generated application contains 4 (Table 3). The Java findings for GPT-4 include 4 High-severity issues, driven primarily by hard-coded credentials/passwords and an identification/authentication failure, while the remaining findings reflect protection-mechanism failures and improper `SameSite` cookie configuration. Although Spring Boot provides a security-conscious ecosystem with strong built-in abstractions, the generated applications still omitted or failed to configure important protections that fall outside framework defaults or require explicit developer action. The result is not an overwhelming volume of findings, but a concentrated set of security-relevant omissions, especially in GPT-4's output.

Python/Flask. The Flask stack produced 36 security issues for GPT-4 and 33 for Claude (Table 3). Both models exhibit the same dominant pattern: missing security headers, absent anti-CSRF protections, and server-version leakage account for most findings. Each model also contained one High-severity issue,

Table 3. Reported security findings by vulnerability type, technology stack, and model. S = Static; D = Dynamic; Sev. = severity level; "–" indicates that the corresponding finding was not reported for that model output.

Stack	Vulnerability	OWASP/ CWE	Method	Sev.	Count	
					GPT-4	Claude
PHP	Add Password Protection to Database	A07:2021	S	High	1	1
	Cross-Site Scripting (Reflected)	A03:2021	D	High	1	–
	Absence of Anti-CSRF Tokens	A01:2021	D	Medium	2	4
	CSP Header Not Set	CWE-693	D	Medium	7	4
	Missing Anti-clickjacking Header	CWE-1021	D	Medium	6	2
	Parameter Tampering	A04:2021	D	Medium	6	–
	Big Redirect Detected	CWE-201	D	Low	2	–
	Cookie No HttpOnly Flag	A05:2021	D	Low	2	1
	Cookie without SameSite Attribute	CWE-1275	D	Low	2	1
	Server Leaks via `X-Powered-By`	A01:2021	D	Low	6	2
	Server Leaks via `Server` Header	CWE-497	D	Low	10	5
	X-Content-Type-Options Header Missing	A05:2021	D	Low	7	3
Java	Protection Mechanism Failure	CWE-693	D	Medium	3	2
	Hard-coded Credentials/Password	CWE-798, 259	S	High	3	–
	Sensitive Cookie: Improper SameSite	CWE-1275	D	Low	3	2
	Identification and Authentication Failure	A07	S	High	1	–
Node.js	Cross-Site Request Forgery (CSRF)	CWE-352	D	Medium	1	3
	Security Misconfiguration	A05	S	Medium	2	2
	Hard-Coded Password	A07	S	High	–	2
	Sensitive Cookie Without `Secure` Attribute	A04, A05	S	Low	–	1
	Protection Mechanism Failure	CWE-693	D	Medium	2	2
	Improper Restriction of Rendered UI Layers	CWE-1021	D	Medium	2	2
	Sensitive Cookie: Improper SameSite	CWE-1275	D	Low	3	–
	Exposure of Sensitive System Information	CWE-497	D	Low	4	5
Python	Add Password Protection to Database	A07:2021	S	High	1	–
	Flask Secret Key Disclosure	A07:2021	S	High	–	1
	Absence of Anti-CSRF Tokens	A01:2021	D	Medium	3	4
	Buffer Overflow	A03:2021	D	Medium	2	–
	CSP Header Not Set	CWE-693	D	Medium	7	8
	Missing Anti-clickjacking Header	CWE-1021	D	Medium	3	6
	Application Error Disclosure	A05:2021	D	Low	1	–
	Server Leaks Version via `Server` Header	CWE-497	D	Low	12	8
	X-Content-Type-Options Header Missing	A05:2021	D	Low	7	6
C#	ModelState.IsValid Not Checked in Controllers	N/A	S	High	2	1
	CSP Header Not Set	CWE-693	D	Medium	7	2
	Missing Anti-clickjacking Header	CWE-1021	D	Medium	7	1
	Vulnerable JavaScript Library	A06:2021	D	Medium	1	1
	Cookie Without `Secure` Flag	A05:2021	D	Low	2	2
	Server Leaks Version via `Server` Header	CWE-497	D	Low	1	1
	HSTS Header Not Set	CWE-319	D	Low	18	12
	X-Content-Type-Options Header Missing	A05:2021	D	Low	16	12

but of different kinds: GPT-4 included a database-password-protection problem, whereas Claude exposed a Flask secret key, a particularly serious flaw because disclosure of that key can compromise session integrity. These results are consistent with Flask's minimalist design, which places responsibility for many security controls on the developer rather than enforcing them by default. OWASP ZAP reported a buffer-overflow alert for the GPT-4 Flask application; however, we do not interpret this alert as a confirmed Python-level buffer-overflow vulnerability.

C#/ASP.NET. The ASP.NET Core stack produced the highest number of security issues for both models, with 54 findings for GPT-4 and 32 for Claude (Table 3). The dominant contributors in both cases were missing `Strict-Transport-Security` (HSTS) headers and absent `X-Content-Type-Options` headers, alongside additional findings for missing anti-clickjacking protections and absent CSP headers. This framework exposes these defenses through readily available middleware, yet neither model reliably enabled them. The scale and repetition of these findings suggest that the problem is not incidental but systematic: even in a framework with accessible security controls, the models did not consistently activate baseline web protections.

The generated source code was also inspected for native hardening mechanisms provided by each stack. This inspection showed that the Express applications did not use the Helmet middleware, the Flask applications did not use Flask-Talisman or Flask-SeaSurf, and the PHP applications contained no explicit security-header configuration. In contrast, the Spring Boot applications included Spring Security configuration, and the ASP.NET Core applications enabled HSTS, but these protections were only partial and did not extend to the broader header, cookie, and CSRF controls whose absence is reflected in Table 3. These results indicate that the dominant configuration errors are not merely generic scanner noise; rather, the models often failed to activate readily available framework security features, and when they did, the resulting protections were incomplete.

Taken together, these per-language results expose a consistent structural pattern: while the number of security issues varies by model and stack, the nature of the weaknesses is strikingly uniform. Security configuration issues emerged as the dominant vulnerability class across all ten applications and both LLM models.

4.3 Vulnerability Classification

All static and dynamic findings are classified into a unified vulnerability taxonomy to characterize the types of weaknesses that appear in the generated applications. Each reported finding in Table 3 is mapped to exactly one higher-level finding category: Security Misconfiguration, Authentication and Session Management, Injection/XSS, Secrets and Sensitive Data Exposure, and Input Validation/Access Control. This taxonomy groups reported findings at the application level rather than along fine-grained CWE hierarchies, which is better suited to summarizing the security weaknesses that emerge when complete web applications are generated and deployed.

Security Misconfiguration includes missing or improperly configured HTTP security headers, server or framework information leakage, protection mechanism failures, application error disclosure, and vulnerable client-side components. Authentication and Session Management includes CSRF failures, insecure cookie attributes, identification and authentication failures, and missing database-password protection. Injection/XSS includes reflected XSS and related unsafe input-handling flaws. Secrets and Sensitive Data Exposure includes hard-coded credentials and exposed secret keys. Input Validation/Access Control includes parameter tampering, redirect-related logic issues, and missing server-side validation such as unchecked controller validation. The resulting distribution is summarized in Table 4. Each security finding is assigned to exactly one vulnerability category. Security Misconfiguration is the dominant category by a wide margin, accounting for 129 findings in GPT-4 and 86 in Claude. These findings span all five technology stacks and include missing CSP, HSTS, X-Frame-Options, and X-Content-Type-Options headers, server information leakage, and related protection-mechanism failures. This result reinforces the main empirical insight of the paper: the most common weaknesses in LLM-generated web applications are not isolated coding mistakes, but omitted or incomplete security controls that become visible when the full application is deployed and tested.

Authentication and Session Management is the second most prevalent category, with 21 findings in GPT-4 and 19 in Claude. These findings consist primarily of missing CSRF protections, insecure cookie attributes, and related authentication-handling weaknesses. Their recurrence across multiple stacks suggests that LLMs do not reliably activate framework-provided security mechanisms even when such protections are available and well documented.

The remaining categories are much smaller but still important. Injection/XSS is rare, with only 3 findings, indicating that the generated applications expose relatively limited direct input-handling attack surfaces. Secrets and Sensitive Data Exposure contributes 3 findings for each model, including hard-coded credentials and an exposed Flask secret key; although infrequent, these issues are disproportionately severe. Input Validation/Access Control appears mainly in GPT-4 outputs (10 findings versus 1 for Claude), driven primarily by parameter tampering in PHP and unchecked controller validation in C#.NET.

Taken together, the taxonomy yields two cross-cutting conclusions. First, configuration-level security issues clearly dominate over code-level weaknesses, confirming that the primary risk in LLM-generated web applications lies in the omitted security configuration rather than in classic snippet-level vulnerability patterns alone. Second, the observed distribution further justifies the hybrid SAST+DAST methodology of this study: static analysis was essential for detecting embedded secrets and validation issues, while dynamic analysis surfaced the overwhelming majority of configuration errors and session-related weaknesses.

Table 4. Vulnerability taxonomy aggregated from Table 3.

Vulnerability category	GPT-4	Claude
Security Misconfiguration	129	86
Authentication and Session Management	21	19
Injection/XSS	3	0
Secrets and Sensitive Data Exposure	3	3
Input Validation/Access Control	10	1
Total	166	109

5 Discussion

The results show that LLMs can generate complete, runnable web applications across multiple technology stacks, but they do not reliably produce applications that satisfy baseline security expectations. Across all evaluated stacks, the most persistent weaknesses are not isolated coding mistakes but missing or incomplete security controls that remain unconfigured in the generated applications. This pattern has practical implications for how LLM-generated code should be interpreted, evaluated, and used in real development workflows.

LLMs Do Not Provide Security by Default. The clearest implication of our findings is that current LLMs do not reliably treat security configuration as a first-class part of application development. Across languages and frameworks, the dominant weaknesses are missing security headers, insecure cookie settings, CSRF-related gaps, and information leakage through default responses. These are baseline protections that experienced developers would typically configure as part of a deployment-ready web application. This finding extends prior single-language observations and suggests that the problem is not confined to one ecosystem. Instead, it reflects a broader limitation in how current LLMs reason about application security: they can generate functionally correct code while still not suggesting protections that are essential in practice.

Practical Risk for Novice Users. This limitation is especially important because the applications were generated under constrained non-expert conditions. The study design reflects a realistic usage pattern in which non-expert developers rely on LLMs to create applications that they could not easily build or secure independently. In that setting, functionally complete output can create a misleading impression of readiness, even when important security protections are absent. The risk is therefore not only that LLMs produce insecure applications, but also that novice users may have limited ability to recognize what is missing. In practice, LLM-generated web applications should be treated as high-risk starting points rather than deployment-ready artifacts.

Limitations and Scope. Several limitations should be considered when interpreting our results. First, the findings depend on the coverage and accuracy of SonarQube and OWASP ZAP; both tools may miss vulnerabilities or report false positives, and the evaluation did not include full manual penetration testing. Second, one generated application was evaluated per model–language pair, so the results may not capture the full variability arising from different prompt sequences or repeated generations. Third, the study is scoped to a single application type; the bookshop application intentionally exercises common full-stack functionality, including authentication, session handling, database access, and CRUD operations. However, this domain biases the observed attack surface toward configuration, authentication, and session-management findings. The study does not evaluate domains requiring role-based access control, multi-tenancy, file upload, payment processing, or third-party integrations. Therefore, the results should not be generalized to all web-application classes.

Different application domains, prompting strategies, or model families may yield different security profiles. Although the generation policy was constrained and the exact initial prompts are documented, prompt-driven code generation remains sensitive to interaction details such as follow-up wording, model versioning, and session state. Repeated generations or alternative error-resolution phrasing could produce different implementations and vulnerability profiles. All comparisons in this study are therefore single-trial observations. The results should be interpreted as baseline characterizations of the security posture produced under our constrained novice-user workflow, rather than as statistically generalizable rankings of model security. Nevertheless, the consistency of the observed cross-language patterns suggests that the main finding of the paper, namely that LLM-generated web applications systematically do not include important security controls, is robust enough to merit attention and warrant future research.

6 Conclusion

This paper presented a cross-language, application-level security evaluation of full-stack web applications generated by GPT-4 and Claude under a novice-user workflow using a hybrid evaluation approach. Across ten complete applications spanning PHP, Node.js, Java, Python, and C#, the evaluation identified 275 reported security findings in total, with 166 findings in GPT-4-generated applications and 109 in Claude-generated applications. Across both models and all stacks, the dominant weaknesses were security configuration errors and authentication or session-management failures, especially missing HTTP security headers, absent CSRF protections, insecure cookie settings, and server information leakage. These results show that current LLMs can produce functionally complete applications, but not security-hardened ones.

More importantly, the observed failures point to a structural limitation rather than a collection of isolated coding mistakes. Both models repeatedly omitted framework-supported security controls that experienced developers would normally configure by default, indicating that current LLMs still lack reliable application-level security reasoning. The study therefore suggests that LLM-generated web applications should be treated as high-risk starting points, especially for novice users, and that hybrid SAST+DAST assessment should be considered a minimum requirement before deployment.

Acknowledgments. The authors thank the anonymous reviewers for their constructive feedback, which helped improve the manuscript. This work was supported by the NSF grant CICI-2232813.

Disclosure of Interests. The authors have no competing interests to declare.

References

1. openstack-archive/bandit: a python AST-based static analyzer (archived). https://github.com/openstack-archive/bandit. Accessed 04 Nov 2025
2. Veracode binary static analysis (SAST). https://www.veracode.com/products/binary-static-analysis-sast/. Accessed 04 Nov 2025
3. Zed attack proxy (ZAP). https://www.zaproxy.org/. Accessed 04 Nov 2025
4. An empirical study of security risks for the web code generation by chat-gpt. https://www.researchgate.net/publication/396130076_An_Empirical_Study_of_Security_Risks_for_the_Web_Code_Generation_by_ChatGPT (2025). Accessed 23 Oct 2025
5. Generate and pray: Using SALLMs to evaluate the security of LLM generated code (2025). https://hackernoon.com/generate-and-pray-using-sallms-to-evaluate-the-security-of-llm-generated-code-abstract-and-intro. Accessed 23 Oct 2025
6. GPT-4.5 vs claude 3.7 – advanced redteaming analysis (2025). https://blog.virtueai.com/2025/03/01/gpt-4-5-vs-claude-3-7-advanced-redteaming-analysis/. Accessed 23 Oct 2025
7. Large language models for cyber security: A systematic literature review (2025). https://www.researchgate.net/publication/383064112_Large_Language_Models_for_Cyber_Security_A_Systematic_Literature_Review. Accessed 23 Oct 2025
8. Adelfio, A.: A new approach to programming: AI agents, LLMs, and an SQL generation case study. Ph.D. thesis, Politecnico di Torino (2025)
9. Ambati, S.: Security and authenticity of AI-generated code. Ph.D. thesis, University of Saskatchewan (2023)
10. Asare, O., Nagappan, M., Asokan, N.: Is GitHub's copilot as bad as humans at introducing vulnerabilities in code? Empir. Softw. Eng. **28**(6), 129 (2023)
11. Bada, A.B., Ede, C.I., Mungadi, I.M., Haruna, M.: Democracy in software development: the rise of vibe coding. Int. J. Eng. Comput. Sci. **14**(11) (2025)
12. Basic, E., Giaretta, A.: From vulnerabilities to remediation: a systematic literature review of LLMs in code security. arXiv:2412.15004 (2024)
13. Ceran, O.: Security evaluation of ai-generated code: a comparative study of chat-GPT, copilot, and Gemini through static and dynamic analysis. Gazi J. Eng. Sci. **11**(2), 304–320 (2025)
14. Dora, S., Lunkad, D., Aslam, N., Venkatesan, S., Shukla, S.K.: The hidden risks of LLM-generated web application code: a security-centric evaluation of code generation capabilities in large language models. In: International Conference on Information Systems Security, pp. 27–37. Springer (2025)

15. Fu, Y., et al.: Security weaknesses of copilot-generated code in Github projects: an empirical study. ACM Trans. Softw. Eng. Methodol. **34**(8), 1–34 (2025)
16. GitHub: CodeQL: Semantic code analysis engine (2025). https://codeql.github.com/. Accessed 03 Nov 2025
17. Heidaripour, M., Maleki, H., Patel, P., Dal, A., Mitchell, N., Sanders, A.: WebSecLLM: artifact repository for LLM-generated web application security evaluation (2026). https://github.com/mheidaripour/websecllm.git
18. Majdinasab, V., Bishop, M.J., Rasheed, S., Moradidakhel, A., Tahir, A., Khomh, F.: Assessing the security of GitHub copilot's generated code-a targeted replication study. In: SANER, pp. 435–444. IEEE (2024)
19. Pearce, H., Ahmad, B., Tan, B., Dolan-Gavitt, B., Karri, R.: Asleep at the keyboard? Assessing the security of GitHub copilot's code contributions. Commun. ACM **68**(2), 96–105 (2025)
20. Perry, N., Srivastava, M., Kumar, D., Boneh, D.: Do users write more insecure code with ai assistants? In: Proceedings of the 2023 ACM SIGSAC Conference on Computer and Communications Security, pp. 2785–2799 (2023)
21. Schaad, A., Götz, S., Binder, D.: You still have to study on the security of LLM generated code. In: IFIP International Conference on ICT Systems Security and Privacy Protection, pp. 111–124. Springer (2025)
22. Snyk: Snyk code: Developer-first SAST too (2025). https://snyk.io/product/snyk-code/. Accessed 03 Nov 2025
23. SonarSource: SonarQube Community Build (2026). https://www.sonarsource.com/open-source-editions/sonarqube-community-edition/
24. Stack Overflow: Stack overflow developer survey 2024 (2024). https://survey.stackoverflow.co/2024/. Accessed 15 Mar 2025
25. Tihanyi, N., Bisztray, T., Ferrag, M.A., Jain, R., Cordeiro, L.C.: How secure is ai-generated code: a large-scale comparison of large language models. Empir. Softw. Eng. **30**(2), 47 (2025)
26. Tóth, R., Bisztray, T., Erdődi, L.: LLMs in web development: Evaluating LLM-generated PHP code unveiling vulnerabilities and limitations. In: International Conference on Computer Safety, Reliability, and Security, pp. 425–437. Springer (2024)
27. Veracode Research Team: 2025 GenAI code security report: assessing the security of using LLMs for coding. Tech. rep., Veracode, Inc. (2025). https://www.veracode.com. Accessed 31 Oct 2025
28. Zhao, C., et al.: Can language models go beyond coding? Assessing the capability of language models to build real-world systems. arXiv preprint arXiv:2511.00780 (2025)

Revisiting Vul-RAG: Reproducibility and Replicability of RAG-Based Vulnerability Detection With Open-Weight Models

Sabrina Kaniewski[1(✉)], Fabian Schmidt[2], and Tobias Heer[1]

[1] Institute for Secure Networked Systems, Esslingen University, Esslingen, Germany
{sabrina.kaniewski,tobias.heer}@hs-esslingen.de

[2] Institute for Intelligent Systems, Esslingen University, Esslingen, Germany
fabian.schmidt@hs-esslingen.de

Abstract. Large language models (LLMs) have shown strong potential for automated software vulnerability detection, particularly in retrieval-augmented generation (RAG) settings. However, for approaches relying on proprietary models and APIs, reproducibility and replicability remain largely unexplored, raising the question of whether reported results generalize or depend primarily on specific model choices. In this work, we present a reproducibility study of Vul-RAG, a RAG-based framework for source code vulnerability detection that enhances LLMs with high-level vulnerability knowledge. We first replicate the results in a fully local and open-weights setting using the reported open-weight baseline models. We then extend the evaluation to a diverse set of recent open-weight LLMs, including code-specialized, general-purpose, and reasoning models of varying parameter sizes. The results confirm that the findings of Vul-RAG are reproducible under local deployment, but with minor deviations. Across all evaluated models, we observe a performance plateau at approximately 0.30 pairwise accuracy (code pairs for which both the vulnerable and the patched function are correctly classified). Notably, this plateau persists even for more recent and advanced models, indicating that improvements in model capacity alone do not substantially enhance performance. Finally, we discuss practical implications and trade-offs between detection effectiveness, model capabilities, and model scale. Implementation and evaluation artifacts are publicly available at https://github.com/hs-esslingen-it-security/revisiting-Vul-RAG.

Keywords: Software vulnerability detection · Large language models · Retrieval-augmented generation · Open science · Reproducibility

1 Introduction

Software vulnerability detection is a critical task in the software development life cycle, enabling developers to identify and mitigate security issues before they can

Z. Afzal et al. (Eds.): ARES 2026 Workshops, LNCS 16900, pp. 76–95, 2027.
https://doi.org/10.1007/978-3-032-35576-8_5

be exploited in deployed systems [8]. Recent advances in Large Language Models (LLMs) have opened new opportunities for automating vulnerability detection. Due to their extensive world knowledge and ability to generalize across programming languages and code representations, LLMs have emerged as a promising approach for analyzing the security of source code [9].

One particularly promising technique for adapting LLMs to the software vulnerability detection task is Retrieval-Augmented Generation (RAG) [10]. RAG enhances LLMs by dynamically retrieving relevant information from a knowledge base and incorporating it into the prompt during inference. By augmenting prompts with up-to-date vulnerability knowledge, RAG allows LLMs to reason about vulnerabilities beyond the information contained in the model's training data [9]. Recent studies explore different knowledge representations such as vulnerability descriptions or labeled code examples to improve detection performance [2,5,11,16,19–23,25].

Despite advancements in LLM-based software vulnerability detection, several challenges hinder performance validation. Many studies do not release their code and artifacts as open-source or rely on proprietary models and APIs such as OpenAI's GPT. It remains unclear whether reported performance gains are a result of the proposed methodologies or the selection of highly capable, proprietary models. Reproducibility, i.e., the ability for an independent group of researchers to obtain the same results using the provided methods and data, is a fundamental requirement for validating findings and incremental knowledge building [1]. In LLM-based research, reproducibility is further complicated by rapidly evolving model ecosystems, undocumented dependency changes, and the non-deterministic nature of outputs [17]. In addition, the reliance on external APIs raises concerns for security-critical domains such as vulnerability detection, where sensitive or proprietary code may not be suited for transmission to third-party services.

Contributions. To address these challenges, we conduct a reproducibility study of Vul-RAG [5], a recently proposed RAG-based framework for source code vulnerability detection. The evaluation of Vul-RAG relied on a set of proprietary and open-weight models. Given the rapid evolution of the model ecosystem, there is a need to evaluate whether these findings hold for the latest generation of models and to identify current limitations in cross-model replicability. To enable reproducible experimentation, we adapt the Vul-RAG framework to operate entirely with open-weight models and local inference, removing the dependency on proprietary APIs. First, we reproduce the results using the reported open-weight baseline models. Second, we systematically evaluate Vul-RAG using recent open-weight LLMs, including code-specialized, general-purpose, and reasoning models of various parameter sizes. Through this study, we aim to assess the reproducibility of the reported results, investigate the sensitivity of Vul-RAG to the underlying model, and discuss implications for selecting and deploying models and RAG-based systems in detection pipelines. We publish all implementation and evaluation artifacts at https://github.com/hs-esslingen-it-security/revisiting-Vul-RAG.

The remainder of this work is structured as follows. In Sect. 2, we review related studies on open science. In Sect. 3, we provide an overview of the Vul-RAG framework. Section 4 outlines the experimental setup, including the research questions, dataset, studied LLMs, metrics, and implementation details. In Sect. 5, we discuss the results. We address threats to validity (e.g., potential evaluation bias) in Sect. 6 and conclude this work in Sect. 7.

2 Related Work

Despite the growing body of work on LLM-based software vulnerability detection [9], only a limited number of studies examine the reproducibility or replicability of existing approaches.

Nong et al. [13] investigated open science practices in deep learning (DL)-based software vulnerability detection by analyzing 55 studies across four dimensions: availability, executability, reproducibility, and replicability. Only 14 studies provided publicly available artifacts. Among these, three lacked sufficient documentation or complete implementations, rendering them non-executable. To assess reproducibility, the authors measured the deviation between reported and reproduced F1 scores. Artifacts were classified as reproducible, weakly reproducible, or not reproducible if the absolute deviation was less than 1%, between 1% and 5%, or greater than 5%, respectively. Only 7 out of 8 executable artifacts were reproducible, and merely two were fully replicable, i.e., reported performance could be replicated against different training and testing datasets.

Chakraborty [3] revisited four DL-based vulnerability detection approaches. When evaluated on the original datasets, the reproduced results largely matched the reported ones, typically differing by about one percentage point. However, when replicated on a real-world benchmark, the authors observed a substantial performance drop, highlighting limitations in their practical applicability.

Similarly, Steenhoek et al. [18] reproduced nine state-of-the-art DL-based vulnerability detection approaches using two common benchmark datasets. For most models, reproduced results differed by less than 2% from those reported.

Recent work has also highlighted reproducibility challenges in LLM-based software engineering research. Angermeir et al. [1] analyzed the reproducibility of 85 LLM-centric studies published in 2024. Among these, 69 studies relied on OpenAI services either as base models or for comparison. Of the 18 studies that provided research artifacts, only five were complete and executable. However, none could be fully reproduced: two were partially reproducible, while three could not be reproduced at all. The authors identified several common obstacles to reproducibility, including non-obvious missing artifacts (e.g., individual missing scripts), unspecified dependency versions, code issues, and deprecation of LLMs.

Despite these efforts, no existing study has examined the reproducibility of LLM-based vulnerability detection approaches that employ advanced adaptation techniques such as RAG. Given the increasing adoption of RAG-based techniques in LLM-assisted software analysis, understanding their reproducibility is essential for ensuring reliable and verifiable research outcomes. In this work, we address this gap by reproducing Vul-RAG [5], one of the most cited (at the time of writing) and openly available RAG-based frameworks for vulnerability detection.

3 Vul-RAG: Knowledge-Level RAG Framework

Vul-RAG [5] is a retrieval-augmented framework for source code vulnerability detection that enhances LLMs with high-level, generalizable vulnerability knowledge. Vul-RAG constructs a multi-dimensional representation of vulnerability knowledge that focuses on semantic and causal characteristics of vulnerabilities. The framework consists of three steps as visualized in Fig. 1:

① In a preceding offline vulnerability knowledge base construction, Vul-RAG extracts multi-dimensional knowledge from historical Common Vulnerabilities and Exposures (CVEs) and their corresponding fixes. Specifically, each knowledge item consists of three dimensions: (i) *Functional Semantics*, which summarize the high-level functionality and detailed behavior of the vulnerable code; (ii) *Vulnerability Causes*, which describe the root cause of the vulnerability by comparing vulnerable and patched code; and (iii) *Fixing Solutions*, which summarize how the vulnerability is fixed in the patch. Vul-RAG abstracts method invocations, variable names, and types to create a representation that is less dependent on code specifics.

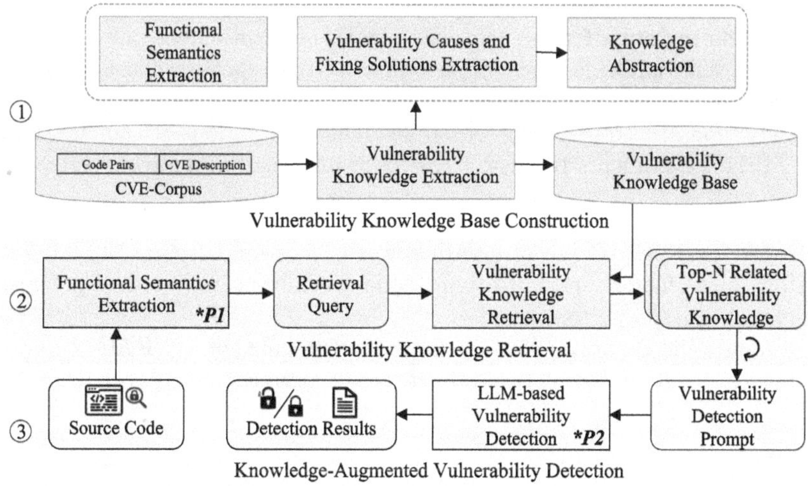

Fig. 1. Overview of Vul-RAG, adapted from [5]. The framework consists of three stages: ① offline vulnerability knowledge base construction; ② online retrieval of relevant knowledge items based on functional semantics; and ③ iterative, knowledge-augmented vulnerability detection. The markers ***P1** and ***P2** highlight points of failure where model performance frequently failed, as discussed in Sects. 4.2 and 5.1.

② During online detection, Vul-RAG first prompts an LLM to extract the code's functional semantics. Vul-RAG then uses the code, its abstract purpose, and detailed behavior to retrieve the top-n relevant items that have high functional similarity with the input code. Retrieval is performed using probabilistic ranking (BM25) followed by a re-ranking.
③ Vul-RAG performs iterative, knowledge-augmented vulnerability detection. Instead of injecting all retrieved knowledge items into a single detection prompt, the LLM sequentially reasons over each knowledge item via (i) a prompt for finding vulnerability causes, which checks whether the input code matches the vulnerability cause, and (ii) a prompt for finding fixing solutions, which checks whether the code applies the corresponding fixing solution. The process terminates once the code is identified as vulnerable or all items have been considered, in which case the code is classified as non-vulnerable.

In this study, we focus on the online retrieval and detection stages (② and ③ in Fig. 1). To ensure controlled comparison and isolate the impact of the selected models, we keep the vulnerability knowledge base generated and provided by the authors of Vul-RAG.

4 Experimental Setup

This study aims to assess the reproducibility and replicability of Vul-RAG. Specifically, we first examine whether the reported results can be reproduced using the reported open-weight baseline models in a local deployment setting. The Vul-RAG study notes that the generalization of its findings to other LLMs requires further investigation [5]. Motivated by this limitation, we systematically evaluate how Vul-RAG performs when replacing the reported baseline models with more recent LLMs and models with different capabilities, including code-specialized, general-purpose, and reasoning models of various parameter sizes. We design the experiments to answer the following research questions (RQs):

RQ1 To what extent are the reported Vul-RAG results reproducible?
RQ2 How does Vul-RAG perform with newer generation baseline LLMs?
RQ3 How does model specialization (code-specialized vs. general-purpose) influence Vul-RAG performance?
RQ4 Do reasoning capabilities improve the performance of Vul-RAG?
RQ5 How does model parameter scale affect the performance of Vul-RAG?

4.1 Benchmark Dataset

We reuse the benchmark dataset introduced in the Vul-RAG study. The dataset consists of pairs of vulnerable and patched functions extracted from real-world CVEs reported for the Linux kernel. Each pair is enriched with Common Weakness Enumeration (CWE) identifiers and descriptions. The dataset comprises 2,903 function pairs covering the ten most prevalent CWEs. It is randomly split in a 1:4 ratio into a test and training set. The test set contains 586 pairs and serves as the evaluation benchmark (PairVul), while the remaining 2,317 pairs form the training set used to construct the knowledge base.

The most prevalent vulnerability types in the datasets are shown in Table 1. We categorize the CWEs according to the CWE-1000 Research View [12], which groups weaknesses into ten high-level research pillars. This categorization enables analysis of Vul-RAG performance across vulnerability classes rather than individual CWEs. The covered CWEs span four of ten pillars, i.e., *Improper Access Control*, *Improper Control of a Resource Through its Lifetime*, *Improper Check or Handling of Exceptional Conditions*, and *Improper Neutralization*. The high coverage of resource-related vulnerabilities is consistent with the Linux kernel setting and its implementation in C, where handling of memory and system resources is a common source of vulnerabilities.

Table 1. Number of vulnerable-patched code pairs per CWE in PairVul and the knowledge base (KB), grouped by CWE-1000 research view pillars [12]: *Improper Access Control* (Access), *Improper Control of a Resource Through its Lifetime* (Resource), *Improper Check or Handling of Exceptional Conditions* (Exceptional), and *Improper Neutralization* (Neutralization).

Set \ *CWE*	**Access**	**Resource**							**Exceptional**	**Neutralization**
	264	*119*	*125*	*200*	*362*	*401*	*416*	*787*	*476*	*20*
PairVul	31	44	35	39	81	26	166	47	71	46
KB	120	173	140	152	320	101	660	187	281	182

CWE-264: Permissions, Privileges, and Access Controls
CWE-119: Improper Restriction of Operations within the Bounds of a Memory Buffer
CWE-125: Out-of-bounds Read
CWE-200: Exposure of Sensitive Information to an Unauthorized Actor
CWE-362: Concurrent Execution using Shared Resource with Improper Synchronization
CWE-401: Missing Release of Memory after Effective Lifetime
CWE-416: Use After Free
CWE-787: Out-of-bounds Write
CWE-476: Null Pointer Dereference
CWE-20: Improper Input Validation

4.2 Studied LLMs

Baseline Models. The Vul-RAG evaluation considered four state-of-the-art LLMs that have been widely used for vulnerability detection [5]: two proprietary models (GPT-4o and Claude Sonnet 3.5) and two open-weight models (DeepSeek-Coder-V2-Instruct and Qwen2.5-Coder-32B-Instruct). While proprietary models are subject to version deprecation and opaque updates (rendering long-term reproducibility difficult), open-weight models remain available, ensuring that experimental results can be verified even as the model ecosystem evolves.

Additional Models. To investigate the impact of different models, we evaluate a broader set of open-weight LLMs. During preliminary experiments, we tested open-weights models of various parameter sizes across the Qwen, DeepSeek, Llama, and OpenAI families, cf. online material. However, some of these models frequently produced outputs that did not consistently follow the given instruction format, i.e., missing `<result>YES</result>` or `<result>NO</result>` tags in ****P2**** (cf. Fig. 1), and, thus, could not be reliably parsed for evaluation. To ensure a stable evaluation pipeline, we restrict the final set of models to those that processed all benchmark items successfully, as summarized in Table 2.

Table 2. Studied LLMs grouped by experiment. Full HuggingFace model identifier, parameter count [B], maximum context length [Token], and knowledge cutoff.

Model Identifier	Parameter	Context	Cutoff
RQ1 Baseline models			
deepseek-ai/DeepSeek-Coder-V2-Instruct [4]	236	131,072	Nov 2023
Qwen/Qwen2.5-Coder-32B-Instruct [7]	32.5	131,072	Feb 2024
RQ2 Newer generation of baseline models			
Qwen/Qwen3-Coder-30B-A3B-Instruct [24]	30.5	262,144	–
RQ3 General-purpose models			
Qwen/Qwen2.5-32B-Instruct [14]	32.5	131,072	–
RQ4 Reasoning models			
deepseek-ai/DeepSeek-R1-Distill-Qwen-32B [6]	32.5	131,072	Jul 2024
Qwen/QwQ-32B [15]	32.5	131,072	Nov 2024
RQ5 Varying model parameter scale			
deepseek-ai/DeepSeek-R1-Distill-Llama-8B [6]	8	131,072	Jul 2024
deepseek-ai/DeepSeek-R1-Distill-Qwen-14B [6]	14	131,072	Jul 2024
Qwen/Qwen2.5-Coder-3B-Instruct [7]	3.09	32,768	Feb 2024
Qwen/Qwen2.5-Coder-7B-Instruct [7]	7.61	131,072	Feb 2024
Qwen/Qwen2.5-Coder-14B-Instruct [7]	14.7	131,072	Feb 2024
Qwen/Qwen3-4B [24]	4	32,768	–
Qwen/Qwen3-8B [24]	8.2	32,768	–
Qwen/Qwen3-14B [24]	14.8	32,768	–
Qwen/Qwen3-30B-A3B-Instruct-2507 [24]	30.5	262,144	–

4.3 Metrics

A challenge in vulnerability detection is that models must reliably distinguish between vulnerable code and its corresponding patch, which often differ only in small but security-relevant details [5]. Misclassifying vulnerable code as safe (false negatives) leaves exploitable weaknesses undetected, while incorrectly flagging safe code as vulnerable (false positives) introduces unnecessary remediation effort and may reduce developer trust in automated tools.

Vul-RAG introduces the *pairwise accuracy* metric, which measures the proportion of code pairs for which both the vulnerable function and its patched counterpart are correctly classified. In addition, the framework introduces *balanced recall* and *balanced precision* (see Equations (1) and (2), respectively) to capture the model's ability to detect vulnerabilities and avoid false alarms. Balanced recall reflects the reliability of identifying vulnerable code, while balanced precision measures the accuracy of predicted vulnerabilities relative to actual weaknesses. In the Vul-RAG study, the best performance was achieved using GPT-4o, with a pairwise accuracy of 0.32, a balanced recall of 0.58, and a balanced precision of 0.63. To put these results in perspective, a random baseline would achieve a recall and precision of 0.50, and a pairwise accuracy of 0.25. These results highlight the complexity of the task even for state-of-the-art models.

$$\text{Balanced Recall} = \left(\frac{\#True_{\text{vul}}}{\#Total_{\text{vul}}} + \frac{\#True_{\text{nvul}}}{\#Total_{\text{nvul}}}\right)/2 \tag{1}$$

$$\text{Balanced Precision} = \left(\frac{\#True_{\text{vul}}}{\#Predict_{\text{vul}}} + \frac{\#True_{\text{nvul}}}{\#Predict_{\text{nvul}}}\right)/2 \tag{2}$$

4.4 Implementation Details

We adapted the Vul-RAG pipeline to use PyTorch and the HuggingFace Transformers library, replacing the original API-based clients with local models. The implementation supports configurable model parameters, such as the maximum number of output tokens (`max_new_tokens=4096`) and temperature, which regulates the randomness of the output by scaling the probability distribution of the next-token prediction; a value close to zero ensures more deterministic and consistent responses. For models without built-in prompt templates, we implemented a fallback formatting routine to standardize inputs. All other components, including source code, input data, prompts, and default Vul-RAG hyperparameter (e.g., `temperature = 0.01`, `max_knowledge = 3`, `retry_times = 5`), remain unchanged.

All experiments were conducted on a high-performance computing cluster. Experiments were executed on NVIDIA L40S 48 GB (for experiments with models with up to 16B parameters) or up to eight NVIDIA H100 80 GB SXM5 GPUs.

5 Results

In this section, we present and discuss the experimental results with respect to the research questions RQ1-RQ5 defined in Sect. 4.

5.1 RQ1 Reproducibility of Vul-RAG

To assess the reproducibility of Vul-RAG, we evaluate the framework using its reported open-weight baseline models: DeepSeek-Coder-V2-Instruct and

Qwen2.5-Coder-32B-Instruct. Following best practices for LLM reproducibility [17], we conducted three independent runs and report the mean performance.

Table 3 compares the reproduced results with the results reported in the Vul-RAG study. For Qwen2.5-Coder-32B-Instruct, the results confirm the reported performance: pairwise accuracy remains identical, and deviations in balanced recall and precision are minor (at most two percentage points, which is negligible considering the reported standard deviation). Examining the CWE-specific pairwise accuracy in Table 4, we observe higher variance: For example, in *CWE-125*, we see a difference of 13% points. However, these discrepancies are likely attributable to output variability.

For DeepSeek-Coder-V2-Instruct, we observe a performance drop across all metrics. DeepSeek-Coder-V2-Instruct in BF16 format requires 8×80GB GPUs for inference according to its HuggingFace model card. Despite executing on eight NVIDIA H100 GPUs, which provide the required resources, the model successfully processed only 565 of 586 pairs. The remaining 21 pairs repeatedly failed due to CUDA out-of-memory (OOM) errors, primarily during the early retrieval phases, e.g., extraction of function purpose and functionality (cf. ***P1*** in Fig. 1). As visualized in Fig. 2, these failures affected all CWE types and were particularly pronounced for long codes. In these cases, the quadratic scaling of the self-attention mechanism exhausts available GPU memory. Due to incomplete processing, Table 3 and Table 4 report only a single run for DeepSeek-Coder-V2-Instruct. The Vul-RAG framework excludes failed items from the evaluation. While excluding these longer and likely more complex items reflects the model's capability on the subset it could successfully process, the results on the remain-

Table 3. Vul-RAG results reported (*) and reproduced (r). We report the mean ± standard deviation for the Qwen baseline, and a single run for the DeepSeek baseline.

LLM		Pair. Accuracy	Recall	Precision
DeepSeek-Coder-V2	*	0.30	0.61	0.62
	r	↓ 0.22	↓ 0.52	↓ 0.53
Qwen2.5-Coder-32B	*	0.26	0.59	0.61
	r	0.26±0.01	0.59±0.01	↓ 0.59±0.01

Table 4. Mean CWE-specific pairwise accuracy for the Vul-RAG results reported (*) and reproduced (r). CWEs grouped by CWE-1000 research view pillars, cf. Table 1.

LLM \ *CWE*		**Access**	**Resource**							**Excep.**	**Neut.**
		264	*119*	*125*	*200*	*362*	*401*	*416*	*787*	*476*	*20*
DeepSeek-Coder-V2	*	0.35	0.30	0.26	0.38	0.25	0.54	0.29	0.32	0.27	0.26
	r	↓ 0.23	0.30	↓ 0.21	↓ 0.14	↓ 0.18	↓ 0.29	↓ 0.21	↓ 0.16	↓ 0.25	0.27
Qwen2.5-Coder-32B	*	0.42	0.23	0.43	0.28	0.22	0.27	0.24	0.21	0.24	0.26
	r	0.49	↓ 0.22	↓ 0.30	↓ 0.26	0.25	↓ 0.26	0.26	0.28	↓ 0.21	↓ 0.20

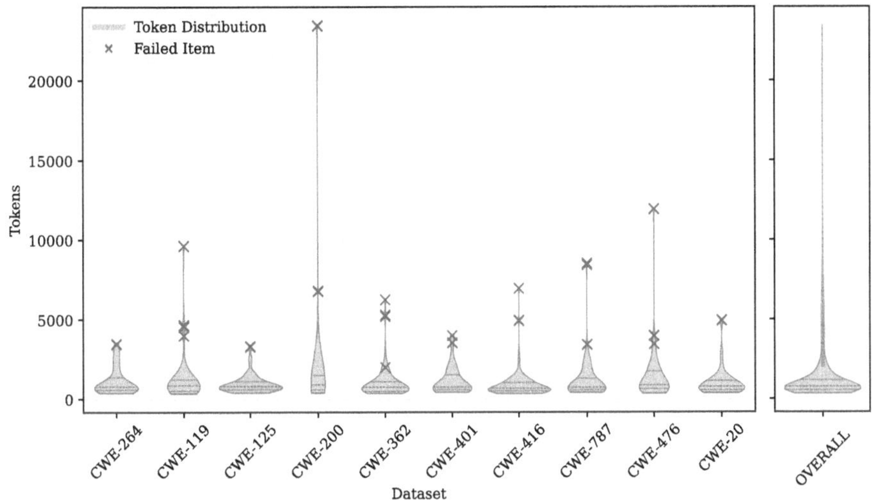

Fig. 2. Distribution of tokens for the detection prompts across the PairVul CWE subsets, calculated using the DeepSeek-Coder-V2-Instruct tokenizer. Red crosses indicate dataset items where the model failed to generate a detection output. (Color figure online)

ing 565 pairs still show a substantial deviation from the reported performance, with a drop of eight percentage points (0.08) in pairwise accuracy and a drop of 9% points (0.09) in both recall and precision.

RQ1 To what extent are the reported Vul-RAG results reproducible?

We were able to reproduce the results for Qwen2.5-Coder-32B-Instruct, with only minor deviations in precision. DeepSeek-Coder-V2-Instruct exhibits a noticeable performance drop and fails to process all input pairs due to OOM errors. Importantly, failed items are excluded from the evaluation; observed discrepancies persist even on the successfully processed subset.

5.2 RQ2 Performance with Newer Generation Models

To assess whether improvements in models translate to enhanced vulnerability detection performance, we evaluate Vul-RAG using the newer generation of the Qwen baseline model, namely Qwen3-Coder-30B-A3B-Instruct. While other newer open-weight models such as DeepSeek-V2.5 and Qwen3-Coder-Next exist, their high parameter counts (236B and 80B, respectively) make them impractical for on-premise deployment; thus, we focus on the 30B-parameter model.

The results are shown in Table 5 row RQ2. Qwen3-Coder-30B-A3B-Instruct achieves a modest increase of two percentage points in pairwise accuracy (0.28 vs.

0.26), while maintaining balanced recall and precision. However, this enhancement remains limited, suggesting that while incremental model updates might provide slight benefits in performance, they do not necessarily overcome the challenges inherent in the detection task.

Table 5. Vul-RAG results reported (*) and reproduced (RQ1-RQ5) using open-weight models. We highlight the **first** , second , and third best reproduced results per metric **across all models for RQ1-RQ4** and the first best **within-family performance for RQ5**. Incomplete item coverage is marked in red. Model names abbreviated.

RQ	LLM	Pair. Accuracy	Recall	Precision	Pairs
*	DeepSeek-Coder-V2	0.30	0.61	0.62	
	Qwen2.5-Coder-32B	0.26	0.59	0.61	
RQ1	DeepSeek-Coder-V2	0.22	0.52	0.53	565/586
	Qwen2.5-Coder-32B	0.26	0.59	0.59	586/586
RQ2	Qwen3-Coder-30B	0.28	0.59	0.59	586/586
RQ3	Qwen2.5-32B	0.25	0.58	0.59	586/586
RQ4	DeepSeek-R1-32B	**0.29**	0.57	0.58	586/586
	QwQ-32B	**0.29**	**0.60**	**0.61**	586/586
RQ5	DeepSeek-R1-8B	0.29	0.57	0.58	586/586
	DeepSeek-R1-14B	0.27	0.56	0.57	586/586
	Qwen2.5-Coder-3B	0.24	0.54	0.54	586/586
	Qwen2.5-Coder-7B	0.08	0.51	0.52	586/586
	Qwen2.5-Coder-14B	0.24	0.57	0.57	586/586
	Qwen3-4B	0.25	0.57	0.58	586/586
	Qwen3-8B	0.24	0.57	0.58	586/586
	Qwen3-14B	0.22	0.58	0.61	586/586
	Qwen3-30B	0.25	0.58	0.60	586/586

RQ2 How does Vul-RAG perform with newer generation baseline LLMs?

Incremental model upgrades yield only modest performance gains, with Qwen3-Coder-30B providing an increase of only two percentage points in pairwise accuracy over the Qwen2.5-Coder-32B baseline.

5.3 RQ3 Code-Specialized Vs. General-Purpose LLMs

To investigate whether strong natural language understanding benefits abstraction-based vulnerability detection, we evaluate Vul-RAG using the general-purpose counterpart of the Qwen2.5-Coder baseline, namely Qwen2.5-32B-Instruct.

The results are shown in Table 5 row RQ3. We observe only a marginal performance decrease of one percentage point in pairwise accuracy and recall compared to the code-specialized baseline. By abstracting code and vulnerabilities into high-level semantic descriptions, Vul-RAG reframes a specialized programming task as a logical reasoning task. The small performance difference suggests that this abstraction can compensate for the absence of explicit code specialization and that, for RAG-based systems relying on high-level knowledge, natural language understanding capabilities may be as critical as domain-specific exposure.

RQ3 How does model specialization influence Vul-RAG performance?

The general-purpose model Qwen2.5-32B shows only a minimal performance drop of one percentage point compared to the code-specialized baseline. The results suggest that Vul-RAG's abstraction allows general-purpose models to compensate for a lack of code-specific training.

5.4 RQ4 Impact of Reasoning Capabilities

To evaluate whether explicit reasoning capabilities improve prediction, we analyze reasoning LLMs from both baseline model families, i.e., QwQ-32B and a distilled variant of the DeepSeek-R1 model (DeepSeek-R1-Distill-Qwen-32B), transferring reasoning patterns into smaller models.

The results are shown in Table 5 row RQ4. The considered reasoning models outperform comparable general-purpose, non-reasoning counterparts (e.g., Qwen2.5-32B-Instruct in RQ3), achieving the highest pairwise accuracy of 0.29, and nearly matching the reported DeepSeek-Coder-V2 baseline of 0.30. However, this performance gain entails a trade-off in computational overhead. As shown in Fig. 3, reasoning models generate substantially more tokens than the non-reasoning Qwen2.5-32B-Instruct. At equal parameter scale, QwQ-32B increases the median output length from 547 to 1385 tokens (+2.53×) and the IQR from 184 to 1035 tokens (+5.63×) compared to Qwen2.5-32B-Instruct. The heavy-tailed output distribution indicates that reasoning models do not merely generate longer outputs but adopt more diverse generation behaviors. Comparing different model families, QwQ shows extensive reasoning traces while DeepSeek-R1 produces more compact outputs.

Further analysis of the iterative retrieval process in Fig. 4 reveals that reasoning models exhibit different conditional success rates (i.e., the proportion of codes that are classified at a specific iteration step). The slight advantage in the first iteration suggests that they are more effective when limited contextual information is available. However, if no decision is reached in the first iteration, subsequent iterations provide only limited additional benefit, suggesting that the advantage of reasoning primarily lies in early-stage decision-making.

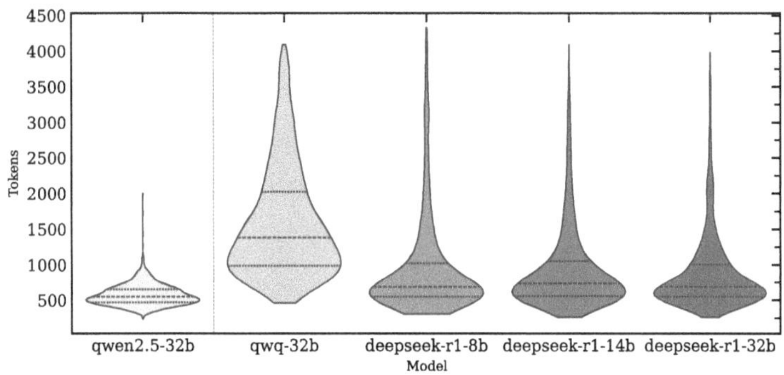

Fig. 3. Comparison of output lengths in tokens between non-reasoning and reasoning models for `max_new_tokens=4096` and individual iterations. Reasoning models exhibit higher token counts and longer tails, reflecting the generation of reasoning chains.

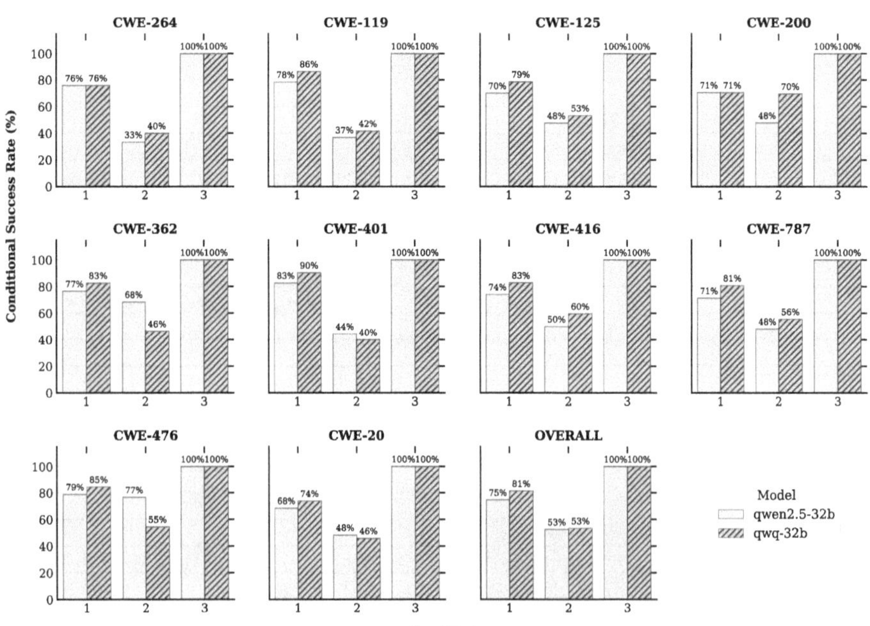

Fig. 4. Conditional success rates for a non-reasoning vs. reasoning model. Values represent the proportion of samples classified at a specific iteration, provided no decision was reached in an earlier iteration. Vul-RAG iterates through up to three items.

RQ4 Do reasoning capabilities improve the performance of Vul-RAG?

Reasoning models achieve the highest pairwise accuracy but incur higher inference costs due to increased token generation. Their advantage in iterative detection is most pronounced in the first iteration, where they more effectively translate retrieved knowledge into a correct prediction.

5.5 RQ5 Impact of Model Parameter Scale

To assess the impact of model parameter scale on performance, we evaluate Vul-RAG across models from RQ1-RQ4 with parameters ranging from 3B to 32B.

The results are shown in Table 5 row RQ5. Overall, we do not observe a consistent relationship between model scale and detection performance. Several smaller models achieve a performance comparable to or exceeding that of larger models. For example, for the Qwen2.5-Coder baseline model (RQ1), pairwise accuracy does not drop significantly when using smaller variants, i.e., with 3B and 14B parameters. While the 7B variant struggled with correctly identifying pairs (biased towards predicting non-vulnerable), the 3B and 14B variants both achieve a pairwise accuracy of 0.24, only two percentage points below the baseline. Similarly, within the Qwen3 model family (RQ2), performance remains largely stable across scales: The Qwen3-4B model achieves a pairwise accuracy of 0.25, matching both Qwen3-30B and Qwen2.5-32B, while Qwen3-14B performs worse with a pairwise accuracy of 0.22. Further, the DeepSeek-R1-Distill-Llama-8B reasoning model (RQ4) reaches a pairwise accuracy of 0.29, matching the best-performing 32B reasoning models, and even outperforms much larger non-reasoning models. These results indicate that architectural and training refinements in newer model generations may have a greater impact than mere parameter count, and that reasoning capabilities can outweigh the benefits of increased parameter scale.

RQ5 How does model parameter scale affect the performance of Vul-RAG?

Increasing model scale does not consistently improve detection performance. Smaller models (e.g., 4B–8B) achieve results comparable to larger 30B–32B models, and in some cases even outperform them. The findings suggest that model capabilities, such as reasoning, are more critical than parameter scale.

5.6 Discussion

The results provide several insights into the current state of RAG-based vulnerability detection and the specifics of Vul-RAG regarding (i) detection effectiveness, (ii) knowledge representation and quality, and (iii) practical deployment.

Table 6. CWE-specific pairwise accuracy across evaluated models. We highlight the **first**, second, third best and worst result per model. CWEs grouped by *CWE-1000* research view pillars, cf. Table 1. Model names abbreviated.

	CWE	**Access**	**Resource**							**Excep.**	**Neut.**
RQ	**LLM**	*264*	*119*	*125*	*200*	*362*	*401*	*416*	*787*	*476*	*20*
RQ1	DeepSeek-Coder-V2	0.23	**0.30**	0.21	0.14	0.18	0.29	0.21	0.16	0.25	0.27
	Qwen2.5-Coder-32B	**0.49**	0.22	0.30	0.26	0.25	0.26	0.26	0.28	0.21	0.20
RQ2	Qwen3-Coder-30B	**0.39**	0.25	0.37	0.23	0.28	0.23	0.25	0.34	0.31	0.28
RQ3	Qwen2.5-32B	**0.45**	0.20	0.23	0.28	0.25	0.27	0.24	0.23	0.24	0.20
RQ4	DeepSeek-R1-32B	**0.55**	0.32	0.31	0.33	0.33	0.23	0.27	0.32	0.23	0.13
	QwQ-32B	**0.48**	0.27	0.37	0.28	0.25	0.46	0.32	0.17	0.20	0.22
RQ5	DeepSeek-R1-8B	0.29	0.30	0.26	0.33	0.25	**0.42**	0.28	0.30	0.32	0.24
	DeepSeek-R1-14B	0.23	0.23	0.34	0.26	**0.36**	0.27	0.27	0.28	0.27	0.20
	Qwen2.5-Coder-3B	0.26	0.20	0.14	**0.36**	0.22	0.35	0.20	0.21	0.27	0.33
	Qwen2.5-Coder-7B	0.06	0.07	0.11	0.10	0.06	**0.15**	0.08	0.06	0.10	0.07
	Qwen2.5-Coder-14B	0.23	0.27	**0.34**	0.21	0.23	0.23	0.24	0.21	0.27	0.17
	Qwen3-4B	0.29	0.25	**0.34**	0.23	0.26	0.27	0.24	0.30	0.20	0.17
	Qwen3-8B	**0.32**	0.30	0.26	0.23	0.22	0.31	0.23	0.23	0.23	0.22
	Qwen3-14B	**0.35**	0.20	0.29	0.18	0.16	**0.35**	0.22	0.26	0.20	0.13
	Qwen3-30B	**0.55**	0.25	0.23	0.23	0.20	0.35	0.23	0.19	0.25	0.20

CWE-264: Permissions, Privileges, and Access Controls
CWE-119: Improper Restriction of Operations within the Bounds of a Memory Buffer
CWE-125: Out-of-bounds Read
CWE-200: Exposure of Sensitive Information to an Unauthorized Actor
CWE-362: Concurrent Execution using Shared Resource with Improper Synchronization
CWE-401: Missing Release of Memory after Effective Lifetime
CWE-416: Use After Free
CWE-787: Out-of-bounds Write
CWE-476: Null Pointer Dereference
CWE-20: Improper Input Validation

Detection Effectiveness. A primary finding across all research questions RQ1-RQ5 is the narrow performance difference despite the diversity of the models evaluated, cf. Table 5. Notably, the highest achieved overall pairwise accuracy of 0.29 is only four percentage points above the random baseline of 0.25. Hence, while the Vul-RAG framework enhances the ability of LLMs to distinguish between vulnerable and non-vulnerable code [5], these capabilities do not scale with model advancement; for instance, Qwen3-4B achieves the same pairwise accuracy (0.25) as Qwen3-30B-A3B-Instruct-2507. The observation of a performance plateau is also evident in the study by Antal et al. [2], where we observe a similar ceiling in the context of Java vulnerabilities. Despite evaluating (proprietary) frontier models with large parameter scales, e.g., DeepSeek-V3.1, GPT-5, and Llama-4-Maverick, the authors reported pairwise accuracies of 16.7%, 23.1%, and 32.4% respectively. The persistence of this plateau across different programming languages, datasets, knowledge bases, and models reinforces the inherent difficulty of the pairwise discrimination task.

Performance also varies considerably across vulnerability types, as shown in Table 6, indicating that certain vulnerabilities are inherently more difficult to capture, even with abstract knowledge representations. Across all models, performance is consistently highest for *CWE-264*, where access control vulnerabilities often follow well-defined patterns that can be captured through semantic descriptions. In contrast, performance is lowest for *CWE-20*. Input validation logic is typically distributed across multiple code locations and depends on broader program context, making it difficult to represent through localized functional semantics. For resource-related CWEs, performance remains inconsistent across models. These vulnerabilities often involve complex interactions or implicit assumptions about program state, which are not easily captured by static knowledge snippets. Notably, reasoning models (RQ4) exhibit more stable performance across CWE categories, suggesting that explicit reasoning helps mitigate some of the limitations of incomplete or imperfect retrieval.

Knowledge Representation and Quality. For reproducibility, we reused the Vul-RAG knowledge base, which was generated using GPT-3.5-turbo-0125. While necessary to ensure a consistent baseline, this choice raises questions about whether system performance is effectively capped by the quality of the initial knowledge extraction. The analysis in Vul-RAG identified that false negatives often stem from non-existent or vague vulnerability descriptions within the knowledge base or from irrelevant retrieval, where the retrieved functional semantics are too different from the input function. Similarly, false positives are frequently triggered by mismatched fixing solutions, particularly when a vulnerability could be addressed by alternative patches not represented in the retrieved context [5]. It remains unclear whether results would improve if the knowledge base were generated by, e.g., a reasoning model. Future research should investigate where model capability matters most (whether in the construction of the knowledge base, the summarization of code semantics, or the final vulnerability prediction) and how to evaluate such model capability regarding effort and quality.

Practical Deployment. We conducted all experiments on a high-performance computing cluster. Such extensive resources are typically unavailable in industrial development environments, where hardware is often more constrained. This discrepancy highlights the importance of the findings regarding model scale: The small performance differences between models suggest that selecting significantly larger models does not necessarily yield proportional gains. Notably, several smaller models achieved comparable performance. Such smaller models are more attractive for on-premise deployment, as they can operate on commodity hardware while maintaining privacy.

Overall, several challenges remain regarding the real-world practicality of RAG-based systems, specifically Vul-RAG. The pairwise accuracy ceiling of approximately 0.30 (and the resulting false positives and false negatives) suggests that Vul-RAG currently serves more as a research framework than a production tool. In addition, its current scope is limited to the Linux kernel and ten CWE types. The non-deterministic nature of LLMs and the strict formatting requirements also pose a challenge for automated integration. Further, the use of a binary output without providing verifiable reasoning makes it difficult for developers to interpret or trust the results. Finally, further benchmarking is required to determine whether these findings generalize to other programming languages and vulnerability types.

6 Threats to Validity

Several factors may impact the validity of the findings.

Data Leakage. A primary threat in LLM-based research is data leakage, i.e., the possibility that a model has seen the evaluation samples during its training and, thus, memorized correct answers rather than performing genuine vulnerability detection. The PairVul dataset was initially published on GitHub in April 2024. Given that several models used in this study were released or updated after this date (cf. Table 2), we cannot rule out the possibility that the evaluation samples were included in their training data. The lack of transparency regarding the training data of LLMs remains an open research challenge.

Bias in Model Selection. Vul-RAG relies on `<result>YES/NO</result>` tags in the model response for automated parsing of the prediction. During preliminary experiments, we excluded several models, as they failed to consistently adhere to this format. A model's failure to follow specific output formats does not necessarily imply an inability to detect vulnerabilities. However, with the setup used by Vul-RAG, such models are penalized, introducing a selection bias towards models with superior instruction-following capabilities. Loosening the evaluation script to handle free-form text might yield different results for less-instructed models but would introduce non-deterministic parsing errors.

Computational Resources and Deployment. Hardware constraints affected the evaluation of DeepSeek-Coder-V2, for which we encountered CUDA out-of-memory errors on an 8×80 GB H100 node. Consequently, the performance reported for this model is not fully representative. More importantly, we highlight a significant gap between research and practice: the infrastructure required to run such large models exceeds the resources available to typical mid-sized organizations, underscoring the necessity for evaluating smaller, more resource-efficient models that can be realistically deployed in industry pipelines.

7 Conclusion

This work presents a reproducibility and replicability study of the Vul-RAG framework in a fully local, open-weights setting. We find that Vul-RAG is reproducible for Qwen2.5-Coder but not for DeepSeek-Coder-V2. Across a diverse set of LLMs, including newer model generations (RQ2), general-purpose models (RQ3), and reasoning models (RQ4) with varying parameter scales (RQ5), we observe only small performance differences. Reasoning models achieve the highest pairwise accuracy of 0.29. In contrast, neither increased model scale nor newer model generations yield substantial improvements. These results consistently indicate a performance plateau in Vul-RAG and highlight the inherent difficulty of the pairwise discrimination task. From a practical perspective, the findings show that large parameter scales are not required for competitive performance, allowing for efficient deployment with smaller models. Future work should focus on improving knowledge base quality and retrieval strategies and investigate where model capability matters most in RAG-based pipelines to overcome the existing performance limitations.

Acknowledgments. This work has been funded by the Federal Ministry of Research, Technology and Space (BMFTR) and the state of Baden-Württemberg (Program: Forschung an HAW, Grant No. 13HAW26PX4), and in part by the German Research Foundation (DFG) under project-ID 528745080 - FIP 68. The authors alone are responsible for the content of this paper. We thank the DACHS data analysis cluster, hosted at Hochschule Esslingen and co-funded by the MWK within the DFG's "Großgeräte der Länder" program, for providing the computational resources necessary for this research.

Disclosure of Interests. The authors have no competing interests to declare.

References

1. Angermeir, F., Amougou, M., Kreitz, M., Bauer, A., Linhuber, M., Fucci, D., et al.: Reflections on the Reproducibility of Commercial LLM Performance in Empirical Software Engineering Studies (2025). arXiv:2510.25506
2. Antal, G., Értekes, L., Szolnoki, N., Hegedűs, P.: Evaluating retrieval-augmented generation for LLM-Based vulnerability detection: an empirical study on real-world java vulnerabilities. IEEE Access **14**, 50878–50891 (2026). https://doi.org/10.1109/ACCESS.2026.3676577
3. Chakraborty, P., Arumugam, K.K., Alfadel, M., Nagappan, M., McIntosh, S.: Revisiting the performance of deep learning-based vulnerability detection on realistic datasets. IEEE Trans. Software Eng. **50**(8), 2163–2177 (2024). https://doi.org/10.1109/TSE.2024.3423712
4. DeepSeek-AI, Zhu, Q., Guo, D., Shao, Z., Yang, D., Wang, P., et al.: DeepSeek-Coder-V2: Breaking the Barrier of Closed-Source Models in Code Intelligence. arXiv:2406.11931 (2024)
5. Du, X., Zheng, G., Wang, K., Zou, Y., Wang, Y., Deng, W., et al.: Vul-RAG: enhancing LLM-based vulnerability detection via knowledge-level RAG. ACM Trans. Softw. Eng. Methodol. (TOSEM) (2026). https://doi.org/10.1145/3797277., Just Accepted
6. Guo, D., Yang, D., Zhang, H., Song, J., Wang, P., Zhu, Q., et al.: DeepSeek-R1 incentivizes reasoning in LLMs through reinforcement learning. Nature **645**(8081), 633–638 (2025)
7. Hui, B., Yang, J., Cui, Z., Yang, J., Liu, D., Zhang, L., et al.: Qwen2.5-Coder Technical Report. arXiv:2409.12186 (2024)
8. Kaniewski, S., Holstein, D., Schmidt, F., Heer, T.: Vulnerability handling of AI-generated code - existing solutions and open challenges. In: Conference on AI,

Science, Engineering, and Technology (AIxSET), Laguna Hills, CA, USA, pp. 145–148 (2024). https://doi.org/10.1109/AIxSET62544.2024.00026
9. Kaniewski, S., Schmidt, F., Enzweiler, M., Menth, M., Heer, T.: A systematic literature review on detecting software vulnerabilities with large language models. ACM Trans. Software Eng. Methodol. (TOSEM) (2026). https://doi.org/10.1145/3815425., Just Accepted
10. Lewis, P., Perez, E., Piktus, A., Petroni, F., Karpukhin, V., Goyal, N., et al.: Retrieval-augmented generation for knowledge-intensive NLP tasks. In: Advances in Neural Information Processing Systems (NeurIPS), vol. 33, pp. 9459–9474 (2020)
11. Lu, G., Ju, X., Chen, X., Pei, W., Cai, Z.: GRACE: empowering LLM-based software vulnerability detection with graph structure and in-context learning. J. Syst. Softw. (JSS) **212**, 112031 (2024)
12. MITRE: CWE-1000: Research Concepts (2026). https://cwe.mitre.org/data/definitions/1000.html Accessed 06 March 2026
13. Nong, Y., Sharma, R., Hamou-Lhadj, A., Luo, X., Cai, H.: Open science in software engineering: a study on deep learning-based vulnerability detection. IEEE Trans. Softw. Eng. **49**(4), 1983–2005 (2023). https://doi.org/10.1109/TSE.2022.3207149
14. Qwen: Qwen2.5-LLM: Extending the boundary of LLMs. https://qwen.ai/blog?id=qwen2.5-llm, Accessed 04 March 2026
15. Qwen: QwQ-32B: Embracing the Power of Reinforcement Learning. https://qwen.ai/blog?id=qwq-32b, Accessed 04 March 2026
16. Safdar, R., Mateen, D., Ali, S.T., Hussain, W.: Real-VulLLM: an LLM Based Assessment Framework in the Wild arXiv:2510.04056 (2025)
17. Sallou, J., Durieux, T., Panichella, A.: Breaking the silence: the threats of using LLMs in software engineering. In: ACM/IEEE International Conference on Software Engineering: New Ideas and Emerging Results (ICSE-NIER), Lisbon, Portugal, pp. 102–106 (2024). https://doi.org/10.1145/3639476.3639764
18. Steenhoek, B., Rahman, M.M., Jiles, R., Le, W.: An empirical study of deep learning models for vulnerability detection. In: IEEE/ACM International Conference on Software Engineering (ICSE), Melbourne, Australia, pp. 2237–2248 (2023). https://doi.org/10.1109/ICSE48619.2023.00188
19. Sun, Y., Wu, D., Xue, Y., Liu, H., Ma, W., Zhang, L., et al.: LLM4Vuln: A Unified Evaluation Framework for Decoupling and Enhancing LLMs' Vulnerability Reasoning arXiv:2401.16185 (2025)
20. Tsai, C.N., Wang, X., Lee, C.H., Lin, C.S.: A sequential multi-stage approach for code vulnerability detection via confidence- and collaboration-based decision making. In: Conference on Empirical Methods in Natural Language Processing (EMNLP), Suzhou, China, pp. 21162–21168 (2025). https://doi.org/10.18653/v1/2025.emnlp-main.1071
21. Tsai, C.N., Xie, J., Lai, C.M., Lin, C.S.: Leveraging intra-and inter-references in vulnerability detection using multi-agent collaboration based on LLMs. Clust. Comput. **28**(15), 1–12 (2025). https://doi.org/10.1007/s10586-025-05721-2
22. Wen, X.C., Wang, X., Chen, Y., Hu, R., Lo, D., Gao, C.: VulEval: Towards Repository-Level Evaluation of Software Vulnerability Detection arXiv:2404.15596 (2024)
23. Wu, Z., Xu, J., Peng, Y., Chong, C.Y., Jia, X.: MulVul: Retrieval-augmented Multi-Agent Code Vulnerability Detection via Cross-Model Prompt Evolution arXiv:2601.18847 (2026)

24. Yang, A., Li, A., Yang, B., Zhang, B., Hui, B., Zheng, B., et al.: Qwen3 Technical Report. arXiv:2505.09388 (2025)
25. Zhu, H., Li, J., Gao, C., Qian, J., Dong, Y., Liu, H., et al.: Specification-Guided Vulnerability Detection with Large Language Models. arXiv:2511.04014 (2025)

Semi-supervised Novel Intrusion Detection via Orthogonal Feature Extraction and Score-Space Meta-Classifier Assembly

Minh-Khanh Vu[1], Cristian Ene[1], Laurent Mounier[1](✉), and Mathias Ramparison[2]

[1] Univ. Grenoble Alpes, CNRS, Grenoble INP, VERIMAG, 38000 Grenoble, France
minh-khanh.vu@etu.univ-grenoble-alpes.fr,
{cristian.ene,laurent.mounier}@univ-grenoble-alpes.fr
[2] Institut Polytechnique de Paris, Telecom Paris (INFRES), LTCI, Paris, France
mathias.ramparison@grenoble-inp.fr

Abstract. Signature-based endpoint detection fails against novel payloads whose behavioral patterns do not match any catalogued specimen. A semi-supervised host-based intrusion detection system is introduced that decomposes each system-call window into three structurally independent views, each trained exclusively on benign traces: frequency and rarity (TF-IDF with a one-class Support Vector Machine), local topology (a 1D convolutional autoencoder), and chronological grammar (a GRU next-event predictor). The three anomaly scalars are assembled into a score-space meta-matrix over which an XGBoost layer learns the final decision boundary without accessing raw syscall sequences or malware signatures directly. On the ADFA-LD 32-bit benchmark, the fusion model achieves Area Under the ROC Curve (AUC) 0.9113, Area Under the Precision-Recall Curve (AUPR) 0.8950, and F1 0.8523 at a full-pipeline latency of 0.2217 ms per window. Per-family evaluation across six attack families yields average AUC 0.9073, and cross-path Pearson correlations of 0.43 to 0.46 indicate that the three views occupy productively distinct operating regimes and increase the number of behavioural constraints an attacker must preserve to evade detection.

Keywords: host-based intrusion detection · system call analysis · orthogonal feature extraction · score-space fusion · semi-supervised anomaly detection · XGBoost

1 Introduction

Host-based endpoint detection and response (EDR) platforms perform reliably when an attack family has been observed and codified as a signature. Against novel payloads *e.g.* variants engineered to differ from any previous specimen,

Z. Afzal et al. (Eds.): ARES 2026 Workshops, LNCS 16900, pp. 96–114, 2027.
https://doi.org/10.1007/978-3-032-35576-8_6

this model breaks: a detector that cannot generalize beyond observed behaviour fails exactly when adversaries carefully avoided matching a known trace.

System call traces offer a promising alternative, because they expose low-level kernel interactions that every process, including novel malware, must eventually perform to read files, spawn shells, or open network connections. A body of prior work has shown that statistical and neural models can learn a manifold of benign execution from unlabeled syscall data and flag departures at inference time [11, 14]; the ADFA-LD corpus [8] provides the standard labelled benchmark against which such detectors are evaluated. A persistent limitation, however, is that each of these systems observes execution through a single analytical lens. Some count which system calls appear and how often (frequency analysis), others check whether nearby calls form familiar patterns (structural analysis), and still others verify that each call follows plausibly from the preceding sequence (sequential prediction). A detector built on only one of these views can be evaded by an attacker who targets that specific dimension while leaving the others untouched.

The existing response to this fragility is ensemble combination, merging multiple classifiers over a shared feature space. However, as established in [27], stacking reduces variance when base classifiers share their feature representation, but cannot recover signals that the shared representation itself fails to capture. A second gap concerns evaluation discipline: sliding-window syscall datasets contain strong inter-window overlap, and mixing windows from the same execution trace across train and test partitions inflates reported performance in a way that cannot be attributed to the detector architecture.

The proposed pipeline addresses both gaps by decomposing system call behaviour into three structurally independent representations before any fusion takes place. Path A extracts frequency and rarity via TF-IDF vectorisation, PCA dimensionality reduction, and a one-class support-vector boundary. Path B captures local topological distortion through the reconstruction error of a 1D convolutional autoencoder operating on learned embeddings. Path C measures chronological plausibility through the per-token negative log-likelihood of a GRU next-event predictor. Each path is trained exclusively on benign traces; no path ingests attack labels during representation learning. The three anomaly scalars are assembled into a score-space meta-matrix $\mathbf{Z} \in \mathbb{R}^{N \times 3}$, over which a supervised XGBoost layer [6] learns the final decision boundary. The threat model assumes the host kernel is intact and the adversary must interact with it via standard system calls; simultaneous evasion across three orthogonal channels increases mimicry cost.

The contributions are fourfold.

1. **Three-path orthogonal feature extraction.** A pipeline over raw system-call windows that assigns frequency/rarity, local geometry, and chronological grammar to three structurally independent anomaly channels, each trained exclusively on benign data.

2. **Score-space meta-classifier.** An XGBoost layer that reasons only over three anomaly scalars, learning to interpret their agreement and disagreement without accessing raw syscall windows or malware signatures directly.
3. **Empirical channel independence evidence.** Cross-path Pearson correlations of 0.43 to 0.46 confirm shared sensitivity to genuine anomalies while indicating no single path subsumes the others; 29,568 attack windows are recovered only because multiple channels complement each other.
4. **Leak-safe trace-level evaluation.** A partitioning scheme that groups windows by source execution trace before splitting, preventing near-duplicate contexts from inflating individual-channel and fusion estimates.

On the ADFA-LD 32-bit benchmark, the XGBoost fusion model achieves AUC 0.9113, AUPR 0.8950, and F1 0.8523, at a full-pipeline latency of 0.2217 ms per window. Per-family evaluation across six attack families yields average AUC 0.9073 and F1 0.7306. Reproducibility artefacts are available online.[1]

2 Related Work

2.1 System Call-Based Intrusion Detection

The use of system call sequences as a behavioral fingerprint was established in [14], which showed that short n-gram windows form a distinctive normality profile for each Unix process. [16] quantified the sensitivity of variable-length windows on the University of New Mexico (UNM) syscall corpus [13]; [28] subsequently showed that Hidden Markov Model (HMM)-based detectors match n-gram detection rates at higher computational cost on the same data. [8] introduced the ADFA-LD benchmark used here, comprising traces from a Linux server subjected to six families of post-exploitation payloads. [30] applied frequency-based evaluation to ADFA-LD, establishing a CNN baseline that highlighted the failure of single-feature representations on multi-stage attack sequences where each individual call is benign in isolation. A common thread across this literature is the reliance on a *single* behavioral paradigm per detector, leaving the system vulnerable to mimicry along the one unmonitored dimension.

2.2 Unsupervised Anomaly Detection

Classical unsupervised detectors model the benign manifold through different geometric assumptions. The OCSVM [25] (One-Class Support-Vector Machine, unsupervised machine learning algorithm for classification and anomaly detection) learns a maximum-margin support boundary in a kernel-induced space. Local Outlier Factor (LOF) [4] computes anomaly as a local density ratio against k-nearest neighbours. Isolation Forest [19] isolates anomalies through recursive

[1] https://anonymous.4open.science/r/Semi-Supervised-Novel-Intrusion-Detection-0A88/README.md.

random partitioning in linear time. [20] applied OCSVM to TF-IDF representations of system call n-grams, showing that frequency features capture distributional anomalies that sequence-only methods miss. As observed in the comprehensive survey of [22], any unsupervised detector is only as discriminative as the representation it receives; none of these methods systematically evaluates what complementarity can be gained by combining representations that are orthogonal in their mathematical assumptions.

2.3 Deep Learning for Behavioral Anomaly Detection

Deep architectures have been widely applied to system call analysis. [2] showed that Variational Autoencoder (VAE) reconstruction probability provides a principled anomaly score. [11] applied Long Short Term Memory (LSTM)-based next-event prediction to system log anomaly detection, showing that sequential plausibility can be learned from benign executions alone. [21] proposed Kitsune, an ensemble of lightweight autoencoders for network traffic, applying the reconstruction-error paradigm at scale. [7] introduced the GRU as a parameter-efficient recurrent alternative used for Path C. Recent hybrid systems attempt to narrow the single-dimension limitation: [3] stacks bidirectional GRU autoencoders with tree ensembles, and [18] combines Isolation Forests with convolutional LSTMs. Yet even these combinations fuse models that largely share the same input representation (sequential embedding) rather than exploiting structurally independent analytical spaces. As noted in the broad time-series anomaly detection survey of [9], no single temporal architecture dominates across all anomaly types, motivating per-paradigm specialisation.

2.4 Ensemble and Fusion Methods

[29] formalised stacked generalisation, in which a meta-learner operates on the predictions of heterogeneous base classifiers. [27] showed that the benefit of stacking depends on the diversity of base-level outputs: when models share the same feature space, the meta-learner mainly corrects calibration bias rather than accessing new discriminative structure. [15] reported F1 gains of 10 to 15% over individual classifiers through adaptive ensemble learning on network intrusion data, but the base models all operated on the same input representation. [26] proposed PROPEDEUTICA, a cascade that routes borderline cases from a lightweight ML classifier to a deep model, achieving 94.34% accuracy with sub-0.1 s detection on CPU, showing the feasibility of heterogeneous latency-aware pipelines, though with multi-class labels rather than benign-only training.

2.5 External Baselines on ADFA-LD

[30] established early frequency-based baselines using k-NN and k-means on system call frequency vectors. [5] trained a bidirectional LSTM autoencoder exclusively on benign traces, reporting an AUC of 0.94. [23] proposed the ALAD

framework combining WaveNet-based next-event prediction with application-level aggregation, reporting an AUC of 99.8% on ADFA-LD. [24] applied stacking ensembles over bag-of-words representations, achieving 97.47% accuracy with a false positive rate as low as 3.34%. [10] proposed GT-FID, a graph-temporal fusion network attaining 96.22% accuracy and a macro-F1 of 0.95.

Among the reviewed baselines, only [5] trains exclusively on benign traces; other systems incorporate attack labels at some stage, which assumes known attack categories unavailable in the novel-intrusion setting addressed here.

2.6 Positioning

Table 1 compares representative prior work, recording whether window-level evaluation and trace-level isolation are enforced; the proposed row uses the trace-isolated test split.

Table 1. Positioning of the proposed approach against representative prior work.

Ref.	Dataset	ROC-AUC	Accuracy	Recall/F1	Window eval.	Trace-isolated
[11]	HDFS/BGL	—	—	Recall 0.96 (F1 0.96)	No	No
[21]	Network pcap	0.99	—	—	No	No
[23]	ADFA-LD	0.998	—	—	Yes	No
[24]	ADFA-LD	—	0.9747	—	Yes	No
[5]	ADFA-LD	0.94	—	—	Yes	No
[10]	ADFA-LD	—	0.9622	Macro-F1 0.95	Yes	No
This work	**ADFA-LD**	**0.9113**	**0.8525**	**Recall 0.9063 (F1 0.8523)**	**Yes**	**Yes**

3 Methodology

The detection pipeline proceeds in five sequential stages: dataset ingestion, sliding-window preprocessing, three structurally independent feature extraction paths, meta-matrix construction, and score-space meta-classification. Figure 1 illustrates the end-to-end architecture. Each stage solves a narrower problem than end-to-end malware classification: the three feature extraction paths each test a different notion of normality trained solely on benign data, while the fusion stage learns how disagreements among those three views correlate with malicious behaviour.

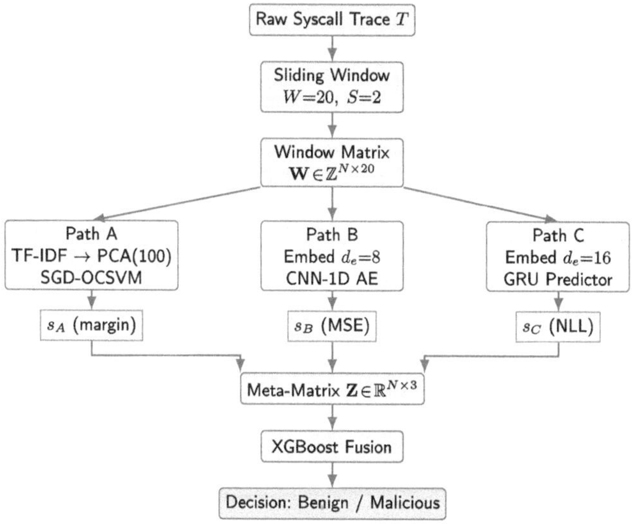

Fig. 1. End-to-end architecture: three orthogonal paths map each window to an anomaly scalar; XGBoost fuses the resulting $\mathbb{R}^3$ score vector into a final binary decision.

3.1 Dataset and Preprocessing

All experiments use the ADFA-LD corpus [8], a widely adopted benchmark for host-based anomaly detection comprising system call traces collected from a Linux server subjected to six attack families: Adduser, Hydra-FTP, Hydra-SSH, Java Meterpreter, Meterpreter, and Web Shell. The corpus provides 833 raw traces for benign training, 4,372 independent benign traces for validation, and 746 attack traces (ten per-variant instances per family).

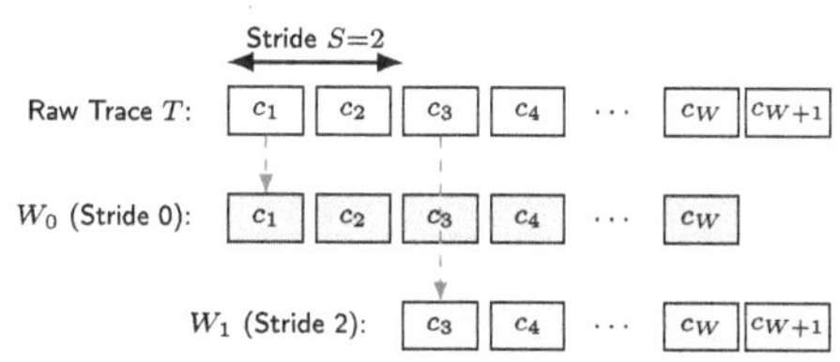

Fig. 2. Sliding-window preprocessing with W=20 and S=2, yielding 90% overlap between adjacent windows.

Let $T=[c_1, c_2, \ldots, c_L]$ denote a raw trace of length L where each $c_i \in \mathcal{V}$, the set of distinct syscall identifiers observed in the corpus, with $|\mathcal{V}|=175$[2].

A fixed sliding window of width W=20 and stride S=2 is applied:

$$W_i = [c_{1+iS}, \, c_{2+iS}, \, \ldots, \, c_{W+iS}], \quad i = 0, \ldots, \left\lfloor \frac{L-W}{S} \right\rfloor \tag{1}$$

[2] The Linux i386 syscall table defines over 340 entries for the kernel version used by ADFA-LD (2.6.38, Ubuntu 11.04); only the 175 identifiers actually invoked by the recorded workloads appear in the corpus vocabulary. The full i386 table is maintained in the kernel source at arch/x86/entry/syscalls/syscall_32.tbl; an interactive reference is available at https://x86.syscall.sh/.

Here W_i is the ith syscall window, c_j is the syscall identifier at position j, L is the trace length, W is the window width, and S is the stride between consecutive windows.

This yields 1,318,389 windows in total (146,321 benign training, 1,020,277 benign validation, 151,791 attack). Width W=20 follows established ADFA-LD practice [8,30]; stride S=2 achieves 90% inter-window overlap, reducing the chance that short attack transitions are split across disjoint windows while keeping the sample count lower than a stride-one scan would produce. Final train/validation/test splits for the score-space fusion stage are formed at the *trace* level (60/20/20) so that no two windows from the same source execution appear on both sides of any partition. Figure 2 illustrates how the fixed-width window advances over the raw syscall trace while preserving strong local overlap between adjacent samples.

3.2 Orthogonal Feature Extraction

A single anomaly paradigm observes execution through one fixed lens. Feature extraction is partitioned into three paths whose input representations are *operationally orthogonal*: each path maps the same raw window through a mathematically distinct pipeline that discards two of the three behavioral dimensions while amplifying the third. Table 2 summarises the three paths. An attacker must simultaneously satisfy the normality criteria of all three to avoid detection.

Table 2. Summary of the three orthogonal feature extraction paths.

Path	Feature transform	Anomaly model	**Score**
A	TF-IDF (uni- and bigrams, 1000 terms) → PCA(100)	SGD-OCSVM (ν=0.01)	Margin s_A
B	Learnable embedding (d_e=8)	1D-CNN autoencoder (k=3)	MSE s_B
C	Learnable embedding (d_e=16)	GRU predictor (h=192)	NLL s_C

Note. d_e: embedding dimension; k: convolutional kernel width; h: GRU hidden state size; ν: OCSVM outlier fraction

Path A: Frequency and Rarity. Each window W_i is treated as a bag of syscall tokens and converted to a TF-IDF vector over unigrams and bigrams (vocabulary capped at 1,000 terms, sublinear TF scaling), then projected to 100 principal components retaining 84.4% of training variance.

A one-class SVM with Stochastic Gradient Descent (SGD) optimisation learns a maximum-margin hyperplane separating benign samples from the origin in the PCA space:

$$f(\mathbf{x}) = \operatorname{sgn}(\mathbf{w}^\top \mathbf{x} - \rho), \quad s_A = -(\mathbf{w}^\top \mathbf{x} - \rho) \tag{2}$$

where $\mathbf{x}$ is the PCA-reduced TF-IDF vector for one window, $\mathbf{w}$ is the learned separating normal, ρ is the offset of the one-class boundary, $f(\mathbf{x})$ is the benign/anomalous decision sign, and s_A is the Path A anomaly score. A larger positive s_A indicates higher anomaly likelihood. Among five candidate unsupervised models tested in the same TF-IDF/PCA space (SGD-OCSVM, Histogram-Based Outlier Score (HBOS), PCA reconstruction error, Isolation Forest, and LOF), SGD-OCSVM was selected as the Path A representative. On the score-space fusion test split used throughout Sect. 4, this channel reaches AUC 0.7754.

Path B: Local Topology. Syscall identifiers are mapped through a learnable embedding table $\mathbf{E} : \mathcal{V} \to \mathbb{R}^8$ before convolution, because syscall numbers are arbitrary kernel-assigned integers (e.g., `read`=3, `write`=4, `open`=5) whose adjacency carries no semantic meaning; the embedding lets the network learn similarity from data rather than from numbering.

A 1D convolutional autoencoder reconstructs the embedded window: the encoder applies two convolutional layers (8→8→4 channels, kernel k=3, stride-2 pooling) yielding a 4×5 bottleneck; the decoder mirrors this with two transposed convolutions. Training minimises Mean Squared Error (MSE) on benign sequences only; the anomaly score is

$$s_B = \frac{1}{W d_e} \sum_{t=1}^{W} \sum_{j=1}^{d_e} (X_{t,j} - \hat{X}_{t,j})^2 \tag{3}$$

where $X_{t,j}$ is the jth embedding coordinate of the syscall at position t, $\hat{X}_{t,j}$ is its reconstruction, W is the window width, d_e is the embedding dimension, and s_B is the mean reconstruction error used as the Path B anomaly score. Kernels of size k=3 implement localised translational invariance: a structurally anomalous three-call span produces a concentrated MSE spike rather than the diffuse residual of a fully connected bottleneck. Among five topology models evaluated (CNN-1D autoencoder, Dense autoencoder, LSTM autoencoder, Variational Autoencoder, and Deep Support Vector Data Description (SVDD)), the CNN-1D model is selected as the Path B representative and reaches AUC 0.7974 on the score-space fusion test split.

Path C: Chronological Grammar. A GRU predictor with embedding dimension d_e=16 and hidden size h=192 is trained on benign windows to predict the next syscall token from the preceding prefix, giving the anomaly score

$$s_C = -\frac{1}{W-1} \sum_{t=2}^{W} \log \hat{P}(c_t \mid c_1, \ldots, c_{t-1}) \tag{4}$$

The score s_C is the mean per-token Negative Log-Likelihood (NLL) over the window, where W=20 is the window width, $c_t \in \mathcal{V}$ is the system call identifier at position t in the window, and $\hat{P}(c_t \mid c_1, \ldots, c_{t-1})$ is the probability assigned by the GRU to the observed call c_t given the preceding prefix. A higher s_C indicates lower chronological plausibility and thus greater anomaly likelihood. The

GRU's update and reset gating preserves multi-step transition context across the 20-token window more efficiently than an LSTM while remaining causally interpretable. Among five chronology models (Markov chain, HMM, LSTM autoencoder, CBOW predictor, and GRU), the GRU is selected as the Path C representative and reaches AUC 0.8307 on the score-space fusion test split, confirming aggressive sensitivity to unlikely transitions.

Operational Orthogonality. Path A destroys token order (bag-of-words), so it cannot detect order-only anomalies. Path B preserves local spatial structure but ignores global ordering, so it cannot detect frequency anomalies that leave topology intact. Path C operates on left-to-right sequence likelihood, so it cannot detect structural motif disruptions that preserve transition plausibility. This complementary blindness increases the number of behavioural constraints an adversary must satisfy simultaneously: preserving benign frequency statistics, local structural motifs, and chronological transition plausibility jointly is a substantially harder optimisation target than evading any single detector. While a sufficiently informed adversary could in principle craft traces that remain near the benign manifold under all three views, doing so requires coordinating perturbations across three structurally distinct spaces, raising the cost and fragility of mimicry. Formal robustness guarantees against fully adaptive adversaries are outside the scope of this work.

3.3 Score-Space Meta-classifier

After scoring all N windows through all three paths, the scalars (s_A, s_B, s_C) are assembled row-wise into a meta-matrix $\mathbf{Z} \in \mathbb{R}^{N\times 3}$. The three scores occupy fundamentally different numeric ranges: s_A spans approximately 0.0254 (signed margin), s_B spans 0.8204 (reconstruction MSE), and s_C spans 14.1177 (negative log-likelihood), giving a scale heterogeneity ratio of $14.1177/0.0254 \approx 556.2$. Arithmetic averaging or fixed distance thresholds applied to this $\mathbb{R}^3$ space introduce systematic bias toward the dominant channel: since s_C is 556 times wider than s_A, a simple average would effectively ignore the frequency-rarity signal. Rank-based normalisation avoids scale bias but discards the shape of each score distribution, losing information about how far a window deviates from the benign cluster within each channel.

An XGBoost ensemble [6] learns the final decision boundary directly on $\mathbf{Z}$:

$$\hat{p} = \text{XGBoost}(\mathbf{z}; \Theta^*), \quad \hat{y} = \mathbb{I}[\hat{p} \geq \tau^*], \quad \tau^* = \arg\max_{\tau} \text{F1}_{\text{val}}(\tau) \tag{5}$$

where $\mathbf{z}=(s_A, s_B, s_C)$ is the three-dimensional score vector for one window, Θ^* denotes the fitted XGBoost parameters, $\hat{p}$ is the predicted attack probability, $\hat{y}$ is the binary decision, $\mathbb{I}[\cdot]$ is the indicator function, and τ^* is the threshold selected by maximising validation F1. Gradient-boosted trees partition score space through ordered threshold comparisons, handling heterogeneous scales natively without requiring shared normalisation. Five meta-classifier architectures were evaluated (logistic regression, random forest, SVM, Multi-Layer Perceptron (MLP), and XGBoost) to confirm that the benefit arises from nonlinear score interaction rather than from adding any supervision. Score-space calibration is the *only* stage where attack labels are used; the three base paths remain benign-only throughout.

3.4 Evaluation Protocol

Windows are partitioned at the *trace* level before any split is formed, *i.e.* all windows extracted from one original execution trace stay in the same split, preventing leakage from overlapping or nearly identical windows across train, validation, and test sets. Performance is reported as AUC-ROC for threshold-free discrimination and F1 at the operating point τ^* that maximises F1 on the validation split; a Savitzky-Golay smoothing pass (polynomial order 2, window length adaptive in $[5, 21]$ and constrained to odd values, both fixed a priori) is applied to the validation precision-recall curve before $\arg\max$ extraction to suppress numerical jitter arising from finite sample size; the smoothing hyperparameters were not tuned per-experiment to inflate the reported F1, and τ^* remains constrained to validation data throughout. All paper-facing metrics are read from exported experiment logs rather than from ad hoc notebook output. All experiments use `random_state=42` throughout.

4 Results

All results are from the 32-bit ADFA-LD pipeline.[3] Table 3 reports the per-path model-selection evidence used to choose the three locked representatives for fusion; fusion, ablation, and ROC values are evaluated on the score-space fusion test split.

4.1 Per-Path Benchmarks

Path A. Panel A of Table 3 compares five unsupervised models after the shared TF-IDF and PCA transform. The reported values come from the Path A sweep over candidate detectors and configurations on the engineering holdout; the table shows model-selection evidence rather than score-space fusion test result. SGD-OCSVM achieves the highest AUC (0.7975) and AUPR (0.3702), confirming that rarity in lexical space is most accurately captured by a support-boundary learner rather than a local-density or partitioning heuristic. The relatively low calibrated F1 (0.2892) reflects the narrow signed-margin distribution (span $\approx$ 0.0254), which makes binary thresholding fragile in isolation; the fusion layer recovers discriminative power by learning an independent split on s_A.

[3] experiments were conducted on an AMD Ryzen 9 6900HX CPU at base clock speed of 3.3 GHz, Radeon 680M graphics, and 32 GB of RAM.

Table 3. Per-path model-selection and score-space fusion benchmarks on the 32-bit ADFA-LD pipeline. Bold: selected/best model in each panel w.r.t. **A**rea **U**nder the **C**urve, **A**rea **U**nder the **P**recision-**R**ecall, F1 scores and **F**alse-**P**ositive **R**ate when the **T**rue-**P**ositive **R**ate is fixed at 95%.

Model	AUC	AUPR	F1	FPR@TPR95
Panel A: Path A (frequency/rarity)				
SGD-OCSVM	**0.7975**	**0.3702**	**0.2892**	0.6782
HBOS	0.7629	0.3291	0.2680	0.7139
PCA-Error	0.7533	0.2660	0.0818	**0.5934**
Isolation Forest	0.7444	0.2866	0.2177	0.6350
LOF	0.6086	0.1746	0.0127	0.6826
Panel B: Path B (local topology)				
CNN-1D AE	**0.7822**	**0.3443**	**0.4599**	**0.7260**
VAE	0.6303	0.2222	0.3746	0.9854
Dense AE	0.6043	0.2046	0.2846	0.8954
LSTM AE	0.5397	0.1890	0.2816	0.8974
Deep SVDD	0.5244	0.1270	0.2467	0.8992
Panel C: Path C (chronological grammar)				
GRU predictor	**0.8151**	**0.3738**	**0.4313**	**0.4217**
Markov	0.7966	0.3331	0.4287	0.4475
CBOW predictor	0.7712	0.7437	0.7624	0.7070
HMM	0.6792	0.2463	0.3138	0.6481
LSTM AE sequence	0.6606	0.1832	0.3174	0.6941
Panel D: score-space fusion				
Logistic Regression	0.8503	0.7787	0.8031	0.2839
Random Forest	0.8877	0.8665	0.8420	0.2382
SVM	0.9004	0.8799	0.8379	0.2236
MLP	0.8952	0.8444	0.8402	0.2105
XGBoost	**0.9113**	**0.8950**	**0.8523**	**0.1953**

Path B. Panel B of Table 3 reports the topology-model sweep used to choose the Path B representative. Each row records the best configuration found for that topology family on the engineering holdout, using the same metric set as Path A. CNN-1D AE is the strongest topology model by both AUC and F1, indicating that local convolutional motif reconstruction captures benign structural regularity more effectively than global compression or hypersphere fitting.

Path C. Panel C of Table 3 reports the chronological-model sweep used to choose the Path C representative. Each row is the best observed configuration for one chronological model family on the engineering holdout. GRU is selected because it has the strongest ranking quality (AUC 0.8151). The high Continuous Bag-of-Words (CBOW) F1 is retained as an engineering reference because it comes from a thresholded holdout snapshot; for score-space fusion, the stronger GRU ranking signal is preferred.

The selected representatives from Table 3 are then carried into the score-space fusion evaluation without changing their model family. Their per-path AUC values in Fig. 4 differ because the figure evaluates the same representatives on the score-space fusion test partition, not on the engineering holdout used for model selection.

4.2 Score-Space Fusion

Panel D of Table 3 compares five meta-classifier architectures over the same $\mathbb{R}^3$ score-space split. The neural baseline is a Multi-Layer Perceptron (MLP), included to test whether a dense nonlinear score-space learner can match boosted trees. XGBoost achieves the strongest performance across all metrics (AUC 0.9113, AUPR 0.8950, F1 0.8523 at τ^*=0.401214, precision 0.8044, recall 0.9063, Matthews Correlation Coefficient (MCC) 0.7110), with a lead of +1.1 pp (percentage point) AUC and +1.5 pp AUPR over the next best supervised model, and the lowest FPR at the operating threshold (0.1953). All supervised meta-classifiers outperform any individual path by a wide margin, indicating that the gain arises from fusing complementary signals rather than from the architecture of any single branch. Figure 4 shows the ROC curves for all three individual paths and the XGBoost fusion on the score-space fusion test split; the fusion dominates at every operating point, with the gain most pronounced in the low-FPR region (FPR $<$ 0.20), where individual paths reach at most TPR $\approx$ 0.70. The per-path AUCs in the ROC legend are therefore score-space fusion re-evaluations of the selected representatives, while Table 3 remains the sweep-based evidence for why those representatives were chosen. At the F1-optimal threshold the XGBoost fusion achieves FPR = 0.1953 (TP = 9,695; FP = 2,357; TN = 9,714; FN = 1,002), compared with Path A's FPR@TPR95 of 0.6782 (false-positive rate when the true-positive rate is fixed at 95%), illustrating the practical gain from score-space fusion over a single unsupervised channel.

Figure 3 plots the score distributions for all three channels on a shared logarithmic density axis, separating benign windows (blue) from attack windows (red). Path A (SGD-OCSVM signed margin) places benign windows near the boundary (mean −0.012, span 0.025); the tight range reflects the one-class formulation, in which all scores fall within a narrow neighbourhood of the training boundary. Path B (CNN-1D AE reconstruction MSE) separates benign (mean 0.052) from attack (mean 0.108) across a span of 0.820, which is approximately 33× wider than Path A. Path C (GRU NLL) shows the largest spread: benign mean 1.22 (std 1.29) vs. attack mean 2.80 (std 1.69), full span 14.12.

The resulting score-span heterogeneity ratio of $14.12/0.025 = 556.2$ renders arithmetic averaging impractical: any fixed scalar weight balancing Path C's NLL against Path A's margin would vary by three orders of magnitude across operating points and suppress one channel entirely. XGBoost learns axis-aligned split thresholds directly in the three-dimensional score space $\mathbb{R}^3$, treating each channel's scale as an independent coordinate and selecting splits invariant to absolute magnitude differences.

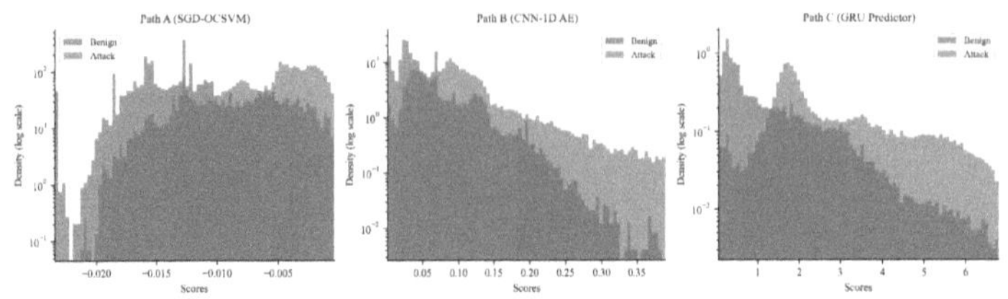

Fig. 3. Empirical score distributions for Path A (SGD-OCSVM margin), Path B (CNN-1D AE reconstruction MSE), and Path C (GRU NLL). The channels occupy different numeric ranges, with a score-span heterogeneity ratio of 556.2, motivating learned score-space thresholding over arithmetic averaging. Axes are clipped at the 99th percentile for readability; full spans are 0.0254, 0.8204, and 14.1177 respectively.

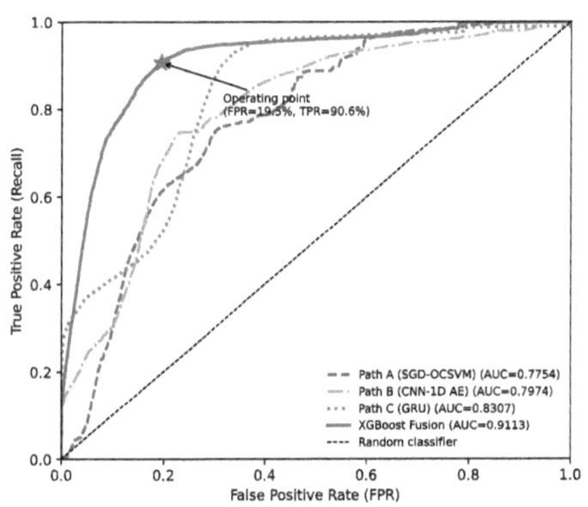

Fig. 4. ROC curves for the three individual anomaly paths and the XGBoost score-space fusion on the ADFA-LD evaluation pool. The fusion model dominates all individual paths across the full operating range; the gain is most pronounced in the low-FPR region (FPR < 0.20), where each individual path reaches at most TPR ≈ 0.70. The star marks the operating point at the val-optimal threshold (τ^*=0.401214): FPR = 0.195, TPR = 0.906. Per-path AUC values in the legend are computed on this score-space fusion split.

4.3 Ablation: Supervised vs. Unsupervised Fusion

Table 4 tests whether XGBoost's advantage stems from access to multiple scores or from learning how to combine them. Replacing XGBoost with the strongest unsupervised percentile-based aggregation rule (Empirical Cumulative Distribution Function (ECDF) + Max, F1 0.7644) costs 8.8 percentage points. Replacing it with a fully unsupervised partition of the three-dimensional score space, either Isolation Forest (F1 0.2045) or Gaussian Mixture Model (GMM) (F1 0.1500), causes catastrophic collapse, confirming that scale heterogeneity ratio 556.2 overwhelms any density- or partition-based rule that lacks label-aware calibration. Complementary orthogonal channels are *necessary* for the performance gain, but learned calibration is *sufficient* to realise it.

Table 4. Fusion ablation: supervised XGBoost vs. unsupervised aggregation alternatives on the 32-bit split.

Method	AUC	F1	Notes
XGBoost (selected)	**0.9113**	**0.8523**	supervised score-space
Isolation Forest baseline	0.8107	0.7937	unsupervised fusion
ECDF + Max	0.6818	0.7644	percentile aggregation
GMM baseline	0.5851	0.7379	density aggregation
IF (score space only)	0.5856	0.2045	unsupervised 3-D partition
GMM (score space only)	0.5796	0.1500	unsupervised 3-D partition

4.4 Per-Family Consistency

Table 5 (Panel A) applies the locked fusion model to each attack family slice independently without retraining. This is a family-sliced consistency diagnostic, not a leave-one-family-out training protocol. AUC stays within a narrow band (0.8979–0.9159) across all six families, and average F1 reaches 0.7306. Meterpreter is the weakest family on F1 (0.6491), consistent with its shorter average trace length and more variable call vocabulary; the remaining five families lie within 0.71–0.78. The consistency across semantically distinct attack types (brute-force, reverse-shell, and web-shell) supports the claim that orthogonal feature extraction generalises across behavioral regimes within this benchmark.

4.5 Orthogonality and Runtime

Table 5 (Panel B) reports pairwise Pearson correlations between benign-window anomaly scores and the detection synergy count. The Pearson correlations of 0.429 to 0.457 in Table 5 (Panel B) place the three score channels in a productive disagreement regime: sufficiently above zero to confirm shared sensitivity to genuine anomalies, and sufficiently below unity to indicate that no single path subsumes the others under linear association. This intermediate regime is where score-space fusion provides maximum benefit: the paths share enough sensitivity to genuine anomaly to reinforce each other, yet they disagree on 29,568 attack windows where at least one channel under-reacts, allowing the fusion layer to recover those windows from the other channels.

Pearson correlation measures linear association only; non-linear statistical dependencies between the three anomaly channels are not excluded by this analysis. More general dependence measures, such as Spearman rank correlation or kernel-based mutual information estimators [17], would provide a fuller characterisation of channel independence and are reserved for future work.

Table 5. Per-family consistency, cross-path orthogonality, and single-thread CPU latency for the 32-bit stack. Panel A reports the locked XGBoost fusion model by attack family; Panel B reports pairwise Pearson correlations, synergy count, and per-window latency.

Panel A: per-family evaluation of the locked XGBoost fusion model on ADFA-LD

Attack family	AUC	AUCPR	F1
Adduser	0.9048	0.6891	0.7093
Hydra FTP	0.9078	0.7311	0.7268
Hydra SSH	0.8979	0.7942	0.7745
Java Meterpreter	0.9159	0.7732	0.7783
Meterpreter	0.9128	0.6988	0.6491
Web Shell	0.9046	0.7757	0.7456
Average	**0.9073**	**0.7437**	**0.7306**

Panel B: cross-path orthogonality and single-thread CPU latency

Correlation pair	Pearson	Latency component	ms/window
Path A vs Path B	0.436	Path A	0.0295
Path B vs Path C	0.457	Path B	0.0140
Path A vs Path C	0.429	Path C	0.1767
Synergy count	29,568	XGBoost fusion	0.0016
		Grand total	**0.2217**

The full-pipeline latency of 0.2217 ms per window on a single CPU thread is computed by summing the three path inference times and the XGBoost meta-classifier step, with Path C (GRU autoregressive prediction) accounting for 80% of the total.

5 Discussion

5.1 Positive Arguments

Channel Independence is Empirically Evidenced, not Merely Assumed. The three paths were designed to occupy different mathematical spaces, but the design intention would be vacuous if the score channels behaved identically at inference time. The Pearson correlations of 0.429 to 0.457 reported in Table 5 place the three pairs in a *productive disagreement regime*: far enough from zero to provide evidence of partial linear independence and shared sensitivity to genuine anomaly, and far enough from unity to indicate that no single path subsumes the others. The synergy count of 29,568 attack windows recovered by at least one path when another under-reacts is a direct measure of the complementary value that this intermediate correlation regime provides.

Score-Space Supervision is Methodologically Justified. The gain from supervised fusion over the best unsupervised aggregation rule (8.8 pp F1 over ECDF+Max) is not an argument against the semi-supervised framing; it is an argument for placing supervision precisely where it is informative. The three base paths remain trained on benign data only, preserving the system's ability to generalise to attack variants outside the training distribution, which is the core requirement for novel-payload detection. The XGBoost layer is exposed only to a three-dimensional score vector; it never observes raw syscall sequences, so it cannot overfit to specific attack signatures. The architecture therefore separates two problems that are frequently conflated: learning what normal behaviour looks like (unsupervised, benign-only) versus learning how to combine anomaly signals into a reliable binary decision (supervised, score-space only).

Operational False-Positive Rate is Substantially Reduced by Fusion. At the F1-optimal threshold (τ^*=0.401214) the XGBoost fusion achieves an FPR of 0.1953 on the trace-isolated test split (FP = 2,357 out of 12,071 benign windows), versus Path A's FPR@TPR95 of 0.6782. For host-based monitors, FPR maps directly to per-host alert volume at the SOC; industry surveys report production FPRs of 40–99% [1], and the fusion model's 0.1953 represents a substantial reduction, though measured on ADFA-LD only and subject to distribution shift in production deployments.

Scale Heterogeneity is a Structural Property, not a Calibration Failure. The anomaly score spans (0.0254 for s_A, 0.8204 for s_B, 14.1177 for s_C) are direct consequences of the three different mathematical objectives (support-boundary margin, reconstruction MSE, and negative log-likelihood) and do not represent miscalibration. Arithmetic averaging would implicitly down-weight s_A by a factor of 556 relative to s_C, discarding the frequency-rarity signal entirely; gradient-boosted threshold partitioning avoids this by learning per-dimension ordered comparisons.

5.2 Limitations and Future Works

Three principal limitations bound the current evidence. First, all evaluation is conducted on a single benchmark, ADFA-LD (Ubuntu 11.04, 2011), which was selected for its trace-level metadata and per-trace boundaries needed for the leak-safe evaluation protocol. A single corpus captures a narrow slice of the attack landscape; cross-dataset validation, particularly on DongTing [12], is the next step to assess generalisation under distribution shift. Second, all three paths assume a stationary benign manifold: a process that changes its normal syscall profile over time (due to software updates, configuration changes, or workload variation) may trigger false alarms that the current protocol cannot distinguish from genuine intrusions, so the benign reference model would need periodic updates as software and workloads evolve. Third, Path C's GRU predictor is stateless at the window boundary: each 20-token window is scored independently, so cross-window temporal dependencies that span multiple stride steps are invisible to the chronological grammar channel; similarly, the reported latency covers only model inference on pre-windowed inputs and does not include kernel-side event capture, buffering, or per-process stream reconstruction in a deployed monitor. Addressing these gaps requires longitudinal benign data collection, domain-adaptation mechanisms, and stateful per-process GRU inference.

6 Conclusion

The results support a simple claim: system call behaviour should be decomposed before fusion. Three structurally independent representations (frequency and rarity, local topology, and chronological grammar) produce anomaly scalars that, when fused by a supervised score-space meta-classifier, outperform every individual single-view branch on the ADFA-LD 32-bit benchmark. The representation layer remains benign-only throughout training, preserving the system's capacity to generalise to novel attack variants; supervision is introduced only at the three-dimensional score-space boundary, where it calibrates agreement and disagreement among the three channels rather than memorising malware signatures.

The XGBoost fusion model achieved AUC 0.9113, AUPR 0.8950, and F1 0.8523 on the refreshed evaluation split. On the same score-space fusion test split, the individual channels achieved AUC 0.7754 for Path A, AUC 0.7974 for Path B, and AUC 0.8307 for Path C, while fusion raised the result to AUC 0.9113. Per-family evaluation across six attack families produced average AUC 0.9073 and F1 0.7306, and cross-path Pearson correlations of 0.43 to 0.46 confirmed that the three views contribute non-redundant evidence at a synergy count of 29,568 recovered attack windows. The full-pipeline latency of 0.2217 ms per window on a single CPU thread establishes an initial feasibility bound within the benchmark setting.

Three directions follow naturally for future work: *i)* integration with an open-source EDR platform such as Wazuh[4], leveraging the measured 0.2217 ms per-window latency for online inference on running Linux processes; *ii)* data collection from real-world deployment alongside a commercial EDR system, using its alerts as an operational reference; and *iii)* evaluation on the DongTing 64-bit corpus [12] to assess cross-dataset robustness.

[4] https://wazuh.com/.

Disclosure of Interests. The authors have no competing interests to declare.

References

1. Alahmadi, B.A., Axon, L., Martinovic, I.: 99 % false positives: a qualitative study of SOC analysts' perspectives on security alarms. In: 31st USENIX Security Symposium (USENIX Security 2022), pp. 2783–2800. USENIX Association, Boston, MA (Aug 2022)
2. An, J., Cho, S.: Variational autoencoder based anomaly detection using reconstruction probability. Tech. Rep. SNUDM-TR-2015-03, SNU Data Mining Center (2015)
3. Babaey, V., Faragardi, H.R.: Detecting zero-day web attacks with an ensemble of lstm, gru, and stacked autoencoders. Computers **14**(6), 205 (2025)
4. Breunig, M.M., Kriegel, H.P., Ng, R.T., Sander, J.: LOF: Identifying density-based local outliers. In: Proc. 2000 ACM SIGMOD International Conference on Management of Data, pp. 93–104. ACM, New York (2000)
5. Chawla, A., Lee, B., Jacob, P., Fallon, S.: Bidirectional LSTM autoencoder for sequence based anomaly detection in cyber security. Int. J. Simul. Syst. Sci. Technol. **20**(5) (2019)
6. Chen, T., Guestrin, C.: XGBoost: a scalable tree boosting system. In: Proc. 22nd ACM SIGKDD International Conference on Knowledge Discovery and Data Mining, pp. 785–794. ACM, New York (2016)
7. Cho, K., van Merrienboer, B., Gulcehre, C., Bahdanau, D., Bougares, F., Schwenk, H., Bengio, Y.: Learning phrase representations using RNN encoder-decoder for statistical machine translation. In: Proc. 2014 Conference on Empirical Methods in Natural Language Processing (EMNLP), pp. 1724–1734. Association for Computational Linguistics, Doha, Qatar (2014)
8. Creech, G., Hu, J.: A semantic approach to host-based intrusion detection systems using contiguous and discontiguous system call patterns. IEEE Trans. Comput. **63**(4), 807–819 (2014)
9. Darban, Z.Z., Webb, G.I., Pan, S., Aggarwal, C.C., Salehi, M.: Deep learning for time series anomaly detection: a survey. ACM Comput. Surv. **57**(1), 1–42 (2024)
10. Do, P.H., Le, T.D., Dinh, T.D., Pham, V.D., Nguyen, T.L.Q.: GT-FID: a graph-temporal fusion network for host-based intrusion detection from system call sequences. In: Proc. 2025 International Conference on Cloud Computing and Internet of Things (CCIOT), pp. 7–14. ACM, New York (2025)
11. Du, M., Li, F., Zheng, G., Srikumar, V.: DeepLog: anomaly detection and diagnosis from system logs through deep learning. In: Proc. 2017 ACM SIGSAC Conference on Computer and Communications Security(CCS), pp. 1285–1298. ACM, NY (2017)
12. Duan, G., Fu, Y., Cai, M., Chen, H., Sun, J.: Dongting: a large-scale dataset for anomaly detection of the linux kernel. J. Syst. Softw. **203**, 111745 (2023)
13. Forrest, S.: Computer immune systems — data sets and software: Sequence based intrusion detection data sets. http://www.cs.unm.edu/~immsec/systemcalls.htm (1998), university of New Mexico (UNM) system call corpus; includes synthetic sendmail (UNM, CERT), live lpr (UNM, MIT), named, xlock, login, ps, inetd, and stide traces
14. Forrest, S., Hofmeyr, S.A., Somayaji, A., Longstaff, T.A.: A sense of self for unix processes. In: Proc. 1996 IEEE Symposium on Security and Privacy, pp. 120–128. IEEE, Piscataway, NJ (1996)

15. Gao, X., Shan, C., Hu, C., Niu, Z., Liu, Z.: An adaptive ensemble machine learning model for intrusion detection. IEEE Access **7**, 82512–82521 (2019)
16. Hofmeyr, S.A., Forrest, S., Somayaji, A.: Intrusion detection using sequences of system calls. J. Comput. Secur. **6**(3), 151–180 (1998)
17. Kraskov, A., Stögbauer, H., Grassberger, P.: Estimating mutual information. Phys. Rev. E **69**(6), 066138 (2004)
18. Kumar, A.: Revolutionising anomaly detection: a hybrid framework for anomaly detection integrating isolation forest, autoencoder, and conv. lstm. Knowl. Inf. Syst. **67**(12), 11903–11953 (2025)
19. Liu, F.T., Ting, K.M., Zhou, Z.H.: Isolation forest. In: Proc. 8th IEEE International Conference on Data Mining, pp. 413–422. IEEE, Piscataway, NJ, USA (2008)
20. Maggi, F., Matteucci, M., Zanero, S.: Detecting intrusions through system call sequence and argument analysis. IEEE Trans. Dependable Sec. Comput. **7**(4), 381–395 (2010)
21. Mirsky, Y., Doitshman, T., Elovici, Y., Shabtai, A.: Kitsune: an ensemble of autoencoders for online network intrusion detection. In: Proceedings of 25th Annual Network and Distributed System Security Symposium (NDSS) (2018)
22. Pang, G., Shen, C., Cao, L., van den Hengel, A.: Deep learning for anomaly detection: a review. ACM Comput. Surv. **54**(2), 1–38 (2021)
23. Ring, J.H., Van Oort, C.M., Durst, S., White, V., Near, J.P., Skalka, C.: Methods for host-based intrusion detection with deep learning. Digit. Threats Res. Pract. **2**(4), 1–29 (2021)
24. Satilmiş, H., Akleylek, S., Yüce Tok, Z.: Development of various stacking ensemble-based HIDS using ADFA datasets. IEEE Open J. Commun. Soc. **6**, 1170–1189 (2025)
25. Schölkopf, B., Platt, J.C., Shawe-Taylor, J., Smola, A.J., Williamson, R.C.: Estimating the support of a high-dimensional distribution. Neural Comput. **13**(7), 1443–1471 (2001)
26. Sun, R., et al.: Learning fast and slow: PROPEDEUTICA for real-time malware detection. IEEE Trans. Neural Netw. Learn. Syst. **33**(6), 2518–2529 (2022)
27. Ting, K.M., Witten, I.H.: Issues in stacked generalization. J. Artif. Intell. Res. **10**, 271–289 (1999)
28. Warrender, C., Forrest, S., Pearlmutter, B.: Detecting intrusions using system calls: Alternative data models. In: Proc. 1999 IEEE Symposium on Security and Privacy, pp. 133–145. IEEE, Piscataway, NJ (1999)
29. Wolpert, D.H.: Stacked generalization. Neural Netw. **5**(2), 241–259 (1992)
30. Xie, M., Hu, J., Yu, X., Chang, E.: Evaluating host-based anomaly detection systems: application of the frequency-based algorithms to ADFA-LD. In: Au, M.H., Carminati, B., Kuo, C.-C.J. (eds.) NSS 2014. LNCS, vol. 8792, pp. 542–549. Springer, Cham (2014). https://doi.org/10.1007/978-3-319-11698-3_44

Proceedings of the Second International Workshop on Cybersecurity and Privacy Risk Assessments (CPRA 2026)

CPRA 2026 Preface

This volume presents the proceedings of the second edition of the Workshop on Cybersecurity and Privacy Risk Assessments (CPRA), held in conjunction with the 21st International Conference on Availability, Reliability and Security (ARES), which took place in Linköping, Sweden on 24–27 August 2026.

CPRA brought together computer scientists, researchers, practitioners, and industry experts to explore emerging approaches for assessing evolving cybersecurity and privacy risks. Discussions addressed the limitations of traditional risk assessment methodologies, particularly their adaptation from the generic IT domain to safety-critical environments. The lack of clear guidance and reproducibility, the extensive manual involvement of experts, and the influence of governmental and standardisation frameworks were also discussed in the context of evolving Cyber Physical System (CPS) technologies. On that note, CPRA emphasised the importance of customising risk assessment methodologies to incorporate safety, Operational Technology (OT), and domain-related factors. The workshop focused on pushing towards more dynamic and proactive approaches, refining standardised methods on top of traditional Threat Analysis and Risk Assessment (TARA), Data Protection Impact Assessment (DPIA), and risk prioritisation techniques. Furthermore, the workshop explored the interplay between regulatory compliance and the impact of heavy risk management processes on Small and Medium-sized Enterprises (SME), particularly in balancing financial, legal, technical, and societal requirements.

The papers of the workshop were grouped into the following topical sections: (i) Risk assessment methodologies for critical and connected systems; and (ii) Risk prioritisation and management frameworks.

The workshop papers included in this volume were selected through a rigorous review process, with an acceptance rate of 50%. Out of ten submissions, five papers were accepted for presentation at the workshop. Manuscripts were double-blind reviewed by at least three experts, assigned based on relevant expertise of program committee members. Evaluation criteria included relevance to the workshop theme, originality of the research, clarity of the methods and results, approach and correctness of the validation, interest to the general, scientific, and practicing public as well as overall quality of the manuscript. All conflicts of interest were declared and verified by the workshop chairs, who ensured that no program committee member served as a reviewer on any paper they co-authored.

August 2026

Meriem Benyahya
Anastasija Collen

CPRA 2026 Organization

Workshop Chairs

Meriem Benyahya	University Mohammed VI Polytechnic, Morocco
Anastasija Collen	University of Applied Sciences and Arts of Western Switzerland (HES-SO Geneva), Switzerland

Program Committee

Tariq Bontekoe	University of Groningen, Netherlands
Don Nalin Dharshana Jayaratne	Swansea University, UK
Sokratis Katsikas	Norwegian University of Science and Technology, Norway
Teri Lenard	University of Medicine, Pharmacy, Science and Technology of Târgu Mureș, Romania
Nico Mexis	University of Passau, Germany
Mohamed Amine Merzouk	Polytechnique Montréal, Canada
Anas Motii	University Mohammed VI Polytechnique, Morocco
Niels Alexander Nijdam	University of Geneva, Switzerland
Narges Rahimi	SHIELD Automotive Cybersecurity Centre of Excellence, University of Windsor, Canada
Jetzabel Serna-Olvera	Cyber4people, IU International University of Applied Sciences, Germany
Michalis Smyrlis	Sphynx Analytics Ltd., Cyprus
Manfred Vielberth	Technische Hochschule Deggendorf, Germany

Systematic Cybersecurity Risk Analysis of European Rail Traffic Management System

Kacper Darowski[1], Sebastian N. Peters[1,2](✉), and Lukas Lautenschlager[1,2]

[1] TUM CIT, Technical University of Munich, Munich, Germany
[2] Fraunhofer AISEC, Garching bei München, Germany
sebastian.peters@aisec.fraunhofer.de

Abstract. European Rail Traffic Management System (ERTMS) is a widely adopted standard unifying train management in the EU. While the standard allows for use cases like fully autonomous driving, cybersecurity has been an afterthought. Risk analysis enables the systematic assessment and prioritization of threats and mitigations. To date, it remains unclear which threats are most significant in ERTMS. This study systematically models components of ERTMS and analyzes their security in light of threats identified in the underlying technologies. The results suggest a concerning state of ERTMS, despite its critical role in railway safety. The use of legacy standards like EuroBalises and GSM - Railway (GSM-R) introduces vulnerabilities that persist across minimal ERTMS implementations, deployments incorporating various optional safety measures, and prospective future evolutions of the system, e.g., adopting Future Railway Mobile Communication System (FRMCS). Fully transitioning to European Train Control System (ETCS) level 2 was identified as the most significant improvement to ERTMS cybersecurity. The results indicate that a shift of ERTMS toward security is required to ensure availability and safe operation. While the chosen methodology proved its feasibility and shows remaining weaknesses of ERTMS, future work is needed to develop railway-centric adaptations to improve the quantification and evaluation of the computed risks.

Keywords: Railway Cybersecurity · Security Risk Analysis · Modular Risk Assessment · ERTMS · ETCS · FRMCS · GSM-R · EuroBalise

1 Introduction

To promote the development and operation of international railways, the EU introduced the European Rail Traffic Management System (ERTMS) [30] to

K. Darowski, S. N. Peters and L. Lautenschlager—These authors contributed equally to this work.

An *extended version* is available at https://doi.org/10.48550/arXiv.2606.11839.

Z. Afzal et al. (Eds.): ARES 2026 Workshops, LNCS 16900, pp. 119–137, 2027.
https://doi.org/10.1007/978-3-032-35576-8_7

establish interoperable signaling, communication, and train management systems. ERTMS enables a number of technologies like standardized signaling, Over-the-air (OTA) communication, and Automatic Train Operation (ATO). Having first become mandatory for new high-speed networks in 2002 [31], and for regular railways in 2004 [32], ERTMS has seen mixed adoption rates ranging from full deployment in Belgium and Luxembourg to a coverage of less than 1% in Germany [55]. ERTMS has even expanded beyond the borders of the EU to countries like Australia or Thailand[1], indicating global trust in the responsible European Union Agency for Railways (ERA). The ERA published the first specification draft in 1996 [30] and subsequently updated it, most recently as "Baseline 4" in 2023 [33]. Nevertheless, this long legacy raises the question to what extent cybersecurity has been part of the standardization process.

In the past decade, various attacks on railway infrastructure have occurred across multiple countries, typically in the form of Denial of Service (DoS) or the release of personal information [53]. Legacy cyber-physical systems, in particular, are vulnerable to low-cost attacks, as was the case with Polish trains being remotely halted by broadcasting a stop command over the radio in 2023 [45]. Apart from attacks carried out for personal gain or targeted service disruptions, concerns about exploitation in military warfare are on the rise amidst heightened geopolitical tensions. While the EU migrating its signaling and train management to highly computerized systems is a necessary step in expanding and unifying its rail networks, the relatively dated nature of ERTMS, compared to the rapid pace of cybersecurity developments, calls for a closer investigation of the status quo. The contributions of this paper are:

C1 We adapt and apply a modular cybersecurity risk assessment approach to systematically model and evaluate ERTMS.

C2 We derive/compare the cybersecurity risk profiles of current/future ERTMS configurations, identifying the assets that expose the largest attack surface.

We summarize related research in Sect. 2 and explain the core concepts of ERTMS in Sect. 3, which are relevant to the system model (Sect. 5) and risk analysis (Sect. 7). Section 4 describes our approach to modeling and analyzing ERTMS. The identified threats and controls are described in Sect. 6. The results of our analysis are shown in Sect. 7 and discussed in Sect. 8. Section 9 concludes our findings.

2 Related Work

This section summarizes the existing literature using the following trichotomy: cybersecurity of generic railway infrastructure, of ERTMS, and risk analysis.

Railway Security: Academic and industrial work agrees that the growing digitalization and connectivity of railway Operational Technology (OT) increases the cyberattack surface of a strategically critical infrastructure [37,38,44,51].

[1] See https://www.ertms.net/deployment-world-map/, Accessed: 2026-06-08.

Surveys highlight safety-security co-engineering, simulation and modeling, and the use of Artificial Intelligence (AI) and blockchain as main research trends, while pointing to gaps in validation, Long-Term Evolution (LTE)/5G security, cybersecurity implementation, and quantitative risk management [34,44]. Technical contributions focus on network-level protections such as segregation via firewalls/gateways, Intrusion Detection Systems (IDSs), Deep Packet Inspection (DPI), AI-based detection, and strong encryption, but also stress practical constraints arising from long asset lifetimes, geographical dispersion, and vendor lock-in, and therefore advocate risk-based and cost-aware security engineering [34,38,40,43,51]. At the normative level, CENELEC TS 50701 and the recent EU Rail System-Pillar specifications provide life-cycle guidance, generic threat scenarios, and baseline cybersecurity requirements for signaling and interlocking systems [1,26–29,38,51]. Our work complements this horizontal view with an independent, technology-aware risk analysis, including explicit attack trees and detailed assessments of Future Railway Mobile Communication System (FRMCS) and ATO.

ERTMS Security: Cybersecurity analyses of ERTMS concentrate mainly on its communication and cryptographic mechanisms. Early work on EuroRadio's "Safety Layer" over GSM-Railway (GSM-R) exposed weak cryptographic primitives (3DES) and problematic key-management practices, and suggested more robust designs [48]. Subsequent studies analyzed denial-of-service and jamming against GSM-R, resource-exhaustion and Pseudo Random Number Generator (PRNG) attacks, and again questioned key management, while calling for systematic vulnerability assessments [36,41]. A second line of work focuses on EuroBalises: simulation-based studies showed that missing integrity protection and remotely modifiable firmware can enable manipulation of automatic train halting; countermeasures include retrofitted authentication tags and anomaly detection [47]. Tests in related Communication Based Train Control (CBTC) systems confirmed that low-cost equipment suffices to jam balise telegrams and also highlighted risks in Wi-Fi-based intra-vehicular communication [57]. More recent contributions discuss system-level mitigations for future ERTMS evolutions, in particular FRMCS, recommending centralized "overarching security mechanisms" (such as Security Operations Centres (SOCs), Maintenance and Data Management (MDM), and a sector-specific Public Key Infrastructure (PKI) and Domain Name System (DNS)) as well as cryptographic agility, continuous mediation, and AI-based observability and "sustained visibility" for already deployed assets [6,42]. These works mostly address individual components or mechanisms; in contrast, we analyze the complete ERTMS, from legacy GSM-R and EuroBalises to FRMCS and ATO, within a unified risk framework.

Cybersecurity Risk Analysis: Methodologically, our work builds on established security risk-assessment approaches. In the automotive domain, Wolf et al. derive risk levels by combining Common Methodology for Information Technology Security Evaluation (CEM)-style attack potentials with damage estimates based on adjusted Safety Integrity Levels (SIL) levels and attack trees [9,61]. Eichler et al. generalize this into the Modular Risk Assessment for the Development of Secure Automotive Systems (MoRA) framework, which supports scalable, function-oriented, and technology-aware analyses [10]. It has been applied before to similar complex use cases, such as autonomous driving [60]. For railways, prior work includes safety-focused risk models [46] and approaches that jointly consider safety and security interactions [2]. Only a few studies apply cybersecurity risk assessment specifically to ERTMS: Bloomfield et al. sketch a methodology for ERTMS-based systems but disclose limited results, while other work concentrates on single mechanisms such as 3DES in EuroRadio or secure ERTMS architectures and key management [8,52,59]. Existing literature thus either remains high-level or focuses on narrowly scoped technical issues. We close this gap by applying MoRA to the full ERTMS specification, including new standardizations such as FRMCS, and by publishing explicit attack trees and detailed, system-wide risk profiles instead of only presenting a methodology.

3 Background

This section explains the current state of ERTMS standards in the scope of this analysis. It introduces the components, interfaces, and cryptographic mechanisms that later form the system model in Sect. 5.

European Train Control System: Within ERTMS, the European Train Control System (ETCS) signaling and control system has the most direct impact on passenger safety. It ensures that no two trains enter the same track segment simultaneously; we consider specification version 4.0.0 [13]. ETCS defines four operational levels: level 0 (no ETCS on the Track-Side (TS)), level "National Train Control (NTC)" (legacy systems connected via a Specific Transmission Module (STM)), level 1 (ETCS train supervision with data from EuroBalises, EuroLoops, Radio Block Centres (RBCs), and Radio Infill Units (RIUs)), and level 2 (continuous radio communication with RBCs, with EuroBalises mainly providing positional data; EuroLoops and RIUs are not used) [13,19,20]. EuroBalises and EuroLoops are spot and semi-continuous track devices that transmit wayside information to the On-Board Unit (OBU) via inductive coupling, while RBCs and RIUs provide radio-based "infill" information [13,19,20]. The pivotal datum is the Movement Authority (MA), which authorizes a train to proceed up to an End of Authority (EOA) or Limit of Authority (LOA); MAs can be extended but not revoked, only cooperatively shortened [13]. Additional data includes emergency stops, temporary speed restrictions, gradients, and further track conditions. Balise linking triggers an emergency halt if expected balises or loops are not detected. This may be suppressed near known interference sources via Big Metallic Masses (BMM) and Virtual Balise Cover (VBC) [13,16]. The ETCS OBU supervises speed and can apply brakes but not traction, which remains with the driver or ATO. Position is computed mainly from odometry referenced to balises, with Global Navigation Satellite Systems (GNSSs) used only as time sources [13,14].

GSM-R and FRMCS: Today, radio communication between train and RBCs/RIUs uses GSM-R, a dedicated mobile network operating in circuit- and packet-switched modes; packet mode relies on standard Transmission Control Protocol (TCP)/Internet Protocol (IP), with the EuroRadio module resolving RBC/RIU addresses via DNS [18]. A "Safety Layer" supplements GSM with traffic encryption and integrity protection using three symmetric keys: `KTRANS` (transport), `KMAC` (authentication) and `KSMAC` (session). Fresh `KSMAC` keys are derived from `KMAC` and nonces via Triple Data Encryption Algorithm (3DES), and a 64-bit Cipher Block Chaining (CBC)-Message Authentication Code (MAC) provides integrity [18]. The upcoming FRMCS replaces GSM-R with a 5G-based system that offers inherent authentication and encryption, plus TLS-protected end-to-end communication. DNS is again used for IP resolution [18,35].

Automatic Train Operation: ATO is an optional subsystem enabling (semi-)autonomous driving and automatic station stops. The ATO OBU receives its data exclusively over FRMCS from the trackside ATO system. Segment Profiles (SPs) describe infrastructure segments (stop points, speed profiles, tunnels, platforms), while a Journey Profile (JP) combines multiple SPs with additional infrastructure and timetable constraints. Internally, the ATO OBU contains three modules: Time Table Speed Management (TTSM), Supervised Speed Envelope Management (SSEM) (respecting ETCS speed supervision), and Automatic Train Stopping Management (ATSM) (accurate stopping at defined points). Their speed recommendations are combined by taking the minimum, and ATO directly controls both traction and brakes, while also having the option to manage door opening/closing according to dwell times and platform data [16]. ETCS remains the safety authority and can override ATO via braking.

Key Management: ERTMS defines a distributed key management architecture for `KTRANS` and `KMAC` [22,23]. Each entity belongs to a key management domain served by a Key Management Centre (KMC), which generates and distributes `KMAC` and handles inter-domain requests. Keys can be provisioned via an off-line, out-of-band interface (using 3DES and a CBC-MAC, with unclear initial secret installation) [22] or via an on-line TLS-protected channel that relies on `KTRANS` and a PKI for certificate-based distribution [13,17,23]. With full transition to FRMCS, legacy `KMAC`/`KSMAC` usage is phased out and all cryptographic material is to be managed by a sector-wide PKI [17].

4 Methodology

The methodology follows four basic steps:

1. **Literature Review:** Identify relevant specification documents and survey existing research on ERTMS, to obtain a detailed understanding.
2. **System Modeling:** Construct an abstract model of the ERTMS.
3. **Risk Analysis:** Perform a risk analysis of the derived system.
4. **Validation:** Compare the results with related work.

The majority of the ERTMS specification is publicly accessible on ERA's website. It is split into multiple documents called "subsets". Due to the large number of these subsets, compiling the information they contain requires substantial effort in cross-referencing the documents. After careful consideration, the previously described MoRA framework has been chosen for the risk analysis for the following reasons: Its **iterative and modular nature** is well-suited for the scale of ERTMS, as granularity can be adapted based on early findings. Establishing the Target of Evaluation (TOE) ensures **completeness** with respect to the selected model and threats, minimizing subjectivity and bias (though not guaranteeing completeness for the real-world system, which depends on the analyst's abstractions). To tackle the scope of the specification in the risk analysis, the following approach to MoRA was chosen:

1. **Creation of TOE**: The system model is formalized into the TOE by identifying system components, connections, and used technologies. Data flows for each connection are modeled at the chosen level of granularity.
2. **Function Assignment**: The data is grouped into "functions" based on their purposes and effects. Any datum can be part of multiple functions. Based on the established data flows, the components and connections are automatically mapped to the same functions.
3. **Quantification of Security Goals**: For each function, the impairment of *Confidentiality*, *Integrity*, and *Availability* is assessed across four damage classes aligned with ISO/SAE 21434 [39]: *Safety*, *Financial*, *Legal (also covering Privacy)*, and *Operational*. Each combination of function and impairment constitutes a security goal. Following MoRA, damages are assessed per function at worst-case severity, as any compromise of a given security goal produces the same downstream consequences regardless of the specific attack vector.
4. **Threat Establishment**: Threats are identified using a subset of Spoofing, Tampering, Repudiation, Information Disclosure, Denial of Service, Elevation of Privilege (STRIDE) (spoofing, tampering, information disclosure, and DoS; repudiation and elevation of privileges are subsumed by spoofing and tampering as ERTMS relies predominantly on physical domain separation, and forged messages inherently deny authentic origin) applied to components or connections. Each threat is rated with a Required Attack Potential (RAP) following CEM [9] across five categories: *Elapsed Time*, *Required Expertise*, *Knowledge of TOE*, *Window of Opportunity*, and *Required Equipment*. According to CEM [9], the RAP levels stem from summed category scores: 0–9 (Basic), 10–13 (Enhanced-Basic), 14–19 (Moderate), 20–24 (High), and $\geq$25 (Beyond High).
5. **Defining Controls**: Different controls that can secure the system are identified through an iterative process. We begin with the set of controls stemming directly from the ERTMS specification and our literature analysis. For each unaddressed threat, further literature is reviewed to identify applicable countermeasures. Next, we identify threats that render some control ineffective; e.g., gaining access to a private key renders a secure channel protected by that key ineffective. Controls beyond those steps are not considered.
6. **Compiling Attack Trees**: For each threat, an attack tree is built recursively. The root represents the threat, and children are "preparation threats"

weakening controls protecting against it. Subtrees that share the same root are duplicated, while paths whose RAP is fully dominated by a shorter path are pruned.

7. **Risk Estimation**: The combined required attack potential of each of the attack trees is calculated by summing each path and multiplying it by the damage levels of the broken security goals, yielding a "risk level" for the tree.
8. **Evaluation of Controls**: Finally, the risks are recalculated for different sets of active controls, to gain an understanding of the effectiveness of various countermeasures. This can then be compared with the claims made by the designers of these controls and other researchers.

5 System Model

This section describes the developed system model as formalized in MoRA's TOE. The identified components can be segregated into four broader categories.

At the core of the On-Board (OB) we find the ETCS OBU, which interfaces with all the other components within a train. For our purposes, we consider the Driver Machine Interface (DMI), the ATO OBU, a representative STM, the On-Board Recording Device (ORD), the EuroRadio module, and the vehicle interface [13]. Some of the abstraction choices include omitting distinct communication modules for EuroBalises and EuroLoops and merging the FRMCS functionality into EuroRadio. All OB components are connected to the ETCS OBU via a physical Ethernet network running PROFINET [13,14]. Historically, Multifunction Vehicle Bus (MVB) and Controller Area Network (CAN) have been used, but we ignore this in our model, as they are no longer permitted in new vehicles. Additionally, the ATO OBU has its own Ethernet connections to the EuroRadio, the DMI, and the vehicle interface (possibly multiple, but this distinction is irrelevant to our analysis).

Our model's TS comprises four train communication systems: the EuroBalise, the EuroLoop, the RBC, and the RIU. It is sufficient to model only one instance of each component. We choose not to model any further components, like Lineside Electronic Units (LEUs), NTC TS, or the interlocking backbone, as these are beyond the scope of ERTMS. For the same reason, we do not model any internal connections on the TS [13]. The TS interfaces transmit messages to the OB via four channels: induction between the EuroBalise and the ETCS OBU, respectively, the EuroLoop, GSM-R between the RBC and the EuroRadio, as well as an equivalent connection with the RIU. We ignore FRMCS here, and view it as a control instead (see Sect. 6) [13].

Some services in ERTMS are accessed via the Internet: PKI, DNS resolver, and ATO TS. We also include a gateway connecting the GSM-R network to the Internet. We form one TCP connection from the PKI to the gateway, the RBC, the RIU, and the ATO TS. The DNS resolver connects to the gateway via User Datagram Protocol (UDP). The train's Internet connectivity is modeled as a GSM-R connection between the EuroRadio and the gateway [16–18].

We define two components relevant to Key Management (KM): a local and an external KMC. The local KMC is connected redundantly via TCP and Out-of-Band (OOB) to the RBC, the RIU, and the external KMC. Both KMCs interface with the PKI over TCP [11,22,23].

Lastly, a Global Navigation Satellite System (GNSS) component with an interface to the ETCS OBU is included for some configurations. Figure 1 illustrates all components and their connections.

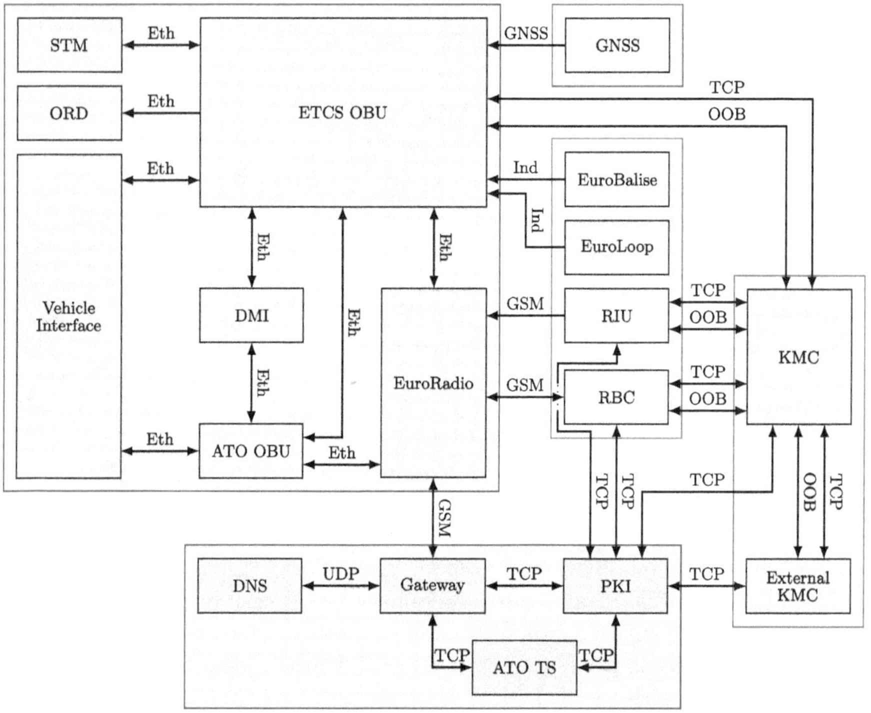

Fig. 1. System components grouped by domain (OB, TS, Internet, KM) and their connections. Edge labels denote the communication technology: Eth = Ethernet, Ind = Magnetic induction, GSM = GSM-R, OOB = Out-of-Band

The data units transferred on each connection were extracted from the relevant specification documents [11–13,15,17,18,21–25]. We omit listing them and instead focus on the identified functions; we define one function related to traction control, one to brake systems, one to MAs, two to the DMI, three to various status reports, five to different track information, one to key management and one to certificate management, three to mode and level transitions, one for door control, as well as one for odometry, current time, version negotiation, communication establishment and termination, logging, acknowledgements, End of Information (EOI), error reporting, safe radio supervision, VBC and balise linking, emergency stops, and NTC each, for a total of 37 functions.

The compromise of the majority of these functions' security goals is associated with a *Very High* or *High* damage level, as it may lead to consequences ranging from section blockages to level-crossing accidents resulting in injuries or fatalities. Security goals with *Moderate* and *Low* damage levels relate to moderate train delays, e.g., due to a broken MA shortening, or passenger comfort, e.g., due to a compromise of air conditioning. Table 1 lists all functions with their security goals and assigned damage severity in each class. For example, the integrity of the function MA yields *Very High* safety damages, as authorizing a train to move into an occupied block can lead to collisions between trains. This also applies to the *High* financial damages caused through potential collisions between trains. Operational damages arise from attacks on the integrity or availability of the MA function—e.g., spoofing a blocked signal or dropping authorization messages—which can prevent train movement authorizations to free blocks, causing significant delays and network blockages.

Table 1. Damage level assessment per function and security goal. Each color represents a severity (■*Very High*, ■*High*, □*Moderate*, □*Low*, □*Very Low*, ▨*No Damages*). An asterisk (*) at the function name indicates that one or more of that function's security goals break a control, e.g., the integrity of the certificate management breaks TLS.

Function	Safety			Financial			Legal			Operational		
	C	I	A	C	I	A	C	I	A	C	I	A
Traction Control	-	VH	VH	-	H	H	-	-	-	-	H	H
Brake Control*	-	VH	VH	-	H	H	-	-	-	-	H	H
Door Control	-	VH	-	-	-	-	-	-	-	-	M	M
Certificate Manag.*	-	-	-	-	-	-	-	-	-	-	H	H
Track Condition	-	VH	-	-	H	-	-	-	-	-	H	H
Movement Authority	-	VH	-	-	H	-	-	-	-	-	H	H
Balise Linking*	-	-	-	-	-	-	-	-	-	-	-	-
Version Negotiation	-	-	-	-	-	-	-	-	-	-	H	H
NTC	-	VH	-	-	H	-	-	-	-	-	H	H
Display	-	-	-	-	-	-	-	-	-	-	-	-
Air Intake	-	L	L	-	-	-	-	-	-	-	VL	VL
Power	-	H	-	-	M	L	-	-	-	-	H	H
Logging	-	-	-	-	-	-	-	H	H	-	-	-
Level Crossing	-	VH	VH	-	M	M	-	-	-	-	H	H
Communication Est.	-	-	-	-	-	-	-	-	-	-	H	H
Key Management*	-	-	-	-	-	-	-	-	-	-	H	H
Mode Transition	-	VH	-	-	M	-	-	-	-	-	H	H
ETCS Transition	-	-	-	-	-	-	-	-	-	-	H	H
Location Reference	-	VH	-	-	M	-	-	-	-	-	H	H
Odometry	-	VH	-	-	H	-	-	-	-	-	H	H
Time	-	H	-	-	M	-	-	-	-	-	H	H
Emergency Stop	-	VH	VH	-	H	H	-	-	-	-	H	-
Acknowledgements	-	-	-	-	-	-	-	-	-	-	H	H
Train Data	-	H	-	-	M	-	-	-	-	-	H	H
Train Status Reports	-	-	-	-	-	-	-	-	-	-	H	H
Shunting	-	-	-	-	-	-	-	-	-	-	M	L
End of Information	-	-	-	-	-	-	-	-	-	-	-	-
Error Reporting	-	M	-	-	-	-	-	-	-	-	H	-
DMI Button Press	-	-	-	-	-	-	-	-	-	-	H	H
BMM*	-	-	-	-	-	-	-	-	-	-	H	H
Safe Radio Supervision*	-	M	M	-	-	-	-	-	-	-	H	H

6 Controls and Threats

This section presents the threats (Sect. 6.1 and 6.4) and controls (Sect. 6.2 and 6.3) identified through our methodology, progressing from basic to advanced. Threats are organized by the underlying technology or communication interface identified in the system model (Sect. 5). For each technology of a connection and component, STRIDE categories are applied (Sect. 4, step 4), informed by known vulnerabilities from the literature. Social engineering is a cross-cutting vector that affects OOB key management procedures. RAP values follow CEM [9]; unless stated otherwise, repeated attacks on cryptographic primitives reduce the RAP to *Basic*, since broken keys can be reused.

6.1 Basic Threats

Magnetic Induction (EuroBalise and EuroLoop): The easiest technology to threaten in ERTMS is the magnetic induction used by EuroBalise and EuroLoop telegrams. Disruption of this communication requires only makeshift equipment [58], and long stretches of the track lack physical protection, resulting in a *Basic* RAP. To spoof telegrams, custom equipment on the tracks can imitate a balise, though an expert level of knowledge and bespoke equipment may be necessary. Furthermore, the attacker may need to spend extended time around the railroad, which could raise suspicion. The RAP rating of this threat is *Moderate*. An alternative spoofing approach involves replay attacks as suggested by Lim et al. [47]. We consider this to be as difficult as the fake balise threat, yielding a *Moderate* RAP. Another concern raised by Lim et al. [47] is firmware modification. Although the specification states that such "test interfaces" are "not required to be integrated in the operational equipment" [19], we still consider firmware reflashing in our analysis. Both physical debug and remote interfaces can be used, creating two potential threats. In either case, bespoke tools and expert knowledge may be required due to vendor-specific equipment. Both threats receive a *High* RAP. Information disclosure is not analyzed here, since telegram data are not secret and their effects can be observed externally.
Ethernet (On-Board Communication): Breaking the availability of an Ethernet conduit is trivial; severing the cable prevents data flow. This is done in negligible time, though physical presence is required, resulting in a *Basic* RAP. Sniffing can be executed with similar difficulty. However, specialized equipment may be necessary to reconnect the cable while allowing data interception. The RAP remains *Basic*. Lastly, we consider data integrity. Spoofing on an Ethernet network has the same prerequisites as sniffing, since a physical device must be patched into the network. We raise the expertise level to proficient, since knowledge of layer-2 spoofing is required. However, the RAP does not increase beyond *Basic*. We do not separately evaluate tampering, since combining the availability and spoofing threats achieves the same goal.
Internet Protocol (IP): IP spoofing is trivial and ranks lowest in each category, earning a *Basic* RAP rating. Again, we do not deem it necessary to analyze tampering attacks separately. Compromising the confidentiality of IP traffic

via sniffing requires an on-path position. For our purposes, we consider a malicious network infrastructure operator. We assume it takes about a week for an attacker with expert knowledge to influence routing protocols in the desired way. The knowledge of TOE should be assumed to be restricted at least, since the IP addresses and ports used are not publicly documented. The necessary equipment should be at least specialized, if not bespoke. The total RAP equates to *Moderate*. Disrupting IP traffic availability can be achieved either by an on-path attacker dropping packets (analogous to the sniffing threat) or via large-scale Distributed Denial of Service (DDoS) attacks. The emergence of "DDoS as a Service" providers enables automated botnet-based flooding for monetary compensation [56], requiring only restricted TOE knowledge. The resulting RAP is *Enhanced-Basic*, potentially lower if cost estimates of \$10/h are accurate [3].

GSM-Railway (GSM-R): Due to the prevalence of GSM in mobile communication, equipment for sniffing, jamming, and spoofing is readily available. The knowledge of the TOE ranges from public to restricted, depending on the details, such as the phone numbers used. Each of these three threats can be executed ad hoc if the attacker is adjacent to the track. The resulting RAP is *Basic* irrespective of the expertise level.

Global Navigation Satellite System (GNSS): Morong et al. [49] demonstrated the ease of GNSS jamming, requiring only a few watts of transmission power, and calculated the jam range to be tens of kilometers, requiring no specialized equipment, no sensitive knowledge, and no time investment. The resulting RAP is *Basic*. Attacking the integrity of GNSS is more involved, as correctly spoofing the transmission requires expert understanding of the involved mathematics and signal theory [54]. Furthermore, given more advanced receivers capable of discerning the direction of the incoming signal, the positioning of the antennas must be more deliberate, and the equipment must be at least specialized. Still, the instantaneous long-range nature of the threat means the RAP does not exceed *Enhanced-Basic*. Tampering with the GNSS signal or the satellites themselves is infeasible or overly complex compared to the jam-and-spoof approach. Information disclosure is not considered, since GNSS data is public.

Social Engineering: In general, the adversary might need to be hired by the respective company to gain physical access to the train (estimated time: 1 month). Since details of the KM procedures at the firm are needed, the required TOE knowledge is restricted. Similarly, the window of opportunity is ranked as difficult. The total RAP is *High*. For repeated attacks, the time required is reduced to under a day, since the person on the inside only needs to get through the hiring process once, reducing the RAP to *Moderate*.

6.2 Basic Controls

Controls Inherent to the Model: To simplify the model (Sect. 5), some of the system properties are expressed as controls. Firstly, the lack of ATO can be viewed as a control, since functions associated with automatic driving cannot be exploited when they are not implemented. This control raises the RAP of threats related to ATO to *Beyond High*. Similarly, using ETCS exclusively in level 2 removes the EuroLoop and the RIU from the model and limits data transmitted by the EuroBalise to location references [13]. Lastly, we model FRMCS as a control on GSM-R technology, since it fully replaces the legacy standard. The control protects against threats to confidentiality and integrity by significantly increasing the time, expertise, and resources required to break state-of-the-art cryptographic primitives, resulting in a RAP of *Beyond High* [6].

Mandatory Controls: The ERTMS specifications contain some mandatory protective measures. At the OB Ethernet level, the PROFINET standard is used. However, it does not introduce any cybersecurity measures and instead relies on "defense in depth". For our use case, we consider a properly separated network, as recommended by PROFINET and ERTMS [14]. We assume that all safety-relevant Ethernet cables are physically difficult for normal passengers to access, thereby increasing the window of opportunity to difficult [50]. Nearly all communication over IP, like between the train and the PKI, is TLS-secured. We assume this has the same effect on IP as FRMCS does on GSM-R [16]. One notable exception is DNS, which uses unencrypted UDP datagrams. Lastly, GSM-R extends the Open Systems Interconnection (OSI) network model by a "safety layer". Despite its wording, this layer is responsible for traffic encryption, and the 3DES primitive used in this layer is considered outdated (see Sect. 3) [4,5,7,48]. For our analysis, we estimate that the safety layer increases the RAP of threats to GSM-R's confidentiality and integrity to *Enhanced-Basic*.

Optional Controls: Two optional safety-related concepts in ERTMS apply to cybersecurity. Firstly, balise linking, described in Sect. 3, can be used as a countermeasure against threats to telegram availability. While it does not change the RAP, the control *transforms* safety-related damages into train delays through induced emergency halts [13]. Secondly, the OB's "safe radio supervision" monitors unannounced interruptions of OTA communication. Upon loss of signal, the train either halts or fails to respond, depending on the configuration [13]. Hence, we consider setting the reaction to a trip (or normal braking) as a control on GSM-R's availability with the same transformative property as balise linking. Moreover, the OB Ethernet network specification mentions that "security functions are expected on higher layers to ensure end-to-end security" [14], though it is not clear how these are to be implemented while maintaining interoperability. We model this as a control that raises the RAP of confidentiality and integrity threats on Ethernet to *Beyond High*.

6.3 Further Controls

Existing Literature: Plenty of research suggests various forms of jamming detection and the use of an Intrusion Detection Systems (IDS) [6,42,47,48,57]. Regrettably, these recommendations tend to be vague, especially regarding the system's response to an alarm. For this reason, we choose not to model these controls. The proposal by Lim et al. to introduce MACs to the telegram format offers a unique approach to hardening the interface without breaking backward compatibility [47]. They suggest reusing the 12-bit scrambling mechanism [19] (a shift-register seeded by a short random value) using derived keys from a shared secret to protect the confidentiality and integrity of balise telegrams [47]. While the proposal is creative, we have doubts about its resilience against cyberattacks. Firstly, the short length of the MACs allows for computationally feasible collisions. Forging telegrams can still prove challenging, as the scrambling can be seen as encryption. However, the telegrams are very short, and scrambling was never intended for this use. Additionally, the plaintext could be inferred by observing the rolling stock's reaction. Based on these concerns, we calculate the RAP increase of threats to telegram confidentiality and integrity to *Enhanced-Basic*.

Original Suggestions: Based on early risk indicators, we have composed a few simple controls against threats seen in Sect. 6.1. The relatively low security of OOB key management, balise debug interfaces, and GNSS leads us to believe that disabling these mechanisms should be considered. Prohibition of "off-line" key management [22] eliminates all discussed social engineering threats. Disabling physical and remote debug interfaces protects balise firmware from modification. Accurate OB time-keeping without reliance on GNSS mitigates attacks on this system. Protected level crossings (LXs) should serve as a second layer of defense in case of ETCS compromise. Transferring the responsibility to stop at LXs to road vehicles eliminates the danger of trains not being able to halt there in time. Since the TLS control does not apply to DNS, its integrity remains vulnerable, leading to massive delays in the best case and advanced impersonation attacks in the worst case. We suggest using Domain Name System Security Extensions (DNSSEC) to eliminate this threat. Lastly, we believe that balise linking, in its current state, is easily circumvented by fake balises and replay attacks. We propose extending this measure to support an (authenticated) Denial of Existence (DoE). In short, the train should react to unannounced balises in the same way as to missed balises, e.g., by tripping. This strategy protects against threats to the integrity of telegrams (other than firmware modification) by transforming safety-related damage scenarios into delay-related ones.

6.4 Further Threats

Considering all controls, we identify one novel threat: balise linking can be broken by triggering the BMM track condition. This is possible through attacks on the integrity of telegrams or GSM-R, but one can also provoke its legitimate issuance, e.g., by scattering large metallic masses along the tracks that interfere with the magnetic field without affecting drivability. We model this as spoofing a BMM datum originating from the DMI. The RAP is *Moderate*, since the attacker needs extended presence at the track and precise calibration of the amount of metal. Other controls are already affected by threats from Sect. 6.1, which we reflect by assigning the affected controls to the functions' security goals, so that their compromise disables the controls. We identified three such relationships. Breaking the confidentiality or integrity of Certificate Management Protocol (CMP) breaks the controls TLS, DNSSEC, and FRMCS. Similarly, breaking the confidentiality or integrity of KM breaks the GSM-R safety layer. The control balise linking depends on the availability or integrity of VBC. There are other functions whose compromise can serve as an entry point to more sophisticated attacks, which we leave for future research (see Sect. 9).

7 Evaluation

Through our methodology, we identified a total of 191 risks. We focus on the most substantial ones. With the most basic control set, i.e., only Sect. 6.2 and no ATO, 17 risks have a *Low* risk level, 44 *Moderate*, 62 *High*, and 68 *Very High*. Much of the *Very High* category stems from the insecurity of EuroBalises, since various forms of spoofing, tampering, and jamming of this technology may easily lead to fatalities. Threats to GSM-R and OB Ethernet buses pose the same danger, except for the edge case of precisely timed cable cuts, which we consider unrealistic. DoS attacks on the IP layer are also ranked as *Very High* due to the potential to temporarily halt the entire rail service, e.g., in a scenario where a KMC or the PKI becomes unavailable. A similar effect can be hypothesized for spoofing and tampering of GNSS. Tampering may also lead to life-threatening injuries, should the OB clock drift enough to significantly overrun an LOA.

When all optional ERTMS controls from Sect. 6.2, including FRMCS, are employed, the numbers of risks in each category shift to 17/82/44/48, respectively. However, only risks related to OB Ethernet and GSM-R spoofing are fully mitigated[2], i.e., reduced to *Moderate* risk. While balise linking and safe radio supervision prevent jamming attacks from causing severe injuries, they instead result in service disruptions, since the controls respond by applying brakes (damage transformation from safety to operational damages). The combination of low RAP and potential line-wide disruptions means the effective risk level remains unchanged. Lastly, tampering of telegrams, attacks on GNSS, and DDoS remain entirely unaddressed. The reader is reminded that the decrease in *Very High* risk attacks from 68 to 48 does not imply full mitigation of the underlying threats, since multiple attack trees may share the same root threat.

Introducing suggestions from Sect. 6.3 shifts the classification to 17/89/58/27. Only attacks on GNSS are fully mitigated, which explains the low increase of the *Moderate* category's cardinality. The three main threats to telegram integrity (replay attacks, fake balises, and firmware reflashing) remain possible (albeit with an increased RAP). However, their damage is transformed from train collisions into delays and cancellations, much as discussed for jamming attacks. Due to the non-trivial RAP, the relevant risk level is reduced from *Very High* to *High*. The jamming and DDoS attacks remain problematic at the *Very High* level.

The three control groups are analyzed once more with the inclusion of an "ETCS level 2 only" control, simulating a complete phase-out of levels 0, NTC, and 1. With only mandatory controls, the risk counts are 17/106/33/35. Including the optional controls in the specifications, we obtain 17/126/23/25. Finally,

[2] Raw output suggests that GSM-R spoofing is possible if IP sniffing is done beforehand, as the former breaks TLS encryption and the latter breaks the GSM-R safety layer. This is a shortcoming of the tooling, which omits dependencies (here, circular) between attack steps, so we ignore this risk.

enabling all controls yields 17/129/36/9. In each case, the stark risk reduction is due to the reduced role of EuroBalises. Still, they are used for train positioning, possibly enabling signal and buffer stop overruns that result in severe injuries by gradually shifting the OB's determined location. This is classified as *Very High*. Implementing the linking DoE measure suggested in Sect. 6.3 reduces the risk to *High* by transforming the damages to train delays. The 9 remaining *Very High* risks refer to previously discussed jamming and DDoS attacks, which can disrupt the service with relative ease. A visualization of the effects of the various control groups on the risk taxonomy is shown in Fig. 2.

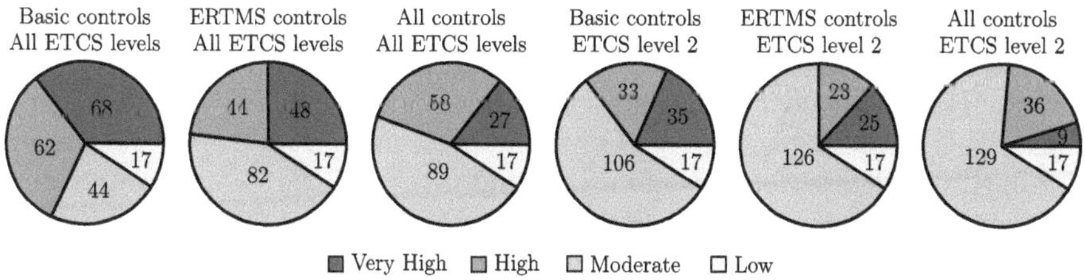

Fig. 2. Total risk count by risk level per active control group set

Lastly, we consider the activation of ATO. This is only valid in conjunction with FRMCS, since ATO over GSM-R is not allowed. In each case, we observe only one additional *High* risk level attack, namely cutting the Ethernet cable between the ATO OBU and the vehicle interface at just the right moment to inhibit the deactivation of traction. Realistically, this is not concerning, as the ETCS OBU's braking system overrides ATO, which our model does not capture [16]. The ATO's low effect on the risks stems from the fact that, if an attacker compromises OB bus connections or the FRMCS network, they can cause catastrophic damage by compromising train brakes even without ATO. With the inclusion of ATO, the attacker could additionally apply full throttle, but that does not change the risk level. Furthermore, the attack surface on ATO is smaller, as all its data is encrypted by TLS.

8 Discussion

The results show that a minimal ERTMS implementation has several vulnerabilities that can lead to fatalities. While additional safety measures defined in the standards, including the upcoming FRMCS, appear to have a significantly positive effect on the estimated security, many concerns remain regarding DoS and EuroBalise tampering. Additional controls from other researchers and this paper address these deficiencies by strengthening wireless interfaces. Nevertheless, the lack of security in telegrams remains a persistent problem. Restricting to ETCS level 2 results in a drastic security improvement by eliminating most EuroBalises' responsibilities, yet attacks on GNSS and telegram forgery remain unaddressed. The ERTMS standard appears to be the weakest link in its cybersecurity defenses, which we attribute to the slow pace of OT system standardization. Even with academic countermeasures, the system's reliability remains vulnerable to remote DoS attacks—consistent with real-life attacks on railway infrastructure. Further defenses must be added to ensure uninterrupted operation by avoiding single points of failure using redundant communication, decentralizing control systems, and enabling Vehicle-to-Vehicle (V2V) communication.

9 Conclusion and Future Work

In this paper, we have performed a risk analysis of the ERTMS suite of standards by systematically translating the specification documents into an abstract system model and subsequently estimating risks using the MoRA framework. By comparing the risk profiles of current and future ERTMS configurations, we identified legacy components, particularly EuroBalises and GSM-R, as the primary source of risk. Fully transitioning to ETCS level 2 and deploying FRMCS significantly improves the cybersecurity posture. Jamming and DDoS remain among the highest risks due to low RAPs.

MoRA allows flexible handling of ERTMS's complexity due to its iterative and modular nature and ensures completeness with respect to the model and selected threats, minimizing subjectivity and bias. This work combines function-level security goals for robustness and defensibility of results with technology-based, asset-level threats to achieve complete coverage. We have identified several limitations in applying MoRA to the railway domain: **(1)** Identified risks are classified as having the highest risk level due to the direct effect that train operations have on human safety. **(2)** Damage transformation (e.g., converting safety hazards into delays) often fails to lower the risk classification when the RAP of the attacks is relatively low. **(3)** Some risks are only reduced to the *Moderate* level, even if the corresponding attacks are determined to be no longer possible. **(4)** Summarizing by count of attack trees may inflate threats with many paths. **(5)** The lack of temporal dependencies between attack-tree nodes renders circular dependencies unresolvable.

A railway-centric risk matrix addresses the points **(1)**–**(3)** as a natural advancement. Further extensions include expanding the model beyond ERTMS, increasing the granularity of specific subsystems (e.g., the attack surface of FRMCS), and validating identified risks through experiments. Results of the risk assessment can be used by the industry to advance ERTMS cybersecurity.

Acknowledgments. Thanks to Patrick Wagner for his advice and review and to Daniel Angermeier for the MoRA tooling (both from Fraunhofer AISEC).

Disclosure of Interests. The authors have no competing interests.

References

1. Abourahim, I., et al.: Interoperability of signaling interlocking and its cybersecurity requirements. In: IRASET, pp. 1–6 (2020)
2. Aktouche, S.R., et al.: Towards reconciling safety and security risk analysis processes in railway remote driving. In: ICSRS, pp. 148–154 (2021)
3. Armor Threat Resistance Unit: The black market report: A look inside the dark web. Technical report, Armor (2018)
4. Barker, E.: Recommendation for key management. Technical report, NIST SP 800-57pt1r5, NIST (2020). https://doi.org/10.6028/NIST.SP.800-57pt1r5
5. Barker, E., et al.: Transitioning the use of cryptographic algorithms and key lengths. Technical report, NIST SP 800-131A Rev. 2, NIST (2019). https://doi.org/10.6028/NIST.SP.800-131Ar2
6. Benjumea, O., et al.: Cyber security for the evolving FRMCS deployment in the European railway sector (2025). https://datacom-ia.eu/wp-content/uploads/2026/01/DIA-RailVert-CS-FRMCS-final.pdf
7. Bhargavan, K., et al.: On the practical (in-)security of 64-bit block ciphers: collision attacks on http over TLS and OpenVPN. In: CCS, pp. 456–467 (2016). https://doi.org/10.1145/2976749.2978423
8. Bloomfield, R., et al.: The risk assessment of ERTMS-based railway systems from a cyber security perspective: methodology and lessons learned. In: Lecomte, T., Pinger, R., Romanovsky, A. (eds.) RSSRail 2016. LNCS, vol. 9707, pp. 3–19. Springer, Cham (2016). https://doi.org/10.1007/978-3-319-33951-1_1
9. Common Criteria Management Board: Common methodology for information technology security evaluation (2022). https://www.commoncriteriaportal.org/files/ccfiles/CEM2022R1.pdf
10. Eichler, J.: Modular risk assessment for the development of secure automotive systems. In: VDI/VW Automotive Security, pp. 21–22 (2015)
11. ERTMS UG: ERTMS/ETCS KMC-ETCS entity off-line KM FIS. SUBSET-114
12. ERTMS UG: ERTMS/ETCS specific transmission module FFFIS. SUBSET-035
13. ERTMS UG: ERTMS/ETCS system requirements specification. SUBSET-026
14. ERTMS UG: ERTMS Data Applications FFFIS part: CCS consist network communication layers. SUBSET-147 (2023)
15. ERTMS UG: ERTMS/ATO ATO-OB / rolling stock FFFIS application layer. SUBSET-139 (2023)
16. ERTMS UG: ERTMS/ATO system req. specification. SUBSET-125 (2023)
17. ERTMS UG: ERTMS/ETCS ERTMS end-to-end security. SUBSET-146 (2023)
18. ERTMS UG: ERTMS/ETCS euro radio FIS. SUBSET-037 (2023)
19. ERTMS UG: ERTMS/ETCS FFFIS for eurobalise. SUBSET-036 (2023)
20. ERTMS UG: ERTMS/ETCS FFFIS for Euroloop. SUBSET-044 (2023)
21. ERTMS UG: ERTMS/ETCS FIS juridical recording. SUBSET-027 (2023)
22. ERTMS UG: ERTMS/ETCS off-line key management FIS. SUBSET-038 (2023)
23. ERTMS UG: ERTMS/ETCS on-line key management FFFIS. SUBSET-137 (2023)
24. ERTMS UG: ERTMS/ETCS train interface FIS. SUBSET-034 (2023)
25. EU Agency for Railways: ERTMS/ETCS ETCS driver machine interface. ERA_ERTMS_015560 (2023)
26. EU Rail: Secure Communication Specification (2026)
27. EU Rail: Secure Component Specification (2026)
28. EU Rail: Security Program Requirements (2026)
29. EU Rail: Shared Cybersecurity Services Specification (2026)

30. European Commission: Council directive 96/48/EC (1996)
31. European Commission: Decision 2002/731/EC (2002)
32. European Commission: Directive 2004/49/EC (2004)
33. European Commission: Commission implementing regulation (EU) 2023/1695 of 10 august 2023. Official J. EU **66**, 381–561 (2023)
34. Fernandes, T., et al.: Cybersecurity in smart railways: exploring risks, vulnerabilities and mitigation in the data communication services. Green Energy Intell. Transp. **4**(4), 100305 (2025). https://doi.org/10.1016/j.geits.2025.100305
35. FRMCS AT Working Group: Future railway mobile communication system requirements specification. FW-AT, p. 7800 (2023)
36. Gabriel, A., et al.: Cyber security flaws and deficiencies in the European rail traffic management system towards cyber-attacks. In: ISCRAM, pp. 17–18 (2018)
37. Gordeychik, S., et al.: Signalling cyber security: the need for a mission-centric approach. J. Civil Struct. Eng. (2016)
38. Ibadah, N., et al.: Securing the future of railway systems: a comprehensive cybersecurity strategy for critical on-board and track-side infrastructure. Sensors **24**(24) (2024). https://doi.org/10.3390/s24248218
39. ISO: ISO/SAE 21434:2021. https://www.iso.org/standard/70918.html
40. Kochan, A.: Cyberbezpieczeństwo systemów sterowania ruchem kolejowym. Inżynier Budownictwa, pp. 71–75 (2021)
41. Kochan, A., et al.: The importance of the cryptographic key management system for the cybersecurity of the ERTMS system. Arch. Transp. Syst. Telem. **12** (2019)
42. Koop, M., et al.: IT-Sicherheitsmaßnahmen für ATO over ETCS. SIGNAL + DRAHT **114** (2022)
43. Koper-Olecka, E., et al.: Cyberbezpieczeństwo systemów kierowania i sterowania ruchem kolejowym (2017)
44. Kour, R., et al.: A review on cybersecurity in railways. Proc. IMechE Part F **237**(1), 3–20 (2023). https://doi.org/10.1177/09544097221089389
45. Kovacs, E.: Train brakes can be hacked over radio—and the industry knew for 20 years (2025). https://www.securityweek.com/train-hack-gets-proper-attention-after-20-years-researcher/
46. Leitner, B.: A general model for railway systems risk assessment with the use of railway accident scenarios analysis. Procedia Eng. **187**, 150–159 (2017)
47. Lim, H.W., et al.: Data integrity threats and countermeasures in railway spot transmission systems. ACM Trans. Cyber-Phys. Syst. **4**(1), 1–26 (2019)
48. Lopez, I., et al.: Cyber security analysis of the European train control system. IEEE Commun. Mag. **53**(10), 110–116 (2015)
49. Morong, T., et al.: Study of the GNSS jamming in real environment. Int. J. Electron. Telecommun., 65–70 (2019). https://doi.org/10.24425/ijet.2019.126284
50. Niemann, K.H.: IT security extensions for PROFINET. In: INDIN, pp. 407–412 (2019). https://doi.org/10.1109/INDIN41052.2019.8972209
51. Nunes, J., et al.: Railway infrastructure cybersecurity: an overview. ECCWS **23**, 331–340 (2024). https://doi.org/10.34190/eccws.23.1.2296
52. Pépin, F., Vigliotti, M.G.: Risk assessment of the 3Des in ERTMS. In: Lecomte, T., Pinger, R., Romanovsky, A. (eds.) RSSRail 2016. LNCS, vol. 9707, pp. 79–92. Springer, Cham (2016). https://doi.org/10.1007/978-3-319-33951-1_6
53. Predescu, S.G., et al.: Cybersecurity in the railway sector. Romanian Cyber Secur. J. **4**(2), 95–104 (2022). https://doi.org/10.54851/v4i2y2022010
54. Psiaki, M.L., et al.: GNSS spoofing and detection. Proc. IEEE **104**(6), 1258–1270 (2016). https://doi.org/10.1109/JPROC.2016.2526658

55. Rico, C., Heyl, B.: The state of the EU's rail infrastructure: investment priorities for more connected and resilient networks. Technical report, Transport & Env. (2025)
56. Santanna, J.: Booters - an analysis of DDoS-as-a-service attacks. In: 2015 IFIP/IEEE IM, pp. 243–251 (2015). https://doi.org/10.1109/INM.2015.7140298
57. Soderi, S., et al.: Cybersecurity considerations for communication based train control. IEEE Access **11**, 92312–92321 (2023)
58. Soderi, S., et al.: Railway cyber-security in the era of interconnected systems: a survey. IEEE Trans. Intell. Transp. Syst. **24**(7), 6764–6779 (2023). https://doi.org/10.1109/TITS.2023.3254442
59. Thomas, R.J.: A systematic development of a secure architecture for the European rail traffic management system (2019). https://etheses.bham.ac.uk/id/eprint/8991/19/Thomas2019PhD.pdf
60. Wagner, P., et al.: Cybersecurity risk analysis of an automated driving system. In: 21st ESCAR Europe. RUB (2023). https://doi.org/10.13154/294-10391
61. Wolf, M., et al.: A systematic approach to a qualified security risk analysis for vehicular it systems. In: Automotive-Safety & Security 2012, pp. 195–210 (2012)

SARA - Situationally Aware Risk Assessment

Jannis Hamborg[1(✉)], Yannik Franke[1,2], Merlin Kling[1,2], and Christoph Krauß[1]

[1] Darmstadt University of Applied Sciences, Darmstadt, Germany
{jannis.hamborg,christoph.krauss}@h-da.de
[2] SVA System Vertrieb Alexander GmbH, Wiesbaden, Germany
{yannik.franke,merlin.kling}@sva.de

Abstract. Automotive systems are increasingly software-intensive and operate in highly dynamic environments, causing risk to vary with the operational context. Existing automotive risk assessment practices based on Threat Analysis and Risk Assessment (TARA) are performed statically at design time and assume worst-case scenarios. While this conservatism ensures homologation compatibility, it limits expressiveness during operation. In this paper, we propose *Situationally Aware Risk Assessment (SARA)*, an extension of ISO/SAE 21434 that facilitates context-driven risk assessment during runtime, enabling the application of appropriate mitigation measures in specific situations. Building on a layered situational awareness model, SARA structures and interprets contextual information to project situation-specific risk while preserving traceability and compatibility with artifacts defined during an initial TARA. The approach preserves traceability and explainability through modular abstractions, supports generalized Threat and Damage Scenarios with situational differentiation, and minimizes overhead by reusing previously assessed information. A proof of concept instantiation demonstrates the feasibility of explainable situational perception using in-vehicle data.

Keywords: Situational Awareness · Risk Assessment · Safety Critical Systems

1 Introduction

Modern vehicles rely on multiple sensors and interconnected Electronic Control Unit (ECUs) to continuously process contextual information. Consequently, safe and secure operation increasingly depends on correctly interpreting dynamic environmental and system conditions. Therefore, automotive systems must undergo structured risk assessment during design [13]. In practice, this is performed statically using methods such as the Threat Analysis and Risk Assessment (TARA) process defined in ISO/SAE 21434. However, these approaches

Y. Franke and M. Kling: These authors contributed equally.

Z. Afzal et al. (Eds.): ARES 2026 Workshops, LNCS 16900, pp. 138–156, 2027.
https://doi.org/10.1007/978-3-032-35576-8_8

typically assume worst-case scenarios, independent of the concrete operational context [36].

While this conservative approach simplifies assessment, it often overestimates risk, as the actual impact of a *Damage Scenario* depends on the current situation, i.e., the combination of environmental and operational conditions at runtime [7]. Furthermore, the reliance on worst-case assumptions results in overly conservative and often inefficient mitigation strategies that neglect situational variability. To enable context-aware, in-vehicle mitigation beyond static measures (e.g., display warnings or deferred servicing [24]), a dynamic understanding of runtime risk is required, forming the core contribution of this work.

In this paper, we propose the Situationally Aware Risk Assessment (SARA) frame-work, a conceptual extension of ISO/SAE 21434 enabling context-driven refinement of risk assessment at runtime. Rather than replacing the TARA, SARA builds on its results and introduces a layered Situational Awareness (SA) model to continuously perceive, comprehend, and project the current situation. The framework structures contextual information into measurable factors, aggregates them into formalized situation representations, and maps them to generalized Threat and Damage Scenarios. This enables runtime differentiation without exhaustive scenario enumeration during design. By grounding all reasoning in design-time artifacts, SARA preserves traceability and compatibility with established practices. Our main contributions are:

(i) The SARA framework, extending ISO/SAE 21434 with context-driven runtime risk estimation.
(ii) The in-advance impact estimation and projection enables preventive mitigation measures, enhancing system resilience through proactive stabilization.
(iii) A proof of concept implementation and instantiation using real Controller Area Network (CAN) data from two test drives with a 2020 Volkswagen ID.3.
(iv) A publicly available artifact[1] containing code for risk calculation, as well as the pre-trained models, recordings and expert estimations.

This work proposes a concept rather than a fully developed implementation. It focuses on the influence of situational context on safety impact, explicitly excluding considerations of attack feasibility and runtime mitigation decisions, already considered in [21,25]. This aligns with situational awareness theory, as such decisions depend on system constraints and organizational factors beyond situational understanding [18]. The evaluation is based on a subset of possible situations and a single vehicle platform, with the primary emphasis placed on validating the conceptual approach rather than achieving exhaustive coverage. The driver state is explicitly excluded to reduce complexity of the proof of concept and avoid highly unpredictable parameters. Consequently, addressing unseen situations, extending feasibility assessment, and integrating decision-making mechanisms are left for future work. Furthermore, the assessment is contingent upon the accuracy and integrity of the onboard sensor data, without cross-validating

[1] https://code.fbi.h-da.de/acsd/artifacts/ares_cpra-2026-sara.

measurements against independent external references. While this may affect the accuracy of our implementation, it does not diminish its conceptual validity.

The remainder of this paper is structured as follows: Sect. 2 reviews related work, Sect. 3 provides background information, Sect. 4 presents the concept of SARA, Sect. 5 describes our preliminary instantiation of SARA, Sect. 6 evaluates the concept and implementation, Sect. 7 concludes with future work.

2 Related Work

Our work builds on the foundational concepts of Situational Awareness (SA) to establish a context-aware automotive risk assessment methodology. Originally introduced by Endsley as a three-level human-centered model of perception, comprehension, and projection [9], SA has since been adopted in domains requiring adaptive decision-making [17] and extended to digital environments [3]. In this context, SA denotes the ability to perceive digital entities, interpret their relevance, and project their future states [5,18].

Achieving SA requires integrating heterogeneous sensor data into a coherent situational representation [2]. A key milestone was the Joint Directors of Laboratories (JDL) model, which introduced a layered taxonomy spanning low-level signal processing to high-level situation estimation [18,30]. Subsequent refinements expanded the model beyond military use and clarified its relation to human cognition [1,4,5,16,27]. Building on these refinements, our research employs the JDL model within a situationally aware risk-assessment framework aligned with the ISO/SAE 21434 TARA method, which provides a structured framework for asset identification, Damage Scenario definition, and threat quantification.

Zelle et al. [37] and Plappert et al. [22] have collaboratively proposed an ISO/SAE 21434-aligned attack-surface assessment based on generic asset identification and a reference architecture. Their approach partially automates attack-path generation to identify critical and feasible paths while capturing dependencies between attack steps and contextual factors such as vehicle location. However, the methodology relies on a static system definition and does not support dynamic adaptation to changing situational contexts.

Existing research has focused predominantly on static, design-phase risk analysis, which restricts its applicability in dynamic environments. To address this, Pathak et al. [21] introduced a method for dynamic trust and risk assessment in decentralized systems based on behavioral analysis of network components. In the automotive domain, Dávid et al. [7,8] proposed a sensor-data-driven method using neural networks to estimate maneuver-specific risk scores, which were later fused into a risk matrix, though uncertainty in unseen situations and limited decision traceability constrain its use in safety-critical contexts. Püllen et al. [24] extend ISO/SAE 21434 toward vehicle operation time by querying a pre-constructed asset dependency graph upon incident detection to identify attack propagation paths and select a compensating safety action from a set of graduated operational degradation measures. However, risk assessment remains reactive and event-driven, and mitigation is realized primarily through controlled degradation rather than continuous, situation-driven preservation of full safety-system functionality. The literature thus indicates that, despite advances toward runtime and context-aware assessments, a generalizable framework for continuous, situation-driven risk refinement grounded in design-time TARA artifacts remains absent. We therefore propose such a conceptual model and demonstrate its applicability through an automotive case study.

3 Background

We outline the conceptual foundations of SARA, emphasizing contextual perception for situation understanding and dynamic risk assessment.

Automotive Risk Assessment. ISO/SAE 21434 defines the TARA process for identifying assets, impacts, and attack feasibility [13]. For each asset, *Damage Scenarios* and *Threat Scenarios* are described, with risk calculated from feasibility F and impact I. SARA adopts these scenarios but replaces the Impact and Attack Feasibility Ratings with designed functions, preserving TARA compatibility.

Situational Awareness. SA requires perceiving and comprehending relevant contextual characteristics to support dynamic risk assessment [18]. In automotive systems, this process relies on fusing environmental, system, and inner-context data acquired via onboard sensors [7], referred to as $\mathcal{L}_0$. According to Endsley's SA model, gathered information is perceived to assess the relevance, characteristics, and status of contextual entities [9], formally defined as $\mathcal{L}_1$ [18]. Perception is achieved through the logical correlation of preprocessed sensor data to infer the state of the vehicle, its surroundings, and the driver. At $\mathcal{L}_2$, individual $\mathcal{L}_1$ entities are aggregated into a multidimensional situation model [7,8], enriched with contextual factors such as road conditions and traffic to facilitate a thorough understanding of the situation [18]. At $\mathcal{L}_3$, this model is used to project future states [18], aiming for a thorough understanding of the states and dynamics of the observed entities. This understanding is then leveraged to form situation-adequate risk mitigation. Consequently, the resulting situational model encapsulates the comprehension of the prevailing driving circumstances, thereby establishing a foundation for conducting dynamic risk assessments.

Situation Reasoning. A situation is defined as a specific combination of circumstances at a given moment [7]. Situation reasoning extracts high-level knowledge from diverse data sources [23] by inferring new knowledge and filtering data to a relevant, precise and information-dense representation [32]. In SARA, $\mathcal{L}_0$-data is reasoned into a refined entity-level understanding at $\mathcal{L}_1$, where entities are treated as stateless and reflect only the current sensor observation. Stumper et al. demonstrated trajectory-based situation reasoning, using fixed-dimension polynomials, based on position, velocity, acceleration, and yaw angle [31], while omitting road surface, weather, and driver state. This limited situation representation is common in related work [7]. Moreover, existing approaches lack auditability, replicability, and formalized risk assessment grounded in defined Threat and Damage Scenarios. SARA addresses these limitations by building upon an initial ISO/SAE 21434-compliant TARA.

4 Concept

In this section, we describe the concept of our SARA framework, which leverages SA to derive situation-specific risk estimations. SARA comprises two phases: an offline, non-recurring *(a) Initialization Phase* and an online, continuous *(b) Runtime Risk Assessment Phase*. The Initialization Phase is comprised of several steps, including the execution of an initial TARA to ensure seamless integration into existing design, risk-analysis, and homologation processes. The Runtime Risk Assessment Phase applies SA processing layers to estimate situation-dependent impact, feasibility, and risk. We divide both phases (excluding the initial TARA) into four layers $\mathcal{L}_0$-$\mathcal{L}_3$ for situation-based risk derivation. Figure 1 illustrates the overall workflow and is described below for each layer.

The Initialization Phase comprises *(0.a)* a manual ISO/SAE 21434-compliant initial TARA and *(0.b)* the framework initialization. During the Runtime Risk Assessment Phase, *1)* $\mathcal{L}_0$*-contextual information* is continuously gathered during vehicular operation and subsequently preceded into entity-related *2)* $\mathcal{L}_1$*-factors* which are aggregated into a *3)* $\mathcal{L}_2$*-situation*. This situation enables the derivation of situationally aware *4a) feasibility* and *4b) impact* estimates for predefined Threat and Damage Scenarios, which are used to update the *5) risk score* per asset. The resulting risk estimation can inform, guide, and prioritize mitigation decisions (e.g., by a human operator). To limit the scope of this paper, we consider only safety impact. Financial, operational, and privacy impact, as well as the mitigation decision phase, are left for future work. Nevertheless, we assume mitigation measures to be automated in-time remediation steps to preserve safety-system functionality. The feasibility of each threat scenario is considered constant, and it is assumed that the overall concept remains easily transferable.

Initial TARA. During the design-phase of a safety-critical system, a manual TARA is performed to meet homologation requirements, yielding *(0.a)* Threat Scenarios $\mathcal{T}$ and Damage Scenarios $\mathcal{D}$. The results are then used *(0.b)* to define SARA-specific parameters and initialize functions. The initialization and runtime phases are described for each layer $\mathcal{L}_0$–$\mathcal{L}_3$ below.

$\mathcal{L}_0$*: Sensing.* We define $\mathcal{C}$ as the set of all measurable context-related information derived from available sensor data. $\mathcal{C}$ is structured into the subsets $\mathcal{C}_{\text{ENVIRONMENT}}$, $\mathcal{C}_{\text{SYSTEM}}$, and $\mathcal{C}_{\text{INNER}}$ to guide parameter selection. However, $\mathcal{L}_1$ perception parameters may be freely chosen from all subsets. These contextual subsets are acquired from a variety of sources available at runtime. In automotive systems, these sources vary depending on several factors such as manufacturer, application, and regulatory constraints. The set of context-related information $\mathcal{C}$ is derived from the initial TARA and used to define contextual

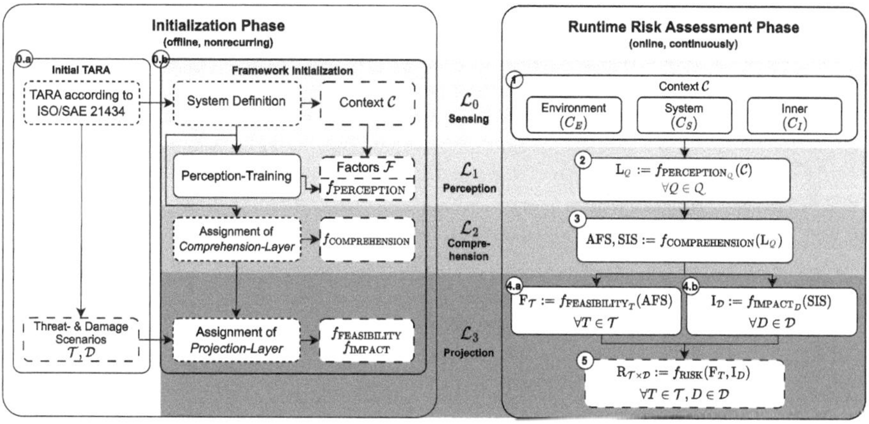

Fig. 1. SARA Overview (dotted border: manual input, solid border: automated processing, dashed border: output).

entities that aggregate related information into higher-level constructs, e.g., clustering all information regarding the current road condition.

$\mathcal{L}_1$*: Perception.* The contextual parameters are surjectively mapped to a set of quality factors $\mathcal{Q}$, representing situation-relevant aspects such as road quality. This set of factors is assigned manually during the Initialization Phase using expert knowledge to account for system-specific characteristics and available context. Consequently, the defined context $\mathcal{C}$ is continuously perceived as a factor $Q \in \mathcal{Q}$, resulting in a factor-specific value L with

$$L_{\mathcal{Q}} := f_{\text{PERCEPTION}_Q}(\mathcal{C}) \quad \forall Q \in \mathcal{Q}, \tag{1}$$

where $L_{\mathcal{Q}}$ denotes the set of factor-specific values. The function $f_{\text{PERCEPTION}}$ may be instantiated with arbitrary perception methods (e.g., linear regression), provided that the defined input and output interface is preserved. The instantiation is done in the *Perception-Training*-Step of the Initialization Phase.

$\mathcal{L}_2$: *Comprehension.* Comprehension of the $\mathcal{L}_2$-situation is predicated on the set of reasoned factor-specific values $L_{\mathcal{Q}}$. We distinguish between *Attack Feasibility Situation* (AFS) and *Safety Impact Situation* (SIS) to derive feasibility- and impact-specific situations, respectively. This is congruent with the principles outlined in [7], yet transferred to multi-dimensionality by

$$\text{AFS, SIS} := f_{\text{COMPREHENSION}}(L_{\mathcal{Q}}), \tag{2}$$

which is instantiated during the Initialization Phase in the *Assignment of Comprehension-Layer*-step to derive both sets (AFS, SIS) from $L_{\mathcal{Q}}$. The function $f_{\text{COMPREHENSION}}$ allows experts to incorporate system specifics and domain knowledge, including subjective assessments of Threat and Damage Scenarios (e.g., road-condition effects). This modular design enables the extension of the set of factors while preserving standardized situation representations.

$\mathcal{L}_3$: *Projection.* Lastly, AFS is projected to the feasibility of a Threat Scenario $T \in \mathcal{T}$, whilst SIS is projected to the impact of a Damage Scenario $D \in \mathcal{D}$, by

$$\mathrm{F}_{\mathcal{T}} := f_{\mathrm{FEASIBILTY}_{\mathcal{T}}}(\mathrm{AFS})\ \forall T \in \mathcal{T}, \qquad \mathrm{I}_{\mathcal{D}} := f_{\mathrm{IMPACT}_{\mathcal{D}}}(\mathrm{SIS})\ \forall D \in \mathcal{D}, \quad (3)$$

where $\mathrm{F}_{\mathcal{T}}$ denotes the set of derived feasibility values per Threat Scenario $T \in \mathcal{T}$ and $\mathrm{I}_{\mathcal{D}}$ the set of derived impact values per Damage Scenario $D \in \mathcal{D}$. During the *Assignment of Projection-Layer*-step the functions $f_{\mathrm{FEASIBILITY}}$ and f_{IMPACT} are instantiated based on the identified Threat and Damage Scenarios, the assigned situation definitions (AFS, SIS), as well as expert knowledge regarding situational influences (e.g., road conditions). This enables the formulation of more generic Threat and Damage Scenarios by eliminating situation-specific contextual aspects. For instance, in ISO/SAE 21434, a Damage Scenario is outlined as follows [13]:

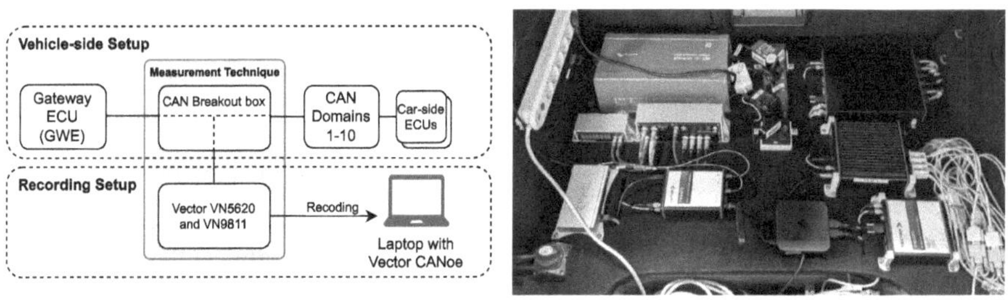

(a) Measurement setup intercepting domain-specific CAN buses.

(b) Recording setup in the trunk of the research vehicle.

Fig. 2. The schematic and real-world measurement setup.

> Front collision with a narrow stationary object (e.g., a tree) was caused by unintended turning-off of headlamp during night driving at medium speed.

Our concept can be used to generalize damage scenarios like this one by removing the context-related parts (underlined), thereby rendering them situation-agnostic. Subsequently, the impact and feasibility values are used to compute a risk score for each assessed combination of Threat and Damage Scenarios $\mathcal{T} \times \mathcal{D}$ by

$$\mathrm{R}_{\mathcal{T}\times\mathcal{D}} := f_{\mathrm{RISK}}(\mathrm{F}_{\mathcal{T}}, \mathrm{I}_{\mathcal{D}}) \quad \forall T \in \mathcal{T}, D \in \mathcal{D}, \quad (4)$$

where f_{RISK} refers to the risk calculation function, defined by the chosen Risk Scoring System (RSS). To transform these numerical values into quantitative values, a mapping matrix is given in Annex H.8 of ISO/SAE 21434 [13]. The resulting risk score can be utilized to ascertain the necessity of mitigation measures.

5 Implementation

In this section, we describe the implementation of the proposed concept and the configuration for aggregating contextual information. The implementation serves as a proof of concept to demonstrate the soundness and feasibility of SARA, rather than aiming for maximum accuracy, with further optimization left for future work. Real-world data was collected using a research vehicle equipped with a dedicated measurement setup. Based on this data, the situation-reasoning steps introduced earlier are applied.

Recording Setup. Our implementation utilizes CAN signals, which are interpreted from CAN messages. These signals are captured from a 2020 Volkswagen ID.3, which is equipped with a self-developed comprehensive measurement setup to capture internal CAN communication. The vehicle is designed following a domain-separated architecture. All CAN domains are connected to a central Gateway ECU (GWE). This configuration facilitates convenient access to the CAN bus by physically intercepting it right before the GWE (cf. Figure 2a). In alignment with [10], our measurement setup is capable of reading and sending messages in compliance with the CAN standard. SARA requires read-only access to the CAN bus, and our measurement setup is configured accordingly. This ensures the safety of driver and passengers, as no potentially critical messages are sent to the CAN bus. Due to the bus topology of CAN, it is possible to capture all messages on the connected bus without interfering with the ongoing communication. To that end, we designed a Breakout Box (BoB) to facilitate the aforementioned objective by establishing relevant connections. Data acquisition is facilitated by a proprietary measurement apparatus situated within the trunk of the research vehicle, as illustrated in Fig. 2b. The device is powered by the vehicle's internal 12V system, enabling continuous recording of messages while driving. For a detailed description, please refer to [10].

Initial TARA and System Definition. During the Initialization Phase, the initial TARA is executed in accordance with the homologation requirements specified in UNECE R 155 [34] and UNECE R 156 [35] and applied by following ISO/SAE 21434 [13]. Next, the system under consideration is defined for our SARA framework building upon the results from the TARA.

a) Initial TARA. The design and evaluation of the proposed framework is conducted in accordance with the ISO/SAE 21434 standard, employing a TARA approach. The identified threat and damage scenarios are designed to be as concrete as possible, while preserving generalizability. This approach is intended to ensure that the scenarios do not become excessively targeted, thereby preserving their applicability to a broader context. The creation of the TARA in the Initialization Phase results in a Threat Scenario $\mathcal{T} := \{T_0\}$ and three Damage Scenarios $\mathcal{D} := \{D_0, D_1, D_2\}$, derived from pre-crash statistics [19], traffic incident data [29] and the example outlined in ISO/SAE 21434 [13][2]. Both, Threat

[2] We intentionally simplify the vehicle TARA to focus on the fundamental mechanics of the SARA framework rather than the granular accuracy of the results.

Table 1. Considered Damage and Threat Scenarios for Evaluation.

	Threat Scenario
T_0	Spoofing of a signal leads to a loss of integrity of the data communication, resulting in an ECU malfunction.
	Damage Scenario
D_0	Front collision with a narrow stationary object (e.g. a tree) was caused by unintended turning-off of the headlamp [13].
D_1	Veering off the road due to a loss of traction caused by unintended disabling of the Electronic Stability Control (ESC) [19].
D_2	Minor collision with a narrow stationary object (e.g. a tree) was caused by unintended turning-off of the windshield wipers [13,29].

and Damage scenarios, are shown in Table 1. We define the set of scenarios as $\mathcal{S} := \{(T_0, D_0), \quad (T_0, D_1), \quad (T_0, D_2)\}$, which are then used in f_{RISK} to ascertain the risk associated with the designated scenario. It is essential to differentiate between *scenario* and *situation*. The former denotes a threat-damage pairing used for risk calculation, while the latter describes the vehicle's current physical environment.

b) System Definition. Driving necessitates significant adaptation to diverse conditions (e.g., weather, road conditions) and scenarios (e.g., construction zones, traffic jams). As this paper aims to establish a comprehensive framework for situational awareness in risk assessment, our primary focus does not lie in encompassing all potential scenarios within the test data. In the context of the present study, two recorded data traces are used, each with a duration exceeding 30 min. These traces encompass a variety of situations, including driving in urban environments, on highways, and on country roads, and different light, road, and, weather conditions.

Ride 0 is characterized by its emphasis on the transition between diverse road and traffic conditions, achieved through the manipulation of audio between jam-packed urban traffic, unobstructed highway passages, and muddy landside roads. The recording of Ride 1 focuses on different driving behaviors and common situations, such as emergency braking, passing crossroads, traffic lights, and construction zones. However, several unanticipated events are included in both rides, including pedestrians walking in front of the car in an urban area as well as in the emergency lane on the highway. During the test drives, we document designated situations (cf. Figures 5 and 6) through manual notes and video recordings, ensuring a reliable baseline for later validation[3]. For our implementation of SARA, context $\mathcal{C}$ is defined exclusively by CAN signals. The interpretation of these CAN signals utilizes the publicly available Comma-AI VW MEB-DBC

[3] The video data is excluded from the dataset due to privacy concerns. The presence of license plates and faces makes robust anonymization infeasible. Moreover, SARA relies exclusively on CAN signals, rendering additional video data unnecessary.

files[4]. We select a context $\mathcal{C}$ of 44 CAN signals (e.g., longitudinal acceleration, speed, and low beam status) based on signal availability and encountered situations. The full list is available in the repository (See Footnote 3).

Context and Factors. In accordance to [33] and the available context information, we assign the following factors:

$$\mathcal{Q} := \{ \underbrace{\text{QoS}}_{\text{Quality of Sight}}, \underbrace{\text{QoR}}_{\text{Quality of Road}}, \underbrace{\text{QoD}}_{\substack{\text{Quality of} \\ \text{Driving Behavior}}} \}$$

Each factor is assigned a value in the interval $[0, 4]$, where 0 denotes the optimal value.

Perception Training. The function $f_{\text{PERCEPTION}}$ is instantiated with the following linear regression

$$y = \sum_{x \in \mathcal{X}} (\beta_x \cdot x) \quad \beta \in \mathbb{R}.$$

The assigned subset of context parameters is employed as the training data $\mathcal{X}$, while the manually assigned expert-estimation of each individual factor at a specific point in time is designated as the target value y.
During training, the β-parameters of the regression function are optimized to minimize the residual sum of squares between the given target y in the dataset and the prediction by the linear approximation [11]. The training data is obtained by selecting the temporally closest data point from the recorded dataset corresponding to the timestamps of the assigned target values. To further optimize the training with expert knowledge, we assign only a factor-specific subset $\mathcal{C}_Q \subset \mathcal{C}$, $Q \in \mathcal{Q}$ to each perception function. For details about the utilized parameters, refer to our repository (See Footnote 3). After training, the function $f_{\text{PERCEPTION}}$ is assigned per factor by

$$f_{\text{PERCEPTION}_{\mathcal{Q}}}(\mathcal{C}_Q) := \sum_{c \in \mathcal{C}_Q} (\beta_c \cdot c) \quad \forall Q \in \mathcal{Q}.$$

A pretrained model, represented by the set $f_{\text{PERCEPTION}_{\mathcal{Q}}}$ consisting of linear regressions, is available in our repository [5].

The decision to employ linear regression as the perception function was made on the basis of its explainability and traceability [26], which are paramount for safety-critical systems. However, the stated set of factors, the considered contextual parameters and the linear regression used as the perception function do not constitute a complete representation of all potential influences. Additional aspects, such as tire condition or inflation level, could also significantly affect the

[4] https://github.com/commaai/opendbc/blob/master/opendbc/dbc/vw_meb.dbc.

[5] The video data is excluded from the dataset due to privacy concerns. The presence of license plates and faces makes robust anonymization infeasible. Moreover, SARA relies exclusively on CAN signals, rendering additional video data unnecessary.

outcome. It is reasonable to assume that there are further factors of this kind that could contribute to more accurate or realistic evaluations. For this exemplary evaluation, the scope is deliberately restricted to the defined subset of factors to ensure methodological clarity and traceability. Nevertheless, integrating and analyzing additional influencing parameters is a promising direction for future work.

The trained model is then factor-wise evaluated using the available CAN signals, which results in the estimation of the respective factor at any given point in time (cf. Figure 3a).

Comprehension Function. The function $f_{\text{COMPREHENSION}}$ is implemented as a static selection of factors for AFS and SIS, respectively:

$$f_{\text{COMPREHENSION}}(\mathrm{L}_{\mathcal{Q}}) := \underbrace{\{\ \emptyset\ \}}_{\text{AFS}}\ ,\ \underbrace{\{\mathrm{L}_{\text{QoS}}, \mathrm{L}_{\text{QoR}}, \mathrm{L}_{\text{QoD}}\}}_{\text{SIS}}$$

In the context of this paper, AFS invariably yields an empty set of factors, as the emphasis is exclusively on the SIS. Consequently, the feasibility remains constant per Threat Scenario for different situations, while the impact is influenced by the factor values.

Projection Functions. The resulting $\mathcal{L}_2$-situations are used to calculate a risk score for the set $\mathcal{S}$ of defined Threat and Damage Scenario combination (cf. Table 1). The function $f_{\text{FEASIBILITY}_{\text{T0}}}$ is instantiated to return $\mathrm{F}_0 = \texttt{MEDIUM := 2}$ for all AFSs based on the defined Threat Scenario. The function f_{IMPACT} is instantiated based on defined Damage Scenarios, as well as expert knowledge informed by extensive traffic incident statistics [19]:

$$\mathrm{I}_0 = f_{\text{IMPACT}_{\mathrm{D}_0}}(\text{SIS}) := (0.6 \cdot \mathrm{L}_{\text{QoS}} + 0.1 \cdot \mathrm{L}_{\text{QoR}} + 0.3 \cdot \mathrm{L}_{\text{QoD}})$$
$$\mathrm{I}_1 = f_{\text{IMPACT}_{\mathrm{D}_1}}(\text{SIS}) := (0.0 \cdot \mathrm{L}_{\text{QoS}} + 0.5 \cdot \mathrm{L}_{\text{QoR}} + 0.5 \cdot \mathrm{L}_{\text{QoD}})$$
$$\mathrm{I}_2 = f_{\text{IMPACT}_{\mathrm{D}_2}}(\text{SIS}) := (0.9 \cdot \mathrm{L}_{\text{QoS}} + 0.0 \cdot \mathrm{L}_{\text{QoR}} + 0.1 \cdot \mathrm{L}_{\text{QoD}})$$

The results of both functions $F_{\text{FEASIBILITY}}$ and f_{IMPACT} align with the feasibility and impact ratings defined in ISO/SAE 21434 Annex H[6] [13] The function f_{RISK} is instantiated according to ISO/SAE 21434 [13] as

$$f_{\text{RISK}}(S_0) := \mathrm{F}_0 \cdot \mathrm{I}_0, f_{\text{RISK}}(S_1) := \mathrm{F}_0 \cdot \mathrm{I}_1, f_{\text{RISK}}(S_2) := \mathrm{F}_0 \cdot \mathrm{I}_2,$$

where $S_0, S_1, S_2 \in \mathcal{S}$. Furthermore, F_T and I_D refer to the feasibility and impact values of the respective Threat and Damage Scenario $S = (T, D)$. Applied to real world data from an automotive system, this results in a continuous risk score $f_{\text{RISK}}(F_T, I_D) \in [0; 16]$ with $F, I \in [0, 4]$ and $R = F \cdot I$, where 0 represents the lowest possible risk. The actual interpretation of these risk values depends on the underlying RSS and the corresponding risk matrix.

[6] Feasibility: $[0, \ldots, 4] \rightarrow$ [`Very Low`, ..., `High`]; Impact: $[0, \ldots, 4] \rightarrow$ [`Negligible`, ..., `Severe`].

6 Evaluation

In this section, we present the evaluation of the SARA framework's conceptual soundness and implementation feasibility. As our implementation serves strictly as a proof of concept, we omit quantitative metrics, as they would not be representative of real-world deployments.

6.1 Conceptual Soundness and Maturity

The conceptual soundness is evaluated with respect to the four quality criteria *coverage*, *traceability*, *effort proportionality*, and *life cycle adaptability*, as derived from [13,25,34,35], and is then assessed for alignment with the aforementioned standards as well as *transferability* to other domains.

Alignment and Coverage. SARA is grounded in the automotive cybersecurity regulatory framework, requiring an ISO/SAE 21434-compliant TARA [13] and aligning with UNECE R 155 and R 156 [34,35]. It preserves the TARA risk estimation model while extending it with proactive, runtime situational differentiation to maintain homologation compatibility. The current scope is limited to safety impact with constant feasibility. Within this scope, however, conformance is maintained because the scenario structures, rating functions, and risk calculations map directly to ISO/SAE 21434. Thus, SARA provides well-bounded coverage, leaving full impact support and dynamic feasibility for future work.

Traceability. In alignment with Rudin et al. [26], who advocate for inherently transparent models over post-hoc explanations in safety-critical contexts, linear regression is selected for $f_{\text{PERCEPTION}}$ to prioritize auditability, essential for UNECE R155 compliance [22,24,34,37]. The resulting coefficients provide explicit, per-signal contributions, enabling full traceability from raw context data to risk estimates through closed-form transformations across all SA layers. The modular decomposition further supports independent inspection of each layer, facilitating targeted validation and identification of latent inter-component dependencies. However, this potential for systematic inspection and refinement is not yet fully realized in the current proof-of-concept implementation.

Effort Proportionality. A central concern in the automotive industry is whether runtime extensions justify their engineering effort [12]. SARA addresses this through artifact reuse, building on the existing TARA, avoiding duplicate work. Additional overhead is limited to framework initialization and perception training, while runtime operation leverages existing vehicle infrastructure. Although expert annotation is required, scalable alternatives exist. Compared to exhaustive scenario enumeration, SARA reduces complexity via situation-agnostic modeling.

Life Cycle Adaptability. ISO/SAE 21434 defines cybersecurity as a continuous life cycle activity [13], which UNECE R 155 operationalizes through post-production monitoring within a Cybersecurity Management System [34]. SARA supports this through a layered decomposition of independently instantiable functions, enabling component-level updates without compromising the framework's overall validity. However, the current implementation lacks mechanisms for updating weighting schemes, scoring functions, or Threat and Damage Scenario catalogs.

Transferability. While evaluated in the automotive domain, the framework naturally extends to other safety-critical systems with long asset life cycles, as reflected in IEC 62443 [14,20] and CLC/TS 50701 [6,15]. Standard agnosticism is achieved through generalized feasibility and impact projection functions, enabling compatibility with established Risk Scoring Systems across domains.

6.2 Viability Evaluation

The proof of concept implementation is evaluated using real-world vehicle data, consistent with recommendations that automotive security concepts be empirically grounded in production systems [7,28]. Accordingly, the evaluation emphasizes practicality and methodological clarity over completeness. Contextual input is derived from internal CAN signals of a 2020 Volkswagen ID.3 using an established measurement setup [10] augmented by expert situation annotations.

Parameter Choice. Signal selection for contextual information is constrained by the available CAN signals of the chosen vehicle platform and guided by Operational Design Domain considerations [33]. While this pre-selection introduces expert subjectivity, it yields a practical and semantically grounded parameterization that exceeds prior approaches limited to positional or lane-geometric abstractions [7,8]. Even under these constraints, the trained models capture meaningful contextual variation (e.g., high beams or sustained braking pressure), that propagates coherently through impact and risk computation.

Situation Transition. The construction-site scenario causes an increase in QoD (cf. Figure 3a), driven by tailgating and adaptive braking, which propagates to elevated impact estimates and risk scores (cf. Figure 3b and 3c). The subsequent red-light event reduces QoD to near zero while environmental factors remain stable, demonstrating coherent and temporally consistent propagation through the pipeline. The figure visualizes the steps from sensing and perceiving contextual information, and then calculating the damage scenario specific impact, and finally the situation specific risk (cf. Figure 3a to 3c, Appendix Figure 4). The purple lines indicate manually assigned situation description, to show the accuracy and timeliness of the algorithmically situation transition. Across the full thirty-minute rides (cf. Appendix Figs. 5 and 6), annotated urban, rural, and highway situations are reflected in structured factor-level responses, confirming that the perception layer provides sufficient abstraction for risk differentiation even from limited context. While the resulting risk dynamics are plausible and aligned with real-world safety indicators, the model lacks the depth for quantitative accuracy analysis, which would require validation against a larger and more diverse labeled dataset .

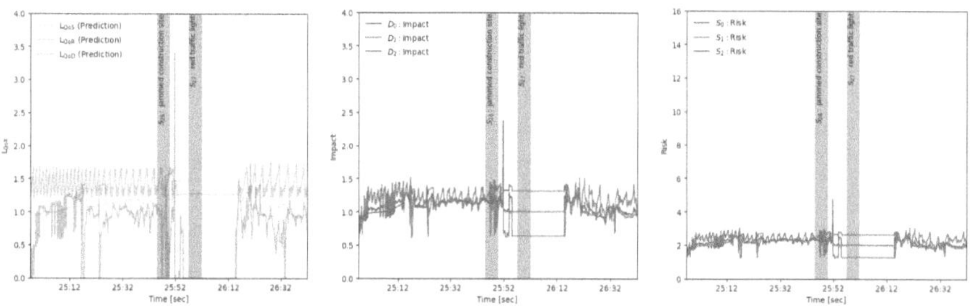

(a) Pred. of QoS, QoR, QoD. (b) Calculated impact. (c) Calculated risk.

Fig. 3. End-to-end reasoning steps of our SARA instantiation for a construction site and following red traffic light scenario. (Color figure online)

Multi-modality. A notable property of the instantiation is its exclusive reliance on signals available from the vehicle's internal CAN bus, requiring no additional control units, external sensors, or dedicated hardware beyond the standard gateway-level read access used for measurement. Despite this constraint, the resulting risk dynamics are meaningful and correlate with real-world safety indicators. However, additional modalities, like Automotive Ethernet, LIN, and information sources, like cameras, LIDAR, or OSINT, could further reduce blind spots and capture greater situational complexity and uncertainty. We explicitly leave this for future work.

Limitations. Beyond the constraints discussed above, several limitations remain. While SARA produces continuous, scenario-specific risk scores, it deliberately does not map elevated risk to concrete mitigation actions. The non-linear relationship between damage severity and appropriate countermeasure while preserving full safety-system functionality renders such a mapping non-trivial, necessitating further evaluation. As feasibility is assumed constant, observed risk dynamics are driven solely by situational impact, which precludes situation-dependent threat modeling. Moreover, the linear regression models underlying $\mathcal{L}_1$ and the expert-weighted impact functions at $\mathcal{L}_3$ aren't accompanied by any uncertainty or error quantification limiting suitability for safety-critical deployments in the current instantiation. Finally, $\mathcal{L}_1$ entities are considered stateless, preventing the framework from reasoning about trends or anticipatory risk escalation.

Overall, the results show that SARA achieves its main objective: a lightweight expert-driven instantiation yields meaningful, structured runtime risk dynamics from live data, demonstrating that preventive situational risk assessment provides added value over static design-time approaches even under simplified assumptions.

7 Conclusion

This work proposes SARA, a situationally aware risk-assessment framework for automotive systems that addresses the limitations of static approaches in ISO/SAE 21434. By leveraging contextual information and situational awareness, SARA enables dynamic runtime risk estimation while maintaining traceability and homologation compatibility. Our preliminary implementation demonstrates the validity of continuous, explainable risk assessment, showing that even lightweight instantiations can improve upon static methods.

Nevertheless, several limitations remain. The proof of concept focuses exclusively on impact estimation, omits feasibility reasoning, and relies on a limited dataset from a single vehicle. Furthermore, while situation abstraction supports generalizability, it may oversimplify complex interactions. Addressing these challenges requires richer sensor modalities, integrated feasibility reasoning, and validation across diverse operational domains. Further research will explore advanced perception models, optimized situation representations, and the inclusion of additional impact dimensions. Decision-making and mitigation strategies remain outside the current scope. Overall, SARA provides a foundation for context-driven, adaptive risk assessment in increasingly complex automotive systems.

Ethical Considerations and Availability

Our artifacts are publicly available (See Footnote 3), including code for training and risk computation, as well as pre-trained models, recordings, expert assessments, and annotated situations from two drives. This study adheres to ethical guidelines and does not involve personal data. All recordings contain only publicly available information and pose no risk of harm or loss to individuals or organizations. The recordings solely contain publicly available information.

Acknowledgments. We acknowledge the German Research Foundation (DFG) for funding our project within the "Resilience in Connected Worlds" (SPP 2378) program - project number 503329135, enabling advancements in our research.

Disclosure of Interests. The authors have no competing interests to declare that are relevant to the content of this article.

A Appendix

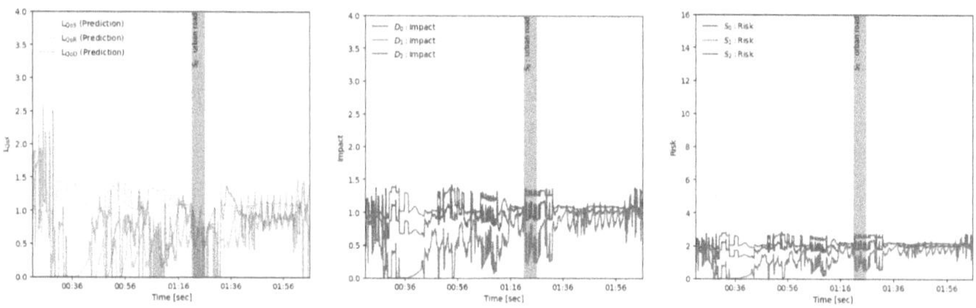

(a) Pred. of QoS, QoR, QoD. (b) Calculated impact. (c) Calculated risk.

Fig. 4. End-to-end reasoning steps for a road type change to urban road.

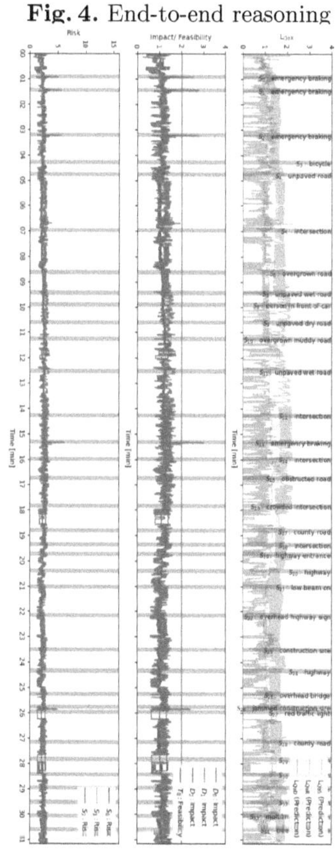

Fig. 5. Factor predictions, Impact, and Risk Estimation of Ride 0.

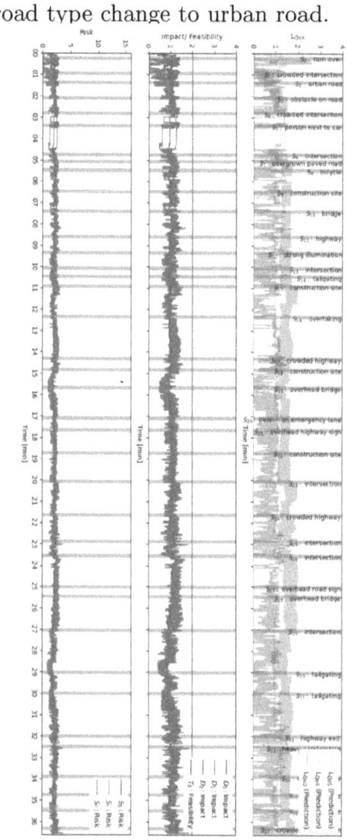

Fig. 6. Factor predictions, Impact, and Risk Estimation of Ride 1.

References

1. Blasch, E.P.: Value-based sensor and information fusion. In: Signal Processing, Sensor/Information Fusion, and Target Recognition XXXIII, vol. 13057, pp. 177–187, SPIE (2024). https://doi.org/10.1117/12.3014177
2. Blasch, E.P.: Situation Awareness Using Fuzzy Analytical Hierarchy Processing. In: 2025 28th International Conference on Information Fusion (FUSION), pp. 1–8 (2025). https://doi.org/10.23919/FUSION65864.2025.11124134
3. Blasch, E.P., Pribilski, M., Daughtery, B., Roscoe, B., Gunsett, J.: Fusion metrics for dynamic situation analysis. In: Signal Processing, Sensor Fusion, and Target Recognition XIII, vol. 5429, pp. 428–438, SPIE (2004). https://doi.org/10.1117/12.542902
4. Blasch, E.P., Salerno, J.J., Tadda, G.P.: Measuring the worthiness of situation assessment. In: Proceedings of the 2011 IEEE National Aerospace and Electronics Conference (NAECON), pp. 87–94 (2011), ISSN 2379-2027. https://doi.org/10.1109/NAECON.2011.6183083
5. Blasch, E.P., et al.: Revisiting the JDL model for information exploitation. In: Proceedings of the 16th International Conference on Information Fusion, pp. 129–136 (2013). https://ieeexplore.ieee.org/abstract/document/6641155
6. DKE: DIN CLC/TS 50701:2024-07 (2024). https://www.dinmedia.de/de/vornorm/din-clc-ts-50701/378603461
7. Dávid, B., Láncz, G., Hunyady, G.: Highway situation analysis with scenario classification and neural network based risk estimation for autonomous vehicles. In: 2019 IEEE 17th World Symposium on Applied Machine Intelligence and Informatics (SAMI), pp. 375–380 (2019). https://doi.org/10.1109/SAMI.2019.8782729
8. Dávid, B., Láncz, G., Hunyady, G.: Real-time Behaviour Planning Concept for Autonomous Vehicles. In: 2019 IEEE 17th World Symposium on Applied Machine Intelligence and Informatics (SAMI), pp. 385–390 (2019). https://doi.org/10.1109/SAMI.2019.8782771
9. Endsley, M.: Toward a theory of situation awareness in dynamic systems. Human Factors J. Human Factors Ergonomics Soc. **37**, 32–64 (1995). https://doi.org/10.1518/001872095779049543
10. Hamborg, J., Lauser, T., Krauß, C.: Rollcan–can-bus based Rolljam-attack. In: Proceedings of the 2nd Cyber Security in CarS Workshop, pp. 1–7 (2025). https://doi.org/10.1145/3736130.3762686
11. Hsieh, W., et al.: A Comprehensive Guide to Explainable AI: From Classical Models to LLMs (2024). https://doi.org/10.48550/arXiv.2412.00800
12. Hunnius, J.P.v.: Overcoming TARA's 5 key challenges in Vehicle Cybersecurity (2024). https://www.cyeqt.com/en/threat-analysis-and-risk-assessment-tara-5-weaknesses/
13. International Organization for Standardization: ISO/SAE 21434: 2021: Road Vehicles: Cybersecurity Engineering. ISO (2021). https://www.iso.org/standard/70918.html
14. International Society of Automation: IEC 62443-4-1: Security for industrial automation and control systems, Part 4-1: Secure product development lifecycle requirements (2018). https://www.isa.org/standards-and-publications/isa-standards/isa-iec-62443-series-of-standards
15. Leander, B., Čaušević, A., Hansson, H.: Applicability of the IEC 62443 standard in industry 4.0 / IIOT. In: Proceedings of the 14th International Conference on Availability, Reliability and Security, ARES '2019, Association for Computing Machin-

ery, New York, NY, USA (2019). ISBN 9781450371643. https://doi.org/10.1145/3339252.3341481
16. Llinas, J., Bowman, C., Rogova, G., Steinberg, A., Waltz, E., White, F.: Revisiting the JDL Data Fusion Model II (2004). https://apps.dtic.mil/sti/html/tr/ADA525721/
17. van de Merwe, K., Mallam, S., Nazir, S.: Agent transparency, situation awareness, mental workload, and operator performance: a systematic literature review. Hum. Factors **66**(1), 180–208 (2024). https://doi.org/10.1177/00187208221077804
18. Munir, A., Aved, A., Blasch, E.P.: Situational Awareness: Techniques, Challenges, and Prospects. AI **3**, 55–77 (2022), ISSN 2673-2688. https://doi.org/10.3390/ai3010005
19. Najm, W.G., Smith, J.D., Yanagisawa, M.: Pre-Crash Scenario Typology for Crash Avoidance Research (2007). https://rosap.ntl.bts.gov/view/dot/6281/dot_6281_DS1.pdf
20. Nunes, J., Cruz, T., Simões, P.: Railway infrastructure cybersecurity: an overview. In: European Conference on Cyber Warfare and Security, vol. 23, pp. 331–340 (2024)
21. Pathak, V., Singh, K., Khan, T., Shariq, M., Chaudhry, S.A., Das, A.K.: A secure and lightweight trust evaluation model for enhancing decision-making in resource-constrained industrial WSNs **14**, 28162 (2024), ISSN 2045-2322. https://doi.org/10.1038/s41598-024-75414-0
22. Plappert, C., Zelle, D., Gadacz, H., Rieke, R., Scheuermann, D., Krauß, C.: Attack surface assessment for cybersecurity engineering in the automotive domain. In: 2021 29th Euromicro International Conference on Parallel, Distributed and Network-Based Processing (PDP), pp. 266–275 (2021). https://doi.org/10.1109/PDP52278.2021.00050
23. Pradeep, P., Krishnamoorthy, S.: The MOM of context-aware systems: a survey. Comput. Commun. **137**, 44–69 (2019), ISSN 0140-3664. https://doi.org/10.1016/j.comcom.2019.02.002
24. Püllen, D., Liske, J., Katzenbeisser, S.: ISO/SAE 21434-based risk assessment of security incidents in automated road vehicles. In: Habli, I., Sujan, M., Bitsch, F. (eds.) SAFECOMP 2021. LNCS, vol. 12852, pp. 82–97. Springer, Cham (2021). https://doi.org/10.1007/978-3-030-83903-1_6
25. Qendah, Y., Hamborg, J., Krauß, C., Katzenbeisser, S.: Adaptive runtime risk assessment with aging-aware feasibility for safety-critical systems. IEEE Access **14**, 30087–30106 (2026). https://doi.org/10.1109/ACCESS.2026.3666222
26. Rudin, C.: Stop explaining black box machine learning models for high stakes decisions and use interpretable models instead. Nat. Mach. Intell. **1**(5), 206–215 (2019). ISSN 2522-5839, https://doi.org/10.1038/s42256-019-0048-x
27. Salerno, J.J., Blasch, E.P., Hinman, M., Boulware, D.M.: Evaluating algorithmic techniques in supporting situation awareness. In: Multisensor, Multisource Information Fusion: Architectures, Algorithms, and Applications 2005, vol. 5813, pp. 96–104, SPIE (2005). https://doi.org/10.1117/12.603825
28. Salfer, M.: Automotive Security Analyzer for Exploitability Risks: An Automated and Attack Graph-Based Evaluation of On-Board Networks. Springer Fachmedien, Wiesbaden (2024)978-3-658-43505-9 978-3-658-43506-6. https://doi.org/10.1007/978-3-658-43506-6
29. Statistisches Bundesamt: Straßenverkehrsunfallstatistik (2025). https://www.destatis.de/DE/Themen/Gesellschaft-Umwelt/Verkehrsunfaelle/_inhalt.html
30. Steinberg, A.N., Bowman, C.L., White, F.E., Blasch, E.P., Llinas, J.: Evolution of the JDL Model (2023). https://isif.org/files/isif/2024-03/ipif-06-01-36.pdf

31. Stumper, D., Knapp, A., Pohl, M., Dietmayer, K.: Towards characterization of driving situations via episode-generating polynomials. In: Schulze, T., Müller, B., Meyer, G. (eds.) Advanced Microsystems for Automotive Applications 2016. LNM, pp. 165–173. Springer, Cham (2016). https://doi.org/10.1007/978-3-319-44766-7_14
32. Tazari, M.R., et al.: The universal Reference Model for AAL. In: Handbook of Ambient Assisted Living, vol. 11, pp. 610–625 (2012). ISBN 978-1-60750-836-6 https://doi.org/10.3233/978-1-60750-837-3-610
33. Thorn, E., Kimmel, S., Chaka, M.: A Framework for Automated Driving System Testable Cases and Scenarios. Technical report DOT HS 812 623, National Highway Traffic Safety Administration (NHTSA), Washington, DC (2018). https://rosap.ntl.bts.gov/view/dot/38824
34. UN Regulation No. 155: Uniform provisions concerning the approval of vehicles with regards to cyber security and cyber security management system (2021) https://unece.org/sites/default/files/2021-03/R155e.pdf
35. UN Regulation No. 156: Uniform provisions concerning the approval of vehicles with regards to software update and software updates management system (2021). https://unece.org/sites/default/files/2021-03/R156e.pdf
36. WITTENSTEIN high integrity systems ltd: Performing the Threat Analysis and Risk Assessment (TARA) Analysis Out Of Contex (2024). https://www.highintegritysystems.com/downloads/white_papers/Performing_the_Threat_Analysis_and_Risk_Assessment_(TARA)_Analysis_Out_Of_Context_White_Paper.pdf
37. Zelle, D., Plappert, C., Rieke, R., Scheuermann, D., Krauß, C.: Threatsurf: a method for automated threat surface assessment in automotive cybersecurity engineering. Microprocess. Microsyst. **90**, 104461 (2022)

Closing the Gap: Empirically Validated Reference Threat Models for Consumer IoT Architectures

Victor Goeman, Stef Verreydt(✉), Tom Cordemans, Laurens Sion, Jorn Lapon, and Vincent Naessens

DistriNet, KU Leuven, 3001 Leuven, Belgium
{victor.goeman,stef.verreydt,tom.cordemans,laurens.sion, jorn.lapon,vincent.naessens}@kuleuven.be

Abstract. The Internet of Things (IoT) connects billions of devices, yet insecure design choices continue to introduce significant security weaknesses. Existing research often studies device-level vulnerabilities but rarely links them back to underlying design choices, and existing threat modeling approaches rarely demonstrate empirical relevance.

In this paper, we introduce reference threat models for three prevalent consumer IoT architectures, highlighting common security threats rooted in the design of such systems. Additionally, we empirically validate these threat models through an in-depth security evaluation of ten representative consumer IoT devices (cameras and doorbells), using a combination of network analysis and firmware reverse engineering. Concretely, this validation shows that vulnerabilities identified in real-world IoT devices correspond to threats captured in the reference threat models.

The publicly available threat models can be used as a reference by developers of consumer IoT devices, lowering the barrier to identifying and mitigating common vulnerabilities at design time. Additionally, by connecting potential threats described in the threat models to actual vulnerabilities encountered in practice, the empirical validation of our threat models provides evidence for the overall effectiveness of threat modeling, which is currently lacking.

Keywords: IoT · Threat modeling · Reverse engineering

1 Introduction

The Internet of Things (IoT) has become deeply embedded in modern life, connecting billions of devices in homes, industries, and critical infrastructure. This rapid expansion has created vast new attack surfaces. The decentralized nature of IoT ecosystems and the heterogeneity of devices operating at the network's edge introduce persistent security challenges that remain difficult to manage. The risks of insecure IoT devices became widely visible in 2016, when the Mirai botnet compromised hundreds of thousands of cameras and routers to launch

Z. Afzal et al. (Eds.): ARES 2026 Workshops, LNCS 16900, pp. 157–174, 2027.
https://doi.org/10.1007/978-3-032-35576-8_9

massive distributed denial-of-service attacks on core internet infrastructure [4]. Nearly a decade later, such large-scale IoT botnets continue to plague the internet [12], underscoring that fundamental design weaknesses remain unresolved.

IoT design choices, often driven by functionality, cost, and user convenience rather than security, are fundamental to a device's security posture. Manufacturers often make these decisions without fully understanding their security implications, inadvertently leaving devices vulnerable to specific attack vectors inherent in their design. For instance, an IoT device designed to operate within a protected internal network, mediated by a dedicated hub, presents a vastly different security profile compared to a device connecting directly to an end user's LAN (our Network model), a crucial distinction that current practices overlook.

While a considerable body of existing research in IoT security focuses on device-centric vulnerabilities and automated detection techniques, such as fuzzing [23,36] or symbolic execution [11,26], fewer studies have examined the architectures of IoT systems and the inherent challenges they face [15]. Furthermore, existing threat modeling studies target specific architectures or domains, or remain theoretical without connecting threats to real-world vulnerabilities [6,8,27].

This paper addresses this gap by creating reference threat models for three prevalent consumer IoT architectures identified from real-world deployments: the Direct, Network, and Gateway models, and evaluating their capability to identify relevant threats. The Direct model represents systems where devices directly connect to the end user (i.e., wearable IoT devices). Devices in the Network model connect to the LAN of the end user, and devices in the Gateway model connect to a dedicated hub that manages multiple IoT devices. This classification is designed to serve as a structured framework for developers to prevent the security risks inherent to these designs.

To demonstrate the validity of the developed threat models, we conducted an in-depth security evaluation of ten representative consumer IoT devices (cameras and doorbells) and mapped the identified vulnerabilities back to threats described in the threat models. In summary, the significant vulnerabilities uncovered through this empirical process consistently matched the threats captured in the threat models, illustrating the validity of the insights captured in these threat models.

By integrating threat modeling with empirical vulnerability assessment, we offer validated reference models as a foundation for security-by-design in consumer IoT development. These reference threat models can be used by developers as a starting point to identify and mitigate vulnerabilities commonly encountered in real-world consumer IoT devices. Furthermore, we derive insights and recommendations for manufacturers, developers, and researchers to proactively address security risks based on their design, contributing to more resilient IoT ecosystems. In summary, our contributions are the following:

(a) We provide reusable reference threat models for dominant consumer IoT architectures (Direct, Network, Gateway);

(b) We empirical validate these threat models by linking architectural threats to real-world vulnerabilities; and
(c) We describe previously unknown vulnerabilities, including four new, high-impact CVEs.

In what follows, we discuss related work and identify gaps in prior studies (Sect. 2), describe the reference threat models (Sect. 3), and present our empirical evaluation, which includes a security analysis of a representative set of consumer IoT devices (Sect. 4), before concluding the paper in Sect. 5.

2 Related Work and Motivation

In this section, we summarize the main concepts of threat modeling before discussing related work on threat modeling and vulnerability assessment of IoT applications. Afterwards, we highlight limitations in prior IoT vulnerability assessment research to motivate the need to perform a novel vulnerability assessment as part of our empirical evaluation, rather than leveraging existing work.

2.1 Threat Modeling Background

Threat modeling is a technique for identifying and addressing security and privacy issues rooted in the design of a system. The first step in threat modeling is constructing a model of the system, usually a data flow diagram (*DFD*). This model is then analyzed to reveal design flaws. A well-known threat modeling acronym that can guide such analysis is STRIDE [29], which stands for *spoofing*, *tampering*, *repudiation*, *information disclosure*, *denial of service* (*DoS*), and *elevation of privilege* (*EoP*). This acronym supports free-form brainstorming sessions or can be applied systematically by iterating over all elements ('STRIDE-per-element') or interactions ('STRIDE-per-interaction') in the system model. Several tools exist that automatically produce lists of threats for a given system model; an overview of contemporary threat modeling tools is provided by Shi et al. [28]. In this context, a threat is the potential harm (what could go wrong), while a vulnerability is a weakness that allows that harm to happen.

2.2 Related Work

Threat Modeling for IoT. Several recent studies introduced novel threat modeling techniques or threat catalogs tailored toward IoT applications. For instance, Casola et al. [6] propose a threat modeling technique and catalog based on IoT ISO standards. De Silva et al. [31] conducted a survey-of-surveys to identify prevalent attacks and countermeasures for IoT systems, illustrating how these can enhance traditional threat modeling approaches, such as STRIDE.

Other research has concentrated on applying threat modeling methodologies to specific IoT application domains rather than actual IoT systems. For example, Seeam et al. [27] applied STRIDE to seven different IoT application domains (smart homes, connected vehicles, etc.), Ficco et al. [8] proposed a meta-model and threat catalog specifically for edge-based IoT systems, Al Asif et al. [1] applied STRIDE to an IoT-enabled agriculture system, and Junejo et al. [19] presented a list of threats for IoT applications in a logistics context.

In contrast to proposing novel threat modeling techniques or domain-specific threat catalogs, our work applies existing threat modeling approaches to create reference threat models that cover three common consumer IoT architectures, which can be leveraged during future development efforts to proactively identify and mitigate common vulnerabilities in such systems. Furthermore, whereas existing threat modeling efforts for IoT applications remain largely theoretical, we provide an empirical validation of our threat models by mapping its contents to vulnerabilities in encountered real-world IoT applications.

Vulnerability Assessments of IoT Devices. Numerous studies have investigated the security of IoT devices, with some considering architectural aspects to varying degrees. Hasija et al. [15] provide a survey that discusses the advantages and disadvantages of distinct high-level IoT architectures, including fog, edge, and cloud architectures, and outlines associated challenges. However, their work remains theoretical and does not investigate how identified threats may be manifested in real-world IoT applications. Ling et al. [20], on the other hand, describe the architecture of an IoT camera application, enumerate its threats, and analyze a single real-world camera system to validate their findings. While this study bridges theoretical architectural considerations with empirical analysis, it is limited in scope, focusing on a single architecture and a single device.

Other empirical studies have introduced frameworks or methodologies for IoT device security assessments. Alharbi et al. [2] applied a novel IoT camera analysis framework to evaluate five IoT cameras. However, their study only considers a single architecture and lacks in-depth vulnerability discovery. Similarly, Stanislav [34] expands upon IoT security frameworks by incorporating a broader range of attack paths and applying them to 40 devices. However, this work emphasized framework application over in-depth device analysis, resulting in a more superficial assessment rather than in-depth, device-specific vulnerability discovery or architectural comparison.

Alrawi et al. [3] conducted a systematization of knowledge (SoK) of IoT security. They proposed a four-component model for IoT deployments – device, mobile application, cloud endpoint, and communication channels – to analyze existing literature and empirically evaluate 45 IoT devices. While evaluating 45 devices is substantial, the depth of analysis is limited to scanning using tools such as Nessus, tackling only known vulnerabilities [35], limiting the depth of the evaluation.

In general, prior work on IoT vulnerability assessment either considers a limited scope in terms of the types of IoT architectures considered or lacks in-depth vulnerability assessment that goes beyond open-source automated scanners. In what follows, we provide a more comprehensive description of related work to further characterize key limitations which make their results insufficient to validate our proposed reference threat models.

2.3 Limitations of Prior Vulnerability Assessment Work

To identify key limitations in existing IoT vulnerability research, we conducted a comparative analysis and mapped the findings of selected studies onto our threat models. We selected studies that (1) performed vulnerability discovery on consumer IoT devices, (2) analyzed a small to medium set of devices (ranging from 5 to 50), and (3) employed analysis techniques beyond basic open-source automated scanners. This approach ensured that we considered studies focused on analysis with sufficient depth, rather than broad, superficial scans. Based on these criteria, we identified nine relevant research papers from 2009 to 2022 (Table 1). Examining these papers revealed several key limitations which hinder using their results to evaluate our proposed reference threat models:

Limited Architectural Variance: The majority of research we examined focuses on a single architecture, and we found a notable lack of empirical studies comparing devices across distinct architectures. In contrast, our proposed reference threat models cover three common IoT architectures (the Direct, Network, and Gateway models, as will be discussed in Sect. 3), and evaluating them thus also requires vulnerability assessments that cover these different architectures.

Limited Breadth of Existing Studies: Our comparison shows that a limited number of attack paths are covered. Some studies prioritize depth, focusing on specific vulnerabilities or a small set of devices. For example, Janes et al. [18] provide an in-depth analysis of a single vulnerability type, authentication flaws in the cloud. This focused approach lacks the breadth to allow linking vulnerabilities to design flaws. Conversely, other studies attempt a broader coverage by analyzing multiple attack types simultaneously. Studies like Stanislav [34], which applied security frameworks across 40 devices, achieve greater breadth but lack depth for linking vulnerabilities to concrete architecture types. These studies do not fully cover the wide range of potential attack paths. Across all reviewed studies, the observed vulnerabilities could only be assigned to seven STRIDE-based threats (Table 1).

In summary, evaluating our proposed reference threat models requires in-depth vulnerability assessments of devices covering multiple IoT architectures, which is not provided by prior work. As such, a separate vulnerability assessment was performed as part of this research, as will be discussed in Sect. 4.

3 Reference Threat Models

To gain an understanding of vulnerabilities in IoT systems stemming from distinct architectural design choices, we developed a set of reference threat models representing the most prevalent *consumer IoT* architectures. More specifically, these reference threat models encompass (1) a data flow diagram that represents

Table 1. Related work mapped to Network threat model in a chronological order

From	Local user → IoT	Cloud User → Cloud	Local User → IoT	IoT → Cloud	IoT → Local User	Local User → IoT	Local User → IoT	
Type[1]	S	S	T	I	I	D	E	Methodology
[5]	●	–	–	–	●	●	●	Hacking web interfaces of cameras
[17]	●	–	●	–	–	●	●	Hacking web interfaces of cameras
[33]	●	–	●	●	●	–	●	Vulnerability analysis of babymonitors
[30]	●	–	●	–	●	–	●	Reverse engineering, bypassing bootloader, and static analysis
[21]	●	–	●	–	●	●	–	Security analysis of customized code
[2]	●	–	●	–	●	–	●	Security Framework for cameras
[3]	–	–	–	●	●	–	●	Scanning devices with Nessus
[18]	–	●	–	–	–	–	–	Authentication after revocation
[34]	●	–	●	–	●	–	–	Security framework evaluated on cameras
Our Study	●	●	●	●	●	●	●	Reverse engineering, network analysis

● threat covered – threat not covered [1] Visualizes only the STRIDE-based threats covered by at least one of the reviewed related work studies.

the high-level architecture and (2) an exhaustive collection of threats, both of which will be discussed in what follows. The full threat models are not included in this paper due to space limitations, but are available online[1].

3.1 Data Flow Diagrams by Architecture

While general IoT literature discusses architectures like edge, fog, and cloud, these do not always correspond to the practical deployments found specifically in consumer IoT ecosystems. In practice, consumer IoT devices typically follow one of three communication models: direct device-to-user communication (e.g., Bluetooth-based devices), devices connected to the local network and optionally the cloud, or devices managed through a dedicated gateway or hub. To capture these models, we constructed the following data flow diagrams:

[1] https://github.com/ku-leuven-msec/IoT-Threat-Models.

- **Direct DFD:** This DFD, visualized in Fig. 1a, represents consumer IoT architectures where devices operate without internet connectivity, relying solely on direct communication to the user over a dedicated network. Examples include devices such as headphones and smartwatches that broadcast Bluetooth networks for direct user connections.
- **Network DFD:** Depicted in Fig. 1b, this DFD represents consumer IoT architectures where devices connect to the internet via the LAN (not using a dedicated hub). Communication with these devices occurs via the local network (local mode) or a cloud platform (cloud mode).
- **Gateway DFD:** Depicted in Fig. 1c, this DFD represents consumer IoT architectures that incorporate a dedicated gateway (DGW) as a central component. Here, the role of the IoT devices is primarily to capture data and transmit it to the DGW, which manages all subsequent operations. Connected to the user's home network, the DGW establishes a dedicated network for IoT devices, effectively isolating the IoT infrastructure. This architecture is frequently found in ecosystems where a central hub controls multiple devices, such as sensor networks or smart lighting systems.

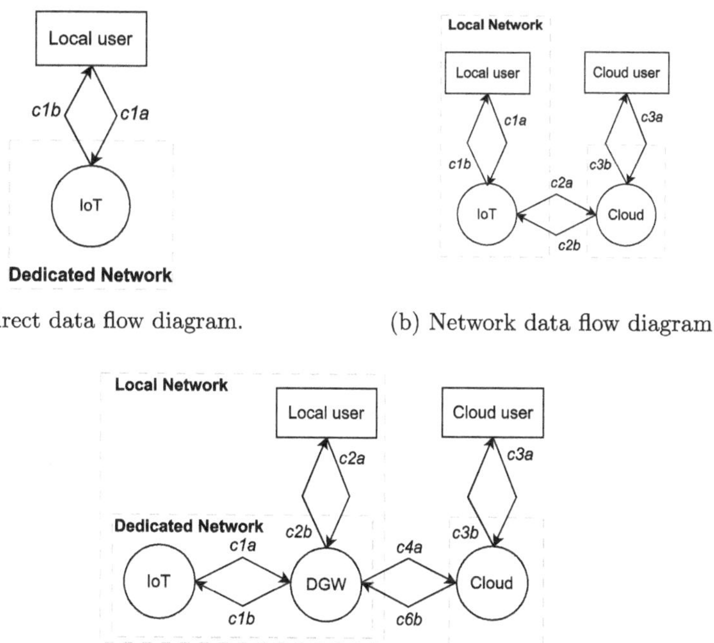

(a) Direct data flow diagram.

(b) Network data flow diagram.

(c) Gateway data flow diagram.

Fig. 1. Data flow diagrams for the three consumer IoT architectures.

Note that these data flow diagrams are deliberately expressed at a high level of abstraction as to cover a wide range of specific applications. Furthermore, limiting the complexity of the models also reduces the amount of security expertise needed to interpret them, lowering adoption barriers. Second, note that home gateways (e.g., routers) are not depicted in the data flow diagrams. The goal of these reference threat models is to provide a starting point for IoT developers to identify and mitigate common threats rooted in their own architectural decisions. In this context, IoT developers have no control over the gateway, and cannot actively mitigate threats targeting gateways, hence their exclusion from the data flow diagrams.

3.2 Threat Elicitation Process

STRIDE threats were systematically identified for each diagram using a STRIDE-per-interaction approach [29]. More specifically, SPARTA [32] was leveraged to automatically elicit an exhaustive set of STRIDE-per-interaction threats for each DFD described above. The generated threats were manually consolidated to remove duplicates and to generalize architecture-specific artifacts. The resulting threat list was then reviewed by multiple authors to ensure consistency and applicability across consumer IoT deployments. Unlike traditional STRIDE applications, which primarily focus on interactions crossing trust boundaries, we explicitly considered all interactions, including those within nominally trusted zones (e.g., LAN, DGW), to reflect that even internal zones may eventually be compromised. In summary, this process yielded 18 potential threats for the Direct DFD, 60 for the Network DFD, and 84 for the Gateway DFD.

These results were manually reviewed to systematically exclude unrealistic threats and threats that are not applicable in a general consumer IoT context. This revision was based on consensus by three of the authors, all of which have extensive expertise in either threat modeling or IoT security research. In particular, the following threats were considered out of scope for this threat model:

- ***Repudiation*-related threats**, as these concern the ability to deny actions and are less relevant in consumer IoT. Put differently, common consumer IoT devices like cameras and doorbells typically do not include measures to provide accountability guarantees, for example access logs. Instead, security measures for these types of devices mostly revolve around preventing unauthorized access, service disruption, and information disclosures, hence the main focus on these types of threats in the threat model.
- **Several threats that target the cloud servers**, as these could not be empirically validated due to legal and technical restrictions.

In summary, this resulted in 13 relevant threats for the Direct DFD, 36 for the Network DFD, and 54 for the Gateway DFD. A complete overview of all threats, including rationales for excluded threats, is provided in the online repository.

4 Evaluation

To evaluate the validity of the threats described in the reference threat models, we performed an in-depth vulnerability assessment on ten consumer IoT devices and mapped the findings to the corresponding threat models. In doing so, we provide evidence that the identified threats are not just theoretical, but can actually be manifest in real-world IoT systems. Furthermore, by mapping vulnerabilities to threats in the threat model, we provide real-world examples which can be leveraged by IoT developers to further inform their threat modeling and vulnerability assessment activities.

4.1 Empirical Analysis

Device Selection Criteria. To establish a representative set of devices, we selected ten popular consumer IoT devices, focusing on smart cameras and doorbells. We specifically chose these types of devices for several key reasons. First, their ubiquity in smart homes positions them as representative of the broader consumer IoT ecosystem. Second, cameras and doorbells integrate diverse functionalities (e.g., video streaming, two-way audio, motion detection, cloud storage) making them representative of complex consumer IoT devices with multiple communication channels and attack surfaces. Finally, and most importantly, these types of devices can be deployed in varying IoT architectures (Direct, Network, and Gateway), enabling a comparison of the security implications across functionally similar devices. The final selection spans multiple manufacturers and price tiers, capturing a realistic cross-section of consumer products.

Methodology. Vulnerability assessment followed a structured approach that combines different analysis techniques. Each device was first assessed to determine its architectures and distinct operational modes. Next, two complementary techniques were applied, namely network analysis and firmware analysis. By combining these complementary techniques, we achieve an in-depth understanding that reveals vulnerabilities rooted in the architecture. This contrasts with automated scanners (e.g., Nessus [35]) or simple comparisons against lists of known vulnerabilities, which lack the depth to identify design flaws.

Network analysis involved examining the device in a controlled environment to assess its communication protocols, network services, and interactions with external services. This was essential for identifying vulnerabilities in data transmission, authentication mechanisms, and network service exposure. We captured and analyzed network traffic using tools such as Wireshark [10], tcpdump [14], and nmap [22], focusing on encryption, communication protocols, and security practices that expose the device to potential attack vectors.

Firmware analysis then provided a deeper understanding of the device's internal design, uncovering vulnerabilities that may not be apparent through network analysis. Specifically, firmware analysis was divided into two stages: *acquisition* and *examination*.

- **Firmware Acquisition:** Firmware was obtained either from the vendor's official website or extracted directly from the hardware using interfaces like UART or SPI. Once obtained, the firmware was unpacked using tools such as Binwalk and Unblob to access and analyze key components, including the kernel, filesystem, and bootloader [16,25].

- **Firmware Examination:** Static and dynamic analysis was employed to identify vulnerabilities. Static analysis involved manually inspecting binaries and configuration files, supported by firmware analysis tools such as EMBA [24], and binary analysis tools like Ghidra [7]. Dynamic analysis involved running the firmware in an emulated environment, allowing us to validate the findings obtained through static analysis and discover additional runtime vulnerabilities.

This comprehensive evaluation process was time-intensive, with each device evaluation cycle taking three weeks. The workload was distributed between two researchers based on domain expertise: one researcher focused on firmware reverse engineering, while the other conducted the network analysis.

Following the vulnerability identification phase, three authors with expertise in IoT security and threat modeling collaboratively and jointly mapped the identified vulnerabilities to five of the six threat categories defined by STRIDE: Elevation of Privilege, Spoofing, Tampering, Denial of Service, and Information Disclosure in the matching threat models. Additionally, the severity of the identified vulnerabilities was assessed using CVSS [9].

Limitations. The relatively limited selection of devices was a deliberate methodological trade-off balancing architectural diversity with the effort required to uncover vulnerabilities. While this sample size precludes a comprehensive survey of the entire IoT ecosystem, which is not the goal of this study, it enabled the granular, manual analysis (firmware reverse engineering and network analysis) required to uncover deep architectural flaws. In other words, our selection of devices allows for a focused assessment of consumer IoT architectures rather than a generalization across all embedded system domains. In any case, we argue that our selection is sufficiently diverse for the purposes of this evaluation, namely the validation of our proposed reference threat models.

Regarding cloud communications, our analysis treats cloud servers as black boxes due to legal and technical restrictions on server-side testing. This constraint limits our findings to device-side observations and potentially contributes to the observed disparity in the number of identified vulnerabilities between local and cloud interfaces.

4.2 Results

Our vulnerability assessment of the ten selected IoT devices revealed several vulnerabilities and insecure practices, summarized in Table 2. Specifically, our analysis identified 53 security weaknesses across the evaluated devices, including four previously unknown high-impact vulnerabilities assigned CVE identifiers[2]:

- **Remote Code Execution via Buffer Overflows:** Buffer overflows leading to remote code execution in the LSC indoor camera (CVE-2024-51347) and the BS Petcam camera (CVE-2024-51348).

[2] Writeups available at https://github.com/ku-leuven-msec/IoT-Threat-Models.

- **Custom Encryption Scheme:** Vulnerabilities in the custom encryption scheme used by the Eufy ecosystem (CVE-2024-51346).
- **Weak WPA2-PSK Key Derivation:** A weak key generation algorithm was identified in the dedicated network of the Eufy ecosystem. The WPA2-PSK derivation scheme enabled attackers within wireless proximity to recover the WPA2-PSK and gain access to the dedicated network [13].

Vulnerabilities related to tampering (firmware acquisition) and denial of service against the IoT device (deauthentication attacks) were consistently present, regardless of the architecture. Common, medium-severity findings included insecure network services, transmission of cleartext data, and hardcoded credentials within the firmware.

Table 2. Vulnerabilities and bad practices per camera

	Firmware Acquisition	*Cleartext Signaling*	*Hardcoded Passwords*	*Hardcoded Authentication Keys*	*Hardcoded Encryption Keys*	*Insecure Networking*	*Insecure Data Transfer*	*Vulnerable to DoS*	*Cleartext Passwords*	*Buffer Overflow*	*Root Shell*	*Firmware Flashing*
BS Petcam Camera	SPI	-	X	-	X	X	X	X	-	X	X	-
Foscam VD1 Doorbell	SPI	X	X	X	X	-	X	X	X	-	-	-
LSC Indoor Camera	UART&SPI	X	X	-	-	-	X	X	-	X	X*	X
LSC PTZ Camera	UART&SPI	X	X	-	-	-	-	X	-	-	-	X
Eufy 2K Doorbell	SPI	X	X	X	X	X	X	X	-	-	X*	-
Unify G4 Doorbell	Online	-	X	X	-	X	X	X	X	-	X	-
Unify Dome Camera	Online	-	X	X	-	X	X	X	X	-	X	-
Digitus Doorbell	SPI	X	-	-	-	-	-	X	-	-	-	X
Sygionix Doorbell	SPI	X	-	-	-	-	-	X	X	-	-	X
Ring Doorbell	SPI	-	-	-	-	-	-	X	-	-	-	-

X: vulnerability found -: no vulnerability found * Physical access required via debug port

4.3 Mapping Vulnerabilities to Threat Models

To assess the validity of our reference threat models, we systematically mapped the vulnerabilities discovered in our vulnerability assessment to the threats defined within each model. This was a collaborative effort by three of the authors with expertise in IoT security and threat modeling.

Note that a single vulnerability can realize multiple threats (e.g., authentication issues may lead to both elevation of privileges and spoofing). As an IoT device might offer multiple operational modes that engage with different attack vectors, this vulnerability mapping considers the specific operational mode in which the vulnerability was exploitable. For instance, a device might offer a direct configuration, a local configuration when operating on the LAN, and a cloud configuration for remote access via the internet. Each operational mode represents a distinct security posture. Accordingly, our validation process iterated through all relevant attack paths for each device configuration to determine which threats were applicable.

In what follows, we summarize the findings for each of the three models.

Direct Threat Model. In the Direct architectural model, devices operate without cloud or gateway connectivity, instead providing a dedicated (often wireless) network for direct user interaction. Within our evaluation set, this architecture was exemplified solely by the BS Petcam, which establishes its own Wi-Fi network for direct user connections. Of the 13 relevant threats described in the reference threat model for this architecture, 12 were actually realized for the BS Petcam device. Specifically, our vulnerability assessment did not reveal any vulnerabilities where device secrets are leaked from the device (i.e., information disclosure on the device).

Table 3 presents a condensed version of the vulnerability to threat mapping, the full mapping table is provided online. The key vulnerabilities include:

- **S - Weak Authentication:** Weak authentication mechanisms were used in the device's dedicated network, enabling *spoofing* attacks.
- **I - Weak Encryption:** Network traffic over the dedicated network was entirely unencrypted, leading to *information disclosure.*
- **E - Insecure Network Services:** Multiple open network services were detected, and vulnerabilities were discovered within these services (e.g., buffer overflow on open HTTP port), which may lead to *elevation of privileges.*

The high percentage of realized threats in the BS Petcam case study gives an indication of the security challenges of this model. For IoT devices that will operate in such architectural context, developers should thus focus on securing the direct communication channel. For instance, implementing robust authentication and encryption during the design phase in the dedicated network would have mitigated the spoofing and information disclosure threats and improved the overall security of the Petcam device.

Table 3. Threats realized in the Direct threat model

Threat Type	From → To	BS Petcam Vulnerability
Spoofing	IoT ⇆ User	Improper Authentication (CWE-287)
Tampering	IoT → User	No Encryption (CWE-319)
Tampering	User → IoT	Firmware Dump (CWE-1202)
Information Disclosure	IoT ⇆ User	No Encryption (CWE-319)
Denial of Service	User → IoT	Deauthentication (CWE-400)
Elevation of Privilege	User → IoT	Buffer Overflow (CWE-121)

Network Threat Model. The Network model encompasses devices that connect directly to the internet (without a dedicated gateway), supporting both local network (LAN) and cloud-based access. In our evaluation set, seven devices fall under this architecture, making it the most prevalent in our study.

Of the 36 threats described in the reference threat model, 15 were realizable in at least one of the inspected devices due to vulnerabilities. A condensed overview of the realized vulnerabilities is provided in Table 4. Threats in the reference threat model which could not be realized in real-world devices were mainly related to a) information disclosure and tampering, as sufficient encryption was leveraged, or b) spoofing, as authentication was present and correctly implemented. As such, the fact that these threats could not be realized during our evaluation does not indicate that they are irrelevant and should be removed from the reference threat model. On the contrary, these threats were not realizable as manufacturers already considered and mitigated them, providing further evidence for their relevance.

In short, the most significant vulnerabilities in the local configuration can be mapped as follows:

- **S - Weak Authentication on Local Services:** Weak authentication mechanisms were observed on the device's local interfaces, mapping to *spoofing* threats (e.g., open RTSP ports without authentication and hardcoded credentials in local interfaces).
- **I - Weak Encryption:** Inadequate or missing encryption was present in LAN communications, leading to *information disclosure.*
- **E - Insecure Network Services:** Several exploitable software vulnerabilities within the local services on the device, resulting in *elevation of privilege.*

Devices operating in cloud-connected configurations exhibited recurring vulnerabilities related to:

- **I - Weak Encryption:** During the setup of remote communication channels, the signaling phase, sensitive information or credentials were leaked, resulting in *information disclosure.*
- **S, E - Authentication Vulnerabilities:** Cloud-related vulnerabilities mapped to *spoofing* and *elevation of privilege* threats concerning cloud authentication.

These findings indicate distinct risk areas for local versus cloud operation modes. Security efforts should focus on hardening interfaces exposed on local networks, mandating standardized, vetted, and encrypted protocols for locally configured devices, while ensuring secure signaling mechanisms and robust authentication protocols for devices that employ a cloud configuration.

Gateway Threat Model. The Gateway model, employed by three devices in our evaluation set, introduces a dedicated gateway (DGW) to manage IoT devices. Although designed to enhance functionality and isolate devices, the gateway adds complexity and more communication interfaces, expanding the overall attack surface. We observed a high number of vulnerabilities, which appear correlated with this additional complexity, and the challenge of securing this extra DGW device.

Table 4. Threats realized in the Network threat model

Threat Type	From $\rightarrow$ To	Local Access			Cloud Access						
		BS Petcam	Foscam VD1	LSC Indoor Camera	Petcam	Foscam VD1	LSC Indoor Camera	LSC PTZ Camera	Digitus Doorbell	Sygionix Doorbell	Ring Doorbell
S	Cloud $\rightarrow$ Cloud user	-	-	-	-	AB	-	-	-	-	-
S	Local user $\leftrightarrows$ IoT*	-	AB	AB	-	-	-	-	-	-	-
T	Local user $\rightarrow$ IoT	FF,FD	FD,FDC	FF,FD	FF,FD	FD,FDC	FF,FD	FF,FD	FD	FF,FD	FD
T	IoT $\rightarrow$ Local user	-	NE	NE	-	-	-	-	-	-	-
I	IoT $\rightarrow$ Cloud	-	-	-	-	NE	NE	NE	NE	NE	-
I	Local user $\leftrightarrows$ IoT*	NE	NE,CC	NE,CC	-	-	-	-	-	-	-
D	Local user $\rightarrow$ IoT	DOS	D	DOS	D	D	D	D	D	D	D
E	Local user $\rightarrow$ IoT	BO	SC	BO	-	AB	-	-	-	-	-

AB: Authentication Bypass (CWE-288) **BO**: Buffer Overflow (CWE-121)
CC: Cleartext Credentials (CWE-200) **D**: Deauthentication (CWE-400) **DOS**: Denial of Service (CWE-400)
FDC: Firmware Decrypt (CWE-200) **FD**: Firmware Dump (CWE-1202) **FF**: Firmware Flashing (CWE-1202)
NE: No Encryption (CWE-319) **SC**: Stolen Credentials (CWE-200)

Of the 54 relevant threats described in the reference threat model for this architecture, 29 were realized due to vulnerabilities in at least one of the evaluated devices. We note that six threats in the reference threat model were not evaluated, specifically those regarding the DGW being spoofed so that the device connects to a malicious DGW, due to technical limitations. In short, other than these six threats, six spoofing threats, ten tampering threats, and three elevation of privilege threats were not realizable due to sufficient mitigations being implemented by the manufacturers.

A summary of the identified vulnerabilities is provided in Table 5. In short, these includes the following:

- **S - Insufficient Authentication on the Dedicated Network:** A recurring issue was that access to the dedicated network was protected with weak or, in some cases, no authentication, which left the network vulnerable to *spoofing* attacks.
- **I, T - Insufficient Encryption on the Dedicated Network:** Inadequate encryption within the dedicated network left the ecosystem vulnerable to *information disclosure* and *tampering* threats (e.g., no encryption between the IoT device and the DGW).
- **S, E - Lack of Network Isolation:** The inclusion of the DGW introduces risks related to improper isolation between the dedicated network and the user's LAN. Failures in segmentation can enable lateral movement, for example, allowing attackers to compromise the dedicated network and pivot into the LAN, bypassing expected security boundaries, leading to *spoofing* and *elevation of privilege.*

The implementation of cloud access within a device impacted the security. The Eufy doorbell serves as an example: accessing the cloud via "Cloud-App" mode led to encryption vulnerabilities that were mitigated when using "Cloud-Web" mode. This variance across modes underscores the impact of their implementations on the security posture.

Overall, these findings indicate the need for manufacturers to secure the dedicated network connecting the DGW and the IoT devices. Developers should therefore ensure secure pairing mechanisms, strong authentication, and encryption within this dedicated network, along with network isolation.

Table 5. Threats realized in the Gateway threat model

Threat Type	From → To	Eufy 2K Doorbell				UniFi (G4 & Dome)	
		Local	Cloud App	Cloud Web		Local	Cloud
S	DGW ⇆ IoT	AB,IE	AB,IE	AB,IE	-	-	-
S	Local user ⇆ DGW	AB,IE	AB,IE	AB,IE	-	ID	ID
T	DGW → IoT	FD,DP	FD,DP	FD,DP	-	FD	FD
T	Local user → DGW	FD,DP	FD,DP	FD,DP	-	FD	FD
I	Cloud user ⇆ Cloud	-	FE	-	-	-	-
I	DGW ⇆ Cloud	FE	FE	NE	-	-	-
I	DGW ⇆ IoT	NE	NE	NE	-	NE	NE
I	Local user ⇆ DGW	NE	-	-	-	NE	-
D	Local user → IoT	D	D	D	-	D	D
D	DGW → IoT	D	D	D	-	D	D
E	IoT ⇆ DGW	-	-	-	-	ID	ID
E	Local user → DGW	-	-	-	-	ID	ID

AB: Authentication Bypass (CWE-288) **D**: Deauthentication (CWE-400)
DP: Debug Port (CWE-1207) **FD**: Firmware Dump (CWE-1202)
FE: Flawed Encryption (CWE-326) **ID**: Insecure Defaults (CWE-453)
IE: Insufficient Entropy (CWE-331) **NE**: No Encryption (CWE-319)

4.4 Discussion

This evaluation highlights how real-world IoT devices embody the threats predicted by our reference models. Across the evaluated devices, we identified 53 security weaknesses, including four previously unknown high-impact vulnerabilities that were assigned CVE identifiers. A large fraction of the threats described in the reference models were realized in practice, demonstrating the practical relevance of the proposed threat models.

A possible reason for this large number of vulnerabilities may be the result of differing trust assumptions between the manufacturers and our models. For instance, Eufy's dedicated network appeared to be treated as inherently trusted: once its weak key generation was exploited, the absence of network isolation enabled a pivot into the LAN. Similarly, the BS Petcam assumed only benign users would connect to its network, yet without proper authentication and encryption, an attacker in range could easily compromise it. Devices in the Network model frequently expose insecure services on the LAN, indicating that vendors assume the local network is safe, an assumption that fails in the presence of other compromised devices, malicious insiders, or network misconfigurations.

These cases demonstrated that broadening threat elicitation beyond strict trust boundaries revealed risks that vendors had overlooked. Not every vulnerability we mapped is equally severe, but the systematic patterns confirm that misplaced trust assumptions open up attack paths.

Finally, we emphasize the scope of our findings. With ten devices, our study demonstrates the practical relevance of the models, though not statistical generality. Moreover, our device-centric methodology provides limited visibility into cloud components, which were treated mostly as black boxes.

Despite these limitations, this evaluation illustrates the validity of the threats described in the reference threat models. Thus, by leveraging the reference threat models, developers can anticipate architecture-specific threats, proactively mitigate them, and reduce the likelihood of vulnerabilities.

Responsible Disclosure: All vulnerabilities identified in this study were responsibly disclosed to the affected vendors prior to publication. Each vendor received a technical summary of the findings, along with suggested mitigations and sufficient time to respond. Our evaluation was conducted in controlled environments without exploiting devices beyond necessary validation, and no user data or production systems were accessed or affected.

5 Conclusion

We introduced three reference threat models for consumer IoT architectures: Direct, Network, and Gateway models, derived from data flow diagrams and a systematic STRIDE-per-interaction approach. By mapping real-world vulnerabilities from ten popular IoT devices onto these models, we showed that the models capture recurring threats and highlight the risks of misplaced trust assumptions, such as treating LANs or dedicated networks as inherently safe.

Our evaluation confirms that uncovered vulnerabilities align with threats that could have been anticipated through threat modeling at design time. The mapping of real-world vulnerabilities back to our models also demonstrated that each architecture presents a distinct security posture. Key findings include the security challenges inherent in the self-managed networks of the Direct model; the distinct local versus cloud threat surfaces of the Network model; and heightened vulnerability potential of the Gateway model due to its complexity.

In summary, our proposed reference threat models describe empirically validated threats for prevalent consumer IoT architectures. These threat models can be consulted by developers of consumer IoT applications, allowing them to anticipate architecture-specific threats and reduce the risk of introducing common vulnerabilities. In addition, these models lower the barrier for adoption of threat modeling in practice, since developers can reuse validated reference models rather than creating them from scratch. This makes threat modeling more accessible to practitioners who may lack deep security expertise.

Acknowledgments. This research was partially funded by the Research Fund KU Leuven, and by the Cybersecurity Research Program Flanders.

Disclosure of Interests. The authors have no competing interests to declare that are relevant to the content of this article.

References

1. Al Asif, M.R.: STRIDE-based cyber security threat modeling for IoT-enabled precision agriculture systems. In: 2021 3rd International Conference on Sustainable Technologies for Industry 4.0 (STI). IEEE (2021)
2. Alharbi, R.: An IoT analysis framework: An investigation of IoT smart cameras' vulnerabilities. In: Living in the Internet of Things: Cybersecurity of the IoT - 2018 (2018). https://doi.org/10.1049/cp.2018.0047
3. Alrawi, O., et al.: SoK: security evaluation of home-based IoT deployments. In: 2019 IEEE Symposium on Security and Privacy (SP) (2019). https://doi.org/10.1109/SP.2019.00013
4. Antonakakis, M.: Understanding the Mirai botnet. In: Proceedings of the 26th USENIX Conference on Security Symposium, SEC 2017. USENIX Association, USA (2017)
5. Bojinov, H.: Embedded management interfaces: emerging massive insecurity. BlackHat USA, p. 14 (2009)
6. Casola, V., et al.: Toward the automation of threat modeling and risk assessment in IoT systems. Internet of Things (2019). https://doi.org/10.1016/j.iot.2019.100056
7. Directorate, N.R.: Ghidra (2025). https://ghidra-sre.org/
8. Ficco, M.: Threat modeling of edge-based iot applications. In: Paiva, A.C.R., Cavalli, A.R., Ventura Martins, P., Pérez-Castillo, R. (eds.) Quality of Information and Communications Technology. Springer, Cham (2021)
9. Forum of Incident Response and Security Teams (FIRST): Common Vulnerability Scoring System (CVSS). https://www.first.org/cvss/
10. Foundation, W.: wireshark (2025). https://www.wireshark.org/
11. Gibbs, W., et al.: Operation mango: scalable discovery of taint-style vulnerabilities in binary firmware services. In: 33rd USENIX Security Symposium (USENIX Security 24). USENIX Association, Philadelphia (2024). https://www.usenix.org/conference/usenixsecurity24/presentation/gibbs
12. GlobalDots: From 2024 to 2025: the evolving DDoS threat landscape (2025). https://www.globaldots.com/resources/blog/ddos-threat-landscape-2025-trends/
13. Goeman, V., De Ruck, D., Cordemans, T., Lapon, J., Naessens, V.: Reverse engineering the Eufy ecosystem: a deep dive into security vulnerabilities and proprietary protocols. In: 18th USENIX WOOT Conference on Offensive Technologies (WOOT 24), pp. 133–147 (2024)
14. Group, T.T.: tcpdump (2025). https://www.tcpdump.org/
15. Hassija, V., et al.: A survey on IoT security: application areas, security threats, and solution architectures. IEEE Access (2019). https://doi.org/10.1109/ACCESS.2019.2924045
16. Heffner, C.: binwalk (2025). https://github.com/ReFirmLabs/binwalk
17. Heffner, C.: Exploiting surveilance cameras like a Hollywood hacker. BlackHat USA (2013)
18. Janes, B.: Never ending story: authentication and access control design flaws in shared IoT devices. In: 2020 IEEE Security and Privacy Workshops (SPW), pp. 104–109 (2020). https://doi.org/10.1109/SPW50608.2020.00033
19. Junejo, A.K., et al.: Threat modeling for communication security of IoT-enabled digital logistics. Sensors **23** (2023). https://doi.org/10.3390/s23239500, https://www.mdpi.com/1424-8220/23/23/9500
20. Ling, Z., et al.: An end-to-end view of IoT security and privacy. In: GLOBECOM 2017 - 2017 IEEE Global Communications Conference (2017). https://doi.org/10.1109/GLOCOM.2017.8254011

21. Liu, M., et al.: Security analysis of vendor customized code in firmware of embedded device. In: Deng, R., Weng, J., Ren, K., Yegneswaran, V. (eds.) Security and Privacy in Communication Networks. Springer, Cham (2017)
22. Lyon, G.: Nmap: discover your network (2025). https://nmap.org/
23. Ma, X., et al.: From one thousand pages of specification to unveiling hidden bugs: large language model assisted fuzzing of matter IoT devices. In: 33rd USENIX Security Symposium (USENIX Security 24). USENIX Association, Philadelphia (2024). https://www.usenix.org/conference/usenixsecurity24/presentation/ma-xiaoyue
24. Messner, M.: EMBA (2024). https://github.com/e-m-b-a/emba
25. Onekey: Unblob (2025). https://github.com/onekey-sec/unblob
26. Redini, N., et al.: Karonte: detecting insecure multi-binary interactions in embedded firmware. In: 2020 IEEE Symposium on Security and Privacy (SP) (2020). https://doi.org/10.1109/SP40000.2020.00036
27. Seeam, A.: Threat modeling and security issues for the internet of things. In: Conference on Next Generation Computing Applications (NextComp) (2019). https://doi.org/10.1109/NEXTCOMP.2019.8883642
28. Shi, Z., et al.: Threat modeling tools: a taxonomy. IEEE Secur. Priv. (2021). https://doi.org/10.1109/MSEC.2021.3125229
29. Shostack, A.: Threat Modeling: Designing for Security, 1st edn. Wiley (2014)
30. Shwartz, O., et al.: Opening pandora's box: effective techniques for reverse engineering IoT devices. In: Eisenbarth, T., Teglia, Y. (eds.) Smart Card Research and Advanced Applications. Springer, Cham (2018)
31. da Silva, L.P., et al.: A comprehensive approach for applying threat modeling to internet of things systems. In: 2022 IEEE 8th World Forum on Internet of Things (WF-IoT) (2022). https://doi.org/10.1109/WF-IoT54382.2022.10152291
32. Sion, L., et al.: SPARTA: security & privacy architecture through risk-driven threat assessment. In: 2018 IEEE International Conference on Software Architecture Companion (ICSA-C) (2018). https://doi.org/10.1109/ICSA-C.2018.00032
33. Stanislav, M., Beardsley, T.: Hacking IoT: a case study on baby monitor exposures and vulnerabilities. Rapid7 2015 (2015)
34. Stanislav, M.A.: Multi-dimensional security integrity analysis of broad market internet-connected cameras. Ph.D. thesis, Dakota State University (2022)
35. Tenable: Tenable nessus (2025). https://www.tenable.com/products/nessus
36. Zheng, Y., et al.: FIRM-AFL: high-throughput greybox fuzzing of IoT firmware via augmented process emulation. In: 28th USENIX Security Symposium (USENIX Security 19). USENIX Association, Santa Clara (2019). https://www.usenix.org/conference/usenixsecurity19/presentation/zheng

A PDCA-Based OT Security Framework for Small and Medium-Sized Enterprises: Design and Preliminary Evaluation

Nico Mexis(✉) and Stefan Katzenbeisser

University of Passau, Innstraße 43, 94032 Passau, Germany
{nico.mexis,stefan.katzenbeisser}@uni-passau.de

Abstract. Small and Medium-sized Enterprises (SMEs) are increasingly reliant on connected Operational Technology (OT), which can include manufacturing machinery, cameras and access control systems, among other things. However, most cybersecurity resources tend to be either too complex or too generic to be of any practical use. This paper presents a concise and practitioner-tested OT security guide designed specifically for SMEs and structured around the familiar Plan-Do-Check-Act (PDCA) cycle. We distilled eight prioritised best practices through a non-systematic and prior systematic literature review, SME surveys, and iterative expert feedback, and iteratively refined and formatively assessed these through a conference workshop, three pilot SMEs, and expert interviews. To help SMEs evaluate and improve their OT security, we also provide a Gantt chart template and five quick self-assessment questions. Our solution's main strength lies in its unique combination of these components.

Keywords: Operational Technology Security · Industrial Control Systems (ICS) · Small and Medium-sized Enterprise (SME) · PDCA Cycle · Cybersecurity Best Practices

1 Introduction

Industrial control systems, programmable logic controllers, and connected machinery, collectively known as Operational Technology (OT), are increasingly present even in small and medium-sized enterprises (SMEs). Although IT security has received considerable attention in recent decades, the security of OT environments remains critically under-explored, particularly among companies that arguably need the most help [1,23]. According to the European Commission [12], an SME is defined as a company that employs less than 250 people and has either an annual turnover that does not exceed EUR 50 million or has an annual balance sheet total that does not exceed EUR 43 million.

SMEs form the backbone of economy, not only representing 99.8% of businesses in Europe, but also employing 64.4% of people and adding 52.5% of

Z. Afzal et al. (Eds.): ARES 2026 Workshops, LNCS 16900, pp. 175–193, 2027.
https://doi.org/10.1007/978-3-032-35576-8_10

value [13,14], face a unique and uncomfortable position when it comes to cybersecurity. They typically lack the dedicated security personnel, budgets, and expertise of larger organisations [23], yet they increasingly rely on internet-connected OT devices, often significantly underestimating the risks [1]. This so-called IT/OT convergence exposes production systems, cameras, access controls, and even ventilation infrastructure to threats that were once confined to the IT world. A successful attack on these systems can halt production entirely, which is a potentially existential threat for smaller companies. Furthermore, the resources that do exist to help SMEs improve their OT security tend to fall into one of two traps: they are either too generic to be actionable, or so technically complex that practitioners already surrender before they begin [29,32]. Our own preliminary interviews with SMEs confirmed this frustration first-hand.

We argue that the primary barrier to OT security adoption in SMEs is not a lack of guidance, but a lack of actionable, appropriately scoped guidance. This paper addresses that barrier directly by providing a structured, prioritised, and practitioner-tested guide. We present a concise, practitioner-tested OT security best practice guide specifically designed for SMEs, structured around the well-known Plan-Do-Check-Act (PDCA) cycle [9,28] – a framework already familiar to most IT professionals. Rather than producing yet another comprehensive standard, our goal was to create something SMEs would actually use. To this end, we make the following contributions:

- Based on literature and expert opinions, we demonstrate empirically that existing frameworks fail SMEs not due to content gaps but due to actionability gaps, and show that PDCA framing and prioritisation measurably reduce adoption friction.
- We validated the guide and its appendices through various phases, including pilot experiments as well as expert and SME interviews.
- We derived five quick self-assessment questions to determine the current level of maturity of SMEs with regard to OT security.

We must emphasise that the real strength and novelty of our proposed solution lies in the validated combination of its individual parts, rather than in the parts themselves. The rest of this work is structured as follows: Sect. 2 introduces the topic of OT security in SMEs, followed by our development and validation methodology using literature reviews and validation approaches in Sect. 3. Then, our guide and its accompanying artefacts are described and evaluated in Sects. 4 and 5, respectively. Finally, Sect. 6 concludes the work and points out possible routes for future work.

2 Background

Even though, SMEs are very heterogeneous, their digital infrastructure can usually be divided into four categories or layers, as illustrated in Fig. 1. Nonetheless, a few devices may belong to either more than one category or to none of the categories. We deliberately depart from the Purdue model, as it presupposes a level of OT architectural maturity with clearly delineated manufacturing zones and defined data flows that most SMEs will never be able to achieve.

The arrows, pointing towards and away from the company, represent the supply chain. These may be connected to other companies, suppliers, service providers, or customers. The first layer within the company consists of mobile devices, which are the "usual" devices that employees work and communicate with, such as smartphones, tablets, laptops etc. The next layer is IT, which communicates directly with these devices. It consists of servers and similar equipment that are responsible for providing the necessary information services.

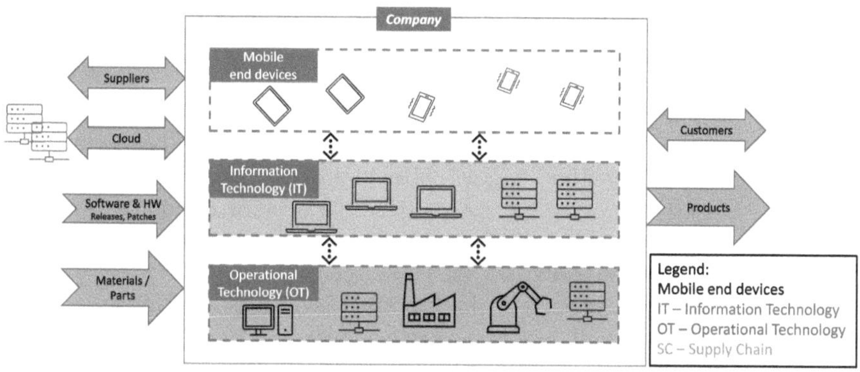

Fig. 1. General and heavily simplified digital structure of a company in terms of the four layers *mobile end devices*, *Information Technology (IT)*, *Operational Technology (OT)*, and *Supply Chain (SC)*, taken from [26].

In this paper, we are mostly interested in the bottom-most layer: the OT. According to our surveys, nowadays the OT environment of SMEs can comprise a wide variety of devices, ranging from cameras to entire manufacturing machines. Building on this, an Industrial Control System (ICS) thus comprises several such control components that work together to achieve a specific industrial objective [31]. However, nowadays, the paradigm presented in Fig. 1 seems to shift: the IT and OT environments tend to unify more and more. This effect is called *IT/OT convergence*. Although better intra- and inter-connectivity could benefit devices, it introduces new risks to the entire ecosystem by allowing adversaries to connect to even more sensitive devices, if proper network segmentation or isolation procedures are inadequate.

SMEs in particular face various challenges in regard to OT cybersecurity. Firstly, according to their definition, they have less money and fewer employees than larger companies, and therefore less expertise. Also, as previous studies and literature reviews identified, due to their heterogeneity, less tailored solutions exist for them [23]. On the other hand, paradoxically, resources that do exist are often not applicable to SMEs because of their complexity, e.g. [29]. This is reinforced by many independent studies that also often point out that existing standards (such as the widely-known IEC 62443 standard) are inapplicable to SMEs due to their complexity [32]. Furthermore, many SMEs are affected by IT/OT convergence, either knowingly or unknowingly, while often remaining unaware of the enormous security risks that come with it [1]. Our best practice guide aims to fill this apparent gap.

3 Methodology

Our development and validation process follows the design science research paradigm [17], in which small-sample, qualitative, iterative evaluation with practitioners is a standard and accepted methodology ("Case Study"). Our general methodology consisted of six main steps. As a first step, we interviewed several SMEs in order to find out which general areas are neglected the most in terms of cyber security. Simultaneously, we used the results of our previous general systematic literature review [23] about cybersecurity-related works specific for SMEs according to the methodology proposed by Kitchenham [20]. This helps us identify the biggest research gaps. As explained in Sects. 3.1 and 3.2, the results have been transferred into five different use cases that have each been researched individually. One of these use cases was "OT security for SMEs".

Subsequently, we extracted all the literature, which is relevant for each use case, and started a second, use-case-specific literature review phase, which is described in Sect. 3.3. This review phase already relied on the specific results from both SME feedback and the systematic literature review. Based on all the knowledge that has been gained about the specific challenges that need to be addressed in our guide, we formulated various expectations for our guide that are explained in detail in Sect. 3.4. Finally, the methodology behind the development of our guide and its evaluation are presented in Sect. 3.5.

3.1 Detailed Assessment Surveys

In order to be able to properly analyse the current state of cybersecurity within SMEs, we conducted detailed interviews with such companies. For this, we prepared a questionnaire that is based directly on the controls from both the CIS Critical Security Controls Version 8 [6] and the CIS Critical Security Controls ICS Companion Guide Version 7 [5], as they have been proven applicable to SMEs in particular by focusing on implementation group 1 [27]. The following data is based on real assessments that has been collected together with a partner institution. However, for reasons of confidentiality, we may only report general trends and no specific values.

The coverage of ICS controls is consistently significantly lower than the coverage of the implementation group 1 of the IT controls. Even when considering implementation group 2 for the IT security results, SMEs perform significantly worse in the ICS controls, highlighting the current imbalance of IT and OT security importance and leading to our decision to provide guidance towards proper OT security in SMEs. It should still be mentioned that these figures should be interpreted as illustrative rather than statistically representative, especially due to the redacted data.

The areas that seemed to be most neglected were inventory management, secure configuration, access control, malware protection, and awareness. Conversely, network segmentation is an example of a rather consistently implemented measure.

3.2 Systematic Literature Review

Our systematic literature review methodology and full results are described in detail in [23]. Briefly, we applied the Kitchenham methodology [20] across seven databases, filtering 1192 papers down to 112. Of these, 108 ($\approx$ 96%) focused on IT security; only 41 addressed OT and 20 addressed supply chain cybersecurity. We argue, however, that the relevant gap is not really the absence of OT security guidance in absolute terms, but the absence of a validated, practitioner-tested, concise guide that combines prioritized best practices, a familiar process structure, a planning template, and self-assessment questions. None of the existing works, including IEC 62443-based summaries, offer this combination in a form confirmed usable by SMEs [32].

3.3 Specific Literature Review

We conducted a non-systematic literature review with a focus on grey literature. Through this process, we were able to identify three grey literature works [3,4, 24] and an additional piece of scientific literature that are not included in the results of the systematic procedure [30]. The latter mostly provided setup guides for honeypots and other open-source software that may help implementing an intrusion detection system that is specifically applicable to SMEs. Alas, it does not focus specifically on the OT environment – parts of it can be referenced as setup guides for OT-specific solutions nonetheless.

On the other hand, [24] contained concise and easy-to-understand descriptions of OT-specific terms, as well as a first set of best practices for ICS. [4] highlighted the importance for SMEs to regularly audit and centrally manage OT assets as part of a unified process. Additionally, best practices are presented and the IEC 62443 standard is briefly summarised. However, the authors acknowledge that most SMEs would find the IEC 62443 standard too complex to understand without help. They recommend referring to summaries to avoid feeling overwhelmed. Finally, [3] contains best practices for basic protection in the OT environment as well as a tailored digital maturity survey.

3.4 Expectations to the Guide

As already described in Sects. 3.2 and 3.3, there are already a number of resources which try to summarise best practices or entire frameworks for OT security. However, in our opinion and the opinion of most SMEs we have asked, many of these frameworks and guides are too comprehensive and hence, can only be applied partially in SMEs with both limited expertise and resources. Because of this, our guide should be as concise as possible, whilst still retaining as much information as possible, without overwhelming SMEs. The challenge is finding a sweet spot between this triad of expectations.

When we originally started to develop our OT security guide for SMEs, the OWASP OT Top 10 list [16] was still in development. Hence, we opted for writing our own guide first and using their list as validation instead. It contains the top 10 pitfalls, according to their research, for OT security. Our guide should not only cover all their ten points but should also contain either ten or less than ten "best practices" for SMEs to follow. We chose the OWASP OT Top 10 as a validation benchmark rather than IEC 62443 precisely because the latter, while authoritative, has been shown to be inapplicable to most SMEs due to its complexity [32].

As already stated in Sect. 2 and reinforced by our SME interviews in Sect. 3.1, most often there is no dedicated staff or roles for OT devices in SMEs, which is why the IT staff usually needs to simultaneously take care of the OT environment, without the proper expertise to account for the specific challenges in this area. Hence, our guide also needs to be comprehensible with as little knowledge as possible about OT in general. We opted for including a short description, motivation, and glossary for OT security in SMEs in our guide. Additionally, our guide follows the Deming cycle, or PDCA (Plan-Do-Check-Act) [9,28] cycle. We selected the PDCA cycle because it is already embedded in widely-used IT management practices and standards familiar to SME IT staff (e.g., ISO 9001 [18] and ISO 27001 [19]), thereby reducing the overhead of adopting a new structural framework and encouraging the continuous improvement mindset that is consistently absent in SME security postures.

Furthermore, many SMEs do not know where to start or how to plan improvements to their cyber security, let alone in their OT environment. For this reason, a preliminary prioritisation of various best practices based on expert feedback is appropriate. Providing an example Gantt chart could also help SMEs plan their security upgrade projects more effectively. Our guide should intentionally not feature specific implementation guides as they significantly increase the length and complexity of the guide and cannot be generalised to fit every SME in every industrial sector.

Finally, we acknowledge that some SMEs may want to delve even deeper into implementing security solutions for their OT environment. For these SMEs, we should also add a list of literature for further reading. This alleviates the need for them to conduct literature reviews on their own to identify tailored solutions for SMEs. Simultaneously, this list can act as a bibliography for the guide itself, as most of our content is based on the same literature as well.

To reiterate, the final guide should

- be as short and concise as possible, i.e., less than 15 pages (in contrast to existing works such as [29]; based on SME feedback, guides exceeding ≈ 15 pages are routinely abandoned),

- contain as much information as possible,
- not overwhelm the SME in question,
- cover all the OWASP OT Top 10 [16], at least to some extent each,
- be as comprehensible as possible, even without proper knowledge about OT-specific challenges,
- contain a prioritisation of best practices in the field,
- have an accompanying example Gantt chart, and
- contain literature for further reading.

3.5 Development and Formative Evaluation of Our Guide

In order to evaluate the validity of our identified best practices as well as the rest of the content that is being presented in our guide, we conducted interviews in three phases, between core steps within the writing process.

First, we fully developed our workshop concept based on the output of the previous phases, as shown in Sect. 4.1. Before transforming the content into the written best practice guide in Sects. 4.2 and 4.3, we validated it during the IKT-Sicherheitskonferenz 2024 (ICT Security Conference 2024) in Vienna, Austria.[1] There, we presented our workshop and asked the participating SMEs and experts specific questions about its content.

The second phase took place after our workshop concept was fully transformed into a written best practice guide. We invited several pilot SMEs to use the guide to improve their OT cybersecurity and asked for feedback during check-in appointments in intervals of a month each. Our pilot SMEs were invited to also ask questions regarding the guide in these scheduled meetings, if any occurred.

The third and last phase consisted of interviews with SMEs and experts about the final state of our OT best practice guide. In total, we conducted five expert interviews and three final SME interviews in order to make last-minute changes to our guide before publishing its final version and to finish the formative evaluation. We present the results of these interviews in Sects. 5.1, 5.2 and 5.3.

4 The OT Security Guide for SMEs

4.1 Accompanying Workshop Concept

To develop a proper workshop concept, we first summarised the most important best practices repeatedly mentioned in the literature and interviews. This yielded a list of the following nine best practices:

1. Network segmentation [2,10,24]
2. Awareness [3,4]
3. Updates [2–4]
4. Backups [3,4,10]

[1] https://web.archive.org/web/20240916124728/https://seminar.bundesheer.at/.

5. Access control [2,24]
6. Plan-Do-Check-Act (PDCA) cycle [11]
7. Security Information and Event Management (SIEM) [4,24]
8. Basic protection [3,4]
9. Standards/documented processes [2–4]

Risk assessment is treated as a prerequisite rather than a discrete best practice: it is implicitly addressed through the inventory phase and self-assessment questions, a design choice made to avoid adding a process that, in our experience, SMEs with limited expertise find too open-ended to execute without dedicated support. We also compiled descriptions and details of possible implementation routes for each best practice, as well as the reasons why each one is important. Furthermore, two open-source assessment tools, namely LARS ICS[2] and CSET[3] have been mentioned in Ehrlich et al.'s work [11]. We subsequently added a section about open-source assessment applications to our workshop. In total, our workshop required approx. 40 min of presentation. The structure can be roughly summarised as follows:

1. Introduction of important terms such as OT, ICS, and IT/OT convergence
2. Definition of OT in SMEs, also using the illustration from Fig. 1
3. Demonstration of the importance of OT security in SMEs by inventing an exemplary company that is being attacked
4. Illustration of differences between IT and OT environments using a simplified version of the CIA triad (confidentiality is the most important factor in IT, whereas availability is the most important factor in OT)
5. Very short summary of five different OT-security related standards and guides and their applicability for SMEs, according to practical evaluations, surveys and the literature
6. Simple open-source assessment software for OT environments
7. Our best practices and a short description, each
8. Questions & Feedback (ref. Section 5.1)

4.2 The OT Security Best Practice Guide

After our workshop concept was successfully validated, we transformed its content into concise full-text. During this process, we decided to organise the best practice guide into the four categories of Plan, Do, Check and Act, according to the PDCA cycle [9,28] with which most IT staff in SMEs should already be familiar. This structure is also well-established since many guides and even standards, such as the ISO 9001 [18], are based upon the same principle. It should be noted that a further division of the "Plan" phase into "Observe" and "Plan" would have been possible, leading to the, also rather well-known, OPDCA cycle. However, we ultimately decided against this.

[2] https://www.bsi.bund.de/dok/7029486.

[3] https://www.cisa.gov/resources-tools/services/cyber-security-evaluation-tool-cset.

The workshop concept initially comprised nine items, including the PDCA cycle itself. However, in this step, PDCA was promoted from a best practice to the organising structure of the entire document. Subsequently, we formulated our eight best practices and added an approximate estimate of the resources (monetary and time-based) required to implement them in the form of "low", "medium", and "high". In addition, we created a template for an inventory list based on real-life examples demonstrated to us during our surveys (ref. Sect. 3.1). We also developed various exemplary test criteria for OT devices. According to the guide, the test criteria should be aggregated device-specifically, in order to be able to evaluate whether the OT security project was successful in the Check phase. In addition to the written guide, there have been only rather few changes (content-wise), such that the workshop can still act as an accompanying learning resource.

The guide opens with an introductory section defining OT, motivating OT security for SMEs, and summarising common pitfalls. A preparatory chapter then covers objective-setting, responsibility assignment, and project planning. The core of the guide follows the four PDCA phases: Plan (inventory, self-assessment, test criteria, improvement planning), Do (piloting on one device), Check (verification against test criteria), and Act (rollout or rollback). The guide closes with a continuous improvement section and appendices including an inventory list template and further reading. The full-text content (excluding cover, ToC, references, and appendices) is under 13 pages.

Emphasis is placed on the preparation and planning phases by design, as we wanted the planning phase to be as comprehensive as possible, in order to avoid issues in the further phases that may affect availability of devices in the context of the CIA triad. As already mentioned, the guide does not feature specific implementation guides, due to the aforementioned reasons and limitations. The guide (original in German) can be found as additional material on our website.[4] Additionally, it was published as part of a larger full-scale cyber security framework for SMEs [8].

4.3 The Gantt Chart

In order to allow SMEs for quick adoption of our proposed workflow, we provided an exemplary Gantt chart that covers all the steps mentioned in our best practice guide (ref. Section 4.2). For better reference, some of the entries in the Gantt chart correspond exactly to separate sections of the guide itself, as illustrated in Table 1. Every task should be handled sequentially, except for T3.1 and T3.2, which run concurrently. Again, the Gantt chart (original in German) can be found as additional material on our website.[5]

4 https://cyseres-kmu.eu/handbuch-ot-security/.

5 https://cyseres-kmu.eu/gantt-chart_cyseres-kmu_ot/.

Table 1. The phases and tasks from our Gantt chart together with their respective durations as well as their visualisation.

Phase	Task	Duration [Weeks]
P0 | Pre	T0.1 - Set Objectives	0.50
	T0.2 - Define Responsibilities	0.50
	T0.3 - Establish Project Plan	0.50
P1 | Plan	T1.1 - Create/Update an Inventory List	1.00
	T1.2 - Identification of Improvement Opportunities	1.00
	T1.3 - Define Test Criteria for Devices	1.00
	T1.4 - Planning the Improvements	2.00
P2 | Do	T2.1 - Improvement of a Selected OT Device	0.20
	T2.2 - Update of the Inventory List	0.20
P3 | Check	T3.1 - Test Phase with Normal Device Operation	10.00
	T3.2 - Continuous Monitoring of the Device	10.00
P4 | Act	T4.1 - General Implementation or Rollback	2.00

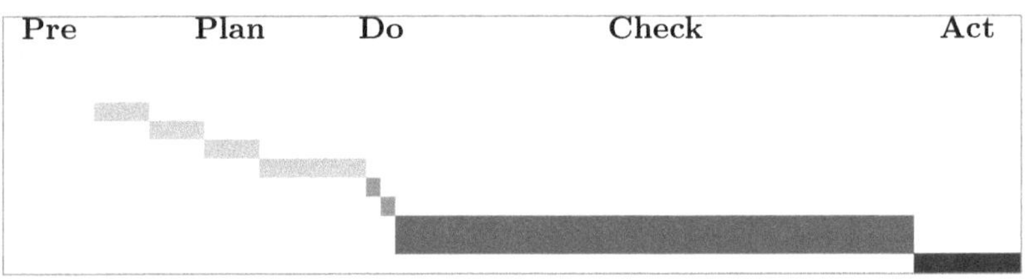

5 Formative Evaluation

5.1 Preliminary Feedback

As already described as part of our validation methodology in Sect. 3.5, we presented the workshop at the IKT-Sicherheitskonferenz 2024 (ICT Security Conference 2024) in Vienna, Austria. Due to our late time slot on the final day, only four SMEs attended; results are therefore indicative rather than confirmatory. The 40-minute presentation generated no questions, suggesting the concepts were conveyed clearly. During the feedback session, participants physically ranked best practices using picture cards (a method recommended by a pedagogy expert). No full consensus was reached, but the discussion yielded a clear directional ranking: network segmentation, awareness, and updates were rated most important. (OT) SIEM, standards, and PDCA were rated least important. Participants also suggested adding documented processes as an explicit best practice, which we incorporated.

5.2 Pilot Experiments

The pilot experiments were the most important phase of our validation process. In total, three SMEs were willing to follow our OT security guide to improve their cybersecurity posture. Two SMEs took general advice from the guide, especially the inventory list, assessment tools and best practices, to check and improve their OT cybersecurity on their own. Still, they gave positive feedback and required little to no help to understand and implement the new cyber security measures.

Alas, only the single remaining SME followed the proposed PDCA-based methodology and Gantt chart. The SME is from the manufacturing sector and has a dedicated IT person who is also responsible for the OT environment. Additionally, the company's Chief Financial Officer (CFO) has considerable expertise in cybersecurity, particularly with regard to SMEs. The company was relatively easy to work with due to their existing familiarity with OT security. They also permitted on-site visits, facilitating exchange and enabling us to witness their actions first-hand.

The company had already begun several initiatives. For example, they were actively inventorying their IT assets using open-source software they had been using for 15 years. Their first initiative was extending their inventory list into the OT space. The first step was to summarise all the interconnected devices within their OT environment on a flip chart. Much to their surprise, this yielded a much longer list than anticipated. As well as production facilities and their controlling computers, it contained their ventilation system, their entire DECT network, access control systems (e.g., barriers), cameras, access points, network switches in their production network, and multiple Raspberry Pi clients managing and monitoring various devices. It took them longer than a week (as suggested by the Gantt chart in Sect. 4.3) to properly detect and document their OT infrastructure and put it into their open-source inventory management system due to their rather strict network segmentation (even with DMZs and micro-segmentation in some places).

The most pressing issues were around access control and OT backups, which is why these best practices were ultimately chosen as the pilot improvements. For the former specific improvement, the test criteria could be kept rather simple: access to specific folders and files on a dedicated file server should still be possible, whilst all other files are blocked. Also, every machine currently has centrally-managed users, which can be used to log in to any other machine as well. Every machine and PC that requires file access should have two dedicated accounts: one for logging in to this specific machine only, and one for accessing a specific folder on the file server exclusively, without being able to log in to any machine itself. For backups, test criteria about the machine's availability and current capabilities were carefully collected. Additionally, test criteria for the backups themselves were documented (restoring should work, specific folders and files should be included etc.). As a last step of the planning phase, open-source solutions towards full system backups tackling the specific challenges of OT environments were searched. Ultimately, the company opted for a PXE boot-based solution, which is said to be capable of backing up the entire system.

Overall, the Preparation and Plan phases took approximately 1.5 months, which is slightly longer than anticipated in the Gantt chart.

In the Do phase, no immediate problems came up and the company was successfully able to implement the best practices. However, due to the large number of devices and accounts that were chosen as pilots, it took them longer than anticipated to apply the improvements properly. During the subsequent Check phase, no problems were identified and in the Act phase, the best practices could be applied everywhere - again without additional problems.

Their conclusion was that, although, a strict project plan/Gantt chart is good as a comparison baseline, certain flexibility in following them worked better for their type of company. They also emphasised that their documentation is poor in general, which they confirmed is a common pattern typical of the German mid tier ("trial and error, little documentation"). Ultimately, we decided not to adjust the pre-defined times on our Gantt chart, as these are just recommendations that can be amended by any SME that wishes to do so. In general, our guide helped this SME improve its OT cybersecurity posture by encouraging them to take an inventory of their OT environment and close critical security gaps regarding access control mechanisms, as well as addressing availability concerns through better user management and backups, respectively.

5.3 Final Interviews

For this, we used the feedback we received in the various evaluation phases. Of course, no consensus has been reached regarding the importance of each individual best practice, but a general trend in the feedback could be observed. Generally, the guide was well-received. Experts found it clear, comprehensible, and appropriately concise for SMEs. The glossary, descriptions of individual measures, and the PDCA structure were consistently praised. One SME noted it had already prompted concrete action in areas like backup and access control.

Chapter 3 (the specific procedures, including the best practices etc.) was consistently identified as the core value of the guide. However, also the glossary, use of links, and the inventory list template were highlighted positively. At 13 pages, most found the length appropriate for SMEs. According to our participants, the guide is best suited for small (10–49) and medium (50–249) companies. Micro-enterprises were seen as unlikely to have OT at all, while larger companies (>250) likely already have more sophisticated approaches. On the other hand, the most frequently raised issues were:

- An introductory section helping readers determine whether they even have OT ("Am I affected?") was suggested.
- The inventory list may be too detailed or complex for first-time users. Also, entries such as "network address" and "contact data" were unclear.
- The standards section was considered too long and too generic. Removing ISO 27k from the OT-specific context was also recommended.
- Currently, the guide is too heavily focused on the "Plan" phase. More content on "Do", "Check", and "Act" would be valuable. For instance, the "Check" phase may be framed more explicitly as a security audit.

- Concrete checklists, a maintenance/review cycle plan, a maturity model (e.g. spider chart for self-assessment), and an FAQ compiled from SME experiences were recurring ideas.

Distributing the guide in PDF format was broadly accepted as pragmatic and appropriate. Several experts mentioned that publishing it as a website would also work well and allow easier navigation. However, short introductory videos (especially for tools like LARS ICS) in addition to the PDF were the most commonly suggested supplementary format. Also, most experts agreed that external support is likely necessary for/during implementation, especially if no dedicated OT staff is present. The guide can serve as a coordination tool, but hands-on implementation typically requires an OT specialist, external consultant or close collaboration with the distributor or maintainer of the respective devices. However, this does not contradict our rationale that the guide is not applicable without external support, as this is a limitation with devices in the OT environment in general.

Finally, we used the final interviews as another phase of retrieving feedback on the prioritisation and description of best practices. Some interviewees mentioned that the approximate cost and time required to implement some of the best practices may need to be adjusted slightly. We took this advice if it was mentioned by at least three experts. For the prioritisation, each expert was asked to reorder the best practices, just like during the preliminary interviews (ref. Sect. 5.1), just with slightly different entries, and applied Borda count aggregation to their answers. While this method has known limitations with small samples and is sensitive to individual ordinal judgements, it provides a transparent and reproducible basis for prioritisation. For this, we converted their rankings to concrete numbers, i.e., the most important best practice is assigned a value of 1, while the least important is assigned a value of 8, and added up those numbers. A Kendall's coefficient of $W \approx 0.485$ indicates moderate inter-rater agreement, which, while not strong, is sufficient to establish a directional consensus given the known sensitivity of ordinal aggregation methods to small samples. The Borda count method yielded the following total ranking:

1. Backups
2. Network segmentation
3. Access control
4. Updates
5. Documented processes
6. Awareness
7. Basic protection
8. Monitoring

5.4 Comparison With Our Expectations

The guide meets all expectations stated in Sect. 3.4. At under 13 pages of full text, it is concise yet complete. Interviewees confirmed it is neither overwhelming nor superficial. The OWASP OT Top 10 [16] items are, each at least partially, covered as follows:

1. Unknown Assets and Unmanaged External Access: *Monitoring*
2. Devices with known Vulnerabilities/Issues: *Updates*
3. Inadequate Supplier/Supply Chain Management: *Inventory List*[6]
4. Loss of Availability: *Updates, Monitoring*
5. Insufficient Access Control: *Access Control*
6. Missing Incident Detection/Reaction Capabilities: *Backups*
7. Broken Zones and Conduits Design: *Network Segmentation*
8. Missing Awareness: *Awareness*
9. Components/Protocols with Insufficient Security Capabilities: *Awareness, Updates*
10. Missing Hardening: *Access Control*

The final expert and SME interviews confirmed that, although some knowledge of either field is still necessary, our guide is comprehensible to IT and OT experts alike. As a result of said interviews, we were also able to refine our prioritisation of best practices. In addition to the guide, an exemplary Gantt chart is available (see Sect. 4.3). The references can also be used as a list of suggested further reading. Thus, we believe that the final version of our OT security guide for SMEs meets all our expectations.

5.5 Comparison with Related Work

While our guide may not contain some pieces of information from bigger frameworks or standards such as the IEC 62443, it still contains the OWASP OT Top 10 [16] items, as demonstrated in Sect. 5.4. Additionally, our guide contains actionable advice as it is structured according to the PDCA cycle and features a dedicated Gantt chart.

In comparison to similar guides such as [3,4,29], our document is much more lightweight. Also, while [4] often just refers to "bigger" frameworks such as RAMI 4.0 or the IEC 62443 standard, our guide contains much more concise descriptions of each control. On the other hand, [3] features a self-assessment questionnaire, which is absent in our guide. Section 5.6 of this article contains pointers in this direction, albeit not in a production-ready format.

Our guide covers most of their controls, only missing a few such as dedicated protection against (D)DoS [3,4] or vulnerability management [29]. It should be noted that some of these controls were intentionally omitted from our guide due to feedback from SMEs who felt that their respective implementations were too burdensome or out of their budget.

5.6 Quick OT Security Self-assessments

As part of a data-driven, SME-tailored cyber security assessment suite that has been published in part separately [25], we set out to derive five central questions

[6] In fact, our guide does not describe the inventory list as one of our best practices, but rather as a prerequisite for any OT security project.

from the best practice guide that SMEs can use to gain an initial understanding of their operational technology (OT) security status. Hence, we consulted our prioritisation results from the interviews in Sect. 5.3. The best practices that were rated among the five most important have then been converted into proper security controls:

- OT backups: Functioning backup systems (emergency devices and data recovery media) are available for the OT environment. These are tested regularly and are ready for use in an emergency.
- OT network segmentation: Our networks are segmented so that there is no direct access from the IT environment to the OT environment. A demilitarised zone (DMZ) separates IT and OT to ensure security.
- OT security measures: If the networks are not segmented, IT and OT security measures are managed as a unified system. If segmentation is in place, dedicated OT security measures are implemented, which are regularly reviewed and updated.
- OT updates: OT systems are updated regularly (i.e., there is documentation on the frequency). The hardware used is supported by the manufacturer, and SLAs are in place with the manufacturers.
- OT standards: OT security measures comply with recognised industry standards and best practices (e.g., ISA/IEC 62443, NIST SP 800-82, VDI/VDE 2182).

The first two questions, as well as the fourth, obviously correspond exactly to their respective best practices. The third and fifth items correspond to access control and documented processes, respectively. Their description differs slightly from their respective original best practice, as we wanted them to also reflect those that were rated less important, at least to some extent. For a proper maturity model, we believe that a 4-point or 6-point Likert scale [7,21,22] may be appropriate in order to avoid bias towards the midpoint [15].

5.7 Limitations and Future Work

While it is already a big step in the right direction, our OT Security Best Practice Guide for SMEs still has some limitations. First of all, as already mentioned as part of the feedback we received from SMEs in Sects. 5.2 and 5.3, our guide does not provide explicit recommendations for either proprietary or open source software or setup guides. This is due to the fact that there is no piece of software (or hardware) that will fit every use case from every SME, due to their heterogeneity. However, in future iterations of the guide, or in a separate summary, various pieces of commonly used software could be summarised. The two assessment tools LARS ICS and CSET are an exception here, as they are specifically designed to be applied to virtually any enterprise.

Furthermore, this paper only provides empirical evidence that the guide is actually helpful for SMEs, due to the low number of SMEs involved in the formalisation and evaluation of the document. More pilot experiments should be conducted to fully prove the adequateness of the presented measures and processes.

OT safety is intentionally out of scope here, as it constitutes a distinct regulatory domain governed by standards such as IEC 62443-4 and ISO 13855. Addressing it adequately would double the scope of the guide and undermine its core design goal of conciseness.

Additionally, our best practice guide is not only written in German, but also based on the experiences of Austrian and German SMEs. Although we believe that our guide could be applicable to a wider geographical area in Europe, it is not yet clear how well its findings can be generalised. Future work could involve an empirical evaluation of the differences between various SMEs in different geographical locations, with the aim of enhancing or revising the best practice guide in this regard.

6 Conclusions

Despite the fact that a successful attack on their operational infrastructure can halt production entirely, posing a potentially existential threat to smaller companies, OT security remains a largely overlooked challenge for SMEs. Current resources are either too technical or too abstract to be of practical use, leaving a clear gap that this work set out to fill.

In this paper, we presented a concise OT security best practice guide for SMEs that has been tested by practitioners and is structured around the familiar PDCA cycle. Drawing on a prior systematic literature review [23], detailed SME surveys and iterative expert feedback, we have distilled the most important OT security measures into eight prioritised best practices. A workshop, three pilot SMEs and a final round of expert and SME interviews provided initial practitioner evidence that it strikes an appropriate balance between conciseness and completeness.

Our pilot experiments showed that SMEs can effectively implement the guide's recommendations, even without dedicated OT security staff. The accompanying Gantt chart and inventory list template further reduce the barriers to getting started. Additionally, we have created five quick self-assessment questions that enable any SME to evaluate their current OT security measures in just a few minutes. We hope this guide serves as a practical first step for SMEs who recognise the need to improve their OT security but are unsure where to start.

Acknowledgments. This work is co-funded by the European Union through INTERREG VI-A Germany/Bavaria-Austria 2021-2027 – INTERREG VI-A Bayern-Österreich 2021-2027, as part of the Project "CySeReS-KMU: Cyber Security and Resilience in Supply Chains with focus on SMEs" (project number BA0100016).

Disclosure of Interests. The authors have no competing interests to declare that are relevant to the content of this article.

References

1. Aoudi, S., Al-Aqrabi, H.: Integrating IoT security practices into a risk-based framework for small and medium enterprises (SMEs). Comput. Stand. Interfaces **97**, 104099 (2026). https://doi.org/10.1016/j.csi.2025.104099
2. Arnarson, H., Kanafi, F.S., Kaarlela, T., Seldeslachts, U., Pieters, R.: Evaluation of cyber security in agile manufacturing: maturity of technologies and applications. In: 2022 IEEE/SICE International Symposium on System Integration (SII), pp. 784–789. IEEE (2022). https://doi.org/10.1109/SII52469.2022.9708888
3. Bundesamt für Sicherheit in der Informationstechnik (BSI): Empfehlungen für betreiber von ics (nd). https://www.bsi.bund.de/dok/6603566. Accessed 09 Feb 2026
4. Bundesministerium für Klimaschutz, Umwelt, Energie, Mobilität, Innovation und Technologie (BMK): Sicherheit für die digitale transformation der produktion. Technical report, Vienna, Austria (2020). https://www.bmk.gv.at/dam/jcr:9d50fe2a-b645-4910-9c1b-1e612a4ee1ff/sisgi_endbericht.pdf
5. Center for Internet Security, Inc. (CIS): CIS Controls Industrial Control Systems Companion Guide. East Greenbush, NY (2018). https://www.cisecurity.org/insights/white-papers/cis-controls-implementation-guide-for-industrial-control-systems. Accessed 16 Feb 2026
6. Center for Internet Security, Inc. (CIS): CIS Critical Security Controls Version 8. East Greenbush, NY (2021). https://www.cisecurity.org/controls/v8. Accessed 16 Feb 2026
7. Chang, L.: A psychometric evaluation of 4-point and 6-point Likert-type scales in relation to reliability and validity. Appl. Psychol. Meas. **18**(3), 205–215 (1994). https://doi.org/10.1177/014662169401800302
8. CySeReS-KMU: Cyber-Security und Resilienz in Supply Chains mit Fokus auf KMU. Technical report, University of Passau (2026). https://doi.org/10.15475/cyseres_kmu.2026
9. Deming, W.E.: Out of the Crisis. MIT Press, Cambridge (1986)
10. Douchek, P., Nedomova, L., Luc, L., Novak, L.: Information security: the glory and penury of SMEs in the Czech and Slovak republics. In: 2020 International Conference on Engineering Management of Communication and Technology (EMCTECH), pp. 1–7. IEEE (2020). https://doi.org/10.1109/EMCTECH49634.2020.9261506
11. Ehrlich, M., Trsek, H., Wisniewski, L., Jasperneite, J.: Survey of security standards for an automated industrie 4.0 compatible manufacturing. In: IECON 2019-45th Annual Conference of the IEEE Industrial Electronics Society, vol. 1, pp. 2849–2854. IEEE (2019). https://doi.org/10.1109/IECON.2019.8927559
12. Commission, E.: Directorate-general for internal market, industry, entrepreneurship and SMEs: user guide to the SME definition. Publications Office (2020). https://doi.org/10.2873/255862
13. European Commission. Statistical Office of the European Union: Key figures on European business - 2024 edition. Publications Office of the European Union (2024). https://doi.org/10.2785/659794
14. European Commission. Statistical Office of the European Union: Key figures on Europe - 2025 edition. Publications Office of the European Union (2025). https://doi.org/10.2785/0857421
15. Garland, R.: The mid-point on a rating scale: is it desirable? Mark. Bull. **2**, 66–70 (1991)

16. Happe, A., Hollerer, S., Rommer, S.: OWASP Operational Technology (OT) Top 10 (2025). https://ot.owasp.org/. Version 2025, Accessed 09 Feb 2026
17. Hevner, A.R., March, S.T., Park, J., Ram, S.: Design science in information systems research1. MIS Q. **28**(1), 75–106 (2004). https://doi.org/10.2307/25148625
18. International Organization for Standardization: ISO 9001 Quality Management Systems. Requirements. ISO, Geneva, Switzerland (2015)
19. International Organization for Standardization: ISO 27001 Information technology - Security techniques - Information security management systems – Requirements. ISO, Geneva, Switzerland (2022)
20. Kitchenham, B.: Procedures for performing systematic reviews. Joint Technical Report TR/SE-0401, Keele University, Keele, UK (2004). https://www.inf.ufsc.br/~aldo.vw/kitchenham.pdf
21. Leung, S.O.: A comparison of psychometric properties and normality in 4-, 5-, 6-, and 11-point Likert scales. J. Soc. Serv. Res. **37**(4), 412–421 (2011). https://doi.org/10.1080/01488376.2011.580697
22. Likert, R.: A technique for the measurement of attitudes. Arch. Psychol. **22**(140), 5–55 (1932)
23. Lill, B., Sauerwein, C., Mexis, N., Langner, K.: A comprehensive review of information security research regarding SMEs and future directions. J. Cyber Secur. Mob. **14**(5), 1245–1288 (2025). https://doi.org/10.13052/jcsm2245-1439.1459
24. Luber, S., Schmitz, P.: Was ist ein industrielles steuerungssystem (ICS)? (2021). https://www.security-insider.de/was-ist-ein-industrielles-steuerungssystem-ics-a-1064736/. Accessed 09 Feb 2026
25. Mexis, N., Katzenbeisser, S.: A data-driven approach for cyber security assessments of SMEs. In: Availability, Reliability and Security, pp. 23–39. Springer, Cham, Switzerland (2025). https://doi.org/10.1007/978-3-032-00639-4_2
26. Mexis, N., Lill, B., Doleh, Y., Katzenbeisser, S.: Exposing the gaps: the state of supply chain coverage in current security standards. In: Information Security Education. Empowering People Through Information Security Education, pp. 203–216. Springer, Cham (2025). https://doi.org/10.1007/978-3-031-94924-1_14
27. Ponsard, C., Massonet, P., Grandclaudon, J., Point, N.: From lightweight cybersecurity assessment to SME certification scheme in Belgium. In: 2020 IEEE European Symposium on Security and Privacy Workshops (EuroS&PW), pp. 75–78. IEEE (2020). https://doi.org/10.1109/EuroSPW51379.2020.00019
28. Shewhart, W.A.: Economic Control of Quality of Manufactured Product. D. Van Nostrand Company Inc., New York (1931)
29. Small Business Standards (SBS): SME guide on information security controls. Tech. rep., Small Business Standards (SBS), Brussels, Belgium (2022). https://sbs-sme.eu/wp-content/uploads/2024/01/SBS-SME-Guide_Information-Security-Controls.pdf. Developed in collaboration with the European DIGITAL SME Alliance
30. Srivastava, P., Seludkar, K.: Implementing Enterprise Cyber Security with Open-Source Software and Standard Architecture: Volume II, chap. 7. River Publishers (2023). https://doi.org/10.1201/9781003426134

31. Stouffer, K., et al.: Guide to operational technology (OT) security. Technical report, NIST Special Publication (SP) 800-82r3, National Institute of Standards and Technology, Gaithersburg, MD (2023). https://doi.org/10.6028/NIST.SP.800-82r3
32. Wagner, P., Hansch, G., Konrad, C., John, K.H., Bauer, J., Franke, J.: Applicability of security standards for operational technology by SMEs and large enterprises. In: 2020 25th IEEE International Conference on Emerging Technologies and Factory Automation (ETFA), vol. 1, pp. 1544–1551. IEEE (2020). https://doi.org/10.1109/ETFA46521.2020.9212126

Experience-Driven Framework for Risk-Priorization in Leased Datacenters

Hadi Chamas[1,2(✉)], Samiha Ayed[1], Alexandre Reiffers-Masson[1], Ranwa Al Mallah[3], and Guillaume Antoine[2]

[1] Lab-STICC, IMT Atlantique, Brest, France
{hadi.chamas, samiha.ayed,alexandre.reiffers-masson}@imt-atlantique.fr
[2] Data4 Group, Paris, France
{hadi.chamas,guillaume.antoine}@data4group.com
[3] Polytechnique Montréal, Montréal, Canada
ranwa.al-mallah@polymtl.ca

Abstract. Leased colocation datacenters have become a critical component of modern digital infrastructure, hosting workloads for hyperscalers, financial institutions, healthcare providers, and cloud platforms. Although much of the cybersecurity literature focuses on tenant-facing cloud services, comparatively little attention has been paid to the operator-managed layer responsible for facility systems, physical security, and critical infrastructure technologies. This layer forms a shared dependency between multiple tenants and can therefore become a source of systemic risk.

This paper proposes a structured framework to prioritize cybersecurity domains in colocation datacenters from the operator's perspective. Grounded in operational experience and feedback from DATA4, a European datacenter operator, the approach integrates established security standards and regulatory requirements into an analytical prioritization model aligned with operational objectives. The framework maps NIST CSF 2.0 subcategories to operator security objectives and evaluates cybersecurity topics through a contextualized risk index and interdependency modeling.

The methodology is applied to four European colocation campuses operating under comparable technical architectures but different regulatory and geopolitical environments. The results highlight a relatively stable hierarchy of core security priorities while revealing contextual variations driven by localization factors. In particular, critical infrastructure protection consistently emerges as the dominant cybersecurity domain. This first practical application of the framework demonstrates its usability for governance-level prioritization in operational colocation environments.

Keywords: Colocation Datacenters · Critical Infrastructure Security · Risk-Based Governance · Multi-Tenant Infrastructure · Cybersecurity Prioritization

Z. Afzal et al. (Eds.): ARES 2026 Workshops, LNCS 16900, pp. 194–211, 2027.
https://doi.org/10.1007/978-3-032-35576-8_11

1 Introduction

1.1 General Context

Digital infrastructures increasingly rely on heterogeneous computing paradigms integrating artificial intelligence workloads, big data analytics, edge computing [12], and GPU-as-a-Service (GPUaaS) architectures [5]. This technological shift has accelerated the transition from monolithic cloud deployments toward distributed, hybrid, and multi-cloud environments driven by cost optimization, resilience, and regulatory requirements.

Within this ecosystem, colocation datacenters have emerged as a strategic infrastructure model. Rather than operating private facilities, organizations lease space, power, and cooling resources while maintaining control over their IT assets. This approach reduces capital expenditure and operational complexity while enabling geographic diversification and scalability. However, the colocation paradigm introduces a layered security model in which operator-managed facility systems coexist with tenant-managed IT environments. Recent industry evidence indicates that cybersecurity incidents affecting datacenter operators are becoming more costly [16], while severe cyberattacks originating from IT and OT supply chains are increasing, often exploiting third parties with access to internal networks. These trends highlight that facility, OT, and supplier-connected systems must be treated as cybersecurity-critical assets within the operator-managed perimeter.

Despite the strategic importance of this perimeter, existing cybersecurity literature predominantly focuses on tenant-facing cloud service layers. The facility and operational technology domains of colocation operators remain comparatively underexplored from a quantitative risk prioritization perspective. This gap motivates the development of a structured, objective-driven framework for identifying and prioritizing cybersecurity domains from the colocation operator's standpoint.

1.2 Main Contributions

This work addresses a structural gap in cybersecurity governance for leased colocation datacenters. Existing risk-analysis approaches typically focus either on enterprise IT environments or on tenant-side cloud services, while the operator-managed infrastructure layer remains comparatively underexplored. In multi-tenant facilities, however, this layer represents a shared dependency whose failure may simultaneously affect multiple organizations.

This paper provides the following practical and methodological contributions grounded in operational experience from colocation datacenter environments:

1. **Reframing cybersecurity from the colocation operator's perspective:** we formalize the operator-managed cybersecurity perimeter of colocation datacenters. We decompose facility, physical, and corporate information systems into structured cybersecurity domains aligned with the NIST Cybersecurity Framework 2.0.

2. **Objective-driven integration of security standards and regulatory frameworks:** we introduce the Objective Risk Index (ORI). We propose a multiplicative risk metric integrating likelihood, impact, exposure, assurance, and site-localization factors to enable contextualized cross-campus risk comparison.
3. **A structured analytical prioritization framework for colocation security:** We introduce a formal methodology that combines objective-level risk indexing, vulnerability-adjusted topic effectiveness, and interdependency modeling to rank cybersecurity domains according to their systemic importance for datacenter operators.
4. **Comparison of insights from multiple European colocation campuses:** Applying the framework to four campuses located in different regulatory and geopolitical contexts highlights both structural security priorities and contextual variations in governance emphasis. These results demonstrate how external conditions influence cybersecurity investment priorities even when infrastructure architectures remain similar.

Together, these contributions provide a governance-level analytical framework that helps operators translate compliance requirements and threat intelligence into structured cybersecurity prioritization decisions. This framework helps establish best practices for operators of colocation data centers, based on real-word experience.

2 Related Work

2.1 Cybersecurity Risk Quantification Models

The Factor Analysis of Information Risk (FAIR) framework [9] introduced a structured quantitative model decomposing risk into frequency and magnitude components. FAIR emphasizes probabilistic reasoning and financial loss estimation, providing one of the earliest formal approaches to cyber risk measurement. Similarly, Gordon and Loeb [4] proposed an economic model for optimal cybersecurity investment, demonstrating that investment levels should not exceed approximately 37% of expected loss. Their work formalized cost-benefit reasoning in security spending.

More recently, Hubbard and Seiersen [6] advocated measurement-driven cyber risk management using calibrated probabilistic estimation techniques. Their approach emphasizes reducing uncertainty through structured estimation rather than qualitative scoring.

While these models provide strong financial and probabilistic foundations, they primarily focus on enterprise IT environments rather than shared multi-tenant infrastructure contexts.

2.2 Multi-criteria Decision and Prioritization Methods

Analytic Hierarchy Process (AHP) has been widely applied to cybersecurity prioritization [13], enabling pairwise comparison of controls, criteria, and strategic objectives. Variants integrating fuzzy logic and TOPSIS methods [1,17] further extend multi-criteria ranking approaches by handling uncertainty and ranking alternatives according to their proximity to an ideal solution. These methods are valuable, but they generally require alternatives, criteria, and weights to be defined upfront and rely substantially on expert preference elicitation.

Instead of directly ranking cybersecurity topics through pairwise preferences or distance from an ideal profile, the proposed framework first derives topics from control-objective mappings and then evaluates them through objective-level risk, structural relevance, vulnerability pressure, expected utility, localization factors, and inter-topic dependencies. Expert judgement is therefore not eliminated, but decomposed into operationally interpretable parameters that are traceable to the operator-managed perimeter and comparable across campuses.

2.3 Cybersecurity in Critical Infrastructure and Datacenters

Critical infrastructure cybersecurity has been widely examined in energy and industrial control systems [7]. These studies emphasize the convergence of IT and OT security and highlight systemic cascading risks.

In cloud environments, security governance models often focus on shared responsibility frameworks [3]. However, the specific operator-managed perimeter of colocation datacenters, covering facility management systems, power distribution, and physical security, remains comparatively underexplored.

Research on datacenter resilience has primarily focused on engineering redundancy, fault tolerance, and energy management. While these studies improve infrastructure reliability, they rarely address cybersecurity governance and risk prioritization at the operator level.

2.4 Standards and Framework Alignment

Several standards and frameworks may support cybersecurity governance in datacenter environments. ISO/IEC 27001 and ISO/IEC 27005 provide an ISMS and risk-management foundation, ISA/IEC 62443 addresses operational technology and industrial automation systems relevant to facility environments, CIS Controls provide prescriptive safeguards against common attacks, and Cloud Security Alliance guidance supports cloud security assurance. These frameworks serve complementary purposes: governance, OT security, technical control implementation, and cloud assurance. In this work, the NIST Cybersecurity Framework (CSF) is selected because it provides a technology–neutral taxonomy of cybersecurity outcomes across Govern, Identify, Protect, Detect, Respond, and Recover functions and can be mapped to other standards. Its 2.0 revision [11] expands governance integration and supply chain considerations. However, the literature does not provide a formal mechanism for aligning NIST CSF 2.0 subcategories with operator-defined objectives in a way that simultaneously ensures compliance traceability and supports quantitative prioritization.

2.5 Positioning of This Work

In contrast to existing approaches, this work focuses specifically on the operator-managed security perimeter of leased colocation datacenters, a domain that remains largely absent from the cybersecurity research literature. Furthermore, the proposed framework integrates three dimensions that are rarely combined in prior studies:

- objective-driven alignment with security standards such as NIST CSF 2.0,
- contextual risk modulation through localization factors reflecting regulatory and geopolitical environments, and
- interdependency modeling capturing systemic interactions between cybersecurity domains.

By combining these elements, the proposed approach enables governance-level prioritization of cybersecurity domains in multi-tenant datacenter infrastructures. While prior work addresses cybersecurity governance, risk quantification, and critical infrastructure protection independently, comparatively few studies explicitly focus on governance-level cybersecurity prioritization for the operator-managed layer of leased colocation datacenters.

3 Background

3.1 Leased Datacenter Overview

Based on the definition of NF EN 50600-1 norm [2] of datacenters and on the definition of ISO/IEC 22237 norm [8] of colocation datacenter service, a colocation data center is a shared facility owned and operated by a provider that leases space, power, and cooling infrastructure to multiple tenants. Each tenant, such as Cloud Service Providers (CSP) and banking institutions, installs and manages its own IT equipment within the shared environment, while the operator oversees and maintains the core infrastructure of the facility, including power, cooling, and physical space. Therefore, from a colocation datacenter point of view, the information system of a datacenter can be divided into three domains:

- **Corporate domain:** It encompasses the administrative, financial, and organizational processes that support the data center's business operations.
- **Physical security domain:** It includes video surveillance (CCTV), access control systems, intrusion detection, and security management platforms.
- **Critical environment domain:** It includes the building Management System (BMS) [10] and associated operational technologies that ensure the continuous availability of infrastructure, including power distribution systems and cooling systems.

These information systems form the core of leased colocation datacenters and constitute the environment in which cloud service provisioning operates across different models (SaaS, PaaS, and IaaS) as shown in Fig. 1.

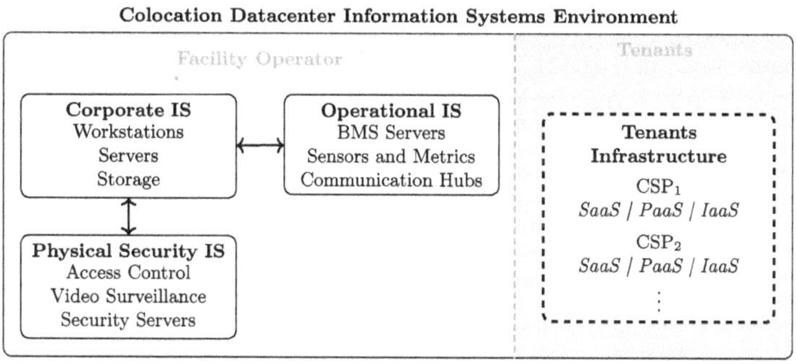

Fig. 1. Conceptual organization of information systems in a colocation datacenter. Three interconnected internal systems support facility operations, while tenant cloud infrastructures remain logically independent.

3.2 Cybersecurity in Colocation Datacenters

Cybersecurity in colocation datacenters can be divided into two complementary domains: *(i)* governance and compliance, and *(ii)* operational security controls. These domains are integrated through the Governance, Risk, and Compliance (GRC) framework, which aligns regulatory requirements, business objectives, and security measures, enabling operators to manage risks while maintaining compliance (Fig. 2).

Governance and Compliance Landscape

Security requirements for colocation datacenters vary across jurisdictions. This paper focuses on European facilities, which must comply with both EU regulations and national legislation. Due to their role in hosting critical and regulated workloads, operators are expected to demonstrate strong security and compliance capabilities.

Customers such as financial institutions, hyperscalers, cloud providers, and healthcare organizations often require compliance with recognized standards. Common frameworks include ISO/IEC 27001 for Information Security Management Systems (ISMS), PCI DSS for payment card security, NIST Cybersecurity Framework 2.0 for risk-based cybersecurity governance, and SOC 2 for assessing service organization controls.

Risk Management and Operational Security

These frameworks rely on structured risk management approaches such as ISO 27005 and EBIOS RM, developed by ANSSI. Beyond voluntary standards, European colocation operators must comply with regulatory requirements including the NIS 2 Directive, GDPR, and, for financial-sector services, DORA.

National regulations may also apply. Examples include HDS certification in France for health data hosting, LOPDGDD and cybersecurity legislation in Spain, and cybersecurity requirements overseen by ACN in Italy.

Together, these obligations can be grouped into three pillars: (i) security management standards (e.g., ISO/IEC 27001), (ii) assurance frameworks (e.g., PCI DSS and SOC 2), and (iii) regulatory requirements (e.g., NIS 2, GDPR, and DORA). To support the remainder of this paper, we focus on ISO/IEC 27001, NIST CSF 2.0, and NIS 2 as representative governance, control, and regulatory frameworks.

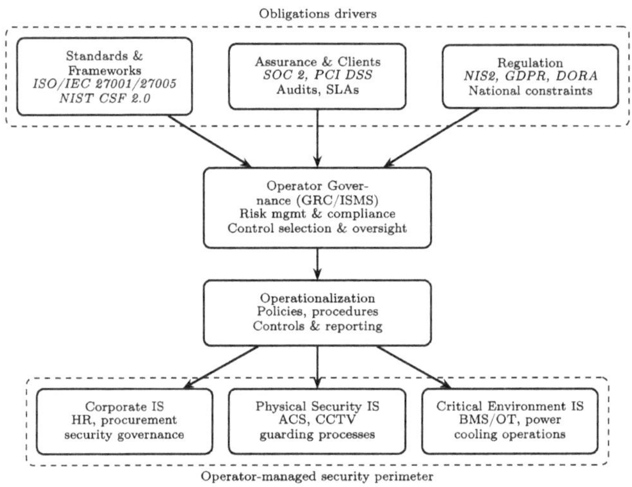

Fig. 2. Governance drivers shaping colocation operator security: standards, assurance demands, and regulations converge into GRC/ISMS and are operationalized across operator-managed domains.

4 Analytical Framework

4.1 Security Threats and Objectives

To ground the model in realistic operational conditions, we synthesize representative risk scenarios observed in European colocation environments and structure them using a scenario-based risk analysis approach. The feared events were derived from the operator-managed perimeter defined in Sect. 3.1, covering corporate information systems, physical security systems, and critical environment systems such as BMS, power, and cooling infrastructures. Following ISO/IEC 27005 and EBIOS RM principles, the analysis starts from adverse consequences affecting the operator's missions, business continuity, contractual obligations, regulatory posture, and customer trust. The analysis was applied to four colocation campuses located in Eastern (E), Southern (S), North-Western (NW), and South-Western (SW) Europe. These sites were selected because they share comparable technical architectures and operator governance structures, while being subject to different local regulatory, customer, and geopolitical conditions.

From the operator's perspective, adverse events may affect business continuity, contractual obligations, and customer trust. Four primary feared events were retained:

- **Interruption of service,** including outages affecting tenant availability due to failures or compromise of power, cooling, connectivity, or management systems;
- **Leak of information,** including disclosure of sensitive operational, customer, or security data;
- **Loss or corruption of information,** including integrity failures impacting logs, configuration baselines, or operational data required for safe operation;
- **Legal or contractual non-compliance,** including failure to meet regulatory duties or customer assurance commitments.

Based on these feared events and in alignment with the operator's control responsibilities, we define four high-level security objectives that represent the strategic protection goals of a colocation datacenter operator:

1. **Ensure infrastructure availability (Av):** preserve continuous service delivery and resilience of critical facility and IT support systems.
2. **Ensure physical safety and security (Phy):** prevent unauthorized physical access and protect people, buildings, and critical assets.
3. **Ensure traceability and auditability (AM):** maintain accountable access control, monitoring, and logging for both physical and logical actions.
4. **Ensure data confidentiality, integrity, and availability (CIA):** protect sensitive data handled by operator systems and ensure trustworthy operational information.

Together, these objectives cover the large majority of operator-managed cybersecurity concerns in leased colocation datacenters and provide the governance layer for the remainder of the framework: the formal mapping identifies which standardized cybersecurity topics contribute to each objective, and the prioritization model ranks these topics based on contextual risk drivers and vulnerability pressure.

4.2 Mathematical Set-Theoretic Model for Topic Extraction

The research follows a two-layered methodological framework combining a **formal mapping model** with a **weighted prioritization model**. The formal model establishes a logical structure linking the NIST CSF 2.0 subcategories with colocation datacenter security objectives and derives, in a systematic manner, the set of relevant cybersecurity topics.

CSF Structure. Let $\mathcal{F}$ denote the set of NIST CSF Functions:

$$\mathcal{F} = \{\text{Govern}, \text{Identify}, \text{Protect}, \text{Detect}, \text{Respond}, \text{Recover}\}$$

For each function $f \in \mathcal{F}$, let $\mathcal{C}_f$ be the set of categories belonging to that function:

$$\forall f \in \mathcal{F} : \mathcal{C}_f = \{c_{f,1}, c_{f,2}, \ldots\}$$

For each category c, let $\mathcal{S}_c$ denote its set of subcategories:

$$\forall c \in \bigcup_{f \in \mathcal{F}} \mathcal{C}_f : \mathcal{S}_c = \{s_{c,1}, s_{c,2}, \ldots\}$$

The universe of all CSF subcategories is:

$$\mathcal{S} = \bigcup_c \mathcal{S}_c$$

Thus, the hierarchical structure is:

$$\mathcal{F} \to \mathcal{C}_f \to \mathcal{S}_c$$

Security Objectives. Let $\mathcal{O}$ be the set of predefined security objectives for a colocation datacenter:

$$\mathcal{O} = \{\text{Av}, \text{Phy}, \text{AM}, \text{CIA}\}$$

Subcategory-to-Objective Mapping. Define a binary relevance relation:

$$\mathcal{R} \subseteq \mathcal{S} \times \mathcal{O}$$

where $(s, o) \in \mathcal{R}$ indicates that subcategory s contributes to objective o.

The set of subcategories relevant to at least one objective is:

$$\mathcal{S}_{rel} = \{s \in \mathcal{S} \mid \exists o \in \mathcal{O} : (s, o) \in \mathcal{R}\}$$

Topic Extraction. Topics are not predefined. Instead, they are derived from the principal subject of each relevant subcategory. In practice, the subject-extraction function ϕ was implemented as a manual, rule-guided expert mapping rather than as an automated natural language processing procedure. Each relevant NIST CSF 2.0 subcategory was assigned to the cybersecurity topic corresponding to its dominant operational subject, using the subcategory wording, its parent CSF category and function, and the operator-managed perimeter defined in Sect. 3.2.

Let

$$\phi : \mathcal{S} \to \mathcal{U}$$

be a subject-extraction function that assigns to each subcategory its principal cybersecurity subject, where $\mathcal{U}$ denotes the universe of possible subjects.

The final set of relevant cybersecurity topics is then defined as:

$$\mathcal{T} = \{\phi(s) \mid s \in \mathcal{S}_{rel}\}$$

Hence, $\mathcal{T}$ represents the set of cybersecurity topics derived exclusively from CSF subcategories that intersect with the datacenter security objectives.

4.3 Risk Index and Objective Weights

Prioritization begins by quantifying the "Objective Risk Index" (ORI) associated with each high level objective of an organization. Risk Index aggregates distinct dimensions of risk into a single scalar. After computing these absolute masses we normalize them to form a probability distribution capturing the relative strategic importance of each objective at a particular site.

Let σ denote a site (campus). For objective o at site σ the Risk Index is defined as

$$R_o^{(\sigma)} = \lambda_o \cdot \iota_o \cdot \epsilon_o \cdot \ell_o^{(\sigma)}, \tag{1}$$

where each symbol stands for:

- **Likelihood ($\lambda_o \in [0, 1]$):** Probability that an adverse event affecting objective o occurs within a reference period. It is estimated from available historical incident information, operational observations, and structured expert assessment when empirical datasets are incomplete or unavailable.
- **Impact ($\iota_o \in [0, 1]$):** The impact parameter represents the normalized severity of adverse consequences to the colocation datacenter operator as a business entity if objective o is compromised. Impact values are estimated using structured business consequence analysis, consistent with enterprise risk management practices such as ISO/IEC 27005 guidelines.
- **Exposure ($\epsilon_o \in [0, 1]$):** The exposure parameter quantifies the degree to which assets supporting objective o are accessible or reachable by potential threat actors. It captures the relative attack surface associated with the objective and is estimated using structural exposure indicators the exposure level of the asset (e.g. external network reachability, degree of remote or privilege access) and the asset criticality and connectivity.
- **Site localization factor ($\ell_o^{(\sigma)} \in \mathbb{R}^+$):** It is a scaling coefficient that adjusts the Risk Index of objective o_i to account to regulatory strictness (e.g., applicability of NIS2, DORA, GDPR, or sector-specific requirements), geographic and environmental constraints (e.g., seismic activity, flood zones, or climate stress), client concentration or critical customer profiles, and the geopolitical context of the host country. Geopolitical factors capture country-level stability, exposure to international sanctions, proximity to armed conflict, state-sponsored cyber activity, sovereignty requirements, and dependencies on foreign supply chains or energy sources at site σ. This localization term is a key differentiator from standard single-site risk scoring approaches: it explicitly models how exogenous regional conditions can shift the strategic importance of objectives even when internal architecture and controls remain comparable. The parameter is defined relative to a reference site σ_0 such that $\ell_o^{(\sigma_0)} = 1$.

Absolute Risk Indexes are calibrated into relative importance via

$$w_o^{(\sigma)} = \frac{R_o^{(\sigma)}}{\sum_{k=1}^{p} R_k^{(\sigma)}} \tag{2}$$

4.4 Area Effectiveness: Blending Relevance and Vulnerability Pressure

Beyond objectives we have the set of topics t as

$$t \in \mathcal{T}$$

defined in Sect. 4.2. Their effectiveness relative to an objective depends both on how relevant the area is semantically and structurally, and on the current vulnerability situation.

We define the per-objective effectiveness of topic t on objective o by

$$\eta_{ot} = \beta\, r_{ot} + (1-\beta)\, v_t\, u_{ot} \tag{3}$$

The parameters are:

- **Base relevance ($r_{ot} \in [0,1]$):** Structural and semantic alignment of topic t with objective o derived from the control-framework mapping and expert consensus. It answers: *'Is this topic fundamentally within the scope of the objective?"*
- **Vulnerability pressure ($v_t \in [0,1]$):** Vulnerability pressure captures the external and systemic threat intensity acting on each security topic. It is defined as a normalized aggregation of vulnerability prevalence, exploitability, and environmental exposure indicators. Estimation is grounded in empirical cybersecurity datasets and threat intelligence sources. The prevalence of vulnerabilities is derived from the relative frequency of publicly disclosed vulnerabilities and incidents assigned to each topic using large-scale repositories such as the NIST National Vulnerability Database (NVD). Exploitability is assessed using observed exploitation likelihood indicators, such as CVSS v3.x exploitability metrics.
- **Objective utility ($u_{ot} \in [0,1]$):** Expected marginal contribution of improving topic t to reducing the risk associated with objective o, derived from scenario reasoning. It answers: *'If we invest in this topic, how much would it reduce objective-level risk in realistic scenarios?"*
- **Blend factor ($\beta \in [0,1]$):** The blend factor $\beta \in [0,1]$ governs the trade-off between framework-driven relevance and vulnerability-driven prioritization. Given the strategic and theoretical scope of the framework, higher values of β are recommended to emphasize structural alignment with security objectives over short-term threat fluctuations, ensuring stability and interpretability at the governance level.

The use of a weighted sum to aggregate structural relevance and vulnerability-adjusted utility is justified by multi-criteria decision analysis (MCDA) theory [15], which addresses the combination of heterogeneous yet complementary evaluation criteria. Structural relevance reflects normative alignment with cybersecurity frameworks and strategic objectives, while vulnerability-pressure-adjusted utility captures empirical threat realism and expected risk reduction. The parameter β therefore acts as a policy-level tuning knob, allowing transparent calibration between compliance-driven prioritization and threat-driven prioritization.

4.5 Interdependency Modeling: Synergies and Overlaps

Cybersecurity topics do not operate in isolation: improvements in one domain may amplify or diminish the effectiveness of others through technical, organizational, or procedural dependencies. To capture these interactions without introducing excessive model complexity, a first-order approximation is employed using a dependency matrix. In this formulation, each matrix coefficient represents the marginal influence of one topic on another, assuming linearity around the current operating point.

Let $\boldsymbol{\eta}_o = [\eta_{o1}, \ldots, \eta_{im}]^\top$ be the vector of effectiveness for all m topics in the objective o. Then

$$\boldsymbol{\eta}_o' = (I + \alpha D)\,\boldsymbol{\eta}_o, \qquad \alpha \in [0,1], \tag{4}$$

where D is an $m \times m$ matrix whose entry $D_{tk} \in [-1,1]$ measures how improving topic k marginally affects topic t. Componentwise,

$$\eta_{ot}' = \sum_{k=1}^{m} (\delta_{tk} + \alpha D_{tk})\,\eta_{ok},$$

where δ_{tk} enotes the Kronecker delta, equal to 1 if t = k and 0 otherwise.

To preserve interpretability of effectiveness as a bounded quantity, we enforce $\eta_{ij}' \in [0,1]$ after applying interdependencies by clipping:

$$\eta_{ot}' \leftarrow \min\{1, \max\{0, \eta_{ot}'\}\}.$$

- **Dependency matrix ($D_{tk} \in [-1,1]$):** Quantifies the marginal effect of improving topic k on the effectiveness of topic t. Positive values represent synergy, negative values represent overlap or diminishing returns. For example, if two topics both fund partially redundant monitoring capabilities (e.g., overlapping logging pipelines implemented under *Security Operations* and *Network Security*), additional investment in one may yield diminishing marginal gains in the other, which can be represented by a negative cross-effect.
- **Interaction strength ($\alpha \in [0,1]$):** The interaction strength $\alpha \in [0,1]$ controls the influence of interdependencies between topics. It is calibrated via sensitivity analysis by progressively increasing α and observing the stability of topic rankings, selecting a value that captures meaningful synergies without inducing excessive amplification or rank volatility.

Expressing dependencies linearly via matrix multiplication is tractable and interpretable; it captures first-order interactions analogous to terms in a Taylor expansion [14]. The identity matrix preserves original effectiveness. The αD term adds net synergy or overlap. Regularizing with $\alpha \leq 1$ prevents runaway effects (Fig. 3).

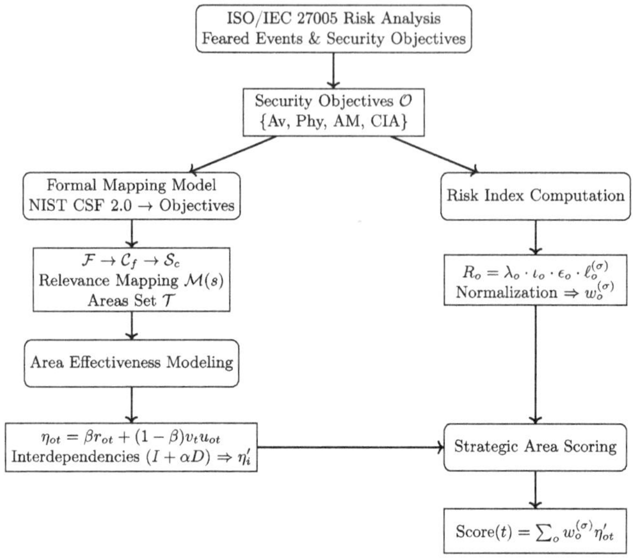

Fig. 3. Logical chart of the proposed cybersecurity prioritization framework

4.6 Scoring and Selection

With normalized objective weights $w_o^{(\sigma)}$ and adjusted effectiveness η'_{ot} we aggregate into a scalar score per topic:

$$\text{Score}(t) = \sum_{o=1}^{p} w_o^{(\sigma)} \, \eta'_{ot}. \tag{5}$$

It sums over objectives the product of how important an objective is ($w_o^{(\sigma)}$) and how effective the topic is for that objective (η'_{ot}).

5 Application and Results

The proposed framework was applied to the four European colocation datacenter campuses mentioned in Sect. 4.1. This directly operationalizes the governance landscape introduced in Sect. 3.2: all campuses fall under common EU-level obligations such as GDPR and NIS2, while national or sector-specific requirements.

This section analyzes the results obtained for these campuses, focusing on how regional, regulatory, and geopolitical contexts shape objective weighting and cybersecurity topic prioritization under a common analytical framework.

Due to the page limitations of the workshop format, detailed numerical examples and full campus-level computation tables are not included in this version. Instead, the paper focuses on the formal definition of the framework, the parameterization process, and the main cross-campus prioritization results. An extended version of this work will provide the complete worked example, including the full set of input parameters, dependency matrices, sensitivity analyses, and reproducibility artifacts.

5.1 Topics Mapping

Based on the mathematical framework of Sect. 4.2, CSF 2.0 subcategories are mapped to operator security objectives and then grouped into a compact set of topics for prioritization. The mapping and grouping process results in ten cybersecurity topics, listed in Table 1.

Table 1. Enumerated cybersecurity areas derived from NIST CSF 2.0 formal mapping for colocation datacenters

Area ID	Cybersecurity Area t_j
T_1	Network Security
T_2	Identity and Access Management (IAM)
T_3	Cryptography
T_4	Security Operations
T_5	Security Awareness & Training
T_6	Critical Infrastructure Security
T_7	Cyber Threat Intelligence
T_8	Risk Analysis
T_9	Physical Security
T_{10}	Supply Chain Security

5.2 Parameterization and Data Sources

In this initial application, parameter estimation primarily relied on structured expert judgment, supported by available operational evidence such as incident records, audit artifacts, and infrastructure inventories. While the framework is designed to incorporate empirical telemetry and large-scale vulnerability datasets when available, such data are not always accessible in operational colocation environments due to confidentiality constraints and heterogeneous monitoring practices across sites.

Consequently, the present study should therefore be interpreted primarily as a practical return-of-experience and an exploratory application of the proposed framework within real operational environments. All parameters were evaluated using bounded scoring scales to ensure consistency and comparability across campuses.

Nevertheless, the framework demonstrates how structured governance-oriented prioritization can still be operationalized under realistic industrial constraints.

5.3 Objective Weight Analysis

Table 2 presents normalized objective weights derived from the Objective Risk Index.

Availability emerges as the dominant objective in three of the four campuses, reaching its highest weight in the South-Western campus (0.55379). This reflects strong regulatory and contractual sensitivity to service continuity. In contrast, the Eastern campus exhibits the highest weight for Physical Security (0.41853), indicating elevated contextual physical or geopolitical exposure.

Access & Monitoring (AM) and CIA objectives remain secondary but non-negligible across all sites, with moderate variation reflecting regulatory posture and tenant profiles.

These results confirm that while the objective set remains invariant, relative strategic emphasis shifts meaningfully with localization factors.

5.4 Topic Prioritization Stability

Across all campuses, T_6 (Critical Infrastructure Security) ranks first. This structural dominance indicates that shared power, cooling, and BMS systems represent the most systemic risk amplifiers in colocation environments.

The second tier of topics varies across campuses:

- Security Operations (T_4) ranks highly in Southern and South-Western campuses.
- Identity and Access Management (T_2) ranks second in the North-Western campus.
- Physical Security (T_9) ranks second in the Eastern campus.
- Network Security (T_1) appears consistently in three sites.
- Supply Chain Security (T_{10}) consistently appears within the top four across all sites.

5.5 Cross-Campus Comparative Insights

Two structural patterns emerge:

1. A universal infrastructure-dependence effect, reflected in the consistent top ranking of Critical Infrastructure Security.
2. A contextual modulation effect, where second-tier priorities shift based on regulatory intensity, geopolitical exposure, or tenant criticality.

Table 2. Comparison of objective weights and top-ranked cybersecurity topics across four European colocation datacenter campuses.

Dimension	E	S	NW	SW
Objective weights $w_i^{(\sigma)}$				
Availability (Av)	0.29895	0.41025	0.36363	0.55379
Physical Security (Phy)	0.41853	0.28717	0.25454	0.22151
Access & Monitoring (AM)	0.15695	0.17948	0.22909	0.11075
Data Security Triad (CIA)	0.12556	0.12307	0.15272	0.11392
Top-ranked cybersecurity topics				
Rank 1	T_6	T_6	T_6	T_6
Rank 2	T_9	T_4	T_2	T_4
Rank 3	T_{10}	T_2	T_4	T_{10}
Rank 4	T_2	T_{10}	T_{10}	T_1
Rank 5	T_4	T_1	T_1	T_2

6 Discussion

The prioritization outcomes reveal both structural invariants and contextual variability within colocation cybersecurity governance.

The dominance of Critical Infrastructure Security across all campuses confirms that shared environmental systems constitute the primary systemic risk vector in multi-tenant datacenters. Power distribution, cooling systems, and building management platforms represent high-impact failure domains capable of cascading across tenants.

Availability-driven weighting reflects contractual and regulatory continuity requirements, while the increased Physical Security emphasis in the Eastern campus illustrates the impact of geopolitical and environmental context on cybersecurity prioritization.

The recurrent importance of Supply Chain Security reflects growing regulatory and operational exposure to third-party dependencies in colocation environments consistent with NIS2, which reinforces obligations related to supply chain risk management, supplier due diligence, and continuous monitoring. Importantly, the framework transforms cybersecurity prioritization from checklist-based compliance toward quantitatively interpretable governance. It allows:

- Cross-campus benchmarking,
- Risk-informed budget allocation,
- Targeted incident simulation planning,
- Transparent tenant-provider risk dialogue.

The observed ranking stability suggests that operator-managed perimeters exhibit intrinsic structural risk hierarchies independent of transient threat fluctuations.

An important insight emerging from the analysis is that the prioritization results diverge from common perceptions within many datacenter security teams. In practice, security investments are often distributed across a wide range of domains without a clear understanding of their relative strategic importance or systemic impact. However, the results of the proposed framework consistently highlights a structural asymmetry in colocation environments: the most consequential failure modes often originate from shared infrastructure technologies such as power distribution, cooling, and building management systems, whose compromise may cascade across multiple tenants.

7 Conclusion

This paper introduced a quantitative, operator-centric framework for cybersecurity prioritization in leased colocation datacenters. By combining formal control–objective mapping, contextualized risk indexing, vulnerability-adjusted effectiveness modeling, and interdependency analysis, the proposed approach provides a structured and reproducible method to support governance-level cybersecurity decision making.

The application of the framework to four European campuses highlights both structural stability and contextual variability in cybersecurity priorities. In particular, Critical Infrastructure Security consistently emerges as the dominant domain across all sites, while objective weighting varies according to regional and operational conditions.

More broadly, the framework contributes to bridging the gap between compliance-driven security standards and risk-informed prioritization practices. By integrating established security frameworks into a quantitative decision model, it offers a systematic approach for interpreting and operationalizing cybersecurity governance in operator-managed datacenter environments. Overall, the proposed methodology provides a foundation for more systematic and context-aware cybersecurity governance in multi-tenant infrastructure environments.

Future work will focus on strengthening the robustness and empirical validation of the proposed framework through sensitivity analysis, Monte Carlo-based uncertainty propagation, and stability assessment of prioritization rankings under parameter variation. Additional research directions include empirical calibration using operational telemetry and incident datasets, benchmarking against alternative multi-criteria decision methodologies such as AHP and TOPSIS, and exploring AI-assisted parameter estimation techniques for large-scale colocation environments.

Disclosure of Interests. The authors have no competing interests to declare that are relevant to the content of this article.

References

1. Çelikbilek, Y., Tüysüz, F.: An in-depth review of theory of the TOPSIS method: an experimental analysis. J. Manage. Anal. **7**(2), 281–300 (2020)
2. CENELEC: EN 50600-1: Information technology – Data centre facilities and infrastructures – Part 1: General concepts. Technical report, European Committee for Electrotechnical Standardization (2018). https://standards.cencenelec.eu
3. Cloud Security Alliance: Security guidance for critical areas of focus in cloud computing v4.0 (2020). https://cloudsecurityalliance.org
4. Gordon, L.A., Loeb, M.P.: The economics of information security investment. ACM Trans. Inf. Syst. Secur. **5**(4), 438–457 (2002). https://doi.org/10.1145/581271.581274
5. Hong, C.H., Spence, I., Nikolopoulos, D.S.: GPU virtualization and scheduling methods: a comprehensive survey. ACM Comput. Surv. **50**(3), 33:1–33:37 (2017). https://doi.org/10.1145/3076251
6. Hubbard, D.W., Seiersen, R.: How to Measure Anything in Cybersecurity Risk. Wiley (2016). https://doi.org/10.1002/9781119085298
7. Humayed, A., Lin, J., Li, F., Luo, B.: Cyber-physical systems security: a survey. IEEE Internet Things J. **4**(6), 1802–1831 (2017). https://doi.org/10.1109/JIOT.2017.2668541
8. International Organization for Standardization, International Electrotechnical Commission: ISO/IEC 22237-1:2021 – Information technology – Data centre facilities and infrastructures – Part 1: General concepts. Technical report, International Organization for Standardization and International Electrotechnical Commission (2021). https://www.iso.org/standard/78550.html
9. Jones, J.A.: An introduction to factor analysis of information risk (FAIR). Technical report, Risk Management Insight LLC (2006). https://www.riskinsight-wavestone.com
10. Joseph, J.: Facility design and process utilities. In: Biopharmaceutical Processing: Development, Design, and Implementation of Manufacturing Processes, pp. 933–986. Elsevier (2018)
11. National Institute of Standards and Technology: Cybersecurity framework (CSF) 2.0. NIST (2024). https://www.nist.gov/cyberframework
12. Ometov, A., Molua, O.L., Komarov, M., Nurmi, J.: A survey of security in cloud, edge, and fog computing. Sensors **22**(3), 927 (2022). https://doi.org/10.3390/s22030927
13. Saaty, T.L.: The Analytic Hierarchy Process. McGraw-Hill, New York (1980)
14. Saltelli, A., et al.: Global Sensitivity Analysis: The Primer. Wiley (2008). https://doi.org/10.1002/97804707252
15. Triantaphyllou, E., Shu, B., Sanchez, S.N., Ray, T.: Multi-criteria decision making: an operations research approach. Encycl. Electr. Electron. Eng. **15**(1998), 175–186 (1998)
16. Weinschenk, R.: Cybersecurity incidents grow costlier amid persistent complexity. Technical report, UII Data Report 185, Uptime Institute Intelligence (2025). https://uptimeinstitute.com, uptime Institute Intelligence Report
17. Zadeh, L.A.: Fuzzy logic. Computer **21**(4), 83–93 (1988). https://doi.org/10.1109/2.53

Proceedings of the First International Workshop on Applied Trust and Cyber Resilience (CyResTrust 2026)

CyResTrust 2026 Preface

The 1st International Workshop on Applied Trust and Cyber Resilience (CyResTrust 2026) was held in conjunction with the 21st International Conference on Availability, Reliability and Security (ARES 2026), August 24–27, 2026, in Linköping, Sweden. CyResTrust focused on practical, deployable, and measurable trust as an enabler of cyber resilience across digital, embedded, and cyber-physical systems. The workshop addressed the growing need to bridge hardware-anchored trust and operational resilience in modern infrastructures. Its scope included Trusted Computing technologies such as Trusted Platform Modules (TPMs), the Device Identifier Composition Engine (DICE), Trusted Execution Environments (TEEs), Confidential Computing, Confidential Containers (CoCo), confidential AI, post-quantum cryptography (PQC), crypto-agility, physically unclonable functions (PUFs), secure and attested update mechanisms, and measurable trust and resilience metrics. The workshop further covered applications in IoT, OT, cloud, HPC, mobility, healthcare, supply chains, safety-critical systems, and critical infrastructures.

CyResTrust 2026 aimed to provide a forum for researchers and practitioners from academia and industry to discuss how computational trust can be established, maintained, measured, and used as an operational foundation for resilient and dependable computing systems. The workshop welcomed original research, applied case studies, and proof-of-concept implementations addressing the interplay between trust, confidentiality, and resilience.

The call for papers attracted 15 submissions. After an initial desk-check phase, 2 submissions were desk-rejected and 13 submissions entered the peer-review process. Each reviewed paper received at least three independent double-blind reviews by members of the Program Committee. Based on the reviews and subsequent discussions among the workshop chairs, 6 papers were accepted for presentation and inclusion in the proceedings. This corresponds to an overall acceptance rate of 40% and an acceptance rate of 46.2% among the reviewed submissions. Conflicts of interest, if any, were handled by excluding conflicted chairs or committee members from the review discussion and decision process.

The accepted papers reflected the breadth of the workshop scope, covering hardware security-based trust anchors for vehicle access control, hierarchical attestation for dynamic workloads, post-quantum privacy-preserving swarm attestation, zero-trust attestation for confidential virtual machines, distributed signature activation for resilient key management, and TEE-based firmware resilience.

The workshop program consisted of an invited keynote presentation, two 90-minute sessions, and a best paper award ceremony. We hope that the CyResTrust 2026 program stimulated fruitful discussions and provided participants with an opportunity to exchange ideas on deployable trust mechanisms, confidential computing, attestation, and cyber resilience across institutions and domains.

We would like to thank all authors for submitting their work to CyResTrust 2026, the members of the Program Committee for their valuable reviews, and the ARES 2026 organizers for their support in hosting the workshop.

August 2026

Michael Eckel
Anirban Basu
Georgios Gkoktsis

CyResTrust 2026 Organization

Workshop Chairs

Michael Eckel Fraunhofer SIT|ATHENE, Germany
Anirban Basu University of Sussex, UK
Georgios Gkoktsis Fraunhofer SIT|ATHENE, Germany

Program Committee

Jean-Michel Cioranesco NXP Semiconductors, Germany
Felix Dörre Karlsruhe Institute of Technology, Germany
Patricia Ehrenreich Fraunhofer SIT|ATHENE, Germany
Florian Fenzl Fraunhofer SIT|ATHENE, Germany
Dominik Roy George KU Leuven, Belgium
Thanassis Giannetsos Technical University of Denmark, Denmark
Janik Gorbracht Fraunhofer SIT|ATHENE, Germany
Björn Grohmann Berlin School of Economics and Law, Germany
Jens Hagemeyer University of Bielefeld, Germany
Konrad-Felix Krentz Fraunhofer SIT|ATHENE, Germany
Torsten Labs Siemens AG, Germany
Cristoffer Leite Eindhoven University of Technology|Jheronimus Academy of Data Science, Netherlands
Ronald Marx Getronics Germany GmbH, Germany
Ludger Peters Fraunhofer SIT|ATHENE, Germany
Andreas Schaad University of Applied Sciences Offenburg, Germany
Savio Sciancalepore Eindhoven University of Technology, Netherlands
Christian Spinnler Friedrich-Alexander University of Erlangen-Nuremberg, Germany

Bootstrapping Secure Next-Generation Vehicle Access Control from a Centralized Hardware Security-Based Trust Anchor

Marco Leeske(✉), Dirk Scheuermann, Ludger Peters, and Christian Plappert

Fraunhofer SIT | Athene, Darmstadt, Germany
{Marco.Leeske,dirk.scheuermann,ludger.peters,
christian.plappert}@sit.fraunhofer.de

Abstract. Access control in vehicles is a critical component of modern automotive security, particularly as vehicles become increasingly connected. Recent cyberattacks have demonstrated that vehicles are vulnerable to cyberattacks, which not only have financial implications but, with the increase in automated driving functions, also pose safety risks for all road users. The Service-Oriented Vehicle Diagnostics (SOVD) standard addresses these issues for next-generation vehicle architectures. However, the standard does not specify how to secure the corresponding security-sensitive credentials. In this work, we propose an enhancement to the SOVD standard, which secures the credentials within a Hardware Security-based Trust Anchor (HTA) concept.

Keywords: Automotive Security · Vehicle Diagnostics · Access Control · Hardware Security · TPM · SOVD

1 Introduction

A secure access management system is essential for connected vehicles due to the increasing interconnectivity within the vehicle and among vehicles, infrastructure, and users. As vehicles become more integrated with advanced technologies, they rely heavily on data exchange for functionalities such as navigation, safety features, and infotainment systems. This interconnectivity exposes vehicles to various cyberthreats, including unauthorized access, data breaches, and potential manipulation of critical systems [5,6,23,27,29,30,37,41,43,44].

Implementing a robust access control management system ensures that only authorized users and devices can access and interact with vehicle systems. It protects sensitive personal information and vehicle data, thereby enhancing user privacy and trust. Furthermore, a secure access control management framework is vital for maintaining the integrity of vehicle-to-vehicle (V2V) and vehicle-to-infrastructure (V2I) communications, which are crucial for safe and efficient transportation.

Z. Afzal et al. (Eds.): ARES 2026 Workshops, LNCS 16900, pp. 217–234, 2027.
https://doi.org/10.1007/978-3-032-35576-8_12

Overall, a secure access control management system is a foundational component in safeguarding the future of connected vehicles, contributing to safer roads and a more secure automotive ecosystem.

Meanwhile, a lot of appropriate security technologies and corresponding technical standards exist to provide more security as well as safety for modern connected vehicles. On the one hand, different sorts of Hardware Security Modules (HSMs), Hardware Security-based Trust Anchors (HTAs) respectively, are available, and solutions have been developed to integrate them into modern vehicles. This also includes first deployment of Trusted Platform Modules (TPMs) [42]. On the other hand, the Service Oriented Vehicle Diagnostics (SOVD) standard [19] provides an efficient solution for standardized diagnostic and communication protocols to handle diagnostic services for interconnected vehicles. However, this standard concentrates on the communication, without taking care for the protection of credentials. Other research activities on this field show open challenges still existing with SOVD, in particular the risks resulting from abuse of diagnostic services [28].

Our main contributions are the followings:

- We develop a security concept for diagnostic services which is based on a combination of SOVD with the usage of HTAs. This also comprises protection mechanisms for the credentials (PIN, password or other access data) needed for accessing the SOVD services.
- We deploy a Trusted Platform Module (TPM) with two core functionalities: It works as Policy Decision Point (PDP) for managing the specified security policies for connecting authorized clients as well as a PEP for token generation and establishing legacy channels.
- Precise security policies for authorization, key distribution and key usage are defined to fulfill specified security requirements.
- We develop an architecture that is vendor-independent and open for integration of many standard protocols.
- Our system is designed in a way to allow a secure and efficient integration of legacy (ECUs) not supporting SOVD.
- We finally evaluate our specified system with a Proof-of-Concept (POC) implementation with selected hardware products already proven for corresponding automotive applications.

The rest of the paper is structured in the following way: In Sect. 2, we illustrate some general background with standards and technologies to be used. Section 3 provides the general design of our solution. A more precise specification of the intended solution is provided in Sect. 4. Section 5 then describes an evaluation of our solution by a realization on selected hardware products. Section 6 provides a comparison with other solutions to realize diagnostic services to highlight the novelties of our solution. The final results are summarized in Sect. 7.

2 Background

This chapter details relevant background information necessary for our work.

2.1 Automotive Domain

Recent advancements aimed at enhancing connectivity and performance, largely driven by the push for automated driving features, have led to a significant increase in the complexity of forthcoming Electrical/Electronic (E/E) architectures. While architectures tend to become more centralized and consolidate more and more former ECU functionality on a few High-Performance Computers (HPCs), the HPCs itself become more complex. Besides the HPCs, the modern centralized automotive architectures also contain Zonal Control Units (ZCUs) to consolidate ECU functionalities with lower power needs and to interact with the HPCs to share the work. An important criterion for HPCs is the operability over Automotive Open System Architecture (AUTOSAR), in particular the Adaptive Platform [3].

2.2 SOVD

The SOVD ISO standard [19–21] is based on an initiative by ASAM and aims to standardize diagnostics and communication protocols within the automotive industry [2].

Its primary purpose is to provide a consistent and interoperable framework for vehicle diagnostics, which is essential for ensuring that different manufacturers and diagnostic tools can effectively communicate and function together. The standard outlines how diagnostic data should be exchanged between vehicles and diagnostic tools, specifying the necessary communication protocols and interfaces. This ensures that various diagnostic protocols, such as On Board Diagnostics (OBD) and Unified Diagnostic Service (UDS) [18], can be integrated and adapted to different vehicle architectures. SOVD is also compatible with AUTOSAR by explicitly foreseeing the usage of the logging format AUTOSAR Diagnostic Log and Trace (DLT). The standard provides guidelines for compliance and testing procedures, ensuring that diagnostic tools meet the required standards for performance and reliability. From a security perspective, SOVD proposes a token-based authentication mechanism for the SOVD clients. The implementation of the tokens is left open, but the standard mentions JSON Webtokens [22] as possible instantiation, which are also used by our implemented SOVD server (see Sect. 5.1).

2.3 TPM 2.0

The TPM library is a cryptographic library openly specified by the Trusted Computing Group (TCG). In its most secure implementation, the TPM library is deployed as discrete hardware chip, the so called Discrete TPM (dTPM), which brings certain additional security features like tamper-protection. In addition, the TPM library can also be deployed as software variant within the host environment, the so-called Firmware TPM (fTPM). To harden fTPMs against cyberattacks, they are typically shielded from the host environment via processor extensions, which create Trusted Execution Environments (TEEs) like TrustZone [35] or Secure Processor [1].

With the new Trusted Platform Module 2.0 (TPM 2.0), specified in 2014 and adopted as an international standard [16], a new family of TPMs is provided with new features and more flexibility. In particular, the new library approach of TPM2 makes the TPM better usable for embedded applications like the automotive domain.

In alignment with TPM2, a new version 2.0 of the TPM Software Stack (TSS) was also specified by the TCG [40].

For accessing a TPM from multiple applications, TCG specified the TPM Access Broker & Ressource Manager (TABRM) [39]. There exists an Open-Source Software (OSS) user land implementation [38] as well as an in-kernel implementation [24]. Additionally, there are some closed-source implementations for proprietary Hypervisor solutions [8,9,36].

3 Design

This chapter presents our system design. Here, we present our asset analysis, system model, and security requirements.

3.1 Notations

This section, as well as the following sections, make use of the following notations. The key pair belonging to an entity X is denoted as X^x and comprises the private (K^X_{Priv}) and public (K^X_{Pub}) key. HK^Xdenotes a handle to X^x (depending on the context K^X_{Priv} or K^X_{Pub}) stored in a secure environment, e.g., Trusted Platform Module (TPM). A cryptographic operation Y using a key K and data Z is denoted as Y(K; Z).

A TPM policy P with 1–N concatenated policy elements E is denoted as $P := E_1[\wedge \cdots \wedge E_N]$. A key K created with a Policy P as authorization value is denoted as K-Template(P). A signed policy with a key K is denoted as P := Auth(K; P).

3.2 Asset Analysis and Threat Model

The basic assets to be considered are the followings: (**1**) User credentials, (**2**) private signature keys and the base derivation key, (**3**) access tokens, (**4**) connected legacy channels, and (**5**) the diagnostic client.

The user credentials are used to authorize different users towards the SOVD server to retrieve their authentication token.

Private signature keys are required for signing token data to generate a valid access token. Furthermore, the Backend uses a private signature key to generate valid client authorization policies. The entities performing the signature process must provide mechanisms for secure storage of these keys and for protection of the keys against unauthorized usage. The base derivation key provides a further asset to be protected in case of using legacy channels.

The access tokens are needed to finally control the access to services, i.e., their misuse or manipulation may disturb the proper usage of diagnosis services. They must be securely transferred to the client, and the client must send them back to the High-Performance Computer (HPC) for activating the access.

Connected legacy channels provide further assets to be protected. They are needed for secure connections to Electronic Control Units (ECUs) that do not support the Service Oriented Vehicle Diagnostics (SOVD) functionalities.

The diagnostic client needs to be considered as an asset to be protected as well, since it may be the victim of an impersonation attack. An unauthorized entity may take the role of the client to get access to the diagnostic service, and it may defraud the Backend.

In this use case, we consider Backend $\mathcal{B}$ and TPM as trustworthy, i.e., the protection of the assets identified above may be based on the proper functionalities of these entities. Therefore entities like $\mathcal{B}$ and TPM as well as the Key Store are trusted in our cyberthreat model and cannot be compromised by remote cyber-attacks. Additionally, TPM is particularly resistant to side-channel attacks and thus provides protection against physical attackers.

However, $\mathcal{H}$ and $\mathcal{E}$ remain vulnerable offline attempts to read cryptographic keys from memory. Due to the remote connection to Backend $\mathcal{B}$, $\mathcal{H}$ is directly exposed to the Internet and therefore vulnerable to remote attacks. Furthermore the $\mathcal{H}$ serves as the central connectivity unit and features a full-fledged, complex POSIX-based operating system. The $\mathcal{H}$ stores and utilizes all vehicle identity keys that are used for authenticating against the backend. Accordingly this target promises the highest revenue for cyberattackers. Since $\mathcal{H}$ comprises a combination of remote connectivity, high attacker incentives, and complex software, it presents the greatest cyberattack surface in our system for both remote and even physical cyberattacks.

$\mathcal{E}$ has a less complex and thus potentially less vulnerable firmware. In addition, $\mathcal{E}$ is not directly connected to the Internet and the Backend $\mathcal{B}$, so only more complex cyberattack chains could target its firmware. $\mathcal{E}$ is not particular hardened against cyberattacks by design, e.g., attacks against sensitive data in flash memory.

3.3 System Model and General Procedure

Our system model is depicted in Fig. 1 and is aligned with the offline authentication and authorization variant described in the SOVD standard. It comprises three basic components, namely (**1**) the vehicle $\mathcal{V}$, (**2**) the backend $\mathcal{B}$, and (**3**) the diagnostic client $\mathcal{C}$. $\mathcal{V}$ provides the major component and is further divided into (**1.1**) the SOVD-enabled HPC $\mathcal{H}$, and (**1.2**) the legacy controller without SOVD-API (e.g., ECU $\mathcal{E}$). The last mentioned ECU may have different configurations, e.g. a modern Zonal Control Unit (ZCU), or even another HPC just not supporting the SOVD-API. $\mathcal{H}$ hosts various apps on top of an isolation layer, e.g., based on hypervisor or OS-level virtualization technology. This includes (**1.1.1**) the vehicle authorization server, (**1.1.2**) an example app, (**1.1.3**) the TPM Access Broker & Ressource Manager (TABRM), and (**1.1.4**) the adapter. All apps on

$\mathcal{H}$ except for TABRM are utilizing the SOVD Application Programming Interface (API) for communication with $\mathcal{B}$ and $\mathcal{C}$. The example app represents an SOVD entity of the type App according to the standard ([2], Sect. 4.2). In addition, Adapter provides a legacy interface to the non-SOVD enabled ECU $\mathcal{E}$. The configuration of Adapter depends on the type of legacy controller and the protocol used. For the case of UDS, a classic diagnostic adapter is specified by the SOVD standard ([2], Sect. 7). $\mathcal{H}$ is additionally equipped with a vehicle TPM as Hardware Security-based Trust Anchor (HTA) of the vehicle.

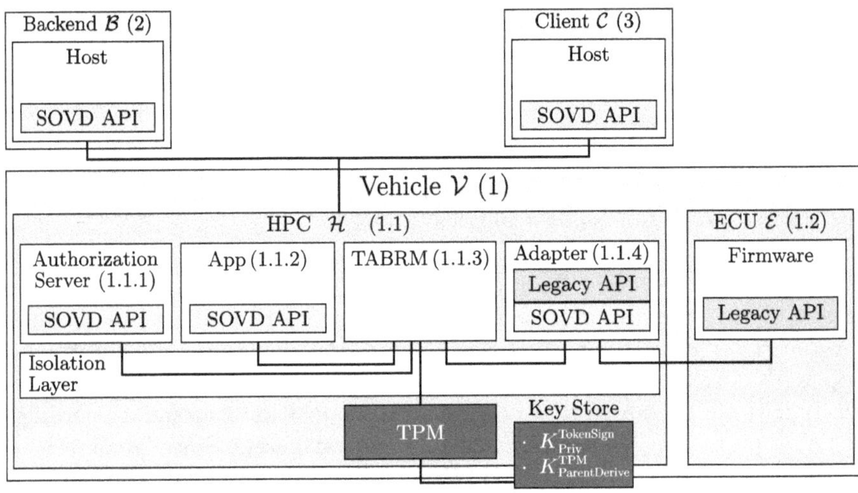

Fig. 1. System Model of TPM-enhanced SOVD

For the general procedure, SOVD is based on a token-based authentication mechanism as described in Sect. 2. A client $\mathcal{C}$ needs to authenticate towards an authorization server, which will then issue a (restricted) authorization token depending on the individual access permissions of the client. Restrictions, or so-called scopes, are encoded into the token and may comprise time or usage limitations for various functions of various vehicle components. The authenticity of the token is ensured by a digital signature created by the authorization server. $\mathcal{C}$ presents the issued tokens to different components in the vehicle to trigger certain functionality. The respective component verifies the signature of the token. Depending on the scope, the component then activates certain functionality.

A special feature of SOVD is the backwards compatibility. With the help of a so-called adapter, SOVD allows accessing features of "legacy" ECUs, which do not implement the SOVD Application Programming Interface (API).

The security of the procedure strongly relies on the secure storage and usage of the token signature key $K_{\text{Priv}}^{\text{TokenSign}}$. With our design, we exclusively store and use it within the TPM. In addition, we bind usage of $K_{\text{Priv}}^{\text{TokenSign}}$ to a strong access control feature using the TPM enhanced authorization mechanism.

Within the TPM, we also store a base derivation key $K^{\text{TPM}}_{\text{ParentDerive}}$ to be used for secure communication with a legacy ECUs. This key is used for derivation of a session key $K^{\text{Access}}_{\text{Shared}}$.

We detail these mechanisms in the next section.

3.4 Security Policy Design

In our system, the usage of the token signing key $K^{\text{TokenSign}}_{\text{Priv}}$ is only unlocked based on certain constraints. Our defined security policy requirements (SPR) are

(SPR1) only an authorized backend is allowed to define our constraints
(SPR2) only an authorized client may authorize unlocking $K^{\text{TokenSign}}_{\text{Priv}}$
(SPR3) access to $K^{\text{TokenSign}}_{\text{Priv}}$ must be actively and passively revocable
(SPR4) access to SOVD service is only granted with a valid token signed with $K^{\text{TokenSign}}_{\text{Priv}}$

In our system, the TPM acts as PDP which only unlocks the necessary token signing key based on our defined constraints. The constraints are modeled by a combination of certain TPM policy commands. The benefit is that the policy decision can now be done completely within the secure environment of the TPM.

Our designed policies are depicted in Eq. 1 with the corresponding notation described in Sect. 3.1. In the following, we detail their functionality.

Regarding SPR1, we build our policies with the basic constraint that all policies are only valid if they are signed by the backend $\mathcal{B}$ with its corresponding backend key $\text{K}^{\text{Backend}}_{\text{Priv}}$. This is enforced by creating all keys in the system with an initial TPM2_PolicyAuthorize policy, which is bound to $\text{K}^{\text{Backend}}_{\text{Pub}}$.

Addressing SPR2, we bind the key unlock to an interactive proof-of-possession of an authentication key $K^{\text{Client}}_{\text{Priv}}$ of client $\mathcal{C}$. This is done with a TPM2_PolicySigned command which is bound to the corresponding public key $K^{\text{Client}}_{\text{Pub}}$. Regarding SPR3, we create an active and passive revocation mechanism by binding a successful policy verification to the state of an Non-Volatile (NV) index in the TPM. Finally, SPR4 is addressed by a verification of the token's signature by the TPM. For the native SOVD app, the corresponding policy just consists of an existing valid signature produced by $K^{\text{TokenSign}}_{\text{Priv}}$.

a) $K^{\text{TokenSign}}_{\text{Priv}}\text{-Template}\big(\text{TPM2\_PolicyAuthorize}(\text{K}^{\text{Backend}}_{\text{Pub}})\big)$

b) $P^{\text{Client}}_{\text{Auth}} := \text{Auth}\big(\text{K}^{\text{Backend}}_{\text{Priv}};\ \text{TPM2\_PolicySigned}(K^{\text{Client}}_{\text{Pub}}) \wedge \text{TPM2\_PolicyNV}()\ \big)$

c) $P^{\text{ECU}}_{\text{Leg}} := \text{Auth}\big(K^{\text{TokenSign}}_{\text{Priv}};\ \text{TPM2\_PolicyAuthValue}() \wedge$
$\text{TPM2\_PolicyTemplate}(\text{Template}^{\text{Fn}}\ ^{*}) \wedge \text{TPM2\_PolicyNV}()\ \big)$

* $\textit{Template}^{Fn} := \textit{Hash(Function)}$

Equation 1. Designed System Policies: a) Key created with initial authorization policy, b) Client-Authorization-Policy $P^{\text{Client}}_{\text{Auth}}$, c) Legacy-Adapter-Policy $P^{\text{ECU}}_{\text{Leg}}$

To access functions of legacy controllers, which do not provide an SOVD-API, i.e., ECU $\mathcal{E}$, Vehicle Authorization Server (VAS) may issue an additional legacy adapter policy $P^{\text{ECU}}_{\text{Leg}}$. It allows the adapter to access the base derivation key $K^{\text{TPM}}_{\text{ParentDerive}}$ and derive a session key $K^{\text{Access}}_{\text{Shared}}$ from it using the input parameter specified by template $\text{Template}^{\text{Fn}}$. TPM2_PolicyTemplate enforces that key derivation is limited to exactly the input $\text{Template}^{\text{Fn}}$ for base derivation key $K^{\text{TPM}}_{\text{ParentDerive}}$. With this construction, a function- and ECU-specific key is derived controlled by VAS and verifiable by ECU $\mathcal{E}$. This is a typical mechanism used in classic automotive protocols like the authentication service (0×29) by UDS [18] and thus ensures backward compliance for legacy ECUs.

4 Specification

This chapter presents our system specification for system provisioning (Sect. 4.1), client registration & policy download (Sect. 4.2), (offline) authorization (Sect. 4.3) and service requests (Sect. 4.4).

Figure 2 shows the sequence of all steps of all subsequent phases after the system provisioning is completed. Each step is detailed in the following.

4.1 System Provisioning

During system provisioning phase, the vehicle is securely provisioned with all relevant keys by backend $\mathcal{B}$. We use secure remote connections directly into the TPM to securely create the key pair $K^{\text{TokenSign}}$ and the base derivation key $K^{\text{TPM}}_{\text{ParentDerive}}$ as well as the NV index used for revocation of access to $K^{\text{TokenSign}}_{\text{Priv}}$ if its state does not fit (see Sect. 3.4). The keys $K^{\text{TokenSign}}$ and $K^{\text{TPM}}_{\text{ParentDerive}}$ are created with our initial authorization policy depicted in Equation 1. a), which enforces that valid policies are at least signed by $\mathcal{B}$.

4.2 Client Registration and Policy Download

During client registration, a client $\mathcal{C}$ registers with backend $\mathcal{B}$ by providing its public key $K^{\text{Client}}_{\text{Pub}}$ over a secure out-of-band channel and proofs possession of the respective private key $K^{\text{Client}}_{\text{Priv}}$. If $\mathcal{B}$ approves $\mathcal{C}$ as valid client, it continues to issue our Client-Authorization-Policy $P^{\text{Client}}_{\text{Auth}}$, which is then downloaded and stored by $\mathcal{C}$.

4.3 (Offline) Authorization

During offline authorization, a registered client $\mathcal{C}$ gets a valid token to access vehicle functions. For this, $\mathcal{C}$ presents its issued policy $P^{\text{Client}}_{\text{Auth}}$, to the VAS. VAS creates raw token data, based on the access permissions of $\mathcal{C}$. To create a valid token, VAS needs to sign the raw token data with the private key $K^{\text{TokenSign}}_{\text{Priv}}$ of key pair $K^{\text{TokenSign}}$. Thus, VAS issues a signing request with key handle $\text{H}K^{\text{TokenSign}}_{\text{Priv}}$

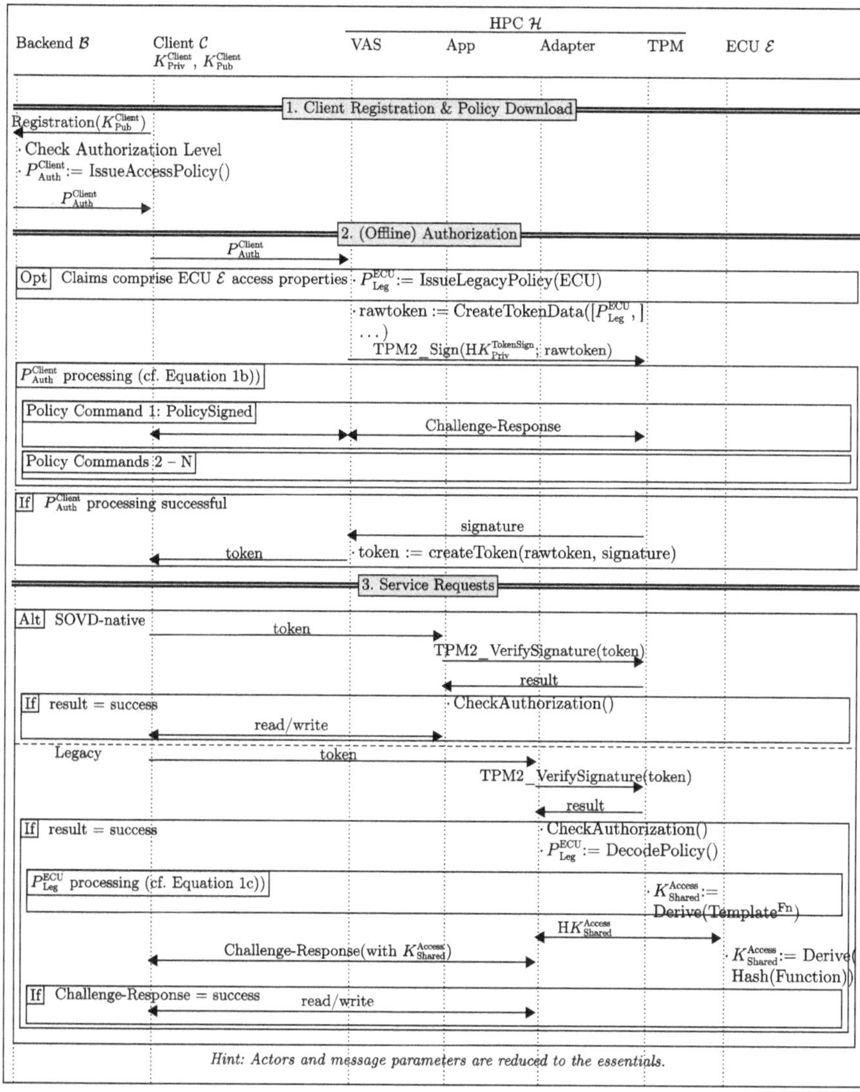

Fig. 2. TPM-Enhanced SOVD concept for SOVD-native and legacy ECUs.

to the TPM via TABRM. Key access of $K^{\text{TokenSign}}_{\text{Priv}}$ is secured by our initial authorization policy. Thus, $\mathcal{C}$ needs to present a valid Client-Authorization-Policy $P^{\text{Client}}_{\text{Auth}}$. The TPM checks all constraints of $P^{\text{Client}}_{\text{Auth}}$, e.g., a valid VAS signature and NV index, and tries to prove possession of the authentication key $K^{\text{Client}}_{\text{Priv}}$ of $\mathcal{C}$ with an interactive challenge-response scheme. If $\mathcal{C}$ can successfully answer the challenge, access to $K^{\text{TokenSign}}_{\text{Priv}}$ is authorized and the token can be signed. The signed token is then returned to $\mathcal{C}$ and can be used to execute service requests.

4.4 Service Requests

The SOVD-native service requests are done according to the standard. The TPM is only used to retrieve public key $K_{\text{Pub}}^{\text{TokenSign}}$ of key pair $K^{\text{TokenSign}}$ to verify the token signature. The SOVD app receives the token from the client and activates the TPM2_VerifySignature command. If the result is ok, the access to the SOVD service is granted.

An exception is the handling of "legacy" controllers, which do not support the SOVD API. They typically support legacy diagnostic protocols, e.g., UDS.

In this case, the adapter takes the task to receive the token and to initiate the signature verification by the TPM. In addition, the legacy-adapter-policy $P_{\text{Leg}}^{\text{ECU}}$ needs to be verified. The great challenge is the need for the $\mathcal{E}$ to verify that $\mathcal{C}$ has access to certain features without an available SOVD API. In the case of UDS, we have several options: The Security Access Service (0×27) may be used with a seed-key handshake that unlocks higher privileges. With the more recent version of the UDS standard, the Authentication Service (0×29) is also available.

5 Evaluation

In this chapter, we evaluate the security and feasibility properties of our solution for the automotive domain based on our POC implementation. It shall be noticed that the chosen hardware products for our practical evaluation only serve for demonstration purpose, whereas the general concept is vendor-independent and not limited to the usage of these products.

5.1 Proof-of-Concept Implementation

For feasibility evaluation of our concept (cf Sect. 5.3), we used a POC implementation, which we describe in the following.

Hardware. For implementation, we used the NXP S32G-VNP-RDB3 [32] as instantiation of the HPC. As DTPM on the HPC, we used the OPTIGA TPM 9672 evaluation board [14].

Software. We implemented our SOVD server in Rust using the Actix-web framework. For communicating with the TPM from both backend and from within the vehicle, we used the Rust wrapper for the TSS 2.0 FAPI [25]. Next to the TPM integration, the SOVD server relies on well-known Rust compilation units (so called crates), e.g., jsonwebtoken, serde, flate2, uuid, simple_encrypt, for cryptographic and serialization tasks. For the FTPM deployment option, we used the reference implementation of the TCG TPM specification [26].

Cryptographic Primitives and Algorithms. For TPM-related operations, we utilize the standard FAPI ECC profile. This results in relying on curve NIST P256-bit curve, ECDSA signing scheme with SHA256. Signing is primarily used for token signing. For encryption, we rely on the symmetric AES-GCM-256 scheme provided by the cryptographic software library of simple_encrypt. The security-sensitive key material is securely sealed by the TPM.

5.2 Security Evaluation

Our major security goal was to enhance the SOVD standard with hardware security, in particular for securing the credentials necessary for accessing the SOVD services. With our concept, the TPM plays a central role to reach this goal.

First of all, it provides a secure storage and usage environment for the signature key to generate and sign the tokens. Hence, a sufficient protection of the important asset $K_{\text{Priv}}^{\text{TokenSign}}$ is provided. Furthermore, the TPM with its security features takes the role of the PEP for token generation and activation of the legacy channel. This takes care for a protection of two further assets, namely the access tokens and the connected legacy channels. The sealing functionalities of the TPM are used to seal the SOVD credential database. This provides a protection of the user credentials as further assets to be considered.

In addition, the TPM works as a PDP to ensure that only authorized clients get access to the diagnostic services. Hence, it also provides a protection of the diagnostic client against impersonation.

With our concept, the general system security is also supported by the Backend as a further important component. By signing the client authorization policies, the Backend prepares the client to be accepted by the PDP. In this way, the protection of the client against impersonation is provided by a cooperation of the Backend and the TPM.

In particular, SPR1 is satisfied by the first step with the client registration: The Backend with a valid key pair $\text{K}^{\text{Backend}}$must become active to enable a successful registration. Next, the Backend and the TPM cooperate to fulfill SPR2. During the registration phase, the Backend checks the authorization of the client with its key pair K^{Client} before issuing the policy $P_{\text{Auth}}^{\text{Client}}$. Within the subsequent authorization phase, the TPM checks the validity of $P_{\text{Auth}}^{\text{Client}}$ before allowing the client the access to the private signature key $K_{\text{Priv}}^{\text{TokenSign}}$. During the authorization phase, the TPM also takes care for fulfillment of SPR3 by also checking the correct NV value before granting access to $K_{\text{Priv}}^{\text{TokenSign}}$. Finally, SPR4 is satisfied during the service access phase with a verification of the token's signature by the TPM and the additional legacy policy $P_{\text{Leg}}^{\text{ECU}}$ in case of legacy channels.

The private keys $\text{K}_{\text{Priv}}^{\text{Backend}}$, $K_{\text{Priv}}^{\text{Client}}$ and $K_{\text{Priv}}^{\text{TokenSign}}$ as well as the base derivation key $K_{\text{ParentDerive}}^{\text{TPM}}$ (for the special case of legacy policies) play the key roles for providing security. All security requirements can be satisfied as long as the keys are not compromised and the algorithms used provide a sufficient security level.

For a modern secure automotive environment, an unsecured SOVD app provides a single point of failure which is overcome by our security solution.

5.3 Feasibility Evaluation

To assess the feasibility of our solution for automotive use cases, we utilized our developed POC for performance measurements. We summarize the results in Table 1.

Table 1. Performance Evaluation of crucial functions regarding execution times. Average values (and standard deviation) from 1000 executions are reported.

Function	Deployment Option					
	dTPM [ms]		fTPM [ms]		Software [ms]	
1. Credential DB Decryption	1981.30	(± 32.93)	946.28	(± 24.70)	907.07	(± 08,17)
1.1 GetKey	1679,79	(± 24,50)	844,95	(± 21,63)	773,33	(± 04,16)
1.2 Decrypt	324,43	(± 11,55)	136,79	(± 31,49)	116,60	(± 02,50)
2. Token Generation	1346,45	(± 22,56)	879,94	(± 07,18)	454,33	(± 20,57)
2.1 GetKey	1157,48	(± 10,45)	702,43	(± 04,21)	221,33	(± 19,22)
2.2 Sign	221,20	(± 25,52)	189,07	(± 20,41)	228,67	(± 18,62)
3. Token Authentication	1344,57	(± 32,93)	958,75	(± 03,74)	641,07	(± 32,78)
3.1 GetKey	1136,00	(± 18,21)	756,06	(± 05,69)	427,33	(± 09,00)
3.2 Verify	201,40	(± 04,33)	172,93	(± 28,86)	187,13	(± 30,47)

We measured the most crucial functions for the deployment options (**1**) dTPM, (**2**) fTPM, and (**3**) a purely software-based SOVD variant without the use of any Hardware Security-based Trust Anchor. We identified the `Token Generation` and `Token Authentication` as most relevant for our performance reporting, since they are time-critical during user interaction and repeatedly done during the runtime of the SOVD application. Additionally, we report measurements of the initial decryption of the credential data base (`Credential DB Decryption`). However, this operation is only done during startup and bringing down of the SOVD application and therefore not as crucial as the token generation and authentication functions. For each functionality (`Credential DB Decryption`, `Token Generation`, and `Token Authentication`), we report the overall execution time for each deployment option, and execution times of time-consuming subprocesses like key loading (`GetKey`) as well as the actual crypto operations decryption (`Decrypt`), signing (`Sign`), verifying (`Verify`).

When executing the listed functions, it becomes apparent that execution times are 1.5 to 2 times longer when using a DTPM than when using an FTPM or the software-based variant. These execution times demonstrate that using a DTPM is a valid solution in this scenario. As shown in Table 1, when using the DTPM, approximately 85% of the runtime for Credential DB Decryption is attributable to the `GetKey` subfunction and approximately 15% to the `Decrypt` subfunction. This distribution also holds true for the Token Generation and Token Authentication functions including their subfunctions. According to the usability studies by Jakob Nielsen [31], the execution times of the time-critical functions `Token Generation` and `Token Authentication` remain within a tolerable range of approximately 1 s, even in the worst-case scenario of a DTPM deployment. As such, they do not significantly disrupt the user experience and the developed system is feasible to be deployed.

6 Comparison to Related Work

In the following, we compare existing approaches for usage of diagnostic services, including SOVD. We thereby use the subsequent categories: (**1**) compliance with standards, (**2**) usage of HTAs, (**3**) existing specification of a protocol, (**4**) provisions for communication security, (**5**) protection against runtime attacks, and (**6**) deployment-readiness. For our solution, compliance with standards is provided by nature since our concept is based on SOVD with special preparations for legacy devices not supporting an SOVD-API. The general system design foresees the usage of a TPM which serves as a standard compliant HTA. Our system specification provides a complete protocol of all steps during the different process phases as illustrated in Fig. 2. Communication security is already provided by the usage of SOVD. If the system is running, i.e. a diagnostic client is accessing the SOVD service, an attacker is still unable to get access without a valid token; hence our solution also provides a protection against runtime attacks. Our security concept may be integrated into already existing implementations of diagnostic clients accessing vehicles; hence our solution is also deployment-ready. Table 2 summarizes our key findings when comparing our system to related work, which we detail in the following.

In 2018, Sawant et al. developed an OBD-II device with special features [34]. A main feature is provided by the possibility of simultaneous usage of CAN and Bluetooth with a special microcontroller as a bridge between the laptop or PC and the OBD port of the vehicle. However, no specific security concepts were added.

A blockchain-enabled identity management framework for intelligent transport systems was developed by Das et al. in 2023 [7]. However, this concept only contains the specification of a protocol for generation, verification, and sharing of Unique Identitys (UIDs), but does not further consider any diagnostic processes.

In 2023, Heithoff et al. [10] developed a scenario with the integration of digital twins into diagnostic scenarios under usage of SOVD. The challenges for the usage of digital twins are discussed, and an application scenario is developed. However, no security concept with a usage of HTAs is visible.

In 2024, Helmy et al. [11] developed a combined solution of UDS and SOVD, and highlighted the novelties against classical UDS solutions. It was based on an implementation of SOVD over Adaptive AUTOSAR [12]. However, no security mechanisms were specified except the standard security provided by the underlying standard Diagnosis over IP (DoIP) [17] (upon which UDS is based on), which means the optional usage of TLS according to Part 2.

Cha et al. considered a combination of Data Distribution Service (DDS) and Diagnosis over IP (DoIP) [4]. Their solution is titled by "Service Oriented

Vehicle Diagnostics", but no SOVD standard is used. It does not contain any specification of security mechanisms except the optional standard mechanisms provided by DOIP [17]. The implementation is done with two NXP S32G boards, i.e., the same product family as used for our implementation, but obviously without any additional Hardware Security Module (HSM).

OPC-UA is a frequently used standard for data communication in the industrial sector, also usable for diagnostic purposes. It exists in parallel as a series of publications by the OPC Foundation [33] as well as a multipart IEC standard [13]. However, it was rarely used in the automotive sector. A first attempt was made by Ioana et al. in 2019 [15]. This contained the development of a gateway between OPC-UA and VSOMEIP, the implementation of Scalable service Oriented MiddlewarE over IP (SOME/IP) provided by the GENIVI Alliance (now called COVESA). However, a clear security concept, in particular with usage of an HTA, is not visible, i.e. only the standard communication security provided by OPC-UA can be guaranteed.

It is obvious that diagnostic standards are already in use for the implementation of identity and access management systems for intelligent vehicles. In particular, the developments of Helmy et al. [11] with the combined UDS-SOVD solution as well as the DDS-DOIP solution developed by Cha et at [4], realized by the NXP boards, show high synergies with our work. However, none of these approaches makes use of TPMs or other sorts of HTAs.

Table 2. Comparison with existing work

Work	Standard Compliance	HTA Usage	Protocol Specification	Communication Security	Runtime Attack Protection	Deployment-readiness
[4]	✗	✗	✓	✓ [1]	✓	?
[7]	✗	✗	✓	✓	?	?
[10]	✓	✗	✗	✗	✗	?
[11]	✓	✗	✓	✓ [1]	✓ [1]	? [2]
[34]	✓	✗	✗	✗	✗	✓ [3]
[15]	✓	✗	✓	✓	?	✓
Our Work	✓	✓	✓	✓	✓	✓

[1]If optional TLS support of DOIP is activated.
[2]Implementation platform unclear.
[3]Only for a special environment (KEAZ128), description of rough algorithm steps only (no protocol) ✓: supported, ✗: not supported, ?: no details given

7 Conclusion and Future Work

In this paper, we design and implement a security concept for enhancing the SOVD standard with hardware security provided by a central HTA. The HTA is realized by a TPM which provides a secure key storage as well as an efficient PDP, and also a PEP for managing the policies for accessing the cryptographic keys as well as the diagnostic services. In addition, we enhance the security of SOVD for embedding legacy ECUs that do not support the SOVD API, in particular with UDS. With our integrated token-based security concept, we assure that a client can only access a diagnostic service with the aid of a valid access token signed by the TPM.

Within our work, we identify specific assets and detailed security policy requirements. A mapping to our bootstrapping concept is elaborated. With a proper handling of the policies and the access tokens, our defined security policy requirements are fulfilled, and the assets are adequately protected as long as the keys in the TPM are not compromised. With the aid of appropriate legacy policies, also based on a key securely stored in the TPM, a secure communication with the legacy ECUs can also be provided.

A comparison with related work in the area of usage of diagnostic services has been performed. To our best knowledge, none of the other approaches provides a similar security level as our concept, in particular due to lack of incorporation of HTAs.

Acknowledgments. This research work was supported by the National Research Center for Applied Cybersecurity ATHENE. In addition, the work was funded by the German Federal Ministries BMWK as part of the project ProSeCA (ID 19A23009F).

Disclosure of Interests. The authors have no competing interests to declare that are relevant to the content of this article.

References

1. Advanced Micro Devices, Inc.: AMD PRO Technologies (2026). https://www.amd.com/en/products/processors/technologies/pro-technologies.html#pro-security
2. ASAM: ASAM SOVD Service-Oriented Vehicle Diagnostics. API Specification Version, (2022). 1.0.0
3. AUTOSAR: Adaptive Platform. https://www.autosar.org/standards/adaptive-platform
4. Cha, S.K., Oh, S.B., Do, Y.S., Choi, H.J., Lim, S.H., Jeon, J.W.: Service-oriented vehicle diagnostics by integrating DDS and DoIP. In: 2025 International Technical Conference on Circuits/Systems, Computers, and Communications (ITC-CSCC), pp. 1–5. (2025). https://doi.org/10.1109/ITC-CSCC66376.2025.11137625
5. Checkoway, S., et al.: comprehensive experimental analyses of automotive attack surfaces. In: Proceedings of the 20th USENIX Security Symposium. USENIX Association (2011)
6. Cho, K.T., Shin, K.G.: Fingerprinting electronic control units for vehicle intrusion detection. In: Proceedings of the 25th USENIX Security Symposium, pp. 911–927. USENIX Association (2016)
7. Das, D., Dasgupta, K., Biswas, U.: A secure blockchain-enabled vehicle identity management framework for intelligent transportation systems. Comput. Electr. Eng. **105**, 108535 (2023). https://doi.org/10.1016/j.compeleceng.2022.108535
8. De Benedictis, M., Jacquin, L., Pedone, I., Atzeni, A., Lioy, A.: A novel architecture to virtualise a hardware-bound trusted platform module. Futur. Gener. Comput. Syst. **150**, 21–36 (2024). https://doi.org/10.1016/j.future.2023.08.012

9. Eckel, M., et al.: Implementing a security architecture for safety-critical railway infrastructure. In: 2021 International Symposium on Secure and Private Execution Environment Design (SEED), pp. 215–226. IEEE (2012). https://doi.org/10.1109/SEED51797.2021.00033, https://ieeexplore.ieee.org/document/9604796/
10. Heithoff, M., Konersmann, M., Michael, J., Rumpe, B., Steinfurth, F.: Challenges of integrating model-based digital twins for vehicle diagnosis. In: 2023 ACM/IEEE International Conference on Model Driven Engineering Languages and Systems Companion (MODELS-C), pp. 470–478 (2023). https://doi.org/10.1109/MODELS-C59198.2023.00082
11. Helmy, M., Hekal, M.: SOVD Fusion: pioneering integration for seamless transition between modern standards and classical protocols in UDS. In: 2024 International Telecommunications Conference (ITC-Egypt), pp. 105–110 (2024). https://doi.org/10.1109/ITC-Egypt61547.2024.10620563
12. Helmy, M., Hekal, M., Emad, Y.: Revolutionizing vehicle diagnostics by new SOVD incorporation and development in adaptive AUTOSAR. In: 2024 14th International Conference on Electrical Engineering (ICEENG), pp. 193–195 (2024). https://doi.org/10.1109/ICEENG58856.2024.10566427
13. IEC: IEC 62541 - OPC Unified Architecture 2025 (2020). multiple parts
14. Infineon Technologies AG: OPTIGA TPM 9672 RPI EVAL (2025). https://www.infineon.com/cms/en/product/evaluation-boards/optiga-tpm-9672-rpi-eval/
15. Ioana, A., Korodi, A.: VSOMEIP - OPC UA gateway solution for the automotive industry. In: 2019 IEEE International Conference on Engineering, Technology and Innovation (ICE/ITMC), pp. 1–6 (2019). https://doi.org/10.1109/ICE.2019.8792619
16. ISO: ISO 11889 – Information technology — Trusted Platform Module Library (multiple parts) (2015)
17. ISO: ISO 13400 – Road vehicles — Diagnostic communication over Internet Protocol (DoIP) (multiple parts) (2016-2025)
18. ISO: ISO 14229 – Road vehicles — Unified diagnostic services (UDS) (multiple parts) (2020-2022)
19. ISO: ISO 17978-1 – Road vehicles — Service-oriented vehicle diagnostics (SOVD) — Part 1: General information, definitions, rules and basic principles (2026)
20. ISO: ISO 17978-2 – Road vehicles — Service-oriented vehicle diagnostics (SOVD) — Part 2: Use cases definition (2026)
21. ISO: ISO 17978-3 – Road vehicles — Service-oriented vehicle diagnostics (SOVD) — Part 3: Application programming interface (API) (2026)
22. Jones, M.B., Bradley, J., Sakimura, N.: JSON Web Token (JWT). RFC 7519 (2015). https://doi.org/10.17487/RFC7519
23. Koscher, K., et al.: Experimental security analysis of a modern automobile. In: 2010 IEEE Symposium on Security and Privacy, pp. 447–462. IEEE (2010). https://doi.org/10.1109/SP.2010.34
24. Linux Kernel Developers: TPM2 In-Kernel Resource Manager (/dev/tpmrm0). https://www.kernel.org/doc/html/latest/security/tpm/tpm_vtpm_proxy.html (2026). available since Linux kernel 4.12
25. Linux TPM2 & TSS2 Software: TSS 2.0 FAPI Rust Wrapper (2025). https://github.com/tpm2-software/rust-tss-fapi
26. Microsoft: MS-TPM-20-Ref: TPM 2.0 reference implementation. https://github.com/microsoft/ms-tpm-20-ref (2019). Accessed 2025
27. Miller, C., Valasek, C.: Remote Exploitation of an Unaltered Passenger Vehicle. Black Hat USA (2015). demonstrated remote access to Jeep Cherokee via cellular network, enabling CAN bus manipulation

28. Miyashita, M., Benchadi, D.Y.M., Takakura, H.: Security-risk-mitigation measures for service oriented vehicle diagnostics SOVD. Int. J. Adv. Sec. **18**, 137–149 (2025). http://www.iariajournals.org/security/sec_v18_n34_2025_paged.pdf
29. Moukahal, L.J., Zulkernine, M., Soukup, M.: Vulnerability-oriented fuzz testing for connected autonomous vehicle systems. IEEE Trans. Reliab. **70**(4), 1422–1437 (2021). https://doi.org/10.1109/TR.2021.3112538
30. Nie, S., Liu, L., Du, Y.: Free-Fall: Hacking Tesla from Wireless to CAN Bus, Black Hat USA (2017). demonstrated remote unauthorized access and control of Tesla Model S/X systems
31. Nielsen, J.: Usability Engineering, Morgan Kaufmann Publishers Inc (1994). https://doi.org/10.1016/C2009-0-21512-1
32. NXP Semiconductors: S32G3 Vehicle Networking Reference Design (2025). https://www.nxp.com/design/design-center/development-boards-and-designs/S32G-VNP-RDB3
33. OPC Foundation: OPC Unified Architecture. https://opcfoundation.org/developer-tools/documents
34. Sawant, P.R., Mane, Y.B.: Design and development of on-board diagnostic (OBD) device for cars. In: 2018 Fourth International Conference on Computing Communication Control and Automation (ICCUBEA), pp. 1–4 (2018). https://doi.org/10.1109/ICCUBEA.2018.8697833
35. Silicon Labs: TrustZone (2026). https://www.silabs.com/security/trust-zone
36. SYSGO: Trusted Platform Module (TPM) in Embedded System Security (2025). https://www.sysgo.com/blog/article/trusted-platform-module-tpm-in-embedded-system-security
37. Thing, V.L.L., Wu, J.: Autonomous vehicle security: a taxonomy of attacks and defences. In: IEEE International Conference on Internet of Things (iThings, pp. 164–170 (2016). https://doi.org/10.1109/iThings-GreenCom-CPSCom-SmartData.2016.52
38. TPM2-Software: TPM2-ABRMD: TPM2 Access Broker and Resource Manager. https://github.com/tpm2-software/tpm2-abrmd (2026)
39. Trusted Computing Group: TSS TAB and Resource Manager. Tech. rep., Trusted Computing Group (2019). https://trustedcomputinggroup.org/resource/tss-tab-and-resource-manager/
40. Trusted Computing Group: TCG TSS 2.0 Overview and CommonStructures Specification, Version 1.0, Revision 10. Tech. rep., Trusted Computing Group (2021). https://trustedcomputinggroup.org/resource/tss-overview-common-structures-specification/
41. Upstream Security: Global Automotive Cybersecurity Report. Upstream Security Ltd. (2024). https://upstream.auto/reports/global-automotive-cybersecurity-report, annual report documenting automotive data breaches, unauthorized access incidents, and attack vectors across the connected vehicle ecosystem
42. Werling, C., Kuehnapfel, N., Jacob, H.N., Drokin, O.: Jailbreaking an Electric vehicle in 2023 or what it means to hotwire tesla's x86-based seat heater (2023). https://www.blackhat.com/us-23/briefings/schedule/index.html#jailbreaking-an-electric-vehicle-in--or-what-it-means-to-hotwire-teslas-x-based-seat-heater-33049

43. Woo, S., Jo, H.J., Lee, D.H.: A practical wireless attack on the connected car and security protocol for in-vehicle CAN. IEEE Trans. Intell. Transp. Syst. **16**(2), 993–1006 (2015). https://doi.org/10.1109/TITS.2014.2351612
44. Zelle, D., Plappert, C., Rieke, R., Scheuermann, D., Krauß, C.: ThreatSurf: a method for automated Threat Surface assessment in automotive cybersecurity engineering. Microprocess. Microsyst. **90**, 104461 (2022). https://doi.org/10.1016/j.micpro.2022.104461

HIEST: Hierarchical Attestation to Support Trusted Dynamic Workloads

Ardhi Putra Pratama Hartono[1(✉)], Andrey Brito[2], and Christof Fetzer[1]

[1] Technische Universität Dresden, Dresden, Germany
{ardhi_pp.hartono,christof.fetzer}@tu-dresden.de
[2] Universidade Federal de Campina Grande, Campina Grande, Brazil
andrey@computacao.ufcg.edu.br

Abstract. Confidential computing leverages VM-based Trusted Execution Environments (TEEs) to protect workloads without modification. However, dynamic workloads, where applications execute atop a Process VM (PVM) such as Python, remain inadequately addressed. Existing solutions, such as Confidential Containers (CoCo), restrict attestation to the first execution layer and deploy workloads using generic micro-VM images, producing identical TEE evidence irrespective of the actual application. This enables an adversary to hijack and reuse an attested environment to run unintended or malicious applications. We propose *HIEST*, a hierarchical attestation mechanism that chains the execution stack, from the Trusted Computing Base (TCB) through the PVM to the application and beyond. Execution is allowed only after successful verification by a trusted remote Key Broker Service (KBS). *HIEST* is runtime-agnostic, supports user-defined constraints, assumes no specific certificate standard or cryptographic algorithm, and extends naturally to additional layers such as data input. Our reference implementation requires no direct PVM modifications and leverages mature components like Kata Containers. Evaluation across multiple use cases demonstrates that *HIEST* mitigates reuse attacks, adding a fixed 12–15 ms of overhead that is negligible as workload durations grows in our setup.

Keywords: confidential virtual machine · hierarchical attestation · certificate chaining · process virtual machine

1 Introduction

Developing confidential computing applications requires careful consideration of their execution model, whether compiled as native binaries or executed dynamically via a Process Virtual Machine (PVM) (e.g., on Python, Java) [34]. Confidential Containers (CoCo) offer a solution for deploying confidential applications as Kubernetes workloads on top of a Trusted Execution Environment (TEE). However, in the context of application in a Process VM, using CoCo alone does not fully resolve the underlying trust for all the components involved.

Z. Afzal et al. (Eds.): ARES 2026 Workshops, LNCS 16900, pp. 235–252, 2027.
https://doi.org/10.1007/978-3-032-35576-8_13

Take Lithops [25], a serverless platform, as an example. As shown in Fig. 1, the application (a *Function/Module*, in this case) is executed on top of a Process VM (a *Runtime*) and is injected by an *Invoker* through the *Worker*. In this case, the application owner needs to fully trust the *Invoker* to correctly spawn the correct Process VM and then inject the application. Despite using state-of-the-art techniques such as CoCo that deploy the Process VM in a trusted manner, we cannot prevent a malicious *Invoker* from injecting malicious code.

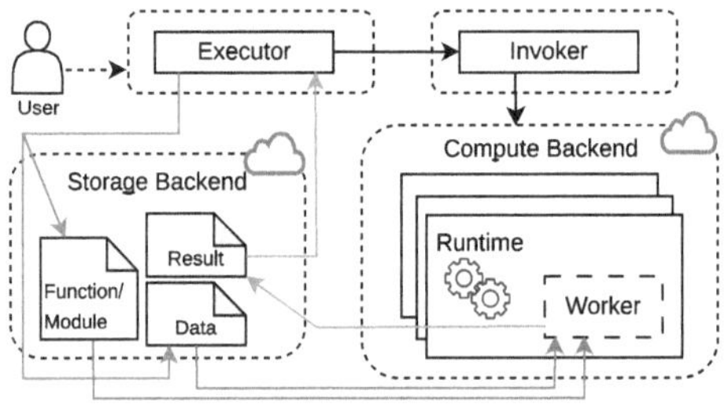

Fig. 1. High-level serverless architecture such as Lithops [25]

As a countermeasure, owners could package the application and Process VM into a single black-box runtime, analogous to a statically linked binary. However, this inflexible approach severely increases deployment overhead, since minor updates necessitate full rebuilds. Alternatively, relying on code signing or cryptographic checksums for integrity introduces significant complexity, as these mechanisms must be independently implemented across both the existing framework (e.g., Lithops components) and the application.

As a concrete example, consider a Machine Learning (ML) pipeline that requires fine-tuning a confidential model. Research suggests that fine-tuning a model of a Large Language Model (LLM) can extract Personally Identifiable Information [4], expose training data [20], or extract the model completely [16]. Moreover, as categorized by OWASP, Artificial Intelligence agents are initially benign; their behaviour is dictated by the data input they receive for continuous learning. The introduction of malicious inputs can transform their behavior in unpredictable ways [22], undermining any safety guarantees in their deployment.

Mitigating these risks requires application-level attestation on top of the Process VM. However, current CoCo frameworks attest only up to the container image level, namely the PVM and its libraries, leaving the dynamic application executing atop this stack and the data it consumes out of scope. This gap exposes both layers to adversarial threats like post-attestation reuse attacks, forcing application owners to implement custom mitigations that vary across platforms.

This work proposes *HIEST* (pronounced '*heist*'), a TEE-based **HIE**rarchical atte**ST**ation framework to support trusted applications on top of Process VMs. *HIEST* attest the application together with the Process VM dynamically. This ensures a unique and verifiable association between them. In a VM-based TEE, the kernel, which is part of the Trusted Computing Base (TCB) and where most of *HIEST* is implemented, signs attestation evidence and anchors the chain of trust to the hardware Root of Trust (RoT). Furthermore, we support a further attestation layer to be created by the application and beyond, flexibly.

2 Research Motivation and Contribution

CoCo is a state-of-the-art framework that protects *Kubernetes workloads* using VM-based TEEs. By leveraging generic micro-VMs, these workloads can be easily deployed with acceptable performance overhead. A *Policy* confines the workload to expected behavior and ensures it connects only to the designated Key Broker Service (*KBS*), which is responsible for the workload's secret.

Challenges arise when an application dynamically executes generic code, as with a *Process VM* (*PVM*) such as a Python interpreter, Java Virtual Machine, or serverless runtime. Throughout this paper, *Application* denotes the main program running atop PVM, with the PVM responsible for verifying the *Application*'s trustworthiness. Unlike a static workload defined by a single binary, a *Dynamic Workload* is identified by the *Application*-PVM pairing. Unfortunately, even CoCo cannot ensure the execution integrity of such workloads, and a single Pod may host multiple workloads that affect one another. Figure 2 shows the relationship between the Kernel, PVM, *Application*, and Kubernetes workload.

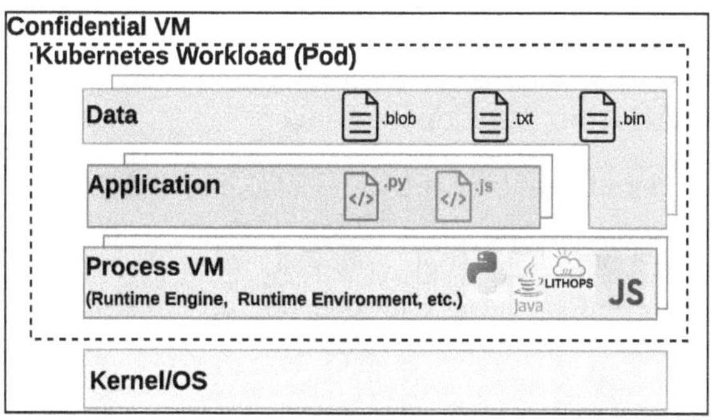

Fig. 2. Architecture of an *Application* with a Process VM in a Confidential VM

Analogously, multi-stakeholder computations present comparable trust challenges when infrastructure, platform, application, and data are distinctly owned. Malicious inputs (e.g., SQL injections, adversarial input for AI, or data rollback) can exploit the application [13], while data owners may require assurance that their assets are processed exclusively by explicitly trusted *Application*-PVM combinations. Platform owners also face collusion threats, where application and data owners conspire to exploit PVM vulnerabilities. All stakeholders thus benefit from a mechanism that explicitly defines and enforces an intended execution chain within the VM, a capability that is still absent in the state of the art.

2.1 Threat Model and Assumptions

We adopt a standard VM-based TEE threat model aligned with CoCo's trust boundaries [5], where the TCB includes the TEE, remote KBS, measured guest environment, and the Kubernetes workload (in our case, a PVM). The Kubernetes operator, *kubelet*, container runtime, *kata-shim*, and storage remain untrusted. Within this model, a highly privileged adversary aims to execute a malicious *Application* inside an already attested PVM. Because CoCo relies on generic VM images, this post-attestation injection remains invisible to the initial attestation evidence, allowing the adversary to bypass existing protections.

Software stack vulnerabilities could theoretically bypass attestation to compromise the *Application*, PVM, or underlying VM. However, mitigating these issues is orthogonal to our work and can be addressed by independent approaches. Also, we consider side-channel attacks, such as CPU bitflips [14] and single-stepping [24], out of scope. Finally, our design cannot prevent an adversary from exploiting existing *Application* or PVM vulnerabilities to extract data or seize control after a successful attestation and execution phase.

Nevertheless, *HIEST* offers mitigations for these challenges. First, its hierarchical attestation can generate a detailed execution record for auditing purposes. In cases of multi-stakeholder collusion, this record is crucial for identifying the responsible party. Second, because *HIEST* is generic and extendable, *Application* owners, with Process VM support, can extend the chain to include *Application* inputs. This way, only trusted/authorized input can be consumed by the *Application*, reducing the risks of exploited vulnerabilities.

2.2 Reuse Attack and Its Consequences

In this section, we detail a Reuse Attack on CoCo, highlighting a security tradeoff introduced by generic micro-VMs for Kubernetes Pods. While such approaches improve deployment efficiency, they create identity provisioning issues: unrelated workloads can impersonate each other and an adversary can still alter the *Application*'s behavior through native Kubernetes APIs, invisible to attestation evidence.

To illustrate the attack mechanics, consider a Python workload inside a Confidential VM that periodically accesses a *ConfigMap* volume. Initially, the VM completes remote attestation via the KBS, and the *kata-agent* enforces the policy, establishing baseline trust. However, the actual *ConfigMap* data resides on the untrusted host node. When the *kata-agent* bridges this content into the guest via the shared *virtio-fs* file system, an adversary can maliciously alter the host-side volume post-attestation. By ingesting this crafted payload, the adversary can fully compromise the *Application* [35] and subsequently hijack the entire VM [17], a vulnerability further amplified if debug modes remain active.

Once an adversary has taken control of the VM, the ability to invoke arbitrary *Applications* undetected within an identical, attested environment poses risks across domains. In the LLMs context, fine-tuning can expose sensitive information [4,12,20], and ML pipelines demand rigorous evaluation even within

TEEs [18]. In serverless platforms, warm-container optimization can leave quasi-persistent vulnerabilities and security leaks [28]. An attacker can also run a collocated malicious application to extract application secrets [29]. Ultimately, these threats highlight the necessity of attesting not only the initial state of the Process VM but also the dynamic application running atop it, and crucially, their combination: the dynamic workload.

Problem Description. Strawman mitigations, such as bottom-up PVM restrictions or top-down data access limits, fail because PVMs cannot evaluate *Application* intent without robust *Application*-PVM identification. Relying solely on state-of-the-art frameworks like CoCo is equally insufficient. Even with a trusted PVM and Kubernetes workload, a powerful adversary can dynamically load a malicious *Application* that bypasses existing attestation and executing a reuse attack. Moreover, even when the *Application* and PVM are statically bound, adversarial inputs (e.g., crafted serverless function arguments or AI agent prompts) can still alter execution behavior. Ultimately, current solutions expose a critical gap by failing to extend the hardware Root of Trust (RoT) through the TEE and PVM to the dynamic *Application* layer, a mechanism strictly necessary for enabling mutual trust verification between *Application* and data owners.

Contribution. We first identify and demonstrate a novel reuse attack exploiting Process VMs and native Kubernetes APIs, describing mitigation strategies unaddressed by current state-of-the-art solutions. To resolve these vulnerabilities, we introduce *HIEST*, a software-based mechanism anchored in hardware TEEs that enables *Application* attestation within Confidential Containers (CoCo). *HIEST* cryptographically binds the *Application* to the previously attested TCB, thereby establishing a remotely verifiable chain of trust.

While initially targeting *Application*-level attestation, our approach is highly flexible. We showcase this versatility via a reference implementation on an unmodified Python runtime, proving the framework can secure subsequent execution layers such as data inputs. Finally, we validate *HIEST*'s practical applicability across diverse real-world use cases. Our performance evaluation demonstrates that the system achieves these robust security guarantees with a negligible latency overhead (10% or less) depending on the workload.

3 Background and Related Works

3.1 Confidential Computing and Its Modern Applications

Confidential Computing aims to protect data-in-use, even in the presence of a powerful adversary, by performing computation inside a TEE. Early efforts that focused on process-based TEEs, such as Intel SGX, can be relatively complex to deploy, despite the availability of frameworks such as SCONE [2] and Graphene [31]. Consequently, VM-based TEEs, coined as *Confidential VM* (CVM), have become increasingly attractive. While this approach expands the TCB to include the guest kernel, it offers significantly easier adoption [17]. The CoCo project [6] leverages this model to integrate TEE capabilities directly with cloud-native applications. Other projects, such as Constellation [8], Veil [1], and Enarx [3] focus on broader usage scenarios that build on CVM to secure the workload.

However, in CoCo, the base VM image is generic, which makes Reuse attack possible as discussed in Sect. 2.2. Although the workload configuration (*Init-Data* [7]) can personalize the attestation report, it only protects the first-level workload that is explicitly specified in the deployment (i.e., the Process VM in our case). Furthermore, Valdez et al. demonstrated that the policy enforcement design, while limiting API access, remains insufficient. Their work highlighted several possible attack variations, including leaking container secrets, manipulating timestamps, and writing to sensitive files [32]. The last attack is particularly relevant as it can also be used to enable the Reuse attack we previously described.

TCB Measurement in Cloud Service Provider. Usually, CVM-based TEE manufacturers, especially in AMD SEV-SNP, designed that TCB measurement can consist of the *initrd*, kernel parameters, kernel, and firmware. Intel TDX, on the other hand, introduces measurement register called RTMR (Runtime Extendable Measurement Register) to extend the measurement [17]. In principle, workload owners should be able to verify these components end-to-end from source or reproducible artifacts. In practice, however, many CSPs often only measure up to the firmware, omitting other components [9]. As a result, CVM instances are indistinguishable since they share identical attestation report, regardless of the guest environment. Even so, only AWS provides open source firmware. GCP provides only a signed binary (so users can verify the signature), whereas Azure publishes only a reference value, which users must ultimately trust [26]. While major CSPs support extending measurements to the OS kernel via a vTPM, the vTPM implementation itself typically resides within unauditable parts, such as the hypervisor [26].

3.2 Trusted Execution of *Applications*atop Process VMs

Prior research has explored the insufficiency of static launch-time measurements, such as in serverless computing [27], and formulated attestation schemes that bind identity to the application rather than the platform [21]. While some approaches focus on intra-enclave environments [1,33,36], Momose et al. enable nested attestation without such isolation [19], and SinClave [11] prevents reuse attacks by instantiating a unique enclave per execution. However, these enclave-centric approaches share the limitation that they require applications to interface with SGX-specific programming models, presenting significant development complexity. Also, unlike *LATTE*'s WebAssembly focus, runtime-agnostic approaches for unmodified Process VMs remain largely unexplored [35].

Another paradigm focuses on flexible attestation within Confidential VMs. While recent frameworks attempt to decouple infrastructure trust [15] or leverage eBPF to mitigate reuse attacks [10], they often remain vulnerable to identical measurement exploits or require non-standard verification mechanisms. Alternative approaches have also emerged, such as leveraging SPIFFE to manage CVM deployment and attestation [23], and extending the TEE-agnostic Enarx framework to attest user applications [3]. However, a common limitation across these solutions is that they assume the attestation target resides only one abstraction layer removed from the TEE. By prioritizing transparency, they hide attestation primitives from the guest workload, effectively preventing the support of attestation-aware applications or further layered environments.

While combining a virtual TPMs with Integrity Measurement Architecture (IMA) can verify file-level integrity, existing vTPM deployments problematically extend trust to the cloud provider [26] or require complex modifications such as on hypervisor [30,37]. Furthermore, relying solely on IMA is inadequate for dynamic *Application*-PVM execution, as it cannot measure fileless workloads or natively attest the exact execution combination order.

4 Design

The *HIEST* architecture consists of the following primary components.

- **Kernel Module** provides the in-kernel attestation interface. It enforces certificate chain construction semantics, generates ephemeral key pairs, and exposes entry points for user-space processes to request attestation services. Additionally, the kernel is responsible for securely maintaining the cryptographic keys used to sign the chain across the various layers.
- `Init` **Process** is an implementation-specific routine executed early in the VM lifecycle. It bootstraps the *HIEST* workflow, including VM attestation and root-certificate generation.
- **The Key Broker Service (KBS)** acts as a remote authority that verifies attestation evidence. It validates the integrity of not only VM but also the certificate chain before authorizing the execution to proceed.
- **User-Space Logic** resides within the PVM or the *Application*, typically implemented as a linked library or a direct code modification. It is responsible for triggering *HIEST* operations, communicating with the KBS, and storing or presenting the certificates associated with the current execution layer.

The hierarchical attestation process operates across three stages: VM, PVM, and *Application*. It begins at the VM level, where the `init` program fetches cryptographic evidence generated by the TEE and submits it to a remote verifier (KBS). This phase generates an ephemeral key and exchanges a nonce, resulting in the kernel holding a certificate signed by a private key whose public key is bound to the TEE evidence. When the PVM launches, it is registered as a new trust layer above the kernel, with the kernel signing its certificate and generating a dedicated ephemeral key pair for this layer. Similarly, before executing an *Application*, the kernel acts on behalf of the PVM to generate an ephemeral key pair for the *Application* and sign its certificate. Each layer is verified by the KBS, establishing a hierarchical chain of trust from the hardware root through every software layer. As listed in Table 1, most core *HIEST* operations reside within the kernel, which is part of the TCB. User-level applications access these functions via the `ioctl` interface, optionally assisted by a library, whereas network communication with the KBS and invocation logic remain in user space.

Table 1. *HIEST* kernel functions and their description

Function name	Short description
`HIEST_INIT`	Initialize the root layer (i.e., kernel)
`HIEST_ATT`	Perform *HIEST* for a target layer
`HIEST_SELF`	Perform *HIEST* for the callee layer
`HIEST_SIGN`	Signing arbitrary data on behalf of the callee
`HIEST_GEN_KEY`	Generate new ephemeral key for a layer

4.1 Attestation Stages with *HIEST*

The core principle of *HIEST* is to provide each execution layer within the Confidential VM a certificate. This certificate demonstrates that the execution conforms to the intended configuration and measured state. Each certificate is signed by the immediately preceding layer, which itself must undergo the same attestation process, establishing a verifiable chain of trust. The chain terminates at a root certificate anchored in the kernel and bound to TEE evidence, which attests to kernel's integrity and establishes the trust foundation for subsequent layers.

While *HIEST* does not assume a specific certificate standard or format, each layer's certificate must contain the following fields: ❶ the public key of the layer's ephemeral keypair, ❷ the layer's measurement, ❸ the additional data describing the certificate in *options*, and ❹ a hash of the preceding certificate in the chain. This requirement is depicted in Fig. 3. To maintain the chain of trust, each certificate is digitally signed by the preceding layer. Furthermore, *HIEST* remains agnostic to the choice of key generation and signature algorithms, allowing flexibility in the implementation.

VM Attestation. The first stage, VM attestation, operates independently of *HIEST*. In CoCo, this process is executed by an Attestation Agent (AA) that launches after the *kata-agent* spawns. Alternative implementations, such as in Azure's Confidential VM architecture, VM attestation is performed immediately as a post-boot script. Regardless of the mechanism used, we refer to this component as the `init` process. During `init`, *HIEST* extends the baseline attestation flow by invoking `HIEST_GEN_KEY` and `HIEST_INIT`. It first sends a challenge request to the KBS, which responds with a nonce. The routine then invokes `HIEST_GEN_KEY` to retrieve the TEE evidence and binds both the public key component and the nonce to the evidence, via `REPORTDATA` field. Finally, this evidence is verified by the KBS, establishing that the VM and kernel are in their intended trusted state.

After the integrity of the VM and kernel has been established, `init` generates a certificate on behalf of the kernel. At the kernel level, `HIEST_INIT` is invoked to obtain a measurement of `init`, construct and sign the certificate, and return it as the root certificate. The resulting artifact, referred to as the root certificate, is self-signed; specifically, the subject public key field correspond to the kernel's public key, which is bound to the TEE evidence. The `init` process then submits this root certificate to the KBS. Only upon successful validation of both certificate and TEE evidence, the process can proceed to the next stages.

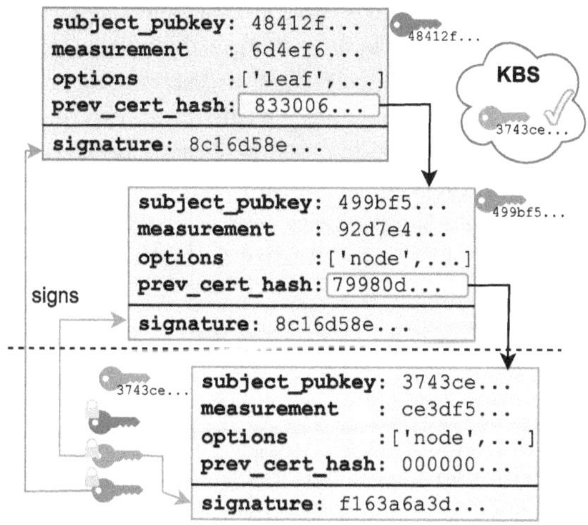

Fig. 3. *HIEST* Certificate semantics

PVM Attestation. After the VM has been successfully attested, a user-defined PVM can be launched, and the kernel assigns it a unique process identifier (PID). Upon launch, the PVM invokes HIEST_SELF , triggering the kernel to generate an ephemeral key pair using HIEST_GEN_KEY . The kernel then constructs and signs a certificate that includes the PVM's both measurement and public key, and returns the resulting certificate to the PVM. The PVM then submits this certificate to the KBS and proceeds with execution only after the KBS successfully verifies it. While *HIEST* is designed with PVMs in mind, it is applicable to any arbitrary application with a valid PID. A key distinction of *HIEST* from other attestation mechanisms is that it can be used to attest dynamic components, such as an *Application* on top of the PVM instance or an input, by treating them as additional layers in the chain.

Application **Attestation**. At runtime, the PVM must execute the target *Application*, such as a Python workload or serverless function. Before the execution, the PVM invokes HIEST_ATT to initiate application-level attestation. By doing so, the kernel measures the *Application* and constructs the corresponding certificate. Alternatively, the PVM may measure the *Application* beforehand and forward it to the kernel. The remaining steps follow the same pattern as in previous layers: the kernel, acting on behalf of the PVM, constructs and signs an *Application* certificate that incorporates the relevant measurements and keys, and the PVM submits this certificate to the remote KBS for verification. Only upon successful remote attestation does the PVM proceed with *Application* execution, ensuring that the entire trust chain from hardware root through kernel, PVM, and *Application* layers has been validated before any untrusted code runs.

Extending the Trust. To ensure generality, *HIEST* supports the attestation of arbitrary layers, such as data inputs, beyond the predefined *VM-PVM-Application* hierarchy. By invoking *HIEST* kernel functions, an *Application* can treat an input as an additional layer and extend the trust chain. This requires that the preceding software stack is fully compatible with *HIEST* and mandates that all intermediate layers are successfully attested prior the interaction with the KBS. Furthermore, *HIEST* permits certificate extensions with user-defined constraints. As illustrated in Fig. 3, certificates can be designated as either a *'node'* or a *'leaf'*. This enables precise policy enforcement; for instance, a *'leaf'* certificate explicitly prevents the generation of subsequent layers, making it ideal for static text files or AI agent inputs. Additionally, this field can store metadata such as algorithm or layer identifiers.

5 Implementation

As described in Sect. 4, *HIEST* main components consist of a kernel module, an `init` process, a KBS, and user-space logic. This section presents a reference implementation of these components. Figure 4 illustrates this architecture with distinct colors representing different architectural layers. In our setup, we use Python interpreter as the PVM and follow the CoCo architecture (including the KBS and using *kata-agent* as `init`). Additionally, we leverage the Integrity Measurement Architecture (IMA) as a means to measure files in the VM. The following section elaborates on each layer in detail. Our reference implementation is open source and available at https://github.com/ardhipoetra/hierarchy-attest-src/.

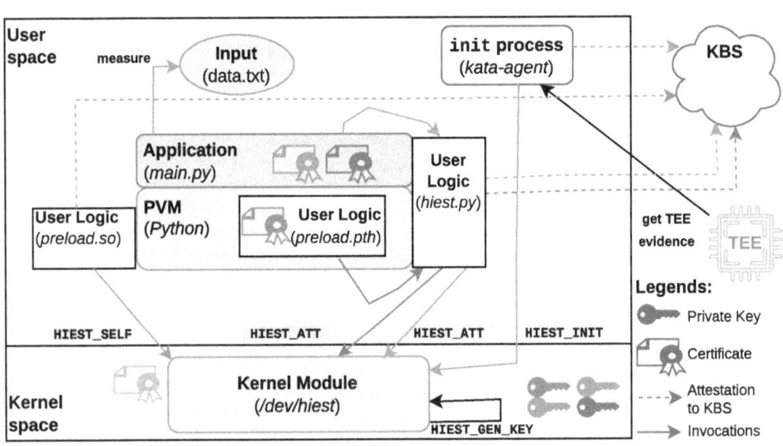

Fig. 4. *HIEST* Reference implementation

Kernel Module and `init` process. We implement the *HIEST* kernel module (KM) as an *in-tree* driver, with creates `/dev/hiest/` as the interface, to ensure flexibility in ABI usage. Our kernel build process is based on the *kata-container* script[1], ensuring alignment with the CoCo ecosystem. In our implementation, we enable the IMA to enforce measurement across the entire VM. Specifically, our IMA policy is configured to measure files upon execution, during library loading (e.g., via *mmap*), and on read operations when the file is owned by root, which matches common container image ownership patterns. As our default algorithm, we employ the Ed25519 digital signature scheme for all ephemeral key pairs, selected for its balance of security and performance. Certificates are encoded in a packed binary format. Their structure and fields are depicted in Fig. 3.

For the `init` process, we reuse the CoCo-style early-boot attestation flow, specifically *kata-agent*, as a practical boilerplate for initiating VM attestation and communicating with the KBS, which also maintains compatibility with various TEE backends to simplify deployment across heterogeneous hardware. The `init` process retrieves KBS details via kernel parameters, which are included in the initial VM measurement and thus attested. The KM, in turn, stores the root certificate and the private keys for all layers in the VM exclusively in kernel memory. KM offers no key-related user-space API exposure, so only kernel code can access them. While stronger security measures like kernel hardening, key deletion, or enclave-style isolation in the CVM [1,33,36] offer enhanced protection, they require substantial software stack modifications. We consider such techniques orthogonal to our primary focus on layered attestation semantics.

Process VM (as Python). In our implementation, the user-space logic is mostly concentrated around the PVM. First, we provide a small preloading library (*preload.so*) that is injected before the PVM starts via the `LD_PRELOAD` environment variable. The library can also be reused for other executables because it is designed to intercept the program entry point (e.g., `main()`). It implements the glue code needed to (i) invoke the API exposed by the KM and (ii) perform communication with the KBS. Most importantly, it triggers `HIEST_SELF` for the loaded executable (e.g., the PVM) to obtain and remotely attest the certificate chain before execution proceeds.

As a reference implementation, specific for Python, we provide a helper mechanism using a *preload.pth* file, a form of Python startup hook, to intercept the PVM's startup sequence prior to executing the *Application*. Once the PVM starts and completes attestation, *preload.so* temporarily holds the resulting certificate until *preload.pth* takes over and makes it accessible to the PVM through a *ctypes* bindings. This helper mechanism is tightly coupled with the *HIEST* library for Python (*hiest.py*). This combination allows us to avoid directly modifying the PVM (e.g., Python) and requires only additional libraries, which can be included in CoCo attestation immediately after starting the VM.

Application (as *main.py*). When the PVM starts an *Application*, *preload.pth* hook triggers the attestation routine defined in *hiest.py*. The routine invokes `HIEST_ATT` to request a certificate for the target *Application*. Since in our example

[1] https://github.com/kata-containers/kata-containers/tree/main/tools/packaging/kernel.

```
import hiest
with open("/data/data.txt", 'r') as f:
  certs = hiest.hiest_att_fd(f.fileno())
  if certs is not None:
    pass            # attestation succeed
  else:
    sys.exit(1)     # attestation failed
```

Listing 13.1. Python application attesting an input example

the *Application* is as a file, the measurement is expected to be obtained via the IMA. At present, our current implementation focuses on file-based execution and does not support Python interactive mode. The library then obtains the certificate chain and verifies it with the KBS. Optionally, depending on the nature of the *Application*, the library may expose the resulting certificate to the *Application*, enabling the attestation of subsequent layers, such as input data.
Input (as *data.txt*). Input data represents a passive layer, meaning although it is an attested artifact, it does not independently utilize the resulting certificate to verify subsequent layers. Nevertheless, the *Application* is responsible for measuring it, either by leveraging existing mechanism (e.g., IMA) or by implementing measurement mechanism internally. In our prototype, the input is a file provided by the orchestrator, therefore we use IMA for simplicity. Interactions with the KM and KBS are performed through the `hiest.py` library by the *Application*, as demonstrated in Listing 13.1.

Key Broker Service (KBS). Each layer in the stack is attested by a remote verifier, a role fulfilled by the KBS. We extend the existing CoCo-KBS implementation, leveraging its compatibility with heterogeneous TEE backends, including for the VM attestation. Our KBS implementation acts as a proof-of-concept verifier for the attestation collateral (the certificate chain). This includes verifying that each certificate is signed by the preceding layer and ensuring that the chain roots in the key established during VM attestation. Furthermore, the KBS enforces user-defined verification policies, allowing users to explicitly specify the expected sequence of layers and their corresponding measurements. This mechanism ensures not only the correctness of individual components but also the structural continuity of the entire execution chain.

6 Evaluation

The experiments were conducted on a server equipped with an AMD EPYC 7313 "Milan" processor and 128 GB of DDR4 RAM. Both the host and guest system runs Linux kernel 6.11 ensuring compatibility with AMD SEV-SNP and Kata Containers (version 3.14, February 2025). Each guest VM was provisioned with 1 vCPU and 2048 MB of memory. The KBS, running CoCo's Trustee version 0.11, was deployed locally on the host. During guest VM attestation, the KBS communicates with AMD's servers to verify the hardware evidence.

6.1 Applying *HIEST*on Various Use Cases

Here we demonstrate how our approach resolves previously identified challenges by detailing specific, practical use cases. In our first use case, we implement the attack scenario described in Sect. 2.2: a Python-based Kubernetes workload that repeatedly opens, reads, and closes a target file backed by a *ConfigMap* volume. The Kubernetes cluster is deployed locally using *k3s*. Acting as an adversary with control over both the host and the operator, we can directly inspect and modify the copy of the target file, which resides at **/var/lib/kubelet/pods/<pod_id>/volumes/kubernetes.io~configmap/voldata/** on the host filesystem. Without *HIEST*, the *Application* blindly consumes the modification and continues execution. In contrast, *HIEST* prevents further execution by first measuring the file, attesting it against the remote KBS, and proceeding only upon successful verification. Later, we evaluate the performance overhead on this scenario.

The second use case highlights the critical need for execution stack integrity. Consider a single container image providing two Python versions (acting as PVMs): 3.10 and 3.11. Suppose *Applications* A and B strictly require Python versions 3.10 and 3.11, respectively. Because both PVMs reside within the same image, a powerful adversary could maliciously swap the environments, i.e., executing *Application* B atop Python 3.10. Such a setup could be advantageous to the adversary if, for example, a known vulnerability exists for that specific combination. *HIEST* prevents this by attesting each execution layer (the PVM and the *Application*) and their exact sequence against a policy that is hosted on the remote, trusted KBS. This policy strictly defines the permitted execution stacks, ensuring each application only runs in its verified, intended environment. In this case, the PVM (i.e., Python 3.10) self-terminates via the preloading library upon failing the attestation of *Application* B.

6.2 Performance Evaluation

We evaluate the performance of our approach at three levels: VM/container, *Application*, and data input. We compare each level's runtime latency against native execution over 10 independent runs and report the average. Both setups are run using a Kata Container and attested to the KBS. After successful verification with AMD's servers, the KBS returns an attestation token to the VM, confirming that the instance is successfully attested and trusted.

We first focus on the latency from the hypervisor spawning the VM until the container is ready. This includes VM initialization followed by container provisioning performed by the *kata-agent* inside the VM. Depicted in Fig. 5a, the overhead introduced by *HIEST* (highlighted in purple) consists of its initialization and attestation with the remote KBS. The difference between the *HIEST* variant and native execution is negligible. The *HIEST* variant incurs an additional overhead of less than 0.03%, primarily due to an extra round-trip communication with the KBS (approximately 12–15 ms), with an average overall boot time of approximately 8200 ms. This minor overhead is vastly outweighed by the baseline VM attestation process itself (which applies to both setups), taking approximately 1200–1300 ms.

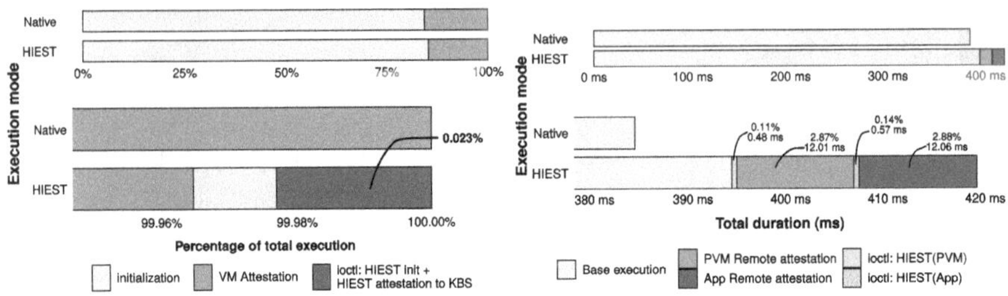

(a) Latency overhead on starting VM/container

(b) Latency overhead on starting *Application*

Fig. 5. Latency overhead for various stages

Next, we direct our focus to *Application*-level performance as shown in Fig. 5b. In both setups, the *Application* simply executes a single line that prints "Hello". However, the *HIEST* variant additionally outputs the certificate obtained from the attestation. Consistent with the previous result, the majority of the overhead stems from communication with the KBS, which in this case occurs twice: once to attest the PVM and once to attest the *Application*, accounting for a total overhead of around 5.6%. Notably, the overhead of kernel operations remains negligible, even though this is where the majority of the implementation resides. The remaining overhead comes from auxiliary operations required to facilitate the *HIEST* mechanism. Overall, the *HIEST* variant incurs an average latency overhead of approximately 8.4% compared to native execution when spawning an *Application*.

Finally, we evaluate the performance of attesting data input, as described in Sect. 6.1. The *Application* repeatedly opens, reads, and closes a target file. We then measure the total execution latency across various file sizes. We observe that the additional operations introduced by *HIEST* incur a near-constant latency (12–14 ms for remote attestation to KBS, 0.6–0.7 ms for kernel operations). When the native execution latency is sufficiently long due to processing a large file, the relative overhead remains marginal (2% for a 32 MB file). Conversely, for smaller files, the shorter native execution time causes the relative overhead to be significantly higher, resulting in a 9× latency increase for a 16 KB file, as illustrated in Fig. 6. This phenomenon aligns with our previous experiments, where the naturally longer baseline durations of booting a VM (8200 ms) and instantiating an application (385 ms) are sufficiently long to absorb the constant overhead latency introduced by *HIEST*. We observe that only experiments with a native execution time of 43 ms or lower incur an overhead exceeding 15%.

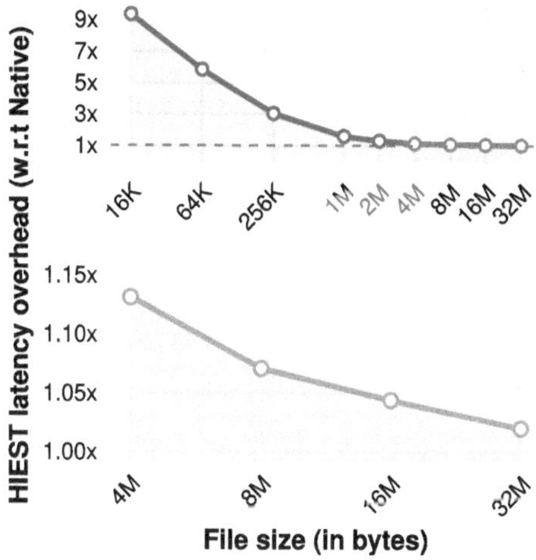

Fig. 6. *HIEST* overhead for input attestation across file sizes

7 Conclusion

Running *Applications* atop a Process VM (PVM) such as Python poses a fundamental challenge for confidential computing. Since state-of-the-art solutions like Confidential Containers (CoCo) deploy workloads using generic micro-VM images, the resulting TEE evidence remains identical across workloads. A skilled adversary can exploit this by reusing an attested environment to execute a malicious *Application* that deviates from the intended specification.

To address this gap, we propose *HIEST*, a hierarchical attestation mechanism for *Applications* running atop a PVM within a VM-based TEE. *HIEST* is runtime-agnostic, flexible through user-defined constraints, independent of any specific certificate standard or algorithm, and extendable to additional layers such as data input. Our approach chains the entire execution stack, from the TCB through the PVM to the application and beyond, using certificates, permitting execution only after successful attestation against policies enforced by a trusted remote Key Broker Service (KBS). By leveraging `LD_PRELOAD` and startup hook files, the reference implementation achieves this without modifying the PVM (e.g., Python), leveraging mature software stacks such as Trustee-KBS and Kata Containers, with critical components residing in the kernel as part of the measured TCB. Through several practical use cases, we demonstrate how *HIEST* prevents reuse attacks by permitting only the intended execution chain. Depending on the workload, *HIEST* introduces less than 10% overhead for the majority of our experiments, while only workloads under 43 ms of execution time incur relative overhead exceeding 15%.

Future Work. Having demonstrated the feasibility of hierarchical attestation for dynamic workloads, our future work will focus on two areas. First, we plan to develop sophisticated policy mechanisms on top of *HIEST* to establish mutual trust in multi-stakeholder environments. For example, confidential data from one owner could be released only after a specific combination of application, platform, and hardware from other owners has been verified. Second, since our reference implementation relies on file-based measurement via IMA, we will explore trusted in-memory measurement to address fileless workloads such as serverless functions, which currently fall outside the scope of our prototype.

Disclosure of Interests. The authors have no competing interests to declare that are relevant to the content of this article.

References

1. Ahmad, A., Ou, B., Liu, C., Zhang, X., Fonseca, P.: Veil: a protected services framework for confidential virtual machines. In: Proceedings of the 28th ACM International Conference on Architectural Support for Programming Languages and Operating Systems, vol. 4, pp. 378–393. ASPLOS '23, Association for Computing Machinery, New York, NY, USA (2024)
2. Arnautov, S., et al.: SCONE: secure linux containers with intel SGX. In: 12th USENIX Symposium on Operating Systems Design and Implementation (OSDI 16), pp. 689–703. USENIX Association, Savannah, GA (2016)
3. Catalano, J., Bravi, E., Sisinni, S., Lioy, A.: Enabling integrity measurement for secure applications in the enarx framework. J. Network Syst. Manage. **34**(1), 7 (2025)
4. Chen, X., et al.: The Janus interface: how fine-tuning in large language models amplifies the privacy risks. In: Proceedings of the 2024 on ACM SIGSAC Conference on Computer and Communications Security, pp. 1285–1299. CCS '24, Association for Computing Machinery, New York, NY, USA (2024)
5. Confidential Container projects: Trust model for confidential containers (2024). https://confidentialcontainers.org/docs/architecture/trust-model/trust-model/
6. Confidential Container projects: confidential containers (COCO) (2026). https://github.com/confidential-containers/
7. Confidential Container projects: init-data at confidential containers (COCO) (2026). https://confidentialcontainers.org/docs/features/initdata/
8. Edgeless Systems: Constellation: the Kubernetes built for confidential computing (2026). https://www.edgeless.systems/products/constellation
9. Eisoldt, J., et al.: A cloudy view on trust relationships of CVMs: how confidential virtual machines are falling short in public cloud. In: 2025 IEEE Annual Computer Security Applications Conference (ACSAC), pp. 440–453 (2025)
10. Galanou, A., Lubitz, F., Jeon, H., Fetzer, C., Kapitza, R.: Full Trust Alchemist: Reforging Attestation for Cloud-based Confidential Workloads. In: Proceedings of the 26th International Middleware Conference. pp. 369–382. Middleware '25, Association for Computing Machinery (2025)
11. Gregor, F., Krahn, R., Quoc, D.L., Fetzer, C.: SinClave: hardware-assisted singletons for TEEs. In: Proceedings of the 24th International Middleware Conference, pp. 85–97. Middleware '23, Association for Computing Machinery (2023)
12. Han, Z., Gao, C., Liu, J., Zhang, J., Zhang, S.Q.: Parameter-efficient fine-tuning for large models: a comprehensive survey (2024). https://arxiv.org/abs/2403.14608

13. Hartono, A.P.P., Brito, A., Fetzer, C.: CRISP: confidentiality, rollback, and integrity storage protection for confidential cloud-native computing. In: 2024 IEEE 17th International Conference on Cloud Computing (CLOUD), pp. 141–152 (2024)
14. Hartono, A.P.P., Fetzer, C.: BROFY: towards essential integrity protection for microservices. In: 2021 40th International Symposium on Reliable Distributed Systems (SRDS), pp. 154–163 (2021)
15. Jing, Y., Steiner, M., Vahldiek-Oberwagner, A., Vij, M., Vilanova, L.: Using recursive attestation to scale trust in modern heterogeneous cloud architectures. In: Proceedings of the 16th ACM SIGOPS Asia-Pacific Workshop on Systems, pp. 185–193. APSys '25, Association for Computing Machinery (2025)
16. Mireshghallah, F., Uniyal, A., Wang, T., Evans, D., Berg-Kirkpatrick, T.: An empirical analysis of memorization in fine-tuned autoregressive language models. In: Goldberg, Y., Kozareva, Z., Zhang, Y. (eds.) Proceedings of the 2022 Conference on Empirical Methods in Natural Language Processing, pp. 1816–1826. Association for Computational Linguistics, Abu Dhabi, United Arab Emirates (2022)
17. Misono, M., Stavrakakis, D., Santos, N., Bhatotia, P.: Confidential VMs explained: an empirical analysis of AMD SEV-SNP and intel TDX. Proc. ACM Meas. Anal. Comput. Syst **8**(3), (2024)
18. Mo, F., Tarkhani, Z., Haddadi, H.: Machine learning with confidential computing: a systematization of knowledge. ACM Comput. Surv. **56**(11) (2024)
19. Momose, A., Qin, K., Sakurai, A., Vij, M.: Securing nested attestation of confidential serverless computing without intra-enclave isolation. Cryptology ePrint Archive. Paper 2025/727 (2025)
20. Oh, M.G., Ahn, H.E., Park, L.H., Kwon, T.: Amplifying training data exposure through fine-tuning with pseudo-labeled memberships (2024). https://arxiv.org/abs/2402.12189
21. Ott, S., Kamhuber, M., Pecholt, J., Wessel, S.: Universal remote attestation for cloud and edge platforms. In: Proceedings of the 18th International Conference on Availability, Reliability and Security. ARES '23, Association for Computing Machinery, New York, NY, USA (2023)
22. OWASP Foundation, Inc: LLM01:2025 Prompt Injection (2026). https://genai.owasp.org/llmrisk/llm01-prompt-injection/
23. Pontes, D., Silva, F., Melo, A., Asadujjaman, A., Falcão, E., Brito, A., Filho, C.: Multi-platform and vault-free attestation of confidential VMs. In: Proceedings of the 13th Latin-American Symposium on Dependable and Secure Computing, pp. 241–251. LADC '24, Association for Computing Machinery, New York, NY, USA (2024)
24. Rauscher, F., Wilke, L., Weissteiner, H., Eisenbarth, T., Gruss, D.: TDXploit: Novel techniques for single-stepping and cache attacks on Intel TDX. In: 34th USENIX Security Symposium (USENIX Security 25), pp. 1207–1222 (2025)
25. Sampé, J., Sánchez-Artigas, M., Vernik, G., Yehekzel, I., García-López, P.: Outsourcing data processing jobs with lithops. IEEE Trans. Cloud Comput. **11**(1), 1026–1037 (2023)
26. Scopelliti, G., Baumann, C., Mühlberg, J.T.: Understanding trust relationships in cloud-based confidential computing. In: Proceedings of the 7th Workshop on System Software for Trusted Execution. SysTEX '24 (2024)
27. Segarra, C., Feldman-Fitzthum, T., Buono, D., Pietzuch, P.: Serverless confidential containers: challenges and opportunities. In: Proceedings of the 2nd Workshop on SErverless Systems, Applications and MEthodologies, pp. 32–40. SESAME '24, Association for Computing Machinery, New York, NY, USA (2024)

28. Song, J., Kim, B., Kwak, M., Lee, B., Seo, E., Jeong, J.: A secure, fast, and resource-efficient serverless platform with function REWIND. In: 2024 USENIX Annual Technical Conference (USENIX ATC 24), pp. 597–613. USENIX Association, Santa Clara, CA (2024)
29. Sorensen, T., Khlaaf, H.: LeftoverLocals: listening to LLM responses through leaked GPU local memory (2024)
30. SUSE: COCONUT-SVSM (2026). https://github.com/coconut-svsm/svsm
31. Tsai, C.C., Porter, D.E., Vij, M.: Graphene-SGX: a practical library OS for unmodified applications on SGX. In: Proceedings of the 2017 USENIX Conference on Usenix Annual Technical Conference, pp. 645–658. USENIX ATC '17, USENIX Association, USA (2017)
32. Valdez, E., Ahmed, S., Gu, Z., de Dinechin, C., Cheng, P.C., Jamjoom, H.: Crossing shifted moats: replacing old bridges with new tunnels to confidential containers. In: Proceedings of the 2024 on ACM SIGSAC Conference on Computer and Communications Security, pp. 1390–1404. CCS '24, Association for Computing Machinery, New York, NY, USA (2024)
33. Wang, W., et al.: The road to trust: building enclaves within confidential VMs. In: Proceedings 2025 Network and Distributed System Security Symposium. Internet Society (2025)
34. Würthinger, T., et al.: Practical partial evaluation for high-performance dynamic language runtimes. SIGPLAN Not. **52**(6), 662–676 (2017)
35. Xu, H., Xiang, J., Huang, Z., Chen, G., Meng, Y., Zhu, H.: Latte: layered attestation for portable enclaved applications. In: 2025 IEEE 10th European Symposium on Security and Privacy (EuroS&P), pp. 339–354 (2025)
36. Zhao, S., Li, M., Zhangyz, Y., Lin, Z.: vSGX: virtualizing SGX enclaves on AMD SEV. In: 2022 IEEE Symposium on Security and Privacy (SP), pp. 321–336 (2022)
37. Zhou, Z., Anjali, Chen, W., Gong, S., Hawblitzel, C., Cui, W.: VeriSMo: a verified security module for confidential VMs. In: 18th USENIX Symposium on Operating Systems Design and Implementation (OSDI 24), pp. 599–614 (2024)

PQ-PRIVÉ: A Post Quantum Privacy-Preserving Swarm Attestation

Nada El Kassem[1(✉)], Stefanos Vasileiadis[2], Evgenia-Niovi Sassalou[3], Georgios Fotiadis[4(✉)], Yalan Wang[1], Ioannis Siachos[4], Liqun Chen[1], Thanassis Giannetsos[4(✉)], Bruno Crispo[2], and Constantinos Patsakis[5]

[1] Surrey Centre for Cyber Security, University of Surrey, Surrey, UK
{nada.elkassem,yalan.wang,liqun.chen}@surrey.ac.uk
[2] University of Trento, Trento, Italy
{stefanos.vasileiadis,bruno.crispo}@unitn.it
[3] Qubitech Ltd., Athens, Greece
nsassalou@q.ubitech.eu
[4] Digital Security and Trusted Computing Group, Ubitech Ltd., Athens, Greece
{gfotiadis,isiachos,agiannetsos}@ubitech.eu
[5] Department of Informatics, University of Piraeus, Piraeus, Greece
kpatsak@unipi.gr

Abstract. In modern large-scale systems, composed of heterogeneous devices, swarm attestation schemes have emerged to address the scalability and efficiency limitations of traditional single-Prover and single-Verifier approaches. While the PRIVÉ swarm attestation scheme represents the first privacy-preserving swarm attestation scheme, its reliance on classical cryptographic techniques renders it vulnerable to quantum attacks. In this paper, we propose PQ-PRIVÉ, a post-quantum (PQ), privacy-preserving, scalable, and accountable swarm attestation scheme. Our design enables anonymous attestation while preserving device attribute privacy, and its quantum-resistant construction ensures suitability for deployment in the post-quantum era. To the best of our knowledge, this work presents the first PQ-secure swarm attestation scheme. Furthermore, we present experimental benchmarking results that demonstrate the efficiency and scalability of the proposed approach.

Keywords: Swarm Attestation · Privacy · Remote Attestation · Hash-based Cryptography

1 Introduction

As modern computing paradigms shift towards highly distributed edge and cloud architectures, critical infrastructures increasingly rely on massive networks of interconnected, resource-constrained devices. Establishing trust in these environments fundamentally relies on Remote Attestation (RA); a cryptographic mechanism enabling a verifier to assess the software and hardware integrity of a

Z. Afzal et al. (Eds.): ARES 2026 Workshops, LNCS 16900, pp. 253–271, 2027.
https://doi.org/10.1007/978-3-032-35576-8_14

remote device [2]. However, traditional single-prover, single-verifier RA protocols impose prohibitive communication and computational bottlenecks when applied at scale. To address this limitation, swarm attestation schemes have emerged to collectively verify the integrity of large device groups, significantly minimizing operational overhead [3].

Despite enhancing scalability, existing swarm attestation schemes struggle to accommodate the inherent heterogeneity of modern IoT ecosystems. Devices within a single swarm frequently originate from diverse supply chains, necessitating the verification of distinct, device-specific configurations. For instance, the integrity of an Intel-based device relies on the validity of its underlying Trusted Computing Base, whereas a device adopting a layered operational model relies on the correctness of its individual components. Consequently, the traditional model of attesting a uniform property across an entire swarm is no longer viable. This architectural evolution is formally recognized by the Internet Engineering Task Force (IETF) Remote ATtestation procedureS (RATS) working group [19], which highlights the inadequacy of monolithic verifiers and advocates for a composite, multi-prover and multi-verifier ecosystem. In this decentralized model, multiple untrusted verifiers (deemed as untrusted, in contrast to the trust model adopted by this work) must interact with varying device manufacturers to enforce heterogeneous appraisal policies. However, this introduces a critical privacy bottleneck: manufacturers possess highly sensitive hardware configurations. Exposing this privileged knowledge to untrusted external verifiers during the device lifecycle constitutes a severe privacy violation, demanding new models that inherently shield these secrets while facilitating distributed verification.

To realize this decentralized architecture without compromising interoperability, a secure swarm attestation protocol must guarantee *public verifiability* and *transparency* while strictly preserving *identity privacy*, and *attribute privacy*. Existing protocols fail to achieve this balance because they typically conflate the roles of manufacturers and verifiers, operating under the restrictive assumption that only privileged entities possessing the exact cryptographic witnesses can verify the swarm's integrity [1,3]. We resolve this limitation by strictly constraining the manufacturer to the role of an *endorser* rather than an active verifier. This decoupling ensures that any untrusted verifier can publicly appraise the swarm without ever requiring access to the underlying secrets. Furthermore, existing privacy-preserving protocols inherently assume the presence of heavyweight trusted components capable of secure non-volatile storage and static evidence tracing—assumptions fundamentally incompatible with the physical realities of low-end IoT devices [17]. Finally, their reliance on classical cryptographic primitives renders the current state-of-the-art critically vulnerable to emerging quantum computing threats, necessitating a rigorous transition to *post-quantum security* [16].

Contributions. In this work, we present PQ-PRIVÉ, the first post-quantum, privacy-preserving, and publicly verifiable swarm attestation scheme that achieves all of the aforementioned properties simultaneously. PQ-PRIVÉ is specifically engineered to support complex, multi-verifier architectures, enabling the transparent verification of an extended set of heterogeneous attributes without leaking the underlying reference values. Our main contributions are summarized as follows. First, we introduce a **post-quantum privacy-preserving swarm attestation** protocol that achieves post-quantum security while guaranteeing identity anonymity, attribute privacy, and public verifiability. Second, we present a **decoupled multi-verifier architecture** aligning with emerging IETF RATS paradigms, which enables multiple untrusted verifiers to securely appraise diverse attributes and allows manufacturers to participate as endorsers without exposing exact reference values, thereby ensuring robust evidence privacy. Third, we establish a **realistic lightweight trust anchor**. Diverging from the reliance on impractical, heavyweight secure elements, PQ-PRIVÉ is instantiated using Physical Unclonable Functions (PUFs) to provide a *true* lightweight hardware root of trust that facilitates on-demand key and evidence generation without vulnerable non-volatile memory, effectively neutralizing physical key-extraction attacks. Finally, through **practical implementation and benchmarking**, we provide a proof-of-concept demonstrating the scheme's efficiency in realistic environments, with experimental evaluations confirming that PQ-PRIVÉ is highly scalable and its performance is bounded primarily by the underlying communication medium rather than cryptographic operations.

Table 1. Comparison with existing swarm attestation protocols

Scheme	Topology	Identity Privacy	Attribute Privacy	Publicly Verifiable	Traceability	Post-Quantum
SEDA [3]	Spanning tree	×	×	×	×	×
SANA [1]	Spanning tree	×	×	✔	✔	×
US-AID [11]	Flat/Decentralized	×	×	×	×	×
PASTA [14]	Flat/Decentralized	×	×	×	×	×
SHeLA [18]	Hierarchy	×	×	×	✔	×
ESDRA [15]	Hierarchy/Distributed	×	×	×	×	×
SPARK [7]	Hierarchy	✔	×	✔	✔	×
PRIVÉ [6]	Hierarchy	✔	×	✔	✔	×
PIRANHAS [8]	Non-Hierarchical	✔	×	✔	×	×
PQ-PRIVÉ (Ours)	**Hierarchy**	✔	✔	✔	✔	✔

2 Related Work

Modern swarm attestation must guarantee scalability, identity and attribute privacy, public verifiability (supporting multiple provers and verifiers), and post-quantum security, all while relying on realistic hardware assumptions. Existing literature fails to satisfy these requirements simultaneously (Table 1).

SEDA [3] introduced scalable spanning-tree attestation, while ESDRA [15], US-AID [11], and PASTA [14] utilized flat or decentralized topologies. SHeLA [18] adopted hierarchical (Verifier→Edge→IoT) architectures for massive swarms. However, these early schemes lack privacy and public verifiability. SANA [1] achieved public verifiability but relied on a heavy trust model with unrealistic assumptions. Crucially, without public verifiability, earlier schemes cannot support the multi-prover, multi-verifier architectures required by modern heterogeneous swarms (as highlighted by recent IETF drafts).

Recent schemes like PRIVÉ [6], SPARK [7], and PIRANHAS [8] provide identity privacy and traceability. However, they inherently assume a monolithic verifier with global knowledge of all device reference values. In reality, reference values (e.g., PUF outputs) are known only to specific manufacturers (endorsers), who will not reveal them to external verifiers during the device lifecycle. Existing schemes fail to provide the *attribute and evidence privacy* necessary for this distributed trust model.

Regarding hardware trust assumptions, existing protocols simulate the behavior of an ideal lightweight trusted component by relying on traditional, heavyweight trusted components (requiring secure non-volatile storage and static evidence tracing), which resource-constrained IoT devices cannot support in real life. In contrast, PQ-PRIVÉ leverages a *true* lightweight trusted component—a Physical Unclonable Function (PUF)—to dynamically generate keys and evidence at runtime, eliminating the need for secure non-volatile storage.

Finally, existing privacy-preserving swarm attestation schemes rely exclusively on classical cryptographic primitives. PQ-PRIVÉ is the first and only scheme to provide post-quantum security alongside identity privacy, attribute privacy, and traceability.

3 Building Blocks

3.1 Modified W-OTS$^+$ One-Time Signatures

W-OTS$^+$ is a Winternitz type OTS scheme, introduced by Hülsing in [10], that follows the W-OTS (hash-based) construction paradigm, originally described in [4]. Since W-OTS$^+$ is an OTS scheme, each private key *must be used only once* to sign a single message, otherwise the scheme becomes insecure [9]. W-OTS$^+$ consists of the usual $(\mathsf{KG}, \mathsf{Sign}, \mathsf{Verify})$ functions for key generation, signing and verification, as described in Algorithm 1. To meet the PQ-PRIVÉ requirements, Algorithm 1 includes a modified KG function, in which the randomness used internally in KG is replaced with external randomness given as input.

Initialization. W-OTS$^+$ is parameterized by the security parameter $\lambda \in \mathbb{N}$, the message length n and the *Winternitz parameter* $w \in \mathbb{N}$, which is typically chosen as a power of 2. The Winternitz parameter determines the time-memory trade-off [10]; a larger value of w results in shorter signatures but slower overall signing operations, while it has little effect on security [9]. According to RFC 8391 [9], typical choices of w are limited to the values 4 and 16, since these choices yield optimal trade-offs and easy implementation. These parameters are used to compute the system values ℓ_1, ℓ_2 and ℓ, such that $\ell_1 = \lceil n/\log_2 w \rceil$, $\ell_2 = \lfloor \log_2(\ell_1(w-1))/\log_2 w \rfloor$ and $\ell = \ell_1 + \ell_2$, which are crucial for the encoding of the message and determine the length of the signature, as well as the size of the private/public signing key pairs.

Algorithm 1: Modified W-OTS$^+$ scheme W-OTS$^+$ = (KG, Sign, Verify).

function KG(R, α, ch):
- $count \leftarrow ch[0,7]$, $ch \leftarrow ch[8,255]$
- **for** $i = 1, \ldots, \ell$ **do**
  - $\text{sk}_i \leftarrow H(R \| count + i)$
- $\text{sk} \leftarrow (\text{sk}_1, \ldots, \text{sk}_\ell)$
- **for** $i = 1, \ldots, w-1$ **do**
  - $r_i \leftarrow H(\alpha \| ch \| count + i)$
- $\boldsymbol{r} \leftarrow (r_1, \ldots, r_{w-1})$, $\text{pk}_0 \leftarrow \boldsymbol{r}$
- **for** $i = 1, \ldots, \ell$ **do**
  - $\text{pk}_i \leftarrow H^{w-1}(\text{sk}_i, \boldsymbol{r})$
- $\text{pk} \leftarrow (\text{pk}_0, \text{pk}_1, \ldots, \text{pk}_\ell)$
- **return** (sk, pk)

function Sign(sk, M, $\boldsymbol{r}$):
- $M \leftarrow (M_1, \ldots, M_{\ell_1}) = \texttt{base\_w}(M)$
- $C \leftarrow \sum_{i=1}^{\ell_1} (w - 1 - M_i)$
- $C \leftarrow (C_1, \ldots, C_{\ell_2}) = \texttt{base\_w}(C)$
- $B \leftarrow (b_1, \ldots, b_\ell) = (M \| C)$
- **for** $i = 1, \ldots, \ell$ **do**
  - $\sigma_i \leftarrow H^{b_i}(\text{sk}_i, \boldsymbol{r})$
- $\sigma \leftarrow (\sigma_1, \ldots, \sigma_\ell)$
- **return** (σ)

function Verify(pk, M, σ):
- $M \leftarrow (M_1, \ldots, M_{\ell_1}) = \texttt{base\_w}(M)$
- $C \leftarrow \sum_{i=1}^{\ell_1} (w - 1 - M_i)$
- $C \leftarrow (C_1, \ldots, C_{\ell_2}) = \texttt{base\_w}(C)$
- $B \leftarrow (b_1, \ldots, b_\ell) = (M \| C)$
- $\text{pk}'_0 \leftarrow \boldsymbol{r}$
- **for** $i = 1, \ldots, \ell$ **do**
  - $\text{pk}'_i \leftarrow H^{w-1-b_i}(\sigma_i, r_{b_i+1, w-1})$
- $\text{pk}' \leftarrow (\text{pk}'_0, \text{pk}'_1, \ldots, \text{pk}'_\ell)$
- **if** $\text{pk} = \text{pk}'$ **then**
  - **return** (1)
- **else**
  - **return** (0)

Key Generation. The KG algorithm of W-OTS$^+$ constructs the secret key as a vector $\text{sk} = (\text{sk}_1, \ldots, \text{sk}_\ell)$ of ℓ random components sk_i. In addition, it constructs a public vector $\boldsymbol{r} = (r_1, \ldots, r_{w-1})$ of $w-1$ random elements r_i. In PQ-PRIVÉ we require two distinct parties to be able to generate the same W-OTS$^+$ keys pairs, which implies that the same randomness must be used in both ends. In Algorithm 1, we present a modified KG function that takes as input the external random values R, α and ch. The value R is the output of a PUF (2331 bits), α is a 256-bit string that describes an attribute, and ch is a random 256-bit challenge. In order to generate $\ell + w - 1$ random values, we implement a *Mask Generation Function (MGF)*, in particular the MGF1 function [13], which allows to expand a random input of variable length to a random output of arbitrary length. This requires the use of a counter *count*, initialized with the same value at both ends that execute the KG function[1]. Following the MGF1 approach, each component of the secret key is constructed as $\text{sk}_i = H(R \| count + i)$, for $i = 1, \ldots, \ell$, while each component of the vector $\boldsymbol{r}$ is generated via $r_i = H(\alpha \| ch \| count + i)$, for $i = 1, \ldots, w-1$. The public key is a vector $\text{pk} = (\text{pk}_0, \text{pk}_1, \ldots, \text{pk}_\ell)$ of $\ell + 1$ components, where $\text{pk}_0 = \boldsymbol{r}$ and $\text{pk}_i = H^{w-1}(\text{sk}_i, \boldsymbol{r})$, for each $i = 1, \ldots, \ell$. The

[1] In our implementation, *count* is initialized with the first 8 bits of ch (i.e., $count \leftarrow ch[0,7]$). These 8 bits are removed from the challenge ch (i.e., $ch \leftarrow ch[8,255]$).

hash function exponentiation is defined as:

$$H^j(\mathrm{sk}_i, \boldsymbol{r}) = \begin{cases} \mathrm{sk}_i, & j = 0 \\ H(H^{j-1}(\mathrm{sk}_i, \boldsymbol{r}) \oplus r_i), & j > 0 \end{cases}$$

which implies that each hashing step is masked with a unique, random value r_i, therefore ensuring randomized hashing. KG outputs the key pair (sk, pk).

Signing. The signature generation requires encoding the n-bit message M into its w-ary representation $M = (M_1, \ldots, M_{\ell_1})$, where each $M_i \in \{0, \ldots, w-1\}$. This is described via the function base_2 in Algorithm 1. The algorithm encodes also the checksum C into its w-ary representation $C = (C_1, \ldots, C_{\ell_2})$. The two w-ary vectors are concatenated to produce the vector $B = (b_1, \ldots, b_\ell) = (M \| C)$, in which case the signature σ corresponds to the ℓ-tuple $\sigma = (\sigma_1, \ldots, \sigma_\ell)$, where $\sigma_i = H^{b_i}(\mathrm{sk}_i, \boldsymbol{r})$ for each $i = 1, \ldots, \ell$ (see Sign function in Algorithm 1).

Verification. On input the message M, the signature σ and the public key pk, the verification process requires the reconstruction of the vector $B = (M \| C)$ in w-ary representation and verifying the equation:

$$\mathrm{pk} \stackrel{?}{=} \left(\boldsymbol{r}, H^{w-1-b_1}(\sigma_1, \boldsymbol{r}_{b_1+1,w-1}), \ldots, H^{w-1-b_\ell}(\sigma_\ell, \boldsymbol{r}_{b_\ell+1,w-1})\right)$$

where $\boldsymbol{r}_{a,b} = (r_a, \ldots, r_b)$ if $b < a$ and $\boldsymbol{r}_{a,b} = \emptyset$, otherwise. If the above equation is satisfied, the Verify function (Algorithm 1) outputs 1, otherwise it outputs 0.

4 System and Thread Models

System Model. We consider a (static) interconnected network of heterogeneous devices comprising v edge devices and K IoT devices, following a hierarchical fog computing structure [12]. The cryptographic material managed by each layer of devices throughout the PQ-PRIVÉ operational workflow is depicted in Fig. 1 and detailed in Sect. 5.

- ***IoT Devices (D).*** IoT devices are untrusted and identified as D_k for $k \in [1, K]$. Each device contains a minimal Trusted Computing Base (TCB) instantiated with Physically Unclonable Functions (PUFs), providing a unique hardware-based identity derived from manufacturing variations. Consequently, even if a device is compromised, its physical characteristics remain difficult to replicate.
- ***Edge Devices (E).*** Edge devices are semi-trusted entities connected to IoT devices. They verify IoT contributions before forwarding aggregated results to an external verifier, validate the authenticity of IoT-generated data, and construct the swarm authentication path. Edge devices can also trace back IoT devices that fail attestation.
- ***Trusted Manufacturer (MF).*** The trusted manufacturer represents the entities responsible for IoT device fabrication. Each manufacturer possesses the long-term PUF-related secret embedded during production, which is used to generate PUF responses for given challenges.

- ***Domain Manager (DM).*** The Domain Manager is a trusted third party acting as the issuer. It defines swarm membership and maintains global knowledge of the IoT devices participating in the system.
- ***Verifier ($\mathcal{V}$).*** The Verifier initiates the attestation process and validates the trustworthiness of the swarm. The verifier is assumed to be honest-but-curious, meaning it follows the protocol correctly while potentially attempting to infer additional information from the received attestation data. The Domain Manager may also act as the verifier.

Table 2. PQ-PRIVÉ notation

Symbol	Description
a_p	Name of attribute p
$\alpha_p/\bar{\alpha}_p$	Golden value/runtime value of attribute a_p
N, P, K, v	Number of challenges, attributes, IoT devices, and Edge devices, respectively
$\mathrm{ak}_i^{k,p}$	W-OTS$^+$ signing key pair $(\mathrm{sk}_i^{k,p}, \mathrm{pk}_i^{k,p})$ for attribute p, challenge i, device k
R_i^k	PUF output for challenge i and device k (2331 bits in our implementation)
ch_i	Random challenge of size 256 bits
$\mathtt{AMT}_i^k$	Attribute Merkle Tree for challenge ch_i and IoT device k
$\mathsf{MerkleTree}(h_1, \ldots, h_n)$	Constructs a Merkle Tree with leaf nodes $h_1, \ldots, h_n$
$\mathtt{root.AMT}_i^k$	Extract the root of the $\mathtt{AMT}_i^k$
AK_i^k	Master one-time attribute key of kth PUF; root of $\mathtt{AMT}_i^k$ Merkle tree
PK_i^k	Low-end one-time public key for IoT device k and challenge ch_i
PK_i	Swarm one-time public key
$\mathtt{SMT}$, mpk	Swarm Merkle Tree with root mpk
$\mathrm{AA} = \mathsf{AuthPath}(\mathtt{AMT}, h)$	Computes the authentication of $\mathtt{AMT}$ for leaf node h
$\Sigma_i^{k,p}$	Attribute Merkle Signature for attribute p, challenge i, device k
$\mathsf{extract}(\mathrm{AA}, h)$	Reconstruct Merkle tree root from authentication path AA and leaf h

Threat Model. We consider three classes of adversaries. First, remote software adversaries (Adv_{SW}) aim to compromise IoT and edge devices by exploiting software vulnerabilities and injecting malicious code. Second, honest-but-curious adversaries (Adv_{HBC}) legitimately participate in the swarm execution while attempting to infer sensitive information, particularly the attribute values associated with IoT devices. Third, network adversaries (Adv_{NET}) can intercept, modify, replay, delay, drop, and forge messages exchanged between communicating entities within the swarm. We assume a standard Dolev–Yao (DY) adversarial model [5], in which the adversary has full control over the communication channels between IoT devices and edge devices, and between edge devices and external verifiers.

5 The PQ-PRIVÉ Protocol

In this section we present the details of the PQ-PRIVÉ protocol and describe its main procedures. In particular, the protocol enables four main phases, namely, the `JOIN`, `ATTESTATION`, `VERIFICATION`, and `REVOKE` phases, of low-end IoT devices within a swarm managed by Edge devices (Table 2).

To support scalable and privacy-preserving swarm attestation, PQ-PRIVÉ organizes cryptographic material in a *Merkle forest* construction. For each IoT device, the MF generates a collection of one-time W-OTS$^+$ attribute keys, based on device-specific PUF responses (to a specific set of (public) challenges that can later be used for the attestation of distinct device properties). The public parts of these attribute keys are arranged into an *Attribute Merkle Tree* (AMT) structure, whose root serves as a commitment to all attested attributes of the target IoT device. The root of each AMT is then used to derive a one-time public key. These one-time public keys for all IoT devices (belonging to a *swarm*) are aggregated to construct a higher-level *Swarm Merkle Tree* (SMT). In this way, the AMTs form the lower-layer of the Merkle forest, while the SMT provides a single swarm commitment that enables the efficient verification of IoT device attribute attestations - even for different sets of attributes per device, thus, achieving intelligent swarm attestation automatically grouping devices by the attested attributes without the need od running multiple (exhaustive) verification processes. Throughout this operation, the MF generates and distributes the (device-specific) cryptographic material; the DM is responsible for composing and publishing the swarm commitment; while the Edge device receives all necessary information to securely interact (through symmetric keys) with the associated (children) IoT devices. Figure 1 illustrates an example of the Merkle forest structure for a swarm consisting of K IoT devices. Each device contributes 8 AMTs, corresponding to 8 different random challenges, where each AMT root is a commitment to 4 attributes. The resulting device-level commitments are aggregated into the SMT that provides a single commitment for the entire swarm.

Setup and Join Phase. Figure 2 illustrates the protocol steps for the `SETUP` and `JOIN` procedures. Assuming the successful enrollment of a high-end device (Edge) to the corresponding domain, the DM can assign low-end devices (IoT) as its child devices. The DM generates $N = 2^n$ random challenges $ch_1, \ldots, ch_N$. The DM sends these challenges, together with the IoT identifiers, to their corresponding manufacturers, along with the identifiers of possible parent edge devices (ID_j) and the set of attributes to be attested a_p, for $p \in [1, P]$.

One-time attribute keys. We define P attributes for low-end devices that are known to external verifiers. Let $a_1, \ldots, a_P$ denote the attribute names, where $p \in [1, P]$ is the attribute identifier. The MF computes one-time attribute (signing) keys using the W-OTS$^+$ KG function (Algorithm 1), which takes as input the kth PUF response R_i^k (derived from challenge ch_i), together with the golden value α_p, representing the expected correct value of an attribute a_p, and a challenge

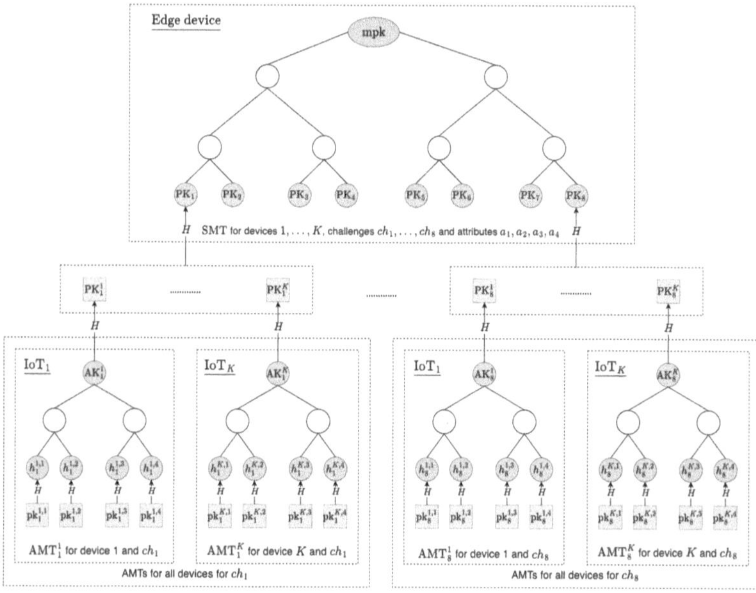

Fig. 1. PQ-PRIVÉ key hierarchy represented as Merkle forest

ch_i. It outputs a $\mathsf{W\text{-}OTS}^+$ attribute key pair:

$$\mathrm{ak}_i^{k,p} = (\mathrm{sk}_i^{k,p}, \mathrm{pk}_i^{k,p}) = \mathsf{KG}(R_i^k, \alpha_p, ch_i).$$

Attribute Merkle Tree (AMT). The MF constructs the kth AMT (denoted by $\mathtt{AMT}_i^k$) for each challenge ch_i, using the hashes of the one-time attribute public keys $h_i^{k,p} = H(\mathrm{pk}_i^{k,p})$, for $p \in [1, P]$ as leaf nodes. This process is denoted by $\mathtt{AMT}_i^k \leftarrow \mathsf{MerkleTree}(h_i^{k,1}, \ldots, h_i^{k,P})$ in Fig. 2. The internal nodes are computed recursively until the root node AK_i^k is obtained (we write $\mathrm{AK}_i^k = \mathtt{root.AMT}_i^k$), which serves as the *master one-time attribute key* of the kth PUF and challenge ch_i. Each attribute key must be uniquely bound to its corresponding attribute domain. Therefore, given the public component of an attribute key pair, any entity should be able to determine the associated attribute domain.

Low-end one-time public keys. For each challenge ch_i, the MF generates the kth *low-end device's one-time public key* PK_i^k using a key derivation function (KDF) with the AMT root node AK_i^k as input. Each MF sends the set of public keys PK_i^k for all $i \in [1, N]$ to the DM.

Swarm one-time public keys. Upon receiving all PK_i^k from different IoT device manufacturers in the swarm, for all $k \in [1, K]$ and $i \in [1, N]$, the DM concatenates them to obtain the *swarm one-time public key* for challenge ch_i, namely $\mathrm{PK}_i = \mathrm{PK}_i^1 \| \ldots \| \mathrm{PK}_i^K$, for $i \in [1, N]$.

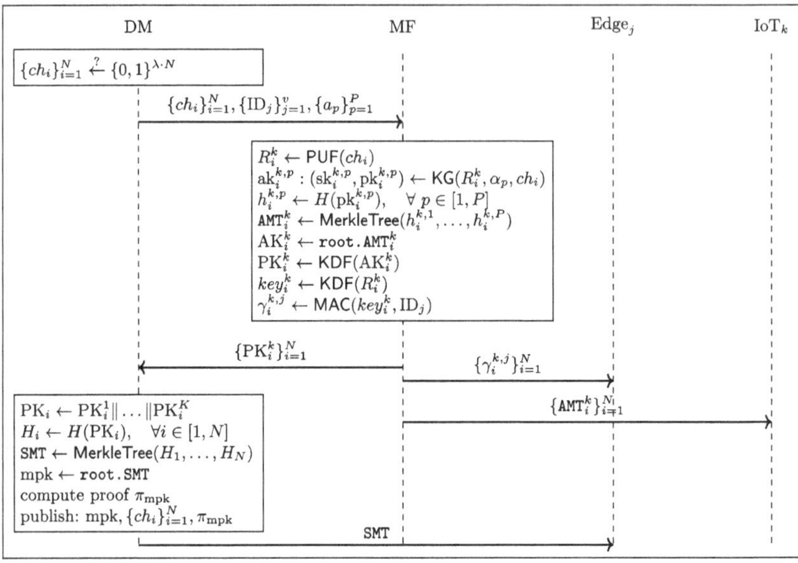

Fig. 2. Join phase.

Authentication key for high-end devices. For the Edge device j associated with the IoT device k, the MF derives a symmetric key key_i^k from the PUF response R_i^k using a KDF. It then computes an authentication tag $\gamma_i^{k,j} = \mathsf{MAC}(key_i^k, \text{ID}_j)$ and sends it to the corresponding Edge device j. These authentication tags allow each IoT to authenticate its corresponding parent edge device before communication. We assume that each Edge device behaves honestly and does not share $\gamma_i^{k,j}$ with other Edge devices. Each MF also sends $\mathtt{AMT}_i^k$ to each IoT k in the swarm. The DM constructs the Swarm Merkle Tree ($\mathtt{SMT}$), using the hash values $H_i = H(\text{PK}_i)$ of the swarm one-time public keys as leaf nodes, for all $i \in [1, N]$. In Fig. 2, this process is denoted by $\mathtt{SMT} = \mathsf{MerkleTree}(H_1, \ldots, H_N)$. The DM publishes the root node mpk of $\mathtt{SMT}$, together with the challenges $\{ch_i\}_{i \in [1,N]}$ and a proof π_{mpk} of mpk construction. It then sends $\mathtt{SMT}$ to Edge device j, and the identity ID_j to each IoT device $k \in [1, K]$.

Attestation and Report Phase. Figure 3 summarizes the `ATTESTATION` and `REPORT` procedures. To initiate a swarm attestation for the enrolled devices in its domain, the DM sends a fresh, previously unused challenge ch_i to the corresponding high-end devices. Each challenge is used only once to prevent replay attacks, with a counter i tracking the challenges. In addition to ch_i, the DM also sends an attribute identifier p specifying which attribute must be attested for each IoT device. Note that the protocol supports heterogeneous attributes within the same swarm under a single challenge.

The high-end device j, with identity ID_j, forwards ch_i together with the corresponding authentication tag $\gamma_i^{k,j}$ and the requested attribute identifier p

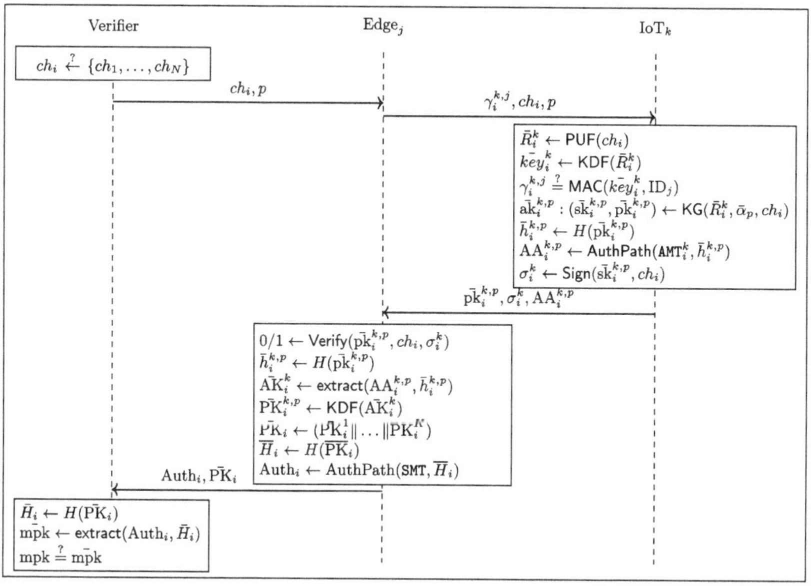

Fig. 3. Attestation/ Verification phase.

to each of its K child IoT devices. The kth IoT device, equipped with a PUF, computes the response $\bar{R}_i^k$ for ch_i and authenticates the high-end device by verifying $\gamma_i^{k,j} \overset{?}{=} \mathsf{MAC}(\bar{R}_i^k, \mathrm{ID}_j)$. Upon receiving ch_i and the attribute identifier p from the DM, each IoT device computes the $\mathsf{W\text{-}OTS}^+$ attribute-specific key corresponding to the current attribute value $\bar{\alpha}_p$, as described in Sect. 3.1:

$$\bar{\mathrm{ak}}_i^{k,p} = (\bar{\mathrm{sk}}_i^{k,p}, \bar{\mathrm{pk}}_i^{k,p}) = \mathsf{KG}(\bar{R}_i^k, \bar{\alpha}_p, ch_i).$$

Using $\mathtt{AMT}_i^k$, the kth IoT computes the *Attribute Authentication path* $\mathrm{AA}_i^{k,p} = \mathsf{AuthPath}(\mathtt{AMT}_i^k, \bar{h}_i^{k,p})$, where $\bar{h}_i^{k,p} = H(\bar{\mathrm{pk}}_i^{k,p})$ is the leaf corresponding to attribute p. Each IoT signs ch_i using its secret attribute key $\bar{\mathrm{sk}}_i^{k,p}$, producing a $\mathsf{W\text{-}OTS}^+$ signature σ_i^k and sends the *Attribute Merkle Signature (AMS)* $\Sigma_i^{k,p} = (\bar{\mathrm{pk}}_i^{k,p}, \sigma_i^k, \mathrm{AA}_i^{k,p})$ to its parent Edge device j that initiated the attestation.

After receiving responses from all K IoT devices, the high-end devices verify each signature σ_i^k with the corresponding key $\bar{\mathrm{pk}}_i^{k,p}$ for all $k \in [1, K]$. If any verification fails, the high-end device aborts the protocol. Otherwise, each Edge device reconstructs the root $\bar{\mathrm{AK}}_i^k$ of $\mathtt{AMT}_i^k$ from the authentication path $\mathrm{AA}_i^{k,p}$ and the leaf hash $\bar{h}_i^{k,p} = H(\bar{\mathrm{pk}}_i^{k,p})$, denoted by $\mathsf{extract}(\mathrm{AA}_i^{k,p}, \bar{h}_i^{k,p})$. Using $\bar{\mathrm{AK}}_i^k$, the high-end device computes $\bar{\mathrm{PK}}_i^k = \mathsf{KDF}(\bar{\mathrm{AK}}_i^k)$ and reconstructs the swarm one-time public key for the challenge ch_i, namely $\bar{\mathrm{PK}}_i = \bar{\mathrm{PK}}_i^1 \| \ldots \| \bar{\mathrm{PK}}_i^K$.

Verification Phase. We distinguish two verification cases in PQ-PRIVÉ, depending on whether the Verifier is the is the DM or an external entity. In the latter case, the Edge device sends the *Swarm Authentication Path* $\text{Auth}_i = \mathsf{AuthPath}(\mathtt{SMT}, H(\bar{\text{PK}}_i))$ and $\bar{\text{PK}}_i$ to the Verifier. The Verifier computes the SMT leaf node $\bar{H}_i = H(\bar{\text{PK}}_i)$ and using Auth_i, it recomputes the root $\bar{\text{mpk}} = \mathsf{extract}(\text{Auth}_i, \bar{H}_i)$, which is compared with mpk. If the two values are equal, the verifier declares the Swarm Merkle Signature as valid; otherwise, it rejects it. Upon successful verification, the Verifier is convinced that each IoT satisfies the attested attribute matches the golden value without knowing the exact current attribute value. This provides *Attribute Privacy.* If the verification and the revocation check pass, then the Verifier outputs 1 (`accept`); otherwise, 0 (`reject`). In the case where the DM acts as a verifier, the Edge device sends only the swarm one-time public key $\bar{\text{PK}}_i$ to the Verifier and the Verifier checks whether the leaf node of SMT corresponding to the challenge ch_i matches $H(\bar{\text{PK}}_i)$.

Revocation. PQ-PRIVÉ supports the revocation of misbehaving IoT devices that consistently fail attestation, which is handled at the Edge device level. To revoke an IoT device, the parent Edge device adds the identity of the IoT to a revocation list RL and informs the DM so that the SMT can be updated for future attestations. Edge devices are assumed to be semi-trusted, therefore, they can also be attested in the same way as IoT devices by incorporating their public keys into PK_i during the join phase and consequently into $\bar{\text{PK}}_i$ during the attestation phase. Furthermore, Edge devices can be attested in a privacy-preserving manner, allowing an external verifier to be convinced that the Edge device is behaving as expected without revealing either its identity or its configuration.

6 PQ-PRIVÉ Security Analysis

This section introduces the security requirements of our protocol. In particular, we define the essential properties that the scheme must satisfy, including correctness, integrity, anonymity, traceability, unforgeability, non-frameability, and attribute privacy. We then analyze how these properties are achieved based on the underlying cryptographic and hardware assumptions, and show that the proposed protocol satisfies all the defined security requirements.

6.1 Security Requirements

In this section, we define the security properties required by our swarm attestation protocol. These properties capture the essential goals of the system, including privacy, correctness, accountability, and unforgeability. The model also guarantees that only legitimate devices can generate valid attestations and that attribute information remains hidden during verification. Together, these properties provide a balanced framework for security, privacy, and controllability in the proposed system.

- ***SP1: Anonymity.*** It should be possible to conceal the identity of IoT devices from the verifier $\mathcal{V}$ via anonymous signatures that hide device identities within the swarm.
- ***SP2: Traceability.*** The opener must be able to trace attestation failures to their source, enabling the identification of compromised IoT devices. A parent edge device can revoke a corrupt child IoT device, ***SP3: Revocation***.
- ***SP4: Correctness.*** Honestly generated signatures are always accepted, and honest devices are never revoked.
- ***SP5: Non-frameability.*** An adversary cannot generate signatures that impersonate honest devices or are traced back to them. In particular, ***SP6: Unforgeability*** ensures that it is computationally infeasible to forge a valid signature σ on a message μ without an honest signer.
- ***SP7: Attribute Privacy.*** A verifier can validate attribute correctness without learning the actual attribute values or their intended reference values.

6.2 Overview of the Security Analysis

To formally establish the security of the proposed swarm attestation protocol, we relate the security requirements defined in Sect. 6.1 to standard cryptographic assumptions underlying the construction. In particular, we show that each requirement is satisfied based on the security of the employed primitives, including the collision resistance of hash functions, the existential unforgeability of the WOTS$^+$ and Merkle signature scheme, the pseudorandomness of the key derivation function, and the unclonability of the PUF.

The analysis proceeds by examining how the protocol enforces integrity, privacy, and authenticity across the Attribute Merkle Tree (AMT) and Swarm Merkle Tree (SMT) structures, as well as how device-specific cryptographic material is bound to hardware-generated secrets. This allows us to argue that only legitimate devices can generate valid attestations, while sensitive attribute and identity information remains hidden from external verifiers.

We then formally state a theorem capturing all required security properties, followed by a unified proof sketch that shows how each property follows from the underlying cryptographic assumptions and construction of the protocol.

Theorem 1 (Security of PQ-PRIVÉ). *Assuming the collision resistance of the underlying hash function, the existential unforgeability of the WOTS$^+$ and Merkle-based signature scheme, the pseudorandomness of the key derivation function, and the unclonability and unpredictability of the PUF, PQ-PRIVÉ satisfies integrity, correctness, anonymity, traceability, non-frameability, unforgeability and attribute privacy against any probabilistic polynomial-time adversary.*

The security of PQ-PRIVÉ follows from the security guarantees of its underlying cryptographic and hardware primitives. Namely, the integrity of the protocol is ensured by the Merkle-based constructions used in both the Attribute Merkle Tree (AMT) and the Swarm Merkle Tree (SMT). Each root value is a hash-based commitment to its leaf values. Due to the collision resistance of the hash function, it is infeasible for an adversary to modify any leaf (such as attribute public keys or device public keys) without changing the corresponding root or producing a hash collision. Hence, all authenticated data structures preserve integrity. Unforgeability follows from the existential unforgeability of the WOTS^+ and Merkle signature scheme. Without access to the corresponding secret keys derived from PUF outputs, it is computationally infeasible for an adversary to produce valid signatures or correct authentication paths. Any successful forgery would therefore contradict the security of the underlying hash-based signature construction.

Correctness follows from the correctness of the WOTS^+ signing and verification algorithms, the Merkle authentication procedures, and the key derivation function. Honest devices executing the protocol always generate signatures and authentication paths that verify successfully at both the edge and verifier levels. Moreover, the PUF produces deterministic and repeatable responses for a given challenge, ensuring consistency between the enrolment phase and the attestation phase. Traceability holds because each device is bound to a unique PUF response, which deterministically defines its signing keys and Merkle structure. Therefore, any valid attestation can be uniquely associated with a single device identity, ensuring one-to-one accountability and enabling the identification of misbehaving devices through their cryptographic material.

Anonymity is achieved because protocol messages do not contain explicit device identifiers, and all cryptographic outputs are derived from fresh challenge-dependent PUF responses and attribute-dependent key material. As a result, external verifiers observing protocol transcripts cannot recover or infer the identity of the underlying IoT device beyond negligible probability. Attribute privacy follows from the pseudorandomness of the key derivation function and the hash-based hiding of attribute keys inside the AMT. During verification, only the validity of the attribute condition is revealed, while the actual attribute values and their underlying representations remain hidden from the verifier.

Non-frameability is guaranteed since producing a valid signature requires knowledge of the correct device-specific secret keys derived from unclonable PUF outputs. An adversary cannot generate valid attestations that can be attributed to an honest device without breaking either the unforgeability of the underlying signature scheme or the security properties of the PUF. Revocation security is ensured by maintaining a revocation list and excluding revoked identities from valid authentication structures. Any revoked device attempting to produce valid attestations would fail verification due to inconsistencies in the Merkle-based authentication structure or mismatches with registered device credentials.

Since all security properties reduce to the security of the underlying primitives, any adversary that breaks one of the stated properties would contradict at least one of the underlying assumptions. Therefore, PQ-PRIVÉ satisfies the stated security properties against any probabilistic polynomial-time adversary.

Table 3. Key/signature size for W-OTS$^+$ and AMTS (in bytes) & number of hash functions.

	W-OTS$^+$			AMTS
value	sk	pk	σ	Σ
size	2144	2624	2144	4832
function	KG	Sign	Verify	AMTS
#hashes	1087	500	500	1505

Table 4. Execution time of W-OTS$^+$ functions on different devices: IoT (Nordic), Edge (RPi) and MF (PC).

W-OTS$^+$ benchmarks (in ms)			
Device	IoT (Nordic)	Edge (RPi)	MF
KG	246.6843	-	0.5707
Sign	110.7840	-	-
Verify	-	8.054	-

7 Complexity Analysis and Performance Evaluation

We present the cost analysis and experimental evaluation of PQ-PRIVÉ, assuming a fixed setup with $P = 4$ attributes (a_1 (secure boot), a_2 (key restriction user policy), a_3 (authenticated tracer) and a_4 (certified PUF)) and $K = 4$ IoT devices. The evaluation considers varying number of challenges $N \in \{2, 4, 8\}$ and excludes fixed overheads added by the PUF (4 s) and the Bluetooth communication (2 s for pairing and 2 s for closing), which are independent of PQ-PRIVÉ. The MF and DM are emulated on a Dell Server with Intel Core i9-1.3GHz . The Edge device is a Rasberry Pi 3 Model B+ and for low-end devices we consider commodity IoT hardware for healthcare applications[2].

W-OTS$^+$. In PQ-PRIVÉ, the W-OTS$^+$ signature scheme is used to sign challenges ch_i of size 256 bits, hence $n = 256$. In addition, we set the Winternitz parameter $w = 16$, so that $\ell_1 = 64$, $\ell_2 = 3$ and $\ell = \ell_1 + \ell_2 = 67$. The corresponding key and signature sizes are reported in Table 3. The computational cost of KG, Sign and Verify is dominated by SHA-256 hash executions. Based on our instantiation, KG requires 1087 hash computations, while Sign and Verify require approximately 500 hashes on average, depending on the w-ary representation $(b_1, \ldots, b_\ell) = (ch_i \| C)$, where C is the checksum (see Sect. 3.1). Table 4 presents the execution time of the W-OTS$^+$ functions measured on the considered three platforms. Although the execution time of KG on the IoT is significantly slower than on the MF, the results confirm the practical feasibility of deploying PQ signatures on low-end devices with acceptable performance overhead.

MF Cost. Figure 4 illustrates the computational and communication overhead incurred by the MF during the Join phase for different numbers of challenges $N \in \{2, 4, 8\}$. The performance results show that the dominant operation is the W-OTS$^+$ KG function, which is executed $8N$ times (for all devices and all attributes), resulting in an execution time ranging from 17.88 to 74.94 ms. In contrast, the construction of the corresponding $8N$ AMTs adds negligible cost in all cases. The evaluation excludes PUF computations, which contribute a fixed overhead of 4 sec per execution, as well as the lightweight cryptographic operations (HMAC, KDF). The communication cost analysis in Fig. 4 shows that

[2] https://www.nordicsemi.com/Products/Development-hardware/nRF52840-DK.

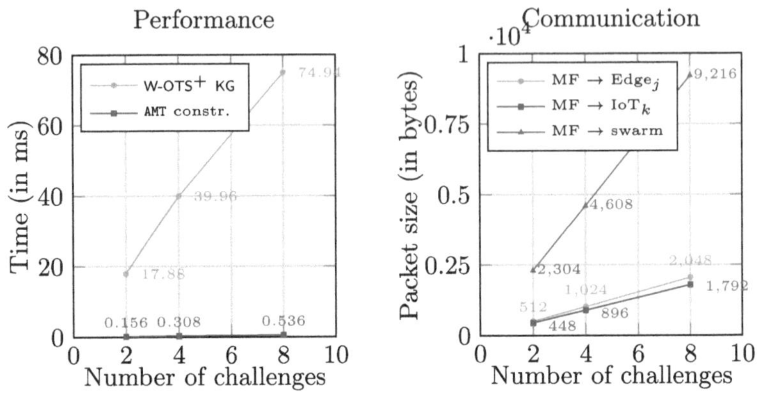

Fig. 4. Execution time of core crypto operations and communication cost for MF.

the packet size transmitted by the MF to the swarm grows linearly in N. During the Join phase, the MF transmits $8N$ HMAC authentication tags of 32 bytes each to the Edge device and $4N$ AMTs of 224 bytes each to the IoT devices, leading to a total swarm communication overhead between 2304 and 9216 bytes.

IoT & Edge Cost. Figure 5 presents the performance of the main cryptographic operations performed by the IoT and Edge during the Attestation phase. On the IoT side, the dominant overhead is introduced by the W-OTS$^+$ KG and Sign processes, with execution times of 246.68 ms and 110.78 ms, respectively, while the HMAC computation incurs only minor cost. The reported values exclude the PUF evaluation, which contributes a fixed overhead of 4 sec per IoT. On the Edge side, the verification of 4 W-OTS$^+$ signatures represents the main computational task (32.216 ms), whereas the the verification of AMTs and the construction of the one-time public keys remain negligible (below 1 ms).

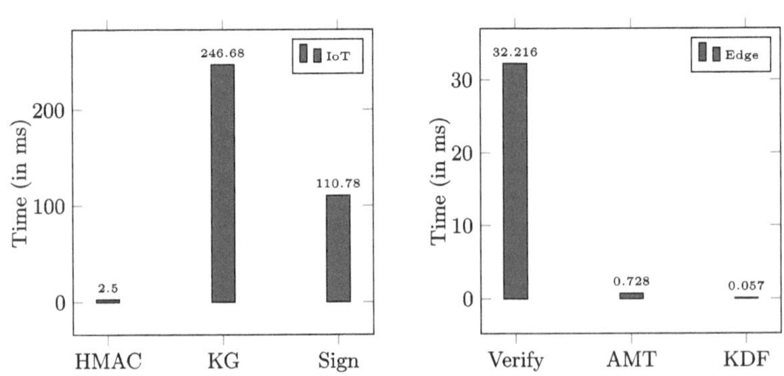

Fig. 5. Execution time of core crypto operations for IoT and Edge devices.

Join & Attestation. Figure 6 summarizes the execution time of PQ-PRIVÉ per phase. Figure 6 (a) shows the cost of the Join phase for the MF and the Edge device under different numbers of challenges $N \in \{2, 4, 8\}$. Since the number of devices and attributes is fixed, the execution time scales mainly with N, resulting in a total cost between 15.42 to 34.2 s. Figure 6 (b) presents the Attestation phase performance per entity (IoT, Edge, Verifier) and per type of operation, namely cryptographic operations, PUF execution, and Bluetooth communication. The results show that each IoT requires approximately 6.34 s in total, with the cryptographic operations contributing only a small fraction of the execution time (5.68%), while most of the overhead derives from the PUF (64.04%) and the Bluetooth communication (30.28%). For the Edge device and the Verifier, the execution time is dominated by communication overhead, while the cryptographic operations add negligible cost (1.69%). Overall, the results imply that the performance of the Attestation phase depends mainly on the hardware and communication constraints, rather than the integration of PQ cryptography.

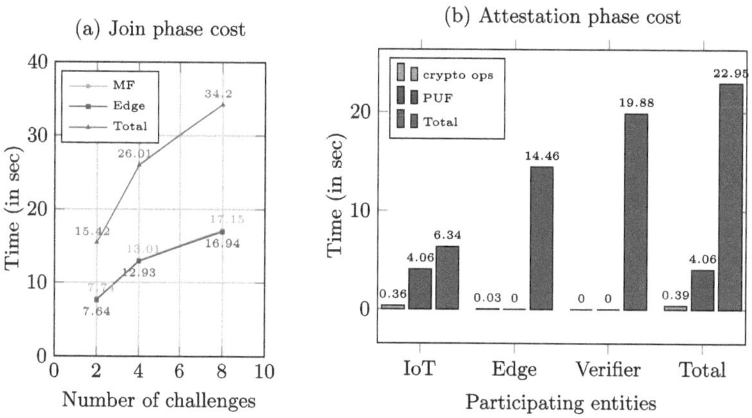

Fig. 6. Total execution time of PQ-PRIVÉ: Join & Attestation.

8 Conclusion

We presented PQ-PRIVÉ, the first PQ swarm attestation protocol, with the innovative features of attribute privacy preservation and accountable attestation, achieved through an enhanced traceable $\mathsf{W\text{-}OTS}^+$ digital signature variant. The protocol is the first concrete solution capable of achieving all requirements specified by the IETF "multiple-prover, multiple-verifier" paradigm in embedded environments, where multiple IoT devices are considered as *composite attesters* and can jointly generate attestation evidence that can be verified by different authorized verifiers. Our novel solution overcomes the limitations of existing schemes, where evidence appraisal can only be achieved by full-trusted verifiers having access to the entire set of reference values, by enabling the concealment of device attributes, even in the case of compromised devices, while also providing the ability to trace back a failed attestation. We conducted a comprehensive mathematical analysis, including formal proofs for all targeted security and privacy requirements, as well as a benchmarking evaluation of the protocol's performance on an experimental testbed incorporating PUF implementation details. Overall, PQ-PRIVÉ provides the necessary level of flexibility to unlock the conundrum for the efficient verification of multiple attesting environments, serving varying subsections of the entire device, without revealing sensitive information of the appraisal policy for evidence beyond the intended owners.

Acknowledgments. This work was supported in part by the EU's Horizon Europe Research & Innovation programme under the projects CASTOR (GA No. 101167904) and ENFORCE (GA No. 101249431).

Disclosure of Interests. The authors have no competing interests to declare that are relevant to the content of this article.

References

1. Ambrosin, M., Conti, M., Ibrahim, A., Neven, G., Sadeghi, A.R., Schunter, M.: SANA: Secure and scalable aggregate network attestation. In: CCS '16 (2016)
2. Ambrosin, M., Conti, M., Lazzeretti, R., Rabbani, M.M., Ranise, S.: Collective remote attestation at the internet of things scale: State-of-the-art and future challenges. IEEE Commun. Surv. Tutorials **22**(4), 2447–2461 (2020). https://doi.org/10.1109/COMST.2020.3008879
3. Asokan, N., et al.: SEDA: scalable embedded device attestation. In: ACM CCS'2015'. pp. 964–975. ACM (2015). https://doi.org/10.1145/2810103.2813670
4. Buchmann, J., Dahmen, E., Ereth, S., Hülsing, A., Rückert, M.: On the Security of the Winternitz One-Time Signature Scheme. In: Nitaj, A., Pointcheval, D. (eds.) AFRICACRYPT 2011. LNCS, vol. 6737, pp. 363–378. Springer, Heidelberg (2011). https://doi.org/10.1007/978-3-642-21969-6_23
5. Dolev, D., Yao, A.: On the security of public key protocols. IEEE Trans. on Inf. Theory **29**(2) (1983)
6. El Kassem, N., et al.: Priv e: Towards privacy-preserving swarm attestation. In: SECRYPT 2025, pp. 247–262 (2025)
7. Hellemans, W., et al.: SPARK: Secure Privacy-Preserving Anonymous Swarm Attestation for In-Vehicle Networks. In: EuroS&P 2025, pp. 903–922. IEEE (2025)
8. Hofmann, J., Lehwalder, P., Ebrahimi, S., Hassanizadeh, P., Faust, S.: PIRANHAS: privacy-preserving remote attestation in non-hierarchical asynchronous swarms. In: NDSS 2026, The Internet Society (2026)
9. Huelsing, A., Butin, D., Gazdag, S.L., Rijneveld, J., Mohaisen, A.: XMSS: eXtended Merkle Signature Scheme. RFC 8391 (2018). https://doi.org/10.17487/RFC8391
10. Hülsing, A.: W-OTS+ – Shorter Signatures for Hash-Based Signature Schemes. In: Youssef, A., Nitaj, A., Hassanien, A.E. (eds.) AFRICACRYPT 2013. LNCS, vol. 7918, pp. 173–188. Springer, Heidelberg (2013). https://doi.org/10.1007/978-3-642-38553-7_10

11. Ibrahim, A., Sadeghi, A.R., Tsudik, G.: US-AID: Unattended scalable attestation of IoT devices. In: IEEE SRDS 2018, pp. 21–30 (2018)
12. IEEE: IEEE standard for adoption of openfog reference architecture for fog computing. RFC 8391 (2018). https://doi.org/10.1109/IEEESTD.2018.8423800
13. Kaliski, B., Staddon, J.: PKCS #1: RSA Cryptography Specifications Version 2.0. RFC 2437 (1998). https://doi.org/10.17487/RFC2437
14. Kohnhäuser, F., Büscher, N., Katzenbeisser, S.: A practical attestation protocol for autonomous embedded systems. In: Euro S&P 2019, pp. 263–278 (2019)
15. Kuang, B., Fu, A., Yu, S., Yang, G., Su, M., Zhang, Y.: ESDRA: An efficient and secure distributed remote attestation scheme for IoT swarms. IEEE Internet Things J. **6**(5), 8372–8383 (2019)
16. Liu, T., Ramachandran, G., Jurdak, R.: Post-quantum cryptography for internet of things: A survey on performance and optimization (2024). https://arxiv.org/abs/2401.17538
17. Marastoni, N., Ceccato, M.: Remote attestation of iot devices using physically unclonable functions: Recent advancements and open research challenges. In: CPSIoTSec '23, pp. 25–36. Association for Computing Machinery, New York, NY, USA (2023). https://doi.org/10.1145/3605758.3623502
18. Rabbani, M., Vliegen, J., Winderickx, J., Conti, M., Mentens, N.: Shela: Scalable heterogeneous layered attestation. IEEE Internet Things J. **PP**, 1–1 (08 2019). https://doi.org/10.1109/JIOT.2019.2936988
19. Richardson, M., Birkholz, H., Deshpande, Y., Fossati, T.: Taxonomy of Composite Attesters. Internet-draft, IETF (2026). https://datatracker.ietf.org/doc/draft-richardson-rats-composite-attesters/04/, work in Progress

Towards Zero Trust Attestation for Confidential VMs in Public Clouds

Simon Ott(✉), Joana Pecholt, Albert Stark, Jonathan Hettwer, and Sascha Wessel

Fraunhofer AISEC, Lichtenbergstr. 11, 85748 Garching, Germany
{simon.ott,joana.pecholt,albert.stark,jonathan.hettwer, sascha.wessel}@aisec.fraunhofer.de

Abstract. Confidential Computing promises to remove the hypervisor from the Trusted Computing Base (TCB), enabling data processing protected from Cloud Service Providers (CSPs). This requires verifying the integrity of the entire software stack running in Confidential Virtual Machines (CVMs), i.e., remote attestation. While an established concept, its potential often remains untapped. One of the main obstacles to practical deployment is that the verifier requires a list of reference hashes for all software running on the proving platform. Given the complexity and frequent updates of software, collecting such a list is a tedious task. In this paper, we analyze the contents of measurement registers in CVMs and demonstrate how to deterministically precompute their values from reproducible software builds, extending supply chain security to the runtime phase. We further evaluate the feasibility by examining the reproducibility of different CVM images, and show that, while precomputation is possible, it remains a tedious process with several practical gaps that need to be addressed. We present a comprehensive evaluation of CVM solutions across major hyperscalers and assess the feasibility of attesting CVMs without implicitly relying on CSP trust, enabling Zero Trust architectures. Based on our findings, we provide recommendations for streamlining measurement register computation.

1 Introduction

The trend of shifting corporate data and applications to public clouds shows no sign of slowing down [12]. At the same time, companies are increasingly concerned about how to protect their sensitive workloads on infrastructure owned by Cloud Service Provider (CSPs). Furthermore, upcoming data protection regulations impose new requirements on how data is stored and protected. This demands solutions to protect sensitive data in the cloud, even from access by the Cloud Service Provider (CSP).

Comprehensive protection requires securing data at rest, data in transit, and data in use. Furthermore, it requires a mechanism to verify the security guarantees of a remote platform, *i.e.* remote attestation. Remote attestation is an important building block for Zero Trust architectures, which assume no implicit

Z. Afzal et al. (Eds.): ARES 2026 Workshops, LNCS 16900, pp. 272–289, 2027.
https://doi.org/10.1007/978-3-032-35576-8_15

trust and therefore require explicit verification of all system components [31]. While protecting data at rest and data in transit can be achieved through Full Disk Encryption (FDE) and the use of secure channel protocols, protecting data in use, can be achieved through using Confidential Computing technologies, such as AMD Secure Encrypted Virtualization - Secure Nested Paging (SEV-SNP), Intel Trust Domain Extensions (TDX), or Arm Confidential Compute Architecture (CCA). They provide hardware-based memory protection for Virtual Machine (VMs), known as Confidential Virtual Machine (CVMs), which protect sensitive data and workloads from the underlying platform, including the hypervisor and thus the CSP.

However, all security guarantees depend on the attestation mechanism and, consequently, on the verifiability of the measurement registers. These registers store cryptographic hashes of artifacts executed during boot and runtime, and form a common building block across all hardware-based attestation technologies. Unfortunately, reliably predicting the register contents is a non-trivial challenge. While it is possible to boot up a reference machine and read the values for later use as reference values, this solution is far from ideal. It captures only a single, non-deterministic snapshot of the system state without a link to the built sources. Furthermore, this process must be repeated for every different hardware configuration and for every single software update, making it infeasible in practice.

To reproducibly allow the assessment of the trustworthiness of the software stack, it is therefore required to reliably precompute the expected measurements of the compiled binaries in the way they are measured. This enables recalculation of the final measurement register values during attestation. We propose to perform the precomputation deterministically as part of a Reproducible Build (R-B) process to link the binaries to the specific source code version, while ensuring scalability across deployments. This allows us to extend supply chain security from the build phase to the runtime phase, since any running artifact can be traced back to a specific source code revision.

Many papers use the remote attestation process of Confidential Virtual Machine (CVMs) as a foundational building block for their system designs, but typically do not describe how trust can be established in a generic and scalable manner [4,10,15,18,29,30]. Our work complements this and potential future system design research through systematically analyzing the complexities of measurement registers in Confidential Computing environments. Based on the analysis, we reliably precompute the measurement registers for heterogeneous software stacks based on reproducible builds. We demonstrate the feasibility of our approach using our own minimal, fully reproducible Confidential Virtual Machine (CVM) images, and assess how far the same approach can be applied to CSP-provided commodity OS CVM images. Since these images originate from the Cloud Service Provider (CSPs), they cannot be implicitly trusted and must therefore also be reproducibly (re-)built to establish trust. Besides the reproducible build process, we introduce a set of open-source tools that facilitate the precomputation.

Furthermore, we provide a detailed evaluation of the current hyperscaler cloud Confidential Computing solutions, focusing on their attestation mechanisms. In our assessment, we explore whether CVMs can be attested without having to inherently trust the CSP. Our findings show that no unified approach to measurement scope and reproducibility currently exists, while closed-source components within the Trusted Computing Base (TCB) partially hinder precomputation and trust establishment via remote attestation. We therefore present recommendations on how existing gaps can be bridged.

2 Background

This section provides background on Trusted and Confidential Computing with a focus on remote attestation. Confidential Computing focuses on protecting data in use by utilizing hardware-isolated and integrity-protected trusted environments. Current technologies enable this by providing on-the-fly confidential and integrity-protected CVMs, where their memory is protected from the untrusted rest of the system, including the hypervisor. A Confidential Computing environment must provide a mechanism to remotely attest to its correct state and the integrity of the software running in it. We additionally include background on Trusted Platform Module (TPMs), as some Confidential Computing technologies closely resemble TPM standards and major cloud providers expose vTPMs inside their CVMs. We focus on the currently available hardware to validate our design and therefore exclude Arm CCA.

2.1 Trusted Platform Modules

In a TPM measured boot, the first and inherently trusted part of the firmware measures itself. Then, bootloader, kernel, command line, and initrd are measured. The kernel can measure applications via the kernel's Integrity Measurement Architecture (IMA). Each measurement (DATA) is recorded into the respective Platform Configuration Register (PCR) via the following *Extend* operation [14]:

$$\texttt{PCR[n]} = \text{HASH}(\texttt{PCR[n]} \,||\, \text{HASH}(\text{DATA})) \tag{1}$$

Platform Configuration Register (PCRs) are initialized to a defined value and can only be reset through a reboot.

The IMA is a kernel subsystem designed to measure the integrity of files accessed by the system, including binaries and configuration files.

2.2 AMD SEV-SNP

SNP enables protection of Virtual Machine (VMs) from the hypervisor and other software components. It enables encryption of memory and CPU register state using hardware-protected unique encryption keys and provides integrity protection. As an optional feature, SNP allows a CVM to further divide its address space into four privilege levels called Virtual Machine Privilege Level (VMPLs), providing an additional layer of isolation [2].

The technology is implemented utilizing the AMD Platform Security Processor (PSP), a secure co-processor within AMD EPYC CPUs. The SP exposes an Application Programming Interface (API) to the hypervisor, as well as an API for the guest. Guests can request an attestation report signed by an asymmetric Versioned Chip Endorsement Key (VCEK), routing back to an AMD Certificate Authority (CA) [2].

2.3 Intel TDX

Intel TDX enables CVMs on Intel platforms, also referred to as Trust Domain (TDs). While its overall design and goals are broadly aligned with AMD's SNP, the specific implementation differs. Intel uses a multi-component architecture comprising Virtual Machine Extension (VMXs), instruction set architecture (ISA) extensions, the Intel TDX module as an intermediary between CVM and Virtual Machine Manager (VMM), as well as Software Guard Extensions (SGX) enclaves for attestation [16]. Comparable to SNP VMPLs, Intel introduced Trust Domain (TD) partitioning to allow nested VMs inside a TD, with a primary Virtual Machine (VM) acting as a privileged hypervisor and up to 3 nested VMs for the workload [7].

The TDX module is measured into the *MRSEAM* register. The initial state of the CVM is measured into the Measurement of Trust Domain (MRTD) register, similar to AMD SNP's measurement register. Additionally, TDX provides runtime measurement registers, the Run-Time Measurement Register (RTMRs), which closely resemble the PCR measurements in a TPM-based measured boot: Each measurement (DATA) is recorded into the respective Run-Time Measurement Register (RTMR) via the following *extend* operation:

$$\texttt{RTMR[n]} = \text{SHA-384}(\texttt{RTMR[n]} \,||\, \text{SHA-384}(\texttt{DATA})) \tag{2}$$

Run-Time Measurement Register (RTMRs) are initialized to zero and can only be reset through a reboot.

3 Threat Model and Requirements

Confidential Computing reduces the TCB by excluding CSP-controlled software, including the hypervisor, leaving only the CVM, its stack, and Confidential Computing-specific hardware and firmware. We do not assume CSP-provided attestation verification services to be trustworthy and therefore implement our own open source verifiers, running in tenant-owned infrastructure.

We assume a powerful attacker with privileged access to the computing platform, including firmware, bootloader, hypervisor, user space software, and potentially other non-confidential virtual machines. Furthermore, we assume an attacker with Dolev-Yao attacker model [9] capabilities, which can read, modify, replay, or relay any transmitted data to and from the CVM. The main goal of the attacker is to get access to the data processed within the Confidential Computing environment.

We assume certain limitations for our attacker. We assume the hardware will work as expected, and that the attacker is not capable of breaking state-of-the-art cryptography. Furthermore, advanced physical and side channel attacks are out of scope, as Confidential Computing technologies do not guarantee protection against such attacks [2,5].

To evaluate the attestability of Confidential VMs in a comparable manner, we define the set of hardware, software, and configuration-level components that must be measured and verified to establish trust in the CVM. We formalize these as the following security requirements:

- SR-I **Confidential Computing state:** This includes hardware, firmware, and microcode versions, the protection mode, and any platform-rooted measurements established by hardware during VM launch.
- SR-II **Boot artifacts:** This encompasses the virtual firmware, bootloaders, the kernel, and any auxiliary binaries that are executed during boot.
- SR-III **Boot configuration data:** Configuration data injected or controlled by the VMM, such as virtual device configuration, ACPI tables, and cmdline.
- SR-IV **Run-time artifacts:** All binaries, libraries, and scripts must be covered and ensured not to leak any sensitive data from the CVM.
- SR-V **Run-time configuration data:** This comprises all system configuration files consumed by privileged software.

4 Precomputing the Measurement Registers

This section outlines our concept for verifiably linking all CVM software artifacts to their sources and build process. It also details the precomputation of the launch and runtime measurement registers for various Trusted and Confidential Computing technologies and software stacks based on reproducible builds.

4.1 Reproducible Build

We craft a transparent and reproducible build to enforce that building given sources and toolchain always generates bit-for-bit identical binaries, leading to fully reproducible CVMs. The artifacts are then measured during the measured boot process and can therefore be linked back to their sources, as shown in Fig. 1. The reproducible build produces all required artifacts running in the CVM, as well as signed reference hashes for all built artifacts. This includes firmware, kernel, initrd, disks, cmdline, and configuration data. The signed reference hashes are then used by the verifier to assess the trustworthiness of the software stack at runtime. With this approach, we extend supply chain security to the runtime phase, enabling source-to-binary correspondence for deployed artifacts.

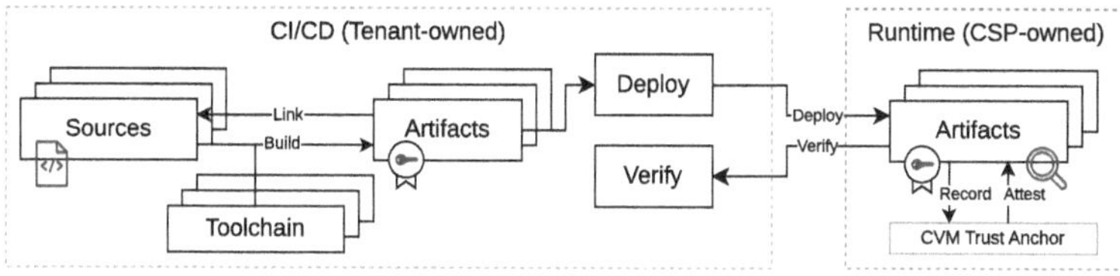

Fig. 1. Reproducible Build

Our reproducible build produces the virtual firmware and minimal, custom CVM images, which can be run on-premises using Kernel-based Virtual Machine (KVM)/QEMU, or in the cloud. For cloud images, we rely on the Virtual Machine Manager (VMMs) and firmware provided by the Cloud Service Provider (CSPs), and rebuild the firmware reproducibly if possible. Furthermore, we craft a reproducible build for commodity OSs offered by the CSPs to evaluate the feasibility of our approach also for stock cloud images.

4.2 TPM

We begin by outlining how to precompute the TPM measurement registers, *i.e.* the Platform Configuration Register (PCRs). This establishes a basis for drawing parallels to the TDX RTMRs later. Furthermore, virtual Trusted Platform Module (vTPMs) are used by CSPs to extend the measurement capabilities of CVMs. We focus on aspects not covered in the specifications [34] and refer to the specification for all documented behavior.

PCR0 is used by the Open Virtual Machine Firmware (OVMF) to measure itself. The Pre-EFI Initialization (PEI) phase measures and extends itself as it resides in RAM, along with the Driver Execution Environment (DXE) phase [34]. To perform the precomputations, we extract the reproducibly built main firmware volume from the OVMF firmware image, extract the PEI and DXE phase and calculate the hashes. *PCR1* contains the Advanced Configuration and Power Interface (ACPI) tables, which depend on the VMM. We precompute minimal static ACPI tables with MMIO-based virtio instead of PCI-based virtio [8] for our CVMs, or, alternatively, dump the tables once via QEMU patches. *PCR1*, depending on the configuration, furthermore contains the SMBIOS tables, which we precompute. Furthermore, *PCR1* contains the Unified Extensible Firmware Interface (UEFI) boot variables [34]. For the precomputation of *PCR1* of our own, minimal CVM images, we can safely assume a single boot entry. *PCR2* and *PCR3* contain UEFI driver code and configuration and are measured according to the specification [22,34]. *PCR4* is used by the OVMF to measure the kernel as a PE/COFF image. The measurement of the PE/COFF is performed in the same way as the *PCR2* UEFI drivers. Furthermore, the image contains the *Real-Mode Kernel Header*, which itself contains several fields that are written by the VMM/bootloader in order to pass information to the kernel. Whether the headers are manipulated depends on the VMM version. Therefore, the precomputation tools must set these fields accordingly, before extending the kernel [6].

PCR5 records the transition from the boot environment to the operating system environment with log strings [34]. If a setup with a GUID Partition Table (GPT) is used, the disk geometry is measured as well, which we precompute bases on the reproducibly built image. *PCR6* is reserved for host platform manufacturer-specific data. For our own images, we do not populate *PCR6*. *PCR7* records the UEFI secure boot variables. If secure boot is activated, we precompute secure boot keys and signatures with the provided variables [34]. *PCR8* is empty for our system configuration with the kernel being booted by the OVMF as EFI-stub without an additional bootloader. If GRUB is used, *PCR8* contains the GRUB commands in GRUB scripting language. The implications are discussed in Sect. 6.5. *PCR9* contains the kernel cmdline and, if present, the initrd as measured by the EFI-stub. *PCR9* further contains the measurements of the bootloader configuration files, if a bootloader is present. *PCR10* contains the IMA measurement of executed user space binaries. This requires the IMA to be activated and configured. The calculation of PCR10 is performed through hashing all binaries and files being read as output by the R-B system.

4.3 Intel TDX

We will describe the measurement register precomputation for Intel TDX in the following section and draw parallels to the TPM computations. Note that the measurements are described for the newest, stable OVMF version. As some measurements changed across versions, we implemented versioning into our pre-computation tools.

The trusted boot chain starts with the Secure Arbitration Mode (SEAM) loader loading the Intel TDX-Module. The TDX-module is open source and can be built reproducibly to calculate the expected *MRSEAM* hash. The correct TDX-module build date, build number, and update version must be passed to the build. The TDX-Module measures the initial content of the CVM and writes the hash into the *MRTD* register. The precomputation tools require the OVMF as input to precompute the MRTD. The process is TDX-specific and therefore differs from the Firmware Volume-granular OVMF measurements in a TPM measured boot. For a detailed algorithm and details on extracting the metadata sections required for precomputation, refer to our open source tools[1].

For runtime measurements, the RTMRs are used. The RTMR precomputation closely resembles the calculation of the PCRs in a TPM-based boot with a SHA-384 hash function and the extend operation as described in Sect. 2.3. *RTMR0* contains the UEFI TD Hand-Off Block (HOB). We precompute the expected hash through parsing the OVMF binary TDVF metadata, specifying the guest RAM size, and then assembling the HOB structures according to the UEFI and TDX specifications [17,35]. Next, the Configuration Firmware Volume (CFV) is measured. The measurement incorporates provisioned data, such as the contents of Secure Boot variables [17]. We extract the CFV from the OVMF

---

[1] https://github.com/Fraunhofer-AISEC/cmc/tree/main/tools/mrtool.

binary and extend it. Then, the UEFI secure boot variables are recorded similarly to the measurements in *PCR7*. Next, the ACPI tables and the UEFI boot variables are measured, similar to the *PCR1* measurements. *RTMR1* contains the Linux kernel PE/COFF image. The calculation is identical to the *PCR4* measurement. Furthermore, the transition from the boot environment to the operating system environment is recorded into *RTMR1*. These calculations are identical to the *PCR5* calculations. *RTMR2* contains the kernel cmdline and initrd similar to *PCR9*. *RTMR3* is empty.

4.4 AMD SEV-SNP

In contrast to Intel TDX and Trusted Platform Module (TPMs), AMD SNP only provides a single measurement register [2] for the measurement of firmware and initial pages by the AMD SP. The SNP firmware measures the CVM launch state before it is started, *i.e.* it constructs a hash chain from the hashes of the pages in the initialized memory of the CVM. In the default configuration, this comprises the OVMF, but neither the kernel nor any user space components.

The measure function takes the provided information on the page type, its contents, and where to store the page in the VM's memory to update the current measurement. The order in which the pages are measured is relevant, as changes to the order result in different measurements, while the final VM still has the exact same memory layout. Furthermore, the VM Safe Area (VMSA) is used to allow for interrupt queuing and event injection into the VM. It has configurations that can vary depending on CPU generation, operating system, and platform configuration. As a result, the contents of the VM Safe Area (VMSAs) must also be known. Finally, the measurement is dependent on the VMM and the CSP, as discussed in Sect. 6.2.

Assessing the trustworthiness of the CVM further requires measuring kernel, cmdline, and initrd, as well as user-space binaries and configuration data. Therefore, we enable measuring kernel, cmdline, and initrd to an additional page during initialization [24]. These hashes are later used by the UEFI to verify the kernel, cmdline, and initrd provided by the hypervisor.

Alternatively, the VMPLs can be used for further intra-CVM privilege separation. This allows to run a virtual Trusted Platform Module (vTPMs) within a Secure VM Service Module (SVSM) at the highest privilege level, providing a mechanism to record runtime measurements into the PCRs [25]. For SVSM-CVM, we adjust our precomputation to include it in the launch measurement. The SVSM-virtual Trusted Platform Module (vTPM) measurements are identical to the VM PCR measurements as described in Sect. 4.2.

5 Implementation

We implemented a set of open-source tools to reproducibly precompute and attest the measurement registers of CVMs for various previously described software stacks based on built artifacts[2]. We implemented and tested the tools on

[2] https://github.com/Fraunhofer-AISEC/cmc.

CVMs with our own images, Ubuntu 24.04 and 25.04, Debian Trixie and Bookworm, and Amazon Linux. We expect them to work with other images as well. We integrated these tools into an R-B system based on buildroot[3] for our own images. The build process produces minimal CVM images with customizations to be able to run on-premises, as well as on the hyperscaler infrastructures.

As we expect many tenants to prefer the commodity OSs as offered by the hyperscalers, we also implemented an R-B system for Ubuntu commodity OSes. We chose Ubuntu, as it is available free of charge on all major hyperscalers. Ubuntu distributes binary packages, which are installed in the CSP's image, as well as the corresponding source packages, which contain the source code from which the package is built. In addition, Ubuntu publishes information about the build environment used to build each binary package. This includes all build dependencies, including their versions, build timestamps, and other information required to reproduce the build. Based on this information, our R-B system attempts to reproduce the build environment and produce a bit-for-bit identical binary package from the source package. We describe the results in Sect. 6.1

6 Evaluation

We evaluated our approach with respect to the reproducibility of both custom and commodity OS images, and the extent to which all relevant artifacts can be precomputed for CVM attestation across different platforms against the requirements defined in Sect. 3. The evaluation covers both on-premises infrastructure and deployments at the major hyperscalers Amazon Web Services (AWS), Google Cloud Platform (GCP) and Microsoft Azure. For the on-premises evaluation, we used 3rd, 4th, and 5th Gen AMD EPYC Servers (AMD EPYC75F3, EPYC9754, EPYC9135), as well as Intel Xeon Scalable processors (XEON SILVER 4510).

6.1 Reproducible Build Evaluation

We successfully verified that our custom images are fully reproducible and capable of running on-premises and across the three major hyperscalers.

We additionally evaluated the feasibility of applying our R-B approach to commodity OSs. Figure 2 shows the results for Ubuntu 24.04 LTS stock CVM cloud images as provided by the hyperscalers, compared to our own images. The packages marked *Reproducible Match* are the packages where we could rebuild each package file so that it is bit-for-bit identical to the version installed in the CVM. Packages marked *Reproducible No Match* are reproducible, but we were unable to recreate the build environment, often because we were not able to retrieve all build dependencies in the version that was used during the build by the OS vendor. This requires installing our self-built versions instead of the shipped versions of those packages for reproducibility. The *Non-Reproducible*

[3] https://buildroot.org/.

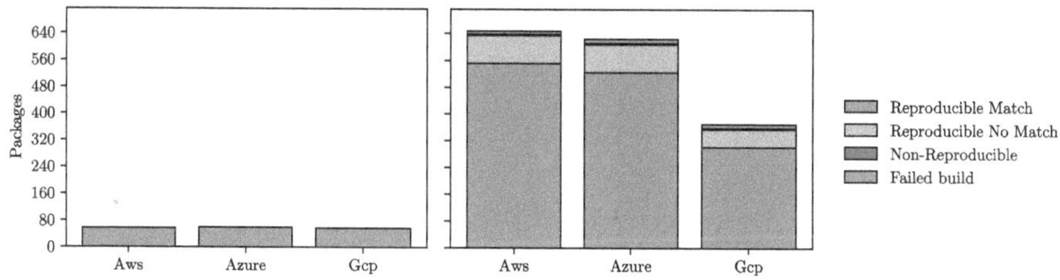

Fig. 2. Reproducible build evaluation: Custom Image (left), Ubuntu (right)

packages require fixing before they can be used in the CVMs. However, these are only 0.5 % on AWS, 0.6 % on Azure and 0.8 % on GCP. The *Failed build* packages, 1.5 % on AWS, 1.9 % on Azure, and 3.2 % on GCP require further manual fixing of the build scripts.

6.2 On-Premises Evaluation

We evaluate the implemented attestation mechanisms for CVMs on-premises regarding attestability and architectural differences.

Intel TDX-Based CVMs. Our software stack comprises the OVMF, kernel, including command line and initrd, and a dm-verity protected rootfs containing user-space applications and configuration files. We were able to precompute all measurements as defined in our requirements `SR-I` - `SR-V`. The runtime measurements closely resemble the TPM measurements.

We observed, however, that the TDX measurement process is not stable across VMM versions. This is because the measurement depends on the sequence of TD calls made by the VMM during guest initialization. We incorporated this in our precomputation tools. Furthermore, in a TDX-measured boot, the TD HOB is measured into RTMR0. This requires specifying the guest RAM size to enable precomputation.

AMD SEV-SNP-Based CVMs. We were able to precompute the expected SNP measurement based on the reproducibly built OVMF, kernel, initrd, and cmdline. As with TDX, the measurement also depends on the VMM, *e.g.* QEMU and AWS EC2 extend the CPUID page at different stages. Furthermore, the measurement depends on the attestation key type, VMM-type, as well as host-specific and CPU-specific information. These dependencies necessitate the generation of a matrix of precomputed measurements to enable the precomputation of the measurement independent of the physical machine and configuration.

For measuring the user space of static, minimal images, we utilize a dm-verity protected rootfs and measure its hash as part of the kernel command line. Where this is not applicable, we utilize an SVSM with vTPM and IMA, as described in the next paragraph.

vTPM-Augmented CVMs. The measurements recorded into the CVM vTPM closely resemble those observed in traditional vTPM-based VMs. We verified that all PCRs can be precomputed and all components are measured according to our requirements. However, several aspects complicate the process and hinder reproducibility:

The OVMF PEI phase is loaded into RAM and initializes modules before measuring itself. The values of global C-code variables of those modules are therefore included in the measurement, as the .data section is part of the measurement. For several versions, we applied patches to remove any code that initializes global variables prior to the self-measurement, ensuring reproducible hashing. The *kernel setup header* is, depending on the VMM version, manipulated before the kernel image is measured into PCR4. Thus, the same modifications must be performed on the built kernel before precomputing the expected hash. The ACPI table precomputation is difficult due to the dynamic and platform-specific nature of ACPI Machine Language (AML) code. Especially if PCI-based virtio is used, the precomputation becomes very difficult. We therefore did not use PCI-based virtio.

6.3 Evaluation of Hyperscaler Implementations

As the primary use case for Confidential Computing is protection from the CSP, we examine the implementation of these technologies in the cloud. We perform the evaluation for the CSPs Amazon (AWS), Microsoft (Azure), and Google (GCP). For the evaluation, we used our own custom images, as well as unmodified Ubuntu CVM 24.04 LTS images as offered by the CSPs. We performed this evaluation in February 2026 and consider this a snapshot, which might be subject to change. We begin with a general evaluation based on observations common across all hyperscalers and then evaluate the individual software stacks, which are shown in Fig. 3.

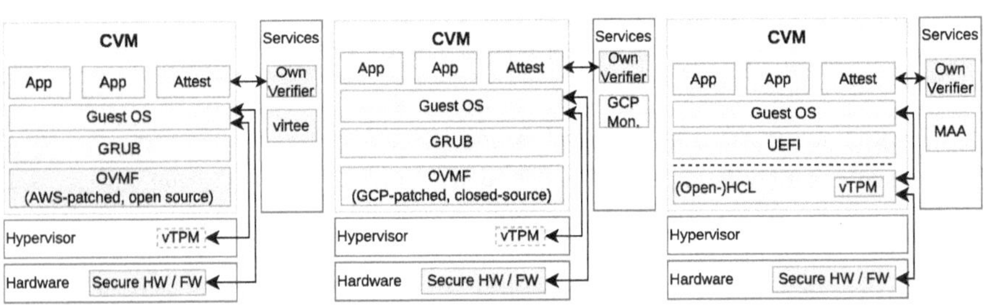

Fig. 3. AWS, GCP, and Azure CVM Implementations from left to right (green: verifiable, orange: non-verifiable) (Color figure online)

Common Findings. *PCR1* contains different and potentially multiple boot entries due to updates. This makes the reliable precomputation difficult. Secure boot is optional on all hyperscalers. All hyperscaler images include custom user space binaries, which can be used by the CSPs to access the CVMs, violating `SR-IV`. They can be removed without breaking CVM functionality.

Amazon Web Services. AWS offers AMD SNP CVMs. The software stack comprises an AWS-patched OVMF, the bootloader GRUB, a guest kernel, and user space applications. The OVMF patches are open source, including a Nix-based reproducible build.

AWS provides direct access to `/dev/sev-guest` to retrieve attestation reports. However, it is not possible to measure the kernel, cmdline, initrd, and user-space [24], or further runtime components and user space applications. Secure boot and a vTPM can be activated for runtime measurements [1]. We observed the following differences compared to on-premises CVMs: *PCR0* contains the OVMF PEIFV and DXEFV measurements. While we could precompute DXEFV, PEIFV differs, potentially due to measured global variables, as described in Sect. 6.2. We realized that ACPI tables are not measured into *PCR1*. We were not able to identify whether these are not used or not measured, which may introduce potential attack vectors [33]. *PCR4* contains the UEFI shim and GRUB bootloader. We precomputed empty *PCR7* secure boot variables for disabled secure boot. *PCR8* contains the GRUB commands. Because of the dynamic nature of GRUB commands, we were not able to precompute *PCR8*. *PCR9* contains boot file measurements, including the ucode, kernel, command line, and initrd.

As the vTPM is not linked to the SNP attestation report and managed by the untrusted hypervisor, it is currently not possible to establish trust with regard to our threat model, as requirements `SR-II` - `SR-V` are violated.

Microsoft Azure. Microsoft Azure offers CVMs with AMD SEV-SNP and Intel TDX technology. Azure uses a different approach compared to AWS and GCP. Instead of utilizing OVMF, they use a custom (Open) Host Compatibility Layer (HCL). OpenHCL offers UEFI and other services, such as a vTPM within the CVM. For privilege separation between the paravisor and the Guest OS, they use the VMPLs on AMD SEV-SNP machines and TD partitioning on TDX machines [23,27]. Attestation reports can be fetched through reading a vTPM-NVIndex, which triggers the generation of a fresh attestation report. The nonce is constructed to include the vTPM Attestation Key (AK) public key to establish a chain of trust between hardware and vTPM measurement.

The Azure firmware does not write the Intel TDX RTMRs. For runtime measurements, Azure relies on the vTPM. We were able to build the OpenHCL firmware from source, but it was not possible to match the precomputed hashes with the running MRTD hash, violating `SR-II`.

We observed the following differences compared to on-premises CVMs: On OpenHCL machines, *PCR2* contains additional driver images. We could confirm this was a temporary issue that has been fixed for the newest OpenHCL version. Similarly, *PCR4* contains an unknown application. *PCR5* records the GPT partition table, which we could not precompute because of a differing measurement by the custom firmware. *PCR6* contains an event recording the DMI table System-UUID, which is CVM-unique and can therefore not be precomputed. We realized that ACPI tables are not measured by the firmware, which again may introduce potential attack vectors [33].

Currently, for AMD SEV-SNP and Intel TDX CVMs, it is not possible to establish trust in the CVM under our threat model. Azure confirmed they are working on reproducible builds. However, they currently use OpenHCL versions with non-public security patches on Azure. This leads to a conflict of the security goals for reproducible builds, enabling verifiable measurements, and the need to apply undisclosed security patches not yet upstreamed into OpenHCL's firmware dependencies.

Google Cloud Platform. GCP offers CVMs with AMD SEV-SNP, as well as Intel TDX. The software stack comprises a GCP-patched OVMF, the UEFI shim bootloader, GRUB, a guest kernel, and user space applications. The OVMF patches are not open source. Instead, GCP only provides reference values for their OVMF, enabling users to verify that a genuine GCP-OVMF instance was launched, but not complying with requirement `SR-II`. The patches do not include mechanisms to measure the kernel, command line, or initrd on SNP machines. Instead, GCP relies on a vTPM, which is, however, managed by the untrusted hypervisor [13]. On TDX-machines, the RTMRs are used to measure kernel command line and initrd. GCP provides access to `/dev/sev-guest` and `/dev/tdx_guest` for attestation report retrieval. However, it is not possible to precompute the SNP measurement or the TDX MRTD.

We were able to precompute the TDX RTMRs, except of the following values: We were not able to precompute the *RTMR0* EFI HOB, the EFI CFV, and the ACPI tables, because of the closed-source firmware. *RTMR1* records the GPT partition table, which we could not precompute because of a differing measurement by the custom firmware. *RTMR2* contains the GRUB commands and files, which we were not able to precompute due to the dynamic nature of GRUB commands. We observed the following vTPM measurement differences compared to on-premises CVMs: For TDX CVMs, the UEFI shim bootloader and the GPT partition table are measured into *PCR2* instead of *PCR4* and *PCR5*, respectively. As the firmware is not open source and the vTPM is controlled by the untrusted hypervisor, it is not possible to establish trust in GCP-CVMs under our threat model.

6.4 Summary

Table 1 shows the attestability of the CVM software stacks. *HW* refers to the Confidential Computing hard- and firmware, *FW* to the virtual firmware, *Cfg* summarizes configuration data exchanged between host and guest, *ACPI* refers to the measurement of ACPI tables, *Vars* refers to the measurement of EFI boot and secure boot variables, *BL* for the bootlader, *Kernel*, *Initrd*, and *Cmdline* summarize the OS, and *Usr* refers to the measurements of user space applications. Items in Grey indicate that the chain of trust was broken on a previous step: On AWS, the kernel and further components are not measured. On GCP and Azure, the firmware is only partially open source and cannot be precomputed as of now.

Table 1. Attestability of CVM software stack across cloud (CoT left to right) ○ Not verifiable, ◐ Verifiable with CSP trust, ● Verifiable via reproducible build.

Environment	HW	FW	Cfg	ACPI	Vars	BL	Kernel	Initrd	Cmdline	Usr
On-Premises	●	●	●	●	●	-	●	●	●	●
AWS	●	●	◐	○	●	◐	◐	◐	●	◐
GCP	●	◐	●	●	●	◐	◐	◐	●	◐
Azure	●	◐	●	○	●	-	◐	◐	●	◐

Table 2 summarizes the contents of the vTPM PCRs of CVMs deployed across the hyperscalers.

Table 2. vTPM PCR usage in hyperscaler CVMs FW FW, Boot Vars, EFI HOB, SecureBoot Vars, ACPI, Driver, EFI-Shim, Grub, Kernel, GPT, System-UUID, Cmdline, Initrd, User Space, MOK-Lists, ? Unknown

PCR	0	1	2	3	4	5	6	7	8	9	10	11	14
On-Prem	FW	Boot Vars, ACPI, EFI HOB	-	-	Kernel	-	-	SecureBoot Vars	-	Cmdline, Initrd	User Space	-	-
AWS SNP	FW	Boot Vars	-	-	EFI-Shim, Grub	GPT	-	SecureBoot Vars	Grub	Grub, Kernel, Cmdline, Initrd	User Space	-	MOK-Lists
Azure SNP	FW	Boot Vars	-	-	EFI-Shim, Kernel, ?	GPT	System-UUID	SecureBoot Vars	-	Cmdline, Initrd	User Space	Cmdline, Initrd, ?	MOK-Lists
Azure TDX	FW	Boot Vars	Driver	-	EFI-Shim, Kernel, ?	GPT	System-UUID	SecureBoot Vars	-	Cmdline, Initrd	User Space	Cmdline, Initrd, ?	MOK-Lists
GCP TDX	FW	Boot Vars, ACPI	GPT, EFI-Shim	-	Grub	-	-	SecureBoot Vars	Grub	Grub, Kernel, Cmdline, Initrd	User Space	-	MOK-Lists
GCP SNP	FW	Boot Vars, ACPI	-	-	EFI-Shim, Grub	GPT	-	SecureBoot Vars	Grub	Grub, Kernel, Cmdline, Initrd	User Space	-	MOK-Lists

6.5 Recommendations

We present recommendations for improving the attestability of CVMs through enhancing the reproducibility of precomputed measurement register values and through reducing the required measurements.

General Improvements. To ensure that measurement registers remain predictable and accurately reflect the reproducible build process, we identify several areas for improvement:

- **VMM-independent measurement generation:** The virtual firmware measurements shall be reproducible, independent of VMM type and version
- **Clean chain-of-trust:** Each component in the boot chain should measure the next component before transferring control. As the firmware is measured by the underlying trust anchor, it does not need to measure itself, which can lead to difficult-to-reproduce measurements. In case it is inevitable that a firmware volume measures itself, global variables should not be included.
- **Simplified HOB calculation**: The Hand-Off Block (HOBs) precomputation mixes static OVMF-derived contents with VMM-declared RAM size, which makes it difficult to precompute.
- **Avoid or simplify ACPI table generation**: ACPI table precomputation is difficult due to the dynamic and platform-specific nature of AML code.
- **Separate kernel and configuration:** As outlined in Sect. 6.2, depending on the VMM, the kernel setup header is modified, complicating reproducibility. This should be avoided.
- **Single boot path:** Multiple boot options lead to multiple boot variables being measured, hindering reproducibility.
- **OS image reproducibility:** OS vendors should publish the build environments used to produce their packages, so that bit-for-bit identical binaries can be reproduced and packages can be linked to their sources. Additionally, OS Vendors could provide reference hashes for the package files.

Hyperscaler-Specific Recommendations. Our evaluation demonstrates that, at present, tenants must still place partial trust in the CSPs, which violates the threat model. However, the remaining steps toward achieving a true zero-trust architecture are relatively minor.

- **Open source and reproducible builds:** All elements of the TCB should be made available as open-source, along with instructions for an R-B.
- **Measurement of runtime artifacts:** Providing a mechanism to measure runtime artifacts is required to ensure runtime integrity. In case a vTPM is used for this purpose, it must reside within the TCB [28].
- **Avoid bootloaders:** Bootloaders introduce additional complexity and result in artifacts being measured redundantly, and should therefore be avoided.
- **CSP user space binaries:** CSP-Binaries providing a channel into the CVM (e.g., to configure SSH keys) should be avoided. Other CSP binaries must be open source and reproducibly buildable.

7 Related Work

Li et al. [19] present a comprehensive analysis of various CVMs and enclave technologies. The work by Niemi et al. [26] offers a systematic investigation into the attestation mechanisms used across different CVM and Trusted Execution

Environment (TEE) frameworks. Similarly, Menetrey et al. [21] provide an evaluation of the attestation mechanisms of several CVMs technologies. We extend this body of research by conducting a detailed analysis of the attestability of the software stack and assessing the deployments in public clouds.

Several studies aim to enhance CVM security by leveraging vTPMs in different configurations but focus on the configuration and use of such vTPMs rather than on the precomputation and verification of measurements [20,25,28]. Recent research has begun to investigate implementations deployed by hyperscalers. In [3], the authors analyze the current CVM offerings in public clouds and show how they are insufficient to provide proper security guarantees based on identified requirements. Scopelliti et al. [32] outline the trust relationships in public cloud Confidential Computing offerings and evaluate the general attestability of AMD SEV-SNP CVMs. Eisoldt et al. [11] present a comprehensive analysis of public cloud CVM offerings. Our work extends this research by providing a detailed examination of the contents of the measurement registers for AMD SNP, Intel TDX, and vTPMs on-premises and in the cloud. Our analysis further assesses the feasibility of reproducibly precomputing all relevant values and providing a set of recommendations on how to improve the reproducibility.

8 Conclusion

Precomputing measurement registers is essential for establishing trust in CVMs, but remains challenging due to platform heterogeneity, undocumented behavior, and the influence of various components on the register values.

We presented a systematic precomputation methodology for CVM measurement registers and open source tools targeting Intel Intel TDX, AMD SNP, and vTPMs.

To demonstrate the feasibility of our approach, we provide fully reproducible images for all evaluated CSPs and show that commodity cloud OS images can be nearly fully reproduced, with less than 1 % packages remaining non-reproducible.

We examine hyperscaler Confidential Computing solutions to assess whether CVMs can be attested without implicitly trusting the CSP, enabling Zero Trust architectures. Our findings show that, as of now, none of the existing solutions fully eliminates trust in the hypervisor. However, the remaining trust assumptions are minimal, suggesting that trust in the CSP could be eliminated with additional work. We conclude with recommendations for closing the gaps.

Acknowledgments. This work is part of the SOVEREIGN project and funded by the Agentur für Innovation in der Cybersicherheit GmbH (Cyberagentur). The Agentur für Innovation in der Cybersicherheit GmbH did not interfere in the research process and its results.

Disclosure of Interests. The authors have no competing interests to declare that are relevant to the content of this article.

References

1. Amazon Web Services: Nitrotpm for amazon ec2 instances (2025). https://docs.aws.amazon.com/AWSEC2/latest/UserGuide/nitrotpm.html
2. AMD: AMD SEV-SNP: Strengthening VM Isolation with Integrity Protection and More. White paper, AMD (01 2020)
3. Asadujjaman, A., Pontes, D., Falcao, E., Brito, A.: Securing confidential VMS in public clouds. In: 2024 IEEE International Conference on Cloud Computing Technology and Science (CloudCom), pp. 55–62. IEEE (2024)
4. Castillo, F., Brito, E., Werner, S., Pullonen-Raudvere, P., Heiss, J.: Towards trusted service monitoring: Verifiable service level agreements, (2025). arXiv preprint arXiv:2510.13370
5. Cheng, P.C., et al.: Intel TDX demystified: a top-down approach. ACM Comput. Surv. **56**(9), 1–33 (2024)
6. Community, K.D.: The linux/x86 boot protocol. https://docs.kernel.org/arch/x86/boot.html
7. Corporation, I.: Intel® trust domain extensions (Intel®tdx) module td partitioning architecture specification (Nov 2024). https://cdrdv2-public.intel.com/839198/intel-tdx-module-1.5-td-partitioning-spec-354807001.pdf
8. Decentriq: Swiss cheese to cheddar: securing amd sev-snp early boot (2022)
9. Dolev, D., Yao, A.: On the security of public key protocols. IEEE Trans. Inf. Theory **29**(2), 198–208 (1983)
10. Eichner, H., et al.: Confidential federated computations. arXiv preprint arXiv:2404.10764 (2024)
11. Eisoldt, J., et al.: SoK: A cloudy view on trust relationships of CVMs - how confidential virtual machines are falling short in public cloud (2025). arXiv preprint arXiv:2503.08256
12. Gartner: (Feb 2022). https://www.gartner.com/en/newsroom/press-releases/2022-02-09-gartner-says-more-than-half-of-enterprise-it-spending
13. Google Cloud: Confidential vm attestation (2025). https://cloud.google.com/confidential-computing/confidential-vm/docs/attestation
14. Group, T.: Trusted platform module library part 1: Architecture. Trusted Computing Group. Tech. Rep. 1 (2019)
15. Hugenroth, D., Lins, M., Mayrhofer, R., Beresford, A.R.: Attestable builds: compiling verifiable binaries on untrusted systems using trusted execution environments. In: Proceedings of the 2025 ACM SIGSAC Conference on Computer and Communications Security, pp. 4514–4528 (2025).
16. Intel: Intel®Trust Domain Extensions. Tech. Rep. 343961-002US, Intel (08 2020)
17. Intel Corporation: TDX Virtual Firmware Design Guide, Revision 004. Intel Corporation, Santa Clara, CA (Dec 2023). https://cdrdv2-public.intel.com/733585/tdx-virtual-firmware-design-guide-rev-004-20231206.pdf
18. Kim, J., Choi, Y., Kim, S.: Attestation-based sbom integrity verification for secure and transparent software supply chains. In: 2025 25th Asia-Pacific Network Operations and Management Symposium (APNOMS), pp. 1–4. IEEE (2025)
19. Li, M., Yang, Y., Chen, G., Yan, M., Zhang, Y.: Sok: Understanding design choices and pitfalls of trusted execution environments. In: Proceedings of the 19th ACM Asia Conference on Computer and Communications Security, pp. 1600–1616 (2024)
20. Mao, J., Zhu, H., Fan, J., Li, L., Chang, X.: Towards trust proof for secure confidential virtual machines (2024). arXiv preprint arXiv:2405.01030

21. Ménétrey, J., et al.: Attestation mechanisms for trusted execution environments demystified. In: IFIP International Conference on Distributed Applications and Interoperable Systems, pp. 95–113. Springer (2022)
22. Microsoft: Uefi secure boot customization for windows (2025). https://github.com/nsacyber/Hardware-and-Firmware-Security-Guidance/blob/master/secureboot/Windows.md#24-create-hashes
23. Microsoft Azure: Azure confidential vms guest attestation (2025). https://github.com/Azure/confidential-computing-cvm-guest-attestation/blob/main/cvm-guest-attestation.md
24. Murik, D.: [RFC PATCH] i386/sev: Support measured direct -kernel boot on SNP (Mar 2022). https://lore.kernel.org/qemu-devel/20220329064038.96006-1-dovmurik%40linux.ibm.com/#r
25. Narayanan, V., et al.: Remote attestation of confidential VMS using ephemeral vTPMs. In: Proceedings of the 39th Annual Computer Security Applications Conference, pp. 732–743 (2023)
26. Niemi, A., Sovio, S., Ekberg, J.E.: Towards interoperable enclave attestation: Learnings from decades of academic work. In: 2022 31st Conference of Open Innovations Association (FRUCT), pp. 189–200. IEEE (2022)
27. OpenVMM: Openvmm tdx.rs (2025). https://github.com/microsoft/openvmm/blob/4851377300ae54aed2580a98da6997b5d93777b7/vm/x86/x86defs/src/tdx.rs#L124
28. Pecholt, J., Wessel, S.: Cocotpm: Trusted platform modules for virtual machines in confidential computing environments. In: Proceedings of the 38th Annual Computer Security Applications Conference, pp. 989–998 (2022)
29. Pontes, D., Silva, F., Melo, A., Asadujjaman, A., Falcão, E., Brito, A., Filho, C.: Multi-platform and vault-free attestation of confidential vms. In: Proceedings of the 13th Latin-American Symposium on Dependable and Secure Computing, pp. 241–251 (2024)
30. Radaljac, T., Miladinović, D., Stanisavljević, Ž., Vuletić, P.: Secure distributed computing in cloud using trusted execution environments. In: 2024 32nd Telecommunications Forum (TELFOR), pp. 1–4 IEEE (2024)
31. Rose, S., Borchert, O., Mitchell, S., Connelly, S.: Zero trust architecture (2020-08-10 04:08:00 2020). https://doi.org/10.6028/NIST.SP.800-207
32. Scopelliti, G., Baumann, C., Mühlberg, J.T.: Understanding trust relationships in cloud-based confidential computing. In: 2024 IEEE European Symposium on Security and Privacy Workshops (EuroS&PW), pp. 169–176. IEEE (2024)
33. Takekoshi, S., Mori, M., Fukai, T., Shinagawa, T.: AML injection attacks on confidential VMS. IIJ Research Laboratory Seminar (2024). https://seminar-materials.iijlab.net/iijlab-seminar/iijlab-seminar-20241217.pdf
34. Trusted Computing Group (TCG): TCG PC client platform firmware profile specification. Technical Report Version 1.06 Rev. 52, Trusted Computing Group (2023)
35. UEFI Forum: UEFI platform initialization (PI) specification version 1.9 (2024)

Decentralizing Trust: Distributed Signature Activation Modules for Resilient Key Management

Stefan Genchev(✉), Veronika Bauer, Sebastian Gallenmüller, and Georg Carle

Chair of Network Architectures and Services, Technical University of Munich, Boltzmannstr. 3, 85748 Garching bei München, Germany
{stefan.genchev,veronika_andrea.bauer, sebastian.gallenmueller,carle}@tum.de

Abstract. Signature Activation Modules (SAMs) are an established security mechanism in key management systems that enforce strict usage control over keys. However, current deployments face multiple challenges, such as overreliance on individual external providers and proprietary protocols. In this paper, we address several constraints of local SAM deployments and introduce a novel architecture for distributed SAMs. A core element of this architecture is an evaluation of authentication and authorization evidence for a signing operation through several independent instances. We strengthen this strategy through hardware-anchored trust, leveraging different Trusted Computing technologies, including HSMs, security microcontrollers, and Trusted Execution Environments on general-purpose CPUs. Thereby, we improve the operational resilience of SAMs and enable their operation in possibly untrusted physical environments. Through a proof-of-concept implementation based on off-the-shelf components, we show the general feasibility of our architecture for a conservative security model. We perform measurements for three relevant data authentication use cases—possibly automated approaches based on symmetric and asymmetric keys as well as human-in-the-loop signing. Our results demonstrate that distributed SAMs are feasible and can support organizations in exercising sovereign control over important key material.

Keywords: SAM · eIDAS · Remote signing · Trusted Computing

1 Introduction

A common strategy for employing hardware protection for key material involves remote Key Management Services (KMSs). KMS solutions, through centrally managed trusted hardware, prevent the extraction of key material to untrusted environments and typically enable transparency through audit logs. An important aspect of key management in this regard concerns usage control. Restricting

Z. Afzal et al. (Eds.): ARES 2026 Workshops, LNCS 16900, pp. 290–307, 2027.
https://doi.org/10.1007/978-3-032-35576-8_16

access to a key bound to an authentication secret (such as a bearer token) represents a first line of defense. More advanced control mechanisms based on a policy and enforced by trusted hardware represent an evolving domain.

Signature Activation Modules (SAMs), as defined in EN 419241-1 [10], are a prominent example of a system enabling such advanced key control in a KMS solution. SAMs build upon a Cryptographic Module (CM), typically a Hardware Security Module (HSM), and ensure that a key in the CM is usable only upon proper authentication and authorization of the holder to whom the key is assigned. In the EU, SAMs are used to protect the signing keys used for creating qualified signatures—which, pursuant to EU Regulation 910/2014 (eIDAS) [8], are legally equivalent to handwritten signatures. SAMs represent a well-established and field-tested key control solution based on trusted hardware.

This work is motivated by our observation that SAMs following EN 419241-1 [10] are predominantly used in highly centralized infrastructures and in the context of eIDAS [8]. We argue that SAM-based KMS solutions can provide significant value beyond this established setting, in particular when deployed closer to the organizations whose keys they protect. A local SAM-based KMS can lower the threshold for organizations to adopt advanced hardware- and policy-based protection for keys. Such a deployment allows organizations to keep direct operational control over their critical key material and reduces their dependence on external providers, thereby strengthening the digital sovereignty of organizations. Document signing, code signing, and authentication of access tokens for high-value systems, among others, can benefit from such advanced protection of the key material involved. Local SAM-based KMS solutions can further better reflect the individual security requirements of different organizations.

To enable such deployments, we investigate strategies to lower adoption barriers and address the security gap that results from operating KMS solutions in possibly untrusted environments. By combining readily available Trusted Computing technologies, we present a practical and deployable KMS architecture that anchors trust in hardware and improves operational, system-level resilience through decentralization. By explicitly placing our work in the context of EN 419241-1 [10], our results can benefit from existing evaluation and operational experience. To the best of our knowledge, this work provides the first study focused on the decentralization of SAMs.

Contributions. Our work makes the following contributions:

1. **Novel SAM architecture**: We propose a novel, generic architecture for SAMs suitable for operation in untrusted environments. Our architecture represents a specialization of the TW4S blueprint defined in EN 419241-1 [10] and, therefore, maintains compatibility with existing systems. We reflect the current state of trusted execution technology and propose a secure composition of different technologies—such as security microcontrollers and Trusted Execution Environments (TEEs) offered by general-purpose CPUs. Through this composition, we address physical attacks and the lack of specialized personnel in our target environments.

2. **Experiments**: We show the feasibility of our architecture through a proof of concept and perform experiments to assess its performance. By exclusively selecting off-the-shelf components for our prototype, we present a practical solution suitable for distributed deployments. We measure a delay of at most 1248 ms per signature transaction for a common use case of human-in-the-loop signing in a minimal setup with a dedicated secure key store.

Paper Structure. Sect. 2 analyzes the problems associated with contemporary SAM solutions and identifies approaches for building more resilient SAMs. Based on this analysis, we define a novel architecture for distributed SAMs in Sect. 3. We report on an implementation and evaluation of our architecture using readily available components in Sect. 4 and our experiments based on this prototype in Sect. 5. Finally, we address related work in Sect. 6.

2 Problem Analysis

Several observations motivate a specialized security architecture for decentralized SAMs. In this section, we critically examine these observations.

Trusted Computing for SAMs. Ensuring the integrity and confidentiality of the application logic and secrets in a SAM is paramount to the security of the composite signing system. Therefore, a SAM must be executed in a trusted environment, prompting the use of specialized hardware. At the same time, we argue that an important prerequisite for a decentralized deployment, as targeted by our work, is the use of off-the-shelf components with open specifications. In this regard, the ability to load custom code without the manufacturer's authorization and documented interfaces that are not subject to confidentiality agreements are important properties that we consider crucial for open source development. This provides organizations with the basis for achieving local KMS deployment independent of individual third-party providers.

Several HSM manufacturers [14,22,25] offer solutions for executing custom code within the trusted (hardware) boundaries of their devices. Both Cryptomathic [9] and Entrust [13] use this capability for the execution of their SAM products. This approach bundles CMs and SAMs physically and enables the use of trusted paths. However, we can identify several limitations. First, HSMs are associated with a high cost factor and require specialized personnel for operation. This renders HSMs unsuitable for highly decentralized deployments, especially for smaller-scale organizations. Second, their interfaces for executing custom application logic are often proprietary and not interoperable. For the HSMs approved for creating qualified signatures in the EU, that is, certified as Qualified Signature Creation Devices [12], at the time of writing, we were not able to find evidence to the contrary. An alternative approach requires a SAM executed in an external, trusted environment to communicate with a CM over a secure channel. Ascertia's SAM [2] adopts this approach. It therefore remains to identify a suitable, dedicated execution environment for the SAM.

Several Trusted Execution Environment (TEE) implementations on general-purpose CPUs are readily available across numerous hardware platforms and can provide an isolated environment for the sensitive computations of a SAM. This includes Intel SGX, Intel TDX, AMD SEV-SNP, and ARM TrustZone, all of which enable the execution of custom application logic without restrictions. However, the operation of such TEEs in untrusted environments requires special attention. TEEs on general-purpose CPUs typically exclude physical attacks from their threat model, the presence of which we must assume in untrusted environments. This is the case for all previously mentioned TEE implementations [1,16]. Through a hardware attack, an attacker may extract key material used for the secure channel with a CM and circumvent the SAM's security functionality. Chuang et al. [6], for example, demonstrate a portable device capable of extracting secrets from popular TEE implementations. Connell et al. [7] propose a two-layered approach addressing this limitation. First, they distribute trust in their protocol across instances running on different TEE implementations to address attacks against individual implementations. Second, they propose an operational distribution of trust among several independent providers (specifically, AWS, Google Cloud, and Azure) as a practical barrier against physical attacks.

Security microcontrollers, in contrast, operate in untrusted environments by default and have specialized security architectures that address such attacks. While the hardware and operating system are often proprietary, several manufacturers support the open JavaCard Runtime Environment (JCRE) [20], which provides a publicly accessible API for applications and for which an open-source simulator [18] exists. The JCRE enables application providers to target multiple hardware platforms with a single code base. Furthermore, there is extensive existing experience in evaluating security products based on security microcontrollers, including advanced hardware attacks [15]. Executing complex protocols or handling many parallel users on a single security microcontroller, however, may not be feasible due to the significant hardware limitations of many off-the-shelf security microcontrollers. A strategy for workload distribution, reflecting this constraint, is required in this case.

Homogenous Implementations. Protection Profile EN 419241-2 [11] highlights the role of SAMs as independent and trustworthy verifiers of authentication and authorization evidence. Per Security Objective *OT.SAP*, SAMs must implement *all* steps of the Signature Activation Protocol (SAP). Threat *T.SAP_BYPASS* further recognizes that non-conformance with the SAP can violate the integrity of the signing system. Consequently, for both direct and indirect authentication [11], SAMs must implement one or more cryptographic protocols within the SAP. This requirement, however, can also introduce a structural weakness due to a reliance on a single software stack in a SAM. Specific concerns in this regard are human errors, vulnerabilities in external dependencies, and supply chain attacks. We argue that an overreliance on the security functionality of SAMs may additionally result from the fact that some SAMs carry a certification, discouraging additional independent security mechanisms in a defense-in-depth strategy.

Formal verification may provide the necessary assurance that a SAM's code implements the SAP and any protocols within the SAP correctly. Chen et al. [5] describe a foundational, practical approach to software reliability with n-version programming. Applied to SAMs, this approach would require SAMs to assess the results of several different *programs* implementing SAP logic, minimizing the risk that errors stemming from a common but incorrect viewpoint within a small, closely collaborating group go unnoticed. A challenge associated with this approach, however, lies in interactive cryptographic protocols—such as protocols based on secure channels rather than verifiable artifacts. We further note that this approach, while similar to the previously discussed distribution of trust among several TEE instances, does not necessarily allow for a 1:1 mapping between a program version and a TEE implementation.

SAP Complexity. A further aspect relevant to the security of SAMs concerns the general implementational complexity of SAPs. Due to the plurality of supported authentication methods and the inherent complexity of authentication protocols, a SAM's code base may increase significantly in size. This complexity directly affects the SAM's Trusted Computing Base, negatively impacting the auditability of SAMs. Considering the example of XML-based assertions (e.g., in the context of SAML), a SAM may need to, inter alia, validate input XML documents against a trusted schema set and include an XML parser. Furthermore, risk-based control of the authentication process, e.g., based on Machine Learning, may not be possible at all due to hardware limitations.

One approach to address this problem is to increase the specialization of SAMs by limiting the number of authentication methods a single SAM supports. However, we recognize that such a restriction may not be commercially viable and may introduce a significant overhead with certification. An existing strategy to enable flexibility with respect to signer authentication in SAMs is through *delegated authentication* [11, Sect. 7.3]. In this case, an external entity (delegated party) performs the authentication procedure and issues an attestation that can be verified by a SAM. Consequently, SAMs must only be able to verify attestations, possibly following a well-defined profile and a fixed algorithm set. With this approach, however, operational measures must ensure the security of the integrated solution [11]. Notably, authentication in this case does not benefit from the security mechanisms of a SAM and is susceptible to attacks on external systems. Entrust's SAM supports a hybrid approach in which the SAM independently enforces a knowledge factor based on a signer's secret in combination with delegated authentication [13].

3 Architecture

Based on our problem analysis in Sect. 2, we proceed to define an architecture for resilient SAMs. We focus on three areas of interest within a signing system.

3.1 Roles

We address the observations from Sect. 2 through two measures that affect the functional profiles of the systems involved in remote signing. First, we propose reducing the Trusted Computing Base of SAMs by **extracting the SAP logic to an external entity**, a *Witness*, that attests to the correct execution of a SAP. Through this measure, similar to delegated authentication, we decouple SAMs from individual authentication methods, facilitate the security evaluation of SAMs, and reduce the computational overhead on SAMs. We borrow the concept of a witness from the field of transparency, reflecting their role as independent control entities. Second, in our architecture, **several Witnesses redundantly verify the Signature Activation Data (SAD)**—that is, the authentication and authorization evidence—and must agree for a signature to be created. We aim to achieve dissimilar redundancy in this way. Overall, we arrive at a distributed system of instances that fulfill a specific function in processing signing transactions:

1. **Witness**: A Witness validates signing requests of signers and issues attestations confirming the legitimacy of individual signing operations. Witnesses may be specialized, supporting only a specific SAP or a subset thereof. Each Witness uses a unique, non-exportable asymmetric key pair for attestations, possibly pinned to a remote attestation of a TEE that the Witness is executed in (see Sect. 3.2). We assume that a trust framework defines the authorization of a Witness to issue attestations for a specific SAP.
2. **Key Store**: A Key Store instance (SCDev per EN 419241-1 [10], CM per EN 419241-2 [11]) securely stores key material and exposes a set of cryptographic operations to authenticated clients. Importantly, we require that Key Stores support a secure channel for communicating with authenticated clients. We expect that Key Stores enable the export and later import of key material under wrap based on an on-device key. Key Stores may be certified according to FIPS 140-3 or EN 419221-5 for compliance with existing regulations.
3. **SAM Kernel**: With the functionality of a Witness extracted, we introduce the role of a SAM Kernel. A SAM Kernel's functionality is largely consistent with that of a SAM as defined in EN 419241-1 [10] in the case of delegated authentication. SAM Kernels represent an authenticated client of Key Stores and terminate secure channels with Key Stores to execute key operations. For each signing request from a signer, a SAM Kernel collects attestations issued by Witnesses until the required number and type of attestations are reached. Once this is the case, the SAM Kernel activates the signer's key and performs the signing operation. In addition, we require SAM Kernels to handle requests for creating new signing key pairs.
4. **Orchestrator**: An Orchestrator is the entry point for signing requests originating from a signing system's back-end[1]. Orchestrators integrate instances with the former three roles and coordinate the necessary communication. For this, Orchestrators can implement the *service registry* pattern, enabling

[1] Specifically, the Server Signing Application (SSA) according to EN 419241-1 [10].

dynamic resolution of the available instances and their roles. The role of the Orchestrator is comparable to the NSSAM Driver proposed by nextsense [19]. Importantly, Orchestrators do not implement a security function. We assume that a malicious Orchestrator can assume the capabilities of an active network-level attacker—incl., creating, modifying, and dropping messages. Without cryptographic involvement in the key generation or signing protocols (described later in Sect. 3.3), a Denial of Service attack vector remains.

3.2 Deployment

In Sect. 2, we discussed the problem of finding a suitable Trusted Computing platform for SAMs. Our role concept from Sect. 3.1 and its targeted separation of duties enables us to follow a hybrid deployment approach. We define two abstract types of TEEs for our architecture, reflecting the varying security characteristics of different TEE implementations:

1. **Type "A" TEE**: Type "A" TEEs protect the integrity and confidentiality of a trusted application's code and data from external influence. Importantly, this TEE type must provide sufficient protection against physical attacks that aim at extracting information from or tampering with the execution of applications. One implementation of this TEE type would be a custom firmware extension on an HSM, as used by Entrust [13] and Cryptomathic [9]. We also consider security microcontrollers as a possible implementation.
2. **Type "B" TEE**: This TEE type represents a relaxation of our requirement for protection against physical attacks. TEEs of this type must only provide logical isolation to trusted applications, including measures to protect the integrity of the executed application logic. For this TEE type, we assume that a remote attestation mechanism exists that can associate a public key with one or more measurements of the executed code. While Intel SGX, Intel TDX, and AMD SEV-SNP provide suitable execution environments with these characteristics, we also consider TPM-measured and attested machines to fulfill our requirements.

SAM Kernels represent a single point of compromise in our security model as they store and process long-lived and session secrets used for secure channels with Key Stores. As previously discussed, an attacker in possession of such secrets can circumvent the protections offered by SAMs. Consequently, we require that SAM Kernels are deployed to a Type "A" TEE to protect these secrets, especially when operated in untrusted environments. In contrast, Witnesses can generally be executed in Type "B" TEEs, since only a single trustworthy instance is required to maintain trust in the system. The (i) number of required Witness versions, (ii) their mapping to one or more TEE implementations of one or both TEE types, and (iii) the physical deployment locations of the TEEs represent control parameters that can be aligned with the specific security needs of a use case.

To maintain sovereign control over its key material, an organization must, as a minimum, operate a SAM Kernel and a corresponding Key Store in a local environment. Since Witnesses may be implemented in a stateless manner and we assume a remote attestation capability for Type "B" TEEs, remote hardware suffices for Witnesses. Connell et al. [7] propose a multi-cloud deployment as a method to distribute trust. In this case, a migration of a Witness from one cloud provider to another can be performed during runtime with remote attestations as a trust anchor, avoiding a dependency on a specific provider. We also envision a purpose-built network of Witnesses operated by Trust Service Providers, such as within eIDAS [8], in a software-as-a-service model. Such a network can explicitly target solutions with regulatory requirements.

We illustrate our architecture in Fig. 1. Section 4 reports on specific instantiations of the two TEE types in our proof-of-concept implementation.

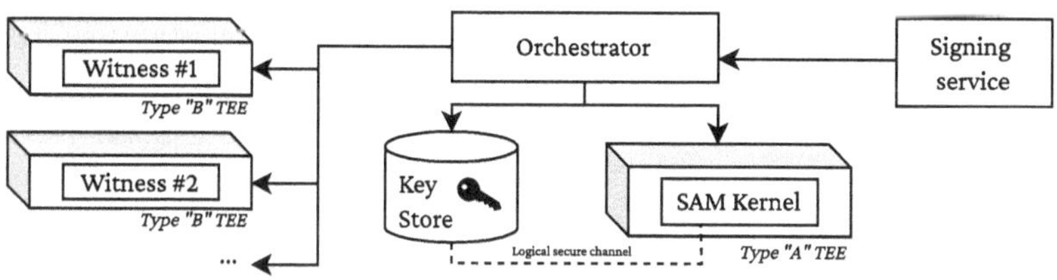

Fig. 1. Proposed architecture for a distributed SAM.

3.3 Protocol

Signer keys are in the center of our architecture. In our design, all keys managed by a SAM are associated with a *signature policy*. A signature policy defines one or more *conditions* under which a key can be used for a signing operation and is specific to a signer. For example, a signature policy may require a human signer to authenticate via Passkey. With Passkeys, an authenticator produces a signature over a challenge that is verifiable using a previously enrolled public key. Therefore, a policy condition tailored for Passkey authentication can bear the credential public key of a specific user. In turn, an automated signer can authenticate via a signed token or a TEE attestation.

In the following sections, we discuss two important phases of a key's lifecycle: key generation and usage.

Key Generation. New signing keys must be requested through the SAM Kernel, since the SAM Kernel maintains a secure channel to a Key Store. Upon generation of a key, the SAM Kernel can either (i) export the key under wrap and delete it from the Key Store memory, (ii) keep the key in the Key Store memory and delete it following a signature transaction, or (iii) keep the key in the Key Store memory without restrictions. The first option enables a potentially unlimited number of signers to use the same Key Store. The second option optimizes one-shot signing with short-lived certificates. The third option is suitable for an organization's credentials.

SAM Kernels must enforce signature policies for keys post-generation. For this purpose, SAM Kernels require knowledge of the association of a specific key with a signature policy. We can identify two approaches to implement this association. With a dynamic assignment, different policies can be assigned to the same key over time. In this case, SAM Kernels require authenticated, rollback-resistant state that scales with the number of signers in order to prevent replay and re-association attacks. Dynamic assignment is necessary to support the practice of key pre-generation [13]. In contrast, a static assignment of a key to a signature policy at generation time can reduce the infrastructure requirements. A SAM Kernel must authenticate the assignment only once. We select the latter approach in order to support plug-and-play deployments.

SAM Kernels can certify the association of a public key with a signature policy through a signature. A SAM Kernel can either use an internally managed key or a key protected by a Key Store. A Certificate Authority can then issue a certificate based on the information in this confirmation. Notably, the Certificate Authority's key can also reside in the same Key Store, with specialized Witnesses controlling the certificate issuance. This approach strongly binds the information in a certificate to the enforced policy.

Signing Protocol. For signing data, we propose the following protocol:

1. A signer transmits Data to be Signed (DTBS) to the signing service. The signing service interacts with the signer for authentication and signature authorization, collecting the SAD. Here, we assume that the SAD is a collection of records verifiable by Witnesses (for brevity, referred to as *evidence*).
2. The signing service prepares and transmits a signing request, which includes the DTBS and the evidence, to the Orchestrator.
3. Based on the information in the signature request, the Orchestrator locates the signature policy associated with the requested key and prepares a *signature proposal*. The signature proposal references, inter alia, the signature policy and the DTBS.
4. Out of its pool of registered Witnesses, the Orchestrator selects a subset that can process the proposal. The Orchestrator then propagates (i) its signature proposal, (ii) the key's signature policy, and (iii) the received evidence to this subset.
5. Each Witness verifies that the signature proposal references the received signature policy and that the signature policy is fulfilled by the received evidence[2]. If this is the case, the Witness signs the received signature proposal.
6. Once the Orchestrator collects the signatures from the specified set of Witnesses, the Orchestrator forwards the signature proposal and the signatures of the Witnesses to a SAM Kernel.
7. The SAM Kernel verifies that the signature policy referenced in the signature proposal corresponds to the policy that the key is associated with. The SAM

[2] We note that EN 419241-1 [10, SRA_SAP.2.3] requires the SAD to reference the DTBS. Therefore, Witnesses also verify that the DTBS in the evidence corresponds to the DTBS in the signature proposal.

Kernel also determines the required number and type of Witness attestations and verifies all received signatures. If all verifications are successful, the SAM Kernel activates the key in its assigned Key Store and performs a signing operation over the secure channel with this Key Store. In case the signer's key was exported under wrap during generation, the SAM Kernel additionally installs the key prior to signature generation and deletes it upon completion.
8. The Orchestrator returns the produced signature to the signer.

We provide an overview of the relationships between the signature policy, the signature proposal, the SAD as evidence, and the DTBS, as introduced in our signing protocol in this section, in Fig. 2. The signature policy is fixed, enforced by a SAM Kernel but evaluated by Witnesses. The remaining records represent transaction data prepared for each signing operation. Reference relationships can be implemented through a digest to reduce I/O requirements.

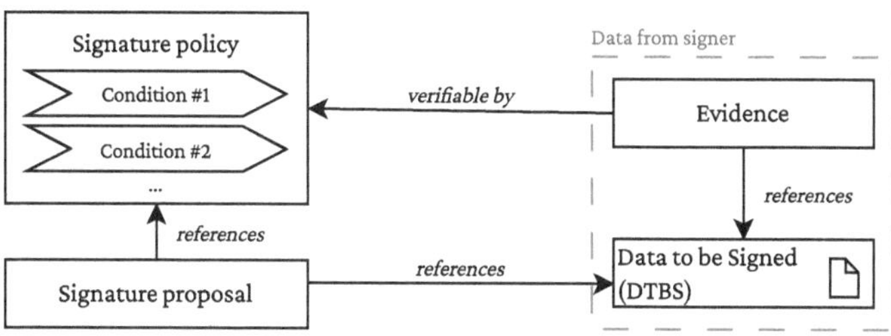

Fig. 2. Relationships of the records used in our signing protocol.

4 Implementation

To demonstrate the feasibility of our architecture, we implemented a proof-of-concept prototype reflecting our considerations. Our goal is to show a cost-effective, yet conservative implementation of our architecture, suitable for decentralized operation. In this section, we report on key implementational aspects of our prototype. We describe a specific component deployment setup in Sect. 5.

As a Key Store, we use a YubiHSM 2 device from Yubico—specifically, its non-FIPS variant with firmware version 2.4. At the time of writing, Yubico offers this device on its website for 773 EUR. YubiHSMs support a version of the SCP03 Secure Channel. We terminate this Secure Channel in our SAM Kernel. YubiHSMs currently support a limited number (256) of objects, which include asymmetric keys. To support the first key handling option described in Sect. 3.3, we can offload signer keys to untrusted storage using the `EXPORT WRAPPED` command and a symmetric wrapping key. We implement command batching to reduce the number of round trips between the SAM Kernel and a YubiHSM. This is possible for two reasons. First, the construction of the SCP03

Secure Channel enables batching in general. Responses that are not known to the SAM Kernel in advance, in the case of batching, do not modify the chaining state required for sending new commands over the channel. Second, the commands used for signing do not need feedback from a response. Signing commands, such as `SIGN ECDSA`, require a key's Object ID, which is returned by the preceding `IMPORT WRAPPED` command. As an optimization, we propose storing a key's Object ID, fixed at generation time, together with its blob. In this way, a `SIGN *` command can be prepared without feedback from an `IMPORT WRAPPED` command.

For implementing the SAM, we use a security microcontroller—a JCOP Integrated Circuit Card (model *J3R180*) in the ISO 7810 ID-1 form factor. We obtained this card for 10 EUR from an Austrian provider. Our selected model *J3R180* provides a JavaCard 3.0.5 runtime environment and implements the v2.3 GlobalPlatform Card Specification. Version 3.0.5 of the runtime environment is the first version to natively support CMAC, required for the SCP03 Secure Channel with the YubiHSM. At applet installation time, we generate two non-exportable keys—an asymmetric attestation key and a symmetric message authentication key. We use the former key to certify the association of a public key with a specific policy. In turn, we use the latter key to seal key records (which include a key's Object ID, associated signature policy, and blob) that are exported to untrusted storage.

We implemented Witnesses in Rust and Java. Both Witnesses can verify assertions from FIDO authenticators.

5 Experiments

We assess the operational characteristics of our architecture applied to the prototype described in Sect. 4 through several experiments. Our evaluation focuses on two aspects concerning the recurring signing process:

1. **End-to-end delay:** The end-to-end delay introduced by a SAM and an HSM represents a lower bound for the delay that signers will experience when signing data. The end-to-end delay is therefore highly relevant to the user experience offered by the system to human signer and any use case-specific real-time requirements. Treating our system as a black box, we measure the processing time of a valid signature request until a signature is available for further processing.
2. **Delay composition:** Our architecture is characterized by a composition of multiple systems with vastly different hardware limitations. To measure the contributions of individual systems to the end-to-end delay in different steps of the signing process, we assume a whitebox view of our system and measure delays from the vantage point of the Orchestrator.

In this section, we present our setup to provide insight into these aspects and report on our findings.

Setup. We use a setup with one Key Store, one SAM Kernel, and three Witnesses (executed in Intel TDX, Intel SGX through Gramine, and on bare metal, respectively) for our measurements. These components have the configurations described in Sect. 4. Our test driver, the Orchestrator, and the Witnesses are executed on the same server platform with a TDX- and SGX-capable Intel Xeon Silver 4514Y CPU and 256 GB RAM. The YubiHSM2 and the J3R180 security microcontroller are connected directly to this server through USB 3.0 ports.

We perform an experiment series with three key configurations. The first two configurations use a single resident key (that is, a key that remains in the persistent memory of the Key Store) and target scenarios for automated authentication of data by an organization. Through (i) a symmetric key and an HMAC based on SHA-256, an organization can authenticate high-value objects for internal use—such as tickets and access tokens. In turn, (ii) through an ECC asymmetric key based on P-384 and an ECDSA signature, an organization can commit to data publicly—for example, through PDF signatures. Our third configuration, in contrast, uses several personalized keys and targets human-in-the-loop (document) signing scenarios. For each signing operation, our test driver iteratively selects a random user from a pool of 25 users, constructs a signature request, and initiates a signing operation. In this case, we use (iii) an ECC asymmetric key based on P-384, imported and deleted prior to and following each signature operation, as well as an ECDSA signature.

In all experiments, we use protocol-compliant FIDO authentication with an authenticator simulated in software. For each unique signer, the test driver (i) assigns a new FIDO authenticator, (ii) prepares a signature policy given a user's unique authenticator public key, and (iii) requests a new key pair from the HSM through the SAM Kernel. During the testing phase, the test driver generates a random 32-byte DTBS and authenticates the request with the respective user's FIDO authenticator.

Results. We plot the measured end-to-end delay and its composition for our three key configurations in Fig. 3. We also provide detailed delay statistics for the third key configuration in Table 1.

At the beginning of the signing process, the Orchestrator obtains signatures from our three Witnesses. Since our implementation of the Orchestrator uses multiple threads for communication with Witnesses, the delay of this step in the signing process corresponds to the longest delay of a Witness. In our measurements, Intel TDX consistently introduces a higher overhead than Intel SGX (see Table 1). However, while TEEs often represent a bottleneck in high-throughput scenarios, here Witnesses contribute a relatively small delay—especially in comparison with the processing times of the SAM Kernel and the YubiHSM2. For our worst-case measurements, this delay accounts for only $\approx$2% of the end-to-end delay (see Table 1).

Both configurations targeting automated use cases achieve an end-to-end delay of less than 266 ms and 421 ms for HMAC/SHA-256 and P-384/ECDSA, respectively. In the 99th percentile, our minimal prototype achieves a through-

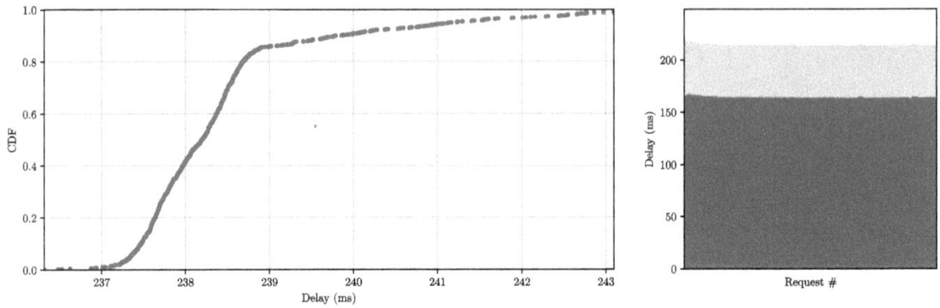

(a) HMAC/SHA-256 operations with resident symmetric key.

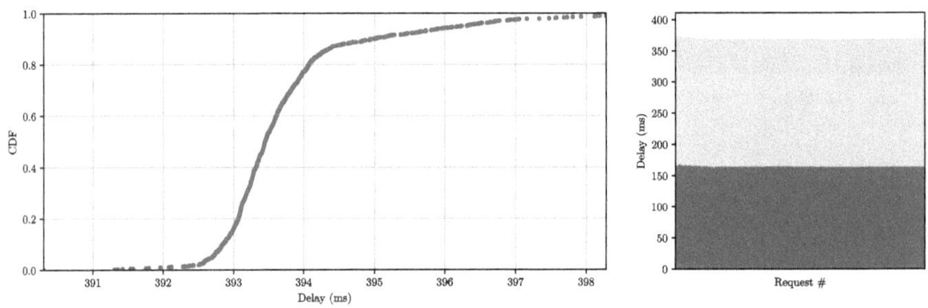

(b) Operations with resident P-384 key.

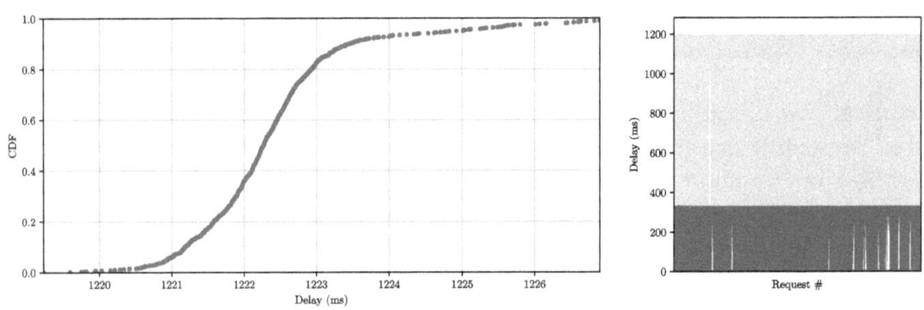

(c) Operations with P-384 keys exported under wrap.

Fig. 3. Plots visualizing the CDF of the end-to-end delay (left hand side) and its composition (right hand side) for (a) a resident HMAC/SHA-256 key, (b) a resident P-384 key and (c) P-384 keys exported under wrap, respectively, for n=1000 measurements per configuration. The CDF is restricted to the 99th percentile for readability. The delay composition shows four components of interest—the Witness verification (dark blue), SAM Kernel command preparation (red), YubiHSM2 command execution (pink) and SAM Kernel response processing (light blue) delays in order from bottom to top.

Table 1. Delay statistics for notable operations within the signing process. All measurements are in milliseconds.

	min.	median	P99	P99.9	max.	SD
Base metal Witness signature	2.87	3.40	5.84	15.30	23.02	0.96
SGX Witness signature	3.33	3.73	6.02	12.91	23.51	0.90
TDX Witness signature	4.14	5.09	7.15	16.56	24.24	0.91
Install sealed record	23.68	23.93	24.05	24.08	24.12	0.06
Verify Witnesses' signatures	121.68	122.47	122.83	122.97	123.07	0.21
Prepare `IMPORT WRAPPED` ↪ command	144.64	144.91	145.12	145.16	145.17	0.10
Prepare `SIGN ECDSA` and ↪ `DELETE OBJECT` commands	60.46	60.70	60.84	60.91	61.26	0.06
Process `IMPORT WRAPPED` ↪ command	569.39	572.32	573.48	576.10	576.72	0.53
Process `SIGN ECDSA` command	148.68	150.29	150.81	151.13	151.88	0.26
Process `DELETE OBJECT` ↪ command	24.96	25.31	25.75	28.99	49.63	0.79
Handle YubiHSM responses	116.33	116.65	116.85	116.90	116.95	0.09
End-to-end delay	1219.24	1222.27	1227.15	1246.97	1248.23	1.72

put of 4.11 and 2.5 transactions per second, respectively. In contrast, the third configuration breaks the one-second-barrier as we record a maximum of 1248 ms.

In Table 1, we can identify a significant overhead caused by operations related to the required import and subsequent deletion of a (non-resident) key. A wrapped P-384 key as produced by the YubiHSM2 exhibits a length of about 230 bytes for a P-384 key, which leads to longer (compared to the short execution times of other commands) processing times in the SAM Kernel for the preparation of the `IMPORT WRAPPED` command. The processing of this command on the YubiHSM2 further contributes the longest recorded delay in the signing process of up to 577 ms. Both operations associated with the `IMPORT WRAPPED` command combined are responsible for up to 58% of the recorded end-to-end delay. The high end-to-end delay of the third key configuration affects both the processing times of individual transactions and the overall throughput of a signing system.

Since personal signatures carry a legal value, the act of signing documents is bound to a human signer's ability to inspect, assess, and approve their contents. This constraint supports two arguments with respect to the real-time requirements of this use case. First, a single signer can only sign a limited number of documents per day. Second, the approval process represents a manual process with a duration in the order of, at least, seconds. We build upon these arguments to argue that an end-to-end delay of $\approx$1200 ms is acceptable for human-in-the-loop signing in decentralized deployments—such as small and medium-sized enterprises hosting a local instance. We further argue that a system based on our prototype may potentially support larger organizations under the assumption of non-bursty usage patterns. Assuming constant utilization and given our worst-case measurement, our minimal setup with off-the-shelf components can produce up to 23,076 signatures in an 8-hour span.

Importantly, we note that our measurements reflect one specific instantiation of our architecture from Sect. 3. Both horizontal and vertical scaling techniques can improve the overall system performance and support use cases with real-time requirements. Horizontal scaling can be achieved by increasing the number of instances that represent a bottleneck. Both our SAM Kernel and Key Store execute resource-blocking operations that introduce extended delays in a signing operation, as evident from our measurements (see Fig. 3). Urien [24] proposes an optimized cluster for security microcontrollers that can be used to distribute workload among several SAM Kernels. In turn, a different hardware platform can support vertical scaling. The use of a high-performance HSM as a Key Store in combination with a firmware extension for the SAM Kernel represents a viable approach that is compatible with our architecture. Nevertheless, one goal of our work is to show that a minimal system based on our prototype is practical for many use cases. By showing this, we argue that this configuration is suitable for a decentralized deployment.

6 Related Work

The field of SAMs is dominated by practical work from the industry [2,9,13,19] rather than academia. This work addresses a research gap in using commodity trusted hardware to support a practical, decentralized operation of SAMs. To the best of our knowledge, we provide the first study in this direction.

SAMs are part of multiple commercially available remote digital signature solutions, including but not limited to [9] and [19]. Contrary to these implementations, our approach aims at local deployment of a KMS. On an abstract level, SAMs enforce a usage policy on key material protected by trusted hardware. Several commercial solutions in the context of crypto wallets exist that provide such functionality. Among those, the use of AWS infrastructure is a common pattern. We can identify three prominent solutions that execute sensitive key operations in AWS Nitro Enclaves and obtain sealing keys for them using the AWS Key Management Service. CubeSigner [4] enables key holders to associate a programmable key policy with a key. In this solution, programmability is achieved through a WebAssembly runtime, which offers significant policy expressiveness. Coinbase [17] and Turnkey [23] similarly offer policy-restricted access to key operations. Importantly, all three solutions handle key material within the boundaries of an AWS Nitro Enclave, raising concerns of side-channel attacks [21]. Our approach, in contrast, accounts for the execution of key operations involving a signer's key material within a purpose-built, possibly certified Key Store (such as an HSM). We further propose a provider-independent architecture in Sect. 3 and show its feasibility through a prototype that can be operated exclusively in a local environment (Sect. 4). We note that our concept of Witnesses bears many similarities with Turnkey's [23]' "Policy Engine Enclave". The "Policy Engine Enclave" accepts, as inputs, information on a transaction and a policy and returns a certified boolean result—exhibiting functional equivalence to Witnesses. In this work, we explicitly address a distribution trust among several program versions and TEE implementations, as opposed to an evaluation of a policy in a single enclave.

One line of work concerns the alternative use of TEEs in general-purpose CPUs to execute sensitive key operations, possibly based on a policy. Aumasson et al. [3] provide an early contribution in this direction. We consider this approach not to be feasible in local deployments, as discussed in Sect. 2.

7 Conclusion

In this work, we investigated how Signature Activation Modules can be operated in a decentralized manner in order to provide advanced key protection for critical key material managed locally. We proposed a generic architecture that accounts for constraints in possibly untrusted (physical) execution environments. A central aspect of this architecture is our novel data-processing model for SAMs, anchored in Trusted Computing. We extract and distribute a SAM's (computationally intensive) evaluation of the legitimacy of signing requests across several independent instances, enabling dissimilar redundancy and reducing the requirements for trusted hardware. At the same time, we map the remaining, limited functionality of a SAM to stronger trusted hardware that can protect long-term and session secrets even in the face of physical attacks. Overall, our architecture can strengthen the operational resilience of SAMs on a system level by removing dependencies on centralized components and enabling distributed stewardship.

To demonstrate the feasibility of our design, we implemented a proof of concept using off-the-shelf components—a YubiHSM2, a JavaCard security microcontroller, and a server with a CPU supporting Intel SGX and Intel TDX. We contribute measurements for several relevant use cases supported by our implementation. Notably, we show an end-to-end delay of at most 1248 ms for human-in-the-loop signing, given a technical setup that can be operated exclusively locally. While our measurements do not suggest that organizations with high-volume or stricter real-time requirements can benefit from our specific setup, our architecture remains generic and we identified both horizontal and vertical scaling techniques to address this limitation, whenever necessary.

Strong protection of key material, including its use, is paramount in the current threat landscape. In this work, we present a practical system providing such protection. We use a combination of both emerging and well-established trusted hardware, achieving a solution with conservative security properties despite operation in untrusted environments. By proposing an accessible and easily deployable setup, our construction can provide an important contribution to the digital sovereignty of organizations.

Acknowledgments. Our work was funded by the Deutsche Forschungsgemeinschaft (DFG, German Research Foundation), projects HyperNIC (503359370) and SLICES-SUSTAINABILITY (566292327), by the EU Horizon Europe programme, project

GreenDIGIT (101131207), by the German Federal Ministry of Research, Technology and Space (BMFTR), project 6G-life (16KIS2414), and by the Bavarian Ministry of Regional Development and Energy, project 6G Future Lab Bavaria. Results presented in this publication were obtained using the SLICES-DE research infrastructure.

Disclosure of Interests. The authors have no competing interests to declare that are relevant to the content of this article.

References

1. Advanced Micro Devices: AMD SEV-SNP: Strengthening VM Isolation with Integrity Protection and More (2020). https://docs.amd.com/v/u/en-US/SEV-SNP-strengthening-vm-isolation-with-integrity-protection-and-more
2. Ascertia Limited: ADSS Server Signature Activation Module (SAM) v7.0.2. Security Target (2022). https://www.commoncriteriaportal.org/nfs/ccpfiles/files/epfiles/st_adss_sam_702_v8.pdf
3. Aumasson, J.P., Merino, L.: SGX secure enclaves in practice, security and crypto review. In: Black Hat USA 2016 - Briefings - August 3 & 4 (2016). https://blackhat.com/docs/us-16/materials/us-16-Aumasson-SGX-Secure-Enclaves-In-Practice-Security-And-Crypto-Review.pdf
4. Brown, F., Stefan, D., Dornseifer, D.P.: Use AWS Nitro Enclaves to build Cubist CubeSigner, a secure and highly reliable key management platform for Ethereum validators and beyond (2024). https://aws.amazon.com/blogs/web3/use-aws-nitro-enclaves-to-build-cubist-cubesigner-a-secure-and-highly-reliable-key-management-platform-for-ethereum-validators-and-beyond/
5. Chen, L., Avizienis, A.: N-version programming: A fault-tolerance approach to reliability of software operation. In: Proceedings of 8th IEEE International Symposium on Fault-Tolerant Computing (FTCS-8), vol. 1, pp. 3–9 (1978)
6. Chuang, J., Seto, A., Berrios, N., van Schaik, S., Garman, C., Genkin, D.: TEE.Fail: breaking trusted execution environments via DDR5 memory bus interposition. In: 47th IEEE Symposium on Security and Privacy (IEEE S&P '26). IEEE Computer Society (2026). https://tee.fail
7. Connell, G., Fang, V., Schmidt, R., Dauterman, E., Popa, R.A.: Secret key recovery in a global-scale end-to-end encryption system. In: 18th USENIX Symposium on Operating Systems Design and Implementation (OSDI 24), pp. 703–719. USENIX Association, Santa Clara, CA (2024)
8. Council of European Union: Regulation (EU) No 910/2014 of the European Parliament and of the Council of 23 July 2014 on Electronic Identification and Trust services for Electronic Transactions in the Internal Market and Repealing Directive 1999/93/EC (2014)
9. Cryptomathic: Cryptomathic Signer SAM v6.0 for Utimaco Cryptoserver CP5 v5.1.0.0. Security Target (2024). https://www.commoncriteriaportal.org/nfs/ccpfiles/files/epfiles/2020-03-ST.pdf
10. DIN EN 419 241-1: Trustworthy Systems Supporting Server Signing – Part 1: General System Security Requirements; German version EN 419241-1:2018. European standard, DIN Deutsches Institut für Normung e. V., Berlin, DE (2018)
11. DIN EN 419 241-2: Trustworthy Systems Supporting Server Signing – Part 2: Protection profile for QSCD for Server Signing; German version EN 419241-2:2019. European standard, DIN Deutsches Institut für Normung e. V., Berlin, DE (2019)

12. Directorate-General for Digital Services, European Commission: eIDAS Dashboard – Qualified Signature/Seal Creation Devices and Secure Signature Creation Devices, https://eidas.ec.europa.eu/efda/browse/notification/qscd-sscd. Accessed 14 Feb 2026
13. Entrust Corporation: Entrust Signature Activation Module. Security Target (2022). https://www.commoncriteriaportal.org/nfs/ccpfiles/files/epfiles/2020-03-ST.pdf
14. Entrust Corporation: nShield5s HSM Security Target (SCCS certification). Security Target (2024). https://www.commoncriteriaportal.org/nfs/ccpfiles/files/epfiles/[DD]%20ST%20nShield5s%20HSM%20Security%20Target%20(SCCS%20certification)-v12.pdf
15. European Union Agency for Cybersecurity: EUCC Scheme: State-of-the-Art Document - Application of attack potential to smartcards and similar devices (2025). https://certification.enisa.europa.eu/document/download/836d47eb-13cf-4415-beb6-df106582f1c1_en
16. Intel Corporation: More Information on Encrypted Memory Frameworks for Intel Confidential Computing (2025). https://www.intel.com/content/www/us/en/developer/articles/news/more-information-encrypted-memory-frameworks.html
17. Jayakumaran, J., Smith, J.: Powering programmable crypto wallets at Coinbase with AWS Nitro Enclaves (2025). https://aws.amazon.com/blogs/web3/powering-programmable-crypto-wallets-at-coinbase-with-aws-nitro-enclaves/
18. Licel Corporation: jCardSim. https://github.com/licel/jcardsim. Accessed 30 April 2026 (commit *aa60a02*)
19. Nextsense: Security Target for Nextsense Remote QSCD Signature Activation Module (SAM) 3.4 for Thales® Luna. Security Target (2024). https://www.commoncriteriaportal.org/nfs/ccpfiles/files/epfiles/st_nssam_3.4_v1.6.pdf
20. Oracle and/or its affiliates: Java Card Platform - Runtime Environment Specification, Classic Edition, (2021). Tech. rep
21. Rammouz, M., Le, Q.D.: Breaking isolation: last-level cache side-channel attacks on AWS nitro enclaves. In: Proceedings of the 9th Workshop on System Software for Trusted Execution, pp. 10–17. SysTEX '26, Association for Computing Machinery, New York, NY, USA (2026). https://doi.org/10.1145/3805690.3805729, https://doi.org/10.1145/3805690.3805729
22. Thales: Thales Luna K7 Cryptographic Module. Security Target (2022). https://www.commoncriteriaportal.org/nfs/ccpfiles/files/epfiles/NSCIB-CC-195307-ST_RevM.pdf
23. Turnkey Team: Turnkey's Architecture. Accessed 03 April 2026 (2025). https://whitepaper.turnkey.com/architecture/
24. Urien, P.: Demonstration Of performance for low cost personal HSM. In: 2023 IEEE 20th Consumer Communications & Networking Conference (CCNC), pp. 879–880 (2023)
25. Utimaco IS GmbH: Security Target Lite for CryptoServer Se-Series Gen2 CP5. Security Target (2025). https://www.commoncriteriaportal.org/nfs/ccpfiles/files/epfiles/NSCIB-CC-2300142-02-ST_lite.pdf

fRE: A TEE-Based Firmware Resilience Engine with Efficient Local Detection and Recovery

Utku Budak[1(✉)], Yigit Arda Ozen[1], Fabrizio De Santis[2], Malek Safieh[2], and Georg Sigl[1]

[1] Chair of Security in Information Technology, Technical University of Munich, Munich, Germany
{utku.budak,yigit.ozen,sigl}@tum.de

[2] Foundational Technologies, Siemens AG, Munich, Germany
{fabrizio.desantis,malek.safieh}@siemens.com

Abstract. Firmware resilience refers to a device's ability to protect its firmware from malicious attacks, quickly detect manipulations, and recover from such attacks to minimize downtime. To enhance firmware resilience, the Trusted Computing Group (TCG) introduced the Resilience Engine (RE), a trusted component designed to remain secure and operational even if the rest of the device firmware is compromised, with the primary role of recovering to a functional state.

This paper presents a firmware RE (fRE) architecture that leverages a Trusted Execution Environment (TEE) to isolate the RE from the rest of the device firmware. The proposed architecture is designed to effectively accelerate both computationally intensive runtime local detection and recovery processes, while addressing on-chip memory constraints through chunkwise firmware verification and stepwise recovery. To demonstrate the feasibility of the proposed architecture, fRE is implemented on an ARM Cortex-M33-based microcontroller unit (MCU) leveraging TrustZone-M. The implementation is also evaluated using various cryptographic hash functions, such as SHA-256, hardware-accelerated SHA-256, SHA-512, Ascon-Hash256, and BLAKE3, to evaluate the runtime overheads of firmware verification and recovery. The implementation results indicate that integrating the proposed architecture into embedded devices with TEE support results in manageable overhead in terms of memory usage and execution time, while enabling faster, efficient firmware verification and recovery.

Keywords: Firmware Resilience · TEE · Resilience Engine · TrustZone

1 Introduction

In today's world, embedded devices are ubiquitous, playing a crucial role in everyday consumer electronics, such as wearables and home appliances, as well

Z. Afzal et al. (Eds.): ARES 2026 Workshops, LNCS 16900, pp. 308–326, 2027.
https://doi.org/10.1007/978-3-032-35576-8_17

as in a wide range of industrial applications [33], including industrial control systems, e.g., the Industrial Internet of Things (IIoT) [30]. These devices might also be integrated into larger systems and are often responsible for controlling critical functions, making them attractive targets for attackers. For instance, attackers can exploit memory corruption vulnerabilities in embedded firmware, such as buffer overflows, to execute various attacks, including return-oriented programming (ROP) [39] and firmware code injection [27]. Hence, ensuring their cybersecurity is an important aspect to consider when designing these devices, as it aims to protect them against cyberattacks and, correspondingly, respond to them, e.g., by improving protection mechanisms upon attack detection. On the other hand, cyber resilience comes with an additional motivation known as "assume breach" [35]. It assumes that a device might be compromised despite all protection efforts and focuses on rapid recovery upon attack detection to restore the device to a functional state [41].

According to the National Institute of Standards and Technology (NIST) [26], which focuses on firmware resilience, a cyber-resilient device shall provide mechanisms that support three main principles: protection, detection, and recovery. To address these principles, the Trusted Computing Group (TCG) has introduced the Resilience Engine (RE) [37]. This engine needs to be well-isolated from the rest of the device firmware, remain active to detect ongoing attacks, and facilitate rapid recovery to a functional state. However, previous literature [13,15,16] indicates that recovery is the most resource-consuming principle, requiring a significant time and memory compared to the other two principles. This is due to the fact that non-volatile memory operations, such as flash erasing and writing, are highly time-consuming on embedded devices. Furthermore, a local recovery process requires additional storage on the device for a recovery image, commonly called the golden copy. On the other hand, an external server is required in a remote recovery to deliver the golden copy over a network connection. Although remote recovery addresses the issue of additional storage, it introduces other drawbacks, such as increased timing overhead and additional complexity for receiving the golden copy remotely. Moreover, the device cannot be recovered if the connection to the server is lost. As a result, enhancing the efficiency of the recovery process by addressing the previously mentioned challenges is essential.

1.1 Contributions

This paper aims to enhance runtime firmware resilience on currently deployed embedded devices without requiring additional hardware components by leveraging only an existing Trusted Execution Environment (TEE) [19] technology. The main contributions of this paper can be summarized as follows:

- **A TEE-based firmware RE (fRE) architecture** to isolate the resources of the RE from the rest of the device firmware;
- **Efficient local detection and recovery mechanisms** to accelerate runtime firmware verification and recovery while considering the memory size;
- **Implementation** of the fRE on an ARM Cortex-M33-based STM32L562QE microcontroller unit (MCU) with ARM TrustZone-M;

- **Performance evaluation** of the fRE with various cryptographic hash functions and the SHA-256 hardware accelerator provided by the selected MCU;

1.2 Paper Outline

The remainder of this paper is organized as follows. Sect. 2 provides background information, including the essential aspects of cyber resilience, firmware resilience, and the basics of TEE, e.g., ARM TrustZone-M. Sect. 3 provides an overview of state-of-the-art RE approaches and other cyber resilience solutions. Thereafter, the attacker model, with the relevant design assumptions, is explained in Sect. 4. In Sect. 5, the design of the fRE is explained, including the architectural details and the workflow. The implementation details, along with the corresponding evaluation results, including memory and execution time overhead for various cryptographic hash algorithms, are presented in Sect. 6. Lastly, the paper concludes in Sect. 7, where potential extensions of the fRE are also presented as future work.

2 Background

This section provides essential background information for the rest of the paper, including brief overviews of cyber resilience, firmware resilience, and TEEs, e.g., ARM TrustZone-M.

2.1 Firmware Resilience

Over the past years, cyber resilience has become a crucial aspect of embedded system design. Although the literature contains various definitions of cyber resilience [26,28,35], this paper primarily follows the NIST definition [26], which focuses on firmware resilience. Hence, NIST presents three principles for building a cyber-resilient device. These are protection, detection, and recovery, which can be correspondingly achieved by authenticated updates [22], local or remote detection mechanisms, e.g., secure boot [25], remote attestation [17], etc., and onboard or remote recovery mechanisms [41]. Following these three principles, TCG has proposed a specification explaining the building blocks of a cyber-resilient system [37], which are depicted in Fig. 1. According to TCG, a cyber-resilient module (CRM) within a device mainly consists of the following two blocks:

- **Resilience Target (RT):** is the mutable part of the device, such as device firmware or configuration, and is assumed to be at risk of compromise by attackers.
- **Resilience Engine (RE):** is often the immutable part of the device that performs services, including protection, detection, and recovery, on the RT to enhance the previously mentioned firmware resilience principles.

TCG has also defined an additional block that might be a remote server or a more powerful device in the same network or system:

- **Resilience Authority (RA):** is a trusted party responsible for managing the RE, e.g., by requesting various services on the RT and receiving corresponding reports. For instance, it might be a backend server, such as an IoT hub, in an IoT system.

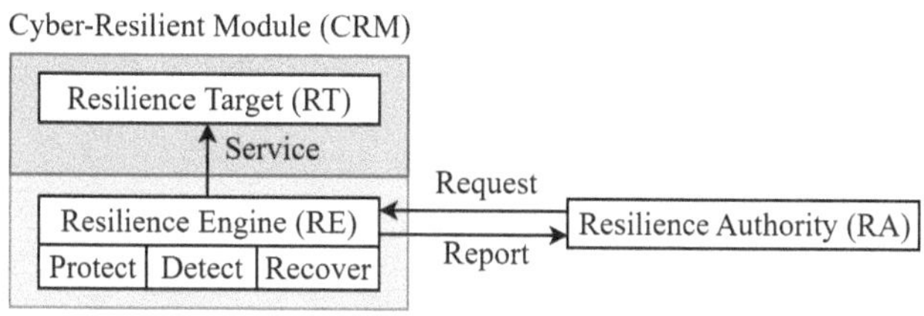

Fig. 1. Relation between the RE, the RT, and the RA, according to TCG [37]. Green indicates a secure environment, whereas red indicates a non-secure environment.

The mentioned TCG specification also emphasizes several essential design aspects to consider when designing the RE [37]. Some of these aspects can be listed as follows:

- **A-I Secure Storage:** The persistent resources of the RE, including its firmware, secrets, and reference values, must be securely stored to prevent RT's access.
- **A-II Secure Execution Environment:** The RE needs to be able to perform its functionalities in a secure environment without interruption from the RT.
- **A-III Control of RT's Storage:** The RE needs access to the RT's storage, including the ability to read and write its content.
- **A-IV Invocation:** The RE must remain active and operational to service the RT, even if the RT is compromised and uncooperative.
- **A-V Attention Signals:** The RE services are triggered by signals, which may originate from an interrupt or be generated by the device firmware, e.g., the RT.
- **A-VI Local Servicing:** The RE needs to locally service the RT, e.g., detect and recover from attacks, even if the network connection to the RA is lost.

2.2 Trusted Execution Environment (TEE)

TEE is a hardware-based security standard supported by GlobalPlatform [19]. It allows secure partitioning of device resources, such as flash, random-access memory (RAM), and other memory-mapped peripherals, into two domains. These are rich execution environment (REE) and TEE. Hence, in a TEE, sensitive applications can be securely executed, and their data can be securely stored and processed. A well-known example of a building block for creating a TEE is ARM's

TrustZone technology, which differs slightly in implementation depending on the processor's version and profile, such as the application class (Cortex-A) or microcontroller class (Cortex-M). TrustZone has been available for Cortex-A processors targeting high-power applications for many years [9]. Following TrustZone in Cortex-A, ARM has introduced TrustZone-M with its microcontroller-class (ARMv8-M) processors, including Cortex-M23 and Cortex-M33, targeting low-power applications [10]. In ARM TrustZone-M, processor execution is divided into two main domains: the secure (S) world, which serves as the TEE, and the non-secure (NS) world, which serves as the REE, as illustrated in Fig. 2.

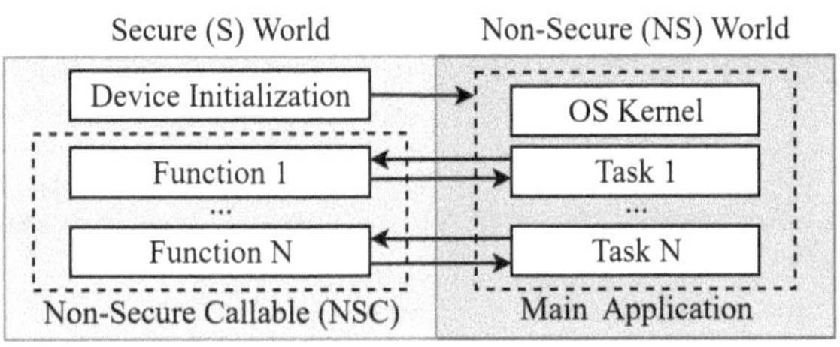

Fig. 2. ARM TrustZone-M for ARMv8-M-based MCUs [10]. Green indicates the secure (S) world, whereas red indicates the non-secure (NS) world.

Once the processor boots up, it first enters the secure world, where the device is initialized, including resource allocation between the secure and non-secure worlds. Then the processor switches to the non-secure world, where the main application, referred to as device firmware in this paper, is executed. The main application can be a real-time operating system (RTOS), such as FreeRTOS [12] or Zephyr RTOS [34], running several tasks, or a simple bare-metal application. The secure world firmware and peripherals can access and modify resources from both worlds, including flash, RAM, and memory-mapped peripherals, whereas the non-secure world firmware and peripherals can access and modify only the resources associated with the non-secure world. Hence, firmware in the non-secure world can access the resources of the secure world only through predefined functions located in a specific region of the secure world called the non-secure callable (NSC). This allows applications in the non-secure world to access secure-world resources only in a secure, controlled manner.

3 Related Work

An architecture employing an RE is described in [18], which aims to enhance firmware resilience at boot time. It includes a hardware-supported code authentication unit responsible for securely booting the application, divided into multiple chunks, and an RE responsible for recovering the individual chunks at boot time from a golden copy stored in secure read-only memory (ROM). In [13], the Device Identifier Composition Engine (DICE) [36] is extended to not only provide remote attestation at boot time but also support secure boot, firmware recovery, and secure firmware updates using only symmetric cryptography.

A runtime RE is presented in [15] for lightweight IoT devices, which could only afford simple processor features, such as a memory protection technology, e.g., memory protection unit (MPU) [5] in ARM and physical memory protection unit (PMP) [6] in RISC-V, and privilege levels. In [16], the architecture presented in [15] is also extended for RTOS use cases. Hence, an RE is integrated into the RTOS kernel to verify the integrity of individual tasks at runtime, checkpoint their stacks, and recover them to a functional state. However, the security guarantees of [15,16] are limited to the selected memory protection technology, e.g., making them vulnerable to direct memory access (DMA)-based attacks [29].

In [40], a trusted computing primitive is proposed, which enables a remote hub to forcibly recover a compromised IoT device via an authenticated watchdog timer (AWDT). In [20], a cyber-resilient IoT architecture is proposed, based on [40] and utilizing ARM TrustZone-M to build a TEE. In that work, an AWDT [37] is implemented in ARM TrustZone-M, which can only be deferred by a ticket issued by a trusted remote IoT hub upon successful attestation. Otherwise, the AWDT forces the device to reboot, and a remote recovery is performed via an update. In [7], the approach presented in [20] is extended to determine whether the disruption is due to a network issue or an attack. Although the approaches in [7,20] offer higher security than those in [15,16] by using TrustZone-M instead of an MPU, making them secure against DMA-based attacks, they do not focus on the TCG design aspect "A-VI Local Servicing" defined in Subsect. 2.1.

Another approach is presented in [24], which targets monitoring and recovering IoT devices, and is further extended in [8], where possible technologies, including TEE, are presented to implement a similar approach. A further firmware resilience solution is provided in [23] and [21], where a Field-Programmable Gate Array (FPGA) detects malicious firmware modifications and recovers from them using a golden copy. Although all referenced solutions target enhancing cyber resilience based on the NIST [26] and TCG [37] requirements, each with its own advantages and disadvantages, they all show that recovery is the most complex and resource-intensive aspect in terms of time and memory, among other principles. As a result, recovery requires in-depth research and evaluation.

4 Attacker Model

This paper primarily focuses on enhancing firmware resilience on embedded devices. The proposed fRE architecture is designed to efficiently detect malicious firmware injections at runtime and recover from them to a functional state without relying on external dependencies. In particular, two types of attackers are considered in the design of the fRE: a basic physical adversary and a remote adversary. A basic physical adversary is limited to replacing the external flash with malicious firmware; however, does not have the capability to modify the internal flash. More sophisticated physical attacks, including debugger-based attacks or side-channel and fault attacks, are also out of scope. A remote adversary can exploit known vulnerabilities in the main application running in the non-secure world of the TEE to inject malicious firmware. This can be achieved by exploiting memory corruption vulnerabilities, such as buffer overflows (e.g., stack overflows), to perform ROP [39], resulting in firmware code injection [27].

5 Design of Firmware Resilience Engine (fRE)

This section describes the architecture and the workflow of the fRE. To ensure practical applicability, fRE leverages a TEE, i.e., ARM TrustZone-M, which is increasingly supported and allows fulfilling the TCG [37] design aspects explained in Subsect. 2.1, as follows:

- TrustZone-M provides secure storage for the resources of the RE and secure execution environment without any interruption from the RT, thereby fulfilling the design aspects **A-I** and **A-II**.
- The RE is located in the secure world and can therefore access the resources of the RT in the non-secure world, thereby fulfilling the design aspect **A-III**.
- To make the RE active and fulfill the design aspects **A-IV** and **A-V**, a secure timer is initialized in the secure world, which cannot be disabled by the non-secure application, and periodically triggers the RE upon its expiration.
- The RE enables efficient local detection followed by a local recovery mechanism without needing external dependencies, e.g., a remote server, thereby fulfilling the design aspect **A-VI**.

5.1 Architecture

The architecture of the fRE is depicted in Fig. 3. The resources of the MCU, including RAM, internal flash, and other peripherals, are divided into two worlds. These are the secure world marked in green, and the non-secure world marked in red. This prevents the resources stored in the secure world from being accessed by the non-secure world.

Secure (S) world includes the RE's resources, such as its firmware, recovery caches, reference hashes, and the counter values of the individual RT chunks referred to as the device firmware, divided into an arbitrary number of chunks. The recovery caches are regions of internal flash in the secure world that are used to accelerate recovery. A portion of RAM is allocated for the RE to securely store and process its runtime data. Additionally, the flash controller is assigned to the secure world, ensuring that access to external flash memory is exclusively controlled by the RE. The external flash is used to store the golden copy of the RT for recovery, considering the limited internal flash capacity. Lastly, a timer is isolated within the secure world, which is mainly responsible for triggering the RE to periodically perform runtime firmware verification on the RT chunks.

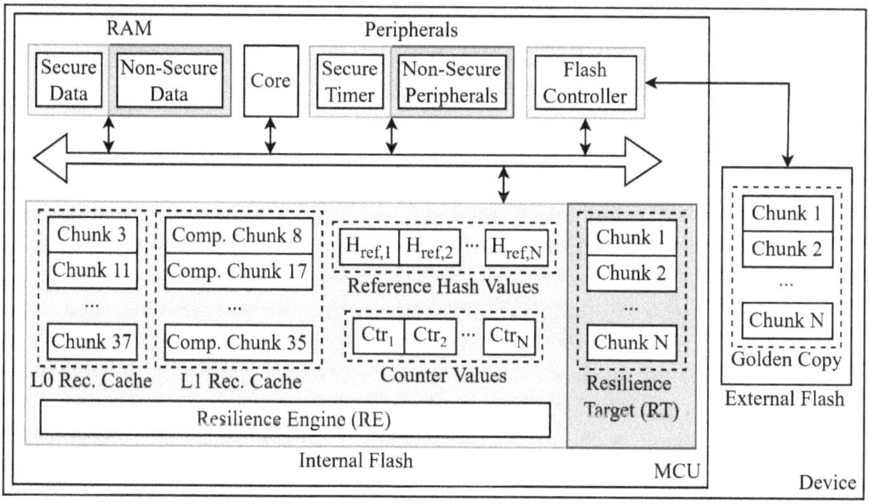

Fig. 3. Top-Level Architecture Design. Green indicates the secure (S) world, whereas red indicates the non-secure (NS) world. (Color figure online)

Non-secure (NS) world includes the RT stored in internal flash and is responsible for executing main device functionality. The RT is divided into multiple chunks, which allows the RE to separately check the integrity of the individual chunks and recover them correspondingly, enabling faster detection and recovery. Other resources used by the RT, including non-secure RAM, peripherals, and interrupt controllers, are also allocated to the non-secure world.

5.2 Workflow

The operation of the fRE is depicted in Fig. 4, which starts with initialization followed by efficient firmware verification and local recovery.

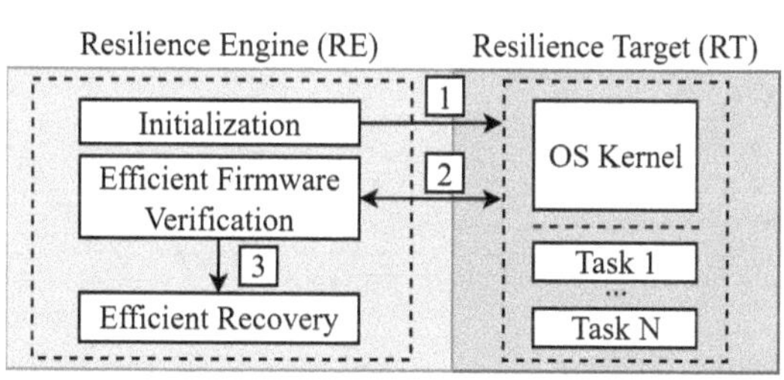

Fig. 4. Workflow of the fRE. Green indicates the secure (S) world, whereas red indicates the non-secure (NS) world. (Color figure online)

5.2.1 Initialization

After a power-on or reset, the device first securely boots up using state-of-the-art secure boot mechanisms [13,14,38], which are not the primary focus of this work. This ensures that the RE's resources are not manipulated at boot time. Then, the device enters the secure world, where the RE performs device initialization. This includes calculating the reference hash values of the individual RT chunks shown in Fig. 3, configuring memory regions, and setting peripheral access permissions to enforce isolation between the secure and non-secure worlds. Additionally, the RE starts a timer in the secure world, where the period, T, of the timer triggering its corresponding interrupt service routine (ISR) is predefined based on the system requirements. For systems prioritizing faster attack detection, the period could be shorter, whereas for systems prioritizing non-violating real-time behavior, it could be longer.

Once initialization is complete, the RE transitions to the non-secure world, where the RT is executed. The RT might be an RTOS-based application that includes an arbitrary number of tasks for different device functionalities.

5.2.2 Efficient Firmware Verification

After the period, T, the secure timer expires and triggers an interrupt that invokes the corresponding ISR shown in Algorithm 1, which is part of the RE located in the secure world. Since interrupts of the secure world have dedicated priority levels, the interrupts originating from the non-secure world cannot interfere with the RE during its execution [11].

Algorithm 1. Chunkwise Firmware Verification (Simplified)

```
global i ← 1                                    ▷ Persistent across interrupts
procedure SECURE_TIMER_ISR()
    H_i ← HASH(CHUNK i)                         ▷ Compute hash of chunk i
    H_ref,i ← READ_REF_HASH(i)                  ▷ Read reference hash of chunk i
    if H_i ≠ H_ref,i then
        STEPWISE_RECOVERY()                     ▷ Shown in Alg. 2
    end if
    i ← i + 1                                   ▷ Advance to next chunk
    if i > N then
        i ← 1
    end if
end procedure
```

Upon being invoked by the secure timer interrupt, the RE performs runtime firmware verification of the RT. To minimize timing overhead and avoid delaying the execution of the RT, the RE verifies the integrity of a single RT chunk during each timer interrupt. To do so, the RE computes the hash of the RT chunk i, H_i, as follows:

$$H_i = \text{Hash}(\text{Chunk } i), \quad i = 1, \ldots, N \tag{1}$$

and compares it with the corresponding reference hash value, $H_{ref,i}$, stored in the secure region of the internal flash. This verification process is performed periodically, with each RT chunk checked in sequence, as shown in Fig. 5.

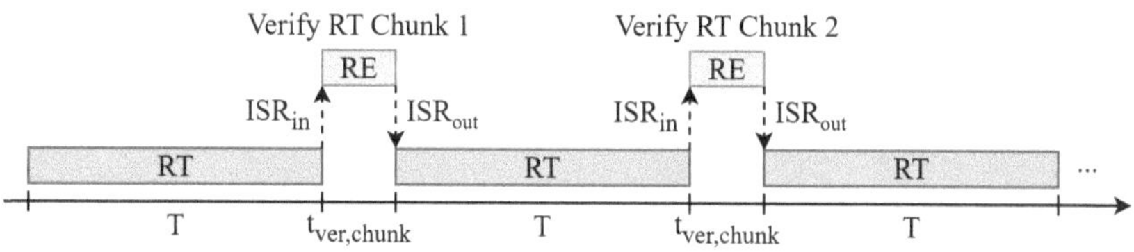

Fig. 5. Chunkwise Firmware Verification of the RT Chunks.

As a result, the integrity of the entire RT is progressively verified over time. If no mismatch is detected during the verification, the corresponding RT chunk is considered valid, and the RT continues executing. The total time needed for the firmware verification of the whole RT to be completed, $t_{ver,total}$, can be calculated as follows:

$$t_{ver,total} = (t_{ver,chunk} + T) \cdot N \tag{2}$$

where $t_{ver,chunk}$ is the time needed for verifying a single RT chunk shown in Algorithm 1 and the T is the period of the timer. The total number of chunks, N, can be calculated by dividing the RT size, s_{RT}, by the selected chunk size, s_{chunk}:

$$N = \left\lceil \frac{s_{RT}}{s_{chunk}} \right\rceil \tag{3}$$

Note that the time needed for switching between the secure and the non-secure worlds, and the context switches of the timer ISR, ISR_{in} and ISR_{out}, are excluded while calculating the $t_{ver,total}$ for simplicity. This is because they are significantly smaller than T and $t_{ver,chunk}$, requiring fewer than a few hundred cycles, and can therefore be neglected. By adjusting s_{chunk} and T based on performance and security requirements, fRE can be flexibly adapted to applications with varying real-time and security constraints. The timing overhead introduced by firmware verification can be easily calculated by setting T to 0. This is due to the fact that T is the time interval during which the RT is executing.

5.2.3 Efficient Local Recovery

Upon detecting a mismatch in an RT chunk, the RE initiates a recovery. Instead of recovering the entire RT, the proposed mechanism targets only the manipulated RT chunks, thereby improving performance by reducing the number of costly flash operations. To further accelerate the recovery process while accounting for internal flash size limitations, the fRE architecture introduces a stepwise recovery approach. This approach provides three different recovery levels, each with its own advantages and disadvantages. These include recovery from L0 and L1 recovery caches, as well as golden copy.

L0 recovery cache is a small region of internal flash in the secure world used to store only a subset of RT chunks. This is because the internal flash often lacks sufficient capacity to store the whole RT, given its large size. Furthermore, once a vulnerability is discovered in one of the RT chunks, the attacker may repeatedly exploit it until it is patched, leading to repeated manipulation of the same RT chunk. Instead of repeatedly recovering the manipulated RT chunks externally, leveraging the L0 recovery cache enables faster recovery. Note that the L0 recovery cache can be updated during execution by replacing less frequently manipulated RT chunks with more frequent ones based on their counter values.

L1 recovery cache is an extension of the L0 recovery cache within the secure world of the internal flash. Note that the content of the L1 recovery cache is defined at boot time, and the RE stores only a set of RT chunks with the highest compression success. The L1 recovery cache lacks an update mechanism due to the irregular sizes of the compressed RT chunks, which adds additional complexity. Here, the compression success depends heavily on both the chosen compression algorithm and the specific RT. If all the compressed RT chunks fit in the internal flash, the L1 recovery cache might also be used to store the whole RT. In this case, there would be no need for the L0 recovery cache or the golden copy stored in an external flash. However, even with compression, storing the entire RT in the internal flash is not feasible in most cases.

Golden copy is a bitwise-identical version of the RT stored in external flash. The external flash provides a large capacity to store the golden copy; however, retrieving RT chunks from it may take a long time, significantly delaying the recovery. Although the external flash controller depicted in Fig. 3 is in the secure world and can only be accessed by the RE, thereby protecting it from the RT, it is physically located outside the MCU. Hence, the external flash must be considered non-secure, as an attacker can simply replace it. Therefore, the integrity of the RT chunks retrieved from the external flash must be cryptographically verified before being used for recovery and later stored in the L0 recovery cache.

The workflow of the stepwise recovery approach is shown in Algorithm 2. At device start-up, the L0 recovery cache is initialized with a predefined or randomly generated state, and the L1 recovery cache with the highest-compressed RT chunks.

Upon detecting a mismatch in one of the RT chunks, the RE verifies the integrity of all other RT chunks, assuming they may have been compromised in the meantime. To recover the manipulated chunks, the RE first checks the L0 recovery cache. If the corresponding RT chunk exists in the L0 recovery cache, it can be immediately recovered from there. Otherwise, the RE next checks the L1 recovery cache and attempts recovery from there. Note that recovering from the L1 recovery cache requires an additional decompression of the RT chunk. If the RT chunk is also missing from the L1 recovery cache, the RE retrieves the corresponding RT chunk from the golden copy stored in the external flash. Subsequently, the RE backs it up in the L0 recovery cache if the counter value of the corresponding RT chunk is higher than the other chunks in the L0 recovery cache. Over time and through repeated attack recoveries, the L0 recovery cache is filled up with the most frequently manipulated RT chunks. The RT chunk to be replaced is selected based on the counter values associated with each RT chunk stored in the secure region of the internal flash shown in Fig. 3. Once all corrupted chunks have been corrected, the RE resets the device to start fresh.

Algorithm 2. Efficient Local Recovery (Simplified)

```
procedure STEPWISE_RECOVERY()
    for i ← 1 to N do
        if VERIFY_RT_CHUNK(i) then
            continue                                  ▷ Skip recovery if chunk i is verified
        end if
        if L0_CACHE_HIT(i) then
            data ← READ_L0_CACHE(i)
            RECOVER_RT_CHUNK(i, data)                 ▷ Recover from the L0
            continue
        else if L1_CACHE_HIT(i) then
            compressed_data ← READ_L1_CACHE(i)
            data ← DECOMPRESS(compressed_data)
            RECOVER_RT_CHUNK(i, data)                 ▷ Recover from the L1
            continue
        else
            data ← READ_GOLDEN_COPY(i)
            if VERIFY(i, data) then
                RECOVER_RT_CHUNK(i, data)             ▷ Recover from the golden copy
                UPDATE_L0_CACHE(i, data)              ▷ Update the L0 content
                continue
            end if
        end if
    end for
    RESET_DEVICE()                                    ▷ Reset the device after recovery
end procedure
```

Internal Flash Resource Distribution. The internal flash size reserved for the L0 and L1 recovery caches, s_{L0} and s_{L1}, can be calculated as follows:

$$s_{L0} + s_{L1} = s_{flash} - (s_{RE} + s_{RT} + s_{hash} + s_{ctr}) \tag{4}$$

Here, the total internal flash size, s_{flash}, is fixed and determined by the selected MCU. The size of the RE, s_{RE}, is also fixed based on the selected MCU and compiler. On the other hand, the size of the RT, s_{RT}, is variable based on the application and decisive, how much storage remains for the recovery caches. The internal flash sizes needed for both the reference hash values, s_{hash}, and the counter values, s_{ctr}, can be calculated as follows:

$$s_{\text{hash}} = \left\lceil \frac{s_{\text{RT}}}{s_{\text{chunk}}} \right\rceil \cdot H, \qquad s_{\text{ctr}} = \left\lceil \frac{s_{\text{RT}}}{s_{\text{chunk}}} \right\rceil \cdot C \tag{5}$$

where H denotes the hash output size (e.g., 32 B for SHA-256), and C denotes the size of each individual counter value (e.g., 1 B). The individual sizes of the L0 and the L1 recovery caches can then be chosen based on the application.

6 Implementation and Evaluation

The proposed fRE architecture is implemented on an STM32L562 discovery kit [31], featuring a single-core 32-bit ARM Cortex-M33-based STM32L562QEI6Q MCU with 512 KB of internal flash memory and operating at 110 MHz. The selected MCU supports TrustZone-M [10] and includes a SHA-256 hardware accelerator [32]. Additionally, the STM32L562 discovery kit includes a secure digital (SD) card slot that serves as external flash memory for storing the golden copy of the RT. To evaluate the performance of the proposed architecture, a 360 KB RT based on FreeRTOS, comprising multiple tasks, is developed and stored in the non-secure world of the internal flash. To enhance timing performance, the implementation is compiled for speed with the `-Ofast` optimization flag. The corresponding memory size overhead of the proposed architecture is presented in Table 1.

Table 1. Memory Size Overhead of the fRE Architecture.

Label	Memory Type	Size (KB)
Resilience Target (RT)	Internal Flash (Non-secure)	360
Resilience Engine (RE)	Internal Flash (Secure)	40
Reference Hashes & Counter Values	Internal Flash (Secure)	4
L0 Recovery Cache	Internal Flash (Secure)	20
L1 Recovery Cache	Internal Flash (Secure)	88
Golden Copy	External Flash (SD Card)	360

An example chunk size of 4 KB is selected, resulting in the RT being partitioned into 90 chunks. For the memory size measurements presented in Table 1, the RE is configured to use SHA-256 as the hash function provided by mbedTLS [2] and the LZ4 [1] lossless compression algorithm to store the compressed chunks in the L1 recovery cache. The resulting RE configuration occupies approximately 40 KB in the secure world of the internal flash. Given a 4 KB chunk size, the internal flash required to store the reference hash and counter values is determined by applying the specified size values to Eq. 5, as follows:

$$s_{\text{hash}} = \frac{360\,\text{KB}}{4\,\text{KB}} \cdot 32\,\text{B} = 2880\,\text{B}, \qquad s_{\text{ctr}} = \frac{360\,\text{KB}}{4\,\text{KB}} \cdot 1\,\text{B} = 90\,\text{B} \tag{6}$$

Accordingly, 4 KB of internal flash is reserved for storing reference hashes and counter values, along with additional metadata, including data for linked-list-based recovery management and status flags required for RE operation. It is also important to note that the memory sizes in Table 1 are aligned to 4 KB boundaries to enable cleaner memory allocation. Consequently, the cumulative size of these auxiliary data structures increases the total storage requirement to 4 KB, explaining why the memory footprint associated with the hash and counter information is larger than initially expected. Hence, the remaining internal flash memory is determined by applying the specified size values to Eq. 4, as follows:

$$s_{L0} + s_{L1} = 512\,\text{KB - } (40\,\text{KB} + 360\,\text{KB} + 4\,\text{KB}) = 108\,\text{KB} \tag{7}$$

The result of Eq. 7 indicates that 108 KB of the internal flash can be allocated for the L0 and L1 recovery caches, where we selected to reserve 20 KB for L0 recovery cache for storing five RT chunks. Hence, the remaining 88 KB is reserved for the L1 recovery cache, where the chunks with the highest compression success are stored until it reaches its full capacity. The corresponding compression results of individual RT chunks for the evaluated RT are shown in Fig. 6. Lastly, the 360 KB golden copy of the RT is stored in the SD card.

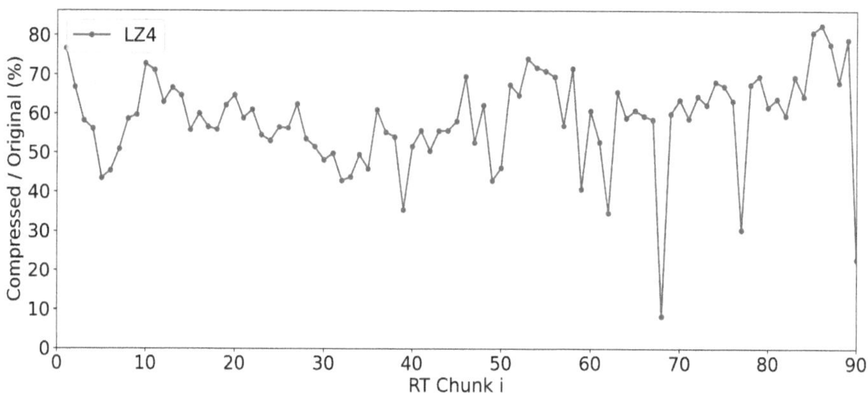

Fig. 6. Compression Results of the 4 KB RT Chunks.

A key function of the fRE is the periodic firmware verification of the RT chunks, triggered by a timer interrupt configured in the secure world during normal device operation. As this verification relies on a hash function, selecting an appropriate cryptographic hash function is crucial for minimizing timing overhead while ensuring strong security. For this purpose, several cryptographic hash algorithms are evaluated, including SHA-256 and SHA-512 from MbedTLS [2], hardware-accelerated SHA-256, Ascon-Hash256 [4], and BLAKE3 [3]. The timing overhead of firmware verification ($t_{\text{ver,chunk}}$) using the aforementioned algorithms is evaluated across different chunk sizes, and the results are summarized in Table 2. As expected, hardware-accelerated SHA-256 achieves the best performance for firmware verification.

Table 2. Timing Overhead of Firmware Verification ($t_{ver,chunk}$) for Various Hash Algorithms and RT Chunk Sizes.

Hash Algorithm	Time (ms)			
	2 KB	4 KB	8 KB	16 KB
SHA-256	0.97	1.89	3.72	7.39
SHA-256 (HW-Accelerated)	0.08	0.16	0.31	0.62
SHA-512	1.91	3.68	7.23	14.30
Ascon-Hash256	1.77	3.48	6.91	13.74
BLAKE3	0.42	0.80	1.56	3.07

For real-time use cases, smaller chunks combined with longer timer periods help reduce runtime overhead. Conversely, in security-critical scenarios, larger chunks and more frequent verification enable faster and more comprehensive detection. The chunk size also directly affects the recovery, determining the latency between attack detection and system reactivation. The recovery time from the golden copy for different chunk sizes is presented in Table 3.

Table 3. Timing Overhead of Recovery from the Golden Copy for Various Hash Algorithms and RT Chunk Sizes, Including Integrity Verification and L0 Cache Backup.

Hash Algorithm	Time (ms)			
	2 KB	4 KB	8 KB	16 KB
SHA-256	130.91	261.55	521.77	1040.85
SHA-256 (HW-Accelerated)	130.07	259.94	518.48	1034.53
SHA-512	131.72	263.13	524.99	1047.49
Ascon-Hash256	131.65	262.85	524.62	1046.97
BLAKE3	130.41	260.48	519.64	1036.79

As shown in Table 3, recovering RT chunks from external flash incurs significant latency, particularly for larger chunk sizes. To address this, the proposed stepwise recovery approach leverages L0 and L1 recovery caches, substantially reducing recovery latency. Table 4 compares the recovery time for chunks retrieved from the L0 and L1 recovery caches. Since no additional verification is required in these cases, the recovery time is independent of the hash algorithm.

Compared to recovery from the golden copy, both L0 and L1 recovery caches significantly reduce recovery latency. L0 consistently achieves the lowest recovery times due to the absence of decompression overhead, while L1 incurs a modest additional delay from decompression but still outperforms external flash-based recovery. Note that the compression success of each RT chunk is application-specific, as some applications are more compressible than others.

Table 4. Timing Overhead of Recovery from L0 and L1 Recovery Caches for Various RT Chunk Sizes, Including Decompression in L1 Recovery.

Time (ms)							
L0 Recovery Cache				L1 Recovery Cache			
2 KB	4 KB	8 KB	16 KB	2 KB	4 KB	8 KB	16 KB
43.78	87.58	175.14	350.16	44.82	89.61	179.23	358.35

7 Conclusion and Future Work

In this paper, a runtime firmware resilience architecture called fRE is proposed that leverages a TEE to isolate the RE from vulnerable device firmware. To enable faster attack detection and local recovery without external dependencies, the proposed architecture employs chunkwise firmware verification and stepwise recovery. To demonstrate its feasibility, fRE is implemented on the STM32L562 discovery kit, featuring an ARM Cortex-M33-based MCU with TrustZone-M. The implementation is evaluated across different RT chunk sizes and hash algorithms for a comprehensive analysis. The results show that the fRE can be effectively integrated into devices with TrustZone-M or a similar technology while introducing manageable memory overhead and configurable runtime overhead.

As part of future work, several directions can be explored. For instance, fRE can be extended with a reporting mechanism that notifies the RA when the counter values of RT chunks exceed a predefined threshold, indicating persistent attacks on specific chunks that require a patch via a firmware update. Additionally, a degraded recovery mode can be incorporated into the proposed stepwise recovery approach to handle cases where the golden copy in external flash is compromised and the corresponding chunk is unavailable in the recovery caches, thereby ensuring continued operation of critical RT functionalities. Finally, the approach presented in [15] can be integrated into fRE, with the RTOS-based RE residing in the non-secure world of TrustZone-M and communicating with the RE proposed in this work to recover RTOS tasks that have been manipulated.

Disclosure of Interests. This work was supported in part by Siemens AG. A patent application covering aspects of the technology described in this article has been filed by the authors and their affiliated institutions. The authors declare no other competing interests relevant to the content of this article.

References

1. Lz4 lossless extremely fast compression algorithm. https://github.com/lz4/lz4. Accessed 2025
2. MBED TLS: An open source TLS library. https://github.com/Mbed-TLS/mbedtls, [Online]. Accessed: 2025
3. The official rust and c implementations of the blake3 cryptographic hash function. https://github.com/BLAKE3-team/BLAKE3, [Online]. Accessed: 2025
4. Reference, highly optimized, masked C and ASM implementations of ascon (NIST SP 800-232). https://github.com/ascon/ascon-c. Accessed: 2025
5. ARM Memory Protection Unit (MPU), chap. 12, pp. 951–974. John Wiley & Sons, Ltd (2015). https://doi.org/10.1002/9781119058397.ch12
6. The RISC-V instruction set manual: Volume ii, privileged architecture, version 20240411 (2024)
7. Al Atiiq, S., Gehrmann, C.: Regaining dominance in cider and Lazarus. IEEE Access **12**, 124589–124603 (2024). https://doi.org/10.1109/ACCESS.2024.3454555
8. Alvarenga, E., et al.: Cyber resilience for the internet of things: implementations with resilience engines and attack classifications. IEEE Trans. Emerg. Top. Comput. **12**(2), 583–600 (2024). https://doi.org/10.1109/TETC.2022.3231692
9. ARM: Trustzone for cortex-a. https://www.arm.com/technologies/trustzone-for-cortex-a. [Online]. Accessed: 2025
10. ARM: Trustzone for cortex-m. https://www.arm.com/technologies/trustzone-for-cortex-m. [Online]. Accessed: 2025
11. ARM: Armv8-m security extension user guide (2025). https://developer.arm.com/documentation/107655/100. [Online]. Accessed: 2025
12. Barry, R.: Mastering the Freertos real time kernel: A hands-on tutorial guide (2016)
13. Budak, U., Safieh, M., De Santis, F., Sigl, G.: A cyber-resilient dice architecture for resource-constrained devices. In: Skopik, F., Naessens, V., De Sutter, B. (eds.) Availability, Reliability and Security, pp. 74–91. Springer Nature Switzerland, Cham (2025)
14. Budak, U., Safieh, M., Ozen, Y.A., De Santis, F., Sigl, G.: An efficient secure boot mechanism leveraging dice as a use case. In: 2026 Design, Automation & Test in Europe Conference (DATE), pp. 1–3 (2026). https://doi.org/10.23919/DATE69613.2026.11539674
15. Budak, U., Santis, F.D., Sigl, G.: A lightweight firmware resilience engine for IOT devices leveraging minimal processor features. In: 2024 IEEE International Conference on Cyber Security and Resilience (CSR), pp. 486–491 (2024). https://doi.org/10.1109/CSR61664.2024.10679408
16. Budak, U., Santis, F.D., Yasar, O., Safieh, M., Sigl, G.: A lightweight firmware resilience engine for real-time operating systems. In: 2025 IEEE International Conference on Cyber Security and Resilience (CSR), pp. 401–406 (2025). https://doi.org/10.1109/CSR64739.2025.11129996
17. Coker, G., et al.: Principles of remote attestation. Int. J. Inf. Secur. **10**, 63–81 (2011)
18. Dave, A., Banerjee, N., Patel, C.: Care: lightweight attack resilient secure boot architecture with onboard recovery for RISC-V based SOC. In: 2021 22nd International Symposium on Quality Electronic Design (ISQED), pp. 516–521 (2021). https://doi.org/10.1109/ISQED51717.2021.9424322
19. GlobalPlatform: Introduction to trusted execution environments (2018). https://globalplatform.org

20. Huber, M., Hristozov, S., Ott, S., Sarafov, V., Peinado, M.: The Lazarus effect: healing compromised devices in the internet of small things. In: Proceedings of the 15th ACM Asia Conference on Computer and Communications Security, pp. 6–19. ASIA CCS '20, Association for Computing Machinery, New York, NY, USA (2020). https://doi.org/10.1145/3320269.3384723, https://doi.org/10.1145/3320269.3384723
21. Intel Corporation: Intel data center block with firmware resilience. https://www.intel.com [Online]. Accessed: 2025
22. Jaouhari, S.E., Bouvet, E.: Secure firmware over-the-air updates for IOT: survey, challenges, and discussions. Int. Things **18**, 100508 (2022). https://doi.org/10.1016/j.iot.2022.100508
23. Lattice: Universal platform firmware resiliency (PFR) – servers. http://www.latticesemi.com/pfr [Online]. Accessed: 2025
24. Medwed, M., Nikov, V., Renes, J., Schneider, T., Veshchikov, N.: Cyber resilience for self-monitoring IOT devices. In: 2021 IEEE International Conference on Cyber Security and Resilience (CSR), pp. 160–167 (2021). https://doi.org/10.1109/CSR51186.2021.9527995
25. Microsoft: Secure boot. https://learn.microsoft.com [Online]. Accessed: 2025
26. National Institute of Standards and Technology (NIST): Special publication 800-193, platform firmware resiliency guidelines. Tech. rep. (2018). https://doi.org/10.6028/NIST.SP.800-193
27. Noman, H.A., Abu-Sharkh, O.M.F.: Code injection attacks in wireless-based internet of things (IOT): a comprehensive review and practical implementations. Sensors **23**(13) (2023). https://doi.org/10.3390/s23136067, https://www.mdpi.com/1424-8220/23/13/6067
28. Ross, R., Pillitteri, V., Graubart, R., Bodeau, D., McQuaid, R.: National institute of standards and technology (NIST) special publication 800–160, volume 2, revision 1, developing cyber-resilient systems: A systems security engineering approach. Tech. Rep. (2021). https://doi.org/10.6028/NIST.SP.800-160v2r1
29. Sensaoui, A.R., Aktouf, O.E.K., Hely, D., Di Vito, S.: An in-depth study of MPU-based isolation techniques. J. Hardw. Syst. Security **3**, 365–381 (2019). https://doi.org/10.1007/s41635-019-00078-6, https://doi.org/10.1007/s41635-019-00078-6
30. Sisinni, E., Saifullah, A., Han, S., Jennehag, U., Gidlund, M.: Industrial internet of things: challenges, opportunities, and directions. IEEE Trans. Industr. Inf. **14**(11), 4724–4734 (2018). https://doi.org/10.1109/TII.2018.2852491
31. STM: Discovery kit with STM32L562QE MCU. https://www.st.com/en/evaluation-tools/stm32l562e-dk.html, [Online]. Accessed: 2025
32. STMicroelectronics: Datasheet ds12736 rev 5: Stm32l562xx (2025). https://www.st.com/resource/en/datasheet/stm32l562ce.pdf
33. Tareq, A., Mostofa, M., Rana, M., Rahman, M.: A comprehensive review of intelligent home automation systems using embedded devices and IOT. Control Syst. Optimiz. Lett. **2**(2), 198–203 (2024). https://doi.org/10.59247/csol.v2i2.110, https://ejournal.csol.or.id/index.php/csol/article/view/110
34. The Zephyr Project: Zephyr RTOs. https://www.zephyrproject.org/ [Online]. Accessed: 2025
35. Tjoa, S., Gafić, M., Kieseberg, P.: Cyber Resilience Fundamentals, pp. 13–21. Springer International Publishing, Cham (2024). https://doi.org/10.1007/978-3-031-52064-8_2, https://doi.org/10.1007/978-3-031-52064-8_2
36. Trusted Computing Group (TCG): Dice layering architecture version 1.0, revision 0.19 (2020). https://trustedcomputinggroup.org

37. Trusted Computing Group (TCG): Cyber resilient module and building block requirements, version 1.0, revision 0.2. Tech. rep. (2022). https://trustedcomputinggroup.org
38. Wang, R., Yan, Y.: A survey of secure boot schemes for embedded devices. In: 2022 24th International Conference on Advanced Communication Technology (ICACT), pp. 224–227 (2022). https://doi.org/10.23919/ICACT53585.2022.9728840
39. Weidler, N.R., et al.: Return-oriented programming on a cortex-m processor. In: 2017 IEEE Trustcom/BigDataSE/ICESS pp. 823–832 (2017). https://doi.org/10.1109/Trustcom/BigDataSE/ICESS.2017.318
40. Xu, M., et al.: Dominance as a new trusted computing primitive for the internet of things. In: 2019 IEEE Symposium on Security and Privacy (SP), pp. 1415–1430 (2019). https://doi.org/10.1109/SP.2019.00084
41. Yao, J., Zimmer, V.: Firmware resiliency: recovery, pp. 163–184. Apress, Berkeley, CA (2020). https://doi.org/10.1007/978-1-4842-6106-4_5

Proceedings of the Fifth Workshop on Cybersecurity in Industry 4.0 and Beyond (SecIndustry 2026)

SecIndustry 2026 Preface

The fourth industrial (Industry 4.0) revolution represents a shift in technology and thinking about value-adding processes. Beyond Industry 4.0, the focus shifts toward Industry 5.0 emphasizing human-centricity, sustainability, resilience, and human–AI collaboration ensuring that advanced automation supports both productivity and societal value. It includes several critical infrastructures, which are needed to make the different technologies come together to create better products and more effective and efficient production processes. It is therefore important to improve the understanding of formal models for adversary placement and interaction in distributed cyber-physical systems. It is also important to look at the human dimensions of security and privacy when undertaking digital transformation. Innovative approaches that promote rapid learning through laboratories, catapult centres, and learning factories are essential for applying theoretical knowledge to real-world challenges. Mini-production lines at Manufacturing Technology Catapult Centres (MTNCs), together with learning factories designed for simulation and testing, can be configured to closely replicate real production environments. This can provide valuable insights into different testing mechanisms and enable a better understanding of the threats and vulnerabilities associated with Industry 4.0 and future manufacturing systems.

The key technologies that boost Industry 4.0 and beyond are the Internet of Things (IoT), Industrial Internet of Things (IIoT), Artificial Intelligence (AI), Cloud computing, Machine Learning, Security, Big Data, Blockchain, Deep learning, Digitalization, Digital Twins, Cyber-physical systems (CPS), Advanced Analytics, Robotics, and Cognitive Computing. These technologies can expand the attack surface of Industry 4.0. Furthermore, as information technology (IT) and operational technology (OT) are being integrated, a new range of security issues can also arise which require the defence of both IT and OT.

The workshop garnered the attention of research communities and fostered novel insights and advancements, with a specific focus on cybersecurity threat detection through AI tools for industrial sectors, security and safety for supply chains, digital twin-driven cyber-resilient supply chains, and emerging EU legislations for industry. The 5th Workshop on Cybersecurity in Industry 4.0 and Beyond (SecIndustry 2026) was held in person. The workshop was organized in conjunction with the 21st International Conference on Availability, Reliability and Security (ARES 2026), August 24–27, 2026, in Linköping, Sweden.

A total of nine submissions were received by the workshop. As a result of an extensive double-blind peer-review process in which submissions received three reviews each on average, five papers were selected to be presented at the workshop. The review process primarily emphasized the quality, scientific novelty, and applicability of the papers to safeguarding critical infrastructure and services. The acceptance rate stood at 55%. The accepted articles encompass a diverse range of techniques addressing, monitoring, and predicting security threats using AI models in AI-based anomaly detection, Industrial

Control Systems, Cyber-Physical Systems, Embedded Systems, and Industrial Internet of Things (IIoT) for industrial sectors.

The workshop showcased one significant and thought-provoking keynote on the topic of "Secure and Resilient IT-OT for Industry 4.0". The workshop was supported by the Center for Research-based Innovation (SFI) of the Norwegian Centre for Cybersecurity in Critical Sectors (NORCICS), the International Alliance for Strengthening Cybersecurity and Privacy in Healthcare (CybAlliance), and Strengthening Resilience in Critical Sectors through IT-OT Integration and Human-Organizational Aspects (ResCri) projects. The organizers would like to thank these projects for supporting the SecIndustry 2026 workshop.

The organizers of the SecIndustry workshop would like to extend their heartfelt appreciation to the SecIndustry 2026 Program Committee for their meticulous and punctual review process, which played a crucial role in bringing the workshop to fruition. We would like to express our gratitude to Linköping University, Linköping, Sweden for hosting the workshop, and extend our appreciation to the ARES 2026 chairs for their invaluable assistance and support.

August 2026

Sandeep Pirbhulal
Habtamu Abie
Halvor Holtskog
Sokratis Katsikas

SecIndustry 2026 Organization

Workshop Chairs

Sandeep Pirbhulal	Norwegian Computing Center, Norway
Habtamu Abie	Norwegian Computing Center, Norway
Halvor Holtskog	Norwegian University of Science and Technology, Norway
Sokratis Katsikas	Norwegian University of Science and Technology, Norway

Program Committee

Cristina Alcaraz	University of Málaga, Spain
Shaukat Ali	Simula Research Laboratory, Norway
Manos Athanatos	Foundation for Research and Technology Hellas, Greece
Sabarathinam Chockalingam	Institute for Energy Technology, Norway
Mauro Conti	University of Padua, Italy
Hervé Debar	Télécom SudParis, France
Sabine Delaitre	GuardedBox, Spain
Joaquin Garcia-Alfaro	Institut Mines-Télécom, France
Martin Gilje Jaatun	University of Stavanger, Norway
Vasileios Gkioulos	Norwegian University of Science and Technology, Norway
Ilias Gkotsis	Satways Ltd., Greece
Dieter Gollmann	Hamburg University of Technology, Germany
Bjørn Axel Gran	Institute for Energy Technology, Norway
Siv Hilde Houmb	Norwegian University of Science and Technology, Norway
Nesrine Kaaniche	Télécom SudParis, France
Stamatis Karnouskos	SAP Research, Germany
Basel Katt	Norwegian University of Science and Technology, Norway
Maryline Laurent	Télécom SudParis, France
Wolfgang Leister	Norwegian Computing Center, Norway
Fabio Martinelli	IIT-CNR, Italy
Vasileios Mavroeidis	University of Oslo, Norway
Aida Omerovic	SINTEF, Norway
Kai Rannenberg	Goethe University Frankfurt, Germany

Reijo Savola	University of Jyväskylä, Finland
Ankur Shukla	Institute for Energy Technology, Norway
Ali Hassan Sodhro	Kristianstad University, Sweden
Mohsen Toorani	University of South-Eastern Norway, Norway
Rita Ugarelli	SINTEF, Norway
Stephen Wolthusen	Norwegian University of Science and Technology, Norway
Christos Xenakis	University of Piraeus, Greece
Shouhuai Xu	University of Colorado Colorado Springs, USA

Structural Blind Spots in AI-Based IIoT Anomaly Detection

Kaan Bilgic[1], Sofiane Aissani[1(✉)], and Mawloud Omar[2]

[1] Université de Technologie de Troyes (UTT), LIST3N, Troyes, France
{kaan.bilgic,sofiane.aissani}@utt.fr
[2] IRISA, University of South Brittany, Vannes, France
mawloud.omar@univ-ubs.fr

Abstract. Unsupervised anomaly detection is widely used in Industrial IoT (IIoT) because labeled attack data is rare. These models are expected to learn normal behavior and flag anything unusual. Still, their behavior is not well understood when attacks are made to look realistic instead of clearly abnormal.

We study this using the Edge-IIoTset dataset and two models: Isolation Forest and an Autoencoder trained only on benign traffic. We apply a progressive feature removal process. Results show a clear pattern. When semantic features (like identifiers or payload information) are available, detection is relatively stable. Once we remove them and keep only geometric features, performance drops a lot. In our case, Isolation Forest recall goes down to about 1.3%, meaning most attacks are missed.

We also test False Data Injection Attacks (FDIA) that follow smooth behaviors such as drift or oscillation. These attacks do not try to look strange. Instead, they stay consistent with normal distributions at each timestep. Because of this, they can remain hidden for long periods. We observe detection delays up to 6700 timesteps, and in some runs, no alert is triggered at all.

To describe this effect, we introduce a simple metric: Time-to-Detection (TTD). We also inspect the Autoencoder latent space. Attack paths often stay inside dense normal regions for a long time, which helps explain the delay.

Overall, our results suggest that anomaly detection strongly depends on feature quality. However, these findings are preliminary and dataset-dependent. When representations are reduced too much, separating normal and malicious behavior becomes difficult and sometimes unclear. This does not invalidate the models, but indicates potential limitations of geometry-only representations in this dataset.

Keywords: Industrial IoT · Intrusion Detection · Anomaly Detection · False Data Injection Attacks · Structural Blind Spots · Adversarial Behavior · Cyber-Physical Systems

Z. Afzal et al. (Eds.): ARES 2026 Workshops, LNCS 16900, pp. 333–350, 2027.
https://doi.org/10.1007/978-3-032-35576-8_18

1 Introduction

Industrial IoT (IIoT) systems increasingly rely on continuous telemetry and AI-based monitoring to supervise critical physical processes. In such environments, small deviations in data streams can propagate into operational failures, production losses, or safety risks. Despite this, most security mechanisms still assume that malicious activity can be detected as a statistical deviation from normal behavior.

Unsupervised anomaly detection is now widely used in this setting [8], as it does not require labeled attack data. Its effectiveness, relies on a key assumption: anomalous behavior is separable from normal activity in the feature space. In this paper, we use Edge-IIoTset instead of BoT-IoT [9,10]. BoT-IoT contains only 0.1% benign traffic, which makes unsupervised learning harder. Edge-IIoTset is more balanced, with about 15% benign traffic.

IIoT data combines semantic attributes (e.g., identifiers, protocol fields) and geometric descriptors (e.g., timing, packet sizes, flow statistics). As a result, detection performance may depend more on the availability of such features than on genuine behavioral modeling.

When these semantic cues are removed or obfuscated, malicious and benign behaviors can overlap within the remaining geometric representation. In this regime, standard anomaly detection methods lose their ability to reliably distinguish system states. We refer to this phenomenon as a *structural blind spot*, where detection fails due to limitations of the description rather than the learning algorithm.

The question is: can anomaly detection remain effective when adversarial behavior is not an outlier, but evolves within the same geometric structure as normal traffic?

To address this question, we adopt an adversarial evaluation framework combining controlled feature ablation, physically consistent attack modeling, and latent space analysis.

Contributions. Our contributions in this paper can be summarized as follows:

- We characterize the notion of *structural blind spots* in IIoT anomaly detection.
- We empirically show that detection collapses under progressive removal of semantic features.
- We design stealthy False Data Injection Attacks that remain geometrically consistent while inducing long-term system deviations.
- We introduce *Time-to-Detection (TTD)* as a metric capturing delayed or failed detection.
- We analyze latent space and show how adversarial trajectories remain embedded within high-density regions.
- We provide initial evidence that these limitations persist even when using temporal models, suggesting that the failure may be influenced by representation constraints rather than being purely algorithm-specific.

The remainder of the paper is organized as follows. Section 2 reviews related work, Sect. 3 formalizes the problem, Sects. 4–6 present experimental results and analysis, and Sect. 7 concludes the paper.

2 Background and Related Work

Unsupervised anomaly detection is widely used in IIoT systems because labeled attack data is rare and quickly outdated. The idea is to learn normal behavior and flag deviations as anomalies. This approach is well established in network security [1,4].

However, it relies on a strong assumption: anomalies are statistically separable from normal traffic. In practice, adversarial behavior can remain within the same distribution. In such cases, performance depends more on feature representation than on the model itself.

2.1 Common Detection Methods and Their Limits

Isolation Forest [2] and autoencoders [3] are standard baselines. Both rely on geometric assumptions.

Isolation Forest assumes anomalies lie in sparse regions. This works when separation is clear, but fails when attacks fall inside dense normal regions.

Autoencoders detect anomalies through reconstruction error, assuming normal data lies on a stable manifold. In practice, they often capture dominant statistical patterns rather than true behavior [1], allowing some attacks to remain undetected.

These limitations have been reported in industrial intrusion detection and graph-based anomaly detection [6,7], but are rarely the main focus.

2.2 Feature Dependence and Dataset Bias

IIoT datasets often include strong semantic features such as IP addresses, ports, or payload-related fields. These act as shortcuts and simplify classification.

This leads to shortcut learning, where models rely on identifiers instead of behavior [4]. While this improves benchmark results, it reduces robustness.

When such features are removed, models must rely only on geometric and statistical structure, which may not be sufficient for reliable separation.

2.3 Adversarial Evaluation and FDIA Models

Most adversarial evaluations in IIoT rely on simple perturbations that do not reflect realistic attacks.

False Data Injection Attacks (FDIA), in contrast, follow physical constraints and evolve gradually [5]. They are therefore more relevant for industrial settings.

However, FDIA-based evaluations remain rare. Most studies use static datasets such as Edge-IIoTset [9] or Bot-IoT [10], where temporal behavior is simplified.

2.4 Representation Limitations in Deep Models

Deep anomaly detection assumes that normal data occupies a compact latent region, while anomalies lie outside [1,8].

In IIoT data, this assumption is weak. Traffic often forms continuous and overlapping regions. As a result, adversarial samples can remain inside high-density areas without being detected.

Similar limitations have been observed in industrial intrusion detection [6].

2.5 Positioning and Research Gap

Table 1 shows how this work differs from previous studies.

Table 1. Positioning of this work with respect to the literature.

Axis	Existing Literature	This Work
Detection Objective	Focus on accuracy	Focus on failure under constraints
Feature Usage	Strong use of semantic features	Separation of semantic and geometric features
Feature Ablation	Rare or partial	Controlled progressive removal
Adversarial Modeling	Simple perturbations	FDIA-inspired temporal attacks
Temporal Aspect	Often ignored	Time-to-Detection analysis
Latent Space View	Limited analysis	Trajectory-based study
Failure Interpretation	Only performance drop	Structural explanation of failure

Most prior work evaluates anomaly detection with rich features and easily separable attacks. Temporal behavior and feature constraints are rarely studied together.

Note that these findings are preliminary and inherently dataset-dependent, FDIA-style attacks, and latent space analysis, with a focus on understanding when detection fails.

3 Structural Blind Spot: Problem Formulation and Experimental Setup

The previous sections highlighted that anomaly detection may fail when feature representations become too constrained. We now formalize this limitation.

Definition (Structural Blind Spot). We define a structural blind spot as a region of the feature space where distinct system states (benign and adversarial) are indistinguishable under the representation mapping, i.e., where the anomaly scoring function is non-injective with respect to the underlying process.

In such regions, the detector cannot reliably distinguish between normal and malicious behaviors, not because of model limitations, but due to insufficient expressiveness of the feature representation. This definition will guide our experimental analysis in the following sections.

3.1 System and Threat Model

We consider an Industry 4.0 environment where IIoT devices continuously generate telemetry streams monitored by a one-class anomaly detection system. The model is trained only on benign data.

Each observation is represented as a feature vector $x \in \mathbb{R}^d$. It contains numerical descriptors such as packet sizes, inter-arrival times, and flow-level statistics. Semantic identifiers (IP addresses, ports, payload content) are removed to avoid trivial separability and to reflect realistic constraints in secured deployments. This setting also approximates scenarios where such information is unavailable or unreliable, for example due to encryption (e.g., TLS or VPN tunnels) or adversarial manipulation such as identifier spoofing. In these cases, detection systems are forced to rely primarily on geometric and statistical properties of the traffic.

The detector outputs an anomaly score $s(x)$ and triggers an alert when $s(x) > \tau$, where τ is calibrated on normal traffic.

Attacker Capabilities. We assume a partial control attacker over the data generation process. The adversary can modify a subset of sensor outputs or network features over time. All modifications must remain physically plausible, i.e., consistent with the underlying system dynamics.

The attack evolves over time through structured perturbations: slow drift, bounded oscillations, or stochastic variations. Each modification is applied incrementally to avoid abrupt changes that would be trivially detected.

Knowledge Assumptions. The attacker operates in a black-box setting. There is no access to model parameters, training data, or the decision threshold τ. Feedback is indirect and limited to observable system behavior after injection.

Attacker Objectives. The goal is not to trigger anomalies, but to modify the system state while staying under the detection threshold.

Formally, the attacker generates a sequence $\{x_t^{adv}\}_{t=1}^T$ such that:

$$s(x_t^{adv}) \leq \tau \quad \forall t,$$

while maximizing deviation from the nominal process.

This is expressed as:

$$\max_{\{x_t^{adv}\}} \mathcal{D}(\{x_t^{adv}\}, \{x_t\}) \quad \text{subject to} \quad s(x_t^{adv}) \leq \tau, \ \forall t,$$

where $\mathcal{D}(\cdot)$ measures cumulative deviation from the expected system behavior.

Discussion. The setting reflects realistic IIoT constraints where attacks unfold as continuous trajectories rather than isolated anomalies. Each observation remains locally plausible, while the global evolution gradually deviates from normal operation. Detection depends entirely on whether the model can separate such trajectories within its learned description.

3.2 Experimental Strategy

We evaluate the system through three steps.

We begin by a feature ablation and study progressively removes semantic information. This isolates the contribution of each feature group and reveals how detection behaves under restricted representations.

then we construct adversarial processes inspired by False Data Injection Attacks. These attacks satisfy three constraints: bounded magnitude, temporal smoothness, and geometric consistency with the normal data manifold. The objective is : remain inside the learned representation while inducing controlled system deviation.

Third, we analyze latent descriptions of both normal and adversarial samples. By projecting embeddings and tracking trajectories, we study how attacks evolve in the learned space and where detection breaks down.

The evaluation follows a simple rule: reduce information, then test whether the remaining structure is still sufficient for detection. We conducted a three-stage ablation study: Scenario A (IP removal), Scenario B (IP and Port removal), and Scenario C (Total sterilization, including payloads). Results show a 'Resilience Plateau' for Scenarios A and B, where performance remains stable. However, a 'Geometric Precipice' occurs in Scenario C, where the removal of textual payloads leads to a drastic drop in F1-Score, proving that the models were over-relying on semantic signatures rather than flow geometry

3.3 Data Engineering Constraints

The experimental pipeline is constrained by realistic hardware limitations (16 GB RAM). The full dataset cannot be processed directly, so we extract 3 million benign samples while preserving statistical diversity.

We also observe a strong imbalance in the data: a single gateway IP dominates the traffic. To prevent bias, we cap the number of samples per source. This ensures that peripheral devices are not underrepresented.

Without this correction, the model would overfit dominant communication patterns, leading to artificially inflated performance.

The final dataset provides a balanced approximation of IIoT traffic, with preserved diversity across devices and communication sources.

To ensure a balanced representation of the industrial fleet, we implemented a per-IP capping strategy (limited to 450,000 rows per source). This prevents the model from being biased by the Gateway's high traffic volume and forces it to learn the behavior of smaller peripheral sensors.

To provide a unified view of our experimental framework and observations, Fig. 1 illustrates the interplay between feature representation, latent space geometry, and detection behavior. As semantic features are progressively removed, the representation becomes increasingly constrained, eventually leading to a geometry-only regime. In this setting, benign and adversarial behaviors overlap within high-density regions of the latent space, creating what we define as a structural blind spot.

Adversarial trajectories, designed to remain smooth and consistent, evolve within these regions for extended periods, delaying or even preventing detection. This effect is captured by the Time-to-Detection (TTD), which highlights the temporal gap between attack onset and detection. The diagram summarizes how detection failure emerges not from model weakness, but from limitations in the underlying representation.

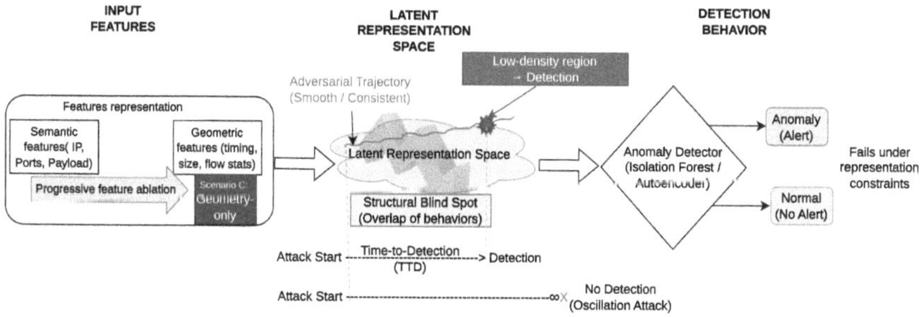

Fig. 1. From Feature Ablation to Detection Failure: A Structural View of Blind Spots in IIoT Anomaly Detection.

4 Feature Dependency Analysis

We do not try to improve performance here. Instead, we try to break it.

The idea is simple: if anomaly detection really captures behavior, it should survive when obvious shortcuts disappear. If it does not, then something else is driving the results.

Rather than tuning models, we directly modify the input space. We remove information step by step and observe what remains. This allows us to separate two possibilities: genuine behavioral learning, or dependence on artifacts hidden in the features.

4.1 Progressive Feature Ablation

We design a structured ablation process. Features are not dropped randomly. They are removed in stages, each step reducing the amount of semantic information available to the model.

We define three scenarios:

- **Scenario A (No IP):** IP addresses are removed. Transport and payload features are still present.
- **Scenario B (No IP + Ports):** both IP addresses and port information are removed. Communication context becomes weaker.

- **Scenario C (Geometry-only):** all semantic features are removed. Only numerical descriptors remain (packet sizes, inter-arrival times, flow statistics).

This progression moves from rich descriptions to minimal ones. In Scenario C, the model has no identifiers, no labels, no context. It only sees distributions. At this point, detection becomes a purely geometric problem.

4.2 Results and Structural Collapse

The results are shown in Fig. 2.

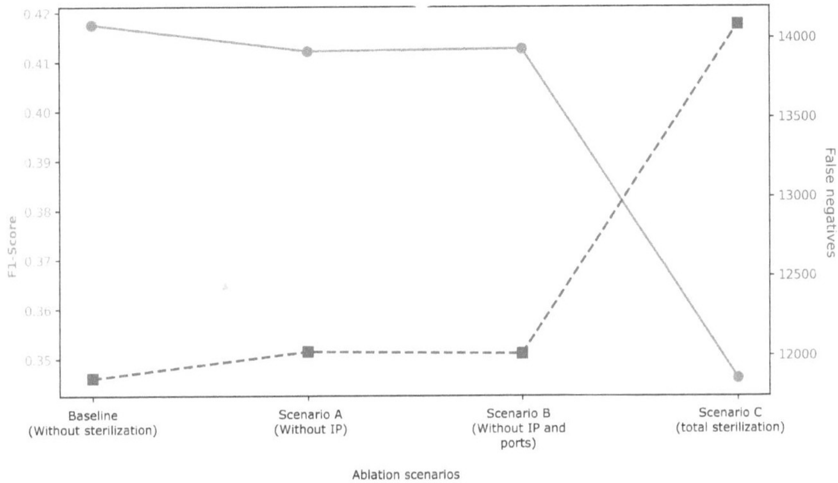

Fig. 2. Impact of progressive feature ablation on detection performance.

Two regimes appear.

From Scenario A to Scenario B, almost nothing changes. Removing IPs and ports has little impact. This is unexpected, but it suggests that these features are not the main drivers of the decision.

The transition to Scenario C is different. Once semantic information disappears completely, performance drops sharply. Not gradually—abruptly. This transition corresponds to the representation collapse illustrated in Fig. 1. The models lose their ability to separate normal and malicious traffic.

This looks less like degradation and more like a break. The decision boundary, which seemed stable before, becomes unclear. Different behaviors collapse into the same regions of the feature space.

In other words, the model can no longer tell things apart.

What looked robust before was partly supported by the representation itself. Once this support is removed, the problem changes.

4.3 Quantitative Comparison

We now focus on Scenario C, the most constrained setting.

Table 2. Crash-test performance under geometry-only representation (Scenario C).

Metric	Isolation Forest	Autoencoder
Accuracy	0.1813	0.5674
Precision	0.6209	0.9977
Recall (%)	1.3	61.4
F1-score	0.0245	0.6439
False Negatives (%)	98.7	38.6
False Positives (%)	3.5	5.1

Hyperparameters were calibrated on the benign validation set (Isolation Forest: 100 estimators, contamination rate 0.05; Autoencoder: three hidden layers with architecture [32, 16, 32], Adam optimizer, MAE loss). Detection thresholds (τ) were set at the 95th percentile of the normal reconstruction or isolation scores. Statistical variability across five independent runs remained below $\pm1.2\%$ for all evaluated metrics. Table 2 makes the situation clear.

For Isolation Forest, detection almost disappears. A recall of 1.3% means that nearly all attacks are missed. This is consistent with the 98.7% false negative rate. The F1-score (0.0245) reflects this collapse.

Interestingly, precision stays at 0.6209. When the model raises an alert, it is often correct. The issue is not randomness. It is lack of sensitivity. Only very strong geometric deviations are detected.

The Autoencoder behaves differently. It keeps a recall of 61.4% and reaches an F1-score of 0.6439. Precision is extremely high (0.9977), meaning that detected anomalies are almost always real.

But this comes at a cost. The model still misses 38.6% of attacks. These correspond to cases where malicious behavior remains too close to normal traffic.

False positives are limited (5.1%), but this is misleading at scale. In an industrial system processing millions of events per hour, this would generate a large number of alerts—far beyond what operators can handle.

The two models fail in different ways. Isolation Forest becomes almost blind. The Autoencoder remains selective, but incomplete.

This asymmetry is important. It shows that failure is not just about accuracy—it is about how the model fails.

4.4 Attack Design Principles

We now build attacks that exploit these weaknesses.

Instead of arbitrary perturbations, we impose strict constraints. The goal is not to create obvious anomalies, but to stay inside what the model considers normal.

We enforce three conditions:

Boundedness. Each perturbation remains small. No single sample should look suspicious.

Temporal Smoothness. Changes are gradual. No abrupt jumps.

In-manifold Consistency. Samples remain in high-density regions of the learned distribution. The trajectory stays geometrically plausible.

This is different from classical adversarial settings. We are not trying to cross a boundary. We are trying to avoid creating one.

Evaluation Dataset. We evaluate on 564,130 samples: 100,000 benign and 464,130 malicious, covering 14 attack types. All data is preprocessed in the same way as the training set.

This setup reflects a difficult but realistic scenario: multiple attacks, no semantic identifiers.

4.5 Temporal Attack Models

We implement three types of temporal attacks.

Slow Drift. We apply a small cumulative change. At each timestep, the signal increases slightly. Concretely, we use a slope of 0.1 per frame on the `tcp.len` feature.

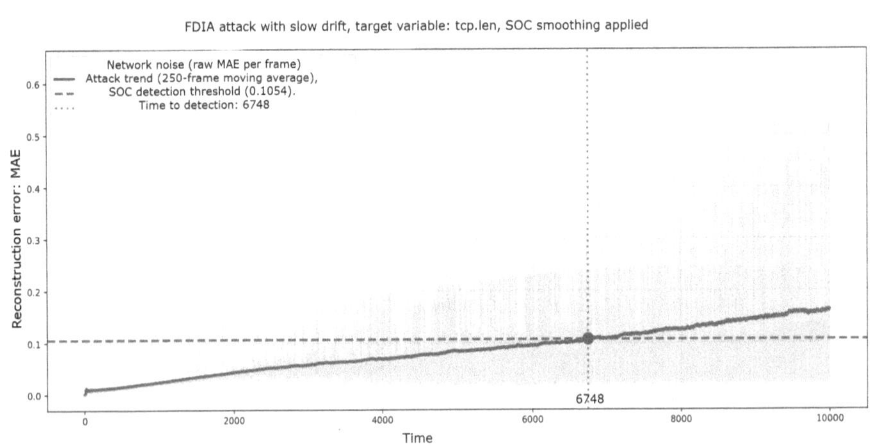

Fig. 3. Reconstruction error under slow drift attack. Detection is delayed despite continuous deviation.

In Fig. 3, the anomaly score rises slowly but stays below the threshold for a long time. Detection eventually happens, but late.

The Time-to-Detection (TTD) reaches several thousand timesteps. During this period, the system processes corrupted data without any alert.

This happens because the model evaluates each sample independently. It does not accumulate evidence over time.

Oscillation. Here, the signal does not drift. It oscillates within a fixed range. We use a sine wave with amplitude 375 and period 4,500 frames.

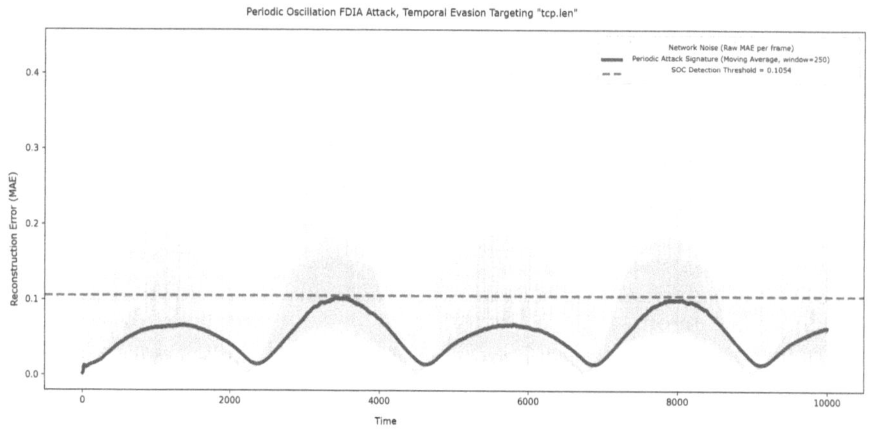

Fig. 4. Reconstruction error under oscillation attack. The signal remains below the detection threshold.

As shown in Fig. 4, the score fluctuates but never crosses the threshold. The attack is never detected.

Because the perturbation is bounded, the system repeatedly returns to dense regions. The detector interprets this as normal variability.

Here, detection is not delayed—it simply does not happen.

Composite Attack. We combine drift with noise to mimic realistic sensor behavior.

In Fig. 5, the signal looks irregular but natural. The noise hides the structure of the attack.

Detection still occurs, but late, as in the drift case. The added randomness makes interpretation harder, both for the model and for a human analyst.

4.6 Takeaway: Beyond Statistical Outliers

The main observation is counter-intuitive.

The most effective attacks are not extreme. They do not stand out. They behave like valid trajectories inside the model's own representation.

At each timestep, everything looks normal. Only the long-term evolution is problematic.

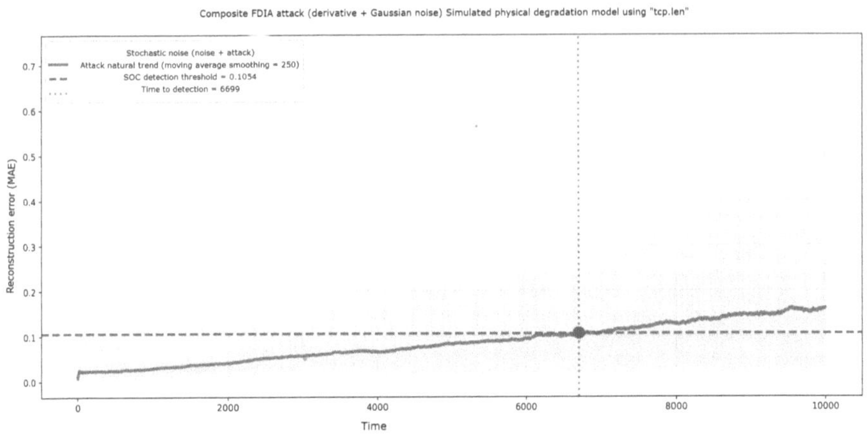

Fig. 5. Reconstruction error under composite attack (drift with noise).

This challenges a common assumption: that malicious behavior is always distinguishable. In our setting, it is not.

To understand why, we need to look at the geometry of the latent space.

5 Latent Space Explanation of Detection Failure

The previous sections established that detection collapses under feature constraints and that this weakness can be actively exploited. We now turn to a more fundamental question: why do these failures occur in the first place?

To answer this, we analyze the internal representations learned by the model. Rather than focusing on input space behavior, we examine how data—and attacks—are structured in the latent space induced by the Autoencoder.

5.1 Learned Representation

The Autoencoder learns a mapping from the input space X_g to a lower-dimensional latent space:

$$z = f(x), \quad z \in \mathbb{R}^h.$$

This transformation is not arbitrary. It defines a compressed representation of the data distribution, often interpreted as an approximation of a manifold $\mathcal{M}$ capturing normal system behavior.

In practice, this manifold is neither discrete nor sharply bounded. Instead, it forms a continuous region of high density, within which variations of normal traffic are smoothly embedded. Reconstruction-based detection relies on the assumption that anomalies lie outside this region and therefore incur higher reconstruction error.

However, this assumption implicitly requires that malicious behavior be separable in the latent space. As we show next, this condition does not hold under realistic constraints.

5.2 Attack Trajectories in Latent Space

To visualize the learned structure, we project latent representations into two dimensions using PCA. Figure 6 illustrates both normal samples and adversarial trajectories.

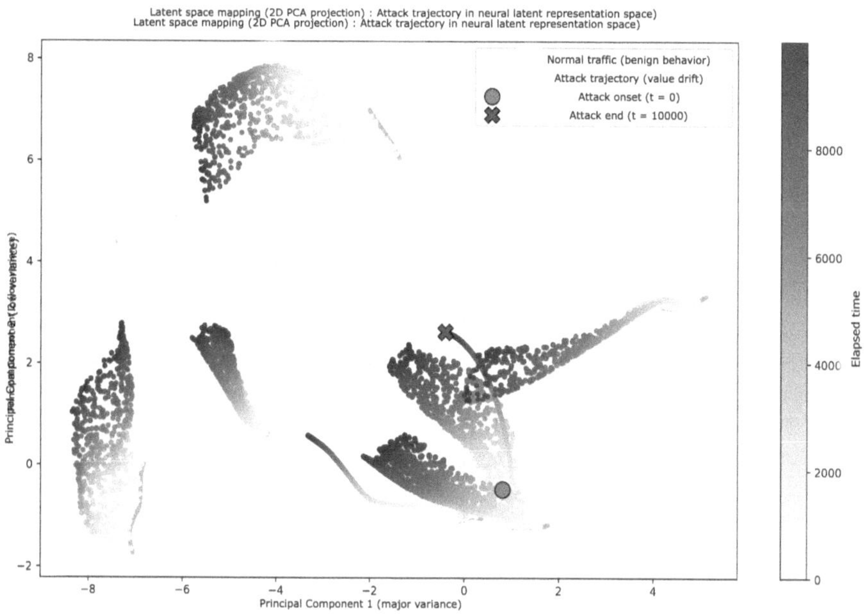

Fig. 6. Projection of latent descriptions. Attack trajectories remain embedded within high-density regions before gradually exiting.

We can make the following observations:

Normal data does not form isolated clusters, but rather a continuous and overlapping region. This reflects the inherent variability of IIoT traffic, where multiple operating modes coexist without clear separation.

Adversarial samples do not appear as isolated points. Instead, they follow smooth trajectories within this region. As shown in Fig. 1, these trajectories remain embedded within high-density areas of the latent space for extended periods, which explains the delayed detection observed in previous sections. For extended periods, these trajectories remain entirely embedded within high-density areas of the latent space. This observation also remains consistent when analyzing temporal embeddings, where adversarial trajectories can still remain within high-density regions over extended periods.

Detection only occurs when the trajectory eventually drifts toward lower-density regions. This explains the delayed detection observed in previous sections: the model does not react to the direction of change, only to its eventual magnitude relative to the learned manifold.

The attack is not initially perceived as anomalous because it remains geometrically consistent with normal data.

5.3 Structural Interpretation

These observations point to a deeper limitation that goes beyond model capacity or training data.

From a functional perspective, the anomaly score defines a mapping:

$$f : X_g \to \mathbb{R},$$

which assigns similar scores to inputs that are close in the latent space. When benign and adversarial samples occupy overlapping regions, this mapping becomes non-injective with respect to the underlying system states.

Distinct behaviors—legitimate and malicious—are projected onto the same regions of the representation space. As a result, the detector cannot reliably distinguish them.

This phenomenon can be understood as a form of topological entanglement. The trajectories induced by attacks are not separated from normal data; they are woven into the same continuous configuration. Temporal smoothness further reinforces this effect by ensuring that transitions remain locally consistent at every step.

Crucially, the failure does not stem from inaccurate modeling, but from the geometry of the representation itself. The detector operates on a space in which adversarial and normal processes are inherently indistinguishable.
suggesting that the issue may lie less in the model itself and more in how the problem is represented. The failure is geometric, not algorithmic.

5.4 Time-To-Detection (TTD)

Standard metrics for anomaly detection—precision, recall, F1-score—treat detection as a static outcome. They answer *whether* an attack is detected, but ignore a more operational dimension: *when* it is detected.

In IIoT settings, this distinction is not cosmetic. A delayed recognition can be functionally equivalent to a failure. An attack that persists unnoticed for thousands of timesteps may already have reshaped system behavior long before any alert is raised.

Definition. To capture this temporal gap, we define *Time-to-Detection (TTD)*. Given an adversarial sequence $\{x_t^{adv}\}_{t=1}^{T}$, we define:

$$\text{TTD} = \min\{t \in [1, T] \mid s(x_t^{adv}) > \tau\}$$

If the condition is never satisfied:

$$\text{TTD} = +\infty$$

TTD measures the delay between attack onset and first system response, as conceptually illustrated in Fig. 1.

Empirical Results. Table 3 reports TTD across attack types.

Table 3. Time-to-Detection (TTD) across attack scenarios

Attack Type	Detection	TTD (timesteps)
Slow Drift	Yes	6700
Oscillation	No	∞
Composite (Drift + Noise)	Yes	$\sim$ 6600

Two regimes emerge. Drift-based attacks are eventually detected, but only after substantial delay. Oscillatory patterns, in contrast, never trigger an alert and remain entirely inside the detector's notion of normality.

Security Implications. TTD exposes a blind spot invisible to classical metrics. High recall does not guarantee operational safety if recognition arrives too late.

In practice, delays of several thousand timesteps correspond to a prolonged exposure window in which system behavior can be progressively altered without interruption. In some cases, detection never occurs, revealing that certain attack classes are not merely difficult to detect—they are structurally unobservable.

TTD therefore complements standard evaluation by adding a temporal axis to detection performance. In industrial security, this axis is not secondary: it often determines whether detection is meaningful at all. Our evaluation of TTD metric reveals a critical security gap. In the Slow Drift scenario, the attacker maintains a window of 6,748 frames before triggering an alert. More alarmingly, the Oscillation attack achieved a permanent evasion ($TTD = \infty$), as the signal mimics natural network fluctuations, remaining entirely invisible to the SOC.

6 Discussion: Rethinking IIoT Anomaly Detection

What we observe in this work is not a corner case. It appears consistently across models, attacks, and settings. The key point is simple: detection depends heavily on what the representation exposes, sometimes more than on the model itself.

6.1 Structural Limitations Observed in Practice

When semantic features are removed, the system behavior changes quickly. This is not a gradual degradation. In our experiments, the transition is abrupt. For example, Isolation Forest drops to around 1.3.

At this point, the issue is no longer low performance. The model can no longer separate the data. Different behaviors start to look the same.

This suggests that part of "learning normality" relies on easy signals. IPs, ports, or payload patterns simplify the task. Once removed, the problem becomes fundamentally different.

We also observe a limitation over time.In our setup, the detector evaluates each sample independently. This works for isolated anomalies, but not for slow changes. In drift scenarios, each point looks normal. The deviation only appears at the sequence level.

Another issue is the overlap between benign and adversarial data. In latent space, this is common when the representation is constrained. PCA projections show that attacks start in dense normal regions and remain there for long periods.

Detection only occurs when the trajectory moves far enough away. In our case, this can take up to 6700 timesteps, which is already too late in practice.

6.2 What This Means for Real Systems

These results have direct implications for real deployments.

First, stealth does not require complex attacks. Simple drift or oscillation patterns are enough, as long as they remain consistent over time.

Second, delay matters. Detection after several thousand timesteps is not a real success. By then, the system may already have deviated significantly.

Third, outputs become harder to interpret. When anomalies look like normal fluctuations, it is difficult to assess whether an alert is meaningful. This creates hesitation for operators.

False positives are also an issue. In our Autoencoder results, the rate is around 5.1.

In practice, no team can handle that volume. This leads to alert fatigue, and alerts may start to be ignored.

Importantly, these failures do not require a strong attacker. The attacks we use are simple and structured, with no need for model access or optimization.

6.3 Why Existing Fixes Are Not Enough

Several approaches have been proposed to improve anomaly detection.

Sequence models add memory and help with abrupt anomalies. However, if the representation already mixes benign and malicious behavior, they do not fully solve the issue and may propagate ambiguity over time.

Adaptive thresholds can adjust sensitivity, but they still rely on the same anomaly score. If the score is not informative, thresholding does not help.

Physics-based constraints are promising, especially for cyber-physical systems. In practice, however, they are difficult to deploy and depend on accurate system knowledge.

Overall, these approaches improve parts of the system, but do not address the core issue: the lack of separability in the feature space.

We also tested temporal models based on LSTM autoencoders. While they improve robustness to abrupt anomalies, they do not resolve the core problem. Attacks that remain geometrically consistent, such as oscillations, can still evade detection. This suggests that the limitation is structural rather than model-specific.

6.4 Limitations of This Study

This work has several limitations.

We rely on a single dataset (Edge-IIoTset), making our findings structurally insightful but dataset-dependent. Furthermore, our current framing lacks a deeper evaluation against broader adversarial machine learning, representation learning, idea drift, or complex physics-informed anomaly detection methods.

The attacks are designed to be controlled and interpretable. They are realistic, but do not cover all strategies.

We also focus on understanding failure rather than fixing it. Designing better representations or detection methods remains an open question.

6.5 Final Perspective

Anomaly detection does not always fail because the model is weak. Sometimes, it fails because the necessary information is not available.

When semantic cues are removed and behaviors overlap, the representation is no longer expressive enough. In this case, improving the model has limited impact.

The problem is therefore not only algorithmic, but also related to how the system is represented.

Improving robustness may require rethinking both the input representation and the evaluation setup, not just building more complex models.

7 Conclusion

This work challenges a central assumption in IIoT security: that anomalies are inherently detectable as deviations from learned normality. Under realistic constraints, this assumption does not hold.

Through feature ablation, FDIA-based attacks, and latent space analysis, we show that detection can collapse abruptly once identifying cues are removed. In this regime, benign and malicious behaviors become indistinguishable, and the problem changes in nature rather than degrading gradually.

The attacks we consider do not rely on strong perturbations. Instead, they exploit continuity: small, consistent changes that remain aligned with the learned distribution. As a result, adversarial trajectories can stay within valid regions for long periods, enabling sustained evasion.

These limitations are not model-specific. When detection relies only on distributional consistency, certain adversarial behaviors cannot be isolated, regardless of the algorithm.

This has direct implications for industrial systems. High benchmark accuracy does not guarantee robustness, especially when attacks evolve over time under physical constraints.

Future work should explore sequence-aware and physics-informed models, along with adaptive mechanisms that capture temporal evolution rather than isolated observations.

Ultimately, the key question is not only whether detection is possible, but whether it remains meaningful in real operational settings.

Disclosure of Interests. The authors have no competing interests to declare that are relevant to the content of this article.

References

1. Ruff, L., Vandermeulen, R.A., Görnitz, N., Binder, A., Müller, E., Müller, K.-R.: A unifying review of deep and shallow anomaly detection. Proc. IEEE **109**(5), 756–795 (2021)
2. Liu, F.T., Ting, K.M., Zhou, Z.-H.: Isolation Forest. In: Proceedings of the IEEE International Conference on Data Mining (ICDM), pp. 413–422 (2008)
3. Sakurada, M., Yairi, T.: Anomaly detection using autoencoders with nonlinear dimensionality reduction. In: Proceedings of the MLSDA Workshop at NIPS (2014)
4. Rezaei, S., Liu, X.: Deep learning for network traffic monitoring and analysis (NTMA): a survey. IEEE Commun. Surv. Tutor. **22**(4), 2292–2327 (2020)
5. Mo, Y., Sinopoli, B.: False data injection attacks against state estimation in electric power grids. ACM Trans. Info. Syst. Secu. **14**(1), 13:1–13:33 (2011)
6. Wolsing, K., Wagner, E., Lux, L., Wehrle, K., Henze, M.: GeCos Replacing experts: generalizable and comprehensible industrial intrusion detection. In: Proceedings of the 34th USENIX Security Symposium (USENIX Security '25), USENIX Association, Seattle, WA, USA (2025)
7. Miliani, A., Touahria, M. Y., Kechad, A., Derdour, H., Kheniche. M. A.: Comparing hyperbolic graph embedding models on anomaly detection for cybersecurity. In: Proceedings of the 20th International Conference on Availability, Reliability and Security (ARES 2025), ACM (2025)
8. Vitale, F., De Vita, F., Mazzocca, N., Bruneo, D.: A process mining-based unsupervised anomaly detection technique for the industrial internet of things. Int. Things **24**, 100993 (2023)
9. Ferrag, M. A.: Edge-IIoTset: Cyber Security Dataset of IoT & IIoT. Kaggle dataset. Available: https://www.kaggle.com/datasets/mohamedamineferrag/edgeiiotset-cyber-security-dataset-of-iot-iiot. Accessed: 25 April 2026
10. Koroniotis, N., Moustafa, N., Sitnikova, E., Turnbull, B.: Towards the development of realistic botnet dataset in the internet of things for network forensic analytics: Bot-IoT dataset. Futur. Gener. Comput. Syst. **100**, 779–796 (2019)

A Hardware-Integrity Architecture for Remote Attestation of Safety-Critical Embedded Systems

Michael Eckel[1](✉), Georgios Gkoktsis[1], Anselm Angert[1], and André Rein[2]

[1] Fraunhofer SIT | ATHENE, Rheinstr. 75, 64295 Darmstadt, Germany
{michael.eckel,george.gkoktsis,anselm.angert}@sit.fraunhofer.de
[2] Mittelhessen University of Applied Sciences, Wiesenstr. 14, 35390 Gießen, Germany
andre.rein@mni.thm.de

Abstract. Remote attestation is a well-established mechanism for verifying the software and firmware state of embedded systems, yet it offers only limited support for assessing hardware integrity. This limitation is particularly relevant for safety-critical embedded and cyber-physical systems, where subtle hardware manipulation, component replacement, or degradation may affect trustworthiness without necessarily changing the measured software state. In this paper, we present a hardware-integrity-aware remote attestation architecture that incorporates analog hardware measurements into established attestation workflows. Our approach integrates such measurements as interoperable attestation evidence within CHARRA- and CEL-based environments, thereby extending existing remote attestation ecosystems rather than replacing them. We describe the architecture, its supporting implementation components, and its integration into a demonstrator on a medical IoMT platform, which serves as a representative safety-critical embedded setting. Furthermore, we evaluate the ability of the approach to distinguish between different hardware configurations and to support appraisal beyond conventional software-centric evidence. The results indicate that analog hardware measurements can complement remote attestation in a practical and structured manner, while also highlighting current limitations in reliably separating highly similar devices. Overall, the paper demonstrates that hardware integrity can be represented and conveyed as reusable attestation evidence, providing a foundation for broader application in healthcare and industrial cyber-physical environments.

Keywords: Remote Attestation · Hardware Integrity · Analog Hardware Measurements · Safety-Critical Embedded Systems · Critical Infrastructure Security

1 Introduction

Embedded and cyber-physical systems increasingly form the technical foundation of safety-critical environments, including medical Internet of Medical Things

Z. Afzal et al. (Eds.): ARES 2026 Workshops, LNCS 16900, pp. 351–369, 2027.
https://doi.org/10.1007/978-3-032-35576-8_19

(IoMT) devices, industrial automation systems, and other critical infrastructure (CI) settings. In such deployments, trust in a device cannot be limited to functional correctness alone. Operators also need mechanisms to verify that devices are genuine, have not been manipulated, and operate in an expected hardware and software state.

Remote Attestation (RA) is a well-established mechanism for providing cryptographically protected evidence about the state of an attested platform. The Internet Engineering Task Force (IETF) Remote Attestation Procedures (RATS) architecture [2], Trusted Platform Module (TPM)-based challenge-response approaches such as CHAllenge-Response based Remote Attestation with TPM 2.0 (CHARRA) [3,7], and standardized event-log formats such as the Trusted Computing Group (TCG) Canonical Event Log (CEL) [20] provide a strong foundation for reporting and appraising software and firmware measurements. However, conventional RA primarily focuses on digital measurements, such as hashes of firmware, boot components, configuration artifacts, or runtime software. Subtle hardware manipulation, component replacement, degradation, or altered electronic components may therefore remain invisible even when the measured software state appears trustworthy. Practical attacks and prior work on hardware Trojans and supply-chain interdiction illustrate that physical manipulation can undermine platform trust without necessarily changing the reported software state [13,16].

Analog hardware measurements provide a promising complementary evidence source. Due to manufacturing tolerances and physical properties of electronic circuits, nominally similar components may exhibit measurable differences in their analog behavior. Such measurements can support the detection of deviations between expected and observed hardware characteristics and have previously been explored for hardware fingerprinting and attestation-related use cases [6,9]. Yet, using analog measurements in practical attestation workflows requires more than measuring a signal: the evidence must be represented, protected, transported, and appraised in a way that is compatible with established RA ecosystems.

This paper presents a hardware-integrity-aware remote attestation architecture for safety-critical embedded systems. By integrating analog hardware measurements into CHARRA- and CEL-based attestation workflows and demonstrating the approach in a medical IoMT platform, we show that hardware integrity can be represented and conveyed as interoperable attestation evidence. The proposed architecture does not replace existing roots of trust or attestation protocols. Instead, it extends them with additional evidence about the physical behavior of hardware components and enables verifier-side appraisal that combines software, firmware, and hardware-related evidence.

We implemented the proposed architecture using a reproducible embedded measurement setup, supporting software components for evidence serialization and CEL integration, and a CHARRA-based attestation workflow. The prototype is evaluated using measurements from multiple microcontroller configurations and is additionally integrated into a medical IoMT demonstrator. While the experimental validation focuses on this demonstrator and microcontroller-based measurements, the architectural principles are applicable to broader industrial and critical-infrastructure settings in which embedded devices require verifiable hardware and software integrity. The main contributions of this paper are:

- A hardware-integrity-aware RA architecture for safety-critical embedded systems that extends software-centric attestation with analog hardware evidence.
- An interoperable integration approach for incorporating analog measurements into CHARRA- and CEL-based workflows and binding them to TPM-protected platform state.
- A prototype implementation and evaluate it using multiple microcontroller configurations and a medical IoMT demonstrator.
- Discussion of the implications, limitations, and threats to validity of using probabilistic analog measurements as complementary attestation evidence.

Our results indicate that analog hardware measurements can support the detection of clear hardware deviations and can be integrated into RA workflows in a practical and structured manner. At the same time, reliably distinguishing highly similar or nominally identical devices remains challenging. We therefore argue that analog hardware measurements should be understood as complementary evidence: they strengthen the appraisal basis of RA, but do not replace software, firmware, device identity, or lifecycle security mechanisms.

The remainder of the paper is structured as follows. Section 2 summarizes the required technical foundations. Section 3 defines the problem statement and threat model. Section 4 presents the proposed architecture, followed by implementation details in Sect. 5 and the evaluation in Sect. 6. Sections 7 and 8 discuss implications, limitations, and related work before Sect. 9 concludes the paper.

2 Background and Technical Foundations

RA enables an attester to provide evidence about its state to a verifier, which appraises this evidence against Reference Values (RVs) and policies and may produce attestation results for a relying party. The IETF RATS architecture defines the corresponding roles and distinguishes evidence, appraisal policies, reference values, and attestation results [2]. In practice, RA is commonly used to establish trust in the software and firmware state of a platform by reporting measurements of boot components, configuration artifacts, or runtime software.

A TPM provides hardware-supported roots of trust for measurement, reporting, and storage. During measured boot, platform events are measured and the resulting digests are extended into Platform Configuration Registers (PCRs), which provide a compact representation of the observed measurement sequence [18,19]. A verifier can request a signed quote over selected PCRs and a freshness value and compare the reported measurements against expected RVs. CHARRA, standardized as RFC 9684, specifies a YANG data model for challenge-response-based RA with TPMs and supports the exchange of TPM-protected evidence and corresponding measurement logs [3].

The TCG CEL specification defines a common and extensible representation for event logs [20]. It separates the abstract information model from concrete encodings, such as Concise Binary Object Representation (CBOR), JSON, or Type-Length-Value, and from content layers that define the semantics of recorded events. In this work, CEL serves as the representation layer for analog hardware measurement evidence, allowing such measurements to be encoded as structured events and processed together with conventional platform measurements.

Analog hardware measurements exploit the fact that electronic components are affected by manufacturing tolerances, aging, environmental influences, and physical properties that can change their analog behavior. Even nominally identical components may therefore exhibit measurable differences when stimulated and observed under controlled conditions. Prior work has explored such measurements for hardware fingerprinting and attestation-related use cases [6,9,11,15]. However, analog measurements differ from digital measurements: unlike firmware hashes, they are affected by noise, temperature, humidity, aging, and measurement setup. Their interpretation is therefore usually probabilistic and may require similarity metrics, classifiers, or policy-defined thresholds.

Safety-critical embedded systems, including medical IoMT devices, industrial controllers, sensor nodes, and embedded systems in CI environments, require trust not only in software and firmware, but also in the authenticity and integrity of the underlying hardware. The architecture proposed in this paper follows this broader view of trust by adding structured analog hardware measurements as complementary evidence within existing RA workflows.

3 Problem Statement and Threat Model

Conventional RA provides strong evidence about the software and firmware state of an attested platform. In TPM-based deployments, measured boot records platform events, extends corresponding digests into PCRs, and enables a verifier to check signed evidence against expected RVs. However, such evidence does not necessarily reflect the physical integrity of hardware components connected to, or embedded within, the attested system. A device may pass software-centric attestation while an attached sensor has been replaced, a microcontroller has been substituted by a functionally similar component, or an analog signal path has been manipulated.

3.1 Problem and Scope

The problem addressed in this paper is how analog hardware integrity measurements can be incorporated into established RA workflows in a practical, interoperable, and cryptographically verifiable manner. The goal is not to replace software- and firmware-oriented attestation, but to complement it with additional evidence about the physical behavior of hardware components.

These requirements follow from the gap between deterministic software measurements and probabilistic analog evidence. First, because analog values are not self-describing, they must be represented in a structured format that captures measurement values, configuration parameters, and relevant environmental context. Second, because measurement records may be transmitted through untrusted software and networks, the resulting evidence must be bound to an attested platform state, for example through TPM-protected PCRs. Third, because the goal is incremental adoption rather than a new attestation protocol, the evidence should be transportable using existing RA mechanisms such as CHARRA. Fourth, because analog evidence is affected by noise, tolerances, and operating conditions, the verifier must appraise it against suitable RVs, reference models, or policies and combine the result with conventional software and firmware appraisal.

We consider safety-critical embedded systems in which the attester collects evidence about both its platform state and selected hardware-related properties. The analog evidence may characterize microcontrollers, sensors, peripheral modules, or other electronic components whose physical integrity is relevant to the system's trustworthiness. We assume that reference measurements or reference models are established during trusted provisioning, commissioning, maintenance, or recalibration phases.

3.2 Threat Model

We assume an adversary who may gain physical or supply-chain access to selected embedded devices or peripheral components. The adversary may attempt to replace a component with a functionally similar one, modify a signal path, exchange a sensor or microcontroller, or introduce hardware that changes the physical behavior of the system while preserving its outward functionality. The adversary's goal is to make the device appear trustworthy to the verifier while altering, degrading, or manipulating the hardware basis on which the system operates.

We further assume that the adversary may observe, delay, replay, or modify network communication between attester and verifier. As in conventional RA, freshness values, signed evidence, and verification of TPM-protected state are used to detect replay or manipulation of reported evidence. The adversary may also attempt to tamper with the software responsible for collecting, encoding, or transmitting analog measurements. Such software components must therefore themselves be covered by conventional software and firmware measurements.

We do not assume that analog hardware measurements provide cryptographic identity by themselves. An adversary with sufficient resources may attempt to emulate analog behavior, reproduce measurement characteristics, or manipulate environmental conditions. The proposed approach is therefore designed to increase the attacker's effort and to provide additional evidence for detecting hardware-level deviations when combined with cryptographic roots of trust and software-centric attestation.

3.3 Security Objectives and Limitations

The proposed architecture aims to preserve the security properties expected from RA evidence while extending the evidence base with hardware-related observations. Analog measurement events must be protected against undetected modification after acquisition, linked to the relevant platform and measurement context, and made available to the verifier in a form that can be appraised together with conventional platform evidence. The architecture should also remain compatible with existing attestation workflows by representing analog measurements as CEL-compatible events and transporting them through a CHARRA-based protocol flow.

Several limitations remain. First, analog measurements cannot be expected to uniquely and reliably identify every individual component under all operating and environmental conditions. Highly similar or nominally identical components may exhibit overlapping measurement characteristics. Second, this paper does not address invasive hardware attacks against trusted reporting components such as the TPM, nor does it define a complete lifecycle process for generating, distributing, and updating hardware RVs. Third, hardware-integrity evidence alone is not sufficient for platform trust. It must be combined with secure boot, measured boot, software attestation, lifecycle management, and operational security controls.

In summary, the threat model motivates an attestation architecture that extends the evidence base beyond software and firmware state while preserving the trust and interoperability properties of established RA. The following section presents such an architecture and describes how analog hardware measurements can be represented, protected, transported, and appraised within CHARRA- and CEL-based workflows.

4 Hardware-Integrity-Aware Attestation Architecture

This section presents the proposed hardware-integrity-aware attestation architecture. The architecture extends conventional RA with analog hardware measurements while preserving compatibility with established attestation workflows. Its main purpose is to represent hardware-related measurements as structured evidence, bind this evidence to a trustworthy platform state, and make it available to a verifier together with conventional software and firmware evidence.

The design follows four goals. First, it should be compatible with existing RA concepts and should not require a new attestation protocol. Second, analog measurements should be represented in a structured format that captures measurement values, configuration parameters, and relevant environmental context. Third, the integrity and ordering of the resulting evidence should be protected by established roots of trust, such as a TPM. Fourth, verifier-side appraisal should remain modular, because analog hardware evidence complements software and firmware evidence but does not provide a standalone proof of platform trust.

4.1 Architecture Overview

Figure 1 illustrates the conceptual architecture and the main processing steps from analog measurement acquisition to verifier-side appraisal. The system consists of five logical components: the component under test, the measurement module, the attester, the verifier, and an optional relying party. The component under test is the hardware whose analog behavior is relevant for the trust decision, such as a microcontroller, sensor, or peripheral module. The measurement module stimulates this component and records an analog response. The attester encodes the resulting data as structured evidence, embeds it into a CEL-compatible event log, anchors it in TPM-protected platform state, and reports it to the verifier. The verifier validates the cryptographic evidence and appraises the analog measurements against RVs, reference models, or policies. A relying party can then use the resulting attestation result to decide whether the device should be accepted, isolated, or inspected further.

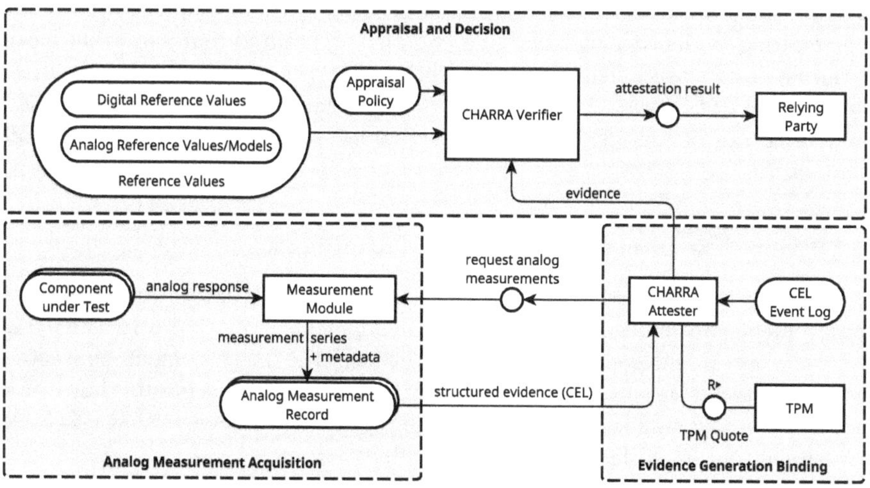

Fig. 1. Architecture of the proposed hardware-integrity-aware remote attestation approach. A measurement module stimulates the component under test and records its analog response together with contextual metadata. The attester encodes the result as structured evidence, embeds it into a CEL-compatible event log, and binds the event to TPM-protected platform state through a PCR extension. During attestation, a CHARRA-based workflow transports the TPM quote and event log to the verifier, which validates the cryptographic evidence and appraises the analog measurement together with conventional software and firmware evidence.

The architecture intentionally separates measurement acquisition, evidence representation, attestation transport, and verifier-side appraisal. This separation allows the same evidence model to be used with different measurement setups, while keeping the attestation workflow compatible with existing CHARRA-based implementations. It also allows appraisal logic to evolve independently from the measurement hardware and transport protocol.

4.2 Measurement Evidence Generation

Analog hardware evidence is generated by stimulating the component under test and recording its response as a measurement series. In the prototype described in this paper, the measured signal is the step response of a microcontroller pin, but the architectural principle is not limited to this signal type. Other analog properties can be integrated as long as they can be represented as structured measurement series and associated with sufficient context information.

Each measurement contains the sampled measurement data, configuration metadata, and environmental metadata. Configuration metadata includes information such as the measurement target, sampling configuration, measurement duration, and signal unit. Environmental metadata, such as temperature or humidity, is relevant because analog measurements are influenced by operating conditions and cannot be interpreted reliably without acquisition context. The resulting evidence is encoded in a compact structured representation based on the analog measurement format introduced in prior work [6] and serialized using CBOR. The format is versioned and extensible, so that additional measurement types or metadata fields can be added without changing the overall architecture.

4.3 Event-Log Integration and TPM Binding

To integrate analog hardware evidence into established attestation workflows, measurements are embedded into a CEL-compatible event-log structure. The CEL acts as an interoperability layer between the measurement subsystem and the attestation protocol. Instead of introducing a separate hardware-measurement log, analog measurements are represented as events that can coexist with conventional platform measurements.

After a measurement event has been generated, the attester computes a digest over the encoded event and extends it into a selected PCR. This links the event log to the TPM-protected platform state. As with conventional measured-boot logs, the verifier can later check whether the received log is consistent with the quoted PCR value. This does not make the analog measurement itself cryptographic; rather, it protects the integrity and ordering of reported measurement events after acquisition. Components that do not understand the analog payload can still process the surrounding CEL structure, while updated verifiers can parse and appraise the additional hardware evidence.

4.4 Attestation and Appraisal Workflow

The proposed workflow follows a conventional challenge-response pattern. The verifier sends an attestation challenge to the attester and requests platform evidence, including the relevant event log. The attester returns a TPM quote over selected PCRs together with the corresponding CEL-based event log. This event log contains both conventional platform measurements and analog hardware measurement events. The verifier checks the freshness of the response, verifies the quote, validates the consistency between the event log and the quoted PCRs, and then appraises the analog measurements.

For the analog evidence, appraisal consists of comparing the reported measurement series against RVs, reference models, or policy-defined thresholds. Depending on the deployment, the verifier may use simple distance metrics, feature extraction, or classification methods. The outcome is not necessarily a binary accept-or-reject decision. A strong mismatch may indicate component replacement, manipulation, measurement failure, or unexpected environmental conditions, while an inconclusive result may require repeated measurements or manual inspection. Thus, hardware-integrity-aware attestation provides an additional confidence signal for risk-based decision making rather than replacing existing trust anchors.

The workflow remains compatible with CHARRA, because CHARRA already supports the exchange of TPM-protected evidence and corresponding measurement logs [3]. The proposed architecture therefore extends the content of the evidence rather than the fundamental protocol structure. Although the implementation and evaluation focus on a microcontroller-based measurement setup and a medical IoMT demonstrator, the architecture is not tied to a specific device class, signal type, or deployment domain. It can be transferred to other safety-critical embedded settings, provided that suitable measurement procedures, RVs, and appraisal policies can be established.

4.5 Scope of the Architecture

The architecture is designed for safety-critical embedded systems in which hardware authenticity and integrity are relevant to operational trust. It is applicable to medical IoMT systems, industrial cyber-physical systems, and other embedded environments in which sensors, microcontrollers, or peripheral components may be exposed to manipulation or replacement. The implementation and evaluation in this paper focus on a microcontroller-based measurement setup and a medical IoMT demonstrator, which serve as concrete validation environments.

At the same time, the architecture is intentionally not tied to a specific device class, measurement signal, or deployment domain. Its core idea is the integration of analog hardware measurements into an existing attestation evidence pipeline. This makes the approach transferable to other safety-critical embedded settings, provided that suitable measurement procedures, reference values, and appraisal policies can be established.

5 Implementation and Demonstrator Integration

We implemented the proposed architecture as a modular prototype that connects analog hardware measurement, structured evidence serialization, CEL-compatible logging, and CHARRA-based attestation. The implementation consists of an embedded measurement setup, two reusable C libraries for evidence handling, and an integration layer that binds analog measurement events to TPM-protected platform state. In addition, the analog evidence layer was ported to a medical IoMT demonstrator to validate that the approach is not tied to a single measurement platform.

5.1 Prototype and Measurement Setup

The main prototype uses a Raspberry Pi as lead attester and coordination platform. It is connected to an external TPM, which is used to extend measurement-event digests into selected PCRs and to produce signed attestation evidence. Analog measurements are acquired by a separate microcontroller-based measurement module built around a NUCLEO-L432KC development board with an STM32L432KC microcontroller and integrated analog-to-digital Converter (ADC). The module stimulates a selected pin of the component under test and records the resulting step response through a separate analog input, following the measurement principle of prior work on analog hardware fingerprinting [6].

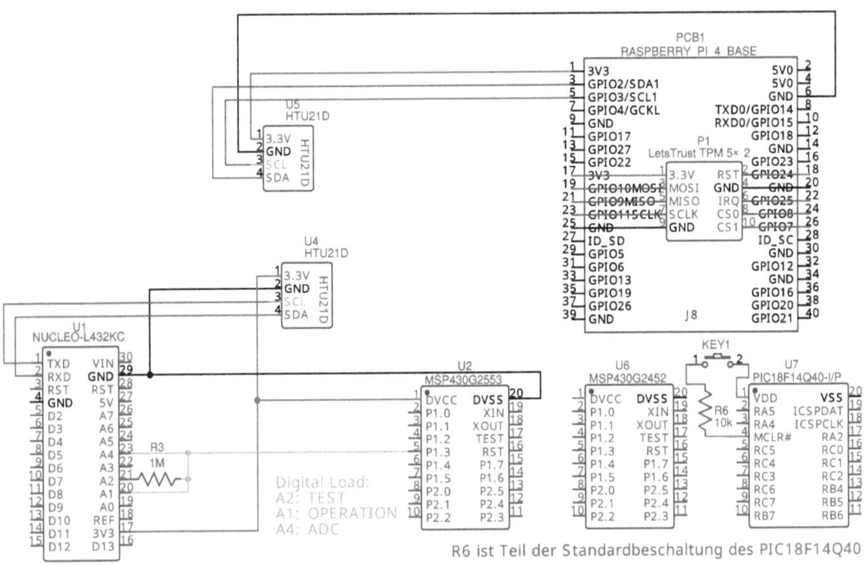

Fig. 2. Schematic of the analog measurement setup. A NUCLEO development board stimulates the component under test and records the resulting step response through its ADC. The Raspberry Pi coordinates measurement processing and anchors the resulting evidence through an external TPM, while environmental sensors provide temperature and humidity metadata for later appraisal.

Figure 2 shows the resulting measurement setup, in which the component under test is mounted in a socket so that different microcontrollers can be measured without changing the surrounding circuit. Each measurement contains the sampled response, measurement configuration, and environmental metadata such as temperature and humidity. This information is required because analog measurements are affected by noise, tolerances, and operating conditions and therefore cannot be interpreted reliably without context.

5.2 Evidence Handling and Attestation Integration

To make analog measurements reusable as attestation evidence, we implemented two C libraries. The first library, `anamsr`, serializes and deserializes analog measurement records, including measurement values, units, configuration parameters, timestamps, and environmental metadata. The second library, `libcel`, embeds these records into CEL-compatible event logs and provides parsing and generation functionality for CBOR-encoded event sequences. Both libraries use QCBOR [12] and follow a modular interface design without hidden global state.

After a measurement event has been encoded, the Raspberry Pi-based attester receives the serialized analog measurement record from the measurement module, stores it in a CEL-compatible event log, computes a digest over the encoded event, and extends this digest into a selected PCR. During attestation, a CHARRA-based workflow transports the TPM quote and the corresponding event log to the verifier. The verifier first performs the conventional cryptographic checks, including freshness validation, quote verification, and consistency checking between the event log and the quoted PCRs. It then extracts the analog measurement events for separate appraisal against RVs, thresholds, or classification models. The classifier is therefore not executed on the measurement module; the module is limited to acquisition and serialization, while the verifier remains the policy decision point.

5.3 Medical IoMT Demonstrator

To validate portability beyond the initial microcontroller-based setup, the analog evidence layer was also integrated into a medical IoMT demonstrator developed in the VE-ASCOT project. The demonstrator uses an field-programmable gate array (FPGA)-based Linux platform with attached analog measurement interfaces. In this setting, measurement acquisition is performed directly on the Linux-capable platform, while the resulting data is serialized as CBOR sequences using the same analog measurement data model.

The demonstrator integration shows that the proposed evidence representation is not tied to the original NUCLEO-based measurement board. Although full CEL and CHARRA integration is implemented in the Raspberry Pi prototype, the medical demonstrator confirms that the measurement and serialization components can be reused across different safety-critical embedded platforms. This supports the broader goal of integrating hardware-integrity evidence into attestation workflows for healthcare and industrial cyber-physical systems.

6 Evaluation

This section evaluates whether analog hardware measurements can provide useful complementary evidence for hardware-integrity-aware RA. The evaluation focuses on three aspects: measurement stability, distinguishability of hardware configurations, and the suitability of different appraisal methods for verifier-side classification.

6.1 Experimental Setup and Dataset

The evaluation uses the microcontroller-based prototype described in Sect. 5. For each device under test, we recorded 100 analog measurement events. Each event contains two consecutively captured measurement series, and each series consists of 20 sampled values representing the observed step response. Environmental metadata, including temperature and relative humidity, was recorded together with each event.

The dataset contains measurements from three microcontroller types and from an empty socket, which represents a missing or disconnected component. In addition, multiple devices from the same microcontroller family were measured to evaluate whether the approach can distinguish not only different hardware classes, but also similar or nominally identical components. One measured microcontroller exhibited a defective voltage pin; we retained this dataset as a realistic fault case instead of removing it as an outlier. Environmental conditions remained largely stable during data collection; therefore, no explicit compensation for temperature or humidity was applied.

The measurement process was stable across all tested configurations. The overall time from triggering a measurement to receiving and processing the resulting data on the attester was approximately 0.3 s. This indicates that analog measurements can be collected without introducing substantial delay into periodic or on-demand attestation workflows. The current prototype prioritizes reproducibility over low-level optimization, leaving room for future improvements in sampling resolution and acquisition overhead.

6.2 Classical Distance Metrics

We first evaluated whether classical distance and similarity metrics are sufficient for distinguishing analog measurement series. The analyzed metrics include cosine distance, root mean square distance, Euclidean and squared Euclidean distance, Manhattan distance, Chebyshev distance, Canberra distance, and Bray–Curtis distance. These metrics were applied to compare measurement series within and across device classes.

The results show that classical distance metrics are well suited to detecting coarse hardware differences. Measurements from the empty socket and from the defective microcontroller clearly deviate from the measurements of intact devices. Similarly, different microcontroller families can be distinguished visually and quantitatively. This confirms that analog hardware measurements can provide useful evidence for detecting missing, defective, or substantially different components.

However, the same metrics are not sufficient for reliable fine-grained classification. Measurements from closely related microcontroller models exhibit strong overlap, and measurements from nominally identical devices do not form clearly separable clusters. In these cases, no robust threshold could be identified that would reliably distinguish all relevant devices. This limitation is important for verifier-side appraisal: simple distance metrics can support anomaly detection, but they should not be treated as sufficient for unique device identification.

6.3 Kernel-Based Classification

To improve distinguishability, we evaluated a kernel-based feature extraction approach inspired by prior work on analog assembly authentication. Random convolution kernels are applied to the measurement series to extract characteristic features from the step response. Candidate kernels are scored using the Fisher score, which favors kernels that assign similar feature values to measurements of the same device while increasing separation between different devices. The extracted features are then classified using a nearest-neighbor approach.

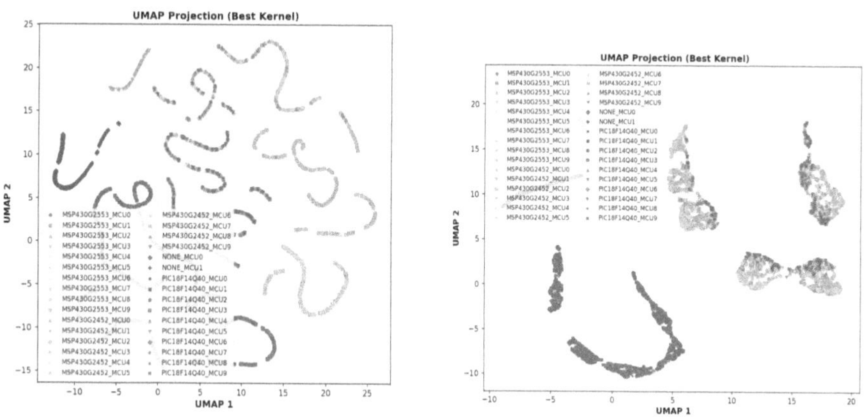

Fig. 3. Two-dimensional UMAP projections of feature vectors extracted from analog measurement series. The left plot uses the mean value as a single feature, while the right plot combines mean, maximum, and standard deviation. The multi-feature representation improves visual separation between hardware classes, while overlaps remain for highly similar devices.

Compared to classical distance metrics, kernel-based feature extraction provides substantially better separation of similar microcontroller models. In particular, combining multiple features, such as the mean, standard deviation, and maximum of the convolved measurement series, reduces previous misclassifications between closely related models. Figure 3 illustrates this effect by projecting the resulting feature vectors into two dimensions.

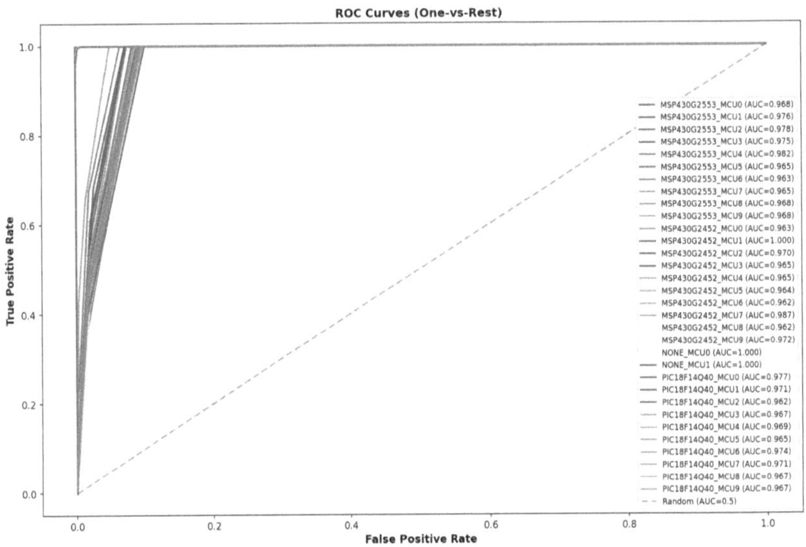

Fig. 4. ROC curves for kernel-based classification using the mean, maximum, and standard deviation of the convolved measurement series as features. AUC values close to 1 indicate strong separability, while lower values indicate overlapping feature distributions and remaining ambiguity.

Figure 4 shows the resulting ROC curves for the multi-feature classifier. The high AUC values for several classes indicate that the extracted features provide a suitable basis for verifier-side appraisal, especially for detecting clearly distinguishable or anomalous hardware configurations. At the same time, the evaluation also shows the limits of the current approach. Distinguishing individual devices from the same production series remains challenging because their feature distributions overlap. The best kernel and feature combinations improved classification, but did not provide reliable unique identification of nominally identical devices.

6.4 Attestation Implications

The evaluation confirms that analog hardware measurements can be integrated into an attestation workflow while preserving the main security properties expected from RA evidence. Each measurement event is serialized, included in a CEL-compatible event log, and cryptographically bound to the attested platform state by extending a digest into a TPM PCR. During verification, the event log can therefore be checked against the quoted PCR value, allowing manipulation of the reported measurement sequence to be detected.

The most important result is not that analog measurements uniquely identify every individual device. Rather, they add an independent evidence dimension to software-centric attestation. They can reveal missing components, defective components, and substantial differences between hardware configurations that would not necessarily be visible in conventional software or firmware measurements. For safety-critical embedded systems, such evidence can support more informed appraisal decisions, for example by triggering re-measurement, isolation, or manual inspection when hardware evidence deviates from expected reference values.

7 Discussion, Implications, and Threats to Validity

The evaluation shows that analog hardware measurements can enrich RA with evidence about the physical behavior of hardware components. The approach is most useful for detecting coarse deviations, such as missing components, defective hardware, or substantially different microcontroller families. Its main implication is therefore not unique device identification, but a broader appraisal basis for safety-critical embedded systems in which hardware manipulation, degradation, or replacement may not be visible in software-centric measurements.

Appraisal Implications. Analog evidence is probabilistic and context-dependent. A verifier should therefore not reject a device solely because one measurement deviates from its RVs. Depending on the deployment, deviations may indicate manipulation, aging, changed environmental conditions, measurement noise, or an unknown hardware variant. Practical policies should combine analog evidence with conventional software and firmware appraisal, device identity, maintenance history, and operational context. Strong deviations may trigger isolation or manual inspection, while weaker or inconclusive deviations may trigger re-measurement or recalibration.

Architectural Boundaries. The proposed architecture separates cryptographic verification from analog appraisal. The verifier first checks freshness, quote validity, and consistency between the CEL log and the quoted PCRs. Only afterwards does it interpret analog measurement events using RVs, thresholds, or classifiers. This keeps the measurement module limited to acquisition and serialization, while preserving the verifier as the policy decision point.

Threats to Validity. The evaluation was conducted under largely stable laboratory conditions. Temperature and humidity were recorded but not yet used for compensation, so long-term robustness under changing environmental conditions remains future work. The dataset covers multiple microcontroller configurations and a realistic fault case, but not the full diversity of embedded hardware used in medical, industrial, or other CI environments. Moreover, highly similar devices still show overlapping feature distributions, which requires explicit thresholds and policies for handling false positives and false negatives. Finally, the prototype prioritizes clarity over optimization; the observed latency is suitable for periodic or on-demand attestation, but not yet evaluated for highly time-critical control loops.

8 Related Work

This work builds on related work in RA, analog hardware fingerprinting, and hardware-integrity mechanisms for embedded systems. The IETF RATS architecture defines the main roles and artifacts of attestation, including attesters, verifiers, relying parties, evidence, RVs, appraisal policies, and attestation results [2]. CHARRA, standardized as RFC 9684, provides a YANG data model for challenge-response-based RA with TPMs [3]. The TCG CEL specification defines an extensible representation for event logs [20], while the TCG Trusted Attestation Protocol information model structures attestation-relevant information independently of a concrete transport protocol [17]. Our work reuses these concepts and extends their evidence base with analog hardware measurements.

Analog hardware fingerprinting has been explored as a way to detect physical manipulation and characterize electronic components. Jäger et al. extended attestation into the analog domain by measuring step responses of embedded circuits in a Device Identifier Composition Engine (DICE)-based setting [9]. Eckel et al. investigated practical hardware fingerprinting for RA, including environmental influences, long-term behavior, and structured measurement representation [6]. Related work on analog sensor characteristics, avionic bus fingerprinting, and analog assembly authentication similarly shows that physical signal properties can support authentication and integrity decisions [5,8,11,15]. In contrast to these works, our contribution is not a new fingerprinting primitive, but an architecture for representing, binding, transporting, and appraising analog hardware evidence within existing CHARRA- and CEL-based RA workflows.

Surveys on RA, system integrity, and embedded-system security emphasize attestation as a key mechanism for establishing trust in distributed and exposed systems [4,10,14]. However, most established approaches remain centered on software, firmware, or configuration state. Our approach adds a complementary hardware-integrity evidence layer while preserving the cryptographic foundations and protocol structure of conventional RA.

9 Conclusions and Future Work

This paper presented a hardware-integrity-aware RA architecture for safety-critical embedded systems. The architecture extends conventional software- and firmware-centric attestation with analog hardware measurements, represents these measurements as structured evidence, embeds them into CEL-compatible event logs, and transports them through a CHARRA-based attestation workflow. A prototype implementation and a medical IoMT demonstrator show that the approach can be integrated into practical embedded settings and is not tied to a single measurement platform.

The evaluation indicates that analog measurements can detect coarse hardware deviations and improve the evidence available to a verifier. Kernel-based feature extraction further improves the separation of similar hardware classes compared to simple distance metrics. However, reliably distinguishing nominally identical devices remains challenging. We therefore conclude that analog hardware measurements are best understood as complementary attestation evidence rather than as a replacement for cryptographic identities, TPM-based roots of trust, or software-centric measurements.

Future work will focus on long-term measurements under varying environmental conditions, improved appraisal methods for highly similar components, and lifecycle management for hardware RVs. Further validation in industrial cyber-physical systems and other CI environments is also required to assess operational robustness beyond the medical IoMT demonstrator. Overall, the results show that hardware integrity can be represented and conveyed as interoperable attestation evidence, providing a practical foundation for stronger trust decisions in safety-critical embedded systems.

Acknowledgments. This research work was funded by the National Research Center for Applied Cybersecurity ATHENE and the German Federal Ministry of Research, Technology, and Space (BMFTR) as part of the project TRUSTnet (ID 16KIS1787). This paper builds on results and findings from Anselm Angert's master's thesis on the practical application of remote attestation for hardware integrity [1].

Disclosure of Interests. The authors have no competing interests to declare that are relevant to the content of this article.

References

1. Angert, A.: On the Practical Application of Remote Attestation for Hardware Integrity. Master's thesis, UAS of Central Hesse (THM), Gießen (2026)
2. Birkholz, H., Smith, N., Voit, E., Pan, W., Wiseman, M.: Remote ATtestation ProcedureS (RATS) Architecture. Technical report 9334, Internet Engineering Task Force (2023). https://doi.org/10.17487/RFC9334, https://datatracker.ietf.org/doc/rfc9334/
3. Birkholz, H., et al.: A YANG Data Model for Challenge-Response-Based Remote Attestation (CHARRA) Procedures Using Trusted Platform Modules (TPMs). RFC 9684, Internet Engineering Task Force (2024). https://doi.org/10.17487/RFC9684, https://datatracker.ietf.org/doc/rfc9684/, proposed Standard
4. Dave, V., Wiseman, Y., Safford, D., et al.: Sedat: security enhanced device attestation with tpm 2.0. arXiv preprint arXiv:2101.06362 (2021). https://arxiv.org/abs/2101.06362
5. Dempster, A., Petitjean, F., Webb, G.I.: ROCKET: exceptionally fast and accurate time series classification using random convolutional kernels. Data Min. Knowl. Disc. **34**(5), 1454–1495 (2020). https://doi.org/10.1007/s10618-020-00701-z

6. Eckel, M., Fenzl, F., Jäger, L.: Towards practical hardware fingerprinting for remote attestation. In: Pitropakis, N., Katsikas, S., Furnell, S., Markantonakis, K. (eds.) SEC 2024. IFIPAICT, vol. 710, pp. 105–118. Springer, Cham (2024). https://doi.org/10.1007/978-3-031-65175-5_8
7. Fraunhofer SIT: CHARRA – challenge response remote attestation with TPM 2.0 (2023). https://github.com/Fraunhofer-SIT/charra
8. Gilboa-Markevich, N., Wool, A.: Hardware fingerprinting for the ARINC 429 avionic bus. In: Chen, L., Li, N., Liang, K., Schneider, S. (eds.) ESORICS 2020, Part II. LNCS, vol. 12309, pp. 42–62. Springer, Heidelberg (2020). https://doi.org/10.1007/978-3-030-59013-0_3, https://doi.org/10.48550/arXiv.2003.12456
9. Jäger, L., Lorych, D.: Remote attestation extended to the analog domain. In: Proceedings of the 16th International Conference on Availability, Reliability and Security (ARES 2021). ACM, Vienna, Austria (2021). https://doi.org/10.1145/3465481.3465762
10. Kuang, Y., Chen, X., Guo, W., Yang, K.: A survey of remote attestation in internet of things: attacks, properties, and challenges. Comput. Secur. **116**, 102675 (2022). https://doi.org/10.1016/j.cose.2021.102675, https://www.sciencedirect.com/science/article/pii/S0167404821003229
11. Lorenz, F., et al.: Fingerprinting analog IoT sensors for secret-free authentication. In: 2020 29th International Conference on Computer Communications and Networks (ICCCN), pp. 1–6 (2020). https://doi.org/10.1109/ICCCN49398.2020.9209643
12. Lundblade, L.: QCBOR: an implementation of nearly everything in RFC 8949 (2018). https://github.com/laurencelundblade/QCBOR
13. Reece, T., Limbrick, D.B., Wang, X., Kiddie, B.T., Robinson, W.H.: Stealth assessment of hardware trojans in a microcontroller. In: 2012 IEEE International Conference on Computer Design (ICCD), pp. 471–474 (2012). https://doi.org/10.1109/ICCD.2012.6378631, https://ieeexplore.ieee.org/document/6378631
14. Sfyrakis, I., Gross, T.: A survey on hardware approaches for remote attestation in network infrastructures. arXiv preprint arXiv:2005.12453 (2020). https://arxiv.org/abs/2005.12453
15. Spinnler, C., Reißland, T., Franchi, N.: AARC-FE: electrical assembly authentication with random convolution kernels and fuzzy extractors. In: Dalla Preda, M., Schrittwieser, S., Naessens, V., De Sutter, B. (eds.) ARES 2025. LNCS, vol. 15992, pp. 257–277. Springer, Cham (2025). https://doi.org/10.1007/978-3-032-00624-0_13
16. Swierczynski, P., Fyrbiak, M., Koppe, P., Moradi, A., Paar, C.: Interdiction in practice–hardware trojan against a high-security USB flash drive. J. Cryptogr. Eng. **7**(3), 199–211 (2017)
17. Trusted Computing Group (TCG): Trusted Attestation Protocol (TAP) Information Model, Version 1.0, Revision 0.36. Technical report, Trusted Computing Group (TCG) (2019). https://trustedcomputinggroup.org/wp-content/uploads/TNC_TAP_Information_Model_v1.00_r0.36-FINAL.pdf
18. Trusted Computing Group (TCG): TCG protection profile for pc client specific tpm, 2.0. Technical report, Trusted Computing Group (TCG) (2021). https://trustedcomputinggroup.org/resource/pc-client-protection-profile-for-tpm-2-0/, conforms to Common Criteria Version 3.1, Revision 5

19. Trusted Computing Group (TCG): TCG PC Client Platform Firmware Profile Specification, Level 00, Version 1.06, Revision 52, Family "2.0". Technical report, Trusted Computing Group (TCG) (2023). https://trustedcomputinggroup.org/wp-content/uploads/TCG-PC-Client-Platform-Firmware-Profile-Version-1.06-Revision-52_pub-3.pdf
20. Trusted Computing Group (TCG): Canonical Event Log Format. Technical report, Trusted Computing Group (TCG) (2024). https://trustedcomputinggroup.org/wp-content/uploads/TCG_IWG_CEL_v1_r0p41_pub.pdf

Evaluation of Trusted Computing Technologies for Cyber-Physical Systems

Dominik Lorych[1(✉)], Georgios Gkoktsis[1], Christoph Krauß[2], Michael Eckel[1], and Christian Plappert[1]

[1] Fraunhofer SIT | ATHENE, Rheinstr. 75, 64295 Darmstadt, Germany
{dominik.lorych,george.gkoktsis,michael.eckel,christian.plappert}@sit.fraunhofer.de

[2] Darmstadt University of Applied Sciences, Schoefferstr. 3, 64295 Darmstadt, Germany
christoph.krauss@h-da.de

Abstract. Cyber-physical systems in domains such as Industry 4.0, autonomous driving, and energy systems face increasing security requirements, including for small embedded controllers and sensors contributing in safety-critical processes. Advanced security mechanisms are often infeasible on these devices due to cost and resource constraints. The Device Identifier Composition Engine (DICE) provides measured boot for such systems, while the DICE Protection Environment (DPE) extends this with an isolated environment for cryptographic secrets. In this paper, we evaluate the security properties of DICE and DPE in the context of resource-constrained cyber-physical systems. We propose an empirical comparative framework that assesses these technologies across multiple criteria. Our methodology is designed to be suitable for many use cases and trust anchors. Our evaluation shows that DICE offers the best performance and lowest hardware cost but weaker protection against SL3/SL4 attackers, while local and remote DPE variants improve protection of long-term secrets at the cost of additional hardware or backend infrastructure.

Keywords: Cyber-Physical Systems · DICE · DPE · Trusted Computing

1 Introduction

Current trends of increased connectivity and automation in cyber-physical systems increase complexity and security requirements of these systems. The advent of Industry 4.0 in manufacturing, autonomous driving, or the digitization of Energy Systems have transformed the nature and operation of engineered systems. The gains in efficiency and new capabilities, which software-controlled cyber-physical systems introduced, come, however, at a cost: They present an attack surface for malicious actors. Even small components, such as sensors

Z. Afzal et al. (Eds.): ARES 2026 Workshops, LNCS 16900, pp. 370–388, 2027.
https://doi.org/10.1007/978-3-032-35576-8_20

and controllers, can be attractive targets whose compromise may cause physical damage, operational disruption, or injury. As these systems integrate into our lives, businesses, and societies, the need to defend them becomes pronounced. In sectors such as energy, regulations (Network Information Security Directive 2 (NIS-2) [26], Cyber Resilience Act (CRA) [7]) and technical recommendations (European Network of Cyber Security (EACS) [11,12]) emphasize the need for more rigor in cybersecurity and trust.

To address these challenges, Hardware Trust Anchors (HTAs) are increasingly used to protect devices, as they provide isolated environments for security-critical data and operations. However, especially for resource-constrained operational environments, it is not immediately, or intuitively clear which trust anchor is the best solution. This disincentivises the broader adoption of HTAs, especially in industrial and OT environments. Advantages and drawbacks of each HTA are influenced by device capability and operational environment. Choosing one option over the other requires a decision-making process, where economic, performance, and security implications are considered.

Previous work has evaluated HTAs for automotive environments [28]. In this work, we provide an evaluation framework for resource-constrained Cyber- Physical Systems (CPS). We have derived evaluation criteria that we use to evaluate each candidate regarding these economic, performance, and security factors. Regarding security, we differentiate both in terms of attacker capabilities and protection goals. We focus our work on options suitable for resource-constrained devices, but our methodology can also be applied to other HTAs. We evaluate the following variants:

Device Identifier Composition Engine (DICE) As it would be used on off-the-shelf microcontrollers.

Local DICE Protection Environment (DPE) A DPE hosted inside a local isolated environment. We assume ARM TrustZone-M [4] to be used here, which is the most prevalent Trusted Execution Environment (TEE) for resource-constrained devices.

Remote DPE A DPE that is hosted in a remote trusted device, connected to the host via a network interface.

We consider only HTAs with concrete specifications, thus treating TEEs as an implementation platform for HTA rather than as freely programmable, standalone HTA. We have designed evaluation criteria to be applicable to a broad range of HTAs, so this could also be applied to e.g. Trusted Platform Modules (TPMs).

The main contributions of this paper are as follows:

- An evaluation mechanism for HTAs for resource-constrained CPS, based on economic, performance, and security criteria and a matrix of attacker types and goals
- A comparative evaluation of DICE, local DPE, and remote DPE using this framework.

The remainder of this paper is organized as follows: We present background in Sect. 2, define our evaluation methodology in Sect. 3 and our evaluation criteria in Sect. 4. Section 5 evaluates each target of evaluation using our methodology using the defined criteria. We present Related Work in Sect. 6 and conclude in Sect. 7.

2 Background

In this section, we present necessary background on the technologies our work is based on. A comparison of DICE and DPE is shown in Fig. 1.

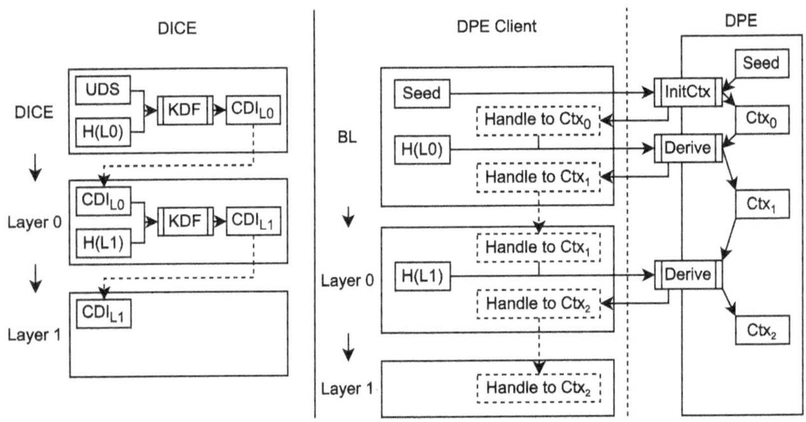

Fig. 1. Comparison of DICE and DPE.

2.1 Device Identifier Composition Engine (DICE)

The DICE architecture [36] generates a chain of cryptographic keys that jointly represent device identity and firmware integrity. Any change to the device or its firmware results in different keys. These keys can be used for Remote Attestation and Sealing, i.e., authenticated encryption of data that is only accessible in a specific system state.

DICE is the root of trust here, seeding the key chain by deriving the first Compound Device Identifier (CDI). The CDI is derived from a key exclusively known to DICE, the Unique Device Secret (UDS), and a measurement of the next firmware layer, typically using Hash-based Message Authentication Code (HMAC). Each following firmware extends the CDI with further firmware measurements, until the last CDI represents all measured firmware layers, as shown in Fig. 1. DICE is not included in these measurements and must therefore be protected by hardware mechanisms.

However, as these CDIs are symmetric, they change after a firmware update and cannot be verified externally. Thus, an intermediate layer can derive asymmetric keys and certificates, enabling verification of updated application firmware [35,40].

The hardware requirements of DICE are minimal. The DICE code must be immutable and always executed first, and DICE must have exclusive access to the UDS [39]. DICE cannot isolate keys from subsequently executed firmware, so keys that are no longer needed (especially during the boot process) must be deleted before control is handed over to the next layer.

2.2 DICE Protection Environment (DPE)

The DPE [38] extends DICE by moving CDI handling into an isolated execution environment, as shown in Fig. 1. This reduces key exposure and offers more flexible usage models. A DPE may run in a local isolated environment (e.g., a secure coprocessor, a Trusted Execution Environment (TEE), or an OS kernel) or in a remote trusted device accessed over an authenticated channel. A DPE is not required to have persistent storage, a True Random Number Generator (TRNG) or a real-time clock.

The DPE manages *contexts*, each containing a CDI and additional purpose-specific keys derived from it. Each context represents a particular system state along the boot chain. Access Control is implemented via *context handles*, which need to be presented to the DPE for access authorization. Except for unsealing data, policies to restrict key access are not included. Apart from context initialization and derivation, the DPE offers functions for key and certificate management (including signing) and sealing/unsealing.

If the DPE is remote, the client must establish a secure channel during early boot. Keys of the DPE can be exported to the client, but this must be indicated in corresponding certificates. For channel establishment, specification recommends using a variant of the Noise protocol [9,34], implementing authenticated key exchange and per-message key rotation to ensure forward and backward secrecy and privacy.

2.3 IEC 62443

IEC 62443 is an international series of standards regarding Industrial Automation and Control Systems (IACS), which can be considered to be a subset of CPS. In IACS environments, safety and 24/7 availability are critical. These requirements are commonly also applicable to general CPS. For this reason, IEC 62443 is applicable to an ever-expanding range of domains and processes like manufacturing, energy systems and transport.

IEC 62443 defines four security levels (SL), on which we base our attacker model. Security requirements are also part of the specification, but these mostly are not applicable to HTA. Instead, we evaluate security by evaluating whether different types of attackers can reach defined attacker goals.

2.4 Academic Work

This section introduces academic works which need to be considered when evaluating the state of the art of evaluated HTAs. Related work to the evaluation effort is presented in Sect. 6.

Hristozov et al. have demonstrated a Time-of-check Time-of-use (TOCTOU) attack on DICE attestation by exploiting a runtime vulnerability [16]. As DICE cannot isolate keys from application code due to minimal hardware requirements, any secret accessible to the application is also available to a runtime attacker, enabling extraction of attestation keys and device impersonation.

Lorych et al. [22] presented techniques for optimizing boot time generation of asymmetric keys, making DICE feasible for environments with limited boot time budget by accelerating the boot. Jäger and Lorych [18], as well as Eckel et al. [10], extended attestation into the analog domain and over long timescales, enabling detection of circuit modifications and integrating these mechanisms with DICE and TPM-based attestation.

As the DPE is quite new, there is currently no scientific work on the DPE. Ongoing industrial efforts aim to integrate DPE into Trusted Firmware-M for Cortex-M [6] and the Open Profile for DICE [14], as well as open Root of Trust projects such as OpenTitan [25] and Caliptra [8]. Current implementations mainly support key derivation for identification and attestation, with sealing and other advanced features only partially covered.

3 Methodology

This section introduces the methodology used to evaluate each HTA using evaluation criteria.

3.1 Evaluated HTA Variants

We make the following assumptions about each HTA in the evaluation:

DICE: We assume asymmetric keys and certificates are generated during the boot for Remote Attestation. Key caching is used for these keys, as demonstrated by Lorych et al. [22].

Local DPE: We assume an implementation in ARM TrustZone for Cortex-M, which is the most prevalent TEE in Microcontroller Units (MCUs).

Remote DPE: We assume that the Remote DPE is implemented in a backend or a local device offering higher security than the typical MCU. We assume that the remote DPE is initialized in a later boot component instead of the root of trust, as this ensures that the root of trust does not need to include a network stack. DICE may be used as the root of trust.

We assume that all systems implement secure boot in addition to the HTA.

3.2 Evaluation Mechanism

We score each HTA variant using evaluation criteria, derived from typical CPS use cases. The criteria fall into three categories: Economics, performance, and security.

We grade each criterion on a four-step scale: ++ (very good), + (good), - (limited), -- (poor). Where required, we define requirements for each step individually per evaluation criterion.

Finally, we use the evaluation results to evaluate the suitability of each HTA for each of our use cases.

3.3 Attacker Types and Attacker Goals

We are evaluating each HTA in its ability to protect the system against different levels of attackers, derived from the security levels of IEC 62443 (refer to Sect. 2.3). We define three attacker levels:

SL2 Attacker: This attacker operates on the SL2 level, meaning that they intentionally violate security using simple means with low resources, generic skills and motivation. An example here is a modification of non-volatile memory of the device, causing attacker-controlled firmware to boot on the device. This can be achieved by exploiting an insecure update mechanism or using exposed debug features.

SL3 Attacker: This attacker operates on the SL3 level, such that they intentionally violate security using sophisticated means with moderate resources, CPS-specific skills and motivation. For embedded systems, the most prevalent attacks on this level abuse memory corruption vulnerabilities to remotely hijack the protected system [16]. These attacks compromise volatile runtime memory, making detection harder. An example for these are Return-Oriented Programming (ROP). Medium complexity physical attacks are also included here, like attacks that (de)solder flash memory to modify memory contents.

SL4 Attacker: Attackers on this level use sophisticated means with extensive resources, CPS-specific skills and high motivation. This attacker type includes side-channel attacks and advanced physical attacks. Examples include voltage glitching, where a chip is operated outside its intended voltage range, and removal of shielding to extract secrets from internal bus systems and subcomponents of the HTA. MCUs are, in general, susceptible to physical side-channel attacks, among others, due to their low physical noise [13]. MCUs can also be vulnerable to remote side-channel attacks [29].

We are not considering attacks that are neither impacted by the HTA nor impact the HTA. For each of those attacker types, we are evaluating whether the attacker can achieve one or multiple of four attacker goals. These goals are general common goals for attackers of IACS and CPS systems. Not all attacker goals require the attacker to compromise the HTA, but HTAs may provide resources to detect or stop attacks on the system which the attacker uses to achieve those goals. We assume that each protected system possesses cryptographic secrets and may also possess general secrets (non-cryptographic data).

Arbitrary Code Execution: This attack goal enables the attacker to execute arbitrary code on the system, interrupting the normal system function. This does not provide the attacker with access to secrets. Usually, this will not require a compromise of the HTA, but an HTA might provide resources to detect or stop such an attack.

Secret Utilization: This enables the attacker to utilize HTA-secured secrets to impersonate and control the device temporarily. This can be achieved through retrieval of access control secrets. As secrets are only usable temporarily while the HTA host device is compromised, secrets do not need to be replaced after recovery.

Secret Deletion: The attacker may delete secrets of the system. If cryptographic secrets of the system have been deleted, new keys need to be rolled out to the system and potentially also peers of the system. Such a process might be costly or might involve manual maintenance. Deletion of non-cryptographic secrets may erase those secrets irrevocably if backup sources are not available. Deletion of secrets without HTA compromise can be possible if secrets of the system are offloaded from the HTA (usually in encrypted form).

Secret Extraction: If the attacker manages to extract secrets, they have permanent access to these secrets, even after the HTA host device has been recovered. Thus, recovery needs to include replacement of all extracted keys. Note that secret extraction implies secret deletion as the secrets are no longer secret then.

To summarize, we are evaluating whether each of three attacker types can achieve each attacker goal. The severity of an attacker achieving a goal is dependent on the use case in which the HTA will be used. Thus, for a final assessment, the evaluation results need to be compared with use case requirements to find the most suitable HTA.

4 Evaluation Criteria Definition

To derive evaluation criteria, we considered various use cases for HTA in resource-constrained applications. These include:

- A battery-powered IoT sensor using a low-power wide-area network like LoRaWAN [20], as an example of a low-criticality device with limited hardware, energy and network resources. Due to widespread distribution and low criticality, physical attacks on individual devices are generally not in scope.
- An automotive Electronic Control Unit (ECU) and sensors embedded in legacy subnetworks, with requirements for quick boot times [22,32], updateability and low operating costs due to long vehicle lifetimes [41] and high cost pressure.
- A central IoT gateway and distributed sensors, with sensors offering only minimal hardware while the gateway offers medium hardware security, for example TrustZone-M-based. This use case requires establishing device identity and integrity, ensuring secure onboarding and continuous integrity.

From these use cases, common and individual requirements can be derived. Generally, different levels of hardware are available, from minimal hardware with no dedicated HTA to TEEs. Depending on cost pressure and number of distributed devices, implementation costs may be important. Operating costs additionally depend on device lifetimes and the business model. Updates may be important.

General performance during operation and/or boot times may be critical. Low-power networks may require minimal network overhead.

Depending on the criticality of the device, operating environment and protection goals, different security levels may be required. For example, devices used in a factory setting usually do not require physical security as the environment is physically secured through security personnel and similar.

From these requirements, we derived evaluation criteria in three categories; economics, performance and security. Each criterion is rated using one of four scores (++, +, -, --).

4.1 Economics

EC1.1: Hardware Cost. The cost of integrating the technology into an existing or upcoming architecture, including required knowledge, also regarding hardware requirements like energy usage and interfaces of the host devices if required.

Ratings are: **++:** HTAs with minimal hardware requirements that usually can be fulfilled by most resource-constrained devices, for example used for low-powered sensor nodes with limited processing capabilities and memory availability. **+:** HTA with increased hardware requirements that still can be met by some resource-constrained devices, for example in form of a TEE for embedded devices. **-:** HTAs requiring separate hardware to the target device, for example in form of a dedicated coprocessor, but in principle also compatible with resource-constrained devices. **--:** HTAs incompatible with resource-constrained devices.

EC1.2: Implementation Costs. The development cost to develop software that implements or integrates a technology into a system and applications. This includes all software required to be implemented. Existing software ecosystems are beneficial for this criterion. The ease of integrating the HTA is also considered, which includes the flexibility of usage and the level of documentation.

Ratings are: **++:** HTA which are easy to implement, with good existing software ecosystems and good documentation to support an implementation. **+:** If one of the above factors is not fulfilled. **-:** If two factors are not given. **--:** If none of these factors is given.

EC1.3: Operating Costs. Operating costs include all the costs during HTA operation. For example, this can include Remote Attestation services that need to be hosted in a trusted environment. For the remote DPE, this includes the operating costs of hosting a DPE in a secure environment.

Ratings: **++:** HTAs which require no services to be hosted externally. **+:** HTAs requiring only simple services to be hosted externally. These services should be simple enough to be executed on a resource-constrained device, for example with a resource-constrained MCU acting as the verifier of the target platform. **-:** If more complex external hosting is needed, suitable for high-powered MCUs and small SoCs, like used on a Raspberry Pi. **--:** If services are required to be hosted on a high-powered computer or server environment due to resource-intensity.

EC1.4: Updatability. This criterion scores if the HTA can be updated to implement new functionality, for example to implement post-quantum cryptography, but also whether the HTA makes updating the host system more complicated.

Ratings are: **++:** HTA that do not limit updatability of the host device, but also can be updated themselves to some extent. Especially the option to implement post-quantum cryptography is important here, but this could also be used to implement new functionality. A deduction by one rank is given if:

- Boot components (except the Root of Trust) cannot be updated easily securely over-the-air, instead usually requiring a secure environment or physical access to the device.
- Update processes are, in general, more complex, for example requiring a migration of sealed/encrypted data.

-: If both factors are given. **--:** If updates to core functionality are not possible.

4.2 Performance

EC2.1: Runtime Speed. For this criterion, the runtime speed of calculations of the HTA during normal operations is the primary factor, in relation to the execution speed of the main Central Processing Unit (CPU).

Ratings are: **++:** If the HTA offers fast runtimes as computations are executed on the CPU or using a cryptographic accelerator, with no limitations on available hardware, compared to a software-only solution. **+:** If some smaller overheads need to be expected when performing computations, for example for frequent context switching in case of a TEE. **-:** If there is a significant overhead to computations, usually because computations are done in a slower external environment.

EC2.2: Boot Overhead. The runtime overhead required for integrating this technology. We assume that either Measured or Secure Boot are required on the system, as hashing operations performed for them already slow down the system. But they are the foundation for most Trusted Computing operations, and hence these are the baseline for our grading. Any additional operations slowing down the boot cause deductions.

Ratings are: **++:** HTA which incur no significant additional overheads compared to the baseline. **+:** HTA which incur significant overhead only in certain situations, usually when updating the system. **-:** HTA that cause significant overhead for every boot. **--:** HTA which cause significant and unreliable overhead, i.e.; which are dependent on some external resource which may be blocked or unreachable.

EC2.3: Network Overhead. This criterion evaluates the amount of network traffic caused by the HTAs. This is supposed to evaluate the usability of HTAs for constrained networks with limited bandwidth or power. The impact of network traffic on performance is not evaluated here, this is included in the two previous criteria.

Ratings are: **++:** Solutions with no or minimal network overhead, based on only symmetric cryptography, which causes significantly smaller overheads than asymmetric cryptography. **+:** If bigger overheads are only caused in certain situations, usually after an update. **-:** If remote attestation is used which causes bigger network overheads, for example regular asymmetric attestation. **--:** If the overhead is significant due to big payload sizes during attestation. The rating additionally gets reduced by one step if communication between the HTA and the host system uses the network interface.

Firmware updates are not accounted for in this criterion as they are usually irregular and less time-critical, commonly not being executed in active operation.

4.3 Security

We evaluate the security of the technologies against three types of attackers and four types of attacker goals, which we have described in the attacker model. The requirements for each rating are the following:

Arbitrary Code Execution. ++: If the attacker cannot execute arbitrary code on the system. **-:** If remote code execution is possible, but the attack can be detected afterward through Remote Attestation. **--:** If the attack can neither be detected nor stopped by the HTA.

Secret Utilization. ++: If the attacker cannot use any secrets protected by the HTA. **+:** If enhanced authorization mechanisms exist that can protect some more critical keys, such that the attacker can only utilize some keys. **-:** If the attacker can use any secrets available to the application. **--:** If the attacker can also use HTA-internal critical keys usually not usable by the application, e.g.; UDS and DeviceID for DICE.

Secret Deletion. ++: If the attacker cannot delete any secrets of the system. **+:** If the attacker can only delete general encrypted data, while not being able to delete any cryptographic secrets. **-:** If the storage for cryptographic keys is limited, such that only a limited number of critical keys can be secured by the HTA, while further keys and general data are offloaded from the HTA in encrypted format (which can be deleted by the attacker). **--:** If all secrets can be deleted by the attacker. Some HTA may allow the attacker to extract secrets but not delete secrets. In this case, we default to the secret extraction rating as the secret can no longer be considered a secret.

Secret Extraction. ++: If secret extraction is not possible. Against an SL4 attacker, this can be achieved using high-strength physical protections and minimal hardened firmware, supported by certification and formal proofs. **+:** If medium-strength protections against the attacker exist. **-:** If no or inadequate protections against the attacker exist, which enables the attacker to extract only secrets that are accessible to the application. **--:** If the attacker can additionally extract HTA-internal secrets that are usually not accessible to the application.

5 Evaluation

Here, we present the evaluation of each HTA variant with concluding summary.

EC1: Economics

EC1.1: Hardware Cost. As DICE is designed for off-the-shelf resource-constrained devices, it has small hardware requirements. Required are hardware protections for DICE firmware and a mechanism to enable exclusive access to the UDS [39]. Rating: ++.

The local DPE has moderate requirements [38] that increasingly often get fulfilled by microcontrollers, usually using ARM TrustZone for Cortex-M, which is the de-facto standard TEE for microcontrollers [17,27,33]. Currently, TrustZone is optionally available on half of all Cortex-M models [5]. However, legacy devices and low-end devices usually do not have access to a TEE, so they can't use this variant. Rating: +.

The remote DPE basically has the same requirements as DICE for the host device, with only the addition of a network interface to connect to the remote DPE [38]. The remote DPE also needs to be hosted and operated, but we score this under Operating Cost. Rating: ++, same as DICE.

EC1.2: Implementation Cost. The implementation of DICE itself is relatively simple, but the integration into existing firmware structures and update systems can cause some additional complexity. One open-source implementation "Open Profile for DICE" by Google exists in production-quality [14], while the remaining ecosystem is fairly small. Rating: +.

As the DPE specification is still quite new, a software ecosystem does not yet exist. Currently, efforts to integrate it into the "Open Profile for DICE" and "Trusted Firmware-M" are ongoing [6,15]. In general, implementing the DPE should be more complex than DICE, but it is also easier to integrate into applications due to a standardized interface and running in a separate environment. Rating: -.

A remote DPE adds some complexity when compared to a local DPE as encryption via the network interface needs to be considered. On the other hand, one instance of a DPE service serving multiple clients will be easier to implement than local DPEs on all devices. Rating: -.

EC1.3: Operating Costs. Both DICE and local DPE require a basic verifier to be hosted for remote attestation services [35,37]. These can be used to check which firmware is currently running on the device and are rather simple to implement and operate. These are simple enough that any relying party can implement such a verification service. Rating: +.

The remote DPE can use the same verification services for remote attestation as the DPE and DICE, but it also requires the DPE itself to be hosted in a remote environment. This needs to be protected sufficiently, as such a service can be a promising attack target, which increases costs. But, also, a single service can serve multiple clients to improve efficiency and reduce costs. Rating: -.

EC1.4: Updatability

In general, the DPE can be easily updated if the environment used to host the DPE offers update capabilities, and updates to the application are also not limited by it. However, some complications can incur for the remote DPE as it requires a network interface in early boot components. The local DPE scores a ++, while the remote DPE scores +. DICE scores a - due to complications updating boot firmware over-the-air and needing to migrate sealed/encrypted data.

EC2: Performance

EC2.1: Runtime Speed. DICE incurs no overheads from context switches or communication with the trust anchor. Cryptographic operations can be executed on the main CPU and on hardware accelerators without limitations [21]. Rating: ++.

A local DPE incurs some overheads from context switching between the DPE client and DPE service. Otherwise, cryptographic operations are usually fast because they are executed on the main CPU in the case of TrustZone-M or some other TEE. Rating: +.

A remote DPE can be implemented on a more powerful device to speed up operations, but communication and encryption over the network cause additional overheads. Also, the DPE service can be blocked if multiple clients send requests at the same time. On the other hand, offloading cryptographic operations to an external device frees up resources locally. Rating: -.

EC2.2: Boot Overhead. To support Measured or Secure Boot on any device, all firmware binaries or files need to be hashed before being loaded. This incurs an overhead, which is the baseline required for every HTA. Deductions are taken for additional operations that slow down the boot.

Asymmetric key generation for DICE can incur some significant overheads during the boot [21]. However, those can be reduced significantly by caching asymmetric keys [22], except for the first boot after an update. Rating: +.

The operations required for the local DPE are equivalent to those required for DICE. Rating: +.

A remote DPE causes significant additional overheads as a network connection needs to be established during the boot, including a key exchange mechanism based on ephemeral keys to get a shared session key. This mechanism also may fail if the service is unavailable or busy. Rating: --.

EC2.3: Network Overhead. DICE and a local DPE both can use remote attestation based on symmetric or asymmetric cryptography [35,37], but the former causes limitations to updatability of the attested application. Hybrid attestation can be used here [23], requiring asymmetric attestation only after an update to the attested application. Rating for both: +.

The remote DPE supports the same remote attestation procedures as DICE and DPE but additionally requires regular communication with the host of the DPE service. Every usage of a key secured in the DPE requires a message and response, secured by a symmetric session key. Keys can be exported to the host device, but this should not be done for critical keys like those used for remote attestation. Rating: -.

EC3: Security

EC3.1: SL2 Attacker. The most prevalent attacks on resource-constrained systems on SL2 are attacks that modify non-volatile memory, causing attacker-controlled firmware to boot on the device. Secure Boot is the best defense against these attacks. All HTAs considered in this paper do not include Secure Boot out of the box, but do include Measured Boot. However, Secure Boot can be implemented for any of them, as it has no requirements on top of those of an HTA. Rating for all of them: ++. Attacks on SL2 generally cannot extract, utilize or delete secrets of HTAs evaluated in this work, so they also receive a ++ for the other criteria.

EC3.2: SL3 Attacker. An SL3 attacker is capable of runtime attacks, where arbitrary code execution on the host system is inherent as their target is the execution of malicious code on the host. They cannot be detected by Measured Boot or stopped by Secure Boot as the compromise happens during the runtime of the device. Rating for all of them: --.

Usually, access control to secrets is implemented by some kind of secret that authorizes the authorized party. These secrets can be extracted by run-time attackers as they need to be available to the host system, which also makes it available to the attacker. However, this only enables the attacker to use application keys, with even more critical boot keys (in case of DICE the UDS and DeviceID) being protected. Also, in some cases remote attestation keys can be erased from the system before such an attacker would get access [16]. Rating for all of them: -.

Arbitrary Code Execution on the host enables the attacker to delete secrets that are not secured internally in the HTA. With DICE, deleted keys can be re-generated with the next boot, but the attacker can extract any key which the application can access, resulting in a rating of -. For both the local and remote DPE, the attacker can delete encrypted data available to the host system, while keys saved in the DPE are protected. An attacker might make keys inaccessible if they can utilize those secrets, but those can be re-generated during a reboot. Rating for all of them: +.

As DICE lacks isolation from the host system, any key accessible to the application also can be extracted [16]. Secret extraction rating: -.

The DPE protects secrets from extraction as they can never leave the HTA, except for specific circumstances defined during key generation. Compromising the DPE itself should not be possible for an SL3 attacker, as the DPE is hosted in a more secure environment than the host system. For example, while ARM TrustZone is vulnerable to advanced physical attacks [2,24,30], simple physical attacks and remote attacks should not be able to compromise ARM TrustZone. Rating for both: ++.

EC3.3: SL4 Attacker. As DICE is usually implemented on devices with constrained resources, which are typically vulnerable to advanced physical attacks [13], DICE also cannot defend against those attacks. Boot keys like the UDS and DeviceID are potentially also vulnerable to advanced physical attacks. Deleted keys may be re-generated after a reboot, but will no longer be secret. Rating for all attacker goals: --.

Regarding a local DPE based on ARM TrustZone-M, the SL4 attacker can fully compromise the non-secure and secure world of ARM TrustZone using advanced physical attacks, as physical attacks are out of scope of TrustZone-M [2]. Consequently, research has found multiple physical attacks on TrustZone [24,30]. For increased physical attack protection, ARM offers extensions like CryptoIsland, which is certified by Common Criteria to protect against various advanced attacks [3]. Rating for all attacker goals: --. If a chip with protections against physical attacks is used (like ARM CryptoIsland-enabled MCUs), a rating of + is possible for secret deletion and extraction.

The same holds true for the remote DPE regarding arbitrary code execution and secret utilization, as the remote DPE has no influence or control over the local device. For extraction or deletion of secrets, we assume that the remote DPE is implemented in a datacenter to which the attacker does not have physical access, or a local device with strong physical security. In this case, we rate the remote DPE at + for both, due to being remote and only offering a minimal defined interface, while certification is missing. If the remote DPE is implemented on a lower-class device, this rating needs to be downgraded (Tables 1 and 2).

Table 1. HTA Economics and Performance Ratings

Evaluation Criterion	DICE	Local DPE	Remote DPE
Hardware Cost	++	+	++
Implementation Cost	+	-	-
Operating Cost	+	+	-
Updatability	-	++	+
Runtime Speed	++	+	-
Boot Overhead	+	+	--
Network Overhead	+	+	-

Possible scores: ++, +, -, --.

Table 2. HTA Security Ratings

DICE					Local DPE					Remote DPE				
	ACE	SU	SD	SE		ACE	SU	SD	SE		ACE	SU	SD	SE
SL2 A.	++	++	++	++	SL2 A.	++	++	++	++	SL2 A.	++	++	++	++
SL3 A.	--	-	-	-	SL3 A.	--	-	+	++	SL3 A.	--	-	+	++
SL4 A.	--	--	--	--	SL4 A.	--	--	--	--	SL4 A.	--	--	+	+

Possible scores: ++, +, -, --. ACE: Arbitrary Code Execution; SU: Secret Utilization; SD: Secret Deletion; SE: Secret Extraction.

5.1 Summary

DICE performs well in terms of economics and performance (except for updatability), but is insecure against SL3 and SL4 attackers.

Local DPE performs slightly worse than DICE in terms of economics and performance (except for updatability) as it requires an isolated execution environment, for example based on ARM TrustZone-M. It offers better security than DICE against SL3 attackers.

Remote DPE offers the best protection of secrets, but causes the highest boot and runtime overheads. It requires a backend or some other trusted environment to host the DPE.

5.2 Use Case Application

Battery-powered IoT sensor. For such a device, hardware and operating costs are to be minimized to achieve minimal cost per device, assuming high numbers of pieces. Network overhead should also be small due to using a low-power long-range network. DICE performs best here.

Automotive ECUs and sensors. Due to the requirement for quick boot times, updatability and low operating costs, the local DPE scores best here. Offloading some secrets to a more powerful in-vehicle device using the remote DPE could also be used if boot overhead is not critical.

Central IoT gateway. As the local DPE offers a good tradeoff of security and cost, it can be used for the gateway. It can also be used to implement a remote DPE for associated sensors.

6 Related Work

Existing work on trusted computing and isolated execution falls into two main categories: (i) systematization and meta-analysis of academic proposals, and (ii) evaluation of industrial standards and platforms. Table 3 provides an overview here, comparing on the types of candidates and application domain, and whether

Table 3. Comparison with Related Work

Work	Topic	Candidate	Domain	System-mization	Criteria Definition	Meta-Analysis	Eval-uation	Scoring
[1]	CF	Academic	×	✓	(✓)	✓	×	×
[42]	TEE	Industry	×	✓	×	(✓)	×	×
[31]	TEE	Both	×	✓	(✓)	(✓)	(✓)	×
[19]	SCP	Academic	×	✓	✓	✓	×	×
[28]	HTA	Industry	Automation	(✓)	✓	×	✓	✓
Our	HTA	Industry	CPS	(✓)	✓	×	✓	✓

CF: Control-Flow Integrity / Attestation; SCP: TEE-based Secure Computation Protocols.

systematization, criteria definition, meta-analysis, evaluation and scoring are performed.

Ammar et al. [1] survey and systematize control-flow integrity and control-flow attestation techniques, relating them to broader runtime protection mechanisms such as memory safety, compartmentalization, and remote attestation. Zhang and Zhang [42] and Schneider et al. [31] analyze hardware-assisted TEEs, classifying their architectural building blocks, usage models, and known attacks, but do not provide a comparative scoring of specific HTAs for constrained CPS. Li et al. [19] review TEE-based secure computation protocols, identify side-channel and state-leakage issues, and highlight that mobile-friendly and multi-party protocols remain underexplored.

Closer to our setting, Plappert et al. [28] evaluate automotive HTAs, comparing legacy automotive modules with modern candidates such as DICE, TPMs, and TrustZone using criteria derived from automotive requirements. Their analysis focuses on the automotive domain.

Our work complements these studies by defining a compact set of economic, performance, and security criteria tailored to resource-constrained CPS, and by applying a transparent scoring procedure to DICE and DPE variants.

7 Conclusion

We presented a framework for evaluating HTAs in cyber-physical applications, focusing on resource-constrained devices, and applied it to DICE and DPE variants. In future work, we intend to address more use cases and HTAs.

In our comparison, DICE usually offers the best performance, but also the worst security, scoring worse than others against attacks on SL3. The local DPE offers improved security at the cost of increased hardware cost. The remote DPE offers the best security and competitive economics, but scores significantly worse for performance. It can be a viable alternative if performance is not critical, especially if a suitable device for hosting the DPE service already exists.

Acknowledgments. This research work was founded by the National Research Center for Applied Cybersecurity ATHENE and the German Federal Ministries BMFTR and BMWE as part of the projects HardShiP (ID 16KIS1860), TRUSTnet (ID 16KIS1787), ProSeCA (ID 19A23009F), and ELISA (ID 19S23002E). This work is based on a master's thesis by Simon Hoffmann "Evaluation of the DICE Protection Environment for Securing Cyberphysical Systems: A Comparison with DICE and TPM".

Disclosure of Interests. The authors have no competing interests to declare that are relevant to the content of this article.

References

1. Ammar, M., Caulfield, A., De Oliveira Nunes, I.: SoK: integrity, attestation, and auditing of program execution. In: 2025 IEEE Symposium on Security and Privacy (SP), pp. 3255–3272 (2025). https://doi.org/10.1109/SP61157.2025.00077
2. ARM Limited: Clarification of Multi-Fault-Injection Attacks on TrustZone enabled Cortex-M based systems
3. Arm Limited: Arm CryptoIsland-300P: Integrated Secure Element Security Target Lite (2022)
4. Arm Limited: TrustZone for Cortex-M (2022). https://www.arm.com/technologies/trustzone-for-cortex-m
5. ARM Limited: Arm Cortex-M Processor Comparison Table (2023). https://documentation-service.arm.com/static/655e085f2c8b3557fee7048f
6. ARM Limited: DICE Protection Environment for TFM (2025)
7. Car, P., De Luca, S.: EU Cyber Resilience Act. EPRS, European Parliament (2022)
8. CHIPS Alliance Project: Caliptra
9. Dowling, B., Rösler, P., Schwenk, J.: Flexible authenticated and confidential channel establishment (FACCE): analyzing the noise protocol framework. In: Public-Key Cryptography – PKC 2020, vol. 12100 (2020). https://doi.org/10.3929/ethz-b-000399156, iACR International Conference on Practice and Theory of Public-Key Cryptography (PKC 2020) (Virtual)
10. Eckel, M., Fenzl, F., Jäger, L.: Towards practical hardware fingerprinting for remote attestation. In: Pitropakis, N., Katsikas, S., Furnell, S., Markantonakis, K. (eds.) SEC 2024. IFIPAICT, vol. 710, pp. 105–118. Springer, Cham (2024). https://doi.org/10.1007/978-3-031-65175-5_8
11. European Network for Cyber Security: Results from the ENCS 2021 Security Programs (2022)
12. European Network for Cyber Security: ENCS and ENTSO-E – Five Years of Collaboration (2023)
13. Fraunhofer Institute for Applied and Integrated Security (AISEC) on behalf of the German Federal Office for Information Security (BSI): A Study on Hardware Attacks against Microcontrollers (2023)
14. Google: Open profile for DICE (2023)
15. Google: Project structure, utilities and traits for a DPE (2023)
16. Hristozov, S., Wettermann, M., Huber, M.: A TOCTOU attack on DICE attestation. In: Proceedings of the Twelveth ACM Conference on Data and Application Security and Privacy. ACM (2022). https://doi.org/10.1145/3508398.3511507

17. Huber, M., Hristozov, S., Ott, S., Sarafov, V., Peinado, M.: The Lazarus effect: healing compromised devices in the internet of small things. In: Proceedings of the 15th ACM Asia Conference on Computer and Communications Security (2020). https://doi.org/10.1145/3320269.3384723
18. Jäger, L., Lorych, D.: Remote attestation extended to the analog domain. In: Proceedings of the 16th International Conference on Availability, Reliability and Security. ARES '21, Association for Computing Machinery, New York, NY, USA (2021). https://doi.org/10.1145/3465481.3465762
19. Li, X., Zhao, B., Yang, G., Xiang, T., Weng, J., Deng, R.H.: A survey of secure computation using trusted execution environments. arXiv abs/2302.12150 (2023). https://api.semanticscholar.org/CorpusID:257102679
20. LoRa Alliance: LoRaWAN 1.1 Specification (2017)
21. Lorych, D., Jäger, L.: Design space exploration of DICE. In: Proceedings of the 17th International Conference on Availability, Reliability and Security. ARES '22, Association for Computing Machinery, New York, NY, USA (2022). https://doi.org/10.1145/3538969.3543785
22. Lorych, D., Jäger, L., Fuchs, A.: Acceleration of DICE key generation using key caching. In: Proceedings of the 19th International Conference on Availability, Reliability and Security. ARES '24, Association for Computing Machinery, New York, NY, USA (2024). https://doi.org/10.1145/3664476.3670869
23. Lorych, D., Plappert, C.: Hardware trust anchor authentication for updatable IoT devices. In: Proceedings of the 19th International Conference on Availability, Reliability and Security. ARES '24. Association for Computing Machinery, New York, NY, USA (2024). https://doi.org/10.1145/3664476.3664479
24. Mahmod, J., Hicks, M.: UnTrustZone: systematic accelerated aging to expose on-chip secrets. In: 2024 IEEE Symposium on Security and Privacy (SP), pp. 4107–4124. IEEE Computer Society, Los Alamitos, CA, USA (2024). https://doi.org/10.1109/SP54263.2024.00069
25. OpenTitan Project: Opentitan. https://opentitan.org/
26. European Parliament and of the Council: Directive (EU) 2022/2555 of the European Parliament and of the Council of 14 (2022)
27. Pinto, S., Santos, N.: Demystifying arm trustzone: a comprehensive survey. ACM Comput. Surv. **51**(6) (2019). https://doi.org/10.1145/3291047
28. Plappert, C., Lorych, D., Eckel, M., Jäger, L., Fuchs, A., Heddergott, R.: Evaluating the applicability of hardware trust anchors for automotive applications. Comput. Secur. **135**, 103514 (2023). https://doi.org/10.1016/j.cose.2023.103514
29. Rodrigues, C., Oliveira, D., Pinto, S.: Busted!!! Microarchitectural side-channel attacks on the MCU bus interconnect. In: 2024 IEEE Symposium on Security and Privacy (SP), pp. 3679–3696 (2024). https://doi.org/10.1109/SP54263.2024.00062
30. Saß, X.M., Mitev, R., Sadeghi, A.R.: Oops..! I glitched it again! How to Multi-glitch the glitching-protections on ARM TrustZone-M. In: 32nd USENIX Security Symposium (USENIX Security 23), pp. 6239–6256. USENIX Association, Anaheim, CA (2023)
31. Schneider, M., Masti, R.J., Shinde, S., Capkun, S., Perez, R.: SoK: hardware-supported trusted execution environments (2022). https://arxiv.org/abs/2205.12742
32. Seyler, J.R., Streichert, T., Glaß, M., Navet, N., Teich, J.: Formal analysis of the startup delay of some/IP service discovery. In: 2015 Design, Automation and Test in Europe Conference and Exhibition (DATE), pp. 49–54 (2015). https://doi.org/10.7873/DATE.2015.0469

33. Tan, X., et al.: SoK: where's the "up"?! A comprehensive (bottom-up) study on the security of arm Cortex-M systems. In: 18th USENIX WOOT Conference on Offensive Technologies (WOOT 24), pp. 149–169. USENIX Association, Philadelphia, PA (2024)
34. Trevor Perrin: The Noise Protocol Framework (2018). https://noiseprotocol.org/noise.html
35. Trusted Computing Group: Implicit Identity Based Device Attestation (2018)
36. Trusted Computing Group: DICE Layering Architecture (2020)
37. Trusted Computing Group: Symmetric Identity Based Device Attestation (2020)
38. Trusted Computing Group: DICE Protection Environment (2024)
39. Trusted Computing Group: Hardware Requirements for a Device Identifier Composition Engine (2024)
40. Trusted Computing Group: DICE Attestation Architecture (2025)
41. United States Department of Transportation: Average age of automobiles and trucks in operation in the united states (2023). https://www.bts.gov/content/average-age-automobiles-and-trucks-operation-united-states
42. Zhang, F., Zhang, H.: SoK: a study of using hardware-assisted isolated execution environments for security. In: Proceedings of the Hardware and Architectural Support for Security and Privacy 2016. HASP '16. Association for Computing Machinery, New York, NY, USA (2016). https://doi.org/10.1145/2948618.2948621

IC3SA Taxonomy: A Safety and Security Awareness Taxonomy for Industrial Control Systems

Fabien Sechi[1(✉)], Gil Ari Agmon[2(✉)], Nadia Saad Noori[1], Ofir Cohen[2], Rami Puzis[2], and Asaf Shabtai[2]

[1] University of Agder (UiA), Agder, Norway
{fabien.e.sechi,nadia.saad.noori}@uia.no
[2] Ben-Gurion University of the Negev, Be'er Sheva, Israel
{gilagm,cofir}@post.bgu.ac.il, {puzis,shabtia}@bgu.ac.il

Abstract. Industrial Control Systems (ICS) increasingly operate as tightly coupled cyber-physical environments where cybersecurity incidents can propagate into operational disruptions and safety consequences. Yet, safety and cybersecurity are still commonly addressed through separate culture, standards, roles, and training practices, leaving stakeholders with limited shared understanding of cross-domain risks, trade-offs, and role-relevant actions. Our work presents a hierarchical, psychologically grounded ICS Safety and Security Awareness Taxonomy that integrates operational safety considerations with cybersecurity awareness under ICS/Operation Technology, real-time and availability, constraints. Building on established Information Security Awareness (ISA) theory, we introduce the IC3SA taxonomy, which structures the domain into Focus Areas (FAs), Sub-Focus Areas, and safety/security topics interpreted through knowledge, attitude, and behavior components (including preventive and confronting behaviors), enabling assessable and role-adaptive awareness constructs. We evaluate the taxonomy through a formative, mixed-method, multi-stakeholder study involving (i) a targeted industry expert group, (ii) a broader practitioner-oriented user group, and (iii) an academic group, using interviews and structured questionnaires. Results indicate strong perceived acceptance across focus areas, while qualitative feedback highlights recurring boundary ambiguities and overlaps—particularly among topics such as governance, continuous improvement, hazard analysis, and threat and vulnerability management—which we used to drive a concrete set of refinement actions applied to the current version of the taxonomy, with structural changes deferred to a planned second version release. Our proposed taxonomy offers an interpretable, standards-aligned framework to support assessment, training design, and enable cross-role communication for improving safety-security awareness in ICS.

Keywords: Industrial Control Systems · Information and Operational Technology · Safety · Cybersecurity · Information Security Awareness · Taxonomy

Z. Afzal et al. (Eds.): ARES 2026 Workshops, LNCS 16900, pp. 389–406, 2027.
https://doi.org/10.1007/978-3-032-35576-8_21

1 Introduction

Industrial Control Systems (ICS) underpin Critical Infrastructures (CIs) such as energy, manufacturing, water, and process industries. Historically, ICS and Operational Technology (OT) were designed as safety-first and largely isolated systems [9]. Today, increasing IT/OT convergence and connectivity expose ICS environments to cyber threats that can directly affect physical processes, availability, and operational safety [23].

Despite this operational reality, cybersecurity and functional safety are still frequently addressed through separate standards, roles, and training practices [20]. In practice the two are intertwined: a cybersecurity breach may disable safety mechanisms or delay operator response, while safety-driven actions may weaken security controls. Decision-making during abnormal situations is distributed across operators, engineers, safety specialists, and security teams acting under uncertainty and operational constraints [1], so response outcomes depend on shared situational understanding as much as on technical controls.

This paper addresses the safety-security gap as a *human awareness* problem. A persistent share of successful incidents involves a human element such as unsafe decisions, misjudgments, configuration errors, or social engineering rather than purely technical flaws [8,16,33]. ICS awareness differs from traditional Information Security Awareness (ISA) because cybersecurity decisions must also respect operational safety, strict availability requirements, and real-time constraints: actions acceptable in enterprise IT may be infeasible or unsafe in OT when they interfere with process continuity. We therefore build on validated ISA taxonomy foundations [5] and adapt them to ICS by incorporating operational safety and OT-specific constraints. Existing standards provide extensive technical and governance guidance [9,34] but offer limited support for assessing whether IT, OT, and safety roles share a coherent understanding of safety-security topics, trade-offs, and role-relevant behaviors.

The objective of this work is therefore to develop and validate an integrated *ICS Safety and Security Awareness Taxonomy (IC3SA Taxonomy)* that structures safety and cybersecurity awareness into hierarchical Focus Areas, Sub-Focus Areas, and topics interpreted through ISA-inspired psychological components, namely knowledge, attitude, and behavior. The taxonomy is intended to support assessment, training design, and bridge communication silos across ICS roles (e.g., in CI operator training and audits) while remaining aligned with established standards relevant to ICS governance and engineering practices.

Our contributions are: (a) a hierarchical, psychologically grounded awareness taxonomy integrating ICS safety and cybersecurity; (b) a mapping of taxonomy elements to established ICS standards and governance frameworks; (c) a multi-method validation combining expert engagement, questionnaires, and scenario-primed workshops; and (d) empirical insights guiding iterative refinement. The work addresses three research questions answered in Sect. 5: **RQ1.** What gaps exist in current ISA approaches when applied to ICS with strong safety and real-time constraints? **RQ2.** How can cybersecurity and safety awareness be structurally integrated into a unified ISA taxonomy for ICS? **RQ3.** How can such a taxonomy be constructed and validated across stakeholders with different roles and expertise?

2 Theoretical Background

Industrial Control Systems (ICS) are socio-technical and cyber-physical environments in which technical infrastructures, organizational processes, and human decisions jointly determine operational dependability. In such systems, cybersecurity incidents may propagate into physical consequences, while safety-driven operational actions may unintentionally affect cybersecurity posture. This theoretical background therefore follows three complementary perspectives: (i) ICS-specific safety-security coupling and situational decision-making, (ii) awareness as a psychological construct through the Knowledge–Attitude–Behavior (KAB) model, and (iii) taxonomies as formal instruments for structuring and assessing awareness across heterogeneous ICS roles.

2.1 ICS Safety–Security Coupling and Situational Decision-Making

ICS span layers from physical processes, field devices, and controllers to supervisory systems and business IT, commonly represented through the Purdue Reference Model (Levels 0–5). Figure 1 positions IC3SA as a human-centered interpretive layer above this stack. Operational constraints, namely availability, timing, and process stability, dominate intervention choices, so enterprise-IT measures such as immediate patching or aggressive isolation may be unsafe or infeasible. Safety and cybersecurity are managed through partially distinct mechanisms (safety instrumented systems vs. segmentation, access control, monitoring, incident response) but interact continuously through shared assets and operational states, making safety-security coupling an operational reality rather than a conceptual issue.

This coupling affects decision-making. Responses depend on distributed interpretation across operators, safety specialists, and cybersecurity teams [2], requiring coordination across strategic, tactical, and operational levels. Failures may emerge from misaligned interpretations, ambiguous responsibilities, or weak cross-role communication, not only from technical weaknesses.

2.2 Awareness as a Psychological Construct: The KAB Perspective

Information Security Awareness (ISA) is commonly conceptualized through the triad of Knowledge, Attitude, and Behavior (KAB) formalized by Kruger and Kearney [19]. KAB is particularly relevant for ICS because safety and cybersecurity decisions involve operational trade-offs: actors must evaluate consequences under time pressure and operational constraints, and awareness reflects whether knowledge, perception, and behavior remain aligned during decision-making rather than merely policy familiarity. ICS environments require interpreting KAB through cyber-physical consequences and operational feasibility, that is, whether actors can select actions that are both secure and safe under real constraints.

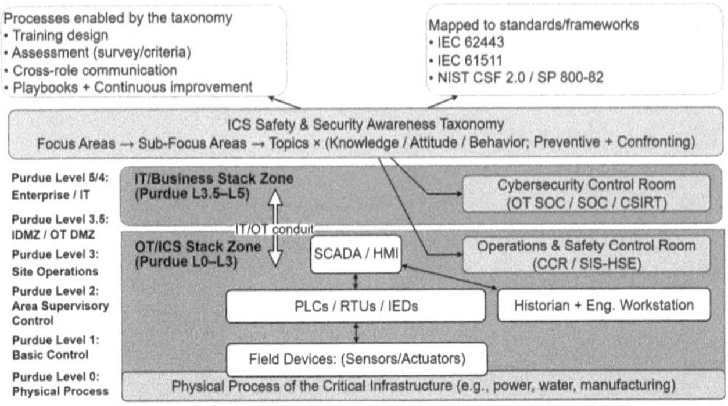

Fig. 1. Conceptual positioning of the IC3SA taxonomy as a human-centered interpretive layer above the ICS/OT stack, supporting coordination across operations, safety, and cybersecurity roles.

Operationalizing KAB. We operationalize each KAB dimension into sub - dimensions consistent with validated ISA instruments [5,26]: *Knowledge* into *declarative* (knowing *that* a control exists) and *procedural* (knowing *how* to apply it); *Attitude* into three perception sub-dimensions rooted in Protection Motivation Theory (*severity*, *probability*, and *usefulness*), which together underlie the HAIS-Q triad [26]; and *Behavior* into *preventive* (proactive adherence under normal conditions) and *confronting* (responsive action under pressure, e.g., refusing an out-of-procedure remote-access request during production pressure). The IC3SA item bank adapts Bitton et al.'s templates [5] and the HAIS-Q item structure; psychometric validation (factor analysis, IRT, test–retest) is deferred to a dedicated instrument-development study (Sect. 5).

2.3 Taxonomies as Structuring Instruments for ICS Awareness

Taxonomies organize complex domains into interpretable categories, stabilize terminology, and, in socio-technical environments such as ICS, act as a shared boundary object between professional communities. For ISA, taxonomies transform abstract KAB dimensions into assessable domain topics, enabling assessment, training design, and cross-role communication.

Positioning Relative to Existing ICS Taxonomies and Ontologies. Several established artifacts structure parts of the ICS domain: threat-oriented taxonomies (MITRE ATT&CK for ICS [22]), control-oriented frameworks (NIST CSF 2.0 [27]; IEC 62443 zones-and-conduits [14]), and functional-safety standards (IEC 61511 [15]). Prior ISA taxonomies in adjacent domains (e.g., mobile security [5]) show how psychological constructs can be operationalized into assessable topics but are not anchored in ICS realities. To our knowledge, no existing artifact integrates safety and cybersecurity at the *awareness* layer with explicit treatment of cyber-physical trade-offs and role-adaptive interpretation. IC3SA is therefore a complementary artifact that reuses concepts from these sources (mapped in Sect. 3.1) and adds a psychologically grounded awareness layer.

Analytical Gap Analysis. Four gaps emerge analytically when established ISA frameworks are transferred to ICS, prior to and independently of our empirical findings (Sect. 5) which corroborate them. *(G1) Safety–security coupling*: the Kruger–Kearney KAB [19] and HAIS-Q [26] operationalize awareness against IT-oriented C/I/A controls; neither represents cyber-to-physical propagation or the reverse, despite its centrality in safety-security co-engineering [1,17,18]. *(G2) IT-centric abstraction*: prior ISA taxonomies anchor topics in personal-computing artifacts (passwords, mobile apps, email [5,26]) that do not transfer to HMIs, engineering workstations, and controllers under real-time and availability constraints [3,28]. *(G3) Lifecycle and supply-chain coverage*: decades-long ICS lifecycles and long vendor relationships [7,11] require firmware authenticity, supplier audits, and integration practices, which are absent from generic ISA. *(G4) Role-adaptive interpretation*: risk perception varies sharply by operator, engineer, safety specialist, security analyst, and manager [10], which single-perspective ISA instruments cannot support. IC3SA addresses G1 through FAs explicitly pairing safety and security topics (FA4, FA8, FA9, FA11); G2 by anchoring topics in OT-specific concepts (safe-state transition, restricted data flow, workstation hygiene); G3 through FA7 and FA10; and G4 through the stakeholder-levels structure (Sect. 3.1) and role-adaptive KAB interpretation.

IC3SA is grounded in IEC 62443 [14], ISA/IEC 61511 [15], NIST CSF 2.0 [27], and NIST SP 800-82r3 [30], but translates them from *required practices and controls* into an awareness-oriented framework of Focus Areas, Sub-Focus Areas, and topics interpreted through KAB dimensions. These three requirements (standards anchoring, cross-role interpretability, and assessable constructs) motivate the two-phase methodology of Sect. 3: construction through standards-driven extraction and ISA-informed structuring, followed by multi-stakeholder validation.

3 Research Methodology

This study adopts a design-oriented methodology with two phases (Fig. 2): (i) taxonomy construction grounded in ICS standards and ISA theory, and (ii) validation through multi-stakeholder evaluation sessions. The research artifact comprises the hierarchical taxonomy and a web-based navigator, targeting operators, engineers, safety professionals, cybersecurity specialists, and managers across the IT/OT spectrum. Our approach builds on prior ISA taxonomy work [5] but deliberately omits the Analytic Hierarchy Process used there to derive global weights: in ICS, perceived importance is role- and situation-dependent (operators vs. security analysts vs. safety engineers), and a single global prioritization may obscure this variability.

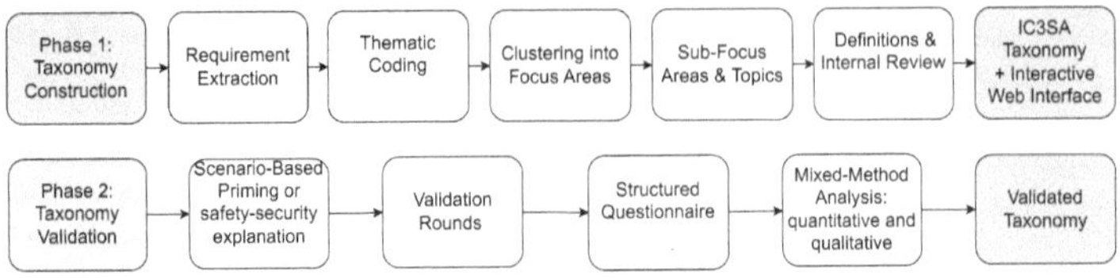

Fig. 2. Research methodology workflow.

3.1 Phase 1: Taxonomy Construction Methodology

The taxonomy was constructed through a structured, iterative process combining standards analysis, thematic coding, and expert judgment, anchored in two methodological references: Nickerson et al. [24], which prescribes iterative cycles alternating empirical-to-conceptual and conceptual-to-empirical refinement, and Noy and McGuinness's *Ontology Development 101* [25] for class, property, and definition construction. Primary sources: IEC 62443, ISA/IEC 61511, and NIST SP 800-82r3, complemented by adjacent ISA taxonomy research [5].

Competency Questions. Following [25], we formulated six competency questions to make explicit what the taxonomy must enable: (CQ1) topics an OT operator must master to recognize and respond to a cyber incident that may propagate into a safety hazard; (CQ2) identification of role-relevant awareness gaps across operators, engineers, safety specialists, and security analysts; (CQ3) which FAs are most affected by IT/OT convergence trade-offs; (CQ4) assessment of shared workforce understanding under abnormal operating conditions; (CQ5) the standards and clauses that underpin each awareness topic; and (CQ6) how preventive and confronting behaviors are distinguished. These were used both as a filter during requirement extraction (clauses with no expressible CQ were excluded) and as an evaluation lens after clustering (each FA must contribute to at least one CQ).

Mapping Criteria. Taxonomy elements were mapped to established ICS standards using (i) semantic correspondence between taxonomy definitions and control statements, (ii) functional intent, and (iii) scope compatibility. When multiple mappings were plausible we preferred the closest functional-intent match and documented overlaps as expected coupling points. The full Focus-Area- and topic-level mapping (with clause references to IEC 62443, ISA/IEC 61511, NIST CSF 2.0, and NIST SP 800-82r3) is exposed through the web interface [13] and in sheet 7 of the workbook [4].

Construction Protocol. The construction process followed five iterative steps, each alternating between empirical-to-conceptual and conceptual-to-empirical refinement [24]: (1) *requirement extraction*: two authors independently extracted safety and security requirements from the standards, retaining only clauses expressible as stakeholder-facing topics covered by at least one competency question; (2) *thematic coding*: open coding informed by KAB dimensions, with disagreements resolved by consensus and unresolved cases escalated to a third author; (3) *clustering into Focus Areas*: themes grouped using Nickerson *ending conditions*, requiring each FA to be concise ($\leq$ 9 Sub-FAs), exhaustive over the themes, and mutually exclusive at the definitional level (overlaps documented in Sect. 4.4); (4) *refinement into Sub-Focus Areas and Topics* validated against the competency questions; (5) *definition and internal review* following the Noy–McGuinness principle [25], with each definition checked for clarity, non-circularity, and standard-clause alignment.

Assignment of elements was guided by thematic alignment, standard section correspondence, expert judgment, and consensus discussion among the authors. The taxonomy draws on ISA principles [5,19] and interprets topics through psychological components, including preventive and confronting behaviors. The five construction steps and their intermediate artifacts are reproduced in full in the accompanying supplementary workbook [4] (sheets 1–7: sources catalogue, requirement extraction, thematic coding, sub-focus-area clusters, focus-area grouping, overlap resolution, and the traceability matrix), supporting independent inspection of every construction-time decision.

To make KAB-based operationalization concrete, we instantiate Sub-FA 1.3 (Regulatory & Compliance Alignment: documentation & reporting for audits): **Knowledge**: *declarative* awareness that audit-ready documentation is required, and *procedural* knowledge of how to maintain logs, diagrams, and incident reports; **Attitude**: *severity* that poor documentation can lead to failed audits, *probability* that inspections may occur unexpectedly, *usefulness* that record-keeping is effective for transparency; **Behavior**: *preventive* actions such as routine record updating, *confronting* actions such as rapidly retrieving documentation during an audit. Equivalent decompositions for the other 148 topics are in sheet 8 of the workbook [4].

The full taxonomy is presented as a 148-row Knowledge–Attitude–Behavior matrix in sheet 8 of the workbook [4]; an interactive navigator is available at [13].

Stakeholder Levels. The taxonomy applies across strategic, tactical, and operational levels as a cognitive lens reflecting distributed, context-dependent ICS decision-making, not a rigid assignment.

3.2 Phase 2: Expert-Based Validation

3.2.1 Objectives

Validation targeted the taxonomy's *conceptual quality* (usability, interpretability, meaningfulness) [29] across three dimensions at the granular Focus-Area level: *completeness and coverage*, *clarity of naming and definitions*, and *boundary distinctness*. Definition-level assessment captured naming suitability and terminology clarity, reflecting the need for shared language across safety, OT, IT, and management roles. The framework combined structured questionnaires, expert interviews, and interactive workshop sessions.

3.2.2 Icebreaker Activity

Rounds 2 and 3 opened with a brief group icebreaker using Microsoft's Elevation of Privilege (EoP) STRIDE cards [21], with the cards loosely contextualized to a smart-grid setting. The icebreaker was intended only to encourage informal discussion among participants who did not know each other and to ease them into the workshop format. Outputs were neither collected nor analyzed, and the activity played no role in the taxonomy evaluation that followed. Rounds 0 and 1 did not include an icebreaker.

3.2.3 Validation Rounds

Round 0: Preliminary Consultation. Initial consultation with eight academic and industry domain experts using prototype questionnaire items; informed refinements to taxonomy and instrument. Round-0 data are not included in the final evaluation.

Round 1: Industry Expert Session - critical energy infrastructures. In-person session with eleven smart-grid ICS practitioners (cybersecurity and safety experts, substantial professional experience). Format: 30-minute taxonomy introduction plus 60-minute structured questionnaire (no icebreaker; participants were working for the same organization). Quantitative scoring covered mainly Focus Area 5 plus one additional FA per participant; Round 1 is therefore interpreted as the primary expert signal, complemented by qualitative feedback.

Round 2: NiKT 2025 Workshop. We conducted a 3-hour interactive workshop at the Norwegian Information Communication and Technology Conference for Research and Education (NiKT 2025), Halden, Norway, with six academic and expert participants (Master's students to professors; one with 10–20 years of industry experience, one with 5–10, four with <5). The session opened with a 60-minute icebreaker activity (Subsect. 3.2.2), followed by a 90-minute block of taxonomy lecture and questionnaire completion.

Round 3: Students' Workshop. Two further sessions followed the same Round-2 structure with nine bachelor's and master's cybersecurity/computer-engineering students with coursework and some professional IT and security experience but no substantial professional ICS experience. Round 3 is framed as an *interpretability probe*: it assesses whether the taxonomy's naming, definitions, and structure remain understandable to less-experienced participants. Participation was voluntary, anonymous, and decoupled from any course evaluation.

Ethical Considerations. All participants provided informed consent; data were anonymous and uncompensated; no personally identifiable information was recorded. Round 3 was administered within a non-credit, voluntary course decoupled from academic evaluation to limit courtesy-bias. Given the low-risk, anonymous, and non-coercive study design, formal ethical approval was not required under the participating institutions' policies for low-risk anonymous research; we acknowledge this as a methodological boundary in Sect. 5.

3.2.4 Validation Instrument and Analysis Strategy

Validation used a structured questionnaire with consent and demographic items (role, sector, ICS/OT years of experience) followed by a per-Focus-Area block of four closed-ended Likert items (1–5; *Naming Suitability*, *Overall Comprehensiveness*, *Sub-topic Comprehensiveness*, *Content Expectation*) and two open-ended items (perceived overlaps; additional comments). FA order was randomized per participant to mitigate ordering effects [6]. The full instrument is reproduced in sheet 10 of the supplementary workbook [4].

Quantitative analysis computed mean scores per Focus Area and assessed internal consistency using Cronbach's alpha, ensuring that related evaluation items coherently captured an underlying perception of taxonomy quality. Qualitative responses were synthesized thematically to identify recurring patterns such as boundary ambiguities, overlap concerns, and suggested refinements. This mixed-method approach supports triangulation by combining structured ratings with contextualized expert reasoning, strengthening construct validity.

To support navigation and reduce cognitive load, we developed an interactive web-based interface [13] integrating the survey instrument with hover- and click-revealed taxonomy definitions; the platform doubled as a data-collection mechanism and a usability probe.

4 Findings

4.1 Taxonomy Structure and Overview of the Focus Areas

The taxonomy follows a hierarchical structure: 11 Focus Areas → 33 Sub-Focus Areas → 74 topics → psychological components → measurable criteria. It defines eleven Focus Areas (FA1–FA11): *FA1 Governance, Risk & Compliance; FA2 System & Network Architecture; FA3 Physical & Access Security; FA4 Operational Resilience & Safe-State Behavior; FA5 Threat & Vulnerability Management; FA6 Incident Response & Recovery; FA7 Supply Chain & Third-Party Security; FA8 Environmental & Human Safety; FA9 Emergency Preparedness & Safety Compliance; FA10 Continuous Improvement & Integrity of Control; FA11 Risk & Hazard Analysis.* Each Focus Area pairs a security and a safety pillar at the Sub-FA and Topic levels. The full hierarchy, with KAB sub-dimensions and measurable criteria for all 148 rows, is provided machine-readably in sheet 8 of the workbook [4]; an interactive navigator is at [13].

4.2 Worked Example: From Focus Areas to Measurable Criteria

We trace one path through the taxonomy: *Focus Area → Sub-Focus Area → Topic → Psychological Component → Measurable Criterion.* We select FA 1 (Governance, Risk, and Compliance) and Sub-FA 1.1 (Policy, Standards, and

Procedures), anchored in IEC 62443-2-1 §4.3.2 and IEC 61511-1 §5. Two complementary topics: *(i) security* TSec1.1.A, namely ICS security policies and SOPs (IEC 62443-2-1 §4.3.2.6); and *(ii) safety* TSaf1.1.A, namely safety policies aligned with ISA/IEC 61511 and HSE principles (IEC 61511-1 §5,§11). The corresponding measurable criteria are: **TSec1.1.A + Confronting behavior**: "the operator refuses a remote-access request that does not follow approved authentication and escalation procedures, even under production pressure"; **TSaf1.1.A + Preventive behavior**: "the operator consistently follows defined safety procedures and does not disable safety interlocks or alarms to restore production more quickly".

From Criterion to Practice. Each KAB sub-dimension yields a concrete instrument: declarative and procedural knowledge items become quiz questions; severity, probability, and usefulness items become Likert pre/post measures of risk perception; preventive and confronting behavior items become observable actions in a tabletop simulation (e.g., did the trainee escalate the remote-access request rather than approve it under production pressure?). An ICS asset owner can sample a fixed number of topics per FA, instrument them with their KAB items, and compute role-segmented scores; divergent scores across roles reveal where shared understanding breaks down (e.g., operators scoring high but SOC analysts scoring low on the same confronting behavior signal an invisible escalation path). Worked KAB instantiations and the topic-level mapping to IEC 62443, IEC 61511, and NIST SP 800-82r3 are in sheets 8–9 of the workbook [4].

4.3 Qualitative and Quantitative Results

The three evaluation rounds (Round 1 industry, $n = 11$; Round 2 NiKT, $n = 6$; Round 3 students, $n = 9$; total $N = 26$) provide converging evidence that ISA for ICS must move beyond IT-centric awareness models toward a socio-technical structure reflecting operational realities. Full per-round Likert scores, combined statistics, instrument items, and headline findings are reproduced in sheet 10 (Validation Results) of the supplementary workbook [4].

Qualitative. Table 1 summarises expert feedback. Participants consistently perceived the proposed Focus Areas as strongly interconnected rather than independent; overlaps were most prominent among FA1, FA5, FA6, and FA11, where risk assessment, monitoring, and response form a continuous lifecycle. Recurring suggestions were to clarify boundaries, simplify terminology, and better articulate the link between patching, firmware authenticity, and asset management; to strengthen supply-chain coverage (FA7); to integrate environmental and human-safety dimensions (FA8); and to consider a dedicated FA on secure development and system integration.

Quantitative. Table 2 reports the per-FA mean Likert score by round and Table 3 the combined statistics. Most FAs score above 4.0, indicating broad acceptance. FA4 (combined Mean = 4.410, SD = 0.766) and FA6 (Mean = 4.360, SD = 0.757)

Table 1. Summary of expert feedback per Focus Area: perceived overlaps and refinement suggestions.

FA	Perceived Overlaps (Q5)	Additional Comments and Suggestions (Q6)
FA1	FA5, FA6, FA8, FA11 (risk/assessment).	Clarify links between lifecycle, patching, firmware authenticity.
FA2	Asset/device mgmt across FAs.	Expand secure-architecture guidance (MACsec/IPsec, proxies); cover local access.
FA3	Some redundancy in sub-focus areas.	Merge/simplify physical access controls (badging/biometrics).
FA4	Limited explicit overlap.	Add safe-state transitions and attack-surface reduction.
FA5	FA2, FA6, FA9, FA11 (monitoring/response).	Clarify scope; separate threat intelligence from monitoring; add threat hunting, inventory integrity.
FA6	Tied to FA5 (monitoring-triggered IR).	Mention redundancy and fault tolerance explicitly.
FA7	Possible link to physical security.	Add vendor audits and supplier-lifecycle assessment.
FA8	—	Terminology unclear ("climate regulations"); use environmental/human-safety phrasing.
FA9	FA6, FA1 (emergency/compliance).	Add safety metrics and training; clarify dual role of emergency routes.
FA10	FA1, FA11.	Inconsistent structure; reframe toward "Integrity of Control".
FA11	FA5, FA1 (threat/vulnerability/risk).	Could integrate asset management; simplify definitions.
General	FAs perceived as interconnected.	Simplify the matrix; possible new FA on secure development/integration.

are the strongest, reflecting agreement on operational resilience and response. FA11 is the lowest (Mean = 3.590, Var = 0.879), quantitatively reinforcing the qualitative ambiguity reported for hazard analysis. Cross-session variability is largest for FA5 (NiKT vs. students), suggesting role-dependent interpretation of monitoring vs. threat-intelligence responsibilities. The Round-1 expert-only column of Table 2 is consistent with the pooled signal: FA1, FA4, FA6 strong; FA8, FA10 mixed; FA9 weak on naming (industry = 3.0; consistent with the dual-role emergency-routes concern). FA7 and FA11 were not scored by Round 1 due to time constraints; their pooled scores should be interpreted with appropriate caution.

Table 2. Per-FA mean Likert score by round (1–5; mean of four metrics). "–" = not evaluated in that round; "Combined" is the unweighted mean of available metrics. Full per-metric scores in sheet 10 of [4].

FA	Industry (n = 11)	NiKT (n = 6)	Students (n = 9)	Combined
FA1	4.88	4.15	4.39	4.35
FA2	4.00	4.58	3.87	4.04
FA3	3.90	3.75	4.08	3.94
FA4	4.50	4.30	4.41	4.39
FA5	4.05	3.48	4.49	4.09
FA6	4.93	4.10	4.35	4.34
FA7	–	3.98	4.30	4.22
FA8	3.75	3.90	4.03	3.97
FA9	3.75	3.83	3.97	3.90
FA10	3.95	3.90	4.08	4.02
FA11	–	2.95	3.85	3.60

Table 3. Per-FA combined statistics across all rounds ($N = 26$); items pooled across the four metrics.

FA	N (scores)	Mean	SD	Var.
FA1	93	4.441	0.580	0.336
FA2	78	4.077	0.786	0.617
FA3	84	3.940	0.734	0.539
FA4	83	4.410	0.766	0.586
FA5	136	4.125	0.764	0.584
FA6	89	4.360	0.757	0.574
FA7	72	4.264	0.556	0.310
FA8	71	3.972	0.676	0.456
FA9	89	3.921	0.801	0.641
FA10	90	4.033	0.800	0.639
FA11	61	3.590	0.938	0.879

4.4 Taxonomy Refinement Based on Validation Feedback

We treated participants' qualitative feedback as actionable design input. Table 4 maps the principal issues from Rounds 1–3 to refinement actions, marking each as *Applied* (incorporated in this version), *Partially applied* (pending further evaluation), or *Planned for v2* (deferred for re-validation). The next-iteration backlog, comprising competency questions, the Ontology-101 self-audit, deferred overlaps, and stakeholder suggestions, is consolidated in sheet 11 of the workbook [4].

Applied refinements target the definitional and terminological clarity identified as the dominant source of perceived overlap; the FAs with the lowest naming and content scores (FA8, FA10, FA11) were those for which participants reported ambiguity rather than missing content, so sharpened definitions address the most acute interpretability issues without altering a hierarchical structure already validated by the high mean scores elsewhere. Structural changes requiring re-validation, namely reframing FA10 toward "Integrity of Control" and a potential secure-development FA, are deferred to v2 and a larger industry-focused study (Sect. 5, Limitations).

Table 4. Mapping of validation feedback to refinement actions. *Applied*: incorporated in this version; *Planned v2*: structural changes deferred for re-validation.

FA	Refinement action	Status
FA1	Definitions tightened to delineate governance scope from operational monitoring (FA5) and incident response (FA6); explicit pointers to lifecycle, patching, and firmware authenticity added in topic descriptions.	Applied
FA2	Sub-Focus on network design extended to reference secure architecture patterns (e.g., MACsec/IPsec, proxies) and local access considerations.	Applied
FA3	Redundancies between physical access topics consolidated; overlapping sub-topics on badging and biometric controls merged into a single physical access control topic.	Applied
FA4	Topics extended to include explicit safe-state transition awareness and attack-surface reduction as preventive behaviors.	Applied
FA5	Scope narrowed to clarify boundary with FA6: monitoring/detection separated from threat intelligence; threat hunting and inventory integrity added as distinct topics.	Applied
FA6	Recovery and resilience topics extended to explicitly include redundancy and fault tolerance as preventive behaviors, complementing post-incident recovery.	Applied
FA7	Supply-chain coverage expanded with vendor audit and supplier lifecycle assessment topics; cross-reference to FA3 added for physical aspects of supplier on-site access.	Applied
FA8	Terminology revised: ambiguous wording (e.g., "climate regulations") replaced with environmental and human-safety phrasing aligned with HSE practice.	Applied
FA9	Definitions clarified to disambiguate the dual role of emergency routes (safety egress vs. physical intrusion vector); safety metrics and safety-training topics added.	Applied
FA10	Internal structure realigned around continuous improvement loops; full reframing toward an "Integrity of Control" perspective.	Planned for v2
FA11	Definitions simplified for readability; partial integration with device/asset management cross-referenced to FA1 and FA2. Full merger with adjacent FAs deferred pending further evaluation.	Partially applied
General	Cross-FA mapping notes added to make safety-security coupling explicit, e.g., between FA5/FA6 (detection–response) and FA1/FA11 (governance–risk). A dedicated Focus Area on secure development and system integration is under consideration.	Planned for v2

5 Discussion

RQ1: Gaps in current ISA for ICS.

Conventional ISA taxonomies developed for enterprise IT often fail to capture the tightly coupled cyber-physical nature of ICS [12]. Four gaps recurred. First, **safety-security coupling**: participants interpreted cyber incidents through their physical consequences and expected ISA to address hazard propagation, fail-safe behavior, and "move-to-safe-state" logic rather than confidentiality or integrity in isolation [18,32]. Second, **IT-centric abstractions** did not match operational mental models: FA5 (Threat & Vulnerability Management) was read as one continuous detection-and-response function, not discrete lifecycle stages, consistent with operational guidance to integrate defensive activities into workflows [30]. Third, **lifecycle and supply-chain realities** (vendor audits, firmware authenticity, long supplier relationships, secure integration) received limited coverage, unsurprisingly, since ICS equipment lifecycles span decades [12]. Fourth, **operational context** (configuration practices, network architecture, physical access) is often excluded from classical ISA training even though ICS staff interpret cybersecurity through engineering practice and procedural knowledge [3,28]. Together, these gaps motivate socio-technical awareness models rather than isolated user-action models [10].

RQ2: Structural integration.

Integration is achievable when ISA is framed relationally rather than as a linear hierarchy [17]. First, the observed **boundary ambiguity among FA1, FA5, FA6, FA10, and FA11** is an empirical feature, not a flaw: practitioners conceptualize safety and security as mutually reinforcing loops in which monitoring informs response, response informs learning, and learning reshapes governance [18]. Second, **operational feedback loops drive acceptance**: the highest-rated FAs (FA4 and FA6, both above 4.3) sit closest to operational continuity, while FA11 (mean 3.59, highest variance) was perceived as abstract rather than rejected [31]. Third, **shared terminology** is a prerequisite for integration: many overlap comments concerned naming mismatches rather than missing content. Fourth, **awareness must be role-adaptive**: relevance varies sharply by operator, engineer, manager, or security analyst [10], requiring multiple interpretive pathways rather than a single perspective.

RQ3: Construction and validation across roles.

The multi-round design demonstrates a practical pathway. **Iterative co-construction** (Round-0 restructuring from a linear questionnaire to randomized FA sections) reduced bias and improved engagement [3]. **Mixed-method validation** captured acceptance through Likert scoring (Cronbach $\alpha = 0.818$) and friction through qualitative responses; dispersion in FA10 and FA11 marks where shared understanding is still emerging [12]. **Heterogeneous sampling** across industry practitioners (Round 1) and academic audiences (Rounds 2–3) surfaced both expert and interpretability signals, supporting cross-stakeholder validation of conceptual quality. Finally, the data support treating the taxonomy as a **living artifact**: refinement through repeated stakeholder engagement [14] rather than static completeness.

Synthesis of Findings and Implications

Participants viewed the taxonomy as comprehensive yet dense; criticisms questioned how explicitly safety-security relationships should be expressed, not whether they should be integrated. The central ISA challenge in ICS is therefore awareness of interdependencies between cyber events and physical hazards, between governance decisions and operational constraints, and between monitoring/ response/ continuous-improvement cycles, rather than of threats in isolation [18].

Three design principles emerge. *(i) Operational grounding*: awareness structures should map to real workflows, not abstract control catalogs [30]. *(ii) Explicit coupling*: safety-security relationships should be visible rather than separated [17]. *(iii) Iterative validation*: heterogeneous stakeholder engagement is needed to sustain alignment over time.

Limitations and Future Work

The evaluation is formative ($N = 26$, workshop-based recruitment): the present evidence supports the taxonomy's conceptual quality and usability rather than its psychometric validity or operational effectiveness, and is sufficient to identify structural patterns and drive a first refinement round (Sect. 4.4) but not to test scalability or long-term usability. Future work: (i) validate the v2 revision (FA10 reframing; potential secure-development FA), (ii) simplify navigation, (iii) explore tool-supported representations [12], and (iv) apply the taxonomy in a real-world case study with an industrial asset owner, embedding it in an operational training and assessment workflow and adapting it to evolving threat landscapes. One methodological limitation: the KAB item bank, adapted from validated ISA instruments [5,26], awaits independent psychometric validation (factor analysis, IRT, test–retest), which we plan to conduct on the data collected in this larger, industry-focused deployment.

6 Conclusion

We introduced and formatively evaluated a psychologically grounded taxonomy integrating safety and security awareness in ICS. Combining standards-driven construction with multi-round expert evaluation, it supports assessment, training design, and cross-role communication. Results indicate positive perceived coverage and strong survey consistency while revealing boundary ambiguities addressed through definitional and scope refinements (Sect. 4.4); structural revisions, prioritizing the FA10 reframing and the lower-scoring FA11 boundaries, are planned for v2. The present evidence supports the taxonomy's conceptual quality and usability; psychometric validation and assessment of operational effectiveness in a real-world deployment are the subject of planned follow-up studies. The accompanying workbook [4] exposes the construction artifacts, the first-iteration taxonomy, and the validation data for reproducibility and Iteration 2 planning.

Acknowledgments. This research was partially supported by both the Energy Center managed by the BIRD Foundation, and the Centre for Integrated Emergency Management of UIA.

Resources. Two supplementary artifacts accompany this paper. *(i) A web navigator* of the taxonomy with hover- and click-revealed definitions for every Focus Area, Sub-Focus Area, Topic, and KAB component, used in the Round 1–3 sessions [13]. *(ii) A construction-and-validation workbook* [4], a single `.xlsx` with twelve sheets in five stages aligned with this paper: *Stage 1* sources catalogue (sheet 1); *Stage 2* ontology construction (sheets 2–7); *Stage 3* the 148-row first-iteration taxonomy with KAB decomposition and worked examples (sheets 8–9); *Stage 4* validation rounds, instrument, and per-FA Likert results (sheet 10); *Stage 5* next-iteration plan with competency questions, Ontology-101 self-audit, and stakeholder suggestions (sheet 11).

Disclosure of Interests. The authors have no competing interests to declare that are relevant to the content of this article.

References

1. Abdo, H., Kaouk, M., Flaus, J.M., Masse, F.: A safety/security risk analysis approach of industrial control systems: a cyber bowtie–combining new version of attack tree with bowtie analysis. Comput. Secur. **72**, 175–195 (2018). https://doi.org/10.1016/j.cose.2017.09.004
2. Andreassen, J., Eileraas, M., Herrera, L.C., Noori, N.S.: InCReASE: a dynamic framework towards enhancing situational awareness in cyber incident response. In: Gjøsæter, T., Radianti, J., Murayama, Y. (eds.) ITDRR 2022. IFIPAICT, vol. 672, pp. 244–258. Springer, Cham (2023). https://doi.org/10.1007/978-3-031-34207-3_16
3. Ani, U.D., Watson, J., He, H., Radanliev, P., Epiphaniou, G.: Minimising cybersecurity risk exposures in industrial control system environments: a techno-human vulnerability analysis approach. J. Cyber Secur. Technol. **10**(1), 1–40 (2026). https://doi.org/10.1080/23742917.2024.2421589
4. Anonymous Authors: IC3SA Taxonomy Workbook (2026). https://github.com/icstaxonomy-web/icstaxonomy/tree/main
5. Bitton, R., Finkelshtein, A., Sidi, L., Puzis, R., Rokach, L., Shabtai, A.: Taxonomy of mobile users' security awareness. Comput. Secur. **73**, 266–293 (2017). https://doi.org/10.1016/j.cose.2017.10.015
6. Boone, H.N., Boone, D.A.: Analyzing Likert data. J. Ext. **50**(2), 1–5 (2012)
7. Canonico, R., Sperlì, G.: Industrial cyber-physical systems protection: a methodological review. Comput. Secur. **135**, 103531 (2023)
8. Cybersecurity and Infrastructure Security Agency (CISA): ICS recommended practices and incident response guidance (2023). https://www.cisa.gov/topics/industrial-control-systems. Accessed 14 May 2026
9. Evans, R.P.: Control systems security center comparison study of industrial control system standards against the control systems protection framework cyber-security requirements. Technical report, Idaho National Laboratory (INL) (2005). https://inldigitallibrary.inl.gov/sites/sti/sti/3480251.pdf. Accessed 03 Mar 2026

10. Evripidou, S., Ani, U.D., Watson, J.D.M., Hailes, S.: Security culture in industrial control systems organisations: a literature review. In: Clarke, N., Furnell, S. (eds.) HAISA 2022. IFIPAICT, vol. 658, pp. 133–146. Springer, Cham (2022). https://doi.org/10.1007/978-3-031-12172-2_11
11. Felser, M., Rentschler, M., Kleineberg, O.: Coexistence standardization of operation technology and information technology. Proc. IEEE **107**(6), 962–976 (2019). https://doi.org/10.1109/JPROC.2019.2913443
12. Humayed, A., Lin, J., Li, F., Luo, B.: Cyber-physical systems security–a survey. IEEE Internet Things J. **4**(6), 1802–1831 (2017). https://doi.org/10.1109/JIOT.2017.2703172
13. ICS Taxonomy Project: ICS taxonomy: Integrated safety and security awareness taxonomy for industrial control systems (2025). https://icstaxonomy.web.app/. Accessed 22 Jan 2026
14. International Electrotechnical Commission: IEC 62443: security for industrial automation and control systems. Technical report, International Electrotechnical Commission, Geneva, Switzerland (2013)
15. International Electrotechnical Commission: Functional safety – safety instrumented systems for the process industry sector – part 1: framework, definitions, system, hardware and application programming requirements. Technical report IEC 61511-1:2016, International Electrotechnical Commission, Geneva, Switzerland (2016)
16. Jeong, J., Mihelcic, J., Oliver, G., Rudolph, C.: Towards an improved understanding of human factors in cybersecurity. In: Proceedings of the 2019 IEEE 5th International Conference on Collaboration and Internet Computing (CIC), pp. 338–345. IEEE (2019). https://doi.org/10.1109/CIC48465.2019.00047
17. Jung, S., Yoo, J., Malek, S.: A systematic co-engineering of safety and security analysis in requirements engineering process. Int. J. Crit. Infrastruct. Prot. **43**, 100642 (2023). https://doi.org/10.1016/j.ijcip.2023.100642
18. Kriaa, S., Pietre-Cambacedes, L., Bouissou, M., Halgand, Y.: A survey of approaches combining safety and security for industrial control systems. Reliab. Eng. Syst. Saf. **139**, 156–178 (2015). https://doi.org/10.1016/j.ress.2015.02.008
19. Kruger, H.A., Kearney, W.D.: A prototype for assessing information security awareness. Comput. Secur. **25**(4), 289–296 (2006). https://doi.org/10.1016/j.cose.2006.02.008
20. Malm, T., et al.: Comparison of cybersecurity and functional safety risk assessments. Technical report VTT-R-00499-24, VTT Technical Research Centre of Finland, Finland (2024)
21. Microsoft: Elevation of privilege (EoP) threat modeling card game (2010). https://www.microsoft.com/en-us/download/details.aspx?id=20303. Accessed 14 May 2026
22. MITRE Corporation: MITRE ATT&CK for ICS (2024). https://attack.mitre.org/matrices/ics/. Accessed 14 May 2026
23. Nankya, M., Chataut, R., Akl, R.: Securing industrial control systems: components, cyber threats, and machine learning-driven defense strategies. Sensors **23**(21), 8840 (2023). https://doi.org/10.3390/s23218840
24. Nickerson, R.C., Varshney, U., Muntermann, J.: A method for taxonomy development and its application in information systems. Eur. J. Inf. Syst. **22**(3), 336–359 (2013). https://doi.org/10.1057/ejis.2012.26
25. Noy, N.F., McGuinness, D.L.: Ontology development 101: a guide to creating your first ontology. Technical report KSL-01-05, Stanford Knowledge Systems Laboratory, Stanford, CA, USA (2001)

26. Parsons, K., Calic, D., Pattinson, M., Butavicius, M., McCormac, A., Zwaans, T.: The human aspects of information security questionnaire (HAIS-Q): two further validation studies. Comput. Secur. **66**, 40–51 (2017)
27. Pascoe, C., Quinn, S., Scarfone, K.: The NIST cybersecurity framework (CSF) 2.0. Technical report, NIST CSWP 29, National Institute of Standards and Technology, Gaithersburg, MD, USA (2024). https://doi.org/10.6028/NIST.CSWP.29
28. Poppleton, A.J.: Special considerations for human factors in industrial control system security. Eng. Technol. Ref. **2016** (2016). https://doi.org/10.1049/etr.2015.0107
29. Reegård, K., Blackett, C., Katta, V.: The concept of cybersecurity culture. In: Proceedings of the 29th European Safety and Reliability Conference (ESREL). Research Publishing Services, Singapore (2019). http://rpsonline.com.sg/proceedings/9789811127243/html/0761.xml. Accessed 03 Mar 2026
30. Stouffer, K., Pillitteri, V., Lightman, S., Abrams, M., Hahn, A.: Guide to operational technology (OT) security. Technical report, NIST Special Publication 800-82 Revision 3, National Institute of Standards and Technology, Gaithersburg, MD, USA (2023). https://doi.org/10.6028/NIST.SP.800-82r3
31. Torkildson, E.N., Li, J., Johnsen, S.O., Glomsrud, J.A.: Empirical studies of methods for safety and security co-analysis. In: Safety and Reliability - Safe Societies in a Changing World (2018). https://doi.org/10.1201/9781351174664-369
32. Torkildson, E.N., Li, J., Johnsen, S.O., Glomsrud, J.A.: Improving security and safety co-analysis of STPA. In: Proceedings of the 29th European Safety and Reliability Conference (ESREL), Research Publishing, Singapore (2019)
33. Verizon Business: 2025 data breach investigations report. Technical report, Verizon (2025). https://www.verizon.com/business/resources/T16f/reports/2025-dbir-data-breach-investigations-report.pdf
34. Wulf, M.: Industrial cybersecurity and process safety: bridging IEC 61511 and IEC 62443 (2024). https://www.ors-consulting.com/industrial-cybersecurity-and-process-safety-bridging-iec-61511-and-iec-62443. Accessed 26 Feb 2026

Honeyfarm: AI-Based Honeypots for Industrial OPC UA Communication via an On-Demand Deployment Architecture

Olaf Sassnick[1,2,3(✉)], Florian Entleitner[1,2], Dalibor Sain[1,2], Thomas Rosenstatter[1,2], Andreas Unterweger[2,3], Simon Hoher[1,2], and Stefan Huber[1,2]

[1] Josef Ressel Centre for Intelligent and Secure Industrial Automation, Salzburg, Austria

[2] Salzburg University of Applied Sciences, Salzburg, Austria
olaf.sassnick@fh-salzburg.ac.at

[3] Paris Lodron University of Salzburg, Salzburg, Austria

Abstract. Cyberattacks against Operational Technology (OT) and Industrial Cyber-Physical Systems (ICPS) are continuously increasing, necessitating advanced defence mechanisms that are robust, adaptive, and resource-efficient. In this context, we propose an AI-based honeypot with an on-demand deployment architecture for ICPS communicating via OPC UA. The proposed system isolates attackers from production systems by dynamically redirecting malicious traffic to a honeypot instance, that continues from the production system state. This redirection allows continued observation without alerting the attacker while protecting the industrial system. At the core of the architecture is a generative AI model that learns ICPS behaviour from OPC UA communication data. In contrast, existing approaches typically require a manually parametrised simulation model. Our proposed approach enables automated creation of medium-interaction honeypot functionality with minimal manual effort. We further discuss generative AI model scopes and identify usable deployment points in the Purdue network model for practical integration. A proof-of-principle implementation is realised using actual industrial hardware and a fully containerised environment for the honeypot. As part of the deployment, two different firewall platforms are evaluated regarding their provided capabilities. Finally, performance results, including switchover time and interaction latency, are presented to demonstrate the practicality of the approach.

Keywords: Industrial Control Systems · Cyber-Physical Systems · Operational Technology · Security · Honeypots · Generative AI

1 Introduction

In recent years, industrial plants have evolved due to Industry 4.0 initiatives and ongoing digitalisation, leading to highly interconnected network structures.

Z. Afzal et al. (Eds.): ARES 2026 Workshops, LNCS 16900, pp. 407–425, 2027.
https://doi.org/10.1007/978-3-032-35576-8_22

This enables a higher degree of automation, allowing for better control and optimisation. Additionally, it facilitates flexible manufacturing, making the mass production of customised products possible.

However, this resulted in a drastically expanded attack surface due to the high interconnectedness of Operational Technology (OT) systems [11], with the number of cyberattacks increasing each year [5]. The motives behind cyberattacks on OT vary, for instance, monetarisation via ransomware, espionage, or sabotage by a targeted manipulation of the industrial process, with the most prominent example being Stuxnet [10]. As a result, more advanced defence mechanisms are required, while still respecting the distinct requirements of OT equipment (e.g., real-time requirements, safety requirements, and minimal downtime).

Honeypots are a well-established security technique for detecting and analysing cyberattacks [1]. On-demand deployment is an alternative to permanent honeypots, where decoy systems are instantiated only during suspected threats or active reconnaissance. This approach shifts the honeypot usage from a detection-oriented mechanism towards an early defence mechanism. It offers the advantage that upon activation, the decoy can be tailored to mimic the targeted OT system for a suspected attacker, while the real OT system is simultaneously isolated from the attacker. Ideally, the attacker's interactions are seamlessly transferred to the honeypot. This strategy provides defenders with time to analyse the attacker's entry methods and activities while continuously monitoring their behaviour, which may also yield insights towards their attack objectives. To make such a deployment effective, the interaction time between the attacker and the honeypot must be maximised. The interaction time depends on the honeypot's level of authenticity, as attackers are likely to abandon the network if they suspect they are interacting with a decoy.

To create authentic honeypots for OT systems, they must also replicate the behaviour of an Industrial Cyber-Physical System (ICPS), which interacts with physical processes. One method to achieve this involves integrating simulations into the honeypot, though this approach requires parametrisation and expert knowledge of the underlying processes. An alternative approach leverages generative AI, offering a scalable solution that demands minimal setup resources. Here, a machine learning model autonomously learns to mimic the behaviour of an observed existing ICPS. This method also provides greater flexibility, as it can mimic any ICPS without requiring domain-specific expertise.

Ultimately, rather than deploying a single honeypot, this work envisions a *honeynet* that replicates a live production environment, as illustrated in Fig. 1. This configuration enables attackers to navigate the network and interact with ICPS as they would in an actual production environment, thereby enhancing the authenticity of the decoy. The approach combines two key security principles: sandboxing for isolation and honeypot technology for deception.

Contributions. This work investigates the potential of AI-based honeypots combined with on-demand deployment strategies. We present a proof-of-principle implementation demonstrating honeypot interactions with attackers via Open Platform Communications Unified Architecture (OPC UA), and discuss considerations for honeypot placement. While Maesschalck et al. [9] survey honeypot fit within Industrial Control System (ICS) security architectures and Honey-PLC [13] discusses honeypot deployment, neither provides a consolidated recommendation framework that simultaneously accounts for interaction level, deployment mode (permanent vs. on-demand), and Purdue model. This work addresses that specific gap. Furthermore, we introduce *Honeyfarm*, an architecture for dynamic honeypot deployment that activates decoy systems upon detection of suspicious activity. Our evaluation examines two *Honeyfarm* variants, which are distinguished by firewall capabilities, to provide comprehensive performance metrics, including system responsiveness.

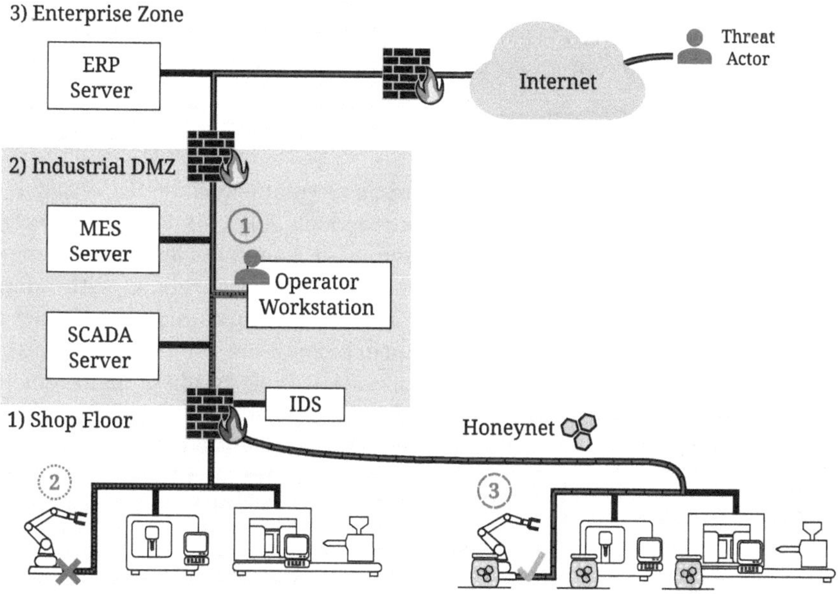

Fig. 1. Overview of a simplified industrial network separated in three zones: the enterprise zone for business operations, the IDMZ as a bridging layer between IT and OT, and the shop floor with a production line. The figure further illustrates the concept of an on-demand honeynet deployment scenario in three steps: (1) an attacker gains remote access to an operator workstation, (2) suspicious interactions by the attacker with the shop floor are detected by an IDS, and (3) the IDS initiates a honeynet and redirects the attacker, as an early response measure, enabling temporary deception and isolation.

2 Background

2.1 Honeypots

Spitzner defines a honeypot as "a security resource whose value lies in being probed, attacked, or compromised" [24]. Depending on the purpose, two types of honeypots exist: research and production honeypots. Research honeypots mainly exist to collect data regarding attacks. Production honeypots, on the other hand, are typically coupled to an Intrusion Detection System (IDS) with the goal to improve the overall attacker detection rate. Commonly, a honeypot is deployed mimicking a valuable asset with low security measures, where consequently any kind of interaction is suspicious. Another way to classify honeypots is the level of possible interaction, where low-, mid-, and high-interaction honeypots (LIH, MIH, HIH) are defined. For a low-interaction type it might be sufficient to replay data streams recorded from the existing real system, while for high-interaction honeypots, the intention is to give the attacker full access to the underlying operating system [24]. In between situated are mid-interaction honeypots, which allow a higher degree of interaction than low-interaction honeypots, but where the interaction with the attacker is intended to be restricted to some kind of fake daemon [18], which later on in our case is represented by an OPC UA server.

2.2 Industrial Networks

ICSs typically adopt zone-based architectures, as recommended by IEC 62443 [7]. The model in this work simplifies the Purdue model [26], a six-level framework, by combining, for instance, the process and basic control layers into a single shop floor level, as illustrated in Fig. 1. This simplification aligns with adaptations of the Purdue model under IEC 62443, where zones may be merged if security requirements are preserved. The **enterprise zone** connects to both the internet and the IDMZ, hosting business operations, like business management software. To retrieve plant data (e.g., production metrics and status updates), these systems access information through the IDMZ [7,8]. The **IDMZ** serves as a secure intermediary zone, hosting the Supervisory Control and Data Acquisition (SCADA) system that monitors, coordinates, and controls shop floor operations. Operators can oversee processes and implement adjustments via Human-Machine Interfaces (HMIs) [7,8]. The **shop floor** contains the ICPSs (i.e., production machines), alongside actuators and sensors. Programmable Logic Controllers (PLCs) in this zone execute real-time control programmes and interface directly with actuators and sensors [8].

Open Platform Communications Unified Architecture. As illustrated in Fig. 1, the communication in the shop floor and to the SCADA system is based on OPC UA. OPC UA is the successor of the OPC standard and standardised in IEC 62541. It has become widely adopted in new products for industrial environments. Reasons for that being that it is platform-independent, secure-by-design and employs a service-oriented architecture. Moreover, OPC UA supports both, client-server and publish-subscriber as communication model allowing to cover a wide range of use cases [15]. The utilised information model is composed of nodes, i.e., objects, variables, methods, and events, including the references that define their relationships. These nodes are structured within the address space of an OPC UA server. The servers expose the information model, which enables access operations such as reading and writing variable values and invoking defined methods. Each OPC UA node is also uniquely identifiable through a combination of its URI and a distinct node identifier [15]. Having this comprehensive way of representing data and the ability to directly interact with named variables and methods allows attackers to gain much faster understanding (compared to Modbus) of the system. Hence, the servers need to be properly secured against unauthorised access and manipulation. OPC UA employs a security model in two layers. The communication layer utilises TCP/IP and TLS to provide basic security requirements like authenticity and confidentiality, and its application layer offers additionally authentication and authorisation for securing the information model [15].

2.3 Existing Works

Existing works relevant to this paper can be grouped mainly into categories: generative AI models for honeypots in OT/ICS environments, and on-demand honeypot deployment approaches. Shan et al. [23] propose NeuPot, a neural network-based ICS honeypot that combines malicious traffic detection with a time-series forecasting model to generate realistic physical-process values. However, the generated process evolves independently of attacker actions, and attacker-induced manipulation of the process state is not considered. Vasilatos et al. [25] employ large language models to emulate industrial protocols, PLC control logic, and physical-process behaviour. Their approach focuses on protocol-level interaction, whereas our work provides interaction at the physical-process level for the attacker. Furthermore, neither work considers automated on-demand deployment within operational OT environments. Regarding on-demand deployment, Park et al. [16] present DVNH, a system that instantiates a new honeypot via NFV and redirects traffic through SDN as soon as a network IDS raises an alert. While conceptually related, DVNH targets IT environments and does not address OT-specific protocols or system state continuity upon switchover. Acosta et al. [2] describe CDES, which redirects live traffic using Open vSwitch and container isolation. Similarly to DVNH, CDES is designed for general-purpose and resource-constrained environments, without consideration of industrial protocols or production system state initialisation. While existing on-demand honeypot approaches do not consider OT-specific requirements such as a transferable system state upon switchover, and AI-based honeypots in the OT-domain have not yet explored on-demand deployment, this work proposes an on-demand architecture for OPC UA-based industrial systems that contributes to both research directions.

3 Research Design

This section describes the research design used to explore the proposed AI-based honeypot approach for an ICPS. Two research questions (RQs) are defined to guide this work:

RQ1 How can an AI-based honeypot be designed for an industrial CPS communicating via OPC UA considering attacks on industrial-process-level?

RQ2 How can the on-demand deployment of an AI-based honeypot be realised in an industrial network?

Overall, the research questions are studied in three stages. First, relevant design considerations are laid out and supported by existing literature. In the second stage, the proposed solutions are described on a conceptual level, while in the third stage, the concrete experimental setup is detailed and results are given. *RQ1* focuses on the design of the AI-based honeypot itself. Design considerations regarding the AI-based model are discussed (Sect. 4.1), followed by a description of the implementation (Sect. 5.1) and a performance evaluation of the deployed generative model is provided (Sect. 7). *RQ2* addresses the deployment of honeypots in industrial network environments such as ICS. First, the placement of honeypots in industrial networks is discussed (Sect. 4.2). Then, a proof-of-principle implementation of an on-demand deployment mechanism is presented (Sect. 5.2) including the details of the hardware and software components used in the experiment setup (Sect. 6). Finally, the proof-of-principle is evaluated focusing on the timing of the deployment process (Sect. 7).

4 Design Considerations

4.1 AI-Based Model Design Spaces for Honeypots

When implementing generative AI models for ICPS honeypots, the intended capabilities for interaction with the attacker must be defined at first. Table 1 provides an overview of the interaction capabilities considered, categorised in four interaction levels ranging from raw network packets to the physical process state. The interaction levels only consider active attacker interactions and malicious system manipulation. Passive reconnaissance and data collection can occur through the same interfaces, but only requires a lower level of interaction.

The capability of a generative model to operate at the adversarial interaction levels listed in Table 1 depends on its design space. The model design space defines the input and output dimensions in which the model operates. Originally, it was proposed in the context of human-computer interaction to categorize interfaces for applications of generative models [14]. In this work, we adapt the concept to the interaction between an attacker and a generative-model-based honeypot. A honeypot model can operate at varying levels of abstraction, ranging from the network-socket level to a closely physics-bound level:

Communication Interface Level. The generative model operates on raw communication exchanges observed at the ICPS interface. Depending on the deployment scenario, they may originate from network traffic (such as TCP/IP and UDP packets), fieldbus communication, serial data frames, etc. The model learns ICPS communication patterns directly from message observations and can be trained and respond to malformed messages, invalid payloads, and other communication-layer attacks. A published work on this level can be found in [25].

Functions such as message encryption, transport mechanisms, integrity checks, and protocol-specific parsing may still be handled externally.

Protocol Level. The generative model processes de-serialised protocol messages such as Modbus, Profibus, or OPC UA. The model can learn protocol semantics based on decoded messages and recognise malicious or invalid protocol interactions, which intend to affect the server logic. Examples include write requests to read-only values, invalid message sequences, or referencing non-existing nodes.

Operational Level. The generative model learns the expected operating behaviour of the ICPS based on the variables exposed through the protocol interface. These variables can represent different types of system state, including purely cyber-state information (for example operating mode, number of produced items, power cycles, or computed wear indicators, firmware version) and as well as values derived from the physical process (for example temperature, actuator voltage, oil pressure, spindle speed). The model learns cross-dependencies between variables and plausible operating ranges. Consequently, its interaction capability with an attacker is to respond plausibly to malicious system inputs. Published implementations can be found in [23] or [21].

Physical Process Level. The generative model learns the underlying behaviour of the physical components present in the ICPS. As such, it operates on variables that describe the physical state of the system. An example would be a honeypot internally based on a NeuralODE [4], which, by learning the derivative of the state-space vector, is naturally well suited to describe physical processes.

Table 1. Active attacker interaction levels that the generative honeypot model can be trained for, ranging from the Communication Interface to the Physical Process level.

Level	Name	Examples
1	Comm. Interface	Malformed messages/packets/frames, invalid payloads
2	Protocol	Invalid requests, forged commands, wrong message sequences
3	Operational	Invalid parameter values, unexpected configuration states
4	Physical Process	Unsafe process trajectories, increased physical system degradation, reduced product quality

Table 2 summarises the input and output dimensions of the presented model spaces and maps them to the possible attacker interaction levels from Table 1. The most universal model can be realised on communication interface level, which however as downside can be expected to have the highest complexity and to require the most training. With each level above the model design space

Table 2. Comparison of input and output dimensions for the different model spaces.

Model Design Space Level	Input	Output	Attacker Interact.
Comm. Interface	Raw communication observations	Raw communication responses	Level 1–4
Protocol	Deserialised message observations	Protocol-specific responses	Level 2–4
Operational	Cyber-physical state observations	Cyber-physical state trajectories	Level 3–4
Physical Process	Physical state observations	Physical state trajectories	Level 4

is shrinking, potentially reducing the model size and increasing its robustness, however also limiting its usage possibilities and requiring additional external components to realise a functional honeypot as also visualized in Fig. 2. Alternatively, instead of a single generative model, combining multiple specialized models may also can be a viable approach. For this work, as focus is on attacks targeting the industrial process level, as indicated by *RQ1*, the model design space at the operational level provides a balance between model complexity and the requirement for additional external components.

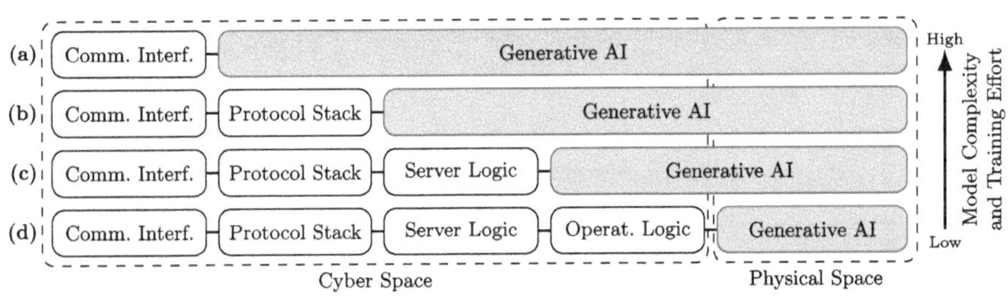

Fig. 2. Illustration of model design space choices for generative AI models as honeypots for cyber-physical systems (CPSs). (a) is at Communication Interface level, (b) operates at Protocol level, (c) at Operational level and (d) at Physical Process level.

4.2 Placement Criteria for Honeypots in Industrial Networks

The placement of honeypots in industrial networks requires careful consideration of visibility to potential attackers, risk to productive operations, and the quality of the data obtained. In this section we investigate the strategic placement of permanent and on-demand honeypots within OT systems (*RQ2*). Honeypots are often located in a segmented area such as the IDMZ, however, this placement does not reflect all scenarios for placing honeypots in a productive environment. For instance, the placement differs when considering on-demand or permanent honeypots as well as when taking their interaction-level into account. In Table 3 we provide a recommendation for the placement of honeypots in industrial networks based on their interaction-level, deployment mode, and location (consolidated Purdue zones).

Permanent Honeypot Deployment. As summarised in Table 3, the suitability of honeypot deployment varies across network zones. In the enterprise zone, low- and medium-interaction honeypots are well suited, e.g., for simulating email or web services [6], whereas HIHs are not recommended due to their lack of OT relevance and increased attack surface. The IDMZ is often described in the literature as the ideal location for low- and medium-interaction honeypots, as it is already designed to detect targeted ICS scans without compromising the production environment [6,13]. High-interaction variants are only acceptable in specific scenarios in which a complex OT system can be mimicked. On the shop floor, LIHs can serve as early warning systems in isolated test zones [22], while medium- and high-interaction honeypots are not recommended.

Table 3. Recommended honeypot placement based on their interaction-level in OT.

Deployment Mode	Location	LIH	MIH	HIH
Permanent	Enterprise Zone	+	+	–
	Industrial DMZ	+	+	o
	Shop Floor	o	–	–
On-Demand	Enterprise Zone	+	o	–
	Industrial DMZ	+	+	o
	Shop Floor	+	+	o

Note: (+) Recommended, (o) Limited suitability, (–) Not recommended.

On-Demand Honeypot Deployment. The placement recommendations for on-demand honeypots (see Table 3) reflect the varying suitability across network zones for on-demand deployments. In the enterprise zone, low-interaction on-demand honeypots can be activated at short notice in response to an increased threat level, while medium-interaction variants should only be deployed selectively. High-interaction variants are not recommended, as their safe deployment requires extensive provisioning, segmentation, and monitoring that cannot be reliably ensured under the time constraints inherent to on-demand activation [2]. The IDMZ is described by several studies [2,17] as the optimal location for forensic analysis and active deception, particularly at a medium level of interaction, with high-interaction honeypots being permissible only under strict monitoring, segmentation, and patching, given the elevated risk of compromise and lateral movement [12] when sophisticated adversaries are already actively present in the network. On the shop floor, low-interaction honeypots may serve as temporary deception systems, medium-interaction variants are only advisable under strict monitoring and thorough segmentation [9]. High-interaction honeypots should be reserved for highly controlled scenarios, such as during an active attack provided that operational isolation is in place as a compromised HIH can be a significant risk to the entire network, especially to the OT systems [19].

5 Implementation

5.1 Generative Model with Operational Level Design Space

As discussed in Sect. 4.1, an AI-based honeypot can be realised in different design spaces. As we previously selected the operational level design space, a multivariate time-series forecasting model can be used to learn the ICPS behaviour. This section provides an overview of the implementation and training procedure for such a honeypot. When implementing a honeypot using the operational level design space, the protocol stack and the system interface are to be provided externally. As protocol stack, any kind of OPC UA library can be used. The system interface can be generated automatically by traversing the interface of the real ICPS.

Consequently, three steps are required. During the first step, **pre-training**, the interface of the real ICPS is traversed and an interface description is constructed. In the **training** step, a dataset is built by monitoring the interface and sampling data at a fixed sampling frequency F_s. The resulting dataset is then used to train the generative model. The **deployment** describes the step in which the real interface is cloned based on the previously generated interface description.

Typically time-series forecasting models receive an input consisting of n time steps with m variables (the *lookback*) and generate an output horizon of h future time steps with the same m variables [3]. As the honeypot operates in isolation after receiving the initial input from the real ICPS, a recursive forecasting strategy is applied. With this strategy, each generated horizon is subsequently reused as part of the next lookback. At the program level, the honeypot can be implemented using a producer-consumer pattern with two threads and a shared queue.

The **producer thread** is responsible for the forecasting process. In this thread, the forecasting model repeatedly generates output horizons of length h and pushes them into the shared queue. The sampling frequency of the training data F_s determines the timing constraints of the system with the required generation frequency given by $F_{gen} = \frac{F_s}{h}$.

In the **consumer thread**, the OPC UA server is concurrently operated. It reads new values from the shared queue at frequency F_s and publishes them to the OPC UA interface.

To enable interaction between an attacker and the generative model, a second shared queue is used as a feedback channel. The consumer thread pushes any received OPC UA method calls into this queue. The producer thread periodically checks this queue at frequency F_{gen} and modifies the lookback window accordingly to incorporate input by the attacker.

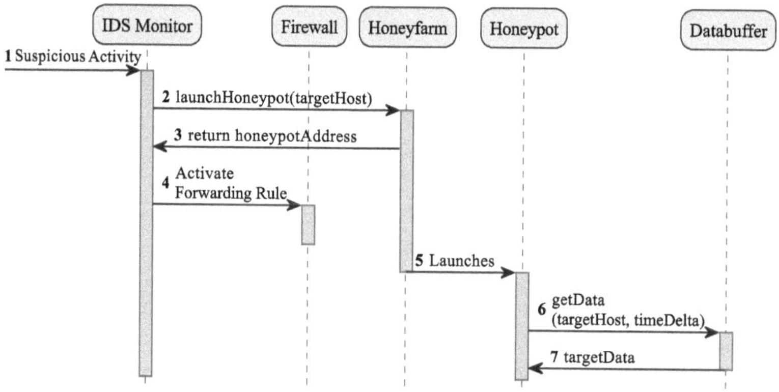

Fig. 3. The deployment sequence for an on-demand honeypot.

5.2 On-Demand Deployment via Honeyfarm

The on-demand deployment of honeypots requires the orchestration of several components. The **IDS monitor** continuously receives all new events logged by the IDS. Once suspicious behaviour towards a target host for which a honeypot is available is received, the IDS monitor can forward the information to the Honeyfarm. The **firewall** dynamically enforces network-level forwarding rules. Via an API, a Destination Network Address Translation (DNAT) rule can be activated, which can be used to replace the destination IP address in network packets. This way suspicious traffic can be redirected to a honeypot. The **Honeyfarm** is the component responsible for managing honeypot instances. It provides an API that allows to request the creation and deployment of a honeypot. The Honeyfarm launches a honeypot instance and manages its lifecycle. Lastly, the **data buffer** provides the recent system state of the real ICPS, which is initially required for the honeypot to resume the behaviour of the real ICPS. The data buffer subscribes to or continuously polls all relevant nodes of the OPC UA interface and maintains a history of the observed ICPS state. The honeypot can retrieve the latest system data through an API in order to initialise its internal state. Figure 3 illustrates the on-demand deployment process as a sequence diagram. It starts with the IDS monitor identifying an attack. The IDS monitor consequently requests a honeypot from the Honeyfarm, including the target host information. The Honeyfarm starts the launching process of the honeypot and returns the honeypot address to the IDS monitor. Consequently, the IDS monitor activates a DNAT rule redirecting the source of the suspicious activity to the honeypot. All other traffic from the source is blocked to guard the network segment. After the honeypot itself is initialised, it requests the latest state from the data buffer, passing along the target host name, as the data buffer can be responsible for multiple ICPS. The data buffer responds with the latest data, which is then forwarded internally in the honeypot to the generative AI model as initial input. In its current implementation, the honeypot needs to be manually stopped upon inspection, and the number of instantiable honeypots is limited by the Honeyfarm to avoid overload.

6 Experiment Setup

The threat model considered in this scenario is an attacker who gains access to an operator workstation located in the IDMZ, e.g., through social engineering or exploiting a vulnerability. The attacker, in turn, tries to gather information about the OPC UA devices located in the shop floor. Thus, the attacker creates an abnormal number of OPC UA connection requests to the OPC UA server, which ultimately triggers the IDS leading to traffic redirection to an instantiated on-demand honeypot. The on-demand activation process for activating the honeypot is evaluated across two different firewalls, which are denoted in the following as firewall A and firewall B. **Firewall A** is combined with an externally hosted Snort IDS, where detection events are relayed to the firewall via a remote REST API. Snort operates on a separate Windows host in the IDMZ and receives traffic via a port mirror on the shop floor switch. In comparison, **firewall B** uses Suricata IDS running directly on the firewall, activating the redirect rule locally. **ICPS1 and ICPS2 with PLCs** simulate the industrial processes being attacked. Both implement the same cyclic procedure and provide an OPC UA interface, where 8 variables are exposed, and additionally method calls are available for the attacker to interact with the Cyber-Physical System (CPS). The cyclic procedure trajectories origin from an actuator resembling a pick-and-place process with two degrees of freedom, and contain actual yaw and pitch angles (Θ, Ψ), actual yaw and pitch angular velocities ($\dot{\Theta}$, $\dot{\Psi}$), and target yaw and pitch angles (Θ_T, Ψ_T), representing the programmed procedure. The **data buffer** is used to collect data from the ICPS1 and ICPS2, which is internally stored in a Redis database. Alternatively, the data could be queried

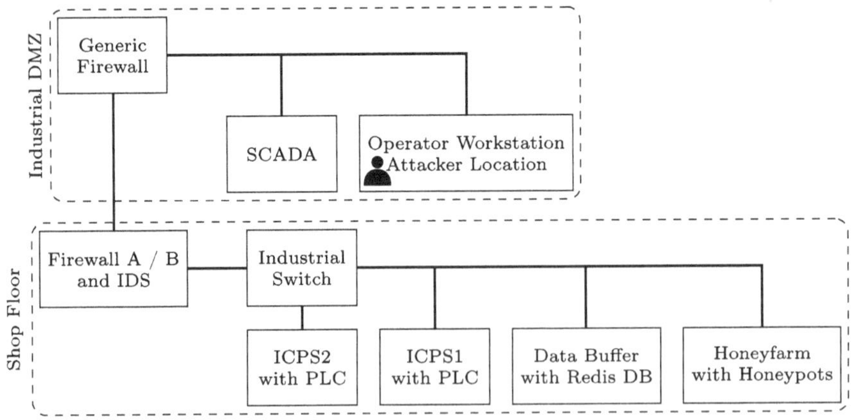

Fig. 4. Overview of the deployment setup of Honeyfarm.

from an existing OPC UA historian. The **honeypot** is implemented according to Sect. 5.1. The training data is sampled at $F_s = 100$ Hz. The generative AI-model is of Crossformer architecture [27] and is configured with 1600 value lookback and 400 value lookahead. It is trained using a two-pass strategy with data augmentation in the second pass, as described in [20], to improve stability. Finally, the **Honeyfarm** manages all Honeypot instances. The deployment setup of the proof-of-principle depicted in Fig. 4 is based on a simplified three layer industrial network (see Sect. 2.2). The Honeyfarm, honeypot, and data buffer share the same host, all running within isolated virtual Docker containers. The host system is equipped with an Intel i5-6400 processor, an NVIDIA RTX A2000 GPU, and a consumer SATA3 SSD. Time synchronisation across all systems is ensured using a network time protocol (NTP).

7 Results and Analysis

The on-demand activation process is evaluated across two different firewall architectures (see Sect. 6). All measurements were collected over $n = 100$ repeated runs per architecture under identical conditions, using an Nmap port scan against the OPC UA port of a PLC. The port scan is only used as an example, as the IDS itself is not in the focus of this work. The on-demand activation process is further separated into six individually timed phases: The *IDS detection delay* spans from the first packet of the Nmap scan until the IDS logs an alert. The *firewall rule triggering* time covers the period from the logged alert until the firewall acknowledges the redirect command. This follows the *DNAT activation time* measuring how long the firewall requires to apply the redirect rule after receiving the command. In firewall A this is the time of receiving a REST API call and internally activating and loading the redirection rule. In firewall B the rule is written directly into an anchor via a local shell command. The *honeypot startup time* spans from the API trigger received at the honeypot until the Docker container has started successfully. The *honeypot setup time* covers the remaining period until the OPC UA endpoint is reachable by the attacker. The *model generation time* measures the duration from the endpoint becoming reachable until the generative AI model finishes initialising and serves the first dynamically generated value. Table 4 presents the mean and standard deviation for each phase in the on-demand activation process over $n = 100$ runs. As the honeypot startup, honeypot setup and model generation time are entirely independent of the firewall architecture in use, the measurements for these three phases are aggregated across both test environments into a combined dataset of $n = 200$ runs. Moreover, three aggregate metrics are derived from these phases (see Table 5). The switchover time is the total duration from IDS alert to honeypot accessibility. The traffic redirection time covers the period from dispatching the DNAT trigger to the honeypot becoming reachable. The overall on-demand process time covers the full span from attack start to honeypot accessibility. All timestamps are synchronised via NTP to allow cross-host correlation.

Table 4. Results of each activation phase for both firewalls ($n = 100$ samples).

Metric	Firewall A (in ms)	Firewall B (in ms)
IDS Detection Delay	$1,942.8 \pm 558.7$	$\mathbf{126.2} \pm 46.3$
Firewall Rule Triggering	650.8 ± 36.1	$\mathbf{200.9} \pm 137.6$
DNAT Activation Time	$3,923.0 \pm 44.1$	$\mathbf{16.7} \pm 0.5$
Honeypot Startup Time	$\mathbf{566.15} \pm 30.42$	
Honeypot Setup Time	$\mathbf{7,608.95} \pm 196.66$	
Model Generation Time	$\mathbf{394.15} \pm 8.5$	

Table 5. Aggregate end-to-end timing metrics for both firewalls ($n = 100$ samples).

Metric	Firewall A (ms)	Firewall B (ms)
Overall On-Demand Process Time	$10,512.2 \pm 594.0$	$\mathbf{8,896.4} \pm 247.1$
Switchover Time	$\mathbf{8,569.5} \pm 202.0$	$8,770.2 \pm 244.4$
Traffic Redirection Time	$\mathbf{7,918.7} \pm 205.2$	$8,569.3 \pm 202.0$

The most significant architectural differences are observed in the IDS detection delay, which reduces from 1,942.8 ms for firewall A to 126.2 ms for firewall B and in the DNAT activation time, dropping from 3,923.0 ms to 16.7 ms. As the honeypot startup, setup, and model generation phases are architecture-independent, they share a combined baseline. Figures 5 and 6 show the on-demand activation process for each architecture, averaged over 100 runs.

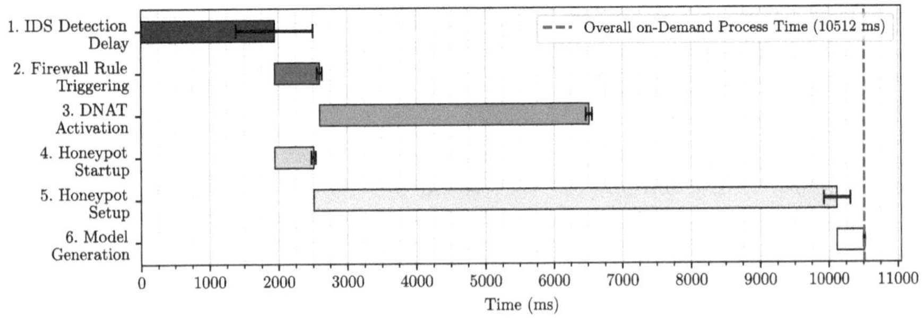

Fig. 5. On-demand activation process for firewall A ($n = 100$ samples).

For variant A the honeypot container and the firewall rule triggering are activated in parallel. The DNAT activation time starts after successful receiving the API call from the external IDS. The honeypot setup phase runs concurrently

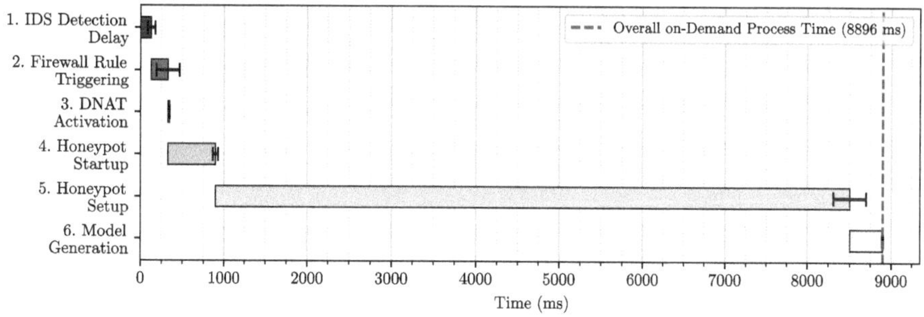

Fig. 6. On-demand activation process for firewall B ($n = 100$ samples).

and takes longer overall, making it the deciding factor for the total process time of $10,512.2 \pm 594.0$ ms. For firewall B, shown in Fig. 6, detection and rule triggering finish within approximately 126 ms and 201 ms respectively. The `pfctl` anchor is written in under 17 ms. In contrast to variant A the redirect in firewall B is activated before the honeypot startup even completes. The overall on-demand process time of $8,896.4 \pm 247.1$ ms is therefore determined almost entirely by the honeypot startup, setup, and model generation phases. Although firewall B achieves a shorter overall on-demand process time, Table 5 shows lower switchover and traffic redirection times for firewall A. This is caused by the architectural differences in the timing of the honeypot trigger. In firewall A, the slow IDS detection and rule triggering phases consume approximately 2.6 s before the DNAT trigger is dispatched. During this time, the honeypot has already been starting, so a significant portion of the startup and setup phases runs before the switchover and traffic redirection clocks even begin. In firewall B, detection and rule triggering complete in under 330 ms, meaning the honeypot has barely started when the DNAT trigger is sent. The full startup, setup, and model generation time therefore falls inside the traffic redirection measurement window. The inference time of the generative model on the host system is on average 0.34 ± 0.11 s ($n = 100$ samples). As interaction input is processed during short idle periods between inference, this also represents the lower bound of the responsiveness of the honeypot.

Visual samples of the generated data trajectories are given in Fig. 7. It shows a sample of the generative model output for the programmed procedure and an interaction sample. In both cases, data trajectories of the real CPS are provided for comparison. While the overall time characteristics remain consistent between both, as also indicated by the low MSE and MAE in Table 6, the real CPS exhibits low amplitude higher-frequency dynamics on the angular velocities ($\dot{\Theta}$, $\dot{\Psi}$), that are not captured by the generative model. A further important aspect is the long-term stability of the generative model. As a recursive forecasting strategy needs to be applied, the generative model is using its previous generated output as input subsequently. For example, a 60 s window of generated trajectories, as shown in Fig. 7 corresponds to 15 recursions. Results regarding

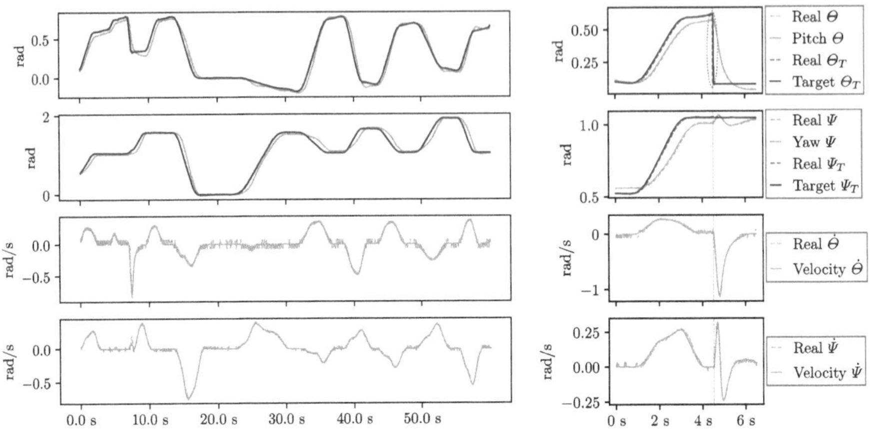

Fig. 7. Visual comparison of the honeypot with the real CPS. **Left:** The programmed procedure defines target angle trajectories Θ_T and Ψ_T. **Right:** The target angle Θ_T is overridden via a method call on the OPC UA interface by the attacker in the circled area. The system response of the real CPS, in a comparable state, is compared to the generated results. With a MAE of 0.217 and a MSE of 0.252 it represents the average quality of the generative model.

Table 6. Evaluation results for honeypot stability and interaction. Errors relative to the real CPS are reported as the mean absolute error (MAE) and mean squared error (MSE), averaged across all normalized variables recorded via an OPC UA client. Each column reports the mean ± standard deviation over $n = 100$ samples. For the stability evaluation, each sample consists of a 60 s recording collected after an increasing honeypot deployment time t_{dp} with random start time. For the interaction evaluation, the immediate response of the honeypot to the real CPS is compared to a manual input of the variable Θ_T.

	Stability			**Interaction**
Metric	$t_{dp} = 0\,s$	$t_{dp} = 200\,s$	$t_{dp} = 2000\,s$	
MAE	0.208 ± 0.005	0.209 ± 0.009	0.220 ± 0.003	0.245 ± 0.094
MSE	0.235 ± 0.014	0.242 ± 0.021	0.263 ± 0.007	0.254 ± 0.127

the stability as MAE and MSE compared to the real CPS over increased operating time are therefore presented in Table 6 as well.

8 Conclusion

This paper introduces *Honeyfarm*, a novel architecture for the on-demand deployment of AI-driven honeypots focused on OPC UA communication in ICPS. It bridges the gap of prior work by integrating generative AI-based emulation with dynamic activation in a unified framework. To address *RQ1*, four model design spaces were characterised, with the operational level design space emerging as the most practical choice for emulating ICPS behaviour without domain-specific process models. The generative model initialises from a live system state, which is provided by a data buffer, enabling seamless behavioural continuity with the real ICPS upon activation. For *RQ2*, placement guidelines were established considering interaction level, deployment mode, and a consolidated network model based on Purdue. The proof-of-principle evaluation of Honeyfarm is conducted with two different firewalls. While the honeypot container initialisation and its configuration dominate the total activation time, rather than firewall rule activation, nevertheless firewall B reduced the total process time from approximately 10.5 s (firewall A) to 8.9 s.

Future Work. While overall the proposed architecture is functional, some limitations are present, which are mainly the result of the dynamic forwarding of the attacker to the honeypot. First, currently no TCP/IP session handling is implemented for the switchover. The TCP/IP session terminates during honeypot switchover, potentially enabling the attacker to detect the redirection. To support common OPC UA security features, for example, the forwarding of existing authentication needs to be realised. Similarly, existing OPC UA node subscriptions need to be forwarded to the launched honeypot. Performance-wise, the system switchover time requires further analysis and optimisation. The primary contributing factor, the honeypot container startup time, could be reduced using higher-performance hardware and storage. An additional optimisation involves forward-streaming the data buffer to bridge the initial model generation time. However, this contributes only marginally to reducing the total switchover time. Also, the scalability of the AI model requires further exploration by deploying the honeypot to replicate more complex ICPS, e.g., a multi-axis industrial robot. Future work also could address the integration of honeypot lifecycle management with incident response workflows, including automated attack-path tracing, isolating further affected assets, and ultimately terminating the interaction with the honeypot.

Acknowledgments. The financial support by the Christian Doppler Research Association, the Austrian Federal Ministry for Digital and Economic Affairs and the Federal State of Salzburg is gratefully acknowledged. The authors would also like to thank Barracuda Networks for providing complimentary firewall licenses, which supported the experimental infrastructure used in this research.

Disclosure of Interests. The authors have no competing interests to declare that are relevant to the content of this article.

References

1. Security and privacy controls for information systems and organizations. Technical report. NIST SP 800-53 Revision 5, National Institute of Standards and Technology (2020). https://doi.org/10.6028/NIST.SP.800-53r5

2. Acosta, J.C., Basak, A., Kiekintveld, C., Kamhoua, C.: Lightweight on-demand honeypot deployment for cyber deception. In: Digital Forensics and Cyber Crime, pp. 294–312. Springer (2022). https://doi.org/10.1007/978-3-031-06365-7_18
3. Bontempi, G., Ben Taieb, S., Le Borgne, Y.-A.: Machine learning strategies for time series forecasting. In: Aufaure, M.-A., Zimányi, E. (eds.) eBISS 2012. LNBIP, vol. 138, pp. 62–77. Springer, Heidelberg (2013). https://doi.org/10.1007/978-3-642-36318-4_3
4. Chen, R.T., Rubanova, Y., Bettencourt, J., Duvenaud, D.: Neural ordinary differential equations. In: NeurIPS (2018)
5. Dragos Inc.: 2026 OT cybersecurity Year in Review: OT/ICS cybersecurity report. Technical report, Dragos (2026)
6. Fraunholz, D., Zimmermann, M., Schotten, H.D.: An adaptive honeypot configuration, deployment and maintenance strategy. In: 2017 19th Int. Conference on Advanced Communication Technology (ICACT), pp. 53–57. IEEE (2017). https://doi.org/10.23919/ICACT.2017.7890056
7. International Electrotechnical Commission: Industrial communication networks – network and system security – part 1-1: Terminology, concepts and models. Technical report. IEC/TS 62443-1-1:2009 (2009)
8. Knapp, E.D., Langill, J.T.: Industrial Network Security: Securing Critical Infrastructure Networks for Smart Grid, SCADA, and Other Industrial Control Systems. Syngress (2011). ISBN 9781597496452
9. Maesschalck, S., Giotsas, V., Green, B., Race, N.: Don't get stung, cover your ICS in honey: how do honeypots fit within industrial control system security. Comput. Secur. **114**, 102598 (2022). https://doi.org/10.1016/j.cose.2021.102598
10. Matrosov, A., Rodionov, E., Harley, D., Malcho, J.: Stuxnet under the microscope – revision 1.31. Technical report, ESET LLC (2011)
11. Miller, T., Staves, A., Maesschalck, S., Sturdee, M., Green, B.: Looking back to look forward: lessons learnt from cyber-attacks on industrial control systems. Int. J. Crit. Infrastruct. Protection **35** (2021). https://doi.org/10.1016/j.ijcip.2021.100464
12. MITRE Corporation: Lateral Movement, Tactic TA0109 – ICS ATT&CK v18 (2025). https://attack.mitre.org/versions/v18/tactics/TA0109/
13. Morales, E.L., et al.: HoneyPLC: A Next-Generation Honeypot for ICS, vol. 89, pp. 145–181. Springer (2023). https://doi.org/10.1007/978-3-031-16613-6_8
14. Morris, M.R., Cai, C.J., Holbrook, J., Kulkarni, C., Terry, M.: The Design Space of Generative Models (2023). https://doi.org/10.48550/arXiv.2304.10547
15. OPC Foundation: OPC unified architecture—part 1: Overview and concepts. Technical report. OPC 10000-1 v1.05, OPC Foundation (2025). https://reference.opcfoundation.org/10000-1/
16. Park, B., Dang, S.P., Noh, S., Yi, J., Park, M.: Dynamic virtual network honeypot. In: 2019 Int. Conference on Information and Communication Tech. Convergence (ICTC), pp. 375–37 (2019). https://doi.org/10.1109/ICTC46691.2019.8939791
17. Pittman, J.M., Hoffpauir, K., Markle, N., Meadows, C.: A taxonomy for dynamic honeypot measures of effectiveness (2020). https://doi.org/10.48550/arXiv.2005.12969
18. Pouget, F., Dacier, M., Debar, H.: White paper: honeypot, honeynet, honeytoken: terminological issues. Rapport technique EURECOM **1275** (2003)
19. Salazar, L., López-Morales, E., Lozano, J., Rubio-Medrano, C., Cárdenas, A.A.: ICSNet: a hybrid-interaction honeynet for industrial control systems. In: Proc. 6th Workshop on CPS&IoT Security and Privacy, pp. 68–79. ACM (2024). https://doi.org/10.1145/3690134.3694813

20. Saßnick, O., Rosenstatter, T., Unterweger, A., Huber, S.: Deep learning-based time series forecasting for industrial discrete process data. In: 8th IEEE Conf. on Ind. CPS (ICPS). IEEE (2025). https://doi.org/10.1109/ICPS65515.2025.11087869
21. Saßnick, O., Schäfer, G., Rosenstatter, T., Huber, S.: A generative model based honeypot for industrial OPC UA communication. In: Computer Aided Systems Theory – EUROCAST 2024 (2024). https://doi.org/10.48550/arXiv.2410.21574
22. Serbanescu, A.V., Obermeier, S., Yu, D.Y.: A flexible architecture for industrial control system honeypots. In: Proc. 12th Int. Conf. Security and Cryptography, pp. 16–26. SCITEPRESS (2015). https://doi.org/10.5220/0005522500160026
23. Shan, Y., Yao, Y., Zhao, T., Yang, W.: Neupot: a neural network-based honeypot for detecting cyber threats in industrial control systems. IEEE Trans. Industrial Informatics **19**(10), 10512–10522 (2023). https://doi.org/10.1109/TII.2023.3240739
24. Spitzner, L.: Honeypots: Tracking Hackers. Addison-Wesley (2003). ISBN 9780321108951
25. Vasilatos, C., Mahboobeh, D.J., Lamri, H., Alam, M., Maniatakos, M.: LLMPot: dynamically configured LLM-based honeypot for industrial protocol and physical process emulation. In: 10th European Symposium on Security and Privacy, pp. 963–979. IEEE (2025). https://doi.org/10.1109/EuroSP63326.2025.00059
26. Williams, T.J.: A Reference Model for Computer Integrated Manufacturing (CIM): A Description from the Viewpoint of Industrial Automation. Instrument Society of America (1989). http://www.pera.net/Pera/PurdueReferenceModel/ReferenceModel.htm. cIM Reference Model Committee, International Purdue Workshop on Industrial Computer Systems
27. Zhang, Y., Yan, J.: CrossFormer: transformer utilizing cross-dimension dependency for multivariate time series forecasting. In: International Conference on Learning Representations (2023)

Proceedings of the First Workshop on Security, Availability, and Fault-Tolerance in Edge AI Systems (SAFE-EDGE 2026)

SAFE-EDGE 2026 Preface

The First International Workshop on Security, Availability, and Fault-Tolerance in Edge AI Systems (SAFE-EDGE 2026) was held in conjunction with the 21st International Conference on Availability, Reliability and Security (ARES 2026) in Linköping, Sweden.

Artificial Intelligence (AI) is increasingly moving from centralized cloud infrastructures toward distributed edge environments to support real-time decision making in cyber-physical systems, Industrial Internet of Things (IIoT), intelligent transportation, healthcare, smart cities, and other critical infrastructures. While edge intelligence offers significant benefits in terms of latency, scalability, bandwidth efficiency, and privacy preservation, it also introduces new challenges related to security, availability, and fault tolerance. Ensuring dependable operation under hardware failures, network disruptions, adversarial attacks, resource constraints, and dynamic operating conditions has therefore become one of the most important research challenges in modern distributed AI systems.

SAFE-EDGE was established to provide a dedicated forum for researchers and practitioners from academia and industry to discuss recent advances in resilient edge intelligence. The workshop focuses on architectural, algorithmic, and system-level approaches for designing secure, trustworthy, and dependable Edge AI systems. The workshop aims to bridge research communities working in distributed systems, cybersecurity, dependable computing, machine learning, and cyber-physical systems. The workshop covers a broad range of topics including secure Edge AI architectures, availability and reliability models, fault-tolerant AI inference, adversarial machine learning, intrusion detection, confidential computing, trusted execution environments, trust management, secure federated learning, privacy-preserving AI computation, self-healing systems, dependable cyber-physical systems, and Edge AI applications for critical infrastructures.

The inaugural SAFE-EDGE workshop received nine submissions. Each submission underwent a rigorous double-blind peer-review process and was independently reviewed by two members of the Technical Program Committee. Based on the reviewers' recommendations, four papers were accepted, four papers were rejected, and one paper was withdrawn, resulting in an acceptance rate of 44.4%. The accepted papers cover secure edge architectures, dependable distributed intelligence, resilient AI deployment, trustworthy cyber-physical systems, and privacy-preserving edge computing.

The workshop program was designed to encourage discussions among researchers working on dependable distributed AI systems and to foster collaborations between the security, distributed systems, and artificial intelligence communities.

We sincerely thank the ARES 2026 General Chairs, Workshop Chairs, the Springer Nature LNCS editorial team, the Technical Program Committee members for their constructive reviews, and all authors for contributing to the success of the inaugural SAFE-EDGE workshop. We hope these proceedings stimulate further research toward secure, available, fault-tolerant, and trustworthy Edge AI systems.

August 2026

Dinesh Kumar Sah
Hossein Fotouhi
Kapal Dev

SAFE-EDGE 2026 Organization

Workshop Chairs

Dinesh Kumar Sah	University of Oulu, Finland
Hossein Fotouhi	Mälardalen University, Sweden
Kapal Dev	Munster Technological University, Ireland

Program Committee

Satish Srirama	University of Hyderabad, India
Sindri Magnússon	Stockholm University, Sweden
Chinmaya Dehury	University of Tartu, Estonia
Naser Hossain Motlagh	University of Helsinki, Finland
Ekaterina Gilman	University of Oulu, Finland
Andrea Morichetta	TU Wien, Austria
Pablo Fernandez	Universidad de Sevilla, Spain
Amir Ali-Pour	ETS Montréal, Canada
Gabriele Morabito	University of Messina, Italy
Jafar A. Alzubi	Al-Balqa Applied University, Jordan
Rani Kumari	Hanken School of Economics, Finland
Amardeep Kumar	University of Oulu, Finland

Adaptive AI Task Partitioning and Safe Offloading in Heterogeneous Edge-Cloud Continuum

Akuen Akoi Deng, Eimantas Butkus, Alfreds Lapkovskis, and Praveen Kumar Donta(✉)

Department of Computer and Systems Sciences, Stockholm University, Borgarfjordsgatan 12, Stockholm, Sweden
{alfreds.lapkovskis,praveen}@dsv.su.se

Abstract. In recent years, the use of artificial intelligence on resource-constrained IoT devices has grown significantly. However, existing approaches to AI task partitioning and offloading across the edge-cloud continuum typically rely on static methods that ignore runtime dynamics. Furthermore, they are often evaluated in simulated environments rather than on real hardware. To address this gap, we propose a framework that dynamically splits neural network layers across the heterogeneous continuum. The framework profiles the model at startup, measures network link conditions between nodes, and periodically re-evaluates the partition to adapt to environmental changes. We created a physical testbed comprising a Raspberry Pi edge device, a laptop fog, and a high-performance desktop PC as the cloud. We evaluated the framework over three widely adopted convolutional neural networks: VGG16, AlexNet, and MobileNetV2. Our results show that the framework achieves reductions in energy and end-to-end latency of 27.09–35.82% and 6.34–22.92%, respectively, compared to a static partitioning baseline. These findings confirm the superiority of adaptive to static partitioning.

Keywords: Model Partitioning · Edge Computing · Distributed Inference · Computing Continuum · Internet of Things · Safe Task Offloading

1 Introduction

In recent years, the widespread adoption of Internet-of-Things (IoT) devices has led to unprecedented growth in the volume, velocity, and variety of data generated [1,6,15]. These devices range from smartphones and wearables to RFID readers and tablets, increasingly supporting applications with strict requirements for latency, energy efficiency, and computational workload [1,14], such

A. A. Deng and E. Butkus—These authors contributed equally to this work.

Z. Afzal et al. (Eds.): ARES 2026 Workshops, LNCS 16900, pp. 431–446, 2027.
https://doi.org/10.1007/978-3-032-35576-8_23

as smart homes, robotics, virtual reality, autonomous driving, and M2M communications [9,15]. Simultaneously, rapid advancements in artificial intelligence (AI), specifically deep neural networks (DNNs), have enabled fast and sophisticated data-driven decision-making across diverse fields [3,18].

Traditionally, AI models have been deployed and executed in a centralized environment, such as the cloud, which provides abundant computational resources. However, this approach introduces significant limitations when applied to IoT systems [1]. In an IoT environment, network latency, privacy concerns, bandwidth constraints, and poor connectivity can significantly degrade real-time system performance [2]. This has driven the research toward a computing continuum spanning cloud, edge, fog, and IoT devices [5], where computing is increasingly distributed across these heterogeneous tiers to meet the demands of modern AI applications [19]. This approach allows some parts of the AI workload to run on edge devices alongside the central cloud servers, a model known as edge-cloud AI, promising to combine the low-latency benefits of edge computing with the scalability of the cloud [15,20,22].

However, designing adaptive and efficient AI systems for resource-constrained edge devices remains challenging due to the inherent heterogeneity of the edge-cloud environment, where devices vary widely in computational capability, energy budget, and network conditions [4,16]. To address this, researchers have explored distributed training, deployment, and inference of AI models across heterogeneous nodes [4,10,12].

In distributed inference, AI workloads are split across edge and cloud devices, allowing latency-critical tasks to execute close to the data source while more computationally intensive operations are offloaded to the cloud [23,24]. However, most current approaches rely on static deployment with predefined inference pipelines that do not adapt to runtime changes. Factors such as fluctuating bandwidth, workload contention, and node mobility make fixed partitioning decisions inefficient in dynamic environments [1], frequently resulting in performance degradation. This motivates the need for an adaptive partitioning and offloading framework that dynamically distributes AI workloads across edge-cloud resources while satisfying stringent latency and energy constraints.

The literature on adaptive AI task partitioning and offloading in heterogeneous edge-cloud networks has expanded significantly in recent years [1,11,17]. Proposed approaches include reinforcement learning-based layer partitioning strategies [17,21], collaborative caching mechanisms [7], and edge-end joint parallel inference architectures [23]. However, a key limitation of many existing solutions is their reliance on simulated environments that assume ideal network conditions [11,13,21], leaving the practical performance of these methods in real-world deployments insufficiently explored.

Li et al. [11] proposed a framework that jointly optimises fine-grained DNN layer partitioning and magnitude-based channel pruning to reduce inference latency, using an LSTM-based controller trained with a policy gradient algorithm and a delay-aware reward function. Despite promising results, the evaluation was conducted entirely through simulation in an MEC environment.

Studies conducted in real environments, e.g., [7], tend to focus on metrics such as task completion time, while overlooking energy consumption and computational load balancing. Fang et al. [8] proposed EdgeDI, which compresses models via structured pruning and a lightweight attention-based convolutional block, then partitions feature-map workloads across industrial IoT devices using an execution-time-aware scheme that accounts for both computation capability and network bandwidth. While EdgeDI achieves notable inference speedups, the work focuses exclusively on inference performance, leaving energy consumption unaddressed.

These examples reflect a consistent trend in the literature: partitioning and offloading frameworks are predominantly evaluated in simulation, and energy consumption is rarely a primary design objective in heterogeneous edge-cloud environments.

This work addresses both gaps through real-world experimentation on resource-constrained hardware, proposing an adaptive partitioning and offloading framework that minimizes energy consumption without violating real-time latency constraints. Our contributions are threefold:

- We propose an adaptive partitioning and offloading framework for DNN inference across a heterogeneous edge-cloud continuum.
- We build a fully functional three-tier testbed comprising a Raspberry Pi edge device, a laptop fog node, and a high-performance PC cloud node, enabling evaluation of vertical offloading strategies on real hardware.
- We conduct real-world experiments over three widely adopted convolutional neural network (CNN) models (VGG16, AlexNet, and MobileNetV2), collecting and evaluating hardware-measured energy and latency metrics across single-device, static partitioning, and adaptive partitioning configurations.

The remainder of this paper is organized as follows. Section 2 presents the proposed adaptive partitioning framework. Section 3 describes the experimental setup and discusses the results. Section 4 concludes the paper.

2 Proposed Framework

We assume a continuum environment with an edge, fog, and a cloud node. In this architecture, inference is initiated on the edge device, intermediate DNN activations are deployed to the fog, and the remaining computations are performed on the cloud. This allows partitioning schemas with $0, \ldots, i$ layers on the edge, $i+1, \ldots, j$ layers on the fog, and $j+1, \ldots N-1$ layers on the cloud, where $1 \leq i < j < N$ are layer indices.

The proposed framework dynamically partitions and offloads CNN inference workloads across nodes to minimize energy consumption without exceeding latency limits. At runtime, the framework periodically evaluates the current partition against available resources. It only reconfigures the workload if real-time computation and communication measurements predict a more optimal split.

The framework follows a five-stage algorithmic pipeline: (i) offline profiling, (ii) two-point link probing, (iii) candidate split estimation, (iv) best candidate search, and (v) adaptive distributed inference scheduling. The following sections detail these stages.

2.1 Offline Profiling

The offline profiler runs once before any partitioning decision is made, producing two lookup tables used throughout the framework. The first is an activation size table, which records the size of the intermediate tensor in bytes at every feature boundary. For a candidate split (i, j), this gives the number of bytes the Raspberry Pi must transmit to the laptop after layer i, and the laptop must transmit to the PC after layer j. The second is a relative compute weight table, where each layer is assigned a normalized fraction of the total inference work based on a single measured execution. These weights serve as a stable reference that allows runtime measurements from a small number of probe splits to be scaled and generalized to estimate the latency and energy of any unseen partition. The offline profiling algorithm is shown in Algorithm 1.

Algorithm 1. Offline profiling of a neural network $\mathcal{N}$

Require: Pretrained network $\mathcal{N}$ with ordered feature children $\mathcal{F} = (f_0, f_1, \ldots, f_{N-1})$ and classifier head H
Ensure: Per-layer activation sizes B and relative compute weights W

$x \leftarrow \text{randn}(1, 3, 224, 224)$
for $k \leftarrow 1$ to 3 **do** ▷ warmup
    $x' \leftarrow H(\mathcal{F}(x))$
end for
$x \leftarrow \text{randn}(1, 3, 224, 224)$
for $i \leftarrow 0$ to $N - 1$ **do**
    $t_0 \leftarrow \text{now}()$
    $x \leftarrow f_i(x)$
    $T[i] \leftarrow \text{now}() - t_0$
    $B[i] \leftarrow \text{numel}(x) \cdot \text{elementSize}(x)$
end for
$t_0 \leftarrow \text{now}()$; $\_ \leftarrow H(x)$; $T[N] \leftarrow \text{now}() - t_0$
$W[k] \leftarrow T[k] \,/\, \sum_j T[j]$ for all $k \in \{0, \ldots, N\}$
return B, W

2.2 Two-Point Link Probing

With activation sizes known, the framework must also estimate the communication cost between nodes. The two-point link probe achieves this by transmitting two payloads of contrasting sizes s_1 and s_2 across each hop, repeating each transmission multiple times and averaging the round-trip times to reduce short-term timing noise. The round-trip time for a payload of size s on hop h is modeled as

Algorithm 2. Two-point link probe

Require: Hop h with round-trip function $\text{rtt}_h(s)$; sizes $s_1 \ll s_2$; repeat count r
Ensure: Link model (ω, β) where ω is fixed overhead and β is throughput in bytes/second

```
1: for s ∈ {s_1, s_2} do
2:     τ[s] ← mean({rtt_h(s) : k = 1, ..., r})
3: end for
4: if τ[s_2] ≤ τ[s_1] then return previous model ▷ malformed probe; keep stale values
5: end if
6: compute β using Eq.(2)
7: ω ← max(0, τ[s_1] − s_1/β)
8: return (ω, β)
```

$$rtt_h(s) = \omega + \frac{s}{\beta}, \tag{1}$$

where ω is the fixed communication overhead and β is the effective throughput in bytes per second. Given the averaged round-trip times $\tau[s_1]$ and $\tau[s_2]$, the throughput is estimated as

$$\beta = \frac{s_2 - s_1}{\tau[s_2] - \tau[s_1]} \tag{2}$$

and the fixed overhead as

$$\omega = \max\left(0, \tau[s_1] - \frac{s_1}{\beta}\right). \tag{3}$$

The resulting pair (ω, β) provides a concrete link model that the framework uses to predict the transfer time of any activation tensor at a given split point, as formalised in Algorithm 2.

2.3 Candidate Split Latency and Energy Estimation

For a candidate split (i, j), where i is the index of the last feature layer executed on the edge node and j is the last feature layer on the fog node, the estimator predicts end-to-end latency and energy consumption before the split is actually run. Latency is computed as the sum of three per-node computation times and two inter-node transfer times, derived from the profiled compute weights, the per-node execution rates, and the fitted link models. Energy is estimated per node by multiplying each node's compute time by its corresponding power or energy rate, where the edge node applies a fixed power model, and the fog and cloud nodes use empirical rates fitted from previous runs. The total system energy is the sum of all three contributions. Since these are estimates rather than measurements, any discrepancy between the predicted and observed values is used to refine the per-node rates in the next re-evaluation cycle, as formalized in Algorithm 3.

Algorithm 3. Estimate latency and energy of a candidate split (i, j)

Require: Candidate (i, j); per-layer compute weights W; per-node speeds $(\sigma_{\text{Pi}}, \sigma_{\text{Lap}}, \sigma_{\text{PC}})$; per-node energy rates $(\rho_{\text{Lap}}, \rho_{\text{PC}})$; link models $(\omega_{pl}, \beta_{pl})$ and $(\omega_{lp}, \beta_{lp})$; payload table B

$w_{\text{Pi}} \leftarrow \sum_{k=0}^{i} W[k]$
$w_{\text{Lap}} \leftarrow \sum_{k=i+1}^{j} W[k]$
$w_{\text{PC}} \leftarrow \sum_{k=j+1}^{N} W[k]$
$t_{\text{Pi}} \leftarrow \sigma_{\text{Pi}} \cdot w_{\text{Pi}}$; $t_{\text{Lap}} \leftarrow \sigma_{\text{Lap}} \cdot w_{\text{Lap}}$; $t_{\text{PC}} \leftarrow \sigma_{\text{PC}} \cdot w_{\text{PC}}$
$t_{pl} \leftarrow \omega_{pl} + B[i]/\beta_{pl}$
$t_{lp} \leftarrow \omega_{lp} + B[j]/\beta_{lp}$
$\hat{L} \leftarrow t_{\text{Pi}} + t_{\text{Lap}} + t_{\text{PC}} + t_{pl} + t_{lp}$
$\hat{E}_{\text{Pi}} \leftarrow P_{\text{Pi}} \cdot t_{\text{Pi}}$ ▷ P_{Pi}: fixed Pi power model (12 W)
$\hat{E}_{\text{Lap}} \leftarrow \rho_{\text{Lap}} \cdot t_{\text{Lap}}$; $\hat{E}_{\text{PC}} \leftarrow \rho_{\text{PC}} \cdot t_{\text{PC}}$
$\hat{E}_{\text{tot}} \leftarrow \hat{E}_{\text{Pi}} + \hat{E}_{\text{Lap}} + \hat{E}_{\text{PC}}$
return $(\hat{L}, \hat{E}_{\text{Pi}}, \hat{E}_{\text{tot}})$

2.4 Best Candidate Split Search

The candidate search evaluates every valid split pair (i, j), where validity requires each node to execute at least one layer, and returns the candidate that minimizes the objective score. For each candidate, the estimator is called to obtain the predicted latency and energies, after which two filters are applied. The first rejects any candidate whose predicted latency exceeds the deadline L_{max}, and the second rejects candidates whose normalized score exceeds that of the static baseline, guaranteeing the adaptive framework never produces a result worse than the baseline it is intended to improve upon. Candidates that pass both filters are scored using the weighted sum

$$S(i,j) \triangleq w_{\text{end}} \frac{\hat{E}_{\text{end}}(i,j)}{n_{\text{end}}} + w_{\text{tot}} \frac{\hat{E}_{\text{tot}}(i,j)}{n_{\text{tot}}} + w_{\text{lat}} \frac{\hat{L}(i,j)}{n_{\text{lat}}}, \tag{4}$$

where w_{end}, w_{tot}, and w_{lat} are user-defined weights, and the normalization anchors n are average values measured from probe splits run at startup. Here, $\hat{E}_{\text{end}}(i, j)$ and $\hat{E}_{\text{tot}}(i, j)$ denote the predicted edge node and total system energy respectively, and $\hat{L}(i, j)$ denotes the predicted end-to-end latency for split (i, j), as estimated by Algorithm 3. Normalization makes the score dimensionless and ensures each weight exerts a comparable influence regardless of the absolute magnitude of the underlying quantities, as formalized in Algorithm 4.

2.5 Adaptive Distributed Inference Scheduling

The adaptive scheduler orchestrates the full runtime loop across two phases, with initialization handled in phase 1 and steady-state operation in phase 2.

In phase 1a, the scheduler runs a user-defined initial split for a fixed number of inferences to record the nodes' latency and energy consumption, establishing the baseline threshold that subsequent candidates must improve upon. In phase

Algorithm 4. Find best candidate split

Require: Rates and link models (as in Alg. 3); weights $\mathbf{w} = (w_{\text{Pi}}, w_{\text{tot}}, w_{\text{lat}})$; normalization anchors $\mathbf{n} = (n_{\text{Pi}}, n_{\text{tot}}, n_{\text{lat}})$; baseline score $S^{\star}$; deadline $L_{\max}$; minimum Pi layers m; current split c

$(s^{\star}_{\text{best}}, S_{\text{best}}) \leftarrow (\textsc{None}, +\infty)$
for $(i, j) \in \{(i, j) : m-1 \leq i < j < N\}$ **do**
  if $(i, j) = c$ **then continue** ▷ exclude currently-running split
  end if
  $(\hat{L}, \hat{E}_{\text{Pi}}, \hat{E}_{\text{tot}}) \leftarrow \textsc{Estimate}(i, j, \ldots)$ ▷ Alg. 3
  if $L_{\max} > 0$ **and** $\hat{L} > L_{\max}$ **then continue** ▷ deadline pre-filter
  end if
  $S \leftarrow w_{\text{Pi}} \cdot \dfrac{\hat{E}_{\text{Pi}}}{n_{\text{Pi}}} + w_{\text{tot}} \cdot \dfrac{\hat{E}_{\text{tot}}}{n_{\text{tot}}} + w_{\text{lat}} \cdot \dfrac{\hat{L}}{n_{\text{lat}}}$
  if $S > S^{\star}$ **then continue** ▷ must beat static baseline
  end if
  if $S < S_{\text{best}}$ **then**
    $(s^{\star}_{\text{best}}, S_{\text{best}}) \leftarrow ((i, j), S)$
  end if
end for
return $s^{\star}_{\text{best}}$

1b, three additional probe splits are run automatically, selected to expose edge-heavy, balanced, and cloud-heavy workload distributions, giving the estimator sufficient data to infer per-node execution rates across a wide operating range. In phase 1c, the collected baseline and probe measurements are used to fit the per-node compute rates, probe both network links, and select the best starting split by evaluating all candidates against the objective score defined in Eq. (4). Energy terms are weighted more heavily than latency, with the edge node energy weight ranging from 0.6 to 0.9, total system energy from 0.2 to 0.3, and latency from 0.1 to 0.3, reflecting the framework's primary objective of reducing energy consumption without violating latency constraints.

In phase 2, the scheduler enters steady-state operation and runs the current split for R_{steady} inferences per window. At the end of each window, it refits the per-node compute rates using both the phase 1 data and the most recent window combined, re-probes both network links, and re-runs the candidate search with the updated parameters. A switch is made if the new candidate improves the objective score by at least 3%. If the latency deadline $L_{\max}$ is violated during a window, the switch is forced regardless of the improvement margin; if no better candidate exists under a deadline violation, the scheduler falls back to the static baseline c_0 as the safest known configuration. This periodic re-evaluation is what makes the framework adaptive, as changes in network bandwidth or node compute load are captured by the re-probing and re-fitting steps and reflected in the next candidate selection, as formalized in Algorithms 5 and 6.

Algorithm 5. Adaptive distributed inference scheduler – Initialization

Require: Model $\mathcal{N}$; initial split c_0; weights $\mathbf{w}$; deadline $L_{\max}$; R_{profile} baseline runs; R_{probe} runs per probe split; R_{steady} runs per re-evaluation window; warmup k_{warm}; switch improvement threshold θ

Phase 1a: baseline run (defines threshold to beat)

$(B, W) \leftarrow$ PROFILE($\mathcal{N}$) ▷ Alg. 1
$\mathcal{D}_{\text{base}} \leftarrow \emptyset$; $c \leftarrow c_0$
for $r \leftarrow 1$ to R_{profile} **do**
  $s \leftarrow$ RUNINFERENCE(c)
  if $r > k_{\text{warm}}$ **then** $\mathcal{D}_{\text{base}} \leftarrow \mathcal{D}_{\text{base}} \cup \{s\}$
  end if
end for
$(b_{\text{Pi}}, b_{\text{tot}}, b_{\text{lat}}) \leftarrow$ mean energies and latency over $\mathcal{D}_{\text{base}}$

Phase 1b: probe reference splits to ground per-layer rates

$\mathcal{P} \leftarrow$ PROBESPLITS(N, m) ▷ 3 splits at fifths of the feature range
$\mathcal{D}_{\text{probe}} \leftarrow \emptyset$
for all $p \in \mathcal{P} \setminus \{c_0\}$ **do**
  for $r \leftarrow 1$ to R_{probe} **do**
    $s \leftarrow$ RUNINFERENCE(p)
    if $r > k_{\text{warm}}$ **then** $\mathcal{D}_{\text{probe}} \leftarrow \mathcal{D}_{\text{probe}} \cup \{s\}$
    end if
  end for
end for

Phase 1c: fit rates, probe links, choose starting split

$\mathbf{n} \leftarrow$ mean energies and latency over $\mathcal{D}_{\text{probe}}$ ▷ normalization independent of c_0
$S^\star \leftarrow w_{\text{Pi}}(b_{\text{Pi}}/n_{\text{Pi}}) + w_{\text{tot}}(b_{\text{tot}}/n_{\text{tot}}) + w_{\text{lat}}(b_{\text{lat}}/n_{\text{lat}})$
$\sigma, \rho \leftarrow$ FITRATES($\mathcal{D}_{\text{base}} \cup \mathcal{D}_{\text{probe}}, W$)
$(\omega_{pl}, \beta_{pl}), (\omega_{lp}, \beta_{lp}) \leftarrow$ LINKPROBE() ▷ Alg. 2
$c \leftarrow$ FINDBEST($\sigma, \rho, \omega, \beta, \mathbf{w}, \mathbf{n}, S^\star, L_{\max}, m$, NONE) ▷ Alg. 4

3 Results and Discussion

This section presents the quantitative evaluation of the proposed adaptive partitioning framework against single-device and static partitioning baselines across three CNN models.

3.1 Experimental Setup

Experiments were conducted on a three-tier heterogeneous testbed representing a typical IoT edge-cloud hierarchy. The edge device is a Raspberry Pi 4 (4-core Arm Cortex-A76, 2.4 GHz, 8 GB LPDDR4X), representing a resource-constrained IoT node. The fog node is a laptop (Intel Core i7-10510U, 16 GB DDR4), and the cloud node is a desktop PC equipped with an NVIDIA RTX 4070 Ti GPU (7680 CUDA cores, 40.09 FP32 TFLOPS, 32 GB DDR5, 12 GB VRAM GDDR6). Nodes were interconnected via Tailscale VPN with ZeroMQ handling inter-node messaging. Network constraints and bottlenecks were simulated using Tailscale's traffic throttling capabilities.

Algorithm 6. Adaptive distributed inference scheduler – Steady state

Require: Current split c; baseline split c_0; weights $\mathbf{w}$; deadline $L_{\max}$; R_{steady} runs per re-evaluation window; warmup k_{warm}; switch improvement threshold θ; Phase-1 data $\mathcal{D}_{\text{phase1}} = \mathcal{D}_{\text{base}} \cup \mathcal{D}_{\text{probe}}$

Phase 2: steady state with periodic re-evaluation

while budget not exhausted **do**
  $\mathcal{W} \leftarrow \emptyset$
  for $r \leftarrow 1$ to R_{steady} **do**
    $s \leftarrow$ RunInference(c)
    if $r > k_{\text{warm}}$ **then** $\mathcal{W} \leftarrow \mathcal{W} \cup \{s\}$
    end if
  end for
  $\bar{L} \leftarrow$ mean latency over $\mathcal{W}$
  $\sigma, \rho \leftarrow$ FitRates($\mathcal{D}_{\text{phase1}} \cup \mathcal{W}$, W) ▷ Phase-1 data keeps rates grounded
  $(\omega, \beta) \leftarrow$ LinkProbe()
  $c' \leftarrow$ FindBest($\sigma, \rho, \omega, \beta, \mathbf{w}, \mathbf{n}, S^{\star}, L_{\max}, m, c$)
  $S_c, S_{c'} \leftarrow$ Score($c, \ldots$), Score($c', \ldots$)
  $\Delta \leftarrow (S_c - S_{c'})/S_c$ ▷ relative improvement

  deadlineHit $\leftarrow (L_{\max} > 0 \wedge \bar{L} > L_{\max})$
  if deadlineHit $\wedge\, c' \neq c$ **then**
    $c \leftarrow c'$ ▷ FORCED switch (deadline violation)
  else if $c' \neq c \wedge \Delta \geq \theta$ **then**
    $c \leftarrow c'$ ▷ NORMAL switch
  else if deadlineHit $\wedge\, c \neq c_0$ **then**
    $c \leftarrow c_0$ ▷ fall back to static baseline
  end if
end while

Three widely benchmarked CNN models were evaluated: VGG16 (138M parameters, 528 MB), AlexNet (61M parameters, 234 MB), and MobileNetV2 (2.2M parameters, 8.8 MB), spanning a broad range of complexity. To isolate computational workload from dataset variability, randomly generated dummy tensors of shape $1 \times 3 \times 224 \times 224$ matching each model's input dimensions were used as inference inputs. Models were implemented in PyTorch.

Energy consumption was measured independently per node: the edge node applied a constant 12 W power model multiplied by measured compute time, the fog node read package energy deltas via Intel RAPL through the Linux powercap interface, and the cloud node integrated instantaneous GPU power readings from NVIDIA NVML over the compute window. Latency was recorded using wall-clock timing. Two primary metrics are reported: total end-to-end inference latency (ms) and total energy consumption (J) across all active nodes.

Each configuration was executed over 500 inference passes, repeated ten times and averaged to ensure measurement stability. We compare three execution strategies: (i) single-device baseline on each node independently, (ii) static partitioning with a fixed split, approximating equal workload thirds across the three nodes, and (iii) the proposed adaptive partitioning algorithm, which dynamically determines split points based on runtime conditions.

The implementation is publicly available on GitHub.[1]

3.2 Single-Device Baselines

Table 1 reports the average per-inference latency and energy consumption for each model running entirely on a single device, with no network transfers or offloading.

Table 1. Average per-inference latency and energy consumption for single-device execution.

Device	Model	Latency (ms)	Energy (J)
Edge	VGG16	666.870	8.002
	AlexNet	132.400	1.589
	MobileNetV2	71.900	0.863
Fog	VGG16	169.908	2.549
	AlexNet	20.988	0.315
	MobileNetV2	15.954	0.239
Cloud	VGG16	1.164	0.037
	AlexNet	0.830	0.024
	MobileNetV2	4.175	0.092

Across all three models, the edge and cloud nodes differ by roughly two orders of magnitude in both latency and energy. The cloud node completes VGG16 in 1.16 ms and AlexNet in 0.83 ms, while the edge node requires 666.87 ms and 132.40 ms respectively, a gap of approximately 570×. MobileNetV2 shows a considerably smaller gap of 17× (71.90 ms vs 4.18 ms), reflecting its design for resource-constrained inference. The fog node sits between the two extremes, with latencies of 169.91 ms, 20.99 ms, and 15.95 ms for VGG16, AlexNet, and MobileNetV2, respectively. The same ordering holds for energy: the edge node consumes 0.86–8.00 J per inference, the fog node 0.24–2.55 J, and the cloud node 0.009–0.037 J. These single-device figures exclude any network transfer cost and therefore represent idealized lower bounds rather than realistic end-to-end performance. In practice, routing all inference to the cloud introduces network latency and bandwidth constraints that make full offloading impractical in real IoT deployments, which is precisely the motivation for adaptive partitioning.

[1] https://github.com/Akuien/DNN-partitioning-and-Offloading-framework-REAP.

3.3 Static Partitioning Baseline

Table 2 reports the per-inference results when the three models are executed across the three-node continuum using a fixed partitioning scheme, with cut points chosen to distribute roughly one-third of the feature extraction work to each node. For VGG16, this corresponds to layers 0–10 on the edge node, layers 11–30 on the fog node, and the classifier head on the cloud node. For AlexNet, layers 0–9 run on the edge node, layers 10–12 together with the adaptive average pooling module on the fog node, and the classifier on the cloud node. For MobileNetV2, the first 10 blocks run on the edge node, the remaining 9 blocks on the fog node, and the pooling and classifier head on the cloud node.

Table 2. Per-inference latency and energy consumption under static partitioning.

Model	Pipeline Latency (ms)	Edge Energy (J)	Fog Energy (J)	Cloud Energy (J)	Total Energy (J)
VGG16	525.142	2.297	2.491	0.905	5.693
AlexNet	78.148	0.237	0.082	0.356	0.675
MobileNetV2	98.457	0.624	0.268	0.027	0.919

Relative to the single-device baseline, static partitioning reduces end-to-end latency for VGG16 by 21.2% (from 666.87 ms to 525.14 ms) and for AlexNet by 41.0% (from 132.40 ms to 78.15 ms). MobileNetV2 behaves differently: the network transfer overhead outweighs the computational benefit, increasing end-to-end latency by 36.9% from 71.90 ms to 98.46 ms. In terms of energy, the total system cost is 5.69 J for VGG16, 0.68 J for AlexNet, and 0.92 J for MobileNetV2. The per-node energy distribution differs markedly across models: for VGG16, the load is spread relatively evenly across all three nodes (2.30 J, 2.49 J, and 0.91 J for edge, fog, and cloud, respectively), while for AlexNet and MobileNetV2 the edge node remains the dominant consumer (0.24 J and 0.62 J), with the fog node contributing considerably less (0.08 J and 0.27 J).

3.4 Adaptive Partitioning

Table 3 reports the same per-inference metrics when the adaptive scheduler controls the split points. The scheduler initializes by running 50 inferences at the static split to establish the baseline threshold, followed by 15 inferences at each of three automatically selected probe splits. It then fits the per-node compute rates and link bandwidth parameters, selects the best starting split, and enters steady-state operation with re-evaluation every 100 inferences.

Under adaptive partitioning, the total system energy is 3.65 J, 0.43 J, and 0.67 J for VGG16, AlexNet, and MobileNetV2 respectively, with end-to-end latencies of 491.86 ms, 60.23 ms, and 84.48 ms. For all three models, the adaptive framework reduces both energy consumption and latency relative to the

Table 3. Average per-inference latency and energy consumption under adaptive partitioning.

Model	Pipeline Latency (ms)	Edge Energy (J)	Fog Energy (J)	Cloud Energy (J)	Total Energy (J)
VGG16	491.855	1.489	1.235	0.930	3.654
AlexNet	60.233	0.078	0.097	0.259	0.434
MobileNetV2	84.479	0.494	0.078	0.099	0.670

static baseline. The per-node energy distribution shifts noticeably between the two configurations: for VGG16, the edge and fog node contributions drop from 2.30 J to 1.49 J and from 2.49 J to 1.24 J respectively. For AlexNet, the edge node contribution drops from 0.24 J to 0.08 J. For MobileNetV2, the edge node drops from 0.62 J to 0.49 J, while the cloud node rises from 0.03 J to 0.10 J, reflecting a shift of heavier computation toward the more energy-efficient cloud node.

3.5 Comparison of Static and Adaptive Partitioning

Table 4 summarizes the improvements achieved by the adaptive framework over the static baseline in terms of percentage reductions in latency and total system energy.

Table 4. Reduction in latency and energy achieved by adaptive over static partitioning.

Model	Latency Reduction (%)	Energy Reduction (%)
VGG16	6.34	35.82
AlexNet	22.92	35.70
MobileNetV2	14.20	27.09

The energy reduction ranges from 27.09% for MobileNetV2 to 35.82% for VGG16, and the latency reduction ranges from 6.34% for VGG16 to 22.92% for AlexNet. Across all three models, the energy reduction consistently exceeds the latency reduction, reflecting the framework's objective weighting. Figures 1 and 2 show the absolute latency and energy values side by side for both configurations, and Fig. 3 shows the relative reductions as percentages.

The three models differ in how the savings are distributed between energy and latency. VGG16 achieves the largest absolute and relative energy reduction (2.04 J, 35.82%) but the smallest latency reduction (33.28 ms, 6.34%), suggesting the scheduler prioritized offloading computation away from the energy-hungry

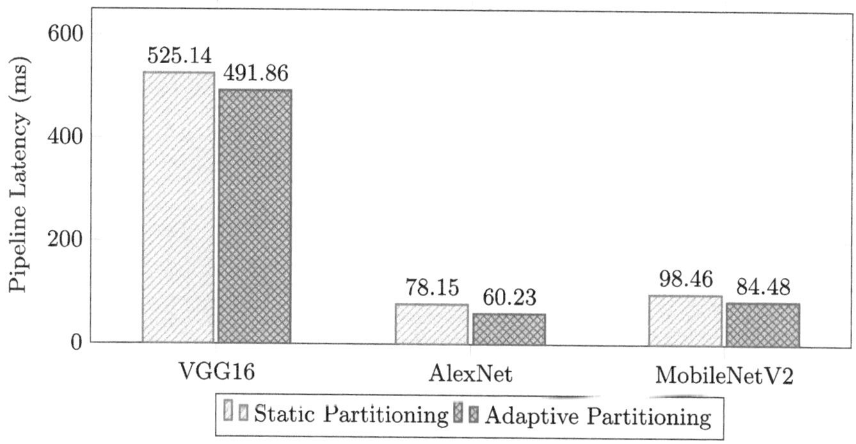

Fig. 1. Pipeline latency under static and adaptive partitioning.

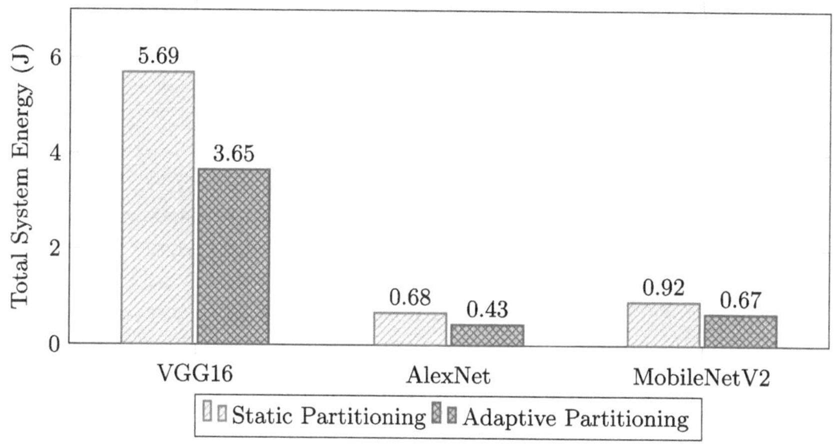

Fig. 2. Total system energy under static and adaptive partitioning.

edge node over minimizing transfer overhead. AlexNet achieves both a large energy reduction (0.24 J, 35.70%) and the largest latency reduction of the three models (17.92 ms, 22.92%). MobileNetV2 shows the smallest energy reduction (27.09%) alongside a moderate latency improvement of 14.20%. Across all three models, energy reductions consistently exceed latency reductions in percentage terms, consistent with the higher weights assigned to energy terms in the objective function.

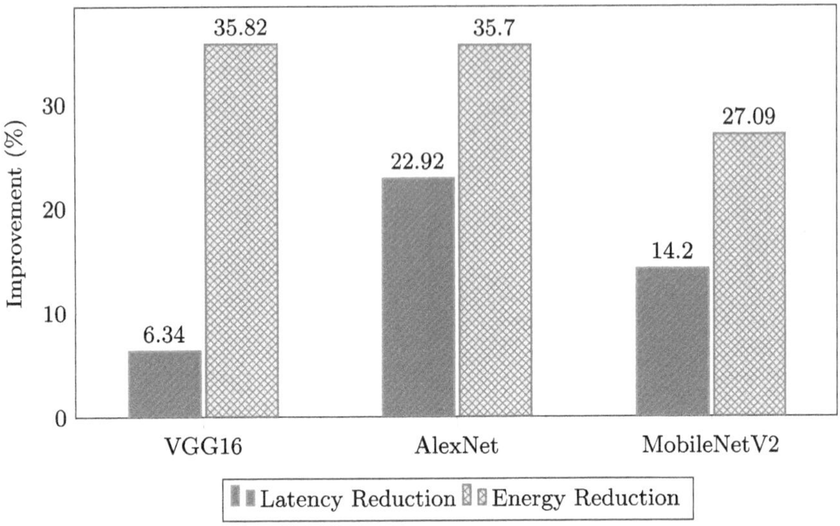

Fig. 3. Reduction in latency and energy achieved by adaptive over static partitioning.

4 Conclusions

This paper presented an adaptive partitioning and offloading framework for distributed DNN inference across a heterogeneous edge-cloud continuum, motivated by the lack of real-hardware evaluation and limited focus on energy consumption in existing works. The framework was validated on a physical testbed comprising a Raspberry Pi edge node, a laptop fog node, and a GPU-equipped cloud node, across three CNN models spanning a broad complexity range. Results show energy reductions of up to 35.82% for VGG16 and AlexNet, and 27.09% for MobileNetV2, alongside latency reductions of up to 22.92%, all relative to a static partitioning baseline. These findings confirm that adaptive partitioning can significantly reduce energy consumption on resource-constrained devices without violating latency constraints, addressing a gap that simulation-based approaches have largely been overlooked.

These results compare favorably with recent related work despite differences in optimisation objective: Li et al. [11] achieved 27.31% latency reduction through joint partitioning and pruning, Chen et al. [2] reported 34.72%–43.52% latency improvements with EdgeCI, and Fang et al. [7] demonstrated substantial power efficiency gains via DRL-based offloading. Our framework achieves comparable improvements while targeting energy consumption over latency, and unlike RL-based or parallel inference approaches, relies on a single weighted objective function evaluated periodically at runtime, making it lightweight and continuously adaptive.

Acknowledgments. This work was partially supported by the MSCA's TALENTS (101299722) project. The computations were enabled by resources provided by the

National Academic Infrastructure for Supercomputing in Sweden (NAISS), partially funded by the Swedish Research Council through grant agreement no. 2022-06725.

Disclosure of Interests. The authors have no competing interests to declare that are relevant to the content of this article.

References

1. Chen, H., Qin, W., Wang, L.: Task partitioning and offloading in IoT cloud-edge collaborative computing framework: a survey. J. Cloud Comput. **11**(1), 86 (2022)
2. Chen, Y., Luo, T., Fang, W., Xiong, N.N.: EdgeCI: distributed workload assignment and model partitioning for CNN inference on edge clusters. ACM Trans. Internet Technol. **24**(2), 1–24 (2024)
3. Dargan, S., Kumar, M., Ayyagari, M.R., Kumar, G.: A survey of deep learning and its applications: a new paradigm to machine learning. Arch. Comput. Methods Eng. **27**(4), 5 (2020)
4. Doan, H.N.T., Nguyen, P.N.T., Bui, B.C., Phan, N.D.: Optimizing edge device routing in edge computing: harnessing the synergy of distributed processing and correlation analysis. In: Proceedings of the 2024 13th International Conference on Software and Computer Applications, pp. 368–372 (2024)
5. Donta, P.K., Murturi, I., Casamayor Pujol, V., Sedlak, B., Dustdar, S.: Exploring the potential of distributed computing continuum systems. Computers **12**(10) (2023). https://doi.org/10.3390/computers12100198. https://www.mdpi.com/2073-431X/12/10/198
6. Edquist, H., Goodridge, P., Haskel, J.: The internet of things and economic growth in a panel of countries. Econ. Innov. New Technol. **30**(3), 262–283 (2021)
7. Fang, C., et al.: AI-driven energy-efficient content task offloading in cloud-edge-end cooperation networks. IEEE Open J. Comput. Soc. **3**, 162–171 (2022)
8. Fang, W., Xu, W., Yu, C., Xiong, N.N.: Joint architecture design and workload partitioning for DNN inference on industrial IoT clusters. ACM Trans. Internet Technol. **23**(1) (2023). https://doi.org/10.1145/3551638. https://doi-org.ezp.sub.su.se/10.1145/3551638
9. Feng, C., Han, P., Zhang, X., Yang, B., Liu, Y., Guo, L.: Computation offloading in mobile edge computing networks: a survey. J. Netw. Comput. Appl. **202**, 103366 (2022)
10. Langer, M., He, Z., Rahayu, W., Xue, Y.: Distributed training of deep learning models: a taxonomic perspective. IEEE Trans. Parallel Distrib. Syst. **31**(12), 2802–2818 (2020)
11. Li, H., Li, X., Fan, Q., He, Q., Wang, X., Leung, V.C.: Adaptive model partitioning and pruning for collaborative DNN inference in mobile edge-cloud computing networks. IEEE Trans. Mobile Comput. (2025)
12. Li, S., et al.: PyTorch distributed: experiences on accelerating data parallel training. arXiv preprint arXiv:2006.15704 (2020)
13. Ma, Y., Wang, Y., Tang, B.: Joint optimization of model partitioning and resource allocation for multi-exit DNNs in edge-device collaboration. Electronics **14**(8) (2025). https://doi.org/10.3390/electronics14081647. https://www.mdpi.com/2079-9292/14/8/1647
14. Ojo, M.O., Giordano, S., Procissi, G., Seitanidis, I.N.: A review of low-end, middle-end, and high-end IoT devices. IEEE Access **6**, 70528–70554 (2018). https://doi.org/10.1109/ACCESS.2018.2879615

15. Pan, J., McElhannon, J.: Future edge cloud and edge computing for internet of things applications. IEEE Internet Things J. **5**(1), 439–449 (2018). https://doi.org/10.1109/JIOT.2017.2767608
16. Sah, D.K., Vahabi, M., Fotouhi, H.: Real-time inference for IIoT using distributed low-power edge clusters. In: 2025 IEEE 11th World Forum on Internet of Things (WF-IoT), pp. 1–3 (2025). https://doi.org/10.1109/WF-IoT64238.2025.11270629
17. Shen, W., Lin, W., Wu, W., Wu, H., Li, K.: Reinforcement learning-based task scheduling for heterogeneous computing in end-edge-cloud environment. Clust. Comput. **28**(3), 179 (2025)
18. Shinde, P.P., Shah, S.: A review of machine learning and deep learning applications. In: 2018 Fourth International Conference on Computing Communication Control and Automation (ICCUBEA), pp. 1–6 (2018). https://doi.org/10.1109/ICCUBEA.2018.8697857
19. Ye, P., Lapkovskis, A., Saleh, A., Zhang, Q., Donta, P.K.: Nesy-edge: neuro-symbolic trustworthy self-healing in the computing continuum, arXiv preprint arXiv:2603.21145 (2026)
20. Yu, W., et al.: A survey on the edge computing for the internet of things. IEEE Access **6**, 6900–6919 (2018). https://doi.org/10.1109/ACCESS.2017.2778504
21. Zhang, Y., Zhang, Z., Zhao, H.: Adaptive DNN partitioning for edge-cloud systems with meta-reinforcement learning. In: Proceedings of the 18th IEEE/ACM International Conference on Utility and Cloud Computing, UCC 2025. Association for Computing Machinery, New York (2026). https://doi.org/10.1145/3773274.3774271. https://doi-org.ezp.sub.su.se/10.1145/3773274.3774271
22. Zhang, Z., Kouzani, A.Z.: Implementation of DNNs on IoT devices. Neural Comput. Appl. **32**(5), 1327–1356 (2020)
23. Zhao, S., Yao, D., Wan, Y., Wu, G., Jin, H.: AdapCP: collaborative inference with adaptive CNN partition on distributed edge servers. ACM Trans. Auton. Adapt. Syst. **20**(4), 1–28 (2025)
24. Zhao, Z., Barijough, K.M., Gerstlauer, A.: Deepthings: distributed adaptive deep learning inference on resource-constrained IoT edge clusters. IEEE Trans. Comput. Aided Des. Integr. Circuits Syst. **37**(11), 2348–2359 (2018)

When We Talk Morse: Lightweight Parameter Encoding for Secure Federated Learning

Huong Nguyen(✉), Amirhossein Ghaffari, and Lauri Lovén

Future Computing Group, University of Oulu, Oulu, Finland
{huong.nguyen,amirhossein.ghaffari,lauri.loven}@oulu.fi

Abstract. Federated Learning (FL) requires clients to send model updates over potentially untrusted networks, creating a need for confidentiality, integrity, and low overhead on resource-constrained edge devices. Existing approaches only partially meet these goals: quantization is lightweight but not cryptographically secure, secure aggregation mainly protects against server-side visibility, and homomorphic encryption (HE) is costly. We propose **MoDuo**, a lightweight FL protection scheme that combines AES-GCM authenticated encryption with a tailored Morse-based and base-32 encoding layer. Compared with HE baselines, including stock FATE and BatchCrypt, MoDuo secures training with negligible impact on accuracy (typically below 1% and in extreme configurations, below 2%), keeps protected payloads within about 4× the original size for a 4.02M-parameter model, reduces cryptographic time by over 187× compared with stock FATE, and saves more than half the cryptographic time compared with BatchCrypt. Compared with direct AES-GCM over decimal-serialized updates, MoDuo reduces the serialized representation size by mapping verbose floating-point values into more compact encoded tokens before encryption, reducing the protected payload by up to 49.3% at the cost of additional encoding time.

Keywords: distributed learning · federated learning · privacy · security · encoding

1 Introduction

In Federated Learning (FL) [16], clients and a central server repeatedly exchange large model updates over potentially untrusted networks. In practice, these updates can be hundreds of megabytes per round and may reveal sensitive information about local data distributions if exposed during transmission. Large and frequent transfers also incur substantial communication and energy costs, especially over wireless or cellular links, and this burden becomes more pronounced as FL moves toward smaller, resource-constrained edge devices. Therefore, a practical protection mechanism for FL communication should satisfy

Z. Afzal et al. (Eds.): ARES 2026 Workshops, LNCS 16900, pp. 447–465, 2027.
https://doi.org/10.1007/978-3-032-35576-8_24

three requirements: *confidentiality*, so that unauthorized external parties cannot inspect updates or infer sensitive information; *integrity*, so that tampering in transit is detected before the model is updated; and *lightweight* operation, so that the protection mechanism does not negate the efficiency of FL.

Existing approaches typically satisfy at most two of these requirements. Gradient compression and quantization techniques [3,12,19] reduce communication overhead and are therefore lightweight, but they do not provide cryptographic confidentiality or integrity by themselves. Compressed raw gradients sent without encryption remain visible and modifiable to an on-path attacker. Secure aggregation (SA) protocols [22,28] are widely used in cross-device FL to hide individual client updates from the server by revealing only an aggregate. However, SA primarily addresses server-side privacy and does not inherently provide channel confidentiality or payload integrity against transmission-line adversaries. In practice, it is often combined with transport-layer protection such as TLS. Homomorphic encryption (HE) schemes such as Paillier [18] and CKKS [5], as well as HE-based FL systems such as BatchCrypt [27] and Poseidon [21], provide strong confidentiality even from an honest-but-curious server by enabling computation over encrypted updates. However, this functionality typically incurs substantial computational and communication overhead, which may be unsuitable for resource-constrained FL clients. These limitations motivate a different design point: *"Can FL payloads be protected against external network adversaries leveraging lightweight authenticated encryption, while using an additional encoding layer to structure and obfuscate the transmitted updates?"* A key consideration is that protection should not only hide the payload but also detect active modification. In HE-based settings, ciphertexts are often susceptible to bit-flipping during transmission; a modified ciphertext may therefore be processed during aggregation and lead to model corruption.

In this paper, we present **MoDuo**, a lightweight protection scheme for FL payloads that combines a tailored encoding layer with AES-GCM-based authenticated encryption [7,15]. MoDuo applies AES-GCM using client-specific symmetric keys, avoiding dependence on a single global key and preventing one client from decrypting or generating valid authenticated messages for another. These keys are assumed to be pre-shared over a secure channel prior to training, such as during device registration or via a TLS-protected handshake. In this design, AES-GCM provides the formal confidentiality and integrity guarantees, while the encoding layer structures and obfuscates the plaintext updates before encryption.

We focus on protecting FL payloads against external transmission adversaries, such as eavesdroppers and man-in-the-middle attackers. Malicious internal clients and malicious servers are important threats in FL, yet are outside the primary scope of MoDuo. Instead, this work aims to provide lightweight confidentiality and integrity against unauthorized interception, modification, and tampering during communication.

Our experimental evaluation shows that MoDuo, when combined with AES-GCM, provides lightweight confidentiality and integrity against external transmission adversaries with significantly lower computational overhead than HE-based protection. By assigning the formal cryptographic protection to fast symmetric authenticated encryption and using the encoding layer for payload structuring and obfuscation, MoDuo offers an efficient design for protecting diverse FL payloads, including model parameters, gradients, and sensitive metadata, in resource-constrained edge environments.

The remaining of the paper is structured as follows: Sect. 2 provides an overview of related works. Section 3 introduces the proposed scheme for the parameter encoding. Section 4 presents experimental details and setup, while Sect. 5 evaluates the efficiency of our proposed method. Finally, Sect. 6 provides a short discussion and summarizes this work.

2 Related Work

FL updates face a recurring three-way tension between (i) *confidentiality* against eavesdroppers, (ii) *integrity* against in-transit tampering, and (iii) *lightweight* overhead suitable for edge deployments. In FL, clients and a central server repeatedly exchange model updates over untrusted networks [16]. Existing lines of work typically emphasize one or two of these goals. A large body of work documents the risks of inference or reconstruction from shared gradients [8,17,29], as well as the broader FL threat surface [1,11]. Poisoning can occur in various ways [14], and if an adversary modifies updates undetected (e.g., via a man-in-the-middle attack), the training process may silently drift or be poisoned [26].

Gradient Compression and Quantization. From an efficiency perspective, a large literature reduces the *lightweight* dimension via compression, but it does not secure the channel. Practical examples include Top-k sparsification with error feedback [13], QSGD [2], SignSGD [3], TLAQC [19], and FedFQ [12]. These techniques are effective for bandwidth reduction but, by design, do not address confidentiality or integrity; adversaries can still read or corrupt compressed updates in transit. Moreover, compression can amplify certain leakage channels without encryption, as reduced redundancy in the transmitted updates can make gradient inversion attacks [8,29] more effective. The survey [1] notes that aggressive sparsification or quantization may remove *noise* that would otherwise obscure sensitive information, thereby easing model or data reconstruction by an adversary.

Secure Aggregation. Complementary to compression, SA focuses on *server-side privacy* of individual updates rather than transport-layer confidentiality or integrity. SA protocols hide each *individual* update from the server while allowing the exact sum to be recovered [4]. A number of follow-ups [10,22,28] aim to improve scalability and verifiability, but SA fundamentally protects only the aggregate; it neither compresses model updates nor detects per-message tampering before aggregation. In addition, SA typically assumes synchronous participation and adds nontrivial protocol overhead compared with simple client–server encryption.

Homomorphic Encryption and Its Limitations. One prominent line of work secures confidentiality by encrypting each client's update with HE so that the server can aggregate without decryption. Representative systems include *Poseidon* [21], which relies on the CKKS approximate-number scheme [5], and *BatchCrypt* [27], which employs the integer-based Paillier cryptosystem [18]. While these methods maintain confidentiality against honest-but-curious servers, they tend to impose significant computational overhead, large ciphertext expansion, and added engineering complexity during training. Importantly, HE by itself does *not* provide authenticity or integrity: a bit-flipped CKKS/Paillier ciphertext still decrypts to some value without any built-in alarm. In other words, if an adversary tampered with a Paillier-encrypted sum or a CKKS ciphertext in transit, the decryptor would simply output a (likely incorrect or garbled) numerical result without detecting that the ciphertext had been modified. This silent failure is problematic in FL, where poisoned or corrupted updates can propagate unnoticed through model aggregation, degrading accuracy or introducing backdoors. Ensuring tamper detection with HE requires wrapping ciphertexts in additional message authentication mechanisms, such as HMAC or digital signatures, which increases bandwidth and computational cost.

As for practicality, BatchCrypt reports communication and speed improvements versus naive Paillier, but its evaluation does not explicitly characterize non-IID client data splits, leaving robustness under realistic heterogeneity unclear [27].

Authenticated Encryption for Transport Security. In contrast to HE and SA, authenticated encryption with associated data (AEAD) schemes such as AES-GCM [7,15] provide confidentiality and integrity in a single pass and are widely deployed in Internet protocols (TLS/QUIC). AEAD does not enable computation over ciphertexts. However, when downstream processing does not require server-side arithmetic on encrypted values, AEAD offers a simple, efficient, well-analyzed building block for securing model-update transport.

Gap and Positioning. Prior approaches typically sacrifice at least one of three goals: confidentiality, integrity, and low overhead. HE offers strong confidentiality but incurs significant computational overhead and ciphertext expansion, requiring additional mechanisms to ensure authenticity. SA hides individual updates from the server but does not, by itself, secure the transport channel, and adds protocol coordination. Compression reduces bandwidth but leaves updates readable and modifiable in transit. MoDuo targets this gap by combining a compact, Morse-inspired binary encoding with duotrigesimal packing and a standard AEAD layer (AES-GCM) that encrypts and authenticates the resulting payload. The result is a lightweight transport protection scheme that keeps updates small, private, and tamper-evident without the computational burden of HE or the coordination cost of SA.

3 Proposed Method

(see Fig. 1).

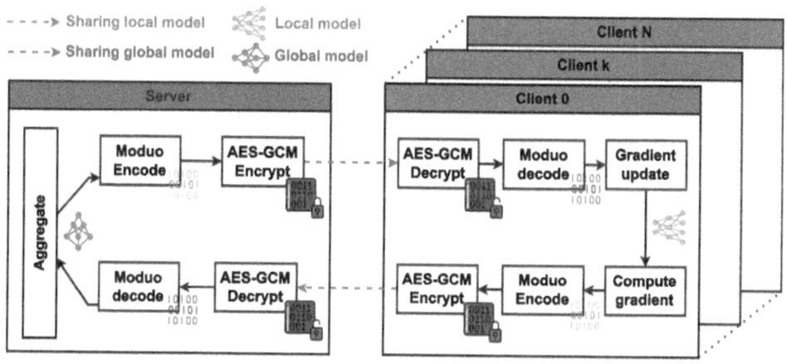

Fig. 1. MoDuo workflow

3.1 MoDuo Encoding

The encoding part in our proposed method introduces an interesting fusion between Morse and the duotrigesimal number system.

Morse and Its Representation: Morse code is one of the earliest digital communication schemes and has been applied across domains [6,23,25]. At its simplest, every letter, digit, and punctuation mark is represented by a sequence of two different signal elements: a short one (called a "dot" or "dit") and a long one (called a "dash" or "dah"). These elements are transmitted as brief or extended bursts of sound, light, or electrical current, and the receiver deciphers each sequence back into the corresponding character. For example, a decimal '5' can be represented as '· · · · ·' or decimal '7' is equal to '– – · · ·' in Morse.

The Bridge to Fusion: Observing that Morse cannot be converted directly into duotrigesimal numbers (base-32), we use an intermediate numbering system that bridges Morse to base-32. Morse code has an inherent property that makes this bridge natural: it relies on only two fundamental symbols to display characters. This fits directly into a binary representation. Inspired by that, we map each dot (·) to the bit *0* and each dash (–) to the bit *1* in our work. For example, the number *5*, written as '· · · · ·' in Morse, becomes '00000' in binary.

At this stage, the Morse-based and duotrigesimal transformation is not intended to provide standalone cryptographic security. Instead, it acts as a deterministic encoding layer that restructures model updates into an intermediate

Algorithm 1: MoDuo

Input : N clients
T communication rounds, E epochs
Encryption keys $K = \{k_0, k_1, \cdots, k_{N-1}\}$
Local weights $W = \{w_0, w_1, \cdots, w_{N-1}\}$
Data partitions $D = \{d_0, d_1, \cdots, d_{N-1}\}$

`// Before FL process`
Share a unique symmetric encryption key k_i between the server and each client i via a secure out-of-band channel prior to training.
`// FL`
SERVER:
$\theta^0 \leftarrow$ Initialize random weights
for $t = 0, 1, \ldots, T$ **do**
  if $t > 0$ **then**
    for $i = 0, 1, \ldots, N-1$ **do**
      ${w^t_i}_{DE} \leftarrow$ `decrypt`(w^t_i)
    end
    $\theta^t = \sum_{j=0}^{N-1} \frac{|D_j|}{|D|} {w^t_j}_{DE}$
  end
  Payload $p \leftarrow$ `encrypt(process(`θ^t, x`))`
  Broadcast p to all N clients
end
CLIENT i:
for $t = 0, 1, \ldots, T$ **do**
  $w_i \leftarrow$ `decrypt`(p)
  for $t = 1, \ldots, E$ **do**
    foreach *batch* $\mathcal{B} = \{x, y\} \subset \mathcal{D}_i$ **do**
      $\mathcal{L} \leftarrow CrossEntropyLoss(\mathcal{F}_{\theta_{DE}}(x), y)$
      $w_i \leftarrow w_i - \eta \nabla \mathcal{L}$
    end
  end
  Send `encrypt(process(`w_i, x`))` to server
end
`// Functions`
Function `encrypt`(v):
  $v_{encode} \leftarrow$ `bin_to_b32(to_morse(`v`))`
  $iv \leftarrow$ Generate nonce
  $v_{encr}, tag \leftarrow$ Encrypt v_{encode} by AES-GCM with k_i and iv
  Put iv, tag, v_{encr} into payload p
  return p
Function `decrypt`(p):
  Extract iv, tag, v_{encr} from p
  $v_{decr} \leftarrow$ Decrypt v_{encr} by AES-GCM with k_i and extracted values
  return `deMorse(b32_to_bin(`v_{decr}`))`
Function `process`$(value, x)$:
  $v \leftarrow$ rounded $value$ up to x digits after decimal point
  $v \leftarrow$ remove decimal points by multiplying by 10^x
  $v_{final} \leftarrow$ Parse v to string type
  return v_{final}

representation before AES-GCM encryption. This representation introduces an additional level of format obfuscation, but the confidentiality and integrity guarantees of the protected payload are provided by AES-GCM.

How it Works: Let `MORSE_BIN` denote the direct mapping from raw characters to their fused Morse-binary representation. In this mapping, the intermediate Morse encoding is combined with its binary form, resulting in a direct translation from character to binary. As a consequence, the mapping includes $\{1 \mapsto 01111, 2 \mapsto 00111, 3 \mapsto 00011, 4 \mapsto 00001, 5 \mapsto 00000, 6 \mapsto 10000, 7 \mapsto 11000, 8 \mapsto 11100, 9 \mapsto 11110, 0 \mapsto 11111, - \mapsto 100001\}$. To convert a binary string to Morse, we define `MORSE_BIN_REV` as the inverse mapping of `MORSE_BIN`. The set is formed with: for every pair $k \mapsto v$ in `MORSE_BIN`, we define a corresponding reversed pair $v \mapsto k$ in `MORSE_BIN_REV`.

Truncation: This step is executed via the `process` function (Algorithm 1, lines 35–39), prior to each encoding step. Starting from the observation that encoding time increases with the number of digits in a value, this process performs truncation and rounds the number after x digits. Via this approximation, we aim to reduce the computational complexity of encoding while maintaining an acceptable level of accuracy.

Encoding: The MoDuo encoding procedure is shown in Fig. 2. Each digit of the decimal value, including the sign, is first mapped to its binary Morse representation using `MORSE_BIN`. The resulting binary string is then converted to base-32 using the `bin_to_b32` function. If the binary length is divisible by 5, the string is split into 5-bit chunks, and each chunk is mapped to one base-32 character. If not divisible, it means the string contains the sign value, and the binary string is first converted to decimal and then encoded in base-32. The resulting base-32 characters are concatenated to form the final encoded value.

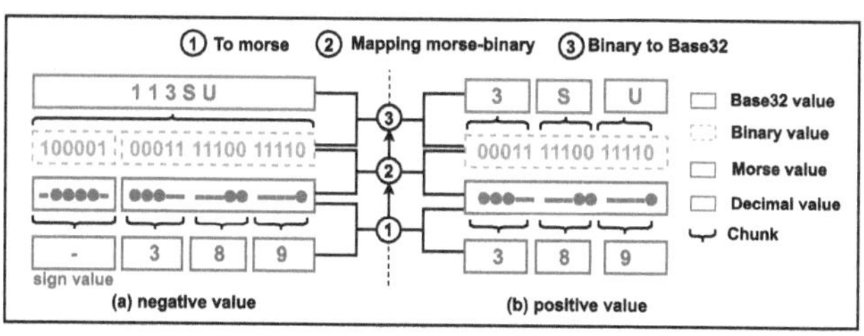

Fig. 2. MoDuo encoding for a negative (−389) and positive value (389).

Decoding: Referred to Fig. 3, is an inverse procedure of encoding, where we reverse from base-32 to binary presentation of Morse using the base-32 to binary function ($b32\_to\_bin$), then from Morse back to decimal value using `MORSE_BIN_REV` in the reversing Morse function ($deMorse$). The trimming step is always needed to present the final binary string, as the negative sign marker (if present), represented by 100001, must appear at the beginning of the binary sequence for correct parsing during the deMorse stage.

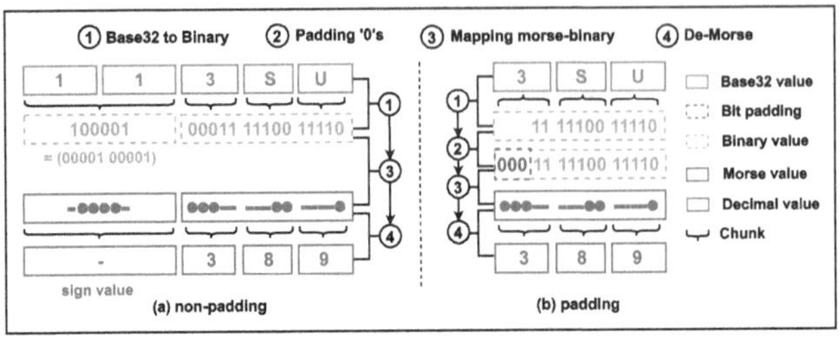

Fig. 3. MoDuo decoding for (a) non-padding and (b) padding cases. In (a), binary string's length not divisible by 5, we search for the sign-value bit: '100001', then chunk every 5 bits to reverse Morse. In (b), as length is not divisible by 5 and does not have '100001' bits at the beginning, zeros are padded to ensure the binary string can be split into 5-bit chunks for reversing Morse.

3.2 Authenticated Encryption with AES Galois Counter Mode

As mentioned regarding the eavesdropping threat in communication between clients and servers, both sides need a secure and efficient operation. In addition, normal encryptions can only ensure confidentiality, yet do not guarantee data integrity. Eavesdroppers may still tamper data by altering one or more bits of the ciphertext before transmitting it to the recipient.

We adopt AES-GCM to encrypt the data between the central aggregator server and participants after encoding it with MoDuo. It computes a universal hash (GHASH) over the ciphertext (and any additional data, e.g., metadata) in the finite field Galois Field GF(2^{128}) to generate a 128-bit authentication tag. From that, when sharing between clients and the server, we not only send the ciphertext of the model, but also need to send along the nonce and tag for authentication and integrity check purposes. On decryption, this tag is recomputed and verified in the same pass. In this way, if an attacker modifies or forges the ciphertext, verification fails, and the receiver can reject the compromised update before it affects aggregation.

Rationale for Choosing AES-GCM We went through below considerations before choosing AES-GCM as our preferred choice for the encryption:

- **Compared to homomorphic schemes:**
  - *Smaller ciphertext:* AES-GCM is more efficient, offering lightweight computation and significantly smaller ciphertexts. While HE methods like Paillier and CKKS support encrypted computation, they incur high overhead and substantial ciphertext expansion, often 10×–100× larger, making them impractical for routine FL tasks. This especially holds true when bootstrapping is used in CKKS to refresh noise.
  - *Authentication feature:* The mentioned homomorphic schemes (CKKS, Paillier) do not integrate any authentication features, but purely focus on enabling computations over encrypted data. This easily allows attackers to tamper with encrypted data, e.g., bit-flipping.

- **Compared to other AES modes:** AES-GCM offers a more efficient and secure solution by combining encryption and authentication in a single pass with minimal additional overhead. Modes like AES-CBC (block cipher mode) or AES-CTR (counter mode) lack built-in authentication, requiring separate and external (hashed) MACs for integrity. This results in additional computational cost and diminished throughput due to double passes and buffering.
- **Compatibility with MoDuo design:** MoDuo's base-32 layer produces a byte string representation, which can be fed directly into AES-GCM. Practically, AES-GCM processes data in 128-bit (16-byte) blocks, and MoDuo encoding does not introduce any bit-level misalignment or additional padding logic requirements.

Encryption: In our FL system, AES-GCM encryption is applied after the entire model weight parameter has been encoded into base-32 format by the sender, which can be either a client or the aggregator. A random nonce is generated for each encryption instance. Upon completion, the process outputs the encrypted value (v_{enc}) along with the corresponding GMAC (tag). These encrypted outputs, together with the nonce, are then transmitted to the receiver, as described in Algorithm 1, lines 25–30.

Decryption: Referred to Algorithm 1, lines 31–34: is the inverse process of encryption. It begins by extracting the received data into nonce, authentication tag, and ciphertext. The ciphertext is then decrypted to get v_{decr}, while simultaneously verifying the tag to ensure data integrity and detect any tampering. At this stage, v_{decr} remains in its encoded form and must be decoded in a final step to retrieve the original weight parameter.

4 Experimental Setup

In our experiments, FL is implemented using the Flower framework[1], involving ten clients and one aggregator, and is conducted over 300 communication rounds.

4.1 Dataset and Partition

Our experiments solely focus on the Non-IID setup on two datasets: CIFAR-10 (60,000 RGB images, 10 classes) and Fashion-MNIST (70,000 grayscale images, 10 classes). To simulate data heterogeneity, we distribute data based on the Dirichlet distribution - Dir(α) - with the smaller α value resulting in a greater skew among clients' data distributions. In this paper, we run $\alpha = 0.1$ (extremely non-IID), 1, 10, and 1000 (nearly IID). No data augmentation was performed for CIFAR-10 in any of the experiments.

[1] https://flower.ai/.

4.2 Model

We use the same model architectures for fair comparisons. The selected models in our experiments are a shallow CNN (cnn), MobileNet-v3-small (mob-v3s) [9], and EfficientNet-B0 (eff-b0) [24], which are used to run on small and constrained devices. The shallow CNN model includes two convolutional layers (followed by one ReLU and one MaxPooling layer), one fully connected layer, one dropout layer, and a final fully connected layer. Each client trains their local model in two epochs with a batch size of 64. We use the Stochastic Gradient Descent (SGD) optimizer with default parameters of learning rate 0.001, no momentum, and no weight decay for both MoDuo and FedAvg [16].

5 Experimental Results

5.1 Training Evaluation

We measured the performance deviations (Δ_{acc}, in %) introduced by MoDuo by comparing it against the baseline FedAvg (without MoDuo encryption) across varying degrees of non-IID data distributions (α) on CIFAR-10 and Fashion-MNIST. These quantitative results are detailed in Table 1 and visualized in Fig. 4 and Fig. 5. We apply Exponential Moving Average (EMA) smoothing in our main plots of these two figures, and focus on rounds 200 to 300 in the inset plots. The EMA smoothing factor is set to 0.15 in this work. Besides, to study the influence of the truncation factor (x), we also evaluate the accuracy difference when running MoDuo with different rounding values $x = \{3, 8, 12\}$ on $\alpha = \{0.1, 1, 10\}$, as shown in Fig. 6.

Table 1. Averaged accuracy differences (%) over all rounds (Δ) between training with and without MoDuo. Red indicates MoDuo underperforms the baseline; green indicates it outperforms.

Setting / Model	CIFAR-10				Fashion-MNIST			
	$\alpha = 0.1$	$\alpha = 1$	$\alpha = 10$	$\alpha = 1000$	$\alpha = 0.1$	$\alpha = 1$	$\alpha = 10$	$\alpha = 1000$
cnn	−1.70	−1.09	−1.52	−1.84	−0.96	−0.79	−1.08	−1.14
mob-v3s	−0.21	−0.97	−0.48	+0.10	−0.65	+0.14	−0.28	+0.09
eff-b0	−0.80	+0.18	+0.23	−0.43	−0.24	−0.14	+0.21	−0.08

Same Rounding Value, Different Settings: As observed, the impact of MoDuo on predictive performance is modest across all settings. The results indicate that MoDuo with x=8 preserves model performance across datasets, architectures, and heterogeneity levels, with accuracy fluctuations remaining minimal relative to the unencrypted baseline (at most roughly 2% and typically within 1%). For the *cnn*, which has the least complexity, MoDuo induces a small degradation,

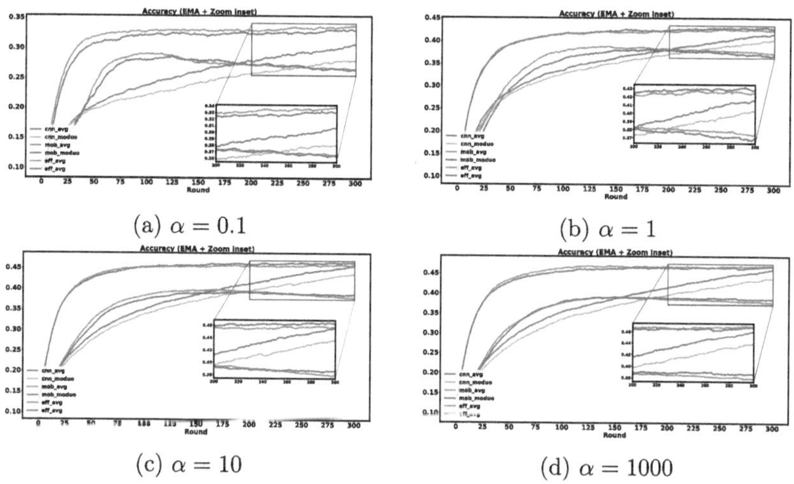

(a) $\alpha = 0.1$

(b) $\alpha = 1$

(c) $\alpha = 10$

(d) $\alpha = 1000$

Fig. 4. Test accuracy on CIFAR10. *cnn* presents the "cnn" model, *mob* presents "mob-v3s", and *eff* is for "eff-b0".

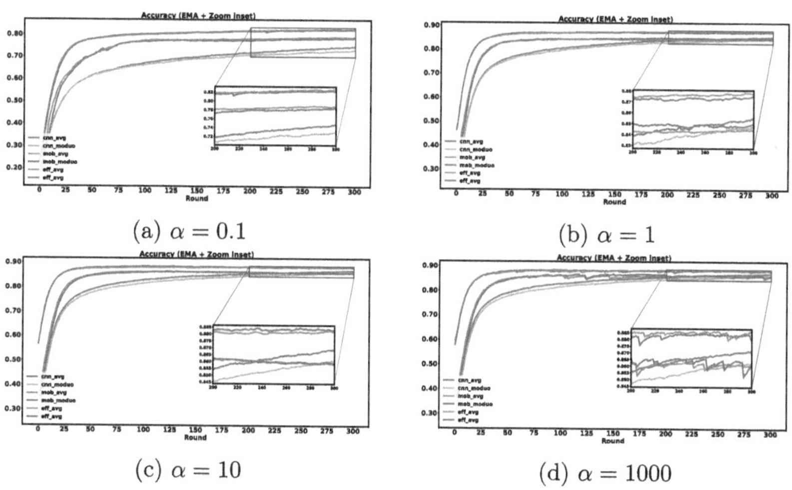

(a) $\alpha = 0.1$

(b) $\alpha = 1$

(c) $\alpha = 10$

(d) $\alpha = 1000$

Fig. 5. Test accuracy on Fashion-MNIST. *cnn* presents the "cnn" model, *mob* presents "mob-v3s", and *eff* is for "eff-b0".

where on CIFAR-10, the average loss ranges from -1.09 to -1.84%, and on Fashion-MNIST from -0.79 to -1.14 points. For the deeper architectures, the effect is substantially smaller. *mob-v3s* exhibits accuracy drops mostly below one point, and even shows slight gains in some settings ($+0.10$ for CIFAR-10 and $+0.14$, $+0.09$ for Fashion-MNIST). The deepest model here, *eff-b0*, shows the best performance on both datasets with almost all Δ_{acc} remaining well below

1%, with multiple positive entries (up to +0.23 on CIFAR-10 and +0.21 on Fashion-MNIST), and the worst degradation is only −0.8%.

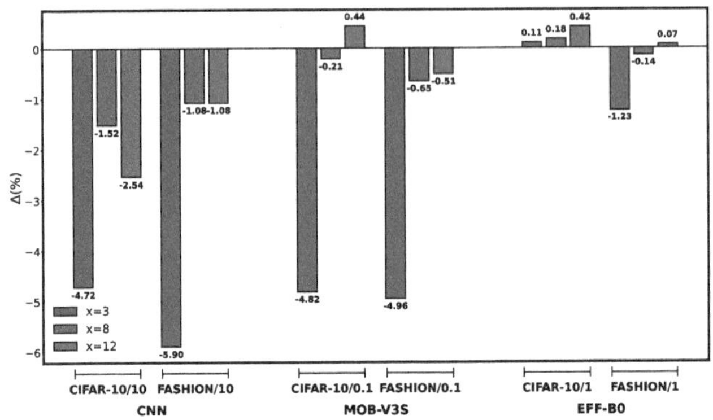

Fig. 6. Δ_{acc} when running the same model on the same setting with different rounding values x. Averaged accuracy differences (%) over all rounds (Δ) between training with and without MoDuo, run with different x values ($x = \{3, 8, 12\}$). The x = 12 achieves the best accuracy in *mob-v3s* and *eff-b0* models, not *cnn*.

Different Rounding Values: Across experimented settings, the fastest and simplest run with $x = 3$ decreases the largest accuracy amount. For the *cnn* under $\alpha = 10$, Δ_{acc} is −4.72 on CIFAR-10 and −5.90 on Fashion-MNIST. These values in *mob-v3s* with $\alpha = 0.1$ are −4.82 to −4.96 on both datasets. Even *eff-b0* at $\alpha = 1$, which is the most complex architecture in our experiments, shows −1.23 on Fashion-MNIST with this rounding value. These numbers indicate that very coarse rounding in MoDuo introduces substantial distortion in the local updates, which the training process cannot fully compensate for.

However, it can be easily seen that increasing x to 8 largely mitigates this effect. For the *cnn*, the degradation shrinks to −1.52 percentage points (%) on CIFAR-10 and −1.08 on Fashion-MNIST. For *mob-v3s*, the Δ_{acc} improves from about −4.82 and −4.96 to −0.21 and −0.65 on CIFAR-10 and Fashion-MNIST, respectively. Regarding *eff-b0*, Δ_{acc} increases slightly as x grows in CIFAR-10, while on Fashion-MNIST the gap shrinks from −1.23 at $x = 3$ to −0.14 at $x = 8$.

For x = 12, *mob-v3s* with $\alpha = 0.1$ moves from −4.82 to −0.21 to +0.44 on CIFAR-10 as x increases from 3 to 8 to 12, and from −4.96 to −0.65 to −0.51 on Fashion-MNIST. *eff-b0* with $\alpha = 1$ exhibits the same trend. On CIFAR-10, Δ_{acc} is +0.11, +0.18, and +0.42 for $x = \{3, 8, 12\}$, and on Fashion-MNIST it goes from −1.23 to −0.14 and then to a small positive +0.07. In contrast, the low complexity *cnn* does not clearly benefit from pushing x beyond 8. Regarding this case, $x = 8$ is consistently better than $x = 3$, while $x = 12$ is similar or slightly worse on CIFAR-10 at $\alpha = 10$.

Overall, we can observe that small x values correspond to overly aggressive rounding in MoDuo, which injects excessive noise into the updates and degrades accuracy, particularly for smaller models. Larger x reduces the rounding error and allows deeper architectures such as *mob-v3s* and *eff-b0* to either tolerate the perturbation or exploit it as a weak form of regularization. Based on this trade-off, we adopt $x = 8$ as the default setting for the rest of our experiments, as it avoids the significant accuracy losses at $x = 3$ while achieving behavior that is close to, and sometimes indistinguishable from, $x = 12$.

5.2 Overhead Evaluation

We evaluate the computational overhead of MoDuo by measuring the runtime of its encoding, encryption, decryption, and decoding operations. To quantify the system-level performance impact of MoDuo, we further analyze these runtimes as a function of model size and complexity.

We compare MoDuo with three baselines. First, we include a direct AES-GCM baseline to capture the minimum runtime of authenticated encryption and isolate the overhead introduced by MoDuo's encoding layer. Second, we compare against Stock and BatchCrypt [27], using their official implementations in FATE [20]. These HE baselines are used as cryptographic cost references rather than threat-model-equivalent baselines. For comparison, we use the largest model supported by all implementations, containing 4.02M parameters.

All experiments are executed on the same hardware. We report computation time only and exclude communication latency, since Flower and FATE use different communication implementations. Table 2 reports the measured overhead across methods and model sizes.

Per-Parameter Cryptographic Time (τ_{pp}): Quantifies the average time required to perform cryptographic operations on one parameter. Here, we separate this metrics into τ_{pp}^{e} and τ_{pp}^{d}, where the "*e*" includes encoding and encryption time, and the "*d*" includes decoding and decryption time. This metric is measured in microseconds per parameter (μs/parameter), where lower values indicate higher computational efficiency of the algorithm.

From Fig. 7, we observe that both the Stock and Batch implementations on FATE take a longer time to encrypt compared to our method with MoDuo encoding. This is mainly due to their use of Paillier-based HE. Batch is around 100× faster than Stock because of its batching HE and low-bit quantization mechanism; however, it still takes over 3.6× longer than our encryption method. Specifically, Stock requires more than 1262 µs, Batch takes 12.607 µs, while MoDuo spends the second-lowest amount of time (3.457 µs) to perform per-parameter encryption. For reference, AES-GCM without MoDuo's additional encoding takes just over 1.5 µs for encryption.

Regarding per-parameter decryption, Stock still exhibits the highest τ_{pp}^{d}, at nearly 400 µs, whereas Batch and MoDuo require substantially less time, and AES-GCM without additional encoding again achieves the lowest operation time with 2.197 µs. As mentioned earlier, Batch benefits more from ciphertext batching for larger models. Unlike encryption, in this decryption comparison, it is the most efficient, with 5.179 µs, closely followed by our MoDuo, which is only

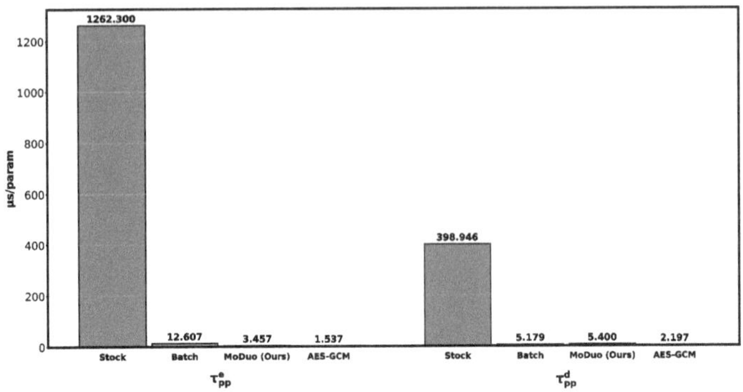

Fig. 7. Per-parameter cryptographic time comparison (τ_{pp}) among BatchCrypt (batch), FATE's stock implementation (stock), MoDuo (ours), and AES-GCM (no extra encoding) on a 4.02M-parameter model.

0.221 µs slower. However, this observation does not hold for smaller and simpler models, as shown in Table 2 where MoDuo clearly outperforms both Batch and Stock in these settings.

Per-Iteration Breakdown Time: Measures the runtime of each individual function, using the built-in `time` library. For MoDuo, the per-iteration breakdown includes the encode, decode, encrypt, and decrypt operations, as shown in Fig. 8. We also report the client's idle time in this figure, defined as the time spent waiting for the server's response. However, as Batch's and Stock's idle time is relatively high due to their geo-distributed deployment, we therefore exclude idle time from the total amount in Fig. 9 and Table 2 to enable a fair comparison.

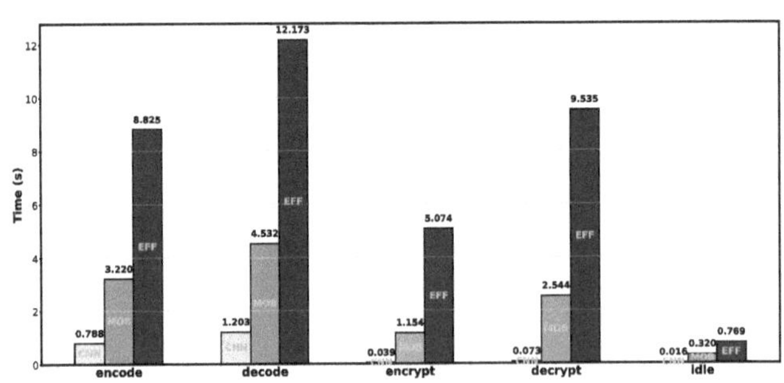

Fig. 8. Breakdown of one FL iteration under MoDuo, averaged over all participants and 1000 independent times. In the plot, *CNN* presents the "cnn" model, *MOB* presents "mob-v3s", and *EFF* is for "eff-b0".

As shown in Fig. 8, decoding and decryption in MoDuo typically take longer than encoding and encryption. This is explained by the additional padding step in MoDuo decoding (Fig. 3), compared to the straightforward encoding procedure (Fig. 2). Additionally, since MoDuo encryption covers serialization and decryption covers deserialization, there is a substantial runtime gap between these two operations. In which decryption takes approximately 2× longer than encryption, despite the comparable computational cost of the underlying AES-GCM. The idle time, although typically small (less than 2.8% of the total iteration time), still contributes to the worker-side runtime and becomes more pronounced with larger models. Beyond this idle, the overall runtime of all functions increases with model size and complexity.

Table 2. Detailed comparison across methods and model parameters. $time^e$ indicates the total time to perform encoding and encryption in one FL iteration, while $time^d$ refers to the time for decoding and decryption.

Method	#params	τ^e_{pp} (μs/param)	τ^d_{pp} (μs/param)	$time^e$ (s)	$time^d$ (s)
AES-GCM	545K	0.202	0.257	0.11 (only encryption)	0.14 (only decryption)
MoDuo		1.517	2.341	0.827	1.276
AES-GCM	1.53M	1.085	1.621	1.66 (only encryption)	2.48 (only decryption)
MoDuo		2.859	4.625	4.374	7.076
AES-GCM	4.02M	1.537	2.197	6.18 (only encryption)	8.83 (only decryption)
MoDuo		3.457	5.400	13.899	21.708
Batch		12.607	5.179	50.680	20.819
Stock		1262.300	398.946	5074.445	1603.762

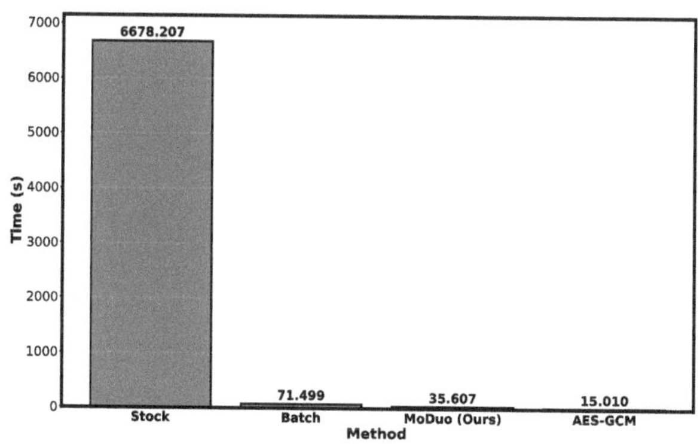

Fig. 9. Per-iteration time comparison among BatchCrypt (batch), FATE' stock implementation (stock), MoDuo (ours), and AES-GCM (no extra encoding) on a 4.02M-parameter model. To ensure fair comparisons, *idle* time is not included, as there are differences between the communication stacks of Flower and FATE.

We also compare the cryptographic time in one iteration of Stock, Batch, MoDuo, and AES-GCM (no extra encoding) as shown in Fig. 9. As our encryption is substantially faster, even when its decryption time is comparable to that of Batch (in *eff-b0* model), MoDuo is overall still the fastest, taking only 35.607 s per iteration for cryptographic operations. Meanwhile, Batch requires double our time, at 71.499 s, and Stock requires 6678 s for a single iteration, corresponding to 93.4× the runtime of Batch and over 187.6× that of MoDuo (excluding training and idle time). This performance gap between Batch and MoDuo is mainly due to their underlying cryptographic primitives, HE (Paillier) in Batch versus a symmetric block cipher (AES-GCM) in our MoDuo. In turn, the significant improvement of Batch over Stock comes from its use of ciphertext batching and low-bit quantization on top of the same Paillier-based design. Besides, as predicted, direct decimal-serialized AES-GCM without any extra steps finishes one iteration in the fastest time of around 15 s.

5.3 Payload Sizes

Table 3 displays the comparison between the size (in MB) of payloads before and after encryption. As the payload is serialized as unsigned 8-bit integer arrays when sending, in this measurement, the total number of bytes in the data is defined as the size of the payload.

Table 3. Payload capacity (in MB): original, via AES-GCM (no extra encoding), and MoDuo

Code	Original	AES-GCM	MoDuo	Size difference (MoDuo vs. Original)
cnn	1.599	9.02	4.570	x2.85
mob-v3s	5.828	35.46	20.426	x3.50
eff-b0	15.334	98.26	60.545	x3.95

As shown in Table 3, MoDuo introduces a controlled payload increase over the original model size. Specifically, the payload size increases by a factor of 2.85× for a small, shallow CNN model (1.6 MB, 0.545M parameters), 3.5× for a medium-sized model (5.8 MB, 1.528M parameters), and just 3.95× for a larger architecture (15.3 MB, 4.02M parameters). It, however, remains more compact than direct AES-GCM over decimal-serialized model values, reducing the protected payload from 9.02 to 4.570 MB (↓49.3%), 35.46 to 20.426 MB (↓42.4%), and 98.26 to 60.545 MB (↓38.4%), respectively.

6 Conclusion

This paper introduces MoDuo, a lightweight protection scheme with an embedded obfuscation layer that enhances standard encoding via a Morse-inspired representation fused with multiple numbering systems. Combined with AES-GCM, MoDuo keeps communication payloads small, private, and tamper-evident, while avoiding both the high computational cost of HE and the coordination overhead of SA. MoDuo is generic and highly usable, supporting diverse payload types, including model parameters, gradients, and sensitive metadata.

Our FL evaluation shows that MoDuo provides a practical trade-off between transmission-level protection and system overhead. It preserves model utility with only minor accuracy drops, typically below 1% and below 2% even under extreme configurations. The minor variations in accuracy are mainly due to rounding precision constraints introduced by the truncation.

Compared with HE-based baselines such as BatchCrypt and stock FATE, MoDuo substantially reduces cryptographic processing time while avoiding encrypted-domain computation. Although slower than direct AES-GCM due to its additional encoding and decoding steps, it reduces the serialized protected payload size and remains significantly lighter than HE-based protection. Overall, MoDuo offers a lightweight design for protecting FL payloads against external transmission adversaries, with acceptable payload growth and practical overhead for resource-constrained edge deployments.

Acknowledgments. This work was supported by the Emerging Projects program, Infotech Oulu; the Research Council of Finland through 6G Flagship program (318927); European Commission (101137711); Business Finland through Neural pub/sub project (diary number 8754/31/2022); the ERDF (project numbers A81568, A91867); and Tauno Tönning Foundation for Huong Nguyen's and Amirhossein Ghaffari's research.

Disclosure of Interests. The authors have no competing interests to declare that are relevant to the content of this article.

References

1. Acar, A., Aksu, H., Uluagac, A.S., Conti, M.: A survey on homomorphic encryption schemes: theory and implementation. ACM Comput. Surv. **51**(4), 1–35 (2018)
2. Alistarh, D., Grubic, D., Li, J., Tomioka, R., Vojnovic, M.: QSGD: communication-efficient SGD via gradient quantization and encoding. In: Advances in Neural Information Processing Systems, p. 30. (2017)
3. Bernstein, J., Wang, Y.X., Azizzadenesheli, K., Anandkumar, A.: signSGD: compressed optimisation for non-convex problems. In: International Conference on Machine Learning, pp. 560–569. PMLR (2018)
4. Bonawitz, K., et al.: Practical secure aggregation for privacy-preserving machine learning. In: ACM Conference on Computer and Communications Security, pp. 1175–1191 (2017)
5. Cheon, J.H., Kim, A., Kim, M., Song, Y.: Homomorphic encryption for arithmetic of approximate numbers. In: Takagi, T., Peyrin, T. (eds.) ASIACRYPT 2017. LNCS, vol. 10624, pp. 409–437. Springer, Cham (2017). https://doi.org/10.1007/978-3-319-70694-8_15
6. Coe, L.: The Telegraph: A History of Morse's Invention and Its Predecessors in the United States. McFarland (2003)
7. Dworkin, M.: Recommendation for block cipher modes of operation: Galois/counter mode (GCM) and GMAC. NIST Special Publication (SP) (2007)

8. Geiping, J., Bauermeister, H., Dröge, H., Moeller, M.: Inverting gradients-how easy is it to break privacy in federated learning? Adv. Neural. Inf. Process. Syst. **33**, 16937–16947 (2020)
9. Howard, A., et al.: Searching for MobileNetV3. In: Proceedings of the IEEE/CVF International Conference on Computer Vision, pp. 1314–1324 (2019)
10. Kadhe, S., Rajaraman, N., Koyluoglu, O.O., Ramchandran, K.: FastSecAgg: scalable secure aggregation for privacy-preserving federated learning. arXiv preprint arXiv:2009.11248 (2020)
11. Kairouz, P., et al.: Advances and open problems in federated learning. Found. Trends Mach. Learn. **14**, 1–210 (2021)
12. Li, H., Xie, W., Ye, H., Ma, J., Ma, S., Li, Y.: FedFQ: federated learning with fine-grained quantization. arXiv preprint arXiv:2408.08977 (2024)
13. Lin, Y., Han, S., Mao, H., Wang, Y., Dally, W.J.: Deep gradient compression: reducing the communication bandwidth for distributed training. arXiv preprint arXiv:1712.01887 (2017)
14. Liu, G., Xu, T., Yang, Y., Abdelmoniem, A.M., Wang, C., Liu, J.: Poisoning as a post-protection: mitigating membership privacy leakage from gradient and prediction of federated models. IEEE Trans. Depend. Secure Comput. (2025)
15. McGrew, D.: An Interface and Algorithms for Authenticated Encryption. RFC 5116, January 2008. https://doi.org/10.17487/RFC5116
16. McMahan, B., Moore, E., Ramage, D., Hampson, S., y Arcas, B.A.: Communication-efficient learning of deep networks from decentralized data. In: Artificial Intelligence and Statistics, pp. 1273–1282. PMLR (2017)
17. Melis, L., Song, C., De Cristofaro, E., Shmatikov, V.: Exploiting unintended feature leakage in collaborative learning. In: IEEE Symposium on Security and Privacy, pp. 691–706. IEEE (2019)
18. Paillier, P.: Public-key cryptosystems based on composite degree residuosity classes. In: Stern, J. (ed.) EUROCRYPT 1999. LNCS, vol. 1592, pp. 223–238. Springer, Heidelberg (1999). https://doi.org/10.1007/3-540-48910-X_16
19. Ren, Y., Cao, Y., Ye, C., Cheng, X.: Two-layer accumulated quantized compression for communication-efficient federated learning: TLAQC. Sci. Rep. **13**(1), 11658 (2023)
20. San, I., At, N., Yakut, I., Polat, H.: Efficient paillier cryptoprocessor for privacy-preserving data mining. Secur. Commun. Netw. **9**(11), 1535–1546 (2016)
21. Sav, S., et al.: POSEIDON: privacy-preserving federated neural network learning. In: 28th Annual Network and Distributed System Security Symposium, NDSS 2021, virtually, 21–25 February 2021. The Internet Society (2021)
22. So, J., et al.: LightSecAgg: a lightweight and versatile design for secure aggregation in federated learning. Proc. Mach. Learn. Syst. **4**, 694–720 (2022)
23. Sushmitha, S., Prasad, H., Sapna, V.: Multi-layer secure authentication using morse code and eye blink detection. In: 2025 9th International Symposium on Innovative Approaches in Smart Technologies (ISAS), pp. 1–8. IEEE (2025)
24. Tan, M., Le, Q.: EfficientNet: rethinking model scaling for convolutional neural networks. In: International Conference on Machine Learning, pp. 6105–6114. PMLR (2019)
25. Tarek, N., et al.: Morse glasses: an IoT communication system based on Morse code for users with speech impairments. Computing **104**(4), 789–808 (2022)
26. Zhang, C., Yang, S., Mao, L., Ning, H.: Anomaly detection and defense techniques in federated learning: a comprehensive review. Artif. Intell. Rev. **57**(6), 150 (2024)

27. Zhang, C., Li, S., Xia, J., Wang, W., Yan, F., Liu, Y.: {BatchCrypt}: efficient homomorphic encryption for {Cross-Silo} federated learning. In: USENIX Annual Technical Conference, pp. 493–506 (2020)
28. Zhou, S., Wang, L., Chen, L., Wang, Y., Yuan, K.: Group verifiable secure aggregate federated learning based on secret sharing. Sci. Rep. **15**(1), 9712 (2025)
29. Zhu, L., Liu, Z., Han, S.: Deep leakage from gradients. Adv. Neural. Inf. Process. Syst. **32** (2019)

Spatio-Temporal Scheduling Prediction Under Backhaul Delay for Resilient Coordinated Beamforming

Prashant Kumar Singh[1,2](✉), Shubham Vaishnav[1], Ahmet Hasim Gökceoglu[2], and Li Wang[2]

[1] Stockholm University, Stockholm, Sweden
{prku7110,shubham.vaishnav}@dsv.su.se
[2] Huawei R&D, Stockholm, Sweden
{ahmet.hasim.gokceoglu1,leo.li.wang}@huawei.com

Abstract. Coordinated beamforming in distributed 5G networks relies on the timely exchange of inter-cell scheduling information, but backhaul latency makes this information stale. Even a single transmission time interval (TTI) of delay can reduce CBF-SLNR performance below the uncoordinated baseline, because the precoder suppresses interference toward users that are no longer active. Coordination on stale information is therefore worse than no coordination at all. To address this, we propose a two-stage predictive framework in which a Spectral Temporal Graph Neural Network (StemGNN) predicts future user equipment (UE) scheduling states from delayed historical observations, and the predictions replace stale inputs to the CBF-SLNR precoder. Evaluated on a three-cell massive MIMO downlink with 60 UEs and 64 antennas per base station under Quadriga Urban Micro (UMi) channels and a proportional fair scheduler, StemGNN achieves a mean scheduling prediction accuracy of 87.57%, outperforming LSTM, GRU, Simple RNN, and Markov chain baselines at all evaluated horizons, with gains of up to 7.71% over LSTM at longer horizons where inter-UE structural dependencies dominate over temporal autocorrelation. When integrated into coordinated beamforming, the predictions recover 57–73% of the sum rate loss caused by one TTI of backhaul delay, improving sum rate by 9.58–14.35% over the no-prediction baseline and recovering up to 83% of the Lag-1 fairness loss for cell-edge users, with fairness gains persisting at higher lag values where throughput gains diminish. These results show that treating backhaul latency as a spatio-temporal forecasting problem is an effective approach for robust inter-cell coordination in delay-constrained networks.

Keywords: Coordinated beamforming · StemGNN · Scheduling prediction · Backhaul delay · Edge AI

1 Introduction

Modern 5G networks, and emerging 6G ones, use coordinated beamforming (CBF) across multiple base stations (BSs) to reduce inter-cell interference and

Z. Afzal et al. (Eds.): ARES 2026 Workshops, LNCS 16900, pp. 466–483, 2027.
https://doi.org/10.1007/978-3-032-35576-8_25

keep spectral efficiency high [5,10,17,27]. In distributed radio access networks, neighboring BSs exchange channel state and scheduling information over backhaul links. These links have limited bandwidth, are often asynchronous, and frequently add delay [3,25]. As a result, the view each BS has of the wider network is almost always out of date, while user activity changes much faster: users enter, leave, or change their scheduling state continuously [15,29]. Standard CBF algorithms such as Weighted Minimum Mean Square Error (WMMSE) optimization [26,27] assume that each BS has fresh, global channel and scheduling information. Once this assumption breaks, the sum rate drops and service quality becomes uneven across cells.

From an edge AI point of view, each BS is an autonomous edge node that has to make real-time, latency-critical decisions using incomplete and partially outdated information about its peers. Backhaul latency, jitter, and asynchronous updates act as a kind of partial fault on the links between nodes: the information a BS needs is not lost outright, it just arrives late and stale. A beamforming controller at the edge therefore needs to stay robust against this kind of information-staleness fault to keep service available and quality of experience consistent across cells.

The trust side of this problem matters too. Each BS feeds its beamformer with scheduling and channel reports it receives from neighbors, and there is no built-in way to tell whether an unusual or late-arriving report reflects genuine network behavior, a backhaul fault, or a tampered message injected somewhere along the path. The more directly a BS depends on raw, last-received neighbor data, the larger this trust surface becomes. A learning-based predictor trained on the legitimate temporal patterns of neighbor scheduling reduces this dependence: the BS can rely on its own predicted view of the neighborhood, and treat late-arriving reports as a correction rather than as ground truth. We do not aim to detect adversarial inputs in this work, but the same prediction step that handles delay also shrinks the attack surface exposed to an attacker on the backhaul.

Despite a lot of progress on CBF and on machine-learning-assisted interference management, most existing work either assumes ideal information exchange, or treats the spatial and temporal sides of the problem separately. Graph Neural Networks (GNNs) capture the spatial structure of wireless networks well by representing BSs and users as nodes in a graph [11,16,35], and recent GNN-based beamforming methods [8,9,13,23] perform strongly but usually assume static user configurations and synchronous information access. On the other side, spectral-temporal forecasting models such as StemGNN [2,31] capture multivariate temporal dependencies but are not connected to physical-layer beamforming decisions. As a result, no existing framework jointly addresses (i) delayed inter-BS information, (ii) a dynamic user population, and (iii) coordinated beamforming in a form that fits an edge deployment.

In this paper, we recast coordinated beamforming under backhaul delay as a prediction-assisted decision problem that runs locally at each BS. Each edge node uses a spectral-temporal GNN, based on StemGNN [2], to predict the current user-equipment (UE) scheduling state of neighboring cells from past, delayed observations, and feeds these predictions into a Signal-to-Leakage-plus-Noise Ratio (SLNR) coordinated beamformer (see Fig. 1 for an overview). To handle the dynamic user populations seen in real networks, we extend the architecture to support a variable number of UEs and a permutation-invariant representation, so the same model still works as users join, leave, or are reordered. The resulting controller suppresses inter-cell interference even when the backhaul is delayed and user activity is stochastic, and gives a concrete example of a fault-tolerant edge AI pipeline for cooperative wireless inference.

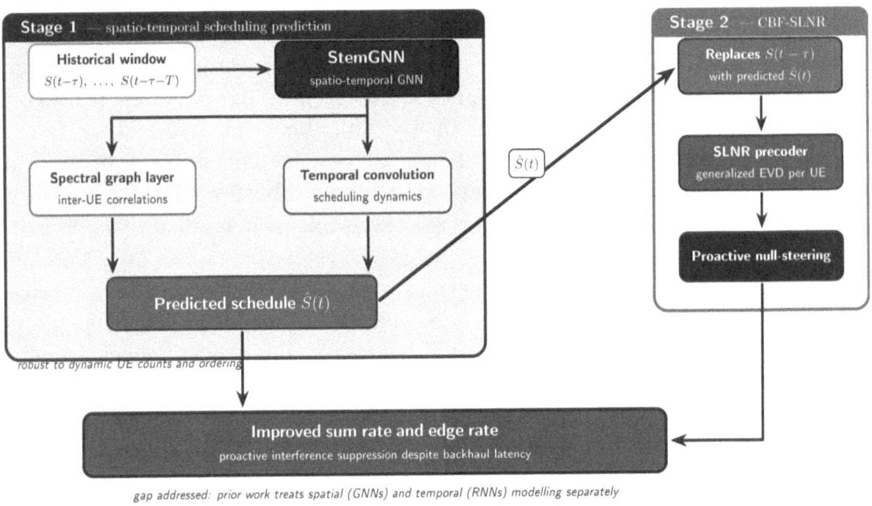

Fig. 1. Proposed prediction-assisted coordinated beamforming framework. Each base station uses a spectral-temporal GNN to predict the current scheduling state of neighboring cells from delayed backhaul observations, and feeds the predictions into an SLNR-based coordinated beamformer.

Contributions. The main contributions of this paper are as follows:

- We formulate inter-BS UE scheduling prediction under backhaul delay as a multivariate binary time-series problem, and benchmark a spectral-temporal GNN against recurrent (RNN, LSTM, GRU) and Markov baselines.
- We extend StemGNN with a permutation-invariant input and output representation that supports a dynamic, variable number of UEs without retraining, making it suitable for realistic edge deployments.
- We integrate the predicted scheduling states into an SLNR-based CBF pipeline and measure the resulting sum-rate gain over conventional beamforming that uses stale information directly, under a range of backhaul delays and dynamic user-activity conditions.

2 Related Work

2.1 Coordinated Beamforming and the Cost of Stale Information

Massive MIMO and coordinated beamforming have become the standard tools for managing interference in dense multi-cell deployments [1,10,17,20,22]. The classical algorithms in this area, mainly WMMSE [27] and fractional programming [26], reach near-optimal sum rate when each base station has accurate and timely channel state and scheduling information from all of its neighbors. In practice this is rarely the case. In cloud and distributed RAN architectures, backhaul links are bandwidth-limited and asynchronous, and the inter-cell information used to drive these algorithms is delayed, partial, or both [3,25]. The repeated matrix inversions and iterative steps in WMMSE and FP also push their computational cost beyond what is reasonable for real-time execution on an edge node such as a base station [20,22]. Decentralized variants reduce some of this burden, but still require frequent inter-cell signaling, which is affected by the same backhaul delays [10,19]. From an edge-deployment standpoint, this points to a clear failure mode: when the data feeding the coordination algorithm is late or incomplete, the algorithm produces a confidently wrong decision, and the system has no fallback.

2.2 Machine Learning Approaches and Their Edge Implications

To work around these limitations, a large body of recent work uses machine learning for wireless resource allocation and interference management [7,12,33]. The general idea is to replace iterative optimization with a learned mapping from network state to control actions, which lowers inference latency and fits the timing budget of edge execution. Reinforcement learning has been applied to beamforming, power allocation, and inter-cell coordination by framing them as sequential decision problems [21,24], though stability under fast-changing conditions remains a concern. Supervised deep-learning models that map channel observations directly to beamforming vectors [28] cut complexity further, but tend to ignore the structural dependencies between cells. From a deployment standpoint, these models also raise questions about trust and robustness: a base station that runs a learned model at the edge inherits the integrity of its training data and the inputs it consumes at runtime, and most of these works do not discuss how the model behaves when those inputs are stale, missing, or tampered with.

2.3 Graph and Spatio-Temporal Models

Wireless networks have a natural graph structure, with base stations and users as nodes and interference relationships as edges. Graph Neural Networks (GNNs) [11,16,30,35] are a good fit for this structure because their message passing is permutation invariant and respects the connectivity of the network. GNN-based beamforming methods, including heterogeneous variants such as

HSTGNN [13,34] and the approaches in [8,9,23], achieve near-optimal sum rate with millisecond-level inference, which is compatible with edge execution. The main limitation across this line of work is the assumption of static, or slowly varying, user configurations. Real cellular traffic does not behave this way: users enter, leave, and change scheduling state on much shorter timescales [5,15,29].

On the temporal side, spectral-temporal models such as StemGNN [2] forecast multivariate time series by jointly modeling temporal dependencies and inter-series correlations in the frequency domain. Graph WaveNet [31] combines graph convolution with dilated temporal convolutions for a similar purpose, and DCRNN and STGCN follow related ideas [18,32]. These models are designed as forecasters, and are not typically connected to a physical-layer decision such as beamforming.

2.4 Positioning of This Paper

Pulling these threads together, three observations stand out for an edge AI deployment in a distributed RAN. Classical CBF assumes information conditions that the edge does not actually have. ML-based beamforming captures spatial structure but treats user activity as static. Spatio-temporal forecasters capture the temporal side but stop short of the beamforming pipeline. To the best of our knowledge, no existing framework jointly addresses (i) the spatial structure of the network, (ii) the temporal evolution of user activity, and (iii) the staleness of inter-base-station information, in a form deployable at the edge. This paper targets exactly that intersection by combining a spectral-temporal GNN predictor for delayed neighbor scheduling with an SLNR-based coordinated beamformer, so that each base station can take a beamforming decision without trusting a possibly faulty or stale neighbor report at face value.

3 System Model and Problem Formulation

3.1 Multi-cell Downlink Model

We consider a downlink Massive MIMO network with B base stations (BSs) operating on the same time–frequency resource, where each BS $b \in \{1, \ldots, B\}$ has M antennas and serves K_b single-antenna user equipments (UEs). The total number of UEs in the network is $K = \sum_{b=1}^{B} K_b$. We denote the channel vector from BS b' to UE k served by BS b as $\mathbf{h}_{b',b,k} \in \mathbb{C}^M$. In our experiments, these channels are generated with the Quadriga Urban Micro propagation model [5], which captures path loss, shadowing, and multipath fading.

At time slot (TTI) t, BS b transmits the linearly precoded signal

$$\mathbf{x}_b(t) = \sum_{k=1}^{K_b} \mathbf{w}_{b,k}(t)\, s_{b,k}(t), \tag{1}$$

where $\mathbf{w}_{b,k}(t) \in \mathbb{C}^M$ is the beamforming vector for UE k in cell b and $s_{b,k}(t) \sim \mathcal{CN}(0,1)$ is the unit-power data symbol. Each BS is subject to a per-cell transmit power constraint $\sum_{k=1}^{K_b} \|\mathbf{w}_{b,k}(t)\|^2 \leq P_{\max}$.

The signal received at UE k in cell b is

$$y_{b,k}(t) = \mathbf{h}_{b,b,k}^H \mathbf{w}_{b,k} s_{b,k} + \sum_{j \neq k} \mathbf{h}_{b,b,k}^H \mathbf{w}_{b,j} s_{b,j} + \sum_{l \neq b} \sum_{j=1}^{K_l} \mathbf{h}_{l,b,k}^H \mathbf{w}_{l,j} s_{l,j} + u_{b,k}, \quad (2)$$

where $u_{b,k} \sim \mathcal{CN}(0, \sigma_u^2)$ is additive Gaussian noise (time index suppressed for readability). The three sums on the right-hand side are, respectively, the desired signal, the intra-cell interference, and the inter-cell interference. The resulting SINR and achievable rate at UE (b,k) are

$$\gamma_{b,k}(t) = \frac{|\mathbf{h}_{b,b,k}^H \mathbf{w}_{b,k}|^2}{\sum_{j \neq k} |\mathbf{h}_{b,b,k}^H \mathbf{w}_{b,j}|^2 + \sum_{l \neq b} \sum_j |\mathbf{h}_{l,b,k}^H \mathbf{w}_{l,j}|^2 + \sigma_u^2}, \quad R_{b,k}(t) = \log_2\left(1 + \gamma_{b,k}(t)\right). \quad (3)$$

3.2 User Scheduling and Backhaul Delay

In each TTI, BS b runs a proportional-fair scheduler [15,29] that selects a subset of its UEs for transmission. We represent this decision by the binary scheduling vector

$$\mathbf{s}_b(t) \in \{0,1\}^{K_b}, \quad s_{b,k}(t) = 1 \iff \text{UE } (b,k) \text{ is active at TTI } t. \quad (4)$$

Only active UEs contribute to the interference terms in (2), so the global scheduling state $\mathbf{s}(t) = [\mathbf{s}_1(t); \ldots; \mathbf{s}_B(t)]$ directly shapes the interference pattern at every UE in the network.

In a distributed RAN, each BS shares its scheduling decisions and channel state with its neighbors over a backhaul link. We model the backhaul as introducing a fixed delay of $\tau \geq 1$ TTIs. At TTI t, each BS therefore observes only

$$\mathbf{s}_{b'}(t - \tau), \quad b' \neq b, \quad (5)$$

about its neighbors. From an edge-deployment perspective, this delay is a structural property of the link between edge nodes, not an occasional event, so any coordination logic running at the BS has to tolerate it by design.

3.3 Coordinated Beamforming with Stale Information

Coordinated beamforming aims to maximize the network sum rate under per-BS power constraints:

$$\max_{\{\mathbf{w}_{b,k}\}} \sum_{b=1}^{B} \sum_{k=1}^{K_b} R_{b,k}(t) \quad \text{s.t.} \quad \sum_{k=1}^{K_b} \|\mathbf{w}_{b,k}\|^2 \leq P_{\max}, \quad \forall b. \quad (6)$$

This problem is non-convex; iterative methods such as WMMSE [27] and fractional programming [26] solve it under the assumption that each BS has timely access to the global channel and scheduling state. Coordinated beamforming via the Signal-to-Leakage-plus-Noise Ratio (SLNR) criterion offers a closed-form per-UE alternative that is well suited to distributed execution at the edge [10]. For UE k in cell b, the SLNR is

$$\mathrm{SLNR}_{b,k}(t) = \frac{|\mathbf{h}_{b,b,k}^{H}\mathbf{w}_{b,k}|^2}{\mathbf{w}_{b,k}^{H}\mathbf{Q}_b(t)\,\mathbf{w}_{b,k} + \sigma_u^2\|\mathbf{w}_{b,k}\|^2}, \tag{7}$$

where the leakage covariance

$$\mathbf{Q}_b(t) = \sum_{l \neq b} \sum_{\substack{j=1 \\ s_{l,j}(t)=1}}^{K_l} \mathbf{h}_{b,l,j}\,\mathbf{h}_{b,l,j}^{H} \tag{8}$$

sums only over UEs that are *currently active* in neighboring cells. The SLNR-maximizing precoder is the dominant generalized eigenvector of the matrix pair $(\mathbf{h}_{b,b,k}\mathbf{h}_{b,b,k}^{H},\ \mathbf{Q}_b(t) + \sigma_u^2\mathbf{I})$, and in practice we use a rank-L approximation of $\mathbf{Q}_b(t)$ to keep complexity within the per-TTI budget of an edge node.

The dependence on the *current* scheduling state $\mathbf{s}_l(t)$ in (8) is the central issue. When the BS has only the stale observation $\mathbf{s}_l(t-\tau)$, it can either (i) plug the stale observation straight into (8), which builds the wrong leakage covariance and steers nulls toward UEs that are no longer active while ignoring UEs that became active in the meantime, or (ii) infer the current scheduling state from the delayed history. We pursue the second option.

3.4 Prediction-Assisted Formulation

Let

$$\mathcal{H}_{b'}(t) = \big[\mathbf{s}_{b'}(t-\tau),\, \mathbf{s}_{b'}(t-\tau-1),\, \ldots,\, \mathbf{s}_{b'}(t-\tau-T_{\mathrm{win}}+1)\big] \in \{0,1\}^{T_{\mathrm{win}} \times K_{b'}} \tag{9}$$

denote the most recent T_{win} delayed scheduling vectors of BS b' as observed at a neighboring BS. Each BS applies a learned per-cell predictor $f_{\theta_{b'}}$ to produce a current-time estimate

$$\hat{\mathbf{s}}_{b'}(t) = \mathbb{1}\big[f_{\theta_{b'}}(\mathcal{H}_{b'}(t)) > 0.5\big] \in \{0,1\}^{K_{b'}}, \tag{10}$$

which replaces $\mathbf{s}_{b'}(t-\tau)$ in (8). The overall design problem then becomes a joint learning-and-control task: learn per-BS predictors $\{f_{\theta_{b'}}\}$ that, when wired into the SLNR precoder of (7)–(8), recover as much as possible of the sum rate in (6) at delay τ.

Two practical constraints follow from the edge setting. First, the predictor must run locally on the BS at TTI granularity, which rules out any centralized or high-latency solution. Second, the predictor should not depend on a fixed UE identity or fixed ordering, since users enter and leave the cell continuously. We therefore require f_θ to be permutation-invariant in the UE dimension, so that the same trained model handles a varying $K_{b'}$ without retraining.

4 Proposed Spatio-Temporal Scheduling Prediction Framework

The proposed framework is a two-stage pipeline (Fig. 1). In Stage 1, each BS trains a spectral-temporal GNN predictor on its own observed history of (delayed) neighbor scheduling. In Stage 2, the trained predictor is wired into the SLNR coordinated beamformer so that the leakage covariance (8) is built from $\hat{\mathbf{s}}_{b'}(t)$ instead of $\mathbf{s}_{b'}(t-\tau)$. Both stages share the same simulator, channel realizations, and proportional-fair scheduler, so the predictor is trained on the same operating regime in which it is later deployed.

4.1 Spectral-Temporal GNN Predictor

We use a StemGNN architecture [2], a spectral-temporal graph neural network originally proposed for multivariate time-series forecasting. The fit is direct: the $K_{b'}$ scheduling sequences of cell b' are correlated through the proportional-fair scheduler that produced them, and StemGNN jointly models temporal and inter-series dependencies in the spectral domain. The network has three components.
Latent Correlation Layer. The input window $\mathbf{X} \in \{0,1\}^{T_{\text{win}} \times K_{b'}}$ is passed through a GRU [4], and a self-attention layer over the hidden states produces a learned adjacency matrix $\mathbf{A} \in \mathbb{R}^{K_{b'} \times K_{b'}}$. This $\mathbf{A}$ captures which pairs of UEs tend to be co-scheduled and is learned from data rather than specified a priori.
StemGNN Block. A Graph Fourier Transform (GFT) using the eigenbasis of $\mathbf{A}$ projects the multivariate input into a spectral domain where inter-UE correlations become orthogonal. A Spectral Sequential Cell then applies a Discrete Fourier Transform along the temporal axis of each (now decorrelated) component, processes the frequency representation with a 1D convolution and a Gated Linear Unit, and inverts back to the time domain. A learned graph convolution and an inverse GFT close the block. Two such blocks are stacked with a residual connection, where the second block learns the reconstruction residual of the first.
Output Layer. A Gated Linear Unit followed by fully connected layers produces per-UE activation logits, which are passed through a sigmoid $\sigma(\cdot)$ and thresholded at 0.5 as in (10) to yield the binary scheduling prediction. Since scheduling prediction is a binary classification task rather than the regression task in [2], we train the network with the binary cross-entropy loss

$$\mathcal{L}(\theta) = -\frac{1}{|\mathcal{D}|} \sum_{(\mathbf{X},\mathbf{y})\in\mathcal{D}} \sum_{k=1}^{K_{b'}} \Big[y_k \log \hat{y}_k + (1-y_k)\log(1-\hat{y}_k) \Big], \tag{11}$$

where $\hat{y}_k = \sigma(f_\theta(\mathbf{X}))_k$ and $\mathcal{D}$ is the training set of (history window, target scheduling) pairs.

4.2 Permutation Invariance and Variable User Population

To meet the second edge constraint above, the input UEs are treated as nodes of the latent graph rather than as fixed positions in a vector. The latent correlation layer infers $\mathbf{A}$ from data on each forward pass, the spectral graph convolution is permutation-equivariant by construction, and the per-UE output head is shared across UE indices. As a result, the same trained model handles a varying number of UEs in cell b' without retraining: UEs that enter the cell are added as new nodes, and UEs that leave are dropped, with no change to the parameters θ.

4.3 Integration with the SLNR Beamformer

At inference time, each receiving BS b runs $B-1$ copies of the trained predictor, one per neighboring cell, on the delayed history $\mathcal{H}_{b'}(t)$ it has on hand. The predicted neighbor scheduling vectors $\hat{\mathbf{s}}_{b'}(t)$ are fed into (8) to build the estimated leakage covariance $\hat{\mathbf{Q}}_b(t)$, and the SLNR precoder of (7) is then computed via a rank-L generalized eigenvalue decomposition. No other change is made to the beamforming algorithm, which keeps the predictor and the beamformer cleanly decoupled and lets the predictor be retrained or swapped without touching the physical-layer code path.

In operational terms, each BS keeps producing a beamforming decision at every TTI even if neighbor reports arrive late, and the decision is no longer a direct function of the most recent received message. The predictor acts as a learned model of expected neighbor behaviour, so a single missing, late, or anomalous report cannot, on its own, drive the beamformer into a faulty state.

4.4 Algorithm

Algorithm 1 summarizes the complete pipeline. Lines 3–5 cover the initial data-gathering phase, during which the BSs run conventional CBF-SLNR with stale scheduling and accumulate a history tensor $\mathcal{H} \in \{0,1\}^{B\times K\times T_{\text{total}}}$. At a fixed TTI t_{train}, each BS trains its own predictor on its accumulated history (lines 16–19). From $t_{\text{train}}+1$ onward, the trained predictor replaces the stale neighbor scheduling in the SLNR precoder (lines 7–10). Training uses the Adam optimizer with learning rate 10^{-3}, mini-batch size 32, gradient clipping at maximum norm 1.0, early stopping on validation loss with patience 15, and a strictly chronological 80/20 train–validation split that avoids any temporal leakage from future to past.

5 Experimental Results

5.1 Experimental Setup

We evaluate the proposed framework on a three-cell Massive MIMO downlink network with 60 single-antenna UEs (22, 20, and 18 in cells 0, 1, and 2 respectively), 64 antennas per base station, and an identical proportional-fair scheduler running at every BS. Channel matrices are generated with the Quadriga Urban Micro (UMi) propagation model [5], which captures path loss, shadowing, and multipath fading under realistic urban conditions and is widely used

```
Input  : Channels H; backhaul delay τ; history window T_win; horizon T_total;
         training trigger t_train.
Output: Beamformers {w_{b,k}(t)}; sum rate; edge rate.
Initialize history H ∈ {0,1}^{B×K×T_total}, PF rate histories r̄_b(t), predictors ← ∅
for t ← 0 to T_total − 1 do
    // Scheduling
    for each BS b do s_b(t) ← PF(H, r̄_b(t)); store in H[·,·,t] // Neighbor
        scheduling estimate
    if predictors = ∅ then
        ŝ_{b'}(t) ← s_{b'}(t − τ) for all b'                      // stale baseline
    else
        for each BS b' do
            H_{b'}(t) ← H[b', ·, t − τ − T_win + 1 : t − τ]
            ŝ_{b'}(t) ← 1[f_{θ_{b'}}(H_{b'}(t)) > 0.5]
        end
    end
    // CBF-SLNR
    Build Q̂_b(t) from {ŝ_{b'}(t)}_{b'≠b} via (8)
    Compute SLNR precoder w_{b,k}(t) via rank-L GEVD of
    (h_{b,b,k} h_{b,b,k}^H, Q̂_b(t) + σ_u^2 I)
    Compute rates R_{b,k}(t) via (3); update r̄_b(t)
    // Train predictors once
    if t = t_train then
        for each BS b' do
            Build D_{b'} from H[b', ·, 0 : t_train] with lag τ, window T_win;
            chronological 80/20 split
            Train f_{θ_{b'}} by minimizing (11) with Adam, BCE loss, gradient
            clipping, early stopping
        end
        predictors ← {f_{θ_{b'}}}_{b'=1}^B
    end
end
return {w_{b,k}(t)}, sum rate, edge rate
```

Algorithm 1: Two-stage prediction-assisted CBF-SLNR pipeline.

in 5G and 6G system-level evaluation. The configuration follows parameters representative of operational Massive MIMO deployments rather than a stylised academic setup. Two subcarrier configurations are evaluated, 1 SC (narrowband) and 48 SC (wideband), which together cover the operating regimes typical of real deployments. Backhaul delays of $\tau \in \{1, 3, 5\}$ TTIs are considered. All models use a 12-step delayed history window ($T_{\text{win}} = 12$).

StemGNN is benchmarked against LSTM [14], GRU [4], Simple RNN [6], third-order Markov chains, and a Simple Moving Average baseline. Two experiments are conducted. **Experiment 1** evaluates standalone scheduling prediction over 2000 TTIs with a 70/20/10 chronological train/validation/test split. **Experiment 2** integrates the trained predictors into the live CBF-SLNR pipeline over 2000 TTIs, with model training triggered at TTI 1600 on the scheduling history accumulated under coordinated beamforming conditions, and performance measured over the final 400 TTIs. The relative improvement of StemGNN over a baseline is reported as $(V_{\text{StemGNN}} - V_{\text{baseline}})/V_{\text{baseline}} \times 100\%$. Results are aggregated across 18 independent operating conditions, namely three cells with different UE populations, two subcarrier configurations, and three backhaul lags, so the trends below reflect consistent behaviour rather than a single favourable run.

5.2 Scheduling Prediction Accuracy

Table 1 reports prediction accuracy at Horizon 1 along with StemGNN's relative improvement over each baseline.

Table 1. Scheduling prediction accuracy (%) at Horizon 1, and StemGNN's relative improvement over each baseline.

Model	BS 0	BS 1	BS 2	Mean	Improv. (%)
Simple Moving Average	66.59	59.36	60.47	62.14	+40.92
3rd Order Markov	86.00	83.53	86.28	85.27	+2.70
Simple RNN	86.19	85.05	86.21	85.82	+2.04
GRU	86.34	85.34	86.33	86.00	+1.83
LSTM	86.24	84.87	86.87	85.99	+1.84
StemGNN (proposed)	**89.71**	**85.71**	**87.30**	**87.57**	—

StemGNN reaches 87.57% mean accuracy at Horizon 1 and leads on every cell. It is ahead of the strongest recurrent baseline (GRU) by 1.83% points, ahead of the third-order Markov chain by 2.70, and ahead of the Simple Moving Average by a much larger 40.92. The recurrent baselines cluster tightly between 85.82% and 86.00%, which suggests that gating mechanisms add little over plain recurrence for short-range binary scheduling dynamics. At Horizon 1, the lead of the spectral-graph predictor over a well-tuned recurrent baseline is modest but consistent across cells.

Table 2 reports accuracy at Horizons 3 and 5.

StemGNN keeps a 3 to 6%-point lead over every recurrent baseline at both longer horizons, and the margin grows with horizon. The advantage over LSTM widens from 1.84% at Horizon 1 to 7.71% at Horizon 3, and the advantage over GRU widens from 1.83% to 5.72% over the same range. As short-range temporal autocorrelation decays at longer horizons, the dominant predictive signal shifts to inter-UE co-scheduling structure, and the spectral graph component of StemGNN captures that structure jointly across all UEs while the recurrent models still process each sequence in isolation.

Table 2. Scheduling prediction accuracy (%) at Horizons 3 and 5, and StemGNN's mean improvement over each recurrent baseline.

Model	Horizon 3				Horizon 5			
	BS 0	BS 1	BS 2	Improv.	BS 0	BS 1	BS 2	Improv.
Simple RNN	77.52	75.29	77.54	+6.38%	76.54	72.68	76.58	+5.40%
GRU	77.44	75.04	78.33	+5.72%	75.43	72.57	76.48	+5.41%
LSTM	76.39	73.47	77.41	+7.71%	74.39	70.91	75.88	+7.44%
StemGNN	**83.00**	**76.00**	**82.00**	—	**80.00**	**75.00**	**79.00**	—

5.3 CBF-SLNR Integration Results

Table 3 reports CBF-SLNR performance under stale scheduling with no ML compensation. This setting isolates what happens when the backhaul fault is left uncorrected.

Table 3. CBF-SLNR performance under backhaul latency without ML prediction. Sum rate and edge rate are in bits/s/Hz.

Configuration	48 SC		1 SC	
	Sum Rate	Edge Rate	Sum Rate	Edge Rate
REZF (uncoordinated)	149.40	1.13	198.61	1.37
CBF-SLNR Lag 0 (ideal)	156.99	1.30	257.11	1.87
CBF-SLNR Lag 1	138.93	1.12	205.89	1.51
CBF-SLNR Lag 3	146.17	1.19	222.80	1.64
CBF-SLNR Lag 5	145.40	1.17	223.61	1.37

One TTI of backhaul delay reduces the 48-SC sum rate by 11.5% and actually pushes performance *below* the uncoordinated REZF baseline (138.93 vs 149.40), which means that running coordinated beamforming on stale inputs is worse than not coordinating at all. At Lag 1, the precoder nulls towards UEs that are no longer scheduled and steers interference towards UEs that are actually active. Lag 3 partially recovers because information several slots old loses its specificity and the precoder degrades towards generic, uncoordinated beamforming, which is harmless by comparison. This is the scenario in which a deployed system needs a fault-tolerance mechanism that activates when fresh information is missing.

Table 4 and Fig. 2 report end-to-end CBF-SLNR performance with ML-predicted schedules at Lag 1, the operating point where the gain is largest.

With the StemGNN predictor in the loop at Lag 1, the 48-SC sum rate climbs from 138.93 to 152.24 bits/s/Hz, recovering 73% of the gap to the ideal Lag-0 upper bound and improving on the no-prediction baseline by 9.58%. In the 1-SC setting, StemGNN recovers 57% of the Lag-1 loss with a 14.35% sum-rate

Table 4. CBF-SLNR performance with ML-predicted schedules at Lag 1. Sum rate and edge rate are in bits/s/Hz, and *Improv.* is StemGNN's relative gain in sum rate over the baseline.

Model	48 SC			1 SC		
	Sum Rate	Edge Rate	Improv.	Sum Rate	Edge Rate	Improv.
No prediction	138.93	1.117	+9.58%	205.89	1.507	+14.35%
LSTM	149.90	1.195	+1.56%	228.79	1.729	+2.91%
GRU	150.74	1.202	+0.99%	228.39	1.723	+3.09%
StemGNN	**152.24**	**1.283**	—	**235.44**	**1.757**	—
Ideal (Lag 0)	156.99	1.300	—	257.11	1.871	—

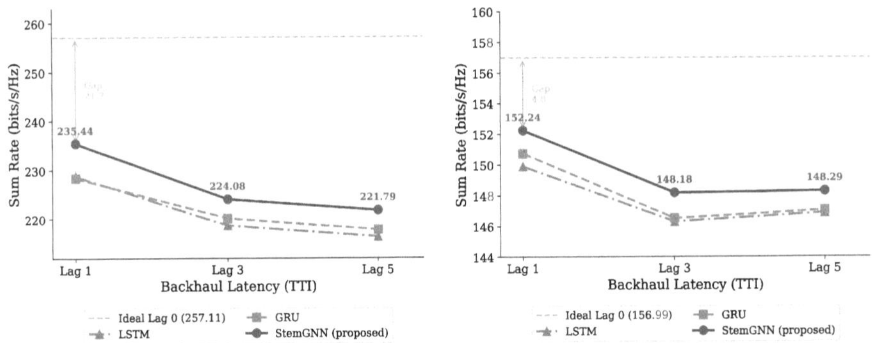

Fig. 2. CBF-SLNR sum rate versus backhaul latency with ML-predicted schedules for 1 SC (left) and 48 SC (right). StemGNN consistently leads at all lag values. The dashed line marks the ideal Lag 0 upper bound.

improvement over the no-prediction baseline. The largest gains land at the Lag-1 operating point, which is the same point at which the uncompensated system is most unsafe to deploy. StemGNN also stays ahead of the recurrent baselines under integration: it beats GRU by 0.99% (48 SC) and 3.09% (1 SC), and LSTM by 1.56% (48 SC) and 2.91% (1 SC). The advantage narrows at higher lags as all models converge towards similar accuracy plateaus, which Fig. 2 shows clearly.

The edge-rate gains are larger in relative terms than the sum-rate gains, and we consider this one of the more important findings for an edge-availability setting. In the 1-SC configuration, StemGNN raises the edge rate from 1.507 to 1.757 bits/s/Hz at Lag 1, a 16.59% improvement, and recovers 83% of the Lag-1 fairness loss. The improvements persist at Lag 3 and Lag 5 even as the sum-rate benefits start to fade, which says that the framework keeps service quality consistent for the cell-edge users who are most exposed to coordination failure [29]. In an edge deployment, this translates directly into more even quality of experience across cells when the backhaul is degraded.

Figure 3 reports prediction accuracy during live CBF-SLNR integration across backhaul latency values. All models drop steeply from Lag 1 to Lag 3, a

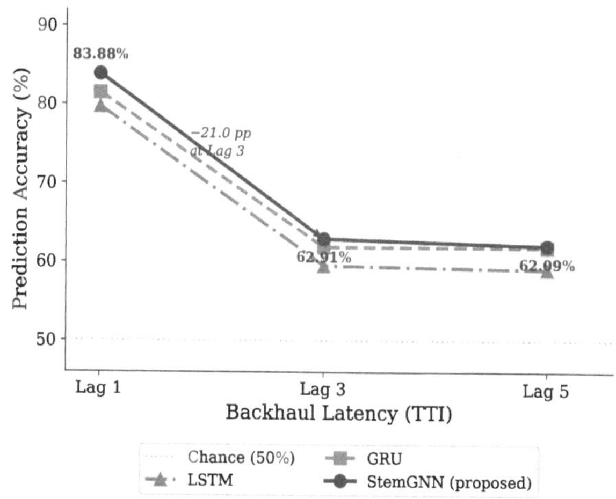

Fig. 3. Scheduling prediction accuracy during CBF-SLNR integration (48 subcarriers). All models drop sharply from Lag 1 to Lag 3 and plateau thereafter. StemGNN leads at Lag 1 with 83.88%.

drop of 21 percentage points for StemGNN (from 83.88% to 62.91%), and plateau thereafter. At Lag 1, StemGNN leads GRU by 2.42 pp and LSTM by 4.19 pp. The collapse in accuracy at Lag 3 directly explains the shrinking sum-rate benefit visible in Fig. 2. The integrated accuracy at Lag 1 (83.88%) is slightly below the standalone accuracy at Horizon 1 (87.57%). This gap reflects a closed-loop distributional shift: the predictor's own influence on the beamformer alters the interference environment and subtly shifts the scheduling dynamics away from the patterns it was trained on. This is a known property of any closed-loop learned controller rather than a defect of the model itself.

5.4 Discussion

Three findings that stand out are as follows:

First, the latency-performance relationship is non-monotonic. Lag 1 is worse than Lag 3 or Lag 5 because the precoder nulls towards users active in the previous slot who may no longer be active, so confident misinformation turns out to be worse than no information at all. The proposed framework directly addresses this failure mode and recovers 57 to 73% of the Lag-1 sum-rate loss with 9.58 to 14.35% improvement over the no-prediction baseline. From a fault-tolerance perspective, this is the worst-case window the edge controller must survive, and it is the window in which the predictor delivers its largest gain.

Second, StemGNN's margin over recurrent baselines grows with prediction horizon, reaching up to 7.71% over LSTM at Horizon 3. This confirms that inter-UE co-scheduling structure becomes the dominant predictive signal once short-range autocorrelation decays. The numbers reported here should be read as conservative estimates. The Quadriga UMi simulator with a proportional-fair scheduler produces scheduling patterns that are more regular than those of a real network with bursty traffic, high user mobility, denser deployments, and many more UEs per cell. In those more realistic conditions, the structural inter-UE dependencies that the spectral graph component captures would carry substantially more predictive value, and we expect the gap over purely temporal recurrent models to widen.

Third, accuracy is high at Lag 1 (83.88% for StemGNN) but drops by roughly 21 percentage points at Lag 3 and plateaus thereafter. Two effects compound here: the growing uncertainty of multi-step forecasting, and the closed-loop distributional shift noted above. This accuracy collapse is the main bottleneck of the current framework and is what limits sum-rate recovery at Lag 3 and Lag 5. The shape of this failure profile is itself useful information for an edge deployment: the system is most reliable exactly at the operating point where it most needs to be reliable, and degrades gracefully towards the uncoordinated baseline as latency grows further, rather than collapsing into a faulty state. Across all 18 operating conditions evaluated, the ranking of StemGNN over the recurrent and statistical baselines remains consistent, indicating that the gains reflect a structural property of the framework rather than an artefact of a specific configuration.

6 Conclusions

This paper addressed the problem of coordinated beamforming under backhaul latency in distributed 5G networks, framed as a fault-tolerance problem for edge AI controllers that must operate on stale information from their peers. We proposed a two-stage predictive framework in which a spectral-temporal GNN predicts future UE scheduling states from delayed historical observations, and the predictions replace stale inputs to the CBF-SLNR precoder without modifying the core beamforming algorithm.

Three conclusions stand out. First, the latency-performance relationship is non-monotonic. One TTI of delay is more harmful than three or five, because the precoder actively suppresses interference toward users that are no longer active. Confident misinformation is worse than no information. Prediction is most valuable at precisely this hardest operating point, where the proposed framework recovers 57 to 73% of the Lag-1 sum-rate loss and brings performance close to the ideal upper bound that assumes zero delay. The framework therefore restores service availability exactly when the system is most exposed to backhaul faults.

Second, spatio-temporal graph modelling captures inter-UE co-scheduling dependencies that purely temporal recurrent models cannot. The advantage grows with prediction horizon, which confirms that structural inter-UE correlations become the dominant predictive signal once short-range autocorrelation decays. The gains reported here are conservative, and in larger and more bursty deployments with greater user mobility, the structural advantage of the spectral graph component is expected to widen.

Third, the performance benefits fall disproportionately on cell-edge users. The framework recovers 83% of the Lag-1 fairness loss in the 1-SC configuration, which makes it a fairness mechanism for the most exposed users as much as a throughput-recovery tool. For an edge deployment, this means more even quality of experience across cells under the same backhaul-fault conditions.

Future work will target the sharp accuracy drop from Lag 1 to Lag 3 through uncertainty-aware prediction, in which the model outputs a confidence estimate that the precoder uses to weight neighbour scheduling states by reliability. This also extends the trust argument from the Introduction by shrinking the surface exposed to late or anomalous reports. Further directions include end-to-end joint training under a task-aware loss, online adaptive learning to handle closed-loop distributional shift, and evaluation on larger network topologies.

Acknowledgments. The authors thank Huawei Sweden R&D for providing the simulation environment and industrial supervision. This work was carried out within the Master's thesis programme at the Department of Computer and Systems Sciences, Stockholm University.

Use of LLMs. Claude (Anthropic) was used for language assistance and drafting under author direction; all technical content is the authors' original work.

Disclosure of Interests. This work was conducted in collaboration with Huawei Sweden R&D. The beamforming and scheduling simulation framework contains proprietary components and was used solely for academic research purposes. Authors A. H. Gökceoglu and L. Wang are employed by Huawei. The authors have no other competing interests to declare.

References

1. Boccardi, F., Heath, R.W., Lozano, A., Marzetta, T.L., Popovski, P.: Five disruptive technology directions for 5g. IEEE Commun. Mag. **52**(2), 74–80 (2014). https://doi.org/10.1109/MCOM.2014.6736746
2. Cao, D., et al.: Spectral temporal graph neural network for multivariate time-series forecasting. In: Advances in Neural Information Processing Systems (NeurIPS), vol. 33, pp. 17766–17778 (2020)
3. Checko, A., et al.: Cloud ran for mobile networks—a technology overview. IEEE Commun. Surv. Tutor. (2015)
4. Cho, K., et al.: Learning phrase representations using RNN encoder-decoder. In: EMNLP (2014)
5. Dahlman, E., Parkvall, S., Sköld, J.: 5G NR: The Next Generation Wireless Access Technology, 1st edn. Academic Press, Oxford (2018)
6. Elman, J.: Finding structure in time. Cogn. Sci. (1990)
7. Farsad, N., Simeone, O.: Deep learning for wireless physical layer: opportunities and challenges. IEEE Commun. Mag. (2018)
8. Ge, J., Liang, Y.C., Joung, J., Sun, S.: Deep reinforcement learning for distributed dynamic miso downlink-beamforming coordination. IEEE Trans. Commun. **68**(10), 6070–6085 (2020). https://doi.org/10.1109/TCOMM.2020.3004524

9. Ge, J., Liang, Y.C., Zhang, L., Long, R., Sun, S.: Deep reinforcement learning for distributed dynamic coordinated beamforming in massive MIMO cellular networks. IEEE Trans. Wireless Commun. **23**(5), 4155–4169 (2024). https://doi.org/10.1109/TWC.2023.3314930
10. Gesbert, D., et al.: Multi-cell MIMO cooperative networks: a new look at interference. IEEE J. Sel. Areas Commun. **28**(9), 1380–1408 (2010). https://doi.org/10.1109/JSAC.2010.101202
11. Gilmer, J., et al.: Neural message passing for quantum chemistry. In: ICML (2017)
12. Giordani, M., et al.: Toward 6g networks: use cases and technologies. IEEE Commun. Mag. (2020)
13. He, C., Lu, Y., Zhang, R., Li, Y., Ai, B., Niyato, D.: GNN-enabled coordinated beamforming design for high speed railway communication systems. IEEE Trans. Mobile Comput., 1–13 (2025). https://doi.org/10.1109/TMC.2025.3649999
14. Hochreiter, S., Schmidhuber, J.: Long short-term memory. Neural Comput. (1997)
15. Kelly, F., Maulloo, A., Tan, D.: Charging and rate control for elastic traffic. Eur. Trans. Telecommun. (1997)
16. Kipf, T., Welling, M.: Semi-supervised classification with graph convolutional networks. ICLR (2017)
17. Larsson, E.G., Edfors, O., Tufvesson, F., Marzetta, T.L.: Massive MIMO for next generation wireless systems. IEEE Commun. Mag. **52**(2), 186–195 (2014). https://doi.org/10.1109/MCOM.2014.6736731
18. Li, Y., et al.: Diffusion convolutional recurrent neural network for traffic forecasting. ICLR (2018)
19. Li, Z., Gamvrelis, T., Ammar, H.A., Adve, R.: Decentralized user scheduling and beamforming in multi-cell MIMO networks. In: ICC 2022 - IEEE International Conference on Communications, pp. 1980–1985 (2022). https://doi.org/10.1109/ICC45855.2022.9839273
20. Lu, L., Li, G.Y., Swindlehurst, A.L., Ashikhmin, A., Zhang, R.: An overview of massive MIMO: benefits and challenges. IEEE J. Sel. Topics in Signal Process. **8**(5), 742–758 (2014). https://doi.org/10.1109/JSTSP.2014.2317671
21. Luong, N.C., et al.: Deep reinforcement learning in wireless communications. IEEE Wirel. Commun. (2019)
22. Marzetta, T.L., Larsson, E.G., Yang, H., Ngo, H.Q.: Fundamentals of Massive MIMO. Cambridge University Press, Cambridge (2016)
23. Mismar, F.B., Evans, B.L., Alkhateeb, A.: Deep reinforcement learning for 5g networks: joint beamforming, power control, and interference coordination. IEEE Trans. Commun. **68**(3), 1581–1592 (2020). https://doi.org/10.1109/TCOMM.2019.2961332
24. Nguyen, T., et al.: Multi-agent reinforcement learning for wireless networks. IEEE Commun. Surv. Tutor. (2020)
25. Park, S.J., Simeone, O., Sahin, O., Shamai, S.: Dynamic coordinated beamforming with limited backhaul capacity. IEEE Trans. Wirel. Commun. (2013)
26. Shen, K., Yu, W.: Fractional programming for communication systems–part I: power control and beamforming. IEEE Trans. Signal Process. **66**(10), 2616–2630 (2018). https://doi.org/10.1109/TSP.2018.2812733
27. Shi, Q., Razaviyayn, M., Luo, Z.Q., He, C.: An iteratively weighted MMSE approach to distributed sum-utility maximization for a MIMO interfering broadcast channel. IEEE Trans. Signal Process. **59**(9), 4331–4340 (2011). https://doi.org/10.1109/TSP.2011.2147784
28. Sun, H., et al.: Learning to optimize for wireless resource management. IEEE Trans. Signal Process. (2018)

29. Tse, D., Viswanath, P.: Fundamentals of Wireless Communication. Cambridge University Press (2005)
30. Wu, Z., et al.: A comprehensive survey on graph neural networks. IEEE Trans. Neural Netw. Learn. Syst. (2020)
31. Wu, Z., et al.: Graph wavenet for deep spatial-temporal graph modeling. In: IJCAI (2019)
32. Yan, S., Xiong, Y., Lin, D.: Spatial temporal graph convolutional networks for skeleton-based action recognition. In: Proceedings of the AAAI Conference on Artificial Intelligence (2018)
33. Zappone, A., Di Renzo, M., Debbah, M.: Wireless networks design in the era of deep learning. IEEE Trans. Commun. (2019)
34. Zhang, C., et al.: Graph neural networks for wireless communications: a survey. IEEE Commun. Surv. Tutor. (2022)
35. Zhou, J., et al.: Graph neural networks: a review of methods and applications. AI Open (2020)

A Learning-to-Rank Framework for AS Prioritization to Support DDoS Attack Mitigation at CDN PoPs

Ryosuke Araki(✉), Yuzo Taenaka, and Youki Kadobayashi

Nara Institute of Science and Technology, 8916-5 Ikoma, Nara, Japan
{araki.ryosuke.ao3,yuzo,youki-k}@is.naist.jp

Abstract. Distributed Denial of Service (DDoS) attacks remain a persistent threat to the availability of cloud-based services, particularly at CDN Points of Presence (PoPs) where mitigation capacity is inherently limited. Because defensive resources cannot be uniformly applied to all traffic sources, accurate ranking of Autonomous Systems (ASes) is beneficial to support DDoS attack mitigation. This paper proposes a framework to rank ASes that are likely to contribute to Layer 7 DDoS attack traffic within the next 15 min. Analysis of real-world attack data from the Cloudflare Radar API reveals pronounced seasonal and trend components in AS-level attack traffic dynamics. Motivated by this observation, we extract temporal features using Seasonal-Trend decomposition based on LOESS. We then reformulate the task as a learning-to-rank problem rather than regression, directly optimizing AS ordering to match operational needs at PoPs. Experimental results show that the proposed method achieves 3.20% lower ranking MAE and 0.43% lower weighted ranking MAE compared to an LSTM regression baseline, with improvements in 23 of 24 test periods (95.83%) for ranking MAE and in 17 of 24 periods (70.83%) for weighted ranking MAE. These findings demonstrate stable and operationally aligned ranking performance for supporting CDN-based DDoS attack mitigation.

Keywords: Learning-to-Rank · AS Prioritization · CDN · Supporting DDoS Mitigation

1 Introduction

DDoS (Distributed Denial of Service) attacks are among the most serious threats to network systems. Attackers primarily attempt to decrease the availability of services by sending malicious requests. This vulnerability is still present in modern services. In 2024, Akamai reported that they received 419 TB of malicious traffic in 24 h [8]. Cloudflare also reported that they observed the largest attack, 31.4 Tbps in 2025 [15]. With the development and spread of hardware, the potential for attack capabilities is increasing. At the same time, the development of deep learning models helps attackers direct their efforts more effectively

Z. Afzal et al. (Eds.): ARES 2026 Workshops, LNCS 16900, pp. 484–501, 2027.
https://doi.org/10.1007/978-3-032-35576-8_26

and explore vulnerable services. Attackers will launch more advanced and more powerful DDoS attacks.

A common solution to these problems is the use of CDN (Content Delivery Network). A CDN operates by connecting users located in different ASes (Autonomous Systems) to nearby PoPs (Points of Presence), which then forward requests to the origin server (Fig. 1). By distributing the load of incoming requests across multiple PoPs, A CDN effectively reduces request times and mitigates the impact of DDoS attacks. This approach prevents excessive traffic from overwhelming the origin server, a benefit that has led many content providers to adopt CDN technology.

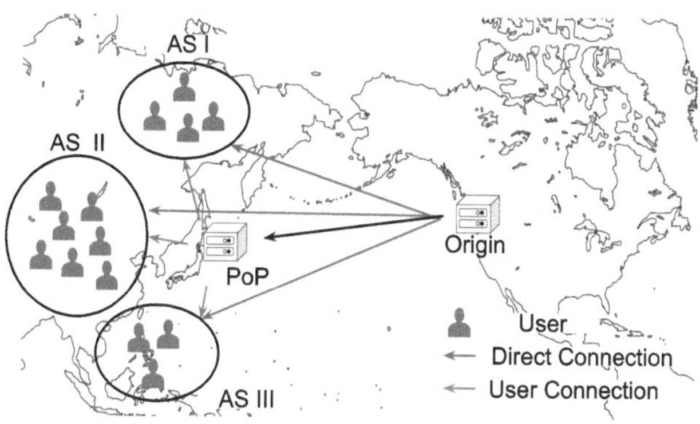

Fig. 1. Overview of a CDN architecture. Users belonging to different ASes are routed to the geographically nearest PoP to minimize service latency.

However, mitigation resources for DDoS attacks in each PoP are inherently limited, particularly for Layer 7 attacks. Unlike volumetric Layer 3/4 attacks that primarily exhaust bandwidth, Layer 7 attacks consume computational resources such as CPU cycles, memory, session tables, and backend application capacity. Even if network-level filtering is in place, excessive application layer requests can overwhelm web servers or backend systems once processing thresholds are exceeded. When such limits are reached, traffic engineering mechanisms can be invoked to redistribute requests across alternative PoPs, scrubbing centers, or other mitigation infrastructures [16]. Although specific traffic engineering policies depend on the CSP (Content Service Provider), they preserve service availability while minimizing additional latency for legitimate users under attack conditions. Naively redirecting all traffic from a particular AS to a scrubbing center, another PoP, or a black hole is often overly coarse-grained and may significantly degrade user experience.

This challenge becomes even more critical when Layer 7 mitigation resources within a single PoP are shared among multiple ASes. Improper or static resource allocation can result in contention at the application layer, causing collateral damage to benign traffic. Previous work has shown that botnet activities exhibit structured behaviors at the AS level, suggesting that AS-level aggregation provides meaningful macroscopic insights into large-scale attack dynamics [2]. This observation motivates the adoption of AS-level control mechanisms to enable scalable mitigation in operational networks, such as dynamically adjusting upper limits for acceptable attack traffic (Fig. 2).

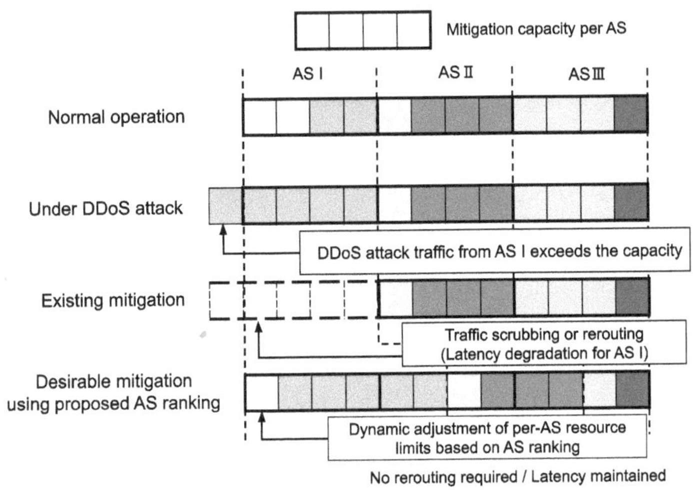

Fig. 2. Conceptual comparison of mitigation strategies. Under normal operation, mitigation capacity is statically allocated per AS. During a DDoS attack, if traffic from a specific AS exceeds its assigned capacity, conventional mitigation relies on traffic scrubbing or rerouting, potentially degrading latency. In contrast, the proposed AS ranking-based mechanism dynamically adjusts per-AS resource limits according to predicted attack ranking, enabling adaptive resource redistribution without rerouting.

To achieve this, it can be beneficial to predict which ASes are likely to contribute attack traffic and to estimate the magnitude of the potential attack. Most existing studies focus on the detection of attack events or the prediction of aggregate traffic and do not directly address resource contention between multiple ASes within a single PoP [9,17]. Such predictive capabilities allow for more proactive resource allocation, effective traffic engineering, and adaptive defense mechanisms that help minimize service disruption. Furthermore, integrating predictive models with real-time monitoring can improve the responsiveness of CDN, thus supporting availability and reducing latency.

In this paper, we propose an AS ranking framework to support DDoS attack mitigation in advance (Fig. 3). The model predicts which ASes are likely to contribute to attack traffic within the next 15 min. Ranking ASes enables CSPs to manage traffic more efficiently. Our ranking-based approach could support a defense mechanism that dynamically adjusts the sliding time window used for the Layer 7 request analysis in addition to dynamic upper limit adjustment (Fig. 2). Specifically, during normal operation, longer time windows are applied to aggregate HTTP requests over extended periods, thereby reducing computational overhead in behavioral inspection. In contrast, for high-ranked ASes during suspected attack periods, shorter time windows are assigned to enable rapid detection of anomalous request patterns such as sudden surges in request rate, abnormal uniform resource identifier concentration, or burst-like session behavior. Because the length of the sliding time window could determine both the temporal resolution of the application layer monitoring and the computational cost of feature extraction, dynamically adjusting the window length allows the inspection capacity to be adaptively redistributed according to the predicted attack likelihood of each AS.

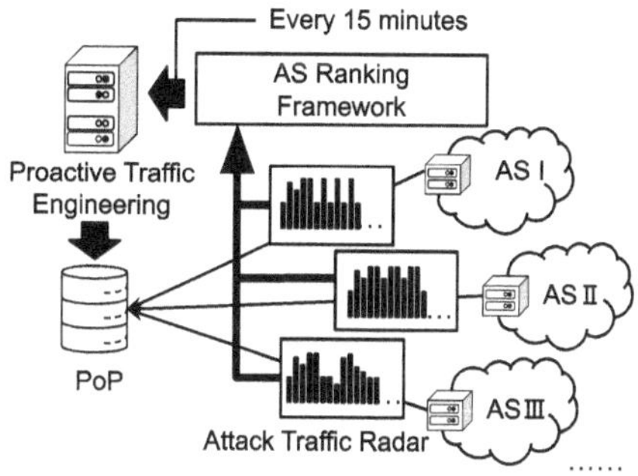

Fig. 3. System overview of the proposed AS ranking framework. Every 15 min, the model analyzes Layer 7 attack traffic observations collected at the PoP (Attack Traffic Radar) and estimates the ranking of each AS. The predicted ranking facilitates proactive traffic engineering and adaptive resource allocation.

To enable this estimation, we leverage attack traffic volume data at the AS-level. By modeling temporal characteristics such as trends, seasonal patterns, and statistical dependencies, the proposed model estimates which ASes are likely to generate attack traffic in the near future. The rapid proliferation of devices connected to the Internet, often deployed with insufficient security configurations, has led to a significant growth in bot populations. These compromised devices can be orchestrated to launch DDoS attacks of varying scales and other malicious activities. Such bot-driven behaviors frequently exhibit temporal regularities, which can manifest as trend and seasonal components in the observed attack traffic. Our approach is designed to capture and exploit these temporal structures. Although extremely large-scale flash-type DDoS attacks that instantaneously overwhelm mitigation capacity fall outside the scope of this study, the proposed method effectively addresses small- to medium-scale attacks that exhibit observable temporal patterns. Specifically, attack events that exceed the total mitigation capacity of a single PoP are not considered in our threat model.

This paper focuses on the ranking formulation of potential attack sources rather than designing mitigation mechanisms themselves. The paper is structured as follows: Sect. 2 addresses the reference gap by providing a comprehensive overview of related works. Sections 3 and 4 introduce our proposed method, along with a detailed analysis of the data. Subsequently, the evaluation of our system is presented in Sect. 5. Finally, Sects. 6 and 7 conclude the paper with a summary of key findings and a discussion of future work.

2 Related Works

In this section, we summarize the related work and relevant techniques.

2.1 AS-Level Protection and Analysis

AS-level control and protection mechanisms against DDoS attacks have been widely studied.

Almazarqi et al. [2] conducted a large-scale Internet measurement study to characterize the AS-level distribution and dynamics of IoT-driven DDoS traffic. Their analysis reveals structural traffic propagation patterns and highlights differences in the relative contribution and impact of individual ASes during large-scale attack events. Complementing this perspective, Almazarqi et al. [3] profiled the propagation patterns of the IoT botnet and identified key ASes that exhibit structural tolerance to DDoS attacks through a case-based analysis. Their findings demonstrate that the distribution of botnets and the latent attack potential differ significantly between ASes, suggesting heterogeneous structural vulnerability within the Internet. These two studies suggest the feasibility of dynamic CAPTCHA challenges depending on AS. Mao et al. [11] study AS-level topology inference under Path-Aware Networking architectures, where packets carry in-band Path Identifiers that expose forwarding paths across AS. Nur [14] proposes a collaborative fair rate throttling mechanism at the AS-level, where victim ASes dynamically compute throttling factors and request upstream ASes to reduce suspicious traffic in a distributed manner. Unlike predictive approaches, their method focuses on reactive rate control once congestion thresholds are exceeded.

Industry practices such as Cloudflare's smart rate-limiting demonstrate the effectiveness of adaptive mitigation mechanisms. However, publicly available descriptions do not provide a formal optimization framework or a predictive resource allocation model. In contrast, our approach explicitly formulates mitigation as a predictive, optimization-driven resource allocation problem and provides a quantitative evaluation of its effectiveness [19].

2.2 Estimation of Attack Traffic and Event

Many studies have investigated methods for predicting network traffic volumes. Fachkha et al. [9] proposed a forecasting model to predict the amount of future DDoS attack traffic. They proposed and evaluated classical statistical methods, including moving average, weighted moving average, exponential smoothing, and linear regression. Ali et al. [1] proposed a deep learning model for predicting DDoS attack traffic. The study showed that the LSTM (Long Short Term Memory) model outperforms both the Recurrent Neural Network and the Gated Recurrent Unit, as well as other classical machine learning algorithms. Alrahman and Elleithy [4] evaluated two modern transformer-based models, FEDformer (Frequency Enhanced Decomposed Transformer) and PatchTST (Patch Time Series Transformer) [13], for network traffic prediction. The evaluation demonstrated that PatchTST achieved higher performance, showing a lower validation loss value compared to FEDformer.

Not only is the prediction of DDoS attack traffic categorized as threat prediction, but DDoS event forecasting is also included in this classification. Falowo and Abdo [10] proposed ARIMA (AutoRegressive Integrated Moving Average) and ETS (Exponential Smoothing State Space) forecasting techniques for the number of DDoS incidents. Wang and Zhang [17] investigated the feasibility of forecasting DDoS events by analyzing text streams from social networks before the occurrence of the attack. Unlike traditional traffic-based detection methods that rely on packet-level anomalies after an attack has begun, their approach monitors Twitter posts related to specific targets and predicts whether a DDoS event is likely to occur on the following day.

2.3 Research Gap

Despite extensive studies on AS-level analysis and DDoS forecasting, several important gaps remain.

First, previous AS-level studies focus primarily on structural analysis, traffic attribution, or reactive mitigation. Measurement-based works reveal heterogeneous AS-level vulnerability and contribution patterns, while collaborative throttling approaches emphasize distributed rate control after congestion is observed. However, these approaches do not provide a predictive mechanism to anticipate the relative contribution of each AS before mitigation resources are saturated. Consequently, resource allocation decisions are typically triggered only after traffic anomalies exceed predefined thresholds. Second, existing traffic forecasting studies aim mainly to predict aggregate attack volume or the number of DDoS incidents. Although statistical, deep learning, and transformer-based models have demonstrated effectiveness in traffic prediction, these approaches generally operate at the global or target level. They do not explicitly model the distribution of attack traffic across ASes, nor do they connect prediction outputs to AS-level mitigation resource allocation. Third, event forecasting approaches based on social networks focus on predicting whether an attack is likely to occur, rather than estimating how attack traffic will be distributed within the network infrastructure. Although such approaches provide early warning signals, they do not address the problem of fine-grained resource adaptation at the PoP or AS-level.

In summary, existing work (i) analyzes AS-level behavior without dynamically modeling future AS-level attack contributions, or (ii) forecasts attack occurrence or traffic volume without modeling AS-level traffic composition and mitigation control. To the best of our knowledge, no prior work addresses AS-level attack traffic ranking for adaptive resource allocation to support DDoS attack mitigation under operational PoP constraints.

3 Attack Data Analysis

This section characterizes the attack traffic data, simultaneously presenting the analysis derived from the data.

3.1 Dataset Collection

We obtain real-world DDoS attack traffic data through the Cloudflare Radar API [7]. Specifically, we collect the volume of Layer 7 DDoS attack traffic associated with selected ASes, as summarized in Table 1. The ASes were selected on the basis of both their scale and their global geographical distribution. Specifically, we select ASes in the central asiaâĂŞeast asia region whose *ASRank* values are closely clustered [5]. CAIDA's *ASRank* represents the scale of AS. The scale of an AS can significantly influence not only the absolute traffic volume, but also the characteristics and patterns of attack traffic. In addition, geographical proximity among ASes affects connectivity efficiency within a CDN architecture. PoPs are often co-located at Internet Exchange Points (IXPs), where multiple ASes interconnect. By deploying PoPs at IXPs, CSPs can transport traffic and mitigate DDoS attacks more efficiently. In real-world deployments, CSPs can selectively monitor and manage traffic from ASes that are directly connected to their PoPs.

Table 1. Collected AS

ASN	*ASRank*	Organization	Country
2516	128	KDDI	JP
17676	129	GIGAINFRA	JP
9318	131	SKB-AS-KR	KR
3786	130	LGDACOM-KR	KR
4788	127	TTSSB-MY	MY
4800	135	LINTASARTA-AS-AP	ID
55836	132	RELIANCEJIO-IN	IN
55410	161	VIL-AS-AP	IN
45820	186	TTSL-MEISISP	IN
18403	183	FPT-AS-AP	VN

The organizational information for each AS was obtained using the *whois* command and *CAIDA ASRank* [5]. It should be noted that DDoS attack traffic detection is entirely based on the Cloudflare detection system, and specific detection algorithms are outside the scope of this paper. The amount of Layer 7 DDoS attacks is represented as time-series data and calculated every 15 min. We collect the time period from January 1, 2022, to January 1, 2026. The value is initially scaled from 0 to 1.

3.2 Preprocess of the Data

We implement the preprocessing of the data as follows.

1. Robust scaling
2. Logarithmic transformation

DDoS traffic data exhibit unique characteristics including irregular spikes and seasonal patterns reflecting temporal trends such as time-of-day or day-of-week effects. This makes the dataset fundamentally different from conventional time-series data, where variations are typically smoother. Traditional models may struggle to capture both seasonality and abrupt anomalies inherent in DDoS traffic.

To prevent extreme spikes from dominating the analysis, we adopted a two-step preprocessing pipeline. First, we used robust scaling using the median and interquartile range (IQR), making it resilient to anomalous data points. Second, we applied the logarithmic transformation to compress the dynamic range. These steps preserve relative traffic differences while capturing seasonal fluctuations and irregular attack patterns, facilitating accurate modeling. An example of the preprocessed data are shown in Fig. 4.

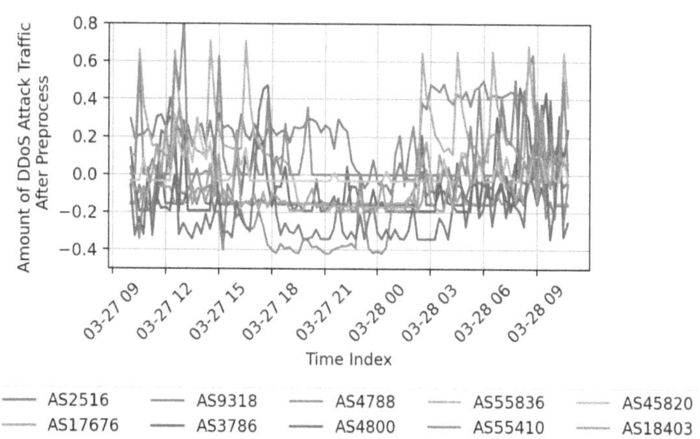

Fig. 4. Comparison of each AS's DDoS attack traffic

The combination of AS selection and IQR-based median normalization in Step.1 brings the preprocessed data closer to enabling a meaningful improvement in relative comparability.

3.3 Seasonality of the DDoS Time-Series Data

Nguyen et al. [12] proposed a source-side DoS attack detection method by adjusting the threshold according to the seasonality of legitimate traffic. Similarly, Yeom et al. [18] proposed a source-side attack detection using a LSTM model with seasonality embedding. As these previous works indicate, developing embedding spaces that accurately capture the seasonality of both legitimate and attack traffic remains a significant challenge. Specifically, the significance of the seasonal components of DDoS attack behavior is still not well studied. To address this, we analyze the trend, seasonality, and residuals of the attack traffic using STL (A Seasonal-Trend Decomposition Procedure Based on LOESS) analysis [6]. By decomposing the time-series data at time t, y_t into these three components (Eqn. 1), we can observe long term growth or decline in attack intensity through the trend term T_t, periodic attack behaviors through the seasonal component S_t, and unpredictable fluctuations or anomalies through the remainder R_t.

$$y_t = T_t + S_t + R_t \tag{1}$$

This decomposition allows for clearer interpretation of how network attack patterns evolve over time. We illustrate the example of seasonality of DDoS attack traffic in Fig. 5.

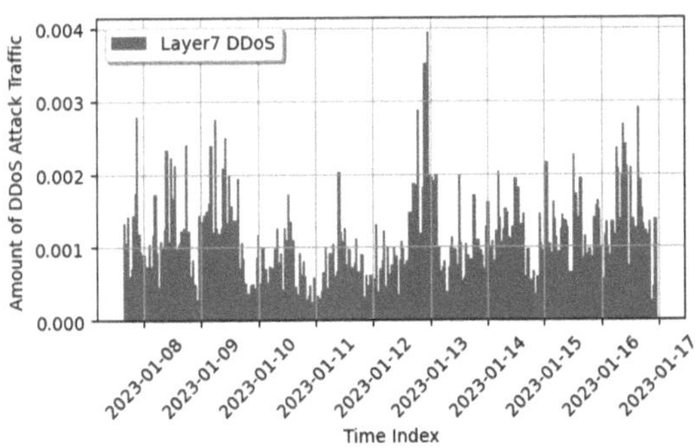

Fig. 5. DDoS attack data of AS2516 which has clear seasonality

As shown in Fig. 5, in some cases, the volume of DDoS traffic clearly exhibits a seasonal pattern. Figure 6 presents the results of the STL analysis. The amount of decomposed DDoS traffic confirms the presence of seasonality, in addition to trend and residuals. The regular interval of traffic change further highlights the inherent seasonality of the data.

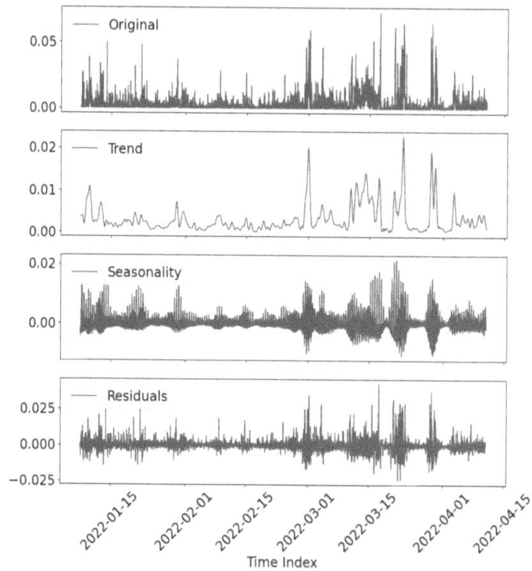

Fig. 6. A subset of DDoS attack traffic data originating from AS3786 with STL analysis

4 Proposal Method

In this section, we introduce our proposal method.

4.1 XGBRanker for AS Ranking

We develop XGBRanker with STL components for AS ranking. Although the underlying structure of XGBRanker is derived from the robust XGBoost (Extreme Gradient Boosting) framework, it is fundamentally a Learning-to-Rank algorithm specifically tailored for optimization tasks where the relative ordering of items is more important than their individual scores. Consequently, a direct input of raw time-series data into XGBRanker is suboptimal, as the model inherently lacks the recurrent or convolutional architecture necessary to process sequences effectively. To bridge this gap and leverage the power of gradient boosting for ranking, we adopt feature engineering. Instead of merely feeding the raw time-series, we extract a comprehensive set of representative statistical features from the raw data and STL analyzed data. We also include raw data from the most recent period as input features (Fig. 7). This simple transformation allows the tree-based XGBRanker to effectively learn the complex, non-linear relationships between the summarized data characteristics and the desired AS ranking.

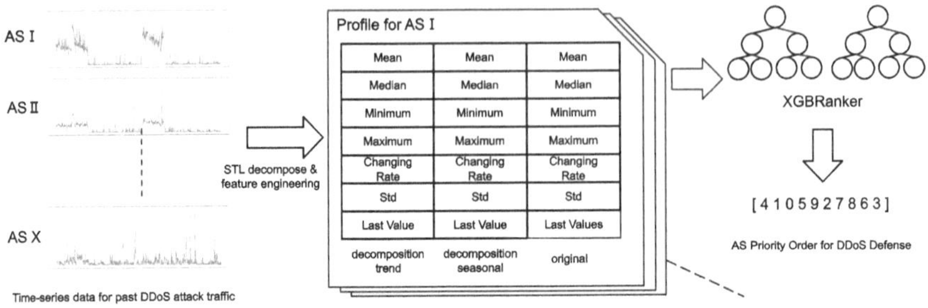

Fig. 7. Model overview of AS ranking framework for DDoS defense

4.2 Profile and Label Generation

For prediction, we employ a profile-based approach. For each AS T_i, we construct its profile step by step using a window size of w. We utilize several statistical features, raw data, and the rate of change, as described in Algorithm 1.

To capture the statistical characteristics of the data, we used μ, med, min, max, and σ from the original, trend and seasonal components from STL components. For the changing rate, we adopt the calculation method proposed in [18]. By applying one-hot encoding to the rate of change, the model can effectively capture the patterns of past variations. We also collect the last values that will affect the predicted value. We set w to 672, corresponding to the weekly window size, so that the model can capture both daily and weekly patterns. This setting is based on the study by Wang and Zhang [17], which uses weekly features as input for DDoS event forecasting. τ is set to 1.0.

After constructing the profile, we generate the prediction labels as described in Algorithm 2. The labels are determined based on the *argsort* of the time index t for each AS T_i. For example, the resulting label sequence may be [4, 1, 0, 5, 9, 2, 7, 8, 6, 3].

5 Evaluation

We evaluate our model against other state-of-the-art techniques. The details of the comparison and the evaluation criteria are presented in this section.

5.1 Comparison and Implementation

We evaluate other models, including the classical method and a state-of-the-art deep learning model. For the classical models, we choose the moving average model and the linear regression model. For the deep learning model, we implement the LSTM model following previous work [1]. For these 3 models, we build the model using the following processes.

1. Building the regression model for each AS class.

Algorithm 1. Profile Generation

```
Require: T = {T_1, ..., T_M}, Time-series data for M ASes,
    where T_i = {x_{i,1}, ..., x_{i,N}}, Window size = w, Threshold = τ
p ← {}
P ← {}
for i = 1 to M do
  for t = w to N do
    data_row_{i,t} ← {x_{i,t-w}, ..., x_{i,t}}
    trend_{i,t} ← STL(data_row_{i,t}).trend
    seasonal_{i,t} ← STL(data_row_{i,t}).seasonal
    component_{i,t} ← (data_row_{i,t}, trend_{i,t}, seasonal_{i,t})
    for component_{i,t} do
      μ_{i,t} ← (1/w) Σ_{s=t-w}^{w} x_{i,s}
      med_{i,t} ← median(data_row_{i,t})
      min_{i,t} ← min(data_row_{i,t})
      max_{i,t} ← max(data_row_{i,t})
      σ_{i,t} ← std(data_row_{i,t})
      last_value_{i,t} ← data_row_{i,t}[-last :]
      rate ← x_{i,t}/x_{i,t-1} - 1.0
      if rate >= 2 * τ then
        rate_status_{i,t} ← {0, 0, 0, 0, 1}
      else if rate >= 1 * τ then
        rate_status_{i,t} ← {0, 0, 0, 1, 0}
      else if rate >= -1 * τ then
        rate_status_{i,t} ← {0, 0, 1, 0, 0}
      else if rate >= -2 * τ then
        rate_status_{i,t} ← {0, 1, 0, 0, 0}
      else
        rate_status_{i,t} ← {1, 0, 0, 0, 0}
      end if
      p ← append(μ_{i,t}, med_{i,t}, min_{i,t}, max_{i,t}, σ_{i,t}, last_value_{i,t}, rate_status_{i,t}})
    end for
    P ← (p_data_row, p_trend, p_seasonal)
  end for
end for
```

2. Predict the amount of attack traffic.
3. Order the class based on the predicted amount of attack traffic.

As rank estimation has not yet been proposed in this domain, this process represents the state-of-the-art approach for the task. Furthermore, to evaluate the effectiveness of the STL components, we also implement an XGBRanker model without them (Simple XGBRanker). The simple XGBRanker utilizes the same features as the full model, excluding the STL components.

Algorithm 2. Label Generation

Require: $T = \{T_1, \dots, T_M\}$, Time-series data for M ASes, where $T_i = \{x_{i,1}, \dots, x_{i,N}\}$

1: $Y_{\text{rank}} \leftarrow \{\}$
2: **for** $t = 1$ to N **do**
3: $data\_column_t \leftarrow \{x_{1,t}, x_{2,t} \dots, x_{M-1,t}, x_{M,t}\}$
4: $rank_t \leftarrow \text{argsort}(data\_column_t)$
5: $Y_{\text{rank}} \leftarrow \text{append}(\{rank_t\})$
6: **end for**

5.2 Test Data

We divide the entire traffic dataset into training and testing sets, using a 50%/50% split. We intentionally limit the amount of training data to encourage the model to learn generalized patterns rather than overfitting to historical attack behaviors. Since DDoS attack patterns continuously evolve over time, a model trained on excessive historical data may become overly specialized to past characteristics and fail to adapt to emerging attack strategies. Therefore, constructing a robust model with a relatively small training set promotes better generalization to unseen attack scenarios. Furthermore, for LSTM, simple XGBRanker, and our proposal, we utilized a subset, specifically 20% of the training data, for their respective validation processes.

5.3 Criteria and Results

The performance of our ranking framework is evaluated using two metrics: ranking MAE (Mean Absolute Error) and weighted ranking MAE. Ranking MAE assesses the discrepancy between the predicted and true orders of the target items. Weighted ranking MAE extends this perspective by assigning larger penalties to errors involving higher-ranked items, inspired by the discounting mechanism used in the Normalized Discounted Cumulative Gain (nDCG) metric widely applied in information retrieval. This weighting strategy reflects the practical assumption that misranking top-ranked items often has a more severe impact than inaccuracies among lower-ranked items. Ranking MAE is formally defined as follows:

$$\text{MAE}_{rank} = \frac{1}{N} \sum_{i=1}^{N} |r_i - \hat{r}_i| \tag{2}$$

where N is the number of ranked items, r_i denotes the true rank of item i, and $\hat{r}_i$ represents the predicted rank. This metric captures the average absolute deviation between the true and predicted rankings. Weighted Ranking MAE introduces rank-dependent weights:

$$\text{WMAE}_{rank} = \frac{1}{N}\sum_{i=1}^{N}\frac{|r_i - \hat{r}_i|}{\log_2(r_i+2)} \tag{3}$$

A larger weight is assigned to errors within higher-ranked items due to their lower denominator $\log_2(r_i+2)$, reflecting their increased importance in the evaluation.

As shown in Table 2, the proposed method achieves a reduction in MAE for both ranking MAE and weighted ranking MAE, at 3.20% and 0.43%, respectively, compared to LSTM. Furthermore, our approach demonstrated lower values compared to a simple XGBRanker. This consistent improvement indicates that the STL components (trend and seasonal) successfully model key data characteristics. Consequently, these findings validate the utility of an approach that learns the ranking relationship based on the comprehensive distribution of the entire class.

Table 2. AS ranking results

Model	Method	Ranking MAE	Weighted Ranking MAE
Traffic Prediction Based	Moving Average	1.9167	0.8316
	Linear Regression	1.5753	0.6690
	LSTM	1.5787	0.6684
Ranking Based	XGBRanker	1.5310	0.6692
	XGBRanker with STL components (ours)	**1.5282**	**0.6655**

To evaluate the temporal stability of our proposed method, we divided the test period into 24 segments and assessed the improvement over LSTM in each period. Figure 8 illustrates the rate of improvement in the period. The proposed method consistently outperformed LSTM in 23 of 24 periods (95.83%) to ranking MAE, with a median improvement of 3.29%. The weighted MAE improved in 17 of 24 periods (70.83%) with a median improvement of 0.77%.

5.4 Experiment Setup and Execution Time

Experiments were conducted on an Apple M2 chip with 16 GB of RAM. Although computational time is not the primary focus of this model, it remains important to assess its efficiency for practical deployment. We measured the computational cost as the average processing time of 100 iterations. The moving average model, linear regression model, LSTM model, and a simple XGBRanker baseline required 0.02 ms, 0.24 ms, 90.42 ms, and 1.23 ms, respectively. Our proposed model, XGBRanker with STL components, recorded 137.31 ms per inference. These results indicate that our model takes longer than the other approaches, yet the processing time remains sufficiently low for the purpose of AS ranking.

6 Limitation and Future Work

In this section, we summarize the limitations of our work and show future directions.

6.1 Performance and Data Limitations

The proposed model underperforms LSTM during the 18th period (Fig. 8), where traffic exhibits stable periodic behavior without significant spikes (Fig. 9). In such conditions, LSTM effectively captures recurring temporal patterns. This suggests that LSTM is well suited for highly periodic traffic, whereas the proposed ranking-based approach is more effective for irregular and non-stationary DDoS traffic.

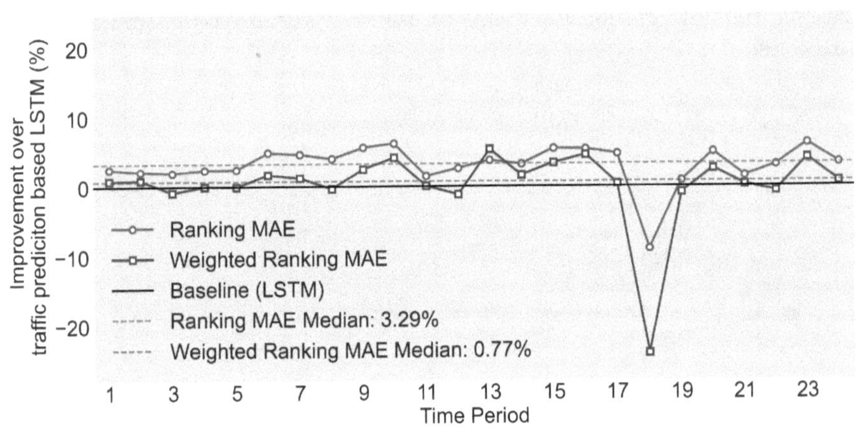

Fig. 8. Temporal consistency of performance: proposed method vs. LSTM model

Although the numerical improvement over LSTM is modest, the main contribution of this work is the reformulation of AS-level attack estimation as a ranking problem aligned with mitigation priorities at CDN PoPs.

Our evaluation relies on pre-scaled Cloudflare data, which limits comparisons of absolute traffic volumes across ASes. Furthermore, the analysis focuses on aggregated traffic volume rather than peak throughput, which is often the practical constraint in operational mitigation systems. Future work will investigate transformer-based architectures and incorporate Layer 3 traffic and peak bandwidth metrics to improve modeling of irregular traffic behavior and mitigation requirements.

6.2 Scope and Scalability

This work focuses on small- to medium-scale DDoS attacks that can be mitigated within a single PoP and excludes large flash-type attacks that immediately

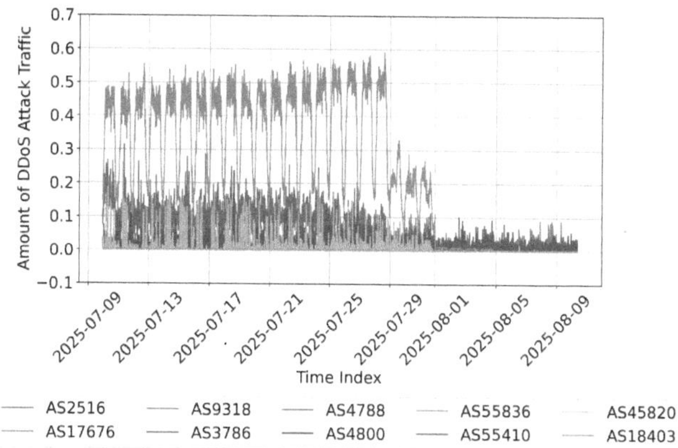

Fig. 9. Traffic patterns during the period where LSTM outperformed the proposed model

exceed mitigation capacity. The proposed approach aims to support adaptive prioritization before resource saturation occurs.

We evaluated the model using 10 AS classes. While larger operational environments may involve substantially more ASes, scalability can be maintained through selective ranking of high-impact ASes and hierarchical grouping strategies. Future work includes validation using a dedicated testbed and evaluation across a broader range of AS types and deployment scenarios.

7 Conclusion

In this paper, we introduce an AS ranking framework for supporting DDoS defense in CDN environments. Unlike traditional regression-based approaches that predict traffic volumes, our method employs XGBRanker with STL components to rank ASes. By extracting statistical and STL-decomposed features from past attack data, our model effectively captures both seasonal patterns and temporal dynamics inherent in DDoS attack traffic. Experimental results demonstrate that our ranking-based approach achieved 3.20% lower ranking MAE and 0.43% lower weighted ranking MAE compared to LSTM model. With an inference time of 137.31 ms, the model is efficient for real-time deployment. This work opens a new avenue for proactive traffic engineering and resource allocation, enabling CSPs to prioritize defensive actions effectively under operational PoP constraints. The implementation code used in this work is publicly available in https://github.com/kyotoor/source_as_ranking_ddos.git.

Acknowledgments. Cloudflare Radar API data was indispensable for this project; we thank the Cloudflare Radar Team. This work was supported by JST SPRING, Japan Grant Number JPMJSP2140.

Disclosure of Interests. The authors have no competing interests to declare that are relevant to the content of this article.

References

1. Ali, D.B., Belaoued, M., Dawaliby, S.: Anticipating cyber threats: deep learning approaches for ddos attacks forecasting. In: 2024 8th Cyber Security in Networking Conference (CSNet), pp. 128–132 (2024). https://doi.org/10.1109/CSNet64211.2024.10851731
2. Almazarqi, H.A., Woodyard, M., Marnerides, A.K.: Macroscopic insights of iot botnet dynamics via as-level tolerance assessment. In: ICC 2024 - IEEE International Conference on Communications, pp. 5244–5249 (2024). https://doi.org/10.1109/ICC51166.2024.10622782
3. Almazarqi, H.A., Woodyard, M., Marnerides, A.K.: Dynamics of large-scale ddos attacks orchestrated by iot botnets. In: 2025 IEEE Symposium on Computers and Communications (ISCC), pp. 1–6 (2025). https://doi.org/10.1109/ISCC65549.2025.11326088
4. Alrahmani, Z.A., Elleithy, K.: Ddos attack forecasting using transformers. In: 2023 IEEE Intl Conf on Dependable, Autonomic and Secure Computing, Intl Conf on Pervasive Intelligence and Computing, Intl Conf on Cloud and Big Data Computing, Intl Conf on Cyber Science and Technology Congress (DASC/PiCom/CBDCom/CyberSciTech), pp. 0911–0915 (2023). https://doi.org/10.1109/DASC/PiCom/CBDCom/Cy59711.2023.10361388
5. CAIDA: Asrank. https://asrank.caida.org/, Accessed 06 March 2026
6. Cleveland, R.B., Cleveland, W.S., McRae, J.E., Terpenning, I.: STL: a seasonal-trend decomposition procedure based on LOESS. J. Official Statist. **6**(1), 3–73 (1990)
7. Cloudflare: Cloudflare radar. https://radar.cloudflare.com/, Accessed 06 March 2026
8. Dummer, S.: Akamai blocked 419 tb of malicious traffic in a 24-hour ddos attack. https://www.akamai.com/blog/security/akamai-blocked-419-tb-of-malicious-traffic, Accessed 06 March 2026
9. Fachkha, C., Bou-Harb, E., Debbabi, M.: Towards a forecasting model for distributed denial of service activities. In: 2013 IEEE 12th International Symposium on Network Computing and Applications, pp. 110–117 (2013). https://doi.org/10.1109/NCA.2013.13
10. Falowo, O.I., Abdo, J.B.: 2019–2023 in review: projecting ddos threats with arima and ets forecasting techniques. IEEE Access **12**, 26759–26772 (2024). https://doi.org/10.1109/ACCESS.2024.3367240
11. Mao, Y., Luo, H., Wang, Z., Zhang, S.: As-level topology inference for path-aware networking. IEEE Trans. Dependable Sec Comput., 1–17 (2025). https://doi.org/10.1109/TDSC.2025.3643435
12. Nguyen, G.T., Nguyen, V.Q., Nguyen, S.N., and, K.K.: Traffic seasonality aware threshold adjustment for effective source-side dos attack detection. KSII Trans. Internet Inform. Syst. **13**(5), 2651–2673 (2019). https://doi.org/10.3837/tiis.2019.05.023
13. Nie, Y., Nguyen, N.H., Sinthong, P., Kalagnanam, J.: A time series is worth 64 words: long-term forecasting with transformers. In: The Eleventh International Conference on Learning Representations (2023). https://openreview.net/forum?id=Jbdc0vTOcol

14. Nur, A.Y.: Combating ddos attacks with fair rate throttling. In: 2021 IEEE International Systems Conference (SysCon), pp. 1–8 (2021). https://doi.org/10.1109/SysCon48628.2021.9447054
15. Omer Yoachimik, J.P., One, C.: 2025 q4 ddos threat report: A record-setting 31.4 tbps attack caps a year of massive ddos assaults. https://blog.cloudflare.com/ddos-threat-report-2025-q4/, Accessed 06 March 2026
16. Rizvi, A.S.M., Bertholdo, L., Ceron, J., Heidemann, J.: Anycast agility: network playbooks to fight DDoS. In: 31st USENIX Security Symposium (USENIX Security 22), pp. 4201–4218. USENIX Association, Boston, MA (Aug 2022). https://www.usenix.org/conference/usenixsecurity22/presentation/rizvi
17. Wang, Z., Zhang, Y.: Ddos event forecasting using twitter data. In: Proceedings of the Twenty-Sixth International Joint Conference on Artificial Intelligence, IJCAI 2017, pp. 4151–4157 (2017). https://doi.org/10.24963/ijcai.2017/580
18. Yeom, S., Choi, C., Kim, K.: Source-side dos attack detection with lstm and seasonality embedding. In: Proceedings of the 36th Annual ACM Symposium on Applied Computing, SAC 2021, pp. 1130–1137. Association for Computing Machinery, New York (2021). https://doi.org/10.1145/3412841.3441987
19. Yoachimik, O.: Defending the internet: how cloudflare blocked a monumental 7.3 tbps ddos attack. https://blog.cloudflare.com/defending-the-internet-how-cloudflare-blocked-a-monumental-7-3-tbps-ddos/, Accessed 06 March 2026

Proceedings of the First Workshop on Sustainable Security and Awareness for Next Generation Infrastructures (SAFER 2026)

SAFER 2026 Preface

The Workshop on Sustainable Security and Awareness For Next Generation Infrastructures (SAFER) was held at Linköping University, Sweden, on August 24–27, 2026, in conjunction with the 21st International Conference on Availability, Reliability and Security (ARES).

Cybersecurity remains a persistent and formidable challenge in our increasingly interconnected society, especially as the Internet of Things and artificial intelligence technologies advance at a rapid pace. Although significant research efforts are directed toward strengthening security measures and many innovations have emerged, there is often a predominant focus on technical improvements without sufficient attention to their broader implications. This narrow approach risks neglecting Environmental, Social, and Governance (ESG) considerations. For instance, the substantial energy consumption of data centers supporting advanced encryption or large-scale neural network training significantly contributes to carbon emissions. Additionally, the high costs associated with robust cybersecurity solutions can disproportionately burden small and medium-sized enterprises, deepening social and economic disparities. On a societal level, certain security technologies—particularly those involving surveillance—may threaten individual privacy and erode public trust. From a governance standpoint, prioritizing security at the expense of civil liberties can open the door to potential abuses. Collectively, these issues underscore the urgent need to re-examine cybersecurity from a holistic perspective. A truly sustainable approach must integrate technological resilience with environmental stewardship, social fairness, privacy safeguards, and sound ethical governance. The workshop provided a platform for researchers and practitioners from diverse disciplines to exchange insights at the crossroads of cybersecurity and Environmental, Social, and Governance considerations. Authors were encouraged to submit manuscripts of up to 18 pages, which underwent a rigorous double-blind peer review. For the 2026 edition, we received nine submissions. With the dedicated efforts of our Program Committee and external reviewers, each paper was assessed by three experts. Following careful evaluation and discussion, four papers were selected for oral presentation at the workshop.

We extend our sincere appreciation to the authors for their outstanding contributions, to the reviewers for their timely and meticulous assessments, and to all participants for their engagement. It is our hope that the collective effort invested in organizing this workshop will advance cybersecurity on a global scale.

August 2026

Daniele Canavese
Mohamed Ali Kandi
Leonardo Regano

SAFER 2026 Organization

Workshop Chairs

Daniele Canavese	CNR-IMATI, Italy
Mohamed Ali Kandi	IRIT-University of Toulouse, France
Leonardo Regano	University of Cagliari, Italy

Program Committee

Cataldo Basile	Politecnico di Torino, Italy
Laurent Bobelin	INSA Centre Val de Loire, France
Luca Caviglione	CNR-IMATI, Italy
Paolo Falcarin	Ca'Foscari University of Venice, Italy
Davide Ferraris	University of Málaga, Spain
Giorgio Giacinto	University of Cagliari, Italy
Youcef Imine	University Polytechnic Hauts-De-France, France
Romain Laborde	IRIT-University of Toulouse, France
Abir Laraba	IRIT-University of Toulouse, France
Davide Maiorca	University of Cagliari, Italy
Luca Mannella	Politecnico di Torino, Italy
Francesco Pagano	Università di Verona, Italy
Rubén Ríos	University of Málaga, Spain
Alessandro Sanna	University of Cagliari, Italy

Additional Reviewers

Matteo Busi
Mohamed Touahria Miliani
Nicola Deidda

An Analysis of the Impact of Psychological Factors and Techniques Across Different Types of Social Engineering

Helin Omer[1] and Daniela Pöhn[2](✉)

[1] Ludwig-Maximilians-Universität München, Munich, Germany
h.omer@campus.lmu.de
[2] University of the Bundeswehr Munich, Neubiberg, Germany
daniela.poehn@unibw.de

Abstract. Phishing is a well-known social engineering (SE) type used to trick individuals into revealing personal information or performing desired actions, like downloading and installing malware. Other SE types, like vishing and smishing, have emerged and are increasingly being used. As SE continues to successfully persuade victims into actions, the questions arise of which SE attack types are most effective for specific psychological factors (PFs) and, conversely, which PFs are most effective for particular attack types. To answer these questions, we conducted a laboratory study with n = 12 participants, in which each participant was shown all 25 stimuli (five PFs and five SE types). The results of this exploratory study show that the most effective SE attack type for authority, trust, and greed was spear-phishing. The most successful combination of PF and attack type was spear-phishing using greed. The least successful combinations were pop-ups using authority, smishing using authority, and vishing using curiosity, each having had no success at all.

Keywords: Social engineering · psychological factors · laboratory study · phishing · human factors · cybersecurity · security culture

1 Introduction

Human factors, including their behaviours, attitudes, and decision-making, influence how individuals manage cybersecurity issues and, ultimately, affect the effectiveness of cybersecurity measures. These human factors are exploited in social engineering (SE) attacks by using psychological factors (PFs) to trick individuals into revealing sensitive information or performing desired actions. Despite decades of innovations and improvements in cybersecurity technologies, humans remain the weakest link in organizational cybersecurity. The 2025 Verizon Data Breach Investigations Report [27] states that the human element is involved in around 60 % of all breaches. In a survey published in 2025, the SANS Institute [24] reveals that 80 % of organizations rank SE as the number one human-related risk, with phishing still leading. The survey further states that

Z. Afzal et al. (Eds.): ARES 2026 Workshops, LNCS 16900, pp. 507–524, 2027.
https://doi.org/10.1007/978-3-032-35576-8_27

SMS-based phishing (smishing) and phone-based voice phishing (vishing) attacks are growing in frequency and sophistication. As email filters have improved, attackers may focus more on other channels [2].

While many existing studies have examined individual aspects of human factors in cybersecurity [25] or have focused on specific SE attacks [19], especially phishing, few have analysed and compared different PFs, such as trust, authority, or curiosity, and PTs, which are strategies used by SE attacks to exploit PFs, e.g., persuasion. Moreover, there is limited research combining PFs and PTs with different SE attacks. By knowing the influence of the PFs/PTs on different SE attacks, better awareness campaigns and other cybersecurity measures can be designed.

This paper aims to bridge this gap by conducting a qualitative laboratory study. The study was conducted by exposing the participants (n = 12) to different SE attacks (n = 5; phishing, spear-phishing, vishing, smishing, and pop-ups) and PFs/PTs (n = 5; authority, fear, greed, trust, and curiosity), resulting in 25 stimuli. The answers were captured on a survey and through the think-aloud method. Our contribution is as follows: (1) comparison of different PFs and PTs for a given SE attack; (2) comparison of different SE attacks for a given PF/PT; (3) best and worst combinations.

The remainder of this paper is as follows: In Sect. 2, we provide the background on SE and psychology. This is followed by a summary of related work in Sect. 3. The study design is outlined in Sect. 4, followed by the presentation of the results in Sect. 5. The results are being discussed in Sect. 6, before we conclude the paper.

2 Social Engineering and Psychology

PFs refer to individual characteristics that can be exploited by adapting the attacker's methods to an individual's personality, aiming at that person's psychological susceptibilities [18]. The Big Five Personality Traits [12] (openness, conscientiousness, extraversion, agreeableness, and neuroticism) is a model in psychology used to describe and assess human personality. Other areas that play a role are cognitive (e.g., dual-process theory [9]) and emotion (e.g., empathy, sympathy, fear, and greed) psychology. Social psychology reflects on how individuals interact with others, focusing on behaviours related to connection, influence, and making or responding to requests. Cialdini [11] describes six principles of persuasion, namely reciprocation, consistency, social validation, liking, authority, and scarcity. Depending on the setting, workplace psychology with factors like stress, busyness, and habituation can play a role.

Longtchi et al. [19] identified 16 PTs, which exploit various PFs: persuasion, attention grabbing, impersonation, pretexting, urgency, visual deception, priming, incentive and motivator, personalization, quid-pro-quo, foot in the door, and decoy effect. The authors conclude that fear, greed, authority, trust, and negligence are most exploited PFs.

SE comprises methods of psychological manipulation that exploit human vulnerabilities to persuade individuals to take specific actions, like downloading and installing malware, or disclose confidential information, like usernames and passwords [22]. There are different email-based attacks, such as generic mass phishing, spear-phishing, clone phishing, and whaling. Other channels are mobile phones (e.g., vishing, smishing, QR code phishing, or app spoofing), online social network (OSN) (e.g., honeytrap, catfishing, angler phishing, or fake profiles), websites (e.g., click-baiting, ad fraud, malvertising, and pop-up attacks), and the physical world (e.g., tailgating, baiting, dumpster diving, and shoulder surfing).

3 Related Work

Some publications generally discuss SE. Mouton et al. [21] provided a more detailed and structured model of SE attacks by extending Mitnick's attack cycle.

Other publications focus on the PFs used in SE. Longtchi et al. [19] investigated why internet-based SE has remained successful despite existing defences by conducting an iterative literature review. The authors identified the gap that attackers exploit more psychological elements than defences addressed at that time. Bullée et al. [5] examined how persuasion principles are employed in SE attacks. The authors concluded that authority is being used most frequently.

Several studies linked personality traits and behaviour to susceptibility, highlighting the influence of conscientiousness and individual differences in information processing. Wall et al. [28] investigated how personality profiles relate to susceptibility to persuasion. Butavicius et al. [7] investigated how the three SE strategies of authority, scarcity, and social proof affect users' judgments of email link safety. Halevi et al. [15] and Alseadoon et al. [1] both investigated how user characteristics shape vulnerability to phishing attacks, whereas Halevi et al. [16] examined factors influencing the susceptibility to spear-phishing. Jun et al. [26] conducted a questionnaire to understand the knowledge, behaviour, experience, and opinion on human factors in cybersecurity. The answers revealed a lack of comprehension of human factors and social engineering. Chrysanthou et al. [10] provided a deep dive into large-scale phishing campaigns aimed at Meta's users. The authors find several poor password choices from the victims.

Longtchi and Xu [18] analysed psychological tactics and techniques in malicious emails using a real-world dataset. They found that certain tactics (e.g., fit and form) and techniques (e.g., attention grabbing) are used most often and often in combination. Burda et al. [6] carried out a systematic literature review on the topic of SE. The authors conclude that the experiments on SE only partially reproduce real attacks and that the attack surface appears larger than the coverage provided by research. For example, attacks conveyed by media other than emails and websites are under-represented, according to the authors. Also, the number of PFs/PTs across studies is limited, with scarcity/urgency, authority, and liking being the most used ones.

Despite the number of publications, there is, to our knowledge, no study that examines the impact of PFs and PTs across different types of SE attacks.

4 Study Design

The laboratory study employed a within-subject 5×5 design to examine how five specific PFs influence twelve participants' susceptibility to five different types of SE attacks. The five PFs are curiosity, greed, trust, authority, and fear. The five SE attack types are phishing and spear-phishing emails, smishing, vishing, and pop-up attacks. This resulted in 25 stimuli, which were presented to each participant in a randomized order to minimize fatigue and order effects. Every PF had their own different scenario. To ensure comparability within each PF, the content was kept constant for the respective PF and was presented only in different formats corresponding to the five attack types (e.g., in an email, SMS, voice message, or pop-up window). This approach ensured that the differences in participants' responses could be attributed to the manipulated variables rather than to content differences. The PFs and SE attack types were the two independent variables, while the participants' response intentions and verbalized reasoning were the main dependent variables.

4.1 Recruitment

A total of 12 participants were recruited through a combination of online and personal outreach strategies in Munich, Germany. They were required to be over 18 years of age. No compensation was given. The gender distribution was skewed towards females (nine female (75 %) and three males (33.3 %)). The ages of the participants ranged from 20 to 50 years, with a median of 22.5 years. Due to the described recruitment method, the sample may have been prone to self-selection bias.

4.2 Procedure

Each participant took part in an individual session lasting approximately 30–60 minutes. The study, including the stimuli and questions, was conducted in German, as this was the native language of the majority of the participants. Before starting with the main part of the study, participants were asked to pretend that their name is Max Mustermann[1], while everything else about them would remain the same. Participants were also encouraged to use the think-aloud method for qualitative insights into cognitive and emotional responses regarding their decisions.

Main Task. After each stimulus, participants were asked to answer the following questions on a tablet:

- "Would you respond to the message/call?" (yes/no)
- "Why or why not?" (open text field)
- "How appealing did you find this message/call ?" (1–4 Likert scale)
- "How urgent did this message/call feel to you?" (1–4 Likert scale)

[1] Equivalent to John Doe in Germany.

Post-Stimulus Questionnaire: After all 25 stimuli were shown, the post-stimulus questionnaire assessed information on participants' socio-demographics, technological affinity, experience, and their handling of unusual messages.

Debriefing: After completing the post-stimulus questionnaire, participants were asked a few reflective questions about their impressions and suspicions. They were then fully debriefed about the study's purpose and informed that all materials were simulated.

4.3 Experimental Setup

The study was conducted in a laboratory environment to ensure consistent conditions for all participants. Each session took place in a testing room, with a tablet placed in front of the participant. All experimental materials, including the stimuli, stimulus-questions, and post-stimulus questionnaire, were presented on that tablet.

PFs. For the PFs, the following impersonations and pretexts were used.

- **Authority:** A person impersonating the CFO of a company asked the recipient to urgently open an attached financial report and confirm its status the same day.
- **Curiosity:** Google was impersonated and the used pretext was receiving access to a shared folder called "Holiday party at the office".
- **Greed:** The used pretext was receiving early access to a Black Friday deal from Amazon.
- **Fear** PayPal was impersonated and the pretext of unusual activity on the recipient's account was given, which allegedly resulted in the account being temporarily frozen. The recipient was asked to confirm their identity through a link.
- **Trust:** Netflix was impersonated and the user was informed of updated account details. To view these details, the user was required to click the provided button.

SE. The following explains the design and creation of the attack examples.

- **Phishing and Spear-Phishing:** Screenshots of simulated phishing emails in an email inbox were presented. The simulated phishing emails were sent from the website canIPhish [8].
- **Smishing:** SMS messages were created with the website iFake [17] and presented as screenshots in a smartphone layout.
- **Vishing:** For this attack type, the website ElevenLabs [13] was used to generate text-to-speech audio using one voice type for all audio to keep consistency among the different PF examples and to avoid different answers based on the voice type.

- **Pop-Ups:** Screenshots of the Wikipedia main page as background with self-created pop-up windows were used. The background remained the same for all pop-up examples to ensure that different behavioural intentions could be attributed to the PF instead of the background.

Material and Stimuli. None of the materials were interactive or contained active links. The stimuli consisted of screenshots or short audio recordings designed to simulate realistic, yet harmless, examples of SE attacks. Two examples can be seen in Fig. 1, with the combinations of phishing and greed (see Fig. 1a) and spear-phishing and trust (see Fig. 1b). Translated, Fig. 1a reads: "Black Friday is just around the corner! Now is the perfect time to get your gifts and avoid the hassle of having to leave your home. With discounts of up to 60 %, you won't want to miss out! Check out the deals!". Figure 1b reads in English: "Hello Max, your Netflix account details have been updated. You can look into your overview through this link: show account overview".

(a) Phishing email using greed.

(b) Spear-phishing email using trust.

Fig. 1. SE examples with different PFs.

4.4 Measurements

Both stimulus and post-stimulus questionnaires were used to assess quantitative and qualitative information.

Quantitative Measures. The post-stimulus questionnaire assessed information on age, gender, study background, prior exposure to phishing, and participants' familiarity with digital means of communications and devices. Participants' behavioural intention to interact with the presented message was measured by their response to the question "Would you respond to the message/call?" (Yes/No). The questions: "How appealing did you find this message?" and "How urgent did this message feel to you?" were asked to obtain an estimation of the urgency and personal appeal to the participants.

Qualitative Measures. Participants' verbalizations from the think-aloud protocol were audio-recorded and transcribed. Written explanations from the stimulus questionnaire ("Why or why not?") were analysed qualitatively to identify reasoning patterns, such as risk awareness, cue utilization, emotional, or personal reactions.

4.5 Limitations

The small sample size and laboratory setting reduce the generalizability of the findings. Because the stimuli were presented as screenshots or audio and involved no real consequences, the ecological validity is limited. The SE attacks can exploit multiple PFs across different PTs. This complexity was not addressed in the study, as this would have exceeded the scope of the thesis. Each PF was represented by a single standardized scenario, which restricts the diversity in which each PF can occur.

5 Results

5.1 Within-PF Design

Authority. The most effective SE type for authority was spear-phishing, with four out of twelve participants tending to interact with the phishing email (33 % yes-votes), followed by phishing. Vishing, smishing, and pop-ups each had success rates lower than 10 %. The overall success rate of authority across the five SE attacks was 13.3 %. When asked why participants would not interact with the stimulus, many answered that the stimulus was delivered on an inappropriate communication channel (in vishing attacks: *"That could/should have been asked in an email."*), that the design seemed illegitimate (*"Does not seem legitimate"*), or that they were sceptical/distrusting (*"Why do I have to download the file immediately?"*).

Curiosity. Curiosity was most successful in the spear-phishing and phishing scenarios, each having had a success rate of 50 %. Pop-ups, smishing, and vishing each had success rates lower than 10 %. The total number of yes-votes for curiosity in the five stimuli was 23.3 %, with spear-phishing and phishing each having a 42.8 % contribution to the total success rate. The most common reason for not interacting with stimuli that use curiosity included "Scepticism / Distrust" (30 % of all reasons for No-votes), followed by "Not interested" (23.9 % of reasons for No-votes). Participants who would interact with any stimuli using curiosity mostly reasoned their answer within the category "Curiosity / Interest" (57.1 % of reasons for Yes-votes), followed by "Seems legitimate".

Fear. Phishing and spear-phishing were the most effective SE attack types for fear, each having had a success rate of 41.6 %. Smishing followed with 25 %, pop-ups with 16.6 % and vishing with 8.3 %. In total, fear had a success rate of 26.6 % across all five scenarios. The most prevalent reason for answering "Yes" was fear (*"PayPal has access to my sensitive information"*, *"It concerns my finances"*, see Fig. 3). This category constitutes 56.2 % of the reasons for answering "Yes". Figure 2 shows that the category "Security concerns" leads the reasons for not interacting with the stimuli (34 % of the reasons for answering "No"). Examples from "Security concerns" are *"I was asked for very sensitive information"* and *"It would make me feel uncertain, but I would check my PayPal app"*.

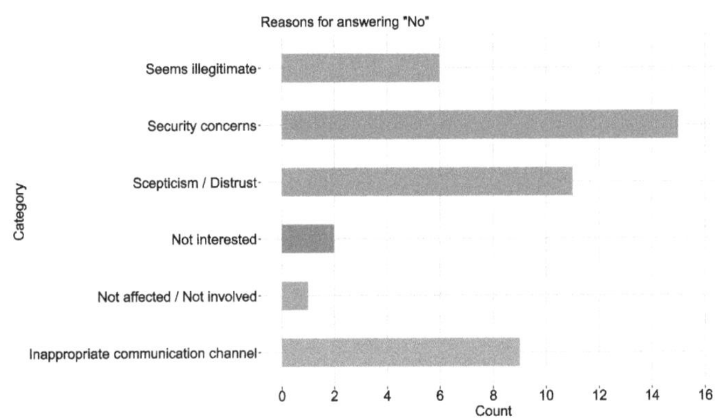

Fig. 2. Reasons for answering "No" in all stimuli using fear.

Greed. The most effective SE attack types for greed were spear-phishing (75 % success rate) and phishing (66.6 % success rate). Both attacks had more "Yes" than "No" answers. Pop-ups followed with a 33.3 % success rate, smishing with 16.6 %, and vishing with 8.3 %. The total Yes-rate of greed in all five attacks was 40 %. The most common reason for answering "Yes" to the greed stimuli was "Financial motivation" (54.1 % contribution to reasons for "Yes"). Examples from "Financial motivation" are *"I like discounts"* and *"There are benefits for me"*. The most prevalent reason for answering "No" to greed stimuli was "Scepticism / Distrust", which occurs strongly in vishing, pop-up, and smishing attacks. An exemplary answer from this category was *"The pretext of being selected for an exclusive access to deals seems odd to me"*.

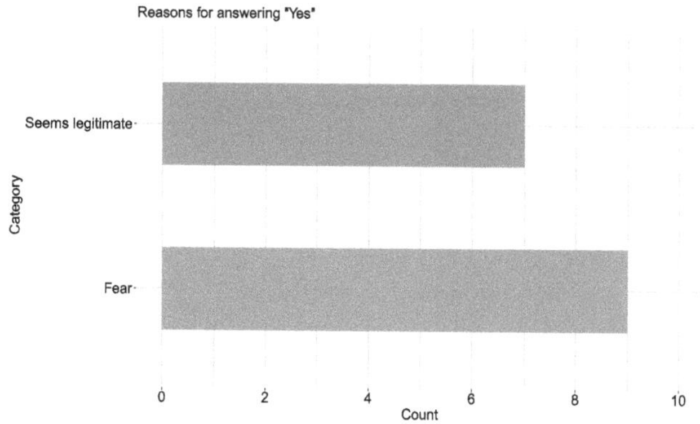

Fig. 3. Reasons for answering "Yes" in all stimuli using fear.

Trust. Trust was most successful in spear-phishing (66.6 % success) and phishing (58.3 % success). The "Yes" answers were more than "No" for these two scenarios. Pop-ups and smishing each had a success rate of 16.6 %, and vishing 8.3 %. The overall success rate of trust in the five SE types was 33.3 %. Reasons for answering "Yes" were mostly in the category "Seems legitimate" (65 % of Yes-vote reasons), followed by "Personal relevance / Relationship" (35 % contribution to Yes-votes). Answers from the category "Seems legitimate" were *"Looks like a normal email from Netflix"* and *"Looks trustworthy"*. An example from "Personal relevance / Relationship" is *"Because I have a Netflix account."* The most common explanation for answering "No" to any stimuli using trust was "Scepticism / Distrust" (42.5 % contribution to No-votes).

5.2 Within-SE Design

Vishing. Vishing had a total success rate of 6.6 % with the PFs authority, fear, greed, and trust each having one out of twelve "Yes" answers (8.3 % success rate each). Vishing using curiosity had no success at all. Most reasons for answering "No" to any of the vishing stimuli were from the category "Scepticism / Distrust", followed by "Inappropriate communication channel". An answer from "Scepticism / Distrust" was *"I generally don't trust phone calls"*. An example from "Inappropriate communication channel": *"This should be sent as an email."*

Phishing. The overall success rate of phishing was 48.3 %. Phishing was most successful by using greed (66.6 % success), followed by trust (58.3 % success), and curiosity (50 % success). Fear in phishing had a success rate of 41.6 % and authority 25 %. The most common reason for answering "Yes" to any phishing stimulus was "Emotional response". This category contributes 58.6 % to the reasons for Yes-votes. Answers from this category included *"Out of curiosity"*, *"I like discounts"*, and *"PayPal has access to my sensitive information."* The most frequently mentioned reasons for answering "No" to any phishing stimulus were

"Scepticism / Distrust" and "Not interested". Answers from the category "Scepticism / Distrust" included *"There is no direct form of address, like 'Good day Mr. Doe'"* and *"There are many fake emails that look like this"*. Figure 4 demonstrates the reasons for answering "No" and shows that the category "Looks illegitimate" occurred this often only in authority.

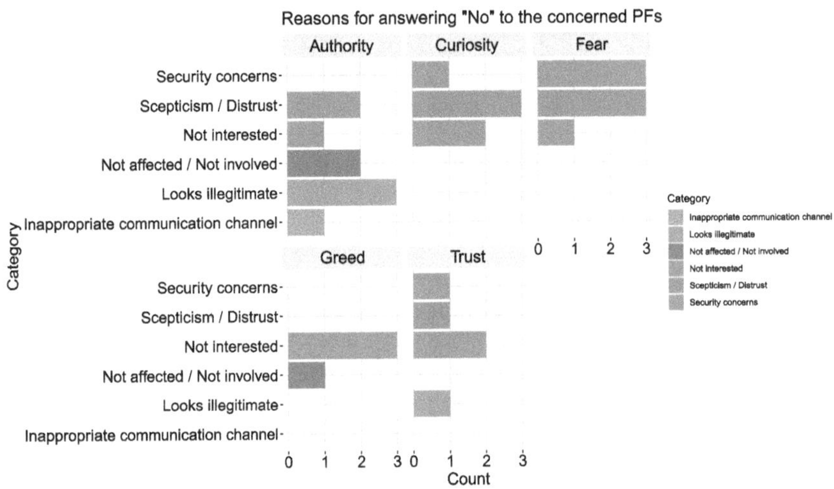

Fig. 4. Reasons for answering "No" to each concerned PF in phishing attacks.

Spear-Phishing. Spear-phishing was most successful by using the PFs greed (75 % success), trust (66.6 % success), and curiosity (50 % success). Spear-phishing using fear had a success rate of 41.6 % and 33.3 % for authority. The overall success rate of spear-phishing constitutes 53.3 %. As seen in Fig. 5, "Emotional response" was the most frequent reason for answering "Yes" to any spear-phishing stimulus (43.7 % contribution to the reasons for yes-votes). Answers from this category included *"It concerns my finances"* and *"I like discounts."* The category "Seems legitimate" follows, and after that comes the category "Felt addressed". The latter category included answers such as *"I was addressed directly by my name and would therefore click on the link without much thought"* and *"My account details, such as my name, are provided."*

Pop-Up. The total success rate of pop-up attacks was 15 %, with greed in pop-ups being the most useful PF (33.3 % success), followed by trust and fear (each 16.6 % success). Curiosity and authority had success rates lower than 10 %. "Emotional response" was the most common reason for answering "Yes". The most common reason for answering "No" was "Scepticism / Distrust", followed by "Inappropriate communication channel". Answers from "Scepticism / Distrust" included *"I don't trust pop-up windows"*, and exemplarily answers from

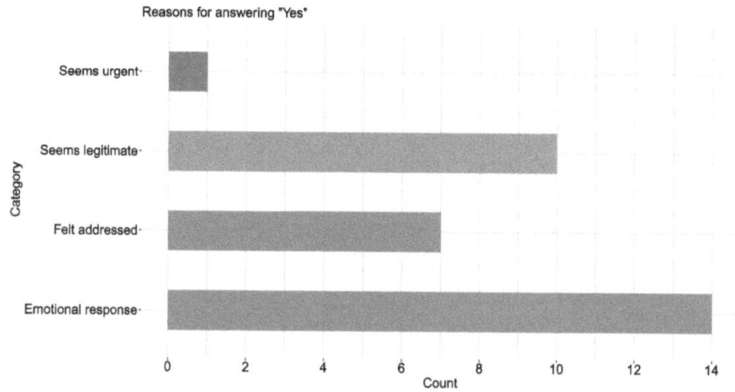

Fig. 5. Reasons for answering "Yes" to all stimuli using spear-phishing.

"Inappropriate communication channel" is *"I would get notified by my app or emails, not through a pop-up."*

Smishing. Smishing was most successful by using fear with an effectiveness rate of 25 %. The overall success rate of smishing was 13.3 %. The most common reason for answering "No" to any smishing stimulus was "Inappropriate communication channel". Answers from that category included *"I'd rather react to an email- an SMS seems strange"* and *"Google wouldn't send me an SMS."*

5.3 Between SE/PF-Design

This section presents the results for all 25 stimuli, alongside the most and least successful combinations of PF and SE attack types (see Fig. 6). Due to the amount of stimuli, the names of the combinations of PFs and SE attacks will be abbreviated. The abbreviation is as follows:

- Authority = AU
- Curiosity = CU
- Fear = FE
- Greed = GR
- Trust = TR
- Vishing = Vi
- Phishing = Ph
- Spear-phishing = SP
- Pop-Up = PU
- Smishing = Sm

The most successful combination of PF and SE attack type was spear-phishing using greed, with a success rate of 75 %, followed by phishing using greed and spear-phishing using trust (each 66.6 % success rate). The third most successful combination was phishing using trust (58.3 % success). The least successful combinations were pop-ups using authority, smishing using authority, and vishing using curiosity, each having had no "Yes" answers at all. Overall, the most successful SE attack type was spear-phishing (53.3 % success), followed by phishing (48.3 % success). The three most effective PFs were greed (40 % success), trust (33.3 % success), and fear (26.6 % success). Figure 6 shows the results for all 25 stimuli.

5.4 Self-rated Digital Risk Awareness

Figure 7 shows the Yes/No answers from participants grouped by their self-rated digital risk awareness. Participants who rated themselves as secure in dealing with digital risks had the highest number of yes-votes (37 yes-votes), followed by the medium group (33 yes-votes). Participants who rated themselves as very secure in dealing with digital risks had the lowest number of yes-votes (3 votes), followed by the insecure group (9 votes).

6 Discussion

6.1 Within-PF Design

Authority. In the laboratory study, authority was not particularly successful in any of the five attack scenarios, with a total yes-vote of 13.3 %. This is contrary to results from previous studies, such as Butavicius et al. [7], where authority was the most persuasive strategy and made phishing harder to detect. Modic and Lea [20] also identified that four key factors, including authority, reliably predict scam compliance. The most frequent reason for answering "No" to any authority stimulus was "Inappropriate communication channel", followed by "Seems illegitimate" (*"It looks fake"*), and "Scepticism / Distrust". Besides "Inappropriate communication channel", the category "Seems illegitimate" is important to consider, since it did not occur as much in the No-vote reasons of other PFs (see Fig. 4 for authority in phishing). Therefore, the limited success of authority may be attributed to two factors: the message content was not appropriate for the used communication channels, and the design/scenario of authority in the emails, SMS, and vishing audio was not convincing enough.

Curiosity. Curiosity had a total Yes-vote of 23.3 % and showed that the most frequently stated reason for answering "No" was within "Scepticism / Distrust", followed by "Not interested". This indicates that the lower Yes-rate could be improved by using more examples that are applicable to more participants, since some may not use Google Drive or are not interested enough in it. The most frequently occurring reason for answering "Yes" was "Curiosity / Interest", which shows that the effect of curiosity, however, did work.

Fear. In previous literature, such as Longtchi et al. [19], fear and greed were the most targeted emotional PFs. In this laboratory study, fear had a total Yes-vote of 26.6 %. Figure 3 and Fig. 2 show the reasons for interacting or not interacting with any fear stimuli. The most prevalent reason for answering "Yes" was fear (*"It concerns my account and finances"*). The most often stated reason

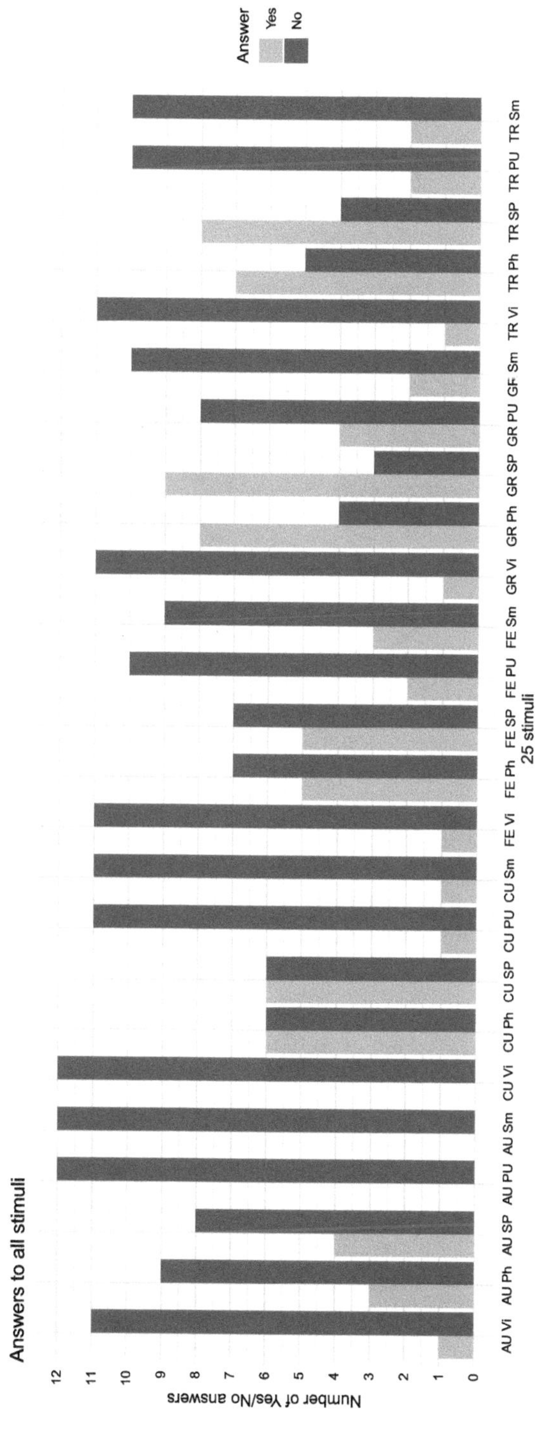

Fig. 6. Results from all 25 stimuli.

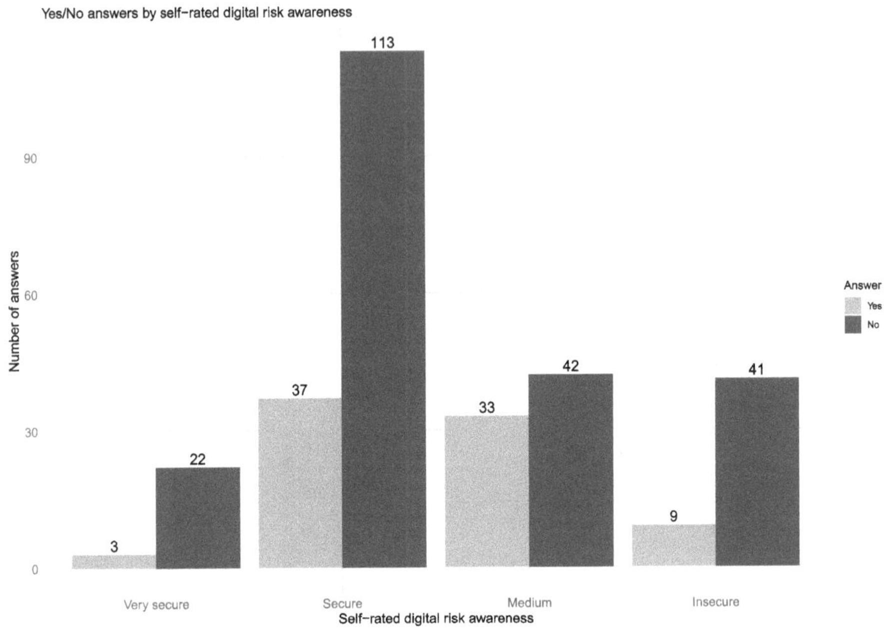

Fig. 7. Yes/No answers by self-rated digital risk awareness

for answering "No" to any fear stimulus was "Security concerns" (*"It concerns my finances"*), which represents fear operating in the opposite direction. Instead of prompting interaction, fear of losing control over sensitive or financial data prevented participants from engaging with the stimulus. This shows that fear was a dominant factor influencing participants' decisions to interact or not to interact with the stimuli. The relatively low Yes-rate for fear can therefore be explained by its counter effect that prevented participants from interacting.

Greed. Atkins and Huang [3] found that advance-fee scams emphasized potential monetary gain, while Longtchi et al. [18] identified that fear and greed were the most targeted emotional PFs. This aligns with our study's results, where greed was successful (40 % success), especially in spear-phishing (75 % success) and phishing attacks (66.6 % success). The most common reason for answering "Yes" to any greed stimulus was "Financial motivation", which supports the effectiveness of greed in the respective stimuli. The category "Seems legitimate" follows after, which shows that the design of the stimuli was convincing.

Trust. Alseadoon et al. [1] found that trust increased compliance, while Longtchi et al. [19] discovered that trust and negligence were the most exploited personality and individual difference (PID) PFs. In this laboratory study, trust had a success rate of 33.3 % and was most successful in spear-phishing (66.6 %

success) and phishing (58.3 % success), which aligns with previous literature. Trust in smishing, pop-ups and vishing however, was not as successful (pop-ups and smishing each had a success rate of 16.6 %, and vishing 8.3 %). Reasons for not interacting with the trust in smishing stimulus were mostly within the category "Scepticism / Distrust", along with trust in vishing and pop-ups. This suggests that these attack types raise more scepticism in general. The most common reason for interacting with any trust stimulus was "Seems legitimate" (65 % contribution to reasons), which in this case translates to the PF trust and demonstrates that trust was accomplished.

6.2 Within-SE Design

Vishing. Previous literature pointed to the steadily growing use of vishing in 2023, with a 260 % increase compared to 2022 Q4 [14]. In 2024 Q1, phone-based phishing continued to grow steadily, with fraudulent phone numbers making up over 20 % of fraud-related assets [2]. This aligns with vishing's low success rate in this study (6.6 %). Due to the significant rise in vishing attacks, individuals' exposure to these calls has increased, which has heightened their distrust towards calls. The most common reason for answering "No" to any vishing stimulus was "Scepticism/Distrust".

Phishing. Phishing via email continues to be one of the most damaging SE attacks [14,19], which is consistent with this study's results (phishing's total success: 48.3 %). Previous studies found that authority and trust were among the most persuasive PFs [1,7] in phishing emails. Contrary to [7], the results of this study showed that authority had the lowest success rate. An explanation for that is seen in Fig. 4; the most common reason for answering "No" to authority in phishing was "Looks illegitimate", which did not occur this often in any of the other four stimuli. This leads to the conclusion that the design of authority in the phishing email was not convincing and led to suspicion. Instead, the most persuasive PFs for phishing were greed (66.6 % success), trust (58.3 % success), and curiosity (50 % success). This aligns with [1], where trust was among the most successful PFs. The main reason for Yes-votes was "Emotional Response", which demonstrates that the PFs were implemented successfully.

Spear-Phishing. Previous research found that authority was the most effective PF for especially spear-phishing emails [7], which is contrary to this study's results, where greed was the most persuasive PF for spear-phishing (75 % success). As discussed before, authority was not particularly successful in any of the five attacks. The most common reason for No-votes to authority in spear-phishing was "Not interested", which did not occur as much in the other PFs. This suggests that the chosen scenario was responsible for the low success rate, rather than the PF authority itself. The most prevalent reason for answering "Yes" to any spear-phishing stimulus was "Emotional Response", which shows that the PFs were successfully implemented. The category "Felt addressed" was the third most common reason for interacting with any spear-phishing stimulus, which demonstrates that the direct address to recipients was noticed and effective.

Pop-Up. Pop-ups were not particularly successful, with an overall success rate of 15 %. The most common reason for answering "No" was "Scepticism/Distrust", followed by "Inappropriate communication channel". This suggests that the content was not suitable for pop-ups and that pop-ups seem to be less trustworthy in general.

Smishing. Blancafor et al. [4] found that trust was the most important PF for smishing attacks, while Rahman et al. [23] found that fear and greed had little difference in their effectiveness in smishing. Our study showed that smishing had the lowest overall success rate (13.3 %), with fear being the most effective PF (25 % success), followed by greed and trust (both 16.6 % success). Overall, smishing was less successful than other attack types because participants viewed SMS as an inappropriate communication channel, while an illegitimate looking design and scepticism also reduced interaction.

6.3 Self-rated Digital Risk Awareness

Halevi et al. found in one study that self-perceived risk did not predict actual behaviour regarding phishing attacks [15], and that participants generally underestimated their own risk [16]. Figure 7 shows that participants who rated themselves as secure and medium in handling digital risks actually overestimated themselves or underestimated their own risk, which aligns with [15,16]. Participants who rated themselves as very secure or insecure were the most cautious, either due to having more knowledge about digital risks or feeling insecure.

7 Conclusion

Human factors are being exploited in SE attacks, with attackers starting to focus on other channels than email. To develop countermeasures like awareness campaigns, it is important to know how effective these attacks are and which PFs and PTs are being most successful. In our study, we exposed the participants with different SE attacks and PFs/PTs. The exploratory results showed that the most effective SE attack type for authority, greed, and trust was spear-phishing. The most effective SE attack types for curiosity and fear were phishing and spear-phishing. Authority was not particularly successful, with a success rate of 13.3 % in comparison with greed (40 %) and trust (33.3 %) that had the highest success rates among the five PFs. The results also show that vishing (8.3 % success rate) was relatively unsuccessful. Overall, the most successful attack types were spear-phishing (53.3 % success rate) and phishing (48.3 % success rate). The most successful combinations were spear-phishing with greed (75 %

success rate), phishing with greed, and spear-phishing with trust (both with 66.6 % success rate). In future work, we want to include more participants, SE attacks, and PFs/PTs, as well as more variations of the combinations to validate and extend our results.

Declarations. The authors have no competing interests to declare that are relevant to the content of this article.

References

1. Alseadoon, I., Othman, M.F.I., Chan, T.: What is the influence of users' characteristics on their ability to detect phishing emails? In: Sulaiman, H.A., Othman, M.A., Othman, M.F.I., Rahim, Y.A., Pee, N.C. (eds.) Advanced Computer and Communication Engineering Technology. LNEE, vol. 315, pp. 949–962. Springer, Cham (2015). https://doi.org/10.1007/978-3-319-07674-4_89
2. APWG: Phishing Activity Trends Report 1st Quarter 2024 (2024). https://docs.apwg.org/reports/apwg_trends_report_q1_2024.pdf
3. Atkins, B., Huang, W.: A study of social engineering in online frauds. Open J. Soc. Sci. **01**, 23–32 (2023). https://doi.org/10.4236/jss.2013.13004
4. Blancaflor, E., Alfonso, A., Banganay, K., Cruz, G., Fernandez, K., Santos, S.: Let's go phishing: a phishing awareness campaign using smishing, email phishing, and social media phishing tools (March 2021). https://doi.org/10.46254/AN11.20211105
5. Bullée, J.W., Montoya, L., Pieters, W., Junger, M., Hartel, P.: On the anatomy of social engineering attacks: a literature-based dissection of successful attacks. Journal of Investigative Psychol. Offender Profiling **15**(1), 20–45 (2018). https://doi.org/10.1002/jip.1482, https://research.utwente.nl/en/publications/on-the-anatomy-of-social-engineering-attacks-a-literature-based-d
6. Burda, P., Allodi, L., Zannone, N.: Cognition in social engineering empirical research: a systematic literature review. ACM Trans. Comput.-Hum. Interact. **31**(2) (2024). https://doi.org/10.1145/3635149
7. Butavicius, M., Parsons, K., Pattinson, M., McCormac, A.: Breaching the Human Firewall: Social engineering in Phishing and Spear-Phishing Emails (2016). https://doi.org/10.48550/arXiv.1606.00887
8. canIPhish: Security Awareness Training | Phishing Simulation | CanIPhish. https://caniphish.com/User/WebPhishing
9. Chaiken, S., Trope, Y.: Dual-process theories in social psychology. Guilford Press (1999)
10. Chrysanthou, A., Pantis, Y., Patsakis, C.: The anatomy of deception: measuring technical and human factors of a large-scale phishing campaign. Comput. Sec. **140**, 103780 (2024). https://doi.org/10.1016/j.cose.2024.103780, https://www.sciencedirect.com/science/article/pii/S0167404824000816
11. Cialdini, R.B.: The science of persuasion. Sci. Am. **284**(2), 76–81 (2001). https://www.jstor.org/stable/26059056
12. Cobb-Clark, D.A., Schurer, S.: The stability of big-five personality traits. Econ. Lett. **115**(1), 11–15 (2012). https://doi.org/10.1016/j.econlet.2011.11.015, https://www.sciencedirect.com/science/article/pii/S0165176511004666
13. ElevenLabs: AI Voice Generator & Text to Speech (2026). https://elevenlabs.io

14. Group A.P.W: Phishing activity trends report, 4th quarter 2023. Technical report, Anti-Phishing Working Group (Nov 2023). https://docs.apwg.org/reports/apwg_trends_report_q4_2023.pdf, zugriff am 19.04.2026
15. Halevi, T., Lewis, J., Memon, N.: Phishing, Personality Traits and Facebook (2013). https://arxiv.org/abs/1301.7643
16. Halevi, T., Memon, N., Nov, O.: Spear-phishing in the wild: a real-world study of personality, phishing self-efficacy and vulnerability to spear-phishing attacks. SSRN Electr. J. (2015). https://doi.org/10.2139/ssrn.2544742, http://www.ssrn.com/abstract=2544742
17. Hess, D.: Fake Text Message | Make Fake Text Conversation (2023). https://ifaketextmessage.com
18. Longtchi, T., Xu, S.: Characterizing the evolution of psychological factors exploited by malicious emails. In: Zhao, J., Meng, W. (eds.) Science of Cyber Security, pp. 158–178. Springer Nature (2025). https://doi.org/10.1007/978-981-96-2417-1_9
19. Longtchi, T.T., Rodriguez, R.M., Al-Shawaf, L., Atyabi, A., Xu, S.: Internet-based social engineering psychology, attacks, and defenses: a survey. Proc. IEEE **112**(3), 210–246 (2024). https://doi.org/10.1109/JPROC.2024.3379855, https://ieeexplore.ieee.org/document/10493072/
20. Modic, D., Lea, S.E.G.: Scam compliance and the psychology of persuasion. SSRN Electr. J. (2013). https://doi.org/10.2139/ssrn.2364464, http://www.ssrn.com/abstract=2364464
21. Mouton, F., Malan, M., Leenen, L., Venter, H.: Social engineering attack framework. Sci. Res. Publishing (2014). https://doi.org/10.1109/ISSA.2014.6950510
22. Pozo, I., Iturralde, M., Restrepo-Calle, F.: Social engineering: application of psychology to information security. In: 2018 6th International Conference on Future Internet of Things and Cloud Workshops (FiCloudW), pp. 108–114 (2018). https://doi.org/10.1109/W-FiCloud.2018.00023
23. Rahman, M.L., Timko, D., Wali, H., Neupane, A.: Users really do respond to smishing (2022). https://arxiv.org/abs/2212.13312
24. SANS Institute: SANS Report Finds Humans Still The Main Attack Vector as 80% of Organizations Flag Social Engineering as Their Number One Risk (2025). https://www.sans.org/press/announcements/security-awareness-report-2025
25. Siddiqi, M.A., Pak, W., Siddiqi, M.A.: A study on the psychology of social engineering-based cyberattacks and existing countermeasures. Appli. Sci. **12**(12) (2022). https://doi.org/10.3390/app12126042, https://www.mdpi.com/2076-3417/12/12/6042
26. Tan Jia Jun, D., Sahban Rafsanjani, A., Aslam, S., Behjati, M.: Human factors in information security: a quantitative study with technical solutions to prevent social engineering attacks. Digital Threats **6**(4) (2025). https://doi.org/10.1145/3767320
27. Verizon: 2025 Data Breach Investigations Report (2025). https://www.verizon.com/business/resources/reports/dbir/
28. Wall, H.J., Campbell, C.C., Kaye, L.K., Levy, A., Bhullar, N.: Personality profiles and persuasion: An exploratory study investigating the role of the Big-5, Type D personality and the Dark Triad on susceptibility to persuasion. Personality Individual Differences **139**, 69–76 (2019). https://doi.org/10.1016/j.paid.2018.11.003, https://linkinghub.elsevier.com/retrieve/pii/S0191886918305865

ABAC-NDN: An Open-Source Security Library for Attribute-Based Access Control in NDN

Ferhat Mecerhed[1,3](✉), Youcef Imine[1], Antoine Gallais[1,2], Stefan Fischer[3], and Mohamed Ahmed Hail[3,4]

[1] LAMIH-UMR CNRS 8201, Université Polytechnique Hauts-de-France, Valenciennes, France
{ferhat.mecerhed,youcef.imine,antoine.gallais}@uphf.fr
[2] INSA Hauts-de-France, Valenciennes, France
[3] Institute of Telematics, University of Lübeck, Ratzeburger Allee 160, Lübeck, Germany
{stefan.fischer,m.hail}@uni-luebeck.de
[4] Kiel University, Hermann-Rodewald-Street 3, Kiel, Germany

Abstract. Named Data Networking (NDN) introduces a data-centric communication paradigm with inherent benefits such as multicast delivery, in-network caching, and built-in integrity. However, it also raises new challenges for data confidentiality and access control. Attribute-based encryption (ABE) has emerged as a powerful cryptographic primitive for enforcing fine-grained access control centered on attributes rather than identities, making it a natural fit for NDN. While several ABE-based access control mechanisms have been proposed in the NDN literature, none, to the best of our knowledge, provide a publicly available implementation nor a detailed description of a reusable library design for NDN.

In this paper, we present ABAC-NDN, the first open-source library implementing a decentralized Attribute-Based Access Control scheme for NDN. The library enables NDN entities to operate as authorities or clients, providing automated configuration of security parameters, key management, and attribute revocation for authorities, while supporting fine-grained access control and secure data exchange for producers and consumers. Its modular architecture enables easy integration with existing NDN applications and supports future extensions, effectively connecting theoretical attribute-based encryption schemes with practical security solutions for NDN. Moreover, the library has been evaluated on a set of heterogeneous devices and a real NDN testbed to provide a benchmark on its performances.

Keywords: Named Data Networking · Security Library · Attribute-based Encryption · Multi Authority

Z. Afzal et al. (Eds.): ARES 2026 Workshops, LNCS 16900, pp. 525–540, 2027.
https://doi.org/10.1007/978-3-032-35576-8_28

1 Introduction

Named Data Networking (NDN) is emerging as a promising evolution of the information-centric Internet architecture, offering solutions to the complex and inefficient content distribution mechanisms of traditional IP models [6,18]. It introduces built-in features such as native multicast communication, in-network caching, multipath forwarding, and enhanced security through data signing [6].

Despite these advantages, ensuring confidentiality in NDN remains a major challenge. This difficulty arises from the decoupling of content from its source identity, as well as the pervasive caching of data in the network. Traditional end-to-end encryption approaches are poorly adapted to this paradigm, since the same content may be retrieved by multiple consumers at different times [5].

Attribute-Based Encryption (ABE) is particularly well suited to address the confidentiality challenge in NDN, as it enforces fine-grained access control directly over content and aligns well with the one-to-many communication paradigm of NDN [8]. Yet, despite its relevance, an open-source security library implementing ABE for NDN is still lacking.

Moreover, existing NDN libraries do not provide integrated confidentiality mechanisms. For example, solutions such as [7,14,15] offer networking primitives for NDN but lack cryptographic access control. Security-oriented NDN libraries mainly address *data integrity* through signatures and trust management [12, 16,19], without supporting confidentiality. Meanwhile, existing access control approaches for NDN rely on identity-based encryption schemes [13,17], which conflict with NDN's content-centric philosophy. This highlights the gap between NDN's confidentiality requirements and existing tools, emphasizing the need for a library that bridges theoretical designs and real-world adoption by enabling the integration of confidentiality into NDN applications.

Therefore, this paper introduces ABAC-NDN [10], a novel practical library that implements the decentralized Attribute-Based Access Control scheme [11] on NDN. To the best of our knowledge, this is the first open-source decentralized attribute-based encryption library publicly available for NDN.

By building on the widely used NDN C++ library (ndn-cxx) [3] and the Pairing-Based Cryptography (PBC) library [9], ABAC-NDN is designed for seamless integration into existing NDN applications and for extensibility through its modular architecture.

The library allows NDN entities to operate either as authorities or as clients. When deployed on an authority, it supports the automated configuration of security parameters, key management, and attribute revocation. When integrated with data producers and consumers, it enables fine-grained access control over data through attribute-based encryption and decryption.

In addition, the library is adapted for multi-authority systems, allowing its use on multiple security authorities within the same network environment. It also automatically manages the underlying NDN communication through the ndn-cxx framework, ensuring secure and transparent data exchange.

Finally, we present a comprehensive benchmark that evaluates the computational performance of the library on heterogeneous hardware platforms, and measures the latency introduced by the encryption scheme through experiments on a real NDN testbed.

The main contributions of this paper can be summarized as:

- We present the first practical library implementing a decentralized fine-grained access control scheme for NDN.
- We provide an in-depth analysis of the library's architecture, enabling researchers and developers to effectively access, extend, and adopt this open-source NDN security framework.
- We propose an ABE implementation for NDN that supports authority and client roles, provide automatic configuration, and enables secure application data exchange.
- We provide a benchmark through experimental evaluation on heterogeneous hardware platforms and a real NDN testbed demonstrates the feasibility and efficiency of the proposed design.

The remainder of this paper is organized as follows: Sect. 2 presents the background on NDN and the MA-ABE scheme for NDN. Section 3 details the architecture of the security library. Section 4 reports performance evaluation results. Finally, we conclude in Sect. 5.

2 Background

2.1 Named Data Networking (NDN)

Named Data Networking (NDN) is an information-centric networking paradigm that shifts the communication model from host-based addressing to data-centric retrieval. Instead of identifying endpoints, NDN focuses on named content as the primary network abstraction. Communication is driven by two fundamental packet types: *Interest* and *Data*. A consumer initiates communication by issuing an Interest packet that carries the hierarchical name of the requested content. This Interest is then propagated through the network until it reaches a node that can satisfy the request. Once the corresponding data is located, the provider returns a Data packet containing the requested content, its name, and a cryptographic signature ensuring integrity and authenticity [18].

To efficiently support this forwarding model, each NDN router maintains three core data structures. First, the *Pending Interest Table (PIT)* records all forwarded Interest packets that have not yet been satisfied, along with the interfaces from which they were received. Second, the *Forwarding Information Base (FIB)* provides name-prefix-based routing information, guiding Interests toward potential data sources through appropriate outgoing interfaces. Third, the *Content Store (CS)* acts as an in-network cache that temporarily stores previously forwarded Data packets, enabling opportunistic reuse and reducing retrieval latency.

Upon reception of a Data packet, an NDN router performs a reverse-path forwarding operation by matching the Data name against existing PIT entries.

If a match is found, the router forwards the Data packet to all recorded downstream interfaces, removes the corresponding PIT entry, and stores a copy of the Data in the Content Store for potential future requests. This in-network caching mechanism, combined with name-based routing, significantly improves bandwidth efficiency and reduces retrieval delay, while simultaneously introducing new security and trust-related challenges [18].

2.2 Bilinear Maps

Let G_1 and G_T be two multiplicative cyclic groups of prime order p. Let g be a generator of G_1 and e be a bilinear map defined as: $e : G_1 \times G_1 \rightarrow G_T$

The bilinear map e has the following properties:

- **Bilinearity**: For all $u, v \in G_1$ and $a, b \in \mathbb{Z}_p$, we have $e(u^a, v^b) = e(u, v)^{ab}$
- **Non-degeneracy**: $e(g, g) \neq 1$.
- **Computability**: An efficient algorithm computes e.

2.3 Decentralized Attribute-Based Access Control for NDN

We briefly outline the cryptographic core of the decentralized attribute-based access control protocol for NDN [11].

Authority Setup. Each authority AA_i, managing a set of attributes S_{AA_i}, needs to generate a set of master keys by randomly choosing for each attribute a set of values $\{\alpha_{i,x}, y_{i,x}, \delta_{i,x}\} \in \mathbb{Z}_q^*$. To generate the public key, each authority generates for each attribute A_x computes:

$$PK_{i,x}^{\mathrm{v}1} = (e(g, g)^{\alpha_{i,x}\delta_{i,x}}, g^{y_{i,x}\delta_{i,x}})$$

Key Generation. To generate a device key, the authority selects a random value $\beta_{i,j,x} \in \mathbb{Z}_q^*$ and calculates the secret key for the attribute as follows:

$$K_{i,j,x} = g^{\alpha_{i,x}\beta_{i,j,x}}.H(GID_j)^{y_{i,x}\beta_{i,j,x}}$$

The authority assigns for the device requesting the key, a random value $L_{i,j} \in \mathbb{Z}_q^*$, this secret value is the second part of the device's key. The authority AA_i also compute an initial public update for the attribute of the device, to allow it to decrypt data. The authority selects a random value $rt_{i,j,x} \in \mathbb{Z}_q^*$ and performs the following:

$$\gamma_{i,j,x}^{\mathrm{v}1} = \frac{\delta_{i,x}}{\beta_{i,j,x} \times H(L_{i,j} + rt_{i,j,x})}$$

Message Encryption. The encryption algorithm takes as input the key material KM, an access tree A, a set of public keys from the authorities, and a subset of relevant nodes $storedNodes$ identified by an optimization algorithm.

At each leaf node of the access tree A, corresponding to attribute x, the secret shares λ and ω are used with a random r_x to compute ciphertext components:

$$C_0 = KM \cdot e(g,g)^s, \quad C_{1,x} = e(g,g)^{\lambda_x} \cdot e(g,g)^{\alpha_x r_x \delta_x},$$

$$C_{2,x} = g^{r_x}, \quad C_{3,x} = g^{y_x r_x \delta_x} \cdot g^{\omega_x} \quad \forall x$$

Message Decryption. The decryption algorithm takes as input the ciphertext CT, the device identity GID_j, a set of valid device keys $SK_{i,j,x}$ satisfying the access tree AT, and the subset of stored nodes $storedNodes$ determined by the optimization algorithm.

For each leaf attribute x, the following value is computed:

$$\frac{C_{1,x} \cdot e(H(\mathrm{GID}_j), C_{3,x})}{e(SK_{j,x}^{v_k}, C_{2,x})} = e(g,g)^{\lambda_x} e(H(\mathrm{GID}_j), g)^{\omega_x}.$$

Using the shares from all satisfied leaves, the algorithm recursively reconstructs the secret by computing:

$$\begin{aligned} & e(g,g)^{\sum_{i=1}^{m} \lambda_i \prod_{j=1, j\neq i}^{m} \frac{x_j}{x_j - x_i}} \\ & \cdot e(H(GID_j), g)^{\sum_{i=1}^{m} \omega_i \prod_{j=1, j\neq i}^{m} \frac{x_j}{x_j - x_i}} \\ & = e(g,g)^s \cdot e(H(GID_j), g)^0 = e(g,g)^s \end{aligned}$$

where x is the index of the child to the current node. The key material KM is calculated as: $\frac{C_0}{e(g,g)^s}$

Attribute Revocation. When an authority revokes an attribute, it generates a new version of the corresponding public key and new device updates to all non-revoked devices. In on-going communications, a new key material is encrypted by the producer using the new public keys, and is decrypted by the consumers using their new updates.

3 Library Design

This section describes our security library that acts as an intermediary layer between NDN applications and the NDN communication stack and enable secure data exchange. It provides a complete framework for initializing the cryptosystem, managing cryptographic material, and supporting secure data production and consumption for NDN applications.

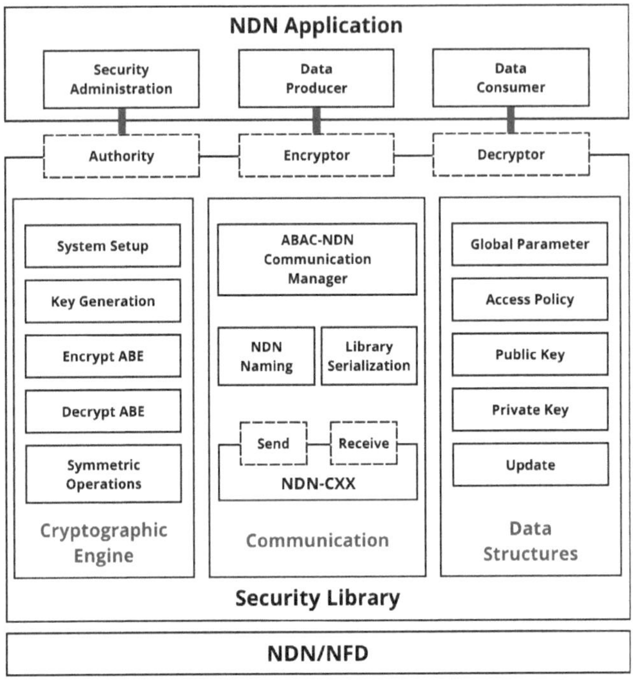

Fig. 1. ABAC-NDN Library Architecture

3.1 Library's Architecture

As illustrated in Fig. 1, the library is organized into three main modules, each responsible for a distinct set of functionalities: a cryptographic engine, a data representation module, and a communication module.

Cryptographic Engine. The cryptographic engine provides a low-level interface to the MA-ABE primitives described in Sect. 2. It supports the main operations of the cryptosystem, including system setup, key generation, client-side encryption, and decryption. The engine operates exclusively on cryptographic objects (system parameters, public and secret keys, access policies, and ciphertexts) and is independent from the underlying network layer. It exposes a well-defined API that is invoked by the communication module to perform cryptographic processing.

Data Structures. This module provides a unified representation of all cryptosystem components, including system parameters, public and secret keys, access policies, and ciphertexts. These data structures serve as the common interface between the cryptographic engine and the communication module. They support the serialization and deserialization of cryptographic objects in order to enable their persistent storage and network exchange between entities.

Communication Component. The communication module is responsible for sending and receiving application data and for exchanging cryptographic components between entities, it utilizes both the Cryptographic Engine and Data Structures.

This section includes the ABAC-NDN Communication Manager that initializes the cryptosystem, orchestrate the exchange of cryptographic components, and ensures secure production and consumption of data provided by the application layer.

The communication section also features the library's naming scheme, which closely follows the NDN naming conventions. As shown in Fig. 2, the library constructs names following the general structure:

`/DomainPrefix/Function/Id[/Option]`. This allows network entities to request global parameters, public keys, device updates, and to receive notifications of attribute revocations.

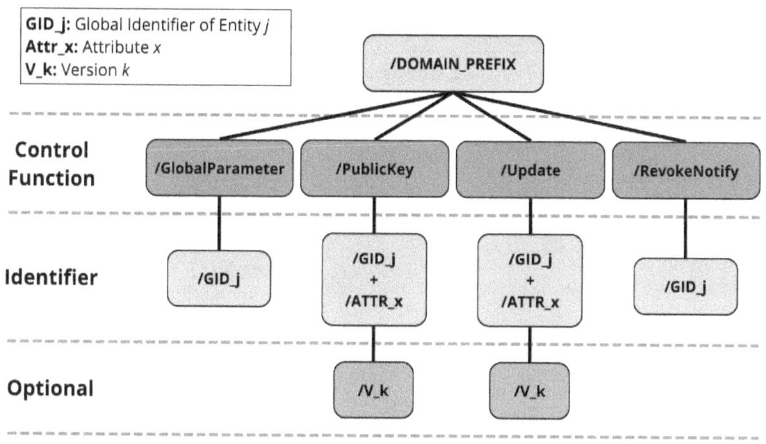

Fig. 2. Hierarchy of the library's naming scheme

3.2 Library's Role Description

By combining the three functional modules, the library enables network entities to operate in two distinct roles. The `Authority` role is responsible for managing global system parameters, issuing attribute keys, and handling revocation. The `Client` role can take one of two forms:

- *Encryptor*, corresponding to a NDN producer, which publishes encrypted data according to an access policy.
- *Decryptor*, corresponding to a NDN consumer, which retrieves and decrypts the encrypted data in accordance with its authorized attributes.

Figure 3 presents the C++ class structure used to implement the roles, together with their main proprieties and methods.

In what follows, we describe how each role is supported by the library and how it can be integrated into an existing NDN application.

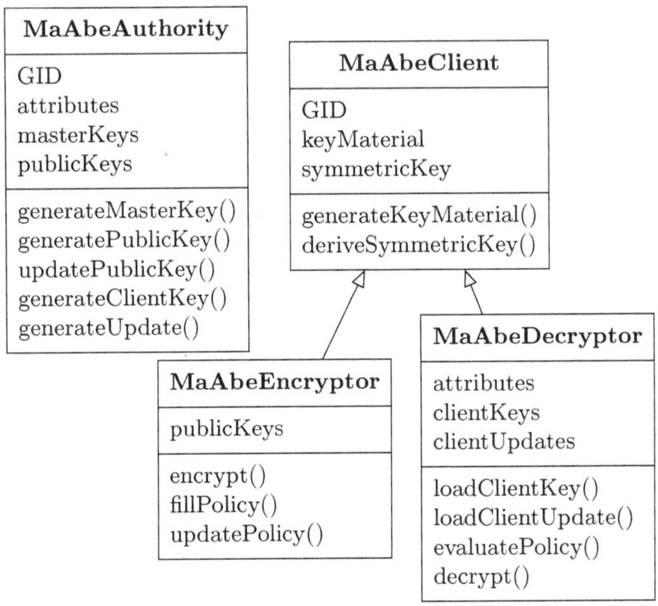

Fig. 3. C++ class diagram of the ABAC-NDN roles

Authority Role. The *Authority* role enables the security administrator to perform authority operations within a specific domain. The library provides a long-running authority application responsible for system setup and the management of requests from other entities. In addition, the application offers an interactive command-line interface that allows client key generation and immediate attribute revocation.

The authority application can be started with the parameters shown in Listing 1. The command requires a global identifier (GID) for the authority and a set of attributes to be managed. Optionally, the `-fetch-gp` flag can be used to specify the content name from which to fetch global parameters from another domain. In that case, the content name to specify takes the form */DOMAIN/-GlobalParameters/AUTH_GID*. If this option is not provided, the authority generates its own global parameters. Starting the authority process initializes the system parameters and generates the master key and the public keys for each defined attribute, as described in Sect. 2.

```
./MaAbeAuthorityNDN
    --gid AUTHORITY_GID
    --attrs ATTR_1,...,ATTR_N
    [--fetch-gp CONTENT_NAME]
```

Listing 1. Start and initialization of the authority

During execution, the authority responds to requests from other entities of the network through the following callbacks:

- *onInterestGlobalParameter*: Responds to requests of the form `/DOMAIN/GlobalParameters/AUTH_GID` by providing the authority's global parameters.
- *onInterestPublickey*: Responds to requests of the form `/DOMAIN/PublicKey/ATTR[/VERSION]` by providing the public key of the specified attribute and version. If no version is specified, the latest corresponding public key is provided.
- *onInterestUpdate*: Responds to requests of the form `/DOMAIN/Update/GID/ATTR[/VERSION]` by generating and providing the update of the specified attribute, user, and version. If no version is specified, the latest corresponding update is provided.

The interactive command-line interface of the authority also supports client key generation and revocation, as shown in Listing 2. The `genkey` command generates a client secret key intended for installation on the decryptor side. The confidentiality of this key must be ensured by the user through a secure transfer mechanism. The `revoke` command launches the revocation procedure for a specified client and attribute. Both client key generation and attribute revocation are described in Sect. 2.

```
authority> genkey CLIENT_GID ATTRIBUTE [OUTPUT_FILE
    ]
authority> revoke CLIENT_GID ATTRIBUTE
```

Listing 2. Authority CLI

Client Role Encryptor. To enable encryption under the access control scheme provided by the library, existing NDN producer applications can take on the role of *Client-Encryptor* role. Using the function shown in Listing 3, The producer can securely publish data provided through a data provider callback under a specified prefix and an access policy expressed in textual form. The *Data Provider* is a user-defined function that supplies the content to be encrypted and published at runtime, allowing the library to retrieve fresh or dynamically generated data on demand. The access policy follows the recursive syntax $k/2(child_1, child_2)$, where k denotes the threshold parameter and 2 is the number of child nodes. The policy node is satisfied when at least k of its two children are satisfied.

```
int publishEncryptedStream(
    ndn::Face& face,
    const ndn::Name& prefix,
    const std::string& accessPolicy,
    std::function<std::istream&(void)> provider);
```

Listing 3. Secure data publication at producer-level

The `publishEncryptedStream` function first initializes a client instance of the library and requests the global parameters from the domain authority by issuing an Interest with the name `/DOMAIN/GlobalParameters/AUTH_GID`. It then constructs an access policy object based on the provided textual representation. For any missing public keys corresponding to the attributes and versions specified in the policy, the function fetches the required keys by querying the authority responsible for each attribute. Specifically, the communication section issues an Interest using the name `/DOMAIN/PublicKey/ATTR[/VERSION]` to retrieve each public key.

The encryptor follows by registering the content prefix with the `ndn::Face`. Following the access control scheme, a symmetric key is generated and encrypted using the ABE policy. This key material is published as the first segment of the stream, only accessible to decryptors satisfying the policy.

For the subsequent data segments, a chunk of plaintext is read from the Data provider function, encrypted with AES using the symmetric key, and published to the NDN network.

Client Role Decryptor. The library allows consumers of the system to take on the role of *Client-Decryptor*. The library expects client secret keys, generated by the authority, to be available in the directory `./.ndn/abe-keys/`. Alternatively, an NDN consumer application can invoke the `installClientKey` utility which moves a given key file into the appropriate directory.

To perform decryption, the library exposes a function shown in Listing 4. Integrating this function into existing consumer NDN application allows the consumption, via a given `ndn::Face`, of a data stream published under a specified `prefix`. If the set of locally installed client keys is sufficient to satisfy the access policy protecting the data, the decrypted data is written into the provided `output` pipeline. Optionally, the NDN consumer application can supply a callback function. It is invoked after the decryption of each segment and receives the plaintext segment as input, allowing the application to perform real-time actions on the data.

```
int consumeEncryptedStream(
    ndn::Face& face,
    const ndn::Name& prefix,
    std::ostream& output,
    std::function<void(const uint8_t* data, size_t
       size)> onSegment = nullptr);
```

Listing 4. Secure data consumption on the consumer side

Internally, the `consumeEncryptedStream` function initializes a `MaAbeDecryptor` instance by first retrieving the global parameters from the domain authority by sending an interest packet named `/DOMAIN/GlobalParameters/AUTH_GID`. It then loads the client keys found in `./.ndn/abe-keys/` and requests the first segment of the stream, which contains the attribute-based ciphertext of the stream's key material. The decryptor evaluates the access policy: if the available keys do not satisfy the policy, the function returns the `AC_NOT_SATISFIED` status code. Otherwise, the decryptor queries the relevant authorities for updates using requests of the name `/DOMAIN/Update/GID/ATTR/VERSION`. These requests allows to obtain updates of the exact versions of the attributes used for encryption.

When valid updates are available, the key material is successfully decrypted. Combined with the nonces embedded in subsequent data packets, it is then derived into a usable symmetric key that enables the decryption of the stream. These operations are described in Sect. 2. The recovered plaintext is written to the specified `output` pipeline, and the optional `onSegment` callback is triggered for each decrypted segment.

4 Performance Evaluation

In this section, we evaluate the performance of our security library and show how to install it. Our goal is to provide a benchmark of its execution times and network performances, rather than to compare it with other solutions. To the best of our knowledge, there is no publicly available NDN-based solution implementing a multi-authority attribute-based access control.

4.1 Installing the Library

The following external dependencies are required for the implementation and operation of our security library:

- **GMP** [2]: Used for large integer arithmetic.
- **PBC** [9]: Provides the bilinear pairing operations required for the ABE scheme implemented in the library.
- **Crypto++** [1]: For symmetric cryptography.
- **ndn-cxx** [3]: The interface to the NDN framework.

- **NFD** [4]: Enable data exchange over an NDN network.

To enable proper communication among the entities within the library, each entity's NFD instance must be configured with the corresponding routes as shown in Listing 5.

```
// Authority
nfdc route add /DOMAIN/RevokeNotify $NEXT_HOP_IP
// Producer
nfdc route add /DOMAIN/GlobalParameter $NEXT_HOP_IP
nfdc route add /DOMAIN/PublicKey $NEXT_HOP_IP
// Consumer
nfdc route add /DOMAIN/GlobalParameter $NEXT_HOP_IP
nfdc route add /DOMAIN/Update $NEXT_HOP_IP
nfdc route add /DOMAIN/Data $NEXT_HOP_IP
```

Listing 5. NFD Routes needed for the library communication

To install the library, we use CMake and the sequence of commands presented in Listing 6:

```
// Install the package
cd NDN-MA-ABE
cmake CMakeLists.txt
make
sudo make install
sudo ldconfig
```

Listing 6. Installation commands of the library

After installation, the library's binaries and headers will be available system-wide, allowing other NDN applications to link against it. The authority can be launched directly via the command-line application `MaAbeAuthorityNDN`. NDN producer and consumer applications can integrate the library by including `MaAbeEncryptorNDN.h` and `MaAbeDecryptorNDN.h`, respectively, in their code.

4.2 Evaluation of the Execution Time

We evaluate our security library by measuring the execution time of its cryptographic operations. Experiments are conducted on three platforms: an ESP32-S3 microcontroller with a dual-core 240 MHz processor and 512 KB RAM, a Jetson Nano with a quad-core ARM Cortex-A57 CPU and 4 GB RAM, and an x86 machine with an AMD Ryzen 7 PRO 4750U processor and 32 GB RAM. The x86 platform is also used to evaluate authority-side operations. Table 1 shows the computation times of each primitive executed on one attribute.

We further evaluate the performance of the proposed cryptographic primitives under different security levels and across the heterogeneous platforms previously presented. In particular, we measure both encryption and decryption execution times under Type A and Type F curve settings with varying

Table 1. Execution times of the library's primitives (in Milliseconds)

Function	ESP32	Jetson Nano	x86
GenerateMasterKey	–	–	0.12
GeneratePublicKey	–	–	1.60
UpdatePublicKey	–	–	1.08
GenerateClientKey	–	–	2.74
GenerateClientUpdate	–	–	0.01
Encrypt	163.60	30.00	3.01
LoadClientUpdate	38.00	4.259	0.87
Decrypt	822.30	16.69	1.28

bit-security strengths. The detailed results for encryption and decryption are presented in Table 2 and Table 3, respectively, highlighting the computational overhead introduced by increased security levels.

Table 2. Encryption execution times across devices and security levels (ms)

Device	Type A			Type F		
	80-bit	112-bit	128-bit	80-bit	112-bit	128-bit
ESP32	163.6	611.86	1339.88	965.24	1515.43	1737.43
Jetson	30.0	112.2	245.7	177.0	277.89	318.6
x86	3.01	11.26	24.65	17.79	27.88	31.97

Table 3. Decryption execution times across devices and security levels (ms)

Device	Type A			Type F		
	80-bit	112-bit	128-bit	80-bit	112-bit	128-bit
ESP32	822.3	4481.5	12161.8	9242.7	14326.1	16174.6
Jetson	16.7	91.0	246.9	187.6	290.8	328.3
x86	1.3	7.0	19.0	14.4	22.3	25.2

4.3 Network Evaluation

The network evaluation was performed using a set of Raspberry Pi 3 B+ nodes connected in a star topology, with a NDN router as central node as shown in Fig. 4. The network was powered by the NDN Forwarding Daemon (NFD)

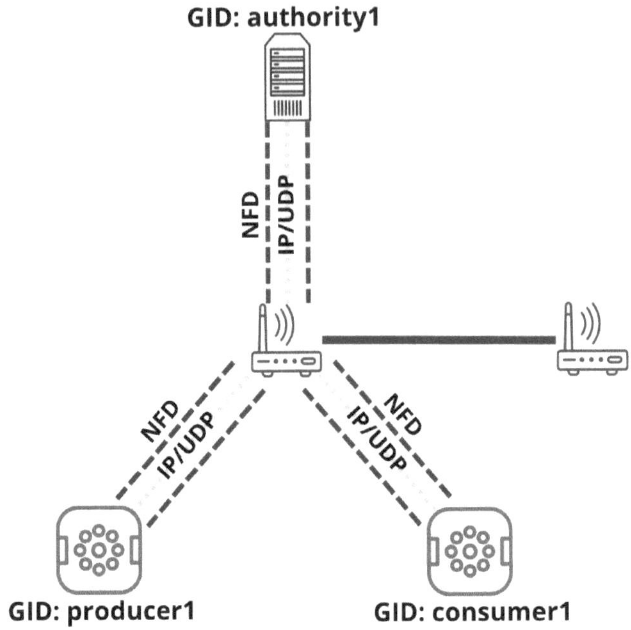

Fig. 4. Single-domain of the evaluation network

Table 4. Data consumption latency using ciphertexts with different numbers of attributes

Number of Attributes in Ciphertext	Latency (ms)
2	147.06
4	267.06
6	388.88
8	511.34
10	632.74

and communication between entities was established over a Wi-Fi network. The cryptographic operations used the *SignatureSha256withECDSA* scheme, which affects packet sizes.

To measure the delay caused by ABAC-NDN on NDN application, we recorded the *data consumption latency*, which is the time from the initial request until the first data packet is decrypted and ready to use. Several measurements were performed using different number of attributes in the ciphertext containing the key material. The results are shown in Table 4.

The results shown in Table 5 include the average packet size of different message types.

Table 5. Packet sizes of different message types

Message	Packet Size (in Bytes)
Global Parameter	132
Public Key	574
Update	107
Key Material (Per attribute)	567

5 Conclusion

In this paper, we presented ABAC-NDN, the first open-source attribute-based encryption library designed to provide fine-grained and decentralized confidentiality for NDN applications. ABAC-NDN aims to bridge the gap between theoretical access control designs and practical solutions for content-centric networking.

We detailed the design and architecture of the proposed library and showed how its modular structure facilitates integration with existing NDN applications, while remaining flexible enough to support extensions. ABAC-NDN enables researchers and developers to experiment with confidentiality mechanisms and to incorporate attribute-based access control into NDN deployments.

Experimental evaluation on a heterogeneous platforms and NDN testbed demonstrated the feasibility and efficiency of the proposed design. As future work, we plan to integrate the security library into NDN simulators.

Acknowledgments. This work was supported by the Franco-German University. The authors would like to thank Nicolas Hawighorst and Thomas Manche for their valuable assistance with the implementation.

Disclosure of Interests. The authors declare that they have no competing interests.

References

1. Crypto++ library 8.9. https://www.cryptopp.com/
2. The gnu mp bignum library. https://gmplib.org/
3. named-data/ndn-cxx: Ndn c++ library (2025). https://github.com/named-data/ndn-cxx
4. named-data/nfd: Named data networking forwarding daemon (2025). https://github.com/named-data/NFD
5. Bilal, M., Pack, S.: Secure distribution of protected content in information-centric networking. IEEE Syst. J. (2019)
6. Carofiglio, G., Muscariello, L., Augé, J., Papalini, M., Sardara, M., Compagno, A.: Enabling icn in the internet protocol: analysis and evaluation of the hybrid-icn architecture. In: Proceedings of the 6th ACM Conference on Information-centric Networking (2019)
7. Junxiao Shi: Ndnts: Ndn libraries for the modern web (2025). https://github.com/yoursunny/NDNts

8. Lewko, A., Waters, B.: Decentralizing attribute-based encryption. In: Paterson, K.G. (ed.) EUROCRYPT 2011. LNCS, vol. 6632, pp. 568–588. Springer, Heidelberg (2011). https://doi.org/10.1007/978-3-642-20465-4_31
9. Lynn, B.: Pbc library. https://crypto.stanford.edu/pbc/
10. Mecerhed, F.: Abac-ndn library. https://github.com/MECERHED-Ferhat/ABAC-NDN
11. Mecerhed, F., Imine, Y., Gallais, A., Fischer, S., Hail, M.A.: An efficient decentralized fine-grained access control for iot ecosystems over ndn. In: 2024 International Conference on Software, Telecommunications and Computer Networks (SoftCOM), pp. 1–6. IEEE (2024)
12. Nichols, K.: Trust schemas and icn: key to secure home iot. In: Proceedings of the 8th ACM Conference on Information-Centric Networking (2021)
13. Shang, W., Afanasyev, A., Zhang, L.: The design and implementation of the ndn protocol stack for riot-os. In: 2016 IEEE Globecom Workshops (GC Wkshps)
14. Shang, W., Thompson, J., Cherkaoui, M., Burkey, J., Zhang, L.: Ndn. js: A javascript client library for named data networking. In: 2013 IEEE Conference on Computer Communications Workshops (INFOCOM WKSHPS)
15. Thompson, J., Burke, J.: Ndn common client libraries. Technical Report NDN-0024, Revision 1. NDN Project (2014)
16. Yu, T., Ma, X., Xie, H., Kocaoğullar, Y., Zhang, L.: A new api in support of ndn trust schema. In: Proceedings of the 10th ACM Conference on Information-Centric Networking (2023)
17. Yu, Y., Afanasyev, A., Zhang, L.: Name-based access control. Named Data Networking Project, Technical Report NDN-0034 (2015)
18. Zhang, L., et al.: Named data networking. ACM SIGCOMM Comput. Commun. Rev. (2014)
19. Zhang, Z., Yu, Y., Afanasyev, A., Zhang, L.: Ndn certificate management protocol (ndncert). NDN, Technical Report NDN-0050 (2017)

Bridging Digitalization Gaps: OCR and NER for Crime Report Automation in the Italian Criminal Justice System

Samuele Yves Cerini[1,2], Nicola Deidda[1,3](✉), Sara Lilli[1,4], Maria Vittoria Zucca[1,4], Giorgio Fumera[3], Giorgio Giacinto[2,3], and Paolo Prinetto[2]

[1] Scuola IMT Alti Studi Lucca, Piazza S. Ponziano 6, 55100 Lucca, LU, Italy
{samuele.cerini,sara.lilli,mariavittoria.zucca}@imtlucca.it
[2] CINI Cybersecurity National Lab, Via Ariosto 25, 00185 Rome, RM, Italy
{samuele.cerini,nicola.deidda,giorgio.giacinto,
paolo.prinetto}@cybersecnatlab.it
[3] Università di Cagliari, Via Università 40, 09124 Cagliari, CA, Italy
{nicola.deidda,fumera,giorgio.giacinto}@unica.it
[4] Scuola Superiore Sant'Anna, Piazza Martiri della Libertà 33, 56127 Pisa, PI, Italy
{sara.lilli,maria.zucca}@santannapisa.it

Abstract. In the Italian judiciary system, Public Prosecutors' Offices still rely on heterogeneous and partially paper-based document workflows, where crime reports and related attachments are often printed, manually signed and annotated, scanned, and finally stored as image-based files. As a consequence, a significant portion of prosecutorial documentation remains only partially machine-readable, limiting the effectiveness of digital case-management systems. In this context, Optical Character Recognition (OCR) and Named Entity Recognition (NER) are enabling technologies that transform unstructured, non-searchable judicial documents into computationally usable legal information. This paper analyzes the technical, organizational, and legal challenges associated with OCR-based processing of crime reports, in the Italian and foreign jurisdictions, and identifies the main methodological requirements for governance-aware NER models used in judicial environments. These include layout-aware document analysis, legal-domain adaptation, human-in-the-loop validation, and privacy-aware processing mechanisms that support pseudonymization and controlled access to sensitive data. Finally, the paper discusses the broader topic of computer-aided judicial digitalization, highlighting the need for reliable, privacy-aware pipelines capable of processing documents at scale in contemporary criminal justice systems.

Keywords: Optical Character Recognition · Named Entity Recognition · Justice System · Privacy-Preserving Data Processing · Crime Reports Classification

S. Y. Cerini, N. Deidda, S. Lilli and M. V. Zucca–These authors contributed equally.

Z. Afzal et al. (Eds.): ARES 2026 Workshops, LNCS 16900, pp. 541–558, 2027.
https://doi.org/10.1007/978-3-032-35576-8_29

1 Introduction

Within the Italian criminal justice system, Public Prosecutors' Offices operate as the entry point of criminal proceedings. They receive *notitiae criminum*, hereafter referred to as crime reports, namely reports of alleged criminal conduct, and oversee the initial organization of investigative activities before any formal prosecution is initiated. This intake phase is operationally critical: each report must be registered, interpreted, assigned to the competent prosecutorial unit, and associated with one or more plausible legal qualifications under the Italian Criminal Code.

Historically, the Italian criminal process has relied on sequential, paper-based document flows centered on the progressive accumulation of a case file. Although this model provides a material form of traceability, it has progressively revealed scalability limits amid growing caseloads, heterogeneous documentation, and increasingly complex investigations. In recent years, the justice sector has therefore undergone a significant digital transformation [12]. This digitalization process has been driven largely by the enforcement of ministerial platforms aimed at ensuring a national, unified management of investigative files.

However, a significant impact of this transition has yet to be observed at the local level, particularly within judicial police units (e.g., Carabinieri, State Police) and the internal structure of Public Prosecutors' Offices. Prior work [1] has shown that Public Prosecutors' Offices continue to face structural and operational challenges, including high document volumes, uneven data quality, heterogeneous formats, and limited automation in preparatory tasks. These issues are particularly evident in the registration and classification of crime reports, which remain largely manual activities requiring substantial interpretative effort by prosecutorial personnel. As a result, the initial processing of criminal reports may become a bottleneck, affecting both timeliness and the quality of downstream information.

The scale of these challenges becomes evident when considering large prosecutorial offices. One of the largest Public Prosecutor's Offices in Italy, according to Ministerial classification and publicly available institutional data, manages an average daily workload of approximately 540 crime reports, totaling more than 200,000 per year. Of these, approximately 150,000 concern proceedings against unknown offenders, while around 50,000 involve identified suspects [22]. In such circumstances, computer-aided automation can efficiently and reliably manage reports while enabling advanced processes, such as automatically correlating crime reports to highlight criminal patterns. The timely classification and assignment of reports to the appropriate prosecutorial group are therefore fundamental operational objectives. However, the challenges previously outlined – particularly those related to non-standardized document formats, unstructured files, and heterogeneous inputs – mandate the need for preprocessing systems primarily based on Optical Character Recognition (OCR) and Named Entity Recognition (NER) models.

The remainder of the paper is organized as follows. Section 2 provides an overview of document management in Law Enforcement Agencies (LEAs) and

Public Prosecutors' Offices in Italy and foreign jurisdictions, highlighting the operational and technical issues that future Artificial Intelligence (AI)-assisted and computer-aided document management systems must overcome. Section 3 summarizes the latest advancements in OCR and NER models, reviewing the methodological requirements and approaches for the analysis of Italian prosecutorial documents. In Sect. 4, we evaluate 3 different families of OCR models on a set of 10 synthetic criminal reports emulating real-world examples. Section 5 discusses security, privacy, and accountability implications, together with the limitations of the proposed analysis. Finally, Sect. 6 concludes the paper and outlines future research directions.

2 Operational Context and Challenges

This section delineates the operational, technical, and legal landscape that constitutes the current electronic processing of criminal complaints by Italian public prosecutors' offices. In doing so, this section aims to highlight recurring issues encountered. Firstly, we describe current document management practices in the context of prosecutorial intake workflows, with a focus on the hybrid paper-digital procedures and the heterogeneity they entail. Secondly, we examine the data-protection implications of computer-aided judicial processing. Finally, we will compare the state of digitalization across different foreign jurisdictions.

Although crime reports are now created and transmitted digitally by LEAs and Public Prosecutors' Offices, their full digital processing is still hindered by reliance on manual internal procedures. Recent exchanges with the Turin Public Prosecutor's Office have led to the identification of three main sources of friction for a proper and effective management of case files:

1. *Document organization and format.* It has been observed that the majority of submitted documents lack a coherent organizational structure. Indeed, within a single complaint, one may find – in no particular order – documents such as police reports, medical certificates, identification forms, photographs, attachments, and other supporting legal materials. In addition, the natural heterogeneity of the judicial offices scattered throughout the jurisdiction of the Public Prosecutor's Office results not only in the aforementioned lack of document standards but also in significant variation in the procedures for creating, managing, and transmitting the documents produced. It is therefore not uncommon for documents obtained by the Public Prosecutor's Offices to appear as PDFs of previously scanned documents. Such formats are therefore devoid of selectable, searchable text and may contain printing errors, handwritten notes, signatures, and stamps. It is evident that the current document management processes pose a significant threat to the integrity of any original machine-readable layer.
2. *Linguistic heterogeneity.* Criminal reports often combine formal legal language, administrative terminology, and narrative descriptions of facts. They may also reproduce statements by complainants, witnesses, or law enforcement officers, leading to colloquialisms, dialectal variants, typographical

errors, and inconsistent references to persons, places, dates, vehicles, or objects. This variability complicates the identification and extraction of legally relevant factual elements and their linking among different procedural cases.
3. *Content and data protection.* Crime reports contain personal and sensitive information in clear text, including names, addresses, telephone numbers, dates of birth, license plates, and other identifiers. Any possible introduction of AI-assisted tools for automated document management must therefore account for confidentiality, access control, minimization of exposed information, and pseudonymization mechanisms compatible with the investigative utility of the documents.

2.1 Document Management in Italian Public Prosecutors' Offices

As previously stated, the reliance on manual procedures by criminal investigation units and prosecutors' offices for the internal management and recording of crime reports significantly undermines the overall effectiveness of subsequent information processing based on the data they yield. Indeed, each of these manual steps introduces an incremental discrepancy between the digital and paper versions, which accumulates through successive modifications.

Despite the theoretical resolution of this discrepancy through a final process requiring the scanning of the paper copy and its reconversion to digital form, errors and semantic uncertainties inevitably accumulate due to the inherent limitations of such print-scan cycles, such as: i) *Print quality*, including variable ink density, smudges, misaligned text, low contrast, and degraded characters; ii) *Storage, transmission and intermediary manipulation* of the paper copy, which induces the presence of accidental stains, signatures and stamps, obscuring the original text, staff annotations and underlining, and the presence of creases and distortions; iii) *Scan quality*, including image resolution, compression artifacts, skewed pages, incomplete scans, and the presence or absence of prior OCR processing.

These issues are not merely technical. In a judicial setting, document format errors may alter names, dates, locations, factual descriptions, or references to legally relevant circumstances. Such errors can propagate to downstream information extraction and legal-classification components. In addition to the risk that they may contain printing defects, current crime reports also lack standardization in the order of embedded documents, their formats, and the total number of pages. Variations can be observed in the templates used and in the file names assigned to each document across different LEA offices. Among the pages that can compose a single complete *notitia criminis* PDF file, one can find, in no fixed order:

1. A **Preliminary Note**, consisting of a single-page landscape-oriented table that summarises the core metadata associated with the report. It may include the date and time of receipt, the date and time of the alleged facts, the reporting LEA office, a preliminary indication of the most plausible offense and

corresponding Criminal Code article, the place of the facts, and identifying information about the complainant.
2. A **Note from the LEA Offices**, usually a multi-page document describing the facts as reconstructed by the officer(s) responsible for the formalization of the complaint. This document often contains the most relevant factual narrative for crime report classification, together with Personal Identifiable Information (PII) concerning the reporting officer, complainant, victim, and possibly the suspect.

Optionally, it may contain (*a*) a **Report or Complaint Regarding a Suspected Crime**, which reports the facts from the perspective of the complainant or other persons involved. There, the presence of PII data is highly expected; (*b*) a **Photographic Identification Report**, containing information on the identification of possible suspects from photographic material; (*c*) a **Medical Report**, documenting medical treatment, diagnosis, or prognosis following the reported event. Such documents contain highly sensitive information; (*d*) a **Request for CCTV Recording**, summarising requests made by LEA officers to obtain videos or images captured near the place of the alleged facts; and (*e*) **Additional Notes**, under varying titles, describing further actions performed by LEA officers or additional procedural information.

From an operational perspective, the current document heterogeneity complicates the transition from document acquisition to case registration. Prosecutorial personnel must identify the legally relevant parts of each file, extract essential metadata, and assign the report to the appropriate internal workflow. Poorly implemented automation can either fail to support this process or introduce errors that require additional human correction, directly affecting workload, timeliness, and the quality of downstream information.

2.2 Processing of Judicial Data

A crime report is a central document in the investigative process as it serves as the foundational piece for the eventual exercise of criminal prosecution. These reports contain a wide array of personal and sensitive data. Indeed, according to the Law Enforcement Directive (LED) (Directive 2016/680), such data includes not only direct identifiers like names and contact details, but also special categories of data as defined by art. 9 of the GDPR, such as information regarding health, criminal convictions, and other aspects of personal life that can reveal highly sensitive characteristics. In accordance with both the GDPR and the LED, all such data must be processed in a way that minimizes the risk of identification. In this regard, the authors have classified judicial data into three categories:

1. **Identifying Data**: refers to data that can directly identify individuals, such as names, dates of birth, and address details. These data points should be replaced with generic pseudonyms (e.g., `COMPLAINANT_1`, `SUSPECT_2`, `VICTIM_3`) to prevent the disclosure of sensitive information. When age is

relevant, it should be grouped into broader categories (e.g., minors under 14 years, adults aged 18–35, etc.) rather than specific ages. Identifying documents (such as ID cards, passports, and health cards) should be replaced by generic identifiers (e.g., `DOC_1`, `DOC_2`) to further minimize exposure.

2. **Sensitive Data**: includes information that, when combined, can identify an individual, such as data related to an individual's health, disability status, or psychiatric conditions. This information must be pseudonymised using non-specific identifiers (e.g., `HEALTH_CONDITION_1`, `DISABILITY_2`, `PSYCHIATRIC_CONDITION_1`). Additionally, professional information should be generalized (e.g., "employee" instead of specifying the company name), and legal proceedings, including precautionary measures or ongoing investigations, should be reported without disclosing personal data (e.g., "precautionary measure in progress", "archiving completed", "conviction").
3. **Technical-Evidentiary Data**: includes items such as phone numbers, social media profiles, IP addresses, and vehicle registration plates, all of which should be replaced with generic codes (e.g., `PHONE_1`, `ONLINE_ACCOUNT_1`, `VEHICLE_1`). Similarly, multimedia files—such as photographs, videos, and medical or technical reports-should either be completely removed if identifiable or pseudonymized using generic identifiers (e.g., `ATTACHMENT_1`, `MEDICAL_REPORT_2`).

Pseudonymization must be calibrated carefully. Legal qualification may depend on the age of a victim, the relationship between parties, the existence of medical consequences, the use of a vehicle, threats, violence, or the value of stolen goods. The goal is therefore not to remove all factual specificity, but to preserve semantic roles and relations while masking unnecessary identifiers.

2.3 The Critical Role of Accurate OCR in Judicial Data Processing

The intake of crime reports in Public Prosecutors' Offices is a document-intensive process in which legal, organizational, and technical dimensions are closely intertwined. Before any downstream analytical or decision-support system can operate, incoming material must be transformed into a reliable representation of the reported facts, the involved subjects, the procedural context, and the plausible legal qualifications.

In this context, OCR acts as the enabling factor for computational judicial data processing. It acts as a key component that dictates whether the contents of a crime report can be searched, indexed, classified, and processed by downstream AI components. The deployment of such systems is only possible if the scans received at a Public Prosecutor's Office are transformed into a structured, machine-readable format, removing the artifacts introduced by print-scan processes without affecting the semantic meaning of the main content. A minor OCR error in a non-relevant word may have little impact. By contrast, an error in a suspect's name, the date of a criminal event, or the description of the alleged conduct will inevitably affect subsequent classification and prioritization. For instance, an error in a date may affect the reconstruction of urgency or limitation periods, while an error in a personal identifier may compromise entity linking across documents.

Following the content's reconversion into a structured format, the focus must shift to extracting legally significant information. This process, which involves identifying facts, persons, places, dates, objects, and relevant circumstances, is an essential component of prosecutorial intake. Such an interpretation of a crime report must uncover a legally meaningful narrative: who did what, where, when, against whom, by which means, and the potential legal consequences. From a personal identifiable data perspective, the use of OCR models changes the risk profile of crime reports and their attachments. Once converted into searchable text, information that was previously difficult to retrieve at scale becomes easier to index, aggregate and reuse. The outputs obtained as byproducts of OCR processing should therefore be treated as a new sensitive data layer rather than mere digitization results.

2.4 Cross-Jurisdictional Relevance of OCR-Based Judicial Intake

Although this work focuses on the operational context of Italian Public Prosecutors' Offices, the underlying challenges are not unique to the Italian judicial system. Across Europe, several criminal-justice systems have progressively introduced digital prosecutorial and judicial case-management systems to improve intake efficiency and reduce procedural fragmentation. In the United Kingdom, the HM Courts and Tribunals Service (HMCTS) reform program introduced the *Common Platform*, a unified digital system shared among courts, prosecutors, police forces, and criminal justice agencies. Official HMCTS documentation nonetheless acknowledges ongoing operational challenges related to legacy systems, the coexistence of paper and digital workflows, and the management of procedural documentation. In Germany, the progressive adoption of the *Elektronische Akte* (electronic legal file) similarly reflects the transition from paper-based prosecutorial and judicial records toward digital criminal-case management systems, while highlighting interoperability and document-standardization issues. Outside the European Union, similar operational pressures emerge in large-scale judicial systems. In India, the *e-Courts Mission Mode Project* explicitly integrates OCR technologies to convert scanned judicial records into searchable, machine-readable text, while academic research highlights persistent challenges with unstructured legal documents, inconsistent formatting, and noisy textual extraction in judicial proceedings [15]. Similarly, in Brazil, the *Justiça 4.0* program promoted the digitalization of judicial proceedings and the adoption of AI-assisted systems for document management and procedural organization, with official documentation identifying OCR-based processing and automated handling of judicial records as central components of prosecutorial and judicial modernization strategies. Overall, these experiences demonstrate that the operational problems addressed by the proposed article represent a broadly shared institutional challenge rather than a jurisdiction-specific issue. Across jurisdictions, digitalization increasingly requires systems that support prosecutors and personnel in the processing, classification, and routing of judicial documentation while preserving accountability and human oversight.

3 Requirements Definition and State of the Art

In this section, we list the necessary requirements that can address the needs and challenges outlined in Sect. 2. From these requirements, a set of functional and non-functional criteria can be derived to identify suitable models that meet our needs. Contextually, the topics of Optical Character Recognition (OCR) and Named Entity Recognition (NER) are introduced.

3.1 Requirements Definition and State of the Art of OCR Models

As highlighted above, a key requirement for preprocessing prosecutorial documents is the ability to handle highly heterogeneous inputs. Traditional OCR systems typically recognize characters or words after segmenting pages into text lines. This is often insufficient for crime reports, which combine zones with distinct legal or administrative functions, including stamps, signatures, handwritten annotations, headers, footers, and tabular forms. Narrative content may also span multiple documents while being interleaved with administrative metadata, making context-aware processing essential. Treating these elements independently or in small chunks may therefore introduce recognition errors that semantic and layout-aware methods could mitigate.

Tabular data poses further challenges, especially when tables use orientations that differ from the rest of the document. These tables often contain legally relevant metadata, such as personal identifiers, dates, locations, references to attachments, and LEA-related information. If their structure is not preserved, extracted values may become detached from their labels, reducing both machine and human interpretability.

OCR systems have evolved from early pattern-matching methods to deep-learning and transformer-based architectures that integrate visual, textual, and structural information [6,14]. CNN- and RNN-based pipelines improved robustness to noise, distortions, and heterogeneous layouts [32]. Tesseract, developed by Hewlett-Packard and released as open source in 2005 [24,25], marked a major step in the diffusion of OCR technologies. More recently, transformer-based models introduced contextual semantic processing [4,10,31], overcoming several limitations of character-level segmentation and improving recognition quality in noisy or structurally complex documents. Recent multimodal OCR architectures, including GOT-OCR 2.0 [33], DeepSeekOCR [34], GLM-OCR [3], LightOnOCR [28], and TextMonkey [11], further extend these capabilities by jointly modeling layout, visual structure, and textual semantics. This makes them particularly suitable for heterogeneous judicial documents affected by degraded scans, printing defects, handwritten annotations, stamps, and mixed layouts.

As reported in Sect. 4, such state-of-the-art OCR models are crucial in our case study, given the substandard print and scan quality of the crime reports routinely received by Italian Public Prosecutors' Offices.

3.2 Requirements Definition and State of the Art of NER Models

NER models provide a crucial bridge between OCR and downstream semantic analysis. By extracting key data from crime reports, they support metadata extraction, document classification, information retrieval, and the organization of judicial materials across the investigative lifecycle, from preliminary investigations to hearings and trials.

Over the past decades, NER has evolved from rule-based and dictionary-driven methods to statistical and transformer-based architectures capable of contextual semantic understanding. Early systems relied on handcrafted rules and pattern matching, often achieving high precision in constrained settings but struggling with linguistic variability. Recurrent architectures such as LSTMs improved the modeling of long-range dependencies [29]. Transformer models such as BERT then introduced self-attention mechanisms that capture contextual relationships between words regardless of distance [2,9,30], establishing the "pre-train and fine-tune" paradigm that now dominates NER research [8].

In our use case, document classification critically depends on the quality of both OCR and NER. Crime reports must be routed to appropriate offense categories and competent working groups based on lexical and semantic cues in the extracted text. Errors in offense-related terminology, personal relationships, locations, or factual descriptions may substantially affect classification outcomes. For example, reports concerning fraud, theft, threats, domestic violence, stalking, bodily harm, and cybercrime may share overlapping terminology while requiring different organizational handling.

The selected NER model must therefore be fine-tuned for Italian legal-domain language, including legal and administrative terminology, procedural abbreviations, and article citations. It must also recognize common personal and administrative identifiers appearing in factual descriptions, such as names, addresses, dates, license plates, tax identification numbers, phone numbers, and other identifiers. Procedural abbreviations and legal citations are especially critical. Expressions such as *c.p.*, *c.p.p.*, *P.M.*, *P.G.*, *G.I.P.*, *G.U.P.*, and *R.G.N.R.*, as well as provisions such as *art. 640 c.p.* and *art. 612-bis c.p.*, are highly sensitive to punctuation, capitalization, and domain conventions. Minor character-level errors may significantly affect legal classification and information retrieval. BERT-based models introduce an additional constraint, as their limited input windows require long documents to be split into chunks [2]. Chunking should therefore use overlapping windows to avoid fragmenting abbreviations or citations across boundaries [23].

From a robustness perspective, over-reliance on NER may propagate uncertainty to downstream classification. In high-volume environments, manually verifying every page is impractical, yet blindly trusting automatically recognized text is inappropriate when errors may affect legal classification, case assignment, or confidentiality. An ideal NER model should provide confidence scores for extracted entities and rank plausible alternatives. This enables selective human validation, reintroducing human oversight at the points where errors are most likely or consequential.

A robust extraction pipeline should also include post-correction methods that detect inconsistencies in structured identifiers by checking expected formats and flagging problematic entries for review. Dates, license plates, telephone numbers, and tax codes typically follow recognizable patterns; for instance, a tax code with invalid length can be flagged rather than passed unchecked to downstream components. In legal domains, however, post-correction must remain conservative, since overly aggressive correction may replace uncommon but valid names, locations, or factual expressions with more frequent terms, thereby distorting the original content.

Finally, privacy-aware OCR and NER processing is essential for crime reports. Transforming images into searchable text increases information availability, but also raises the risk of unauthorized exposure during and after processing. A proper pipeline must therefore protect original documents, extracted text, and all intermediate or derived artifacts. First, given the sensitivity of prosecutorial data, OCR and NER models should be deployed locally within controlled infrastructures subject to institutional oversight. Where external services are unavoidable, strict contractual, technical, and organizational safeguards are required, particularly concerning data location, subcontracting, encryption, logging, and deletion. Second, data minimization should guide the pipeline: no more information than necessary should be retained, and intermediate artifacts should be disposable by default, reducing unnecessary data accumulation and limiting exposure in the event of future data breaches.

4 Contribution and Model Evaluation

In this section, the capabilities of the latest OCR and NER models are analyzed, and their suitability for our use cases is evaluated.

The qualitative tests conducted involved creating 10 distinct synthetic documents to replicate real crime reports with a high degree of fidelity. Beyond the narrative content, the documents incorporated fabricated personal identifiers, temporal references, and chronological data. The final content was then validated by qualified legal experts to ensure a high degree of similarity to real documents. Following digital composition, the documents were output via laser printers with deliberately variable toner quality. Subsequently, signatures, stamps, and handwritten annotations were applied to replicate as closely as possible the distinctive features of authentic files. The process concluded with a multi-stage scanning and reprinting cycle: documents were initially scanned at varying quality parameters and resolutions, then reprinted and rescanned, thereby introducing cumulative degradation.

The aforementioned steps enabled the simulation of the following document lifecycle:

1. The digital creation of the crime report in judicial police offices;
2. The use of stamps and signatures by the head of the judicial police office;
3. The digitization of the document and its upload to the institutional crime report web portal;
4. The printing process and the application of additional stamps, signatures, and handwritten notes, simulating an initial manual classification performed by staff of the public prosecutor's office;
5. A final scan and the uploading of the digital file to the institutional database of reports.

4.1 Testing Procedure and Model Evaluation

During our evaluation, additional tests were conducted in order to assess the computational requirements and the quality provided by the latest OCR models in the presence of possible computational constraints.

An initial evaluation was conducted on a single synthesized two-page crime report, prepared according to the methodology detailed in Sect. 4. The first page represents the tabular form of the "*Annotazione Preliminare*" (preliminary annotation), reported in Fig. 1, whereas the second page includes the summary description of the criminal event, along with fictitious PII data, stamps, and handwritten annotations.

Three different OCR models were tested: DeepSeekOCR [34], GLM-OCR [3] and LightOnOCR [28]. The choice of these models was primarily made to ensure high-quality results even on laptop-grade hardware, resorting to CPU-only computations, with the aim of establishing a lower bound for computational processes while ensuring satisfactory results for future Proof of Concept development and relevant on-field experimentation. Both GLM-OCR and LightOnOCR models were tested in three different quantizations: `F16` [16,19], `Q8_0` [20,27], and `Q4_K_M` [17,26]. All the models tested have been downloaded as GGUF files from the HuggingFace portal [7] and deployed using `llama.cpp` [5], version `b9071-cpu`. This first evaluation used the `hyperfine` benchmarking script [21], which included three warmup runs followed by ten repetitions of the same test (applied to the aforementioned two-page synthetic document). At the end of the testing procedure, the average computing time was collected, so as the standard deviation. All the tests have been conducted on a Dell XPS 9340 laptop, equipped with a Intel Core Ultra 7 155H processor and 32GB RAM, running Fedora Silverblue 44 in performance mode, on the `7.0.8-200.fc44` Linux kernel. The results of these tests are summarized in Table 1.

Finally, a second and final series of evaluations was performed using the same models, quantization settings, and computing conditions across all 10 synthetic crime reports, for a total of 30 pages. The analysis focused exclusively on the summary description section of each report, as this component represents the most informative source for subsequent automated classification tasks. This evaluation aimed to measure the Character Error Rate (CER) and Word Error Rate (WER) for each model variant. Combined with the processing time metrics from the previous evaluation, these measurements enabled a comprehensive assessment of the quality-to-performance trade-off, facilitating the identification of the local OCR model that achieved optimal accuracy relative to computational efficiency. The results obtained are reported in Table 2.

4.2 Results Discussion

The use of state-of-the-art OCR models has proven crucial for our case study: the presence of printing defects, inconsistencies, and structural heterogeneity, as mentioned in Sect. 2, inevitably poses a significant challenge to accurate text recognition. In accordance with prevailing expectations, preliminary tests demonstrated the ineffectiveness and substandard quality obtained by conventional OCR models, particularly those requiring minimal computational resources, such as Tesseract. The analysis revealed substantial limitations in transcription quality in all cases examined. The majority of transcription errors occurred within the descriptive summary section: the most critical part of the entire crime report, especially given its role in the context of a future automated crime report classification pipeline. The models demonstrated considerable sensitivity to printing artifacts and to inadequate contrast in certain scans. The presence of manual annotations and superimposed stamps on the original text has further compounded these challenges, resulting in the complete omission of specific text segments. Additional errors and even the complete absence of relevant data were observed in the identification of tabular forms, which typically compose the opening page of each crime report (see Fig. 1).

As subsequent testing demonstrated, most of these issues can be progressively addressed by leveraging more recent models such as DeepSeekOCR [34], GLM-OCR [3], and LightOnOCR [28]. The majority of these models, based on the latest end-to-end architectures, exhibited adequate robustness and flexibility in the presence of printing defects and stamps, and were capable of producing satisfactory outputs despite numerous inconsistencies in the input images.

With the GLM-OCR and LightOnOCR models, tabular data is correctly parsed and translated from a raw image to a Markdown/HTML tabular structure (an example of the resulting output is shown in Fig. 2). The text reported on stamps is, for the most part, correctly recognized, as are any possible handwritten characters (although spelling errors are present with a token-level granularity). DeepSeekOCR, despite being the fastest model tested, struggled to recognize the entire document in a single pass, producing garbage transcriptions that coincided with the portrait-mode tabular data. Such behavior suggests the need to implement a two-step procedure specific to this model: the first step would aim to convert the descriptive summary of the events, while the second would convert the portrait-oriented table into a final, independent pass.

Regarding the first quantitative evaluation described in the previous Section, Table 1 presents the execution times for each model variant. The results demonstrate that `deepSeek-ocr-Q8_0` achieves the fastest performance with a mean execution time of 41.27 s, while `noctrex-lightonocr-F16` exhibits the slowest performance at 177.13 s. As illustrated in Table 2, quantized variants within

Table 1. Execution times for each model tested. In the table, we detail the average time, the standard deviation, and the average time per page in seconds. For each model, we detail the quantization. In green (red), we highlight the fastest (slowest) models and the lowest (highest) standard deviations.

OCR Model	**Quantization**	**Execution Time**		
		Avg (s)	Std. Dev. (s)	Avg (s/page)
DeepSeekOCR [18]	Q8_0	41.27	6.85	20.66
GLM-OCR [19]	F16	104.42	12.28	52.21
GLM-OCR [20]	Q8_0	92.65	11.80	46.32
GLM-OCR [17]	Q4_K_M	87.11	10.75	43.56
LightOnOCR [16]	F16	177.13	[illegible]	88.56
LightOnOCR [27]	Q8_0	156.68	3.48	78.34
LightOnOCR [26]	Q4_K_M	148.36	4.43	74.19

the same model family (LightOnOCR and GLM-OCR) display highly consistent Word Error Rate (WER) and Character Error Rate (CER) metrics, with transcription quality improving proportionally to the bit-width encoding model weights, as expected. The combined analysis reveals a clear inverse relationship: the fastest model (DeepSeekOCR) produces substantially higher error rates at both character and word levels, whereas LightOnOCR, despite delivering superior transcription accuracy, incurs substantially greater computational overhead. Synthesizing these empirical results, the GLM-OCR model with Q8_0 quantization demonstrates an optimal balance among computational efficiency, execution time, and output quality – particularly noteworthy given that evaluations were conducted on a CPU-only laptop-grade processor. Nevertheless, it is important to acknowledge that future implementations may leverage more sophisticated computing infrastructure and employ increased model complexity, thereby potentially achieving further improvements in transcription accuracy.

In the final stage of our evaluation process, NER models were employed to extract personal and identifying information, dates and times, and legal provisions mentioned in the complaint reports. The `Italian_NER_XXL_v2` [13] model was selected on the basis of it being considered to be one of the most advanced open-source models currently available for the Italian language, capable of recognizing legal entities such as laws, court rulings, attorneys, and courts[1]. The model successfully met the required criteria; however, due to its reliance on BERT, which imposes a maximum window size of 512 tokens, an iterative search and qualitative manual evaluation were necessary to determine the optimal chunking policy for the input documents. At the end of our tests, a window size of 200 tokens and an overlap window of 10 tokens, together with a simple split pol-

[1] For a detailed enumeration of recognized entities, refer to the model's HuggingFace repository.

Table 2. Average CER and WER metrics computed for each model and quantization variant. In green (red) color we highlight the most (least) accurate models.

OCR Model	Quantization	Avg CER (%)	Avg WER (%)
DeepSeekOCR [18]	Q8_0	6.50	12.01
GLM-OCR [19]	F16	2.85	3.48
GLM-OCR [20]	Q8_0	2.98	3.97
GLM-OCR [17]	Q4_K_M	3.42	5.70
LightOnOCR [16]	F16	2.27	[illegible]
LightOnOCR [27]	Q8_0	[illegible]	2.97
LightOnOCR [26]	Q4_K_M	2.27	3.03

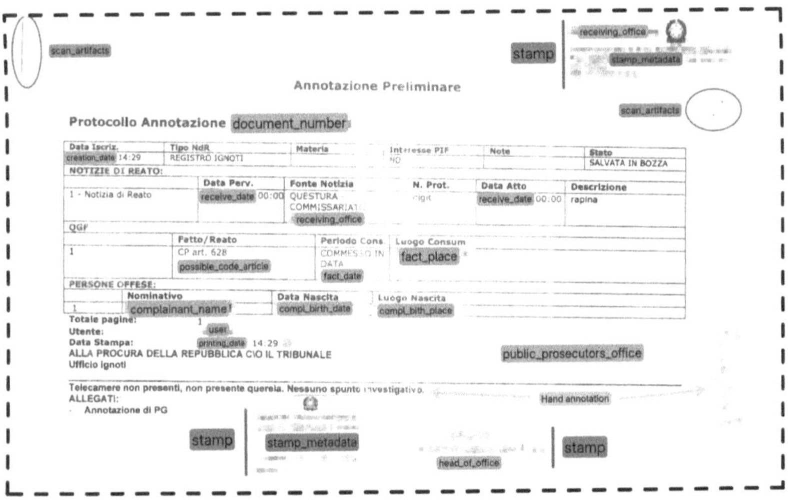

Fig. 1. Fac-Simile of a "Preliminary Note" (see Sect. 2.1). This type of document, scanned and bundled as the first page of a complete crime report file, is presented in landscape mode for readability purposes. Printing and scanning artifacts, along with multiple stamps, signatures, and handwritten notes, often appear.

icy base on newlines and common end-sentence characters (such as '.', '!', '?') proved to be the most effective, allowing to retrieve nearly all entities with a confidence score threshold set to 70%.

5 Discussion

The analysis conducted in this paper shows that OCR should not be treated as a neutral digitization utility, but as a foundational component of prosecutorial intake workflows, with implications across three main dimensions.

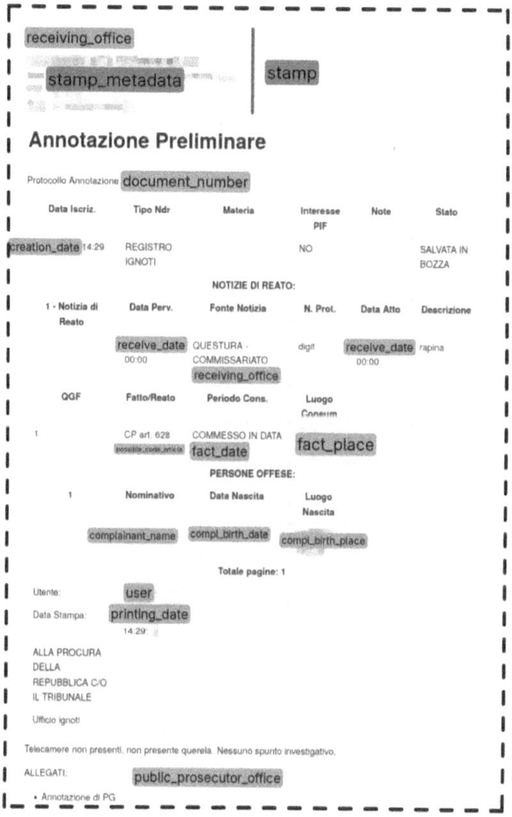

Fig. 2. Rendering of the HTML file obtained as OCR output of the "Preliminary Note" reported in Fig. 1 (obtained using the `staghado/LightOnOCR-2-1B-Q8_0-GGUF:Q8_0` model). All critical entities are recognized correctly, with no spelling errors. All the stamps were clearly identified (only one is visible in this figure). Printing and scanning artifacts, as well as hand annotations, do not affect the final quality.

First, OCR is a critical dependency for downstream AI-based processes, since document classification, legal qualification, and named entity recognition require an accurate and reliable textual layer. Errors affecting offense descriptions, legal references, personal names, addresses, or license plates may propagate through the pipeline, increasing the risk that language models produce plausible but incorrect reconstructions. Accordingly, OCR systems should be evaluated within the broader end-to-end architecture, with explicit error-containment strategies and mandatory human verification for legally material information.

Second, OCR pipeline design has direct security and data-protection implications. Intermediate artifacts, including scanned page images and temporary textual representations, often contain highly sensitive information and therefore require safeguards grounded in data minimization, purpose-limited retention, and access control. Privacy-preserving OCR must also balance two competing objectives: ensuring sufficiently high recall in identifying sensitive entities to prevent confidentiality breaches, while avoiding excessive redaction that could undermine the evidentiary and investigative value of prosecutorial records.

Third, important limitations remain unresolved. In particular, publicly available benchmark datasets for Italian prosecutorial documentation are lacking, and systematic research on the impact of OCR-induced noise on downstream tasks—including classification, entity extraction, privacy-preserving redaction, and document routing—remains limited. These gaps call for future evaluation frameworks capable of defining task-specific OCR quality thresholds and measurable reliability requirements for operational deployment in judicial environments.

6 Conclusion and Future Work

This paper examined the role of OCR in digitizing prosecutorial intake within the Italian criminal justice system. We argued that the registration and preliminary classification of crime reports are constrained by high document volumes, heterogeneous formats, uneven data quality, and limited automation in preparatory tasks. In this context, OCR constitutes a critical layer for transforming non-searchable or partially structured documents into machine-processable information.

OCR quality can significantly affect downstream tasks, including AI-assisted processing, document search, metadata and named entity recognition, crime-report classification, privacy-sensitive redaction, and human review. Transcription errors may propagate through the processing chain, affecting legal interpretation, operational routing, confidentiality, and accountability. Accordingly, OCR in prosecutorial workflows should be evaluated not only through standard metrics such as Character Error Rate and Word Error Rate, but also in terms of legally material errors, layout preservation, entity-role extraction, privacy-sensitive identifiers, and downstream task performance.

We identified several technical requirements for OCR-based processing in this domain: layout-aware recognition, robustness to format and printing defects, support for handwritten and hybrid documents, legal-domain adaptation, uncertainty estimation, and human-in-the-loop validation. We also emphasized that OCR and NER pipelines generate additional artifacts, including text layers, layout annotations, extracted entities, confidence scores, and temporary files. Since these artifacts may contain sensitive data, they require explicit governance rules for access control, retention, deletion, provenance, and auditability.

Future work should proceed in two main directions. First, as shown by the need for synthetic evaluation data, there is a pressing need for datasets of Italian prosecutorial documents that capture both plausible legal content and realistic structural conditions, including heterogeneous layouts, printing defects, and other visually relevant constraints. Second, the evaluation of OCR and NER pipelines should extend beyond conventional metrics such as Character Error Rate and Word Error Rate and adopt task-oriented approaches that assess their impact on legal-domain requirements, including crime-report classification, entity extraction, and privacy-preserving redaction.

Disclosure of Interests. The authors have no competing interests to declare that are relevant to the content of this article.

References

1. Cerini, S.Y., et al.: Integrating human-in-the-loop AI systems in the Italian judicial system. In: CEUR Workshop Proceedings, vol. 4198 (2026). https://hdl.handle.net/11584/479085
2. Devlin, J., Chang, M.W., Lee, K., Toutanova, K.: BERT: pre-training of deep bidirectional transformers for language understanding. In: Proceedings of the 2019 Conference of the North American Chapter of the Association for Computational Linguistics: Human Language Technologies (Volume 1: Long and Short Papers), pp. 4171–4186 (2019). https://doi.org/10.18653/v1/N19-1423
3. Duan, S., et al.: GLM-OCR technical report. arXiv preprint arXiv:2603.10910 (2026)
4. Fujitake, M.: DtrOCR: decoder-only transformer for optical character recognition. In: Proceedings of the IEEE/CVF Winter Conference on Applications of Computer Vision, pp. 8025–8035 (2024). https://doi.org/10.48550/arXiv.2308.15996
5. Gerganov, G., et al.: llama.cpp Official Repository. https://github.com/ggml-org/llama.cpp. Accessed 27 Apr 2026
6. Goodrich, G.L., Bennett, R.R., De L'aune, W.R., Lauer, H., Mowinski, L.: Kurzweil reading machine: a partial evaluation of its optical character recognition error rate. J. Vis. Impairment Blindness **73**(10), 389–399 (1979). https://doi.org/10.1177/0145482X7907301002
7. Hugging Face: Hugging face hub (2026). https://huggingface.co. Accessed 17 May 2026
8. Keraghel, I., Morbieu, S., Nadif, M.: Recent advances in named entity recognition: a comprehensive survey and comparative study. arXiv preprint arXiv:2401.10825 (2024)
9. Koroteev, M.V.: BERT: a review of applications in natural language processing and understanding. arXiv preprint arXiv:2103.11943 (2021)
10. Li, M., et al.: TrOCR: transformer-based optical character recognition with pre-trained models. In: Proceedings of the AAAI Conference on Artificial Intelligence, vol. 37, pp. 13094–13102 (2023). https://doi.org/10.1609/aaai.v37i11.26538
11. Liu, Y., et al.: TextMonkey: an OCR-free large multimodal model for understanding document. IEEE Trans. Pattern Anal. Mach. Intell. **48**(5), 6008–6019 (2026). https://doi.org/10.1109/TPAMI.2026.3653415
12. Ministero della Giustizia: Ricognizione della digitalizzazione del processo civile e penale e della transizione digitale del ministero della giustizia (2021). https://www.giustizia.it/giustizia/page/it/digitalizzazione_del_processo. Accessed 01 Dec 2025
13. Montebovi, M.: Italian_NER_XXL_v2: A Comprehensive Named Entity Recognition Model for Italian (2025). https://huggingface.co/DeepMount00/Italian_NER_XXL_v2
14. Mori, S., Suen, C.Y., Yamamoto, K.: Historical review of OCR research and development. Proc. IEEE **80**(7), 1029–1058 (1992). https://doi.org/10.1109/5.156468
15. Nigam, S.K., Shukla, P.A., Shallum, N., Bhattacharya, A.: Seeing justice clearly: handwritten legal document translation with OCR and vision-language models. arXiv preprint arXiv:2512.18004 (2025)

16. noctrex: LightOnOCR-2-1B-GGUF (F16). Hugging Face Model Hub (2024). https://huggingface.co/noctrex/LightOnOCR-2-1B-GGUF
17. nopesadly: GLM-OCR-Q4_K_M.gguf. Hugging Face Model Hub (2024). https://huggingface.co/nopesadly/GLM-OCR-Q4_K_M.gguf
18. ggml org: Deepseek-ocr-gguf. Hugging Face Model Hub (2024). https://huggingface.co/ggml-org/DeepSeek-OCR-GGUF
19. ggml org: GLM-OCR-GGUF (F16). Hugging Face Model Hub (2024). https://huggingface.co/ggml-org/GLM-OCR-GGUF
20. ggml org: GLM-OCR-GGUF (Q8_0). Hugging Face Model Hub (2024). https://huggingface.co/ggml-org/GLM-OCR-GGUF
21. Peter, D.: hyperfine (2023). https://github.com/sharkdp/hyperfine
22. Procura di Torino: Trasparenza – Procura di Torino. https://procura-torino.giustizia.it/it/trasparenza.page. Accessed 24 Apr 2026
23. Smith, B., Troynikov, A.: Evaluating chunking strategies for retrieval. Technical report, Chroma (2024). https://trychroma.com/research/evaluating-chunking
24. Smith, R.: An overview of the tesseract OCR engine. In: Ninth International Conference on Document Analysis and Recognition (ICDAR 2007), vol. 2, pp. 629–633 (2007). https://doi.org/10.1109/ICDAR.2007.4376991
25. Smith, R.W.: History of the Tesseract OCR engine: what worked and what didn't. In: Document Recognition and Retrieval XX, vol. 8658, p. 865802. SPIE (2013). https://doi.org/10.1117/12.2010051
26. staghado: LightOnOCR-2-1B-Q4_K_M-GGUF. Hugging Face Model Hub (2024). https://huggingface.co/staghado/LightOnOCR-2-1B-Q4_K_M-GGUF
27. staghado: LightOnOCR-2-1B-Q8_0-GGUF. Hugging Face Model Hub (2024). https://huggingface.co/staghado/LightOnOCR-2-1B-Q8_0-GGUF
28. Taghadouini, S., Cavaillès, A., Aubertin, B.: LightOnOCR: a 1B end-to-end multilingual vision-language model for state-of-the-art OCR. arXiv preprint arXiv:2601.14251 (2026)
29. Van Houdt, G., Mosquera, C., Nápoles, G.: A review on the long short-term memory model. Artif. Intell. Rev. **53**(8), 5929–5955 (2020). https://doi.org/10.1007/s10462-020-09838-1
30. Vaswani, A., et al.: Attention is All You Need (2023). https://arxiv.org/abs/1706.03762
31. Vempati, S., Anand, N., Talebailkar, G., Garai, A., Arora, C.: Why stop at words? Unveiling the bigger picture through line-level OCR. arXiv preprint arXiv:2508.21693 (2025)
32. Wang, J.: A study of the OCR development history and directions of development. Highlights Sci. Eng. Technol. **72**, 409–415 (2023). https://doi.org/10.54097/bm665j77
33. Wei, H., et al.: General OCR theory: towards OCR-2.0 via a unified end-to-end model. arXiv preprint arXiv:2409.01704 (2024)
34. Wei, H., Sun, Y., Li, Y.: Deepseek-OCR: contexts optical compression. arXiv preprint arXiv:2510.18234 (2025)

SentiSteg: A Linguistic Steganography System Based on Sentiment Recognition

Bartosz Gutowski, Karolina Gabor-Siatkowska, and Artur Janicki(✉)

Warsaw University of Technology, Warsaw, Poland
Artur.Janicki@pw.edu.pl

Abstract. In this paper, we propose a novel linguistic steganography system called SentiSteg. It is based on generating or forwarding microblog posts (such as former Twitter tweets or X platform posts) so that their sentiment forms a desired binary sequence. We demonstrate a proof-of-concept of SentiSteg and run preliminary experiments using posts from the FIFA World Cup 2022 dataset. We show that the proposed method allows hiding an arbitrary binary message. We discuss the steganographic bandwidth offered by SentiSteg and the detectability of the proposed method.

Keywords: Information hiding · Linguistic steganography · Confidentiality · Privacy · Natural language processing · Sentiment recognition · Large language models · Microblogs

1 Introduction

Microblogging platforms, also called microblogs, such as X (formerly Twitter) or Bluesky, publish hundreds of millions of posts every day. Their audience encompasses hundreds of millions of users. Microblogs are used for instant announcements and for sharing opinions across a variety of domains, such as politics, sports, and culture. The content published on microblogs exhibits a range of emotional flavors, from neutral to emotionally rich, with either positive or negative polarity.

In this paper, we discuss using microblogs to create hidden communication channels. We propose SentiSteg, a linguistic steganography technique that uses microblog posts with different sentiments to convey hidden messages. We will present a proof-of-concept demonstrating that such a method enables correct hidden transmission. We will discuss SentiSteg detectability and ethical aspects. As our work is still in progress, we will also describe the planned next steps.

Our paper is structured as follows. First, in Sect. 2 we briefly present prior work related to our topic. Next, in Sect. 3, we describe the proposed SentiSteg method. In Sect. 4, we present the preliminary experiments conducted and their results. We discuss them in Sect. 5 and conclude the paper in Sect. 6.

Z. Afzal et al. (Eds.): ARES 2026 Workshops, LNCS 16900, pp. 559–573, 2027.
https://doi.org/10.1007/978-3-032-35576-8_30

2 Related Work

In this section, we will show a brief overview of existing linguistic steganography methods, their applications, and also explain the context of text-based sentiment recognition, which will be used in the proposed method.

2.1 Steganography in General

Steganography is a technique of hiding secret information inside other forms of communication or media, such as text, images, or audio. The main focus is on maintaining the confidentiality of the fact that any hidden communication is taking place. When using steganography to hide information, the main concept typically includes the following components:

- a carrier – data which is transmitted overtly, used indirectly to convey hidden information,
- a secret message (payload) – data which has to be hidden,
- an embedding/encoding algorithm – a method used to insert hidden data into the cover signal,
- a stego object (steganogram) – data produced after the embedding process, it should look nearly identical to the original,
- an decoding/decrypting algorithm – a chosen algorithm used by the receiver to recover the hidden message.

Stego objects must be identical to the cover so that they do not reveal the secret message [28]. Nowadays, steganographic techniques have been adapted to a wide range of carrier media, such as images [27], audio [14], video [17], or DNA [33].

The most important attributes of a reliable steganographic system are: security (or detectability), imperceptibility, steganographic bandwidth, and robustness [3,19]. Security refers to a system's ability to remain undetected. Imperceptibility refers to whether changes in the carrier can be perceived by users. Steganographic bandwidth refers to the amount of data that can be hidden within a carrier of fixed size. Finally, robustness describes the ability of the hidden message to withstand distortions, modifications, or attacks while remaining recoverable [4]. When developing new steganographic methods, it is important to maintain these characteristics at a suitable level.

2.2 Text Steganography

Text steganography is a subset of steganographic methods that hides information in text. It can be used to covertly transmit secret messages via an open channel [30]. It is also regarded as one of the most challenging areas of steganography: it requires a deep understanding of the complex linguistic issues involved in the language in which the system is designed to operate. Comparative overviews of text steganography methods are provided in [1,26]. These methods can be divided into three main categories based on how the cover text is processed during embedding [10,38]. Figure 1 shows the main types present in the literature. Below, we describe them with a primary focus on linguistic steganography, as our proposed solution falls within this category.

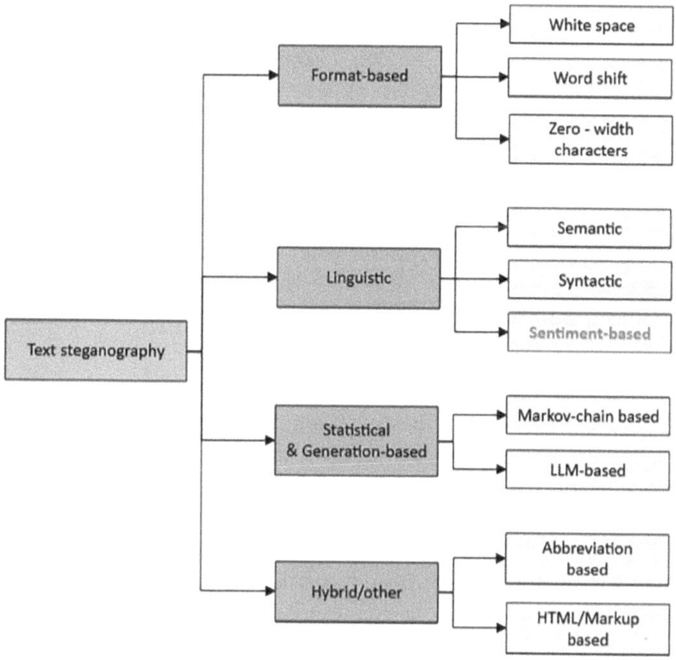

Fig. 1. Types of text steganography, with highlighted sentiment-based steganographic methods.

Format-Based Methods. conceal messages within the formatting of text files, such as word spacing, font size, or text color. By manipulating these formatting properties, secret messages can be embedded without altering the actual file's content. Several representative methods are discussed in the literature [2,32].

Statistical Methods. use the statistical properties of text to hide information, e.g., [22]. The encoding process is based on the fact that certain characters appear more frequently than others in a given language. By using this property, less common character sequences can be replaced with more frequent ones to embed secret information without being noticed by third parties [23].

Linguistic Steganography Methods. conceal information within natural language text [7], typically through techniques such as synonym substitution or word reordering, to encode secret messages within existing content [40]. Linguistic features are manipulated to conceal information, while the resulting text must appear natural and unsuspicious. Only a recipient who knows the exact extraction method can retrieve the hidden message.

However, linguistic steganography faces a fundamental challenge: natural language carries only a few bits per symbol on average [8], leaving little redundant data for message embedding. This makes text the most demanding carrier medium compared to other formats [18]. Despite this limitation, researchers continue to explore methods for embedding secret messages.

Linguistic methods use lexical, syntactic, and semantic properties of text to conceal information. When manipulating these properties, it is important to ensure that the resulting steganogram is grammatically and lexically meaningful, natural, and appropriate to the context. Depending on the origin of the text used, linguistic steganography systems can be divided into modification-based and generation-based systems. When using the first ones, a cover text is needed in advance. In generation-based techniques, the cover text can be skipped; a text carrying secret information for steganography is directly produced [39].

Modification-based methods conceal secret information within the cover text without altering its meaning. The most common approach in this category is lexical substitution [7]. These methods replace words in the cover text with synonyms from resources (e.g., WordNet [21]), which organizes words into sets called 'synsets' (groups of terms sharing the same or similar meaning). The major challenge with these systems is determining the meaning of a word in a given context and selecting the correct synonym when a word has multiple meanings. Even if a word is replaced with a synonym that preserves the meaning of the sentence, there may still be semantic differences between the synonyms [7].

Syntactic methods are less conventional techniques in linguistic steganography. They are based on the idea that a single meaning can be expressed through multiple grammatically different sentence structures. While syntax concerns how words are arranged according to grammatical rules, semantics concerns the meanings of those words. Syntactic transformations exploit the fact that restructuring a sentence does not necessarily alter its meaning. The examples below show these transformations:

- Passivization: Transforming a sentence from active to passive voice.
- Splitting: Converting a complex sentence into a simple one.
- Preposing: Repositioning elements within a sentence; for example, such as moving the object to a position before the subject.

Semantic methods focus on replacing entire sequences of words to ensure that the resulting sequence is correct in every respect. This is a difficult approach because it requires an in-depth understanding of the relationships and meanings of the individual elements within one sentence.

While semantic methods manipulate the linguistic content of a message, other steganographic approaches shift the focus from the text itself to the *behavioral* and *temporal* patterns of communication. An example, therefore, could be timing-based steganography in chat applications, where monitoring behavioral anomalies during conversation is used [24]. In text-based timing steganography messages are sent at very precise moments to encode their hidden information. This shows that steganographic detection is not limited to the content of a message alone, but can also extend to the way it is written and expressed.

The use of text steganography on social media platforms (such as X) has been explored also in earlier works. For example, in 2014, the authors proposed a natural language steganographic system for Twitter, named CoverTweet [36]. It was designed to reproduce the specific language used in the tweets. In that context, it should reflect the language used by the Twitter user who embedded them. Two types of distortion were combined: natural language transformations of the covers during embedding by paraphrasing and a human selecting the 'optimal' stego tweet from a list of possible paraphrases of the cover. This approach differed from previous work, which used general-purpose language models.

Sometimes text steganography methods make generated hidden messages drift semantically from their surrounding context, which makes them easier to detect. Some researchers have therefore explored ways of controlling the emotional tone and context of generated text, with the aim of making hidden messages harder to spot. In [30], the authors propose a steganography system based on an LLM and named entities. The LLM generates stego text, and named entity recognition captures the text around the current context to keep the generated content on topic. Additionally, sentiment analysis is used only to identify sentiment tendencies, so the stego text contains sentiment information.

Another steganographic method targeting social media (especially Twitter and Instagram) is StegHash [5,31]. It focuses on using hashtags for connecting multimedia files (e.g., images, movies or songs) with embedded hidden messages. The main concept is that a set of n hashtags has $n!$ possible permutations, and each permutation can serve as a unique index for a message. With a secret password and a secret transition function, these indexes can be linked together to form a chain of messages that can be accessed one by one, each one carrying hidden content.

2.3 Text-Based Sentiment Recognition

Text-based sentiment recognition involves the automatic identification and classification of the emotional tone or opinion expressed in text as positive, negative, or neutral [29,41]. It is widely used to analyze large volumes of user reviews, social media posts, and customer feedback to understand attitudes, emotions, and satisfaction. Methods used for text-based sentiment recognition can be classified according to several criteria, such as the methodological approach or the type of textual data analyzed. Below, the most common approaches are presented, along with their respective advantages and disadvantages.

Lexicon-Based Methods. use the analysis of the text's semantic and grammatical patterns. To determine the sentiment of the analyzed text, comprehensive dictionaries (e.g., SentiWordNet [9]) and grammatical structures are used to infer meaning. When analyzing a text fragment, a separate emotional tone is determined for each word using the dictionary. The overall polarization of each sentence is then calculated and aggregated for all sentences in the analyzed fragment. The main advantage of this approach is its ease of implementation and low computational resource requirements. The core steps involve text tokenization, dictionary-based sentiment lookup, and result aggregation. However, these methods are vulnerable to grammatical errors in the analyzed text and cannot detect more complex semantic properties (e.g., irony). Therefore, they are not adequate for analyzing social media content. It is important to note that the quality of the dictionary significantly impacts the outcome. Since it may be subject to human error, it may give unsatisfactory outputs.

Machine Learning-Based Methods. enable the classification of the text sentiment using the grammatical and linguistic relationships within the processed texts. As classifiers, e.g., logistic regression, decision trees, and naive Bayes classifiers are employed. These models must first be trained on large, well-preprocessed datasets, from which they learn the relationships between words for a given text type [12]. Unlike lexicon-based methods, machine learning algorithms can be trained to recognize contextual information (e.g., sarcasm), which is their significant advantage. They also produce more accurate outputs. Unfortunately, these algorithms are prone to errors caused by artifacts (e.g., slang or misplaced punctuation), which significantly reduce their accuracy and require more computational resources due to the large volume of data processed during training.

Hybrid Methods. combine the advantages of the lexical approach with machine learning techniques to improve the efficiency of sentiment analysis.

3 Proposed SentiSteg Method

The main concept of the proposed SentiSteg method for embedding hidden data into microblog posts is presented in Fig. 2 and as a pseudocode in Algorithm 1. A microblogger publishes a series of posts, e.g., on platform X, as shown in the figure, named *Post 1*, *Post 2*, etc. These posts are analyzed using a SentiSteg algorithm, which first classifies the sentiment of consecutive posts' text into neutral, positive, or negative classes. Next, we encode them binarily. We propose assigning "0 s" to neutral posts and "1 s" to emotionally flavored posts, i.e., either with positive or negative sentiment.

Next, a SentiSteg encoder analyzes the secret binary sequence to be transmitted. Assuming that one post carries a single bit, the encoder tries to match the posts with the secret. If the message bit matches the bit encoded by the post's sentiment, the steganographic blogger directly reposts it (see *Post 3* in Fig. 2). If not (as in the case with *Post 1*), the post is kept on hold in a buffer and the first post with the matching bit (here *Post 2*) is transmitted first. The waiting posts are transmitted at the first opportunity, when the respective bits match.

Algorithm 1: Concept of the proposed SentiSteg method.

```
Encoding process;
Input: Post queue PQ, Post P, Secret binary sequence SNB
buffer ← [];
P_b ← [];
foreach P in PQ do
    P_s ← sentiment classification {pos, neg, neutral};
    if P_s = {neutral} then
        P_enc ← 0;
    else
        P_enc ← 1;
foreach bit_snb in SNB do
    P ← GET next post FROM PQ;
    bit_p ← GET bit FROM P_enc;
    if P_enc = bit_snb then
        repost P;
    else
        buffer ← append buffer with P;
    foreach P_b in buffer do
        if P_enc (of P_b) = bit_snb then
            repost P_b;
            buffer ← remove P_b from buffer;
            break;
    if buffer is full then
        P ← find earlier P WHERE P_enc = bit_snb;
        repost P;
```

If the waiting queue becomes too long, it means that there are not enough posts with the required sentiment. In such a case, an earlier post with the correct bit can be repeated instead. The whole process continues until there are no more bits of the secret message left.

The decoding process is very simple: the recipient observes the steganographic blogger and analyzes their posts with the very same sentiment recognizer. Neutral posts would denote "0 s", the remaining ones would denote "1 s". Their sequence directly represents the secret.

4 Experiments and Their Results

4.1 Sentiment Recognition Setup

First, we will describe our experiments with setting up the text-based sentiment recognition. Next, we will present our work on the proof-of-concept of the actual SentiSteg algorithm.

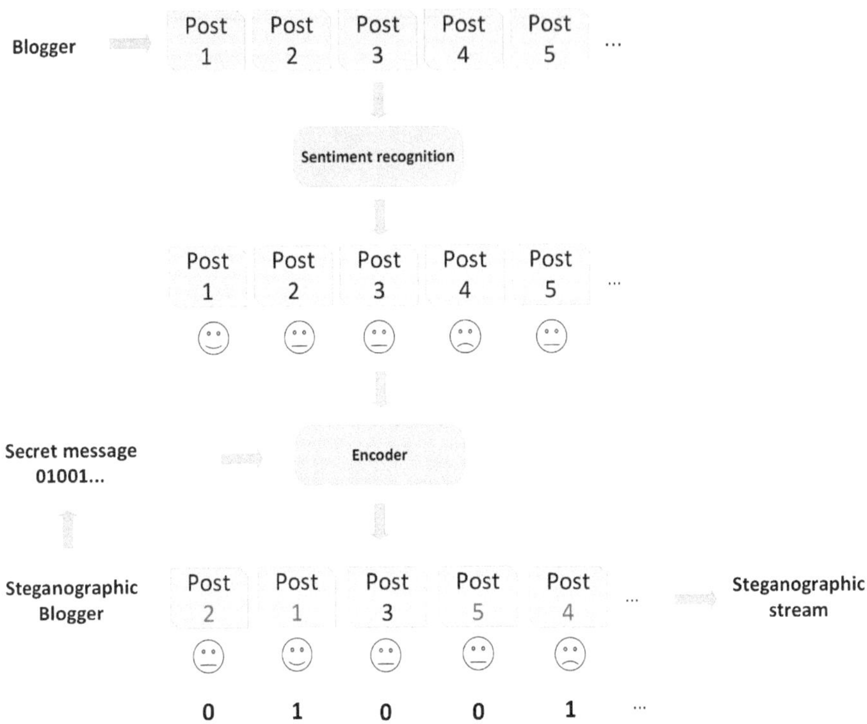

Fig. 2. Idea of SentiSteg encoding process, embedding "01001" message into a steganographic stream of microblog posts (red color denotes reordered posts).

Datasets Used for Sentiment Re cognition. The sentiment recognition module was trained using two corpora. First, we took CORpus of Translated Emotional teXts (CORTEX) [41], which is a parallel (English and Polish) corpus containing over 25k labeled emotional phrases collected with the initial aim of training empathetic dialogue systems [11,16]. In this study, we used only the English part of CORTEX.

Since the preliminary sentiment recognition results trained on CORTEX were unsatisfactory for microblog posts, we also added samples from the EPL Teams – Twitter Sentiment Dataset [35], which contains tweets about the Premier League. They are labeled with polarity in the range of $[-1, 1]$, calculated using the Vader Model from the NLTK Python library – see sample data in Table 1. We mapped this polarity into neutral/positive/negative classes, treating posts with polarity $[-0.05, 0.05]$ as neutral, posts with polarity $(0.05, 1]$ as positive, and posts with polarity $[-1, -0.05)$ as the ones with negative sentiment. As the EPL Teams dataset contains over a million posts, we selected only a fractional random subset to maintain a reasonable balance between general-domain CORTEX data and sport-domain EPL data. By combining these two datasets, we obtained a training corpus comprising 16k neutral, 8k negative and 8k positive posts.

Table 1. Sample from the EPL Teams dataset used for training the sentiment recognition module.

created _at	file _name	search _query	text	pola-rity	user-name
2020-09-23 18:39:34	Crystal Palace	#Crystal -Palace OR #CPFC	Onto Week 2 of Premier League Stars of the Week, where I analyse the highest scoring weekend in Prem...	0.0	TW
2020-09-23 18:39:18	Crystal Palace	#Crystal -Palace OR #CPFC	Our palace team will put our hearts out for our fans because we don't have billions of fans we have ...	0.1531	crystal palace-dan
2020-09-23 18:28:15	Crystal Palace	#Crystal -Palace OR #CPFC	Chelsea v Palace kick-off time changed and TV information confirmed https://t.co/ ktPCyqCcri #CPFC	0.0	Crystal Palace News
2020-09-23 18:28:15	Crystal Palace	#Crystal -Palace OR #CPFC	Academy redevelopment update: Exclusive footage shows new site progression https://t.co/ wQeyi9tk5H #...	0.128	Crystal Palace News
2020-07-09 11:27:39	Liver-pool	#liverpool-fc OR #YNWA OR #LFC	RT @JamesPearceLFC: Mohamed Salah the match-winner but fuming with himself at the end for missing th...	-0.7469	Adebayo Segun Emmy

Training the Sentiment Recognition Module. The training data was preprocessed by converting to lowercase, removing email addresses, removing URLs, removing multiple white characters, etc., and then tokenized. For that purpose, we used the *BertTokenizerFast* tokenizer from the Hugging Face *transformers* library. The `distilbert-base-uncased` BERT model from *Transformers* library was fine-tuned for sentiment recognition using the ADAM optimizer [15] with a learning rate equal $5e-5$, epsilon equal $1e-8$ and batch size equal 16. The training process ended with an accuracy of 92.2% on the validation data and 94.0% on the training data.

4.2 Proof-Of-Concept of SentiSteg Steganographic System

We conducted several experiments with embedding secret messages into a stream of microblog posts. Our objectives were as follows:

- verify if SentiSteg allows accurate transmission of hidden messages;
- evaluate SentiSteg's steganographic bandwidth, i.e., capacity of the created hidden channel.

The next paragraphs describe the dataset used and the results achieved.

Dataset Used for Testing SentiSteg. To imitate a real-life scenario, we decided to use the FIFA World Cup 2022 Tweets corpus [25], containing 22.5k Twitter posts from the first day of the 2022 football world championship. The

Table 2. Data sample from FIFA World Cup 2022 dataset.

Date Created	No. of Likes	Source	Post	Senti-ment
2022-11-20 23:59:21	4	Twitter Web App	What are we drinking today @TucanTribe @MadBears_ @lkinc_algo @al_goanna #WorldCup2022 https://...	neutral
2022-11-20 23:59:01	3	Twitter for iPhone	Amazing CanadaSoccerEN #WorldCup2022 launch video. Shows how much the face of Canada and our men's...	positive
2022-11-20 23:58:41	1	Twitter for iPhone	Worth reading while watching #WorldCup2022 https://t.co/ 1SQrNa2dYU	positive
2022-11-20 23:58:33	1	Twitter Web App	Golden Maknae shinning bright https://t.co/ 4AyZbzGTX4 #JeonJungkook #Jungkook #JK #GoldenM...	positive
2022-11-20 23:58:28	0	Twitter for Android	If the BBC cares so much about human rights, homosexual rights, and women rights then why not say th...	negative

corpus contains tweets with their creation date, No. of likes, source device, content and their sentiment. An event like the football World Cup was well-suited for our PoC, as such events provoke numerous posts with diverse sentiments that SentiSteg can forward in the desired order. Table 2 shows an excerpt from this dataset.

SentiSteg Testing Results. Our experiments showed that SentiSteg allows for embedding any sequence of secret messages and their correct decoding. The only condition is the availability of a sufficient number of posts with sentiment encoded as "0" and "1" (in this case, they were posts of neutral and positive/negative sentiment, respectively).

When applied to the posts from the FIFA World Cup 2022 dataset, the trained BERT-based sentiment recognition module assigned more posts to the neutral class than the original labels (see Table 3). The sentiment recognition accuracy, calculated for the 3-class case using the original dataset labels as the ground truth, was 57.4% (with 33.3% as the chance level), which was not high. However, from the point of SentiSteg operation, the accuracy of sentiment recognition is not critical, as long as the same detection is used in the steganographic encoder and decoder. What is more important is the balance between emotional and neutral classes (i.e., between "1 s" and "0 s"). From this point of view, the trained classifier performed very well, achieving a 45%–55% class distribution, which was much better than for the original labels. Such proportions will allow much easier selection of suitable posts that carry either “0” or “1” (Table 4).

Table 3. Test results of sentiment recognition module for the FIFA World Cup 2022 dataset (22,524 posts in total).

	Positive	Negative	Neutral	Emotional vs. Neutral Ratio
Dataset labels	8489	5784	8251	73.4% vs. 36.6%
Recognized	7682	2410	12432	44.8% vs. 55.2%

As for steganographic bandwidth, so far we have tested using one microblog post per bit. It means that if we consider an intensive microblog that (re)posts one message every minute, we achieve a hidden channel with a capacity of 60 bits/hour. It would allow sending about seven ASCII chars per hour. This, of course, is not an impressive result, compared, e.g., to VoIP steganography, such as that based on transcoding (TranSteg) [20], which achieved channel rates exceeding 40 kb/s [13]. However, in terms of linguistic steganography, the achieved results are satisfactory and sufficient for some applications.

In linguistic steganography methods, much lower embedding rates can be achieved. According to [6], authors of a syntactic transformation method claim around 0.5 to 1.0 bits per sentence were calculated, others mention also 1 bit per sentence [34]. In another work [37] focused mainly on linguistic steganographic method for tweets, an embedding rate of approximately 2.8 bits per tweet was achieved.

5 Discussion

5.1 Detectability

SentiSteg is very difficult to detect because it does not alter the content of the microblog posts used for embedding a hidden message. In contrast, the SentiSteg encoder alters the order of forwarded posts, forming its stream according to the desired binary sequence. However, it is impossible to determine if a given sequence of posts is a result of the SentiSteg operation or is a result of someone’s (re)posting activity.

One method that could help detect the presence of SentiSteg channels is to analyze microblog statistics. Any anomaly in post frequency, unusual sentiment distribution, or repetition of certain posts may indicate that SentiSteg has been used. Machine learning-based anomaly detectors are natural candidates that could help here.

Another potential detection method can be based on the analysis of coherence between consecutive posts. Naturally, posts from the same source should be coherent in their content, e.g., they are often part of a story or some narration. Also, since many microblog contributors comment on, e.g., sports or political events in near real time, it should be possible to detect their unusual relationship with actual events (e.g., a late reaction to a goal in a football match).

Table 4. Sample sequence of microblog posts from the FIFA World Cup 2022 dataset, with SentiSteg encoded binary sequence 0110 0101 (decimal: 101, ASCII: "e")

Post	Encod-ed bit
Enner Valencia during match against Qatar #QatarWorldCup2022 #WorldCup2022 #QATECU https://t.co/F9lpZQiOwx	0
The Ecuadorian supporters are doing the World proud right now. #WorldCup2022 #Qatar2022 https://t.co/wkMehBjMeg	1
Wtf how is that goal disallowed?? #WorldCup2022	1
Get in. Surely no issues with that #WorldCup2022	0
Give this a read #VoyageursFamily! #CanMNT #WorldCup2022 #CanWNT/#CanXNT https://t.co/Kv9GE5UwlH	0
#WorldCup2022 #QATEQU @BBCSport presenters moaning while their snouts are in the trough - don't like it? Come home and give your fee back.	1
Not a fan of Football, but I like World Games. #WorldCup2022 #FIFAWorldCup #VaiBrasil	0
Good start to the #WorldCup2022 ! The hosts get a ridiculous #VAR decision in their favour. https://t.co/SuuJAbhdl1	1

5.2 Ethical Considerations

Like every steganographic method, SentiSteg can also be used for malicious purposes, e.g., for command-and-control communication in a botnet. An important objective of this paper was to make the cybersecurity community aware that hidden channels based on similar, sentiment-based techniques may already exist. The previous subsection on detectability enumerated sample methods of detecting SentiSteg. We hope that future studies will propose effective steganalytic methods to detect sentiment-based hidden channels.

6 Conclusions and Future Work

In this paper, we presented a work-in-progress on a linguistic steganography that uses text-based sentiment recognition. We proposed a method, named SentiSteg, that embeds an arbitrary binary message into microblog posts. In our proof-of-concept, as a carrier, we used tweets sent during the first day of the FIFA World Cup 2022 in Qatar.

We ran a series of preliminary experiments with encoding and decoding hidden messages. Since our sentiment recognition module assigned "0 s" and "1 s" to the FIFA World Cup posts in a fairly uniform manner (neutral category assigned to 55% of posts, and positive or negative emotions to 45% of posts), the SentiSteg encoding algorithm could easily embed any binary sequence (also with a fairly balanced "0 s" and "1 s"), which was then correctly decoded using the same BERT-based sentiment recognizer.

Future work can focus on a more thorough analysis of SentiSteg's operation, considering various data to be embedded and accounting for different encoding schemes, such as Huffman encoding, to increase steganographic bandwidth. Also, microblog posts other than sports can be tested, e.g., to see whether sentiment recognition would be similarly effective across other domains. A deeper analysis of steganalytic methods capable of detecting sentiment-based steganographic transmission is also strongly recommended to increase resilience against similar sentiment-based methods.

Disclosure of Interests. The authors have no competing interests to declare that are relevant to the content of this article.

References

1. Agarwal, M.: Text steganographic approaches: a comparison. Int. J. Netw. Secur. Appli. **5** (2013). https://doi.org/10.5121/ijnsa.2013.5107
2. Al-Nofaie, S., Gutub, A., Al-Ghamdi, M.: Enhancing Arabic text steganography for personal usage utilizing pseudo-spaces. J. King Saud Univ.- Comput. Info. Sci. **33**(8), 963–974 (2021). https://doi.org/10.1016/j.jksuci.2019.06.010
3. Aljughaiman, A., Alrawashdeh, R.: Content-adaptive LSB steganography with saliency fusion, ACO dispersion, and hybrid encryption with ablation study. Sci. Rep. **16**, 3829 (2026). https://doi.org/10.1038/s41598-025-33920-9
4. Bamanga, M.A., Babando, A.K., Shehu, M.A.: Recent advances in steganography. In: Mayer, J. (ed.) Steganography - The Art of Hiding Information, chap. 2. IntechOpen,, London (2024). https://doi.org/10.5772/intechopen.1004521
5. Bieniasz, J., Szczypiorski, K.: Methods for information hiding in open social networks. J. Univ. Comput. Sci. **25**(2), 74–98 (2019)
6. Chang, C.Y., Clark, S.: Adjective deletion for linguistic steganography and secret sharing. In: Proceedings of COLING 2012, pp. 493–510 (2012)
7. Chang, C.Y., Clark, S.: Practical linguistic steganography using contextual synonym substitution and a novel vertex coding method. Comput. Linguist. **40**(2), 403–448 (2014)
8. Dai, F., Cai, Z.: Towards near-imperceptible steganographic text. In: Korhonen, A., Traum, D., Màrquez, L. (eds.) Proceedings of the 57th Annual Meeting of the Association for Computational Linguistics, pp. 4303–4308. Association for Computational Linguistics, Florence, Italy (2019). https://doi.org/10.18653/v1/P19-1422, https://aclanthology.org/P19-1422/
9. Esuli, A., et al.: SENTIWORDNET: a publicly available lexical resource for opinion mining. In: Tapias, D. (ed.) Proceedings of the Fifth International Conference on Language Resources and Evaluation (LREC'06). European Language Resources Association (ELRA),, Genoa, Italy (2006)

10. Farooq Ahmed Adeeb, O., Kabudian, S.J.: StegGPT: a novel foundation-model-based character-level linguistic steganography method utilizing large language models. IEEE Access **13**, 89915–89925 (2025). https://doi.org/10.1109/ACCESS.2025.3568339
11. Gabor-Siatkowska, K., et al.: Therapeutic spoken dialogue system in clinical settings: initial experiments. In: 30th International Conference on Systems, Signals and Image Processing, pp. 1–5. IEEE, Ohrid, North Macedonia (2023). https://doi.org/10.1109/IWSSIP58668.2023.10180265 IWSSIP 2023
12. Ghatora, P.S., Hosseini, S.E., Pervez, S., Iqbal, M.J., Shaukat, N.: Sentiment analysis of product reviews using machine learning and pre-trained LLM. Big Data Cognit. Comput. **8**(12) (2024). https://doi.org/10.3390/bdcc8120199, https://www.mdpi.com/2504-2289/8/12/199
13. Janicki, A., Mazurczyk, W., Szczypiorski, K.: Influence of speech codecs selection on transcoding steganography. Telecommun. Syst. **59**(3), 305–315 (2014). https://doi.org/10.1007/s11235-014-9937-9
14. Kadhim, I.: A new audio steganography system based on auto-key generator. AL-Khwarizmi Eng. **8**, 27–36 (2012). https://doi.org/10.3390/app112110146
15. Kingma, D.P., Ba, J.: Adam: a method for stochastic optimization (2014). arXiv:1412.6980 arXiv preprint
16. Kozłowski, M., Gabor-Siatkowska, K., Stefaniak, I., Sowański, M., Janicki, A.: Enhanced emotion and sentiment recognition for empathetic dialogue system using big data and deep learning methods. In: International Conference on Computational Science (ICCS 2023), pp. 465–480., Prague, Czechia (2023)
17. Limkar, S., Nemade, A., Badgujar, A., Kate, R.: Improved data hiding technique based on audio and video steganography. In: Smart Computing and Informatics, pp. 581–588 (2018)
18. Majeed, M.A., Sulaiman, R., and, Z.S.: New text steganography technique based on part-of-speech tagging and format-preserving encryption. KSII Trans. Int. Info. Syst. **18**(1), 170–191 (2024). https://doi.org/10.3837/tiis.2024.01.010
19. Majeed, M.A., Sulaiman, R., Shukur, Z., Hasan, M.K.: A review on text steganography techniques. Mathematics **9**(21) (2021). https://doi.org/10.3390/math9212829
20. Mazurczyk, W., Szaga, P., Szczypiorski, K.: Using transcoding for hidden communication in IP telephony. Multimedia Tools Appl. **70**(3), 2139–2165 (2014). https://doi.org/10.1007/s11042-012-1224-8
21. Miller, G.A.: Wordnet: a lexical database for English. Commun. ACM **38**(11), 39–41 (1995)
22. Ning, W., Poli, S., Jin, F., Zhongliang, Y., Weibo, M., Zhenru, L.: Coverless text steganography based on maximum variable bit embedding rules. J. Phys.: Conf. Ser. **1237**(2) (2019). https://doi.org/10.1088/1742-6596/1237/2/022078
23. Ning, W., et al.: STBS-STEGA: coverless text steganography based on state transition-binary sequence. Int. J. Distrib. Sens. Netw. **16**(3) (2020). https://doi.org/10.1177/1550147720914257
24. Okello, M.O.: Steganalysis of chat based steganography. Int. J. Info. Appl. Math. **6**(1), 29–39 (2023)
25. Ozkip, E.: FIFA World Cup 2022 Tweets. https://www.kaggle.com/datasets/tirendazacademy/fifa-world-cup-2022-tweets (2022)
26. Por, L.Y., Ang, T., Beh Mei Yin, D.: WhiteSTEG: a new scheme in information hiding using text steganography. WSEAS Trans. Comput. **7** (2008)

27. Płachta, M., Krzemień, M., Szczypiorski, K., Janicki, A.: Detection of image steganography using deep learning and ensemble classifiers. Electronics **11**(10) (2022). https://doi.org/10.3390/electronics11101565
28. Rabie, T., Baziyad, M., Kamel, I.: Secure high payload steganography: a model-based approach. J. Info. Secur. Appl. **63**, 103043 (2021). https://doi.org/10.1016/j.jisa.2021.103043
29. Ren, F., Wang, L.: Sentiment analysis of text based on three-way decisions. J. Intell. Fuzzy Syst.: Appl. Eng. Technol. **33**(1), 245–254 (2017). https://doi.org/10.3233/JIFS-161522
30. Shi, H., Guo, W., Gao, S.: Emotionally controllable text steganography based on large language model and named entity. Technologies **13**(7) (2025). https://doi.org/10.3390/technologies13070264
31. Szczypiorski, K.: STEGHash: new method for information hiding in open social networks (2016). arXiv:1611.00306 arXiv preprint
32. Taha, A., Hammad, A.S., Selim, M.M.: A high capacity algorithm for information hiding in Arabic text. J. King Saud Univ.- Comput. Info. Sci. **32**(6), 658–665 (2020). https://doi.org/10.1016/j.jksuci.2018.07.007
33. Vinodhini, R.E., Malathi, P., Kumar, T.G.: A survey on DNA and image steganography. In: 4th International Conference on Advanced Computing and Communication Systems (ICACCS 2017), pp. 1–7 (2017). https://doi.org/10.1109/ICACCS.2017.8014670
34. Vybornova, O., Macq, B.: A method of text watermarking using presuppositions. In: Security, Steganography, and Watermarking of Multimedia Contents IX, vol. 6505, p. 65051R. SPIE (2007). https://doi.org/10.1117/12.702871
35. William, J.: EPL teams - twitter sentiment dataset. https://www.kaggle.com/datasets/wjia26/epl-teams-twitter-sentiment-dataset (2020)
36. Wilson, A., Blunsom, P., Ker, A.D.: Linguistic steganography on Twitter: hierarchical language modeling with manual interaction. In: Alattar, A.M., Memon, N.D., Heitzenrater, C.D. (eds.) Media Watermarking, Security, and Forensics 2014, vol. 9028, p. 902803. International Society for Optics and Photonics, SPIE (2014) https://doi.org/10.1117/12.2039213
37. Wilson, A., Ker, A.D.: Avoiding detection on twitter: embedding strategies for linguistic steganography. Electron. Imaging **28**, 1–9 (2016)
38. Xiang, L., Wang, R., Yang, Z., Liu, Y.: Generative linguistic steganography: a comprehensive review. KSII Trans. Internet Inf. Syst. **16**(3) (2022). https://doi.org/10.3837/tiis.2022.03.013
39. Yang, T., Wu, H., Yi, B., Feng, G., Zhang, X.: Semantic-preserving linguistic steganography by pivot translation and semantic-aware bins coding. IEEE Trans. Depend. Secure Comput. **21**(1), 139–152 (2023)
40. Ziegler, Z., Deng, Y., Rush, A.: Neural linguistic steganography. In: Inui, K., Jiang, J., Ng, V., Wan, X. (eds.) Proceedings of the 2019 Conference on Empirical Methods in Natural Language Processing and the 9th International Joint Conference on Natural Language Processing (EMNLP-IJCNLP), pp. 1210–1215. Association for Computational Linguistics, Hong Kong, China (2019). https://doi.org/10.18653/v1/D19-1115
41. Zygadło, A., Kozłowski, M., Janicki, A.: Text-based emotion recognition in English and Polish for therapeutic chatbot. App. Sci. **11**(21) (2021). https://doi.org/10.3390/app112110146

Proceedings of the First Workshop on Security, Privacy, and Identity Management for the Digital Transformation (SPIMDT 2026)

SPIMDT 2026 Preface

Recent years have witnessed rapid advances in digital technologies, increased data collection, and the widespread adoption of artificial intelligence systems. While these developments deliver significant societal and economic value, they also pose critical challenges related to responsible data governance, privacy protection, ethical AI use, and regulatory compliance. Organizations increasingly struggle to design digital systems that comply with legal frameworks such as the GDPR and the EU AI Act while maintaining transparency, fairness, and trust.

As one of these developments, the identity environment has evolved into a complex and dynamic ecosystem that demands seamless interoperability, stronger security measures, and user-centric experiences in an increasingly interconnected digital world. As digital transformation accelerates across sectors, the challenges surrounding digital identity systems have grown in scope and complexity. Addressing these difficulties necessitates collaboration among scholars and practitioners from diverse disciplines, establishing an interdisciplinary approach critical for shaping the future of identity management.

The Workshop on Security, Privacy, and Identity Management for the Digital Transformation (SPIMDT) aims to foster dialogue, share emerging research, and catalyse innovative solutions. It explores the evolving digital transformation landscape by engaging with various topics—ranging from data governance frameworks to privacy-enhancing technologies and interoperability standards.

SPIMDT accepted 4 manuscripts out of a total of 11 submissions. At least three reviewers followed a double-blind approach to peer review the manuscripts. The reviewers, who were part of the Program Committee, were composed of 20 experts in digital identities. Based on their valuable reviews, 4 papers were accepted to be published in this LNCS volume by Springer and presented at the workshop.

We thank all the participants, including the authors, the reviewers, and the attendees, for their valuable work and significant efforts, which contributed to the workshop's success. We hope that this workshop will advance the development of security, privacy, and identity management for the digital transformation.

August 2026

Mansoor Ahmed
Nils Gruschka
Markus Helfert
Muhammad Irfan Khalid
Daniela Pöhn
Amir Sharif

SPIMDT 2026 Organization

Workshop Chairs

Mansoor Ahmed	Maynooth University, Ireland
Nils Gruschka	University of Oslo, Norway
Markus Helfert	Maynooth University, Ireland
Muhammad Irfan Khalid	University of Agder, Norway
Daniela Pöhn	Universität der Bundeswehr München, Germany
Amir Sharif	Fondazione Bruno Kessler, Italy

Program Committee

Ahmed Ali	COMSATS University Islamabad, Pakistan
Andre Büttner	University of Oslo, Norway
Andrea Flamini	University of Potsdam, Germany
Erisa Karafili	University of Southampton, UK
Francesco Buccafurri	Università degli Studi Mediterranea di Reggio Calabria, Italy
Giada Sciarretta	Fondazione Bruno Kessler, Italy
Guido Schmitz	Lancaster University Leipzig, Germany
Ibtisam Ehsan	University of Chinese Academy of Sciences, China
Julien Bringer	Smart Valor, France
Marco Pernpruner	Fondazione Bruno Kessler, Italy
Mariia Bakhtina	Masaryk University, Czech Republic
Michael Kubach	Fraunhofer IAO, Germany
Pieter Philippaerts	Katholieke Universiteit Leuven, Belgium
Roberto Carbone	Fondazione Bruno Kessler, Italy
Saif Ur Rehman Malik	Trinity College Dublin, Ireland
Sara Lazzaro	Università degli Studi Mediterranea di Reggio Calabria, Italy
Simone Onofri	World Wide Web Consortium, USA
Stefan More	Graz University of Technology, Austria
Tamas Bisztray	University of Oslo, Norway
Umair Yousuf	University of Calabria, Italy

Secure and Privacy-Preserving Global Revocation for FIDO2-Based Systems

Nirav Pistolwala and Peter Ebinger(✉)

Frankfurt University of Applied Sciences, Frankfurt am Main, Germany
nirav.pistolwala@gavyoma.com, peter.ebinger@fra-uas.de

Abstract. The widespread adoption of Fast Identity Online 2 (FIDO2) introduces new challenges, including the efficient revocation of compromised authenticators across multiple services. This paper bridges the existing gap by presenting effective strategies for global revocation, thereby ensuring a secure and convenient authentication experience while safeguarding against potential privacy and security risks.

Our contribution is a simple public-private key pair-based approach for efficient global revocation of FIDO2 authenticators, with (1) seamless integration with existing FIDO2 protocols, (2) privacy guarantees by providing strong unlinkability, and (3) protection against impersonation attacks and unauthorized revocation by revocation key protection. We demonstrate the feasibility of our method through a proof-of-concept implementation, ensuring compatibility with the FIDO2 ecosystem.

The proposed solutions are not limited to FIDO2 and can be applied to other protocols that need revocation, making them a valuable contribution to the broader field of authentication.

Keywords: FIDO2 · Revocation · Unlinkability · Privacy

1 Introduction

The growing need for secure and user-friendly authentication has led to the emergence of Fast Identity Online 2 (FIDO2) as a promising solution [2,3]. FIDO2 is a challenge-response protocol that enables passwordless authentication, leveraging public key cryptography to ensure secure access to online services. By shifting the focus from "something you know" to "something you have" passwordless authentication enhances security and convenience.

In a FIDO2-based system, a user's token (authenticator) generates a pair of keys: a private key stored on the authenticator and a public key shared with the server. When a user attempts to access a service, the server sends a challenge to the authenticator, which responds with a signed assertion using the private key. This challenge-response mechanism ensures that only authorized authenticators can access the service, thereby providing strong authentication and protection against phishing and replay attacks.

Z. Afzal et al. (Eds.): ARES 2026 Workshops, LNCS 16900, pp. 579–596, 2027.
https://doi.org/10.1007/978-3-032-35576-8_31

However, the widespread adoption of FIDO2 also introduces new challenges [7,9,13,15,16] that must be addressed. A significant challenge is the efficient revocation of compromised authenticators across multiple services.

In FIDO2-based systems, users usually enroll a single authenticator with multiple services, necessitating a standardized approach for global revocation. The lack of such an approach has significant implications for security, convenience, and user experience. Currently, users and organizations face difficulties in efficiently responding to security incidents and maintaining user trust due to the absence of a robust revocation mechanism.

To address this issue, it is necessary to simultaneously revoke *all keys* associated with the authenticator without requiring manual login to each related service. This procedure is called *global revocation* [10].

This paper aims to address the research question: "What strategies can be employed to enable efficient global revocation of FIDO2 authenticators, balancing user convenience with robust privacy and security?" Resolving this challenge is essential for the broad adoption of FIDO2 [9], as it will facilitate simple and efficient revocation of authenticators by users.

A global revocation procedure for FIDO2 was introduced by Hanzlik et al. [10]. However, this procedure has limitations in terms of achieving unlinkability, as it provides only weak unlinkability. The revocation process can potentially be used to link different credentials associated with the same authenticator. This allows an adversary to link credentials created by the same authenticator after the revocation key has been published.

This limitation in achieving complete unlinkability is a significant concern, because it compromises the anonymity and privacy of users. Specifically, when a revocation key is published, an adversary can exploit this information to link multiple credentials that were created using the same authenticator. This means that even if a user attempts to maintain separate identities or personas, an attacker can still correlate these credentials and potentially deanonymize the user. Furthermore, this limitation may have implications for scenarios where unlinkability is crucial, such as in high-stakes authentication or sensitive transactions. As a result, the solution may not be suitable for applications that require strong anonymity guarantees, highlighting the need for further research to address this limitation and achieve more robust unlinkability.

This study seeks to advance the current understanding of FIDO2 by introducing methods for implementing global revocation in FIDO2-based systems. Our proposed approach utilizes public-private key pair-based technique to facilitate efficient revocation of compromised authenticators, while minimizing potential privacy and security risks. Furthermore, these solutions incorporate strong unlinkability properties, ensuring that user identities remain protected and anonymous. The proposed method is designed to be seamlessly integrated into the existing FIDO2 ecosystem, enabling straightforward and non-disruptive implementation by vendors and users alike.

2 Contributions

In this paper, we present a secure and privacy-preserving approach for revocation of FIDO2 authenticators. According to a usability study by Lyastani et al. [9], it is essential to enable efficient revocation of compromised authenticators across multiple services, which becomes impractical through manual means. To address this issue, we propose a simple, user-friendly global revocation procedure that revokes a FIDO2 authenticator for multiple Relying Parties (RPs) without requiring manual log in to each related RP. Furthermore, the same authenticator will not be usable for registering with any RP. This procedure relies on publishing revocation information that is then noticed by all RPs. The revocation information must be stored securely offline by the user, on a piece of paper. In terms of usability, adoptability, security, and privacy, we achieve three key properties:

1. **Seamless Integration**: We present a solution for global revocation which is compatible with the existing FIDO2 ecosystem, enabling easy integration and minimizing user disruption. A proof-of-concept implementation demonstrates the compatibility and interoperability of the proposed solution with the existing FIDO2 ecosystem.
2. **Privacy and Strong Unlinkability before and after Revocation**: The proposed solution ensures privacy by ensuring that all credentials and RPs are unlinkable before and after revocation information is published, as revocation information is generated at random and independently for each registration, providing no structural relationships.
3. **Protection against Impersonation Attacks and Unauthorized Revocation**: In our solution, an attacker cannot revoke an authenticator on behalf of a user because the revocation key is securely stored on the authenticator itself and is only accessible to the user once, during initialisation.

By achieving these properties, our approach ensures a secure and private revocation mechanism for FIDO2 authenticators. The design and implementation of our solution also provides protection against malicious clients [14].

Our approach utilizes a public-private key pair, which is generated once and stored on the FIDO2 authenticator, referred to as the revocation public-private key pair (pk_{revoc}, sk_{revoc}). For each new registration process with an RP, the authenticator generates a public-private credential key pair (pk_{cred}, sk_{cred}).

The authenticator then generates revocation information as follows: First, a random nonce, referred to as the revocation nonce RN, is generated. Then a Key Encapsulation Mechanism (KEM) is used to generate the encrypted revocation information[1]. The encapsulation algorithm $(k, c) := Encap(sk_{revoc})$ is applied using the private key sk_{revoc} to produce a randomly chosen secret key k and the encapsulation ciphertext c. The revocation information consists of a

[1] Please note: In the proposed scheme a modified REVERSE-KEM is used as described in more detail in Sect. 4.2.

triple (v, w, c), where $v := Hash(pk_{cred}, RN)$. $w := Enc(k, RN)$ and c is the encapsulation ciphertext.

When a user wants to revoke an authenticator, pk_{revoc} is published to the global revocation server (GRS). The GRS announces the newly available information. Each RP asks the GRS for proof that it has the related pk_{revoc} by sending the pair (w, c). The response from the GRS is then validated by the RP. The GRS creates a proof using pk_{revoc} and its encapsulation ciphertext c to decrypt w. The GRS uses the public key pk_{revoc} and the encapsulation c to retrieve the encapsulated secret key $k' := Decap(pk_{revoc}, c)$. The secret key is then used to decrypt w to retrieve the proof $RN' = Dec(k', w)$. The GRS responds back to the RP with the proof RN'. The RP calculates $v' = Hash(pk_{cred}, RN')$ and verifies that $v' = v$.

3 Related Work

Global revocation techniques have been extensively studied in various contexts, including anonymous credentials and group signatures. For instance, Camenisch et al. introduced the concept of dynamic accumulators, which enable efficient hashing of large sets of inputs into a single value, while allowing for dynamic addition and deletion of values at a cost independent of the number of accumulated values [6]. They provided a construction of dynamic accumulators and an efficient zero-knowledge proof of an accumulated value, proven secure under the strong RSA assumption. Notably, their work enabled revocation of anonymous credentials, as well as membership revocation for recent group signature and identity escrow schemes.

Building on this foundation, Boneh et al. constructed a short group signature scheme that supports verifier-local revocation (VLR), where revocation messages are only sent to signature verifiers, eliminating the need to contact individual signers upon revocation [4]. Their scheme is based on the Strong Diffie-Hellman assumption and the Decision Linear assumption in bilinear groups, and features signatures as short as standard RSA signatures with comparable security.

Furthermore, Camenisch et al. presented a scalable revocation scheme for privacy-enhancing attribute-based credentials (PABCs), enabling efficient proof generation using offline constrained devices and verification of proofs and revocation status in logarithmic time [5]. Their scheme utilizes n-times unlinkable proofs. As an additional contribution, they designed an efficient proof of knowledge of weak Boneh-Boyen signatures that eliminates the need for pairing computations on the prover side.

Hanzlik et al. [10] introduced a revocation procedure for FIDO2-based on the BIP32 (Bitcoin Improvement Proposal 32) standard used in cryptocurrency wallets. One limitation of using BIP32 for revocation is that it may not provide complete unlinkability, as the revocation process can potentially be used to link different credentials associated with the same authenticator.

4 Global Revocation: Design and Architecture

The following section presents the cryptographic concept of global revocation using a public-private revocation key pair. This affects the FIDO2 registration process, but not the authentication process. Therefore, the authentication process is omitted in the following sections. This is followed by a description of the inverse usage of public key and private key in KEM in our proposed system. The section concludes with a privacy analysis with respect to unlinkability and a security analysis of different attack scenarios.

4.1 Cryptographic Concept to Global Revocation

The current FIDO2 protocol lacks a mechanism for revoking compromised authenticators. This section aims to formally define a process for the global revocation of FIDO2 authenticators, enabling users to easily and efficiently revoke their compromised authenticators across all registered RPs (see Fig. 1).

Design Objectives. The design objective is to prevent two colluding RPs from linking the revocation information of a user who registered with both RPs before or after revoking an authenticator and the corresponding credentials. Therefore, we introduce the GRS to hide this relationship from any colluding RPs or an attacker who gains access to the revocation information.

Only the GRS should know the revocation public key pk_{revoc} of an authenticator after a user has revoked it, and pk_{revoc} should be hidden from any other party, including any RP. Upon a user's request to revoke an authenticator for all credentials, the GRS computes revocation proofs without being able to tell whether the proof is valid or not. Calculating the proof should not reveal any information about which credentials may belong to the same user.

The GRS ecosystem could adopt a governance and operational model similar to that of the public PKI infrastructure (Browser Forum, certification authorities, ...). A central body, such as the FIDO Alliance, could define general technical standards, security requirements, operational policies, and audit criteria for GRS operators. These independent GRS operators would then be responsible for collecting, processing and distributing revocation information in accordance with the specified requirements. In order to establish a transparent, interoperable and accountable revocation infrastructure, web service platform providers, RPs and FIDO2 authenticator vendors would only cooperate with trusted and compliant GRS operators.

Assumptions. The following assumptions are made for the cryptographic primitives and algorithms employed in our concept. Cryptographic outputs should appear random, independent and non-correlatable across executions. Encryption, hashing and key exchange operations should not reveal any hidden structural, relational or identifying information. Furthermore, implementations should not leak exploitable information through timing, metadata, errors, or observable computational behavior.

The assumptions about the capabilities of the attacker are that they can control multiple RPs and correlate information across websites. This enables them to view messages exchanged via the network between the authenticator, the client and the values stored on the RPs, including the revocation information triple (v, w, c). The attacker does not have access to the public revocation keys pk_{revoc}. The authenticator is assumed to be cryptographically trusted and does not reveal the stored private revocation key sk_{revoc} to an attacker.

As a trusted third party, the GRS is assumed to provide a reliable service. It does not reveal any information about public revocation keys pk_{revoc}, correctly calculates revocation proofs and provides them to the RPs.

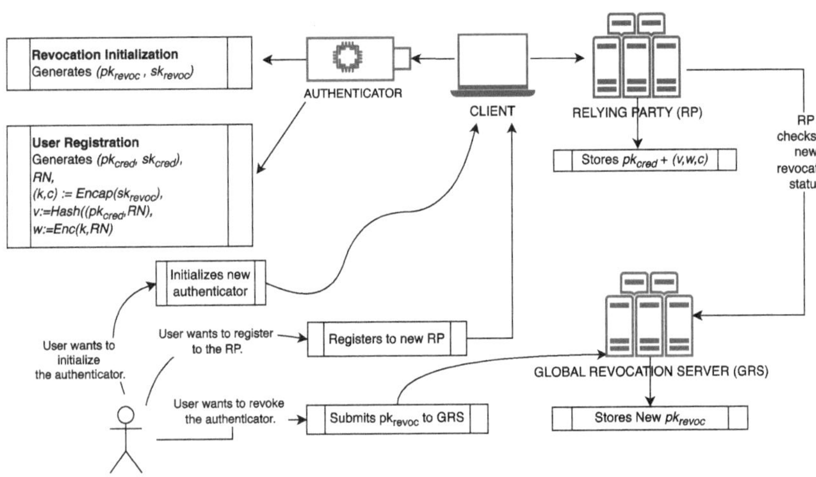

Fig. 1. Global revocation concept using public-private revocation key pair.

(1) Revocation Initialisation. The global revocation mechanism utilizes a public-private key pair, where the authenticator generates a unique revocation key pair and securely stores the private key sk_{revoc} in its internal storage. The corresponding public key pk_{revoc} serves as the global revocation key. Note that sk_{revoc} remains confined to the authenticator and is never exposed or extractable, whereas pk_{revoc} is accessible only once to the user, who is instructed to store it safely offline, e.g., on a piece of paper. By limiting access to pk_{revoc}, we enable a security property that prevents an attacker from gaining access to it, even if the authenticator is compromised.

(2) User Registration. When a user registers with an RP, the authenticator generates a credential key pair (pk_{cred}, sk_{cred}) and securely stores the private key sk_{cred} on its internal storage. The corresponding public key pk_{cred} will be sent to the RP together with revocation information (v, w, c), which are then validated and stored by the RP.

Upon registering new credentials with an RP, the authenticator additionally generates a cryptographically secure random nonce, denoted as the revocation nonce (RN).

Then the encapsulation algorithm $(k, c) := Encap(sk_{revoc})$ is applied using sk_{revoc} to produce a randomly chosen secret key k and the encapsulation ciphertext c. The revocation information consists of a triple (v, w, c), where $v := Hash(pk_{cred}, RN)$. $w := Enc(k, RN)$ and c is the encapsulation ciphertext.

A unique triple of randomly generated values (v, w, c) is employed for each new credential registration. This preserves user privacy and ensures strong unlinkability between different registrations and RPs. This property prevents an attacker from linking multiple registrations or identifying users across different RPs.

(3) Authenticator Revocation. To initiate authenticator revocation, the user submits the corresponding global revocation public key pk_{revoc} to the Global Revocation Server (GRS).

In order to mitigate denial-of-service attacks against the GRS, it is possible to employ rate limiting, challenge-response mechanisms and submission fees to increase the temporal, computational and economic cost associated with revocation submissions. Submission fees should be implemented using privacy-preserving cryptocurrencies or equivalent anonymous payment mechanisms, to avoid creating a link between the payer and the corresponding revocation request.

(4) Revocation Checking. Each RP requests proof from the GRS that it has the related pk_{revoc} by sending (w, c). The GRS creates a proof using pk_{revoc} and the encapsulation c to decrypt w. The GRS takes the public key pk_{revoc} and the encapsulation c to retrieve the encapsulated secret key $k' := Decap(pk_{revoc}, c)$. The secret key is then used to decrypt w and to retrieve the proof $RN' = Dec(k', w)$. This way GRS computes revocation proofs without being able to determine their validity. The calculation process always terminates successfully without revealing any information (see Sect. 4.2).

The GRS responds back to the RP with the proof RN'. The RP calculates $v' := Hash(pk_{cred}, RN')$ and verifies that $v' = v$. If true, the RP revokes access related to that credential.

The components involved in the revocation concept and their knowledge scope are outlined in Table 1.

4.2 Inverse Usage of Public Key and Private Key in KEM

The following explains why a KEM is required for the proposed system, and why standard KEMs are not suitable.

Table 1. Breakdown of components and knowledge scope.

Component	Knowledge Scope
Authenticator	(pk_{revoc}, sk_{revoc}), (pk_{cred}, sk_{cred}), (v, w, c)
RP	pk_{cred}, (v, w, c)
GRS	pk_{revoc}, (w, c)

1. *Necessity of a KEM:* The direct use of an asymmetric encryption scheme would enable the GRS to detect whether a proof is valid, since invalid proofs would cause decryption to fail due to padding errors, whereas valid proofs would succeed. Therefore, a KEM is used instead, which prevents this distinction and preserves unlinkability, as the GRS cannot determine whether the revocation proof it provides to an RP is valid.
2. *Publication of global revocation public key for revocation:* In asymmetric encryption schemes, the public key can typically be derived from the private key, but not vice versa. Therefore the global revocation private key sk_{revoc} remains securely stored on the authenticator and never leaves it, whereas the global revocation public key pk_{revoc} is published during revocation. This way, publishing the global revocation public key information does not compromise the secrecy of the corresponding key.

For these reasons *REVERSE-KEM* is introduced, which reverses the roles of the public and private keys in the encapsulation and decapsulation steps of the KEM compared to those in common implementations and recommendations (cf. [1,11]). The presented implementation uses RSA public-private key encryption. However, the scheme can be adapted for other cryptographic algorithms.

If an attacker could generate revocation information that appears cryptographically valid, the system records could contain revocations that were not initiated by the legitimate user. However, as the private revocation key sk_{revoc} is securely stored on the authenticator and never leaves it, it is impossible to carry out an impersonation attack. This remains true even after the revocation information has been published. Therefore, REVERSE-KEM is needed so that the public key is published instead of the private key.

4.3 Strong Unlinkability

We use a separate public-private key pair for revocation, as it can be managed independently of each credential's keys. This also has the benefit that even if the revocation private key is compromised by an attacker, the attacker cannot use it to log into any account. By design, the revocation information serves only to lock access to an account, not to gain access. The revocation public-private key pair (pk_{revoc}, sk_{revoc}) is generated randomly and independently on each authenticator, therefore the revocation information of different authenticators cannot be linked.

In our concept a revocation information triple (v, w, c) is used to provide strong unlinkability:

- $v := Hash(pk_{cred}, RN)$ is the hash value of a random number RN (which is different for each user registration with an RP).
- $w := Enc(k, RN)$ is the encryption of this random number RN with a randomly chosen secret key k.
- c is the encapsulation ciphertext of a randomly chosen secret key k.

Distributing revocation keys directly to the RPs for self-calculation of revocation proofs would compromise unlinkability. Specifically, if the global revocation public key pk_{revoc} is known, an attacker could link credentials used across multiple RPs if the attacker gains access to the revocation information (v, w, c) stored on two or more RPs.

Therefore, the GRS is used to ensure the secrecy and privacy of the pk_{revoc}. By design, the proofs generated by the GRS can be validated by each RP independently, without revealing pk_{revoc} to them. Consequently, even if the same authenticator is used with multiple RPs, it is impossible to link them. Even if the same authenticator is used for multiple registrations at the same RP the registration information remains unlinkable, as a different random nonce RN is used for each registration.

In our approach, strong unlinkability is preserved even after the revocation key is published, as each entity, including the RP and the GRS, only possesses the information necessary for its intended function as outlined in Table 1. Specifically, the revocation public key pk_{revoc} is exclusively known to the GRS, which ensures that it remains confidential and is not shared with any RP.

4.4 Security Analysis

The security and unlinkability property of the proposed revocation scheme and its implementation are analysed in more detail below, considering different attack scenarios.

Scenario 1: Eavesdropping on Revocation Messages. Consider a scenario in which an attacker intercepts revocation messages transmitted over the network between the GRS and the RP. Even in this case, the user registration credential remains unlinkable due to the use of a random nonce, which is unique for each user credential, including those generated by the same authenticator used for multiple registrations on the same RP.

Furthermore, all communications involving the publication of the pk_{revoc} are secured using standard Transport Layer Security (TLS) encryption. Specifically, this means that all interactions between the user and the GRS are protected, thereby preventing any potential linkage of credentials.

Scenario 2: Compromised RP Servers. Consider a scenario in which an attacker gains access to credential information stored on the RP servers. Even in this case, the credentials remain unlinkable because w is an encrypted nonce that varies with each registration. Moreover, without access to pk_{revoc}, it is impossible for the attacker to link the credentials. This highlights the importance of our design choice, where the RP is never granted access to or knowledge of pk_{revoc}, thereby ensuring the unlinkability of user credentials.

Scenario 3: Resilience to Timing Attacks. Consider a scenario in which an attacker has access to multiple RPs and attempts to launch a timing attack by tracking the exact time of revocation on one RP and searching for corresponding revocations on other RPs. However, even in this case, our system remains unlinkable due to the inherent properties of a large-scale revocation ecosystem. Specifically, with numerous pk_{revoc} potentially being published simultaneously, it becomes increasingly difficult for an attacker to identify a unique correlation between revocations across different RPs. Furthermore, the frequency of checking revocations may vary significantly across RPs, making it even more challenging for an attacker to synchronize their observations and launch a successful timing attack.

The cornerstone of our approach lies in ensuring that the GRS never discloses revocation keys to any entity, with particular emphasis on secure storage and management of these keys on the server. This means that the GRS must implement robust security measures to prevent unauthorized access, leakage, or exposure of revocation keys, thereby safeguarding the integrity of the system.

5 Extending FIDO2 for Global Revocation: Proposed Technical Specification

We present an implementation of global revocation as a standard-conformant FIDO2 extension [8,17,19]. This allows credential revocation to be facilitated by leveraging the existing framework. The presented specifications of the extension are in accordance with the FIDO2 standard. This extension needs to be utilized solely during the revocation initialisation and credential registration processes. It enables the RP to request and retrieve information regarding global revocation from the authenticator.

As an authenticator extension [19], *all processing occurs exclusively on the authenticator itself.* The client or platform serves merely as a passive intermediary, relaying information between parties without requiring any additional action beyond facilitating the exchange of the revocation information (v, w, c) from the authenticator to the RP.

Upon initial use of the authenticator, a unique global revocation public-private key pair (pk_{revoc}, sk_{revoc}) shall be generated. This key pair must be stored securely within the authenticator's trusted storage environment. Throughout the authenticator's entire lifetime, until it undergoes a reset, the same pk_{revoc} and sk_{revoc} will remain in effect. The authenticator must ensure that access to the sk_{revoc} is strictly restricted and entirely unreadable by any means. Furthermore, neither the authenticator nor the client platform shall be able to disclose or provide the RP with direct access to pk_{revoc}.

pk_{revoc} can be accessed by the user through a display directly attached to the authenticator or a specific platform/client command, as described in Sect. 5.2.

Notably, the retrieval of pk_{revoc} is a one-time operation; once generated and accessed, it cannot be retrieved again. This ensures that pk_{revoc} remains securely protected and its disclosure is strictly restricted.

5.1 Proposed CTAP2 Extension: Public-Private Key Pair-Based Global Revocation

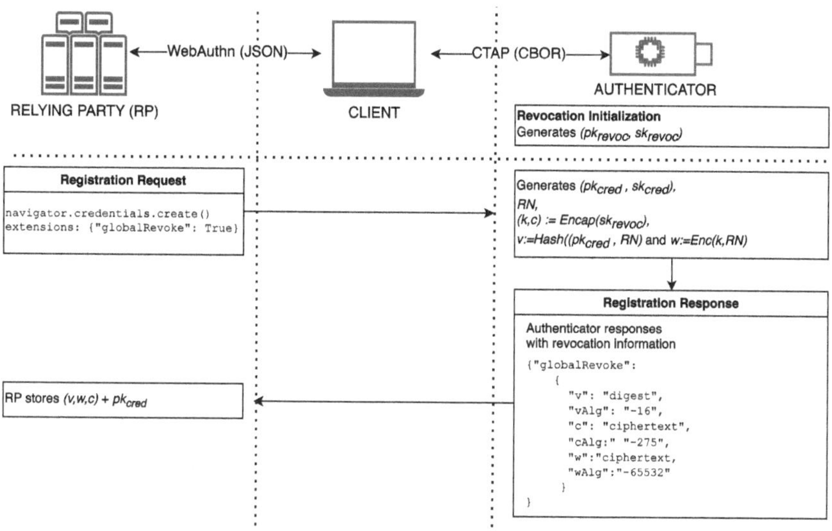

Fig. 2. Global revocation extension process.

A proof-of-concept extension is defined, intended for implementation across the entire FIDO2 stack, including web applications (RPs), client applications (browsers and platforms), and authenticators.

Global Revocation Extension. The `globalRevoke` extension is defined as an authenticator extension [8,19], which enables the authenticator to provide revocation information to the RP. This extension takes a boolean input value, indicating whether the authenticator should process the extension. The output contains the revocation information. Notably, this extension does not require special client-side processing, as the client can simply pass through all inputs and outputs to and from the authenticator as shown in Fig. 2. The authenticator's processing of this extension involves constructing the revocation information and returning it as output. Our globalRevoke extension is identified by the identifier `globalRevoke` in both the CTAP and WebAuthn protocols.

Extension Processing. RP initiates a credential registration request using the browser API, specifically by calling `navigator.credentials.create()`. This function takes a parameter object with a `publicKey` member, which, accepts an extensions attribute. The extensions attribute contains the extension identifier, along with inputs, such as `extensions: "globalRevoke": true`.

Web browsers, being the most common FIDO2 client, are the next component in the FIDO2 stack. They receive the registration request from the RP and facilitate communication with the authenticator. Note that communication between the RP and FIDO2 client occurs in JSON format, while communication between the FIDO2 client and authenticator occurs in CBOR format. To facilitate this, the WebAuthn standard [19] defines conversion rules between JSON and CBOR. After the extension has been successfully processed by the browser and authenticator, the outputs of the extension can be accessed using `credential.getClientExtensionResults()`, which returns an object with extension identifiers as keys and the corresponding extension outputs as values.

Importantly, although the client processes these extension data, all extension data is signed by the authenticator using credential private key sk_{cred}. Consequently, any attempt by a malicious client to tamper with the extension data will be detected by the RP, and registration will be denied. This protects our solution against attacks by the malicious client [14].

Note that, although the WebAuthn specification permits the pass-through of unknown extensions, current major client browsers do not support pass-through extensions [17] without prior registration in the official registry [12]. However, our proof-of-concept overcomes this limitation by leveraging the fact that the RP is unable to send unknown extensions to the authenticator, whereas the authenticator is capable of sending unknown extensions to the RP. So, we have implemented a default behaviour in the authenticator, whereby revocation information is sent to the RP on each registration, effectively hardcoding this functionality into the authenticator.

Cryptographic Implementation. Our proposed solution employs an RSA Key Encapsulation Mechanism (KEM) combined with AES-CTR, using a 256-bit key for encryption. The authenticator generates a 32-byte random revocation nonce (RN) and computes $v := Hash(pk_{cred}, RN)$, $(k, c) := Encap(sk_{revoc})$ and $w := Enc(k, RN)$. If the authenticator successfully generates (v, w, c), it responds with the CBOR map entry in the `extensions` fields to the platform.

Note that in Fig. 2, algorithm number `-275` is used as an example, since this cryptographic algorithm (REVERSE-KEM) is new and currently not registered in the registry [18]. AES-CTR is listed as deprecated in the registry [18] as it lacks integrity protection. However, it remains a secure choice for our proposed use case, as we only require confidentiality and want to avoid key integrity protection as described in Sect. 4.

5.2 Proposed CTAP2 Command: Retrieve Global Revocation Key

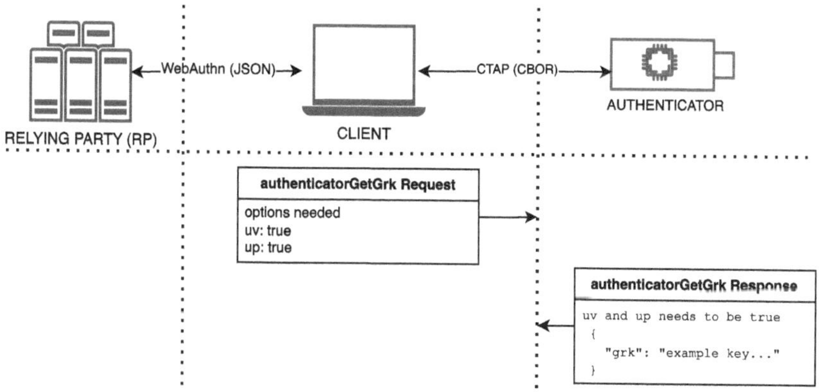

Fig. 3. Retrieval Process for Global Revocation Keys.

To globally revoke the authenticator, the user must publish pk_{revoc} to the GRS. To achieve this, it is essential to store pk_{revoc} externally (e.g., on a piece of paper) so that it remains accessible even if access to the authenticator is not possible.

There are two methods for obtaining the revocation key from the authenticator. To mitigate potential security risks, pk_{revoc} should be retrievable only once from the authenticator. This strict one-time retrieval policy applies uniformly across both methods, and any subsequent attempts to retrieve pk_{revoc} using either method will be explicitly blocked.

- If the authenticator has a display attached to it, pk_{revoc} should be displayed strictly one-time as a QR code, providing an easy-to-scan visual representation of the key.
- Alternatively, the client/platform can retrieve pk_{revoc} strictly one-time via a CTAP2 command `authenticatorGetGrk` as shown in Fig. 3.

The `authenticatorGetGrk` command should only be processed if both User Verification (UV) and User Presence (UP) flags are set to true, and pk_{revoc} has never been displayed/fetched before. This additional security measure prevents unauthorized access to the key.

The source code for our proof-of-concept implementation can be accessed online[2].

Figure 4 illustrates the setup of the RP2040 microcontroller chip, specifically the Raspberry Pi Pico H Board, as an FIDO2 authenticator with an attached display. An expander board connects the microcontroller, the display, and the

[2] https://grs-code.gavyoma.com.

Fig. 4. Proof-of-Concept FIDO2 Authenticator with Global Revocation Capability.

microcontroller debugger. The microcontroller is connected to the client via a Micro-USB cable. In this configuration, the microcontroller features a button that serves as a user presence indicator, enabling the user to register or log in to an RP. The attached display shows the revocation public key pk_{revoc} as a QR code, facilitating easy visualization and scanning.

6 Usability

We recommend using a QR code for revocation initialisation to allow for simple usability. This ephemeral QR code contains only pk_{revoc} and is displayed until the authenticator is disconnected from the host platform. This design intentionally limits exposure time, mitigating risks of accidental sharing, phishing, or unauthorized copying, while enforcing the critical principle that sensitive cryptographic material must be secured before the device becomes operational. Smartphone scanning enables straightforward copy-pasting (as demonstrated in our proof-of-concept), while users may alternatively photograph and archive pk_{revoc} in a secure vault or printed medium-options. If the one-time retrieval is missed entirely, the recommended fallback is to reset the authenticator to regenerate pk_{revoc}, reinforcing that operational use should never precede successful capture.

For display-less hardware, the authenticator may use CTAP2 command for retrieval of pk_{revoc} as described in Sect. 5.2.

Users can easily submit their revocation key to the GRS for authenticator revocation via a standard web browser, receiving explicit confirmation upon successful server-side validation and acceptance.

7 Complexity and Scalability Analysis

The following analysis considers the complexity and scalability of the system in terms of computation cost and network communication requirements.

- for each step
- on a specific component

when introducing the global revocation concept into the FIDO2 ecosystem.

Table 2. Cost analysis for each individual global revocation steps

Step	Computational Cost (# Operations)	Communication Cost (Amount of Data)
(1) Revocation Initialisation	$O(1)$	–
(2) User Registration	$O(revkeys)$	$O(1)$
(3) Authenticator Revocation	$O(1)$	$O(1)$
(4) Revocation Checking on GRS		
RP Requests	$O(rps \cdot newkeys)$	$O(rps \cdot newkeys)$
GRS Proof Calculation	$O(rps \cdot newkeys)$	–
Proof Distribution	$O(rps \cdot newkeys)$	$O(rps \cdot newkeys)$

newkeys: Average number of newly registered keys per RP
revkeys: Total number of revoked keys
rps: Total number of RPs

The analysis considers the computing and communication required when a specific step is executed as part of regular ongoing operations. Therefore, in each step only information (delta) needs to be processed that is newly created or changed.

Previous results remain locally stored: revocation keys that have already been processes on the GRS, and revocation proofs that have already been calculated on each RP. This means that the evaluation only calculates the delta for newly available information and assumes that the results of previously processed revocation information are already available on RP and GRS.

Table 2 provides a summary of the cost analysis for each individual step of the global revocation concept:

- The steps *Revocation Initialisation* and *Authenticator Revocation* are performed only once at all. They require a *fixed number* of operations and no or a *fixed amount* of communication messages between to the user and the GRS.
- The step *User Registration* is performed only once for each registration. Therefore, this requires a *fixed number* of operations on the client and the RP. However, for each newly registered key it should also be checked using

the GRS if the authenticator used was already revoked before. The number of operations on the GRS is proportional to the total number of proofs that must be newly created, which is equal to the total number of already revoked keys. A *fixed amount* of communication messages is required between to the user and the GRS.
- The *Revocation Checking on the GRS* consists of three steps:
  - *RP Requests:* The GRS receives the (w, c) pairs for each newly registered public key pk_{revoc} from all RP in order to check for a new revocation proof. The number of operations is proportional to the total number of RPs multiplied by the number of newly registered keys per RP. The amount of communication data is proportional to the number of RPs multiplied by the average number of newly registered keys per RP.
  - *GRS Proof Calculation:* GRS creates a proof by decrypting w. The number of operations is proportional to the total number of proofs that must be created, which is equal to the number of RPs multiplied by the average number of newly registered keys per RP. This is an internal calculation process that does not require any external communication.
  - *Proof Distribution:* GRS sends the complete list of proofs to all RPs. The number of operations is proportional to the total number of RPs multiplied by the average number of newly registered keys per RP. The amount of communication data is proportional to the number of RPs multiplied by the average number of newly registered keys per RP.

In summary, the computation cost and network communication requirements for a given instance are at most constant for two of the steps. The GRS requires the maximum computation cost for the calculation of the proofs. For user registration, these costs are proportional to the total number of revoked keys. For revocation checking, the cost is proportional to the number of RPs multiplied by the average number of newly registered keys per RP. The maximum communication cost is required for proof requests from the RPs to the GRS, as well as the respective responses. This cost is also proportional to the number of RPs multiplied by the average number of newly registered keys per RP.

Therefore, the proposed system scales well in terms of maximum computation and communication, which are linear in respect to the total number of revoked keys for user registration and proportional to the number of RPs and the average number of newly registered keys per RP for revocation checking.

8 Conclusion and Future Work

In this paper, we presented and analysed an effective and secure implementation of a global revocation solution for FIDO2 authenticators. Our solution protects user privacy by providing strong unlinkability. It is based on a public-private key pair approach that can be integrated directly as an extension into the FIDO2 standard without any modification to the existing standard being required. We provided a technical specification for implementation and demonstrated our implementation in a proof of concept.

Future work will focus on the formal analysis and verification of the proposed revocation protocol, particularly the unconventional use of the KEM primitive. This includes developing a formal security model and proving the claimed security and unlinkability properties under well-defined cryptographic assumptions.

The implementation presented in this paper is based on a reverse KEM which uses RSA as an asymmetric cryptographic scheme. Future work should also investigate adopting this using new post-quantum algorithms and KEM mechanisms such as Kyber (ML-KEM), in order to achieve post-quantum resistance and improved performance.

Disclosure of Interests. The authors have no competing interests to declare that are relevant to the content of this article.

References

1. Alagic, G., et al.: NIST Special Publication 800–227. Recommend. Key-Encap. Mech. (2025). https://doi.org/10.6028/NIST.SP.800-227
2. Barbosa, M., Boldyreva, A., Chen, S., Warinschi, B.: Provable security analysis of FIDO2. In: Malkin, T., Peikert, C. (eds.) Advances in Cryptology - CRYPTO 2021, pp. 125–156. Springer International Publishing, Cham (2021). https://doi.org/10.1007/978-3-030-84252-9_5
3. Bindel, N., Cremers, C., Zhao, M.: FIDO2, CTAP 2.1, and WebAuthn 2: provable security and post-quantum instantiation. In: 2023 IEEE Symposium on Security and Privacy (SP), pp. 1471–1490. (2023). https://doi.org/10.1109/SP46215.2023.10179454
4. Boneh, D., Shacham, H.: Group signatures with verifier-local revocation. In: Proceedings of the 11th ACM Conference on Computer and Communications Security, pp. 168–177. CCS '04, Association for Computing Machinery, New York, NY, USA (2004). https://doi.org/10.1145/1030083.1030106
5. Camenisch, J., Drijvers, M., Hajny, J.: Scalable revocation scheme for anonymous credentials based on N-times unlinkable proofs. In: Proceedings of the 2016 ACM on Workshop on Privacy in the Electronic Society, pp. 123–133. WPES '16, Association for Computing Machinery, New York, NY, USA (2016). https://doi.org/10.1145/2994620.2994625
6. Camenisch, J., Lysyanskaya, A.: Dynamic accumulators and application to efficient revocation of anonymous credentials. In: Yung, M. (ed.) Advances in Cryptology — CRYPTO 2002, pp. 61–76. Springer Berlin Heidelberg, Berlin, Heidelberg (2002). https://doi.org/10.1007/3-540-45708-9_5
7. Farke, F.M., Lorenz, L., Schnitzler, T., Markert, P., Dürmuth, M.: "You still use the password after all" – exploring FIDO2 security keys in a small company. In: Sixteenth Symposium on Usable Privacy and Security (SOUPS 2020), pp. 19–35. USENIX Association (2020). https://www.usenix.org/conference/soups2020/presentation/farke
8. FIDO Alliance: Client to authenticator protocol (CTAP) (2025). https://fidoalliance.org/specs/fido-v2.2-ps-20250714/fido-client-to-authenticator-protocol-v2.2-ps-20250714.html. Accessed 05 Mar 2026
9. Ghorbani Lyastani, S., Schilling, M., Neumayr, M., Backes, M., Bugiel, S.: Is FIDO2 the Kingslayer of user authentication? A comparative usability study of

FIDO2 passwordless authentication. In: 2020 IEEE Symposium on Security and Privacy (SP), pp. 268–285 (2020). https://doi.org/10.1109/SP40000.2020.00047
10. Hanzlik, L., Loss, J., Wagner, B.: Token meets wallet: formalizing privacy and revocation for FIDO2. In: 2023 IEEE Symposium on Security and Privacy (SP), pp. 1491–1508. (2023). https://doi.org/10.1109/SP46215.2023.10179373
11. Housley, R., Turner, S.: Use of the RSA-KEM algorithm in the cryptographic message syntax (CMS). RFC 9690 (2025). https://doi.org/10.17487/RFC9690
12. Jones, M., Mandyam, G.: Web authentication (WebAuthn). https://www.iana.org/assignments/webauthn/webauthn.xhtml (2023). Accessed 05 Mar 2026
13. Kepkowski, M., Machulak, M., Wood, I., Kaafar, D.: Challenges with Passwordless FIDO2 in an enterprise setting: a usability study. In: 2023 IEEE Secure Development Conference (SecDev), pp. 37–48 (2023). https://doi.org/10.1109/SecDev56634.2023.00017
14. Kuchhal, D., Saad, M., Oest, A., Li, F.: Evaluating the security posture of real-world FIDO2 deployments. In: Proceedings of the 2023 ACM SIGSAC Conference on Computer and Communications Security, pp. 2381–2395. CCS '23, Association for Computing Machinery, New York, NY, USA (2023). https://doi.org/10.1145/3576915.3623063
15. Lassak, L., Hildebrandt, A., Golla, M., Ur, B.: "It's stored, hopefully, on an encrypted server": mitigating users' misconceptions about FIDO2 biometric WebAuthn. In: 30th USENIX Security Symposium (USENIX Security 21). pp. 91–108. USENIX Association (2021). https://www.usenix.org/conference/usenixsecurity21/presentation/lassak
16. Owens, K., Anise, O., Krauss, A., Ur, B.: User perceptions of the usability and security of smartphones as FIDO2 roaming authenticators. In: Seventeenth Symposium on Usable Privacy and Security (SOUPS 2021), pp. 57–76. USENIX Association (2021). https://www.usenix.org/conference/soups2021/presentation/owens
17. Putz, F., Schön, S., Hollick, M.: Future-proof web authentication: bring your own FIDO2 extensions. Presented at the (2021). https://doi.org/10.1007/978-3-030-93747-8_2 Emerging Technologies for Authorization and Authentication
18. Schaad, J.: IANA CBOR Object Signing and Encryption (COSE) Algorithms Registry. https://www.iana.org/assignments/cose/cose.xhtml#algorithms. Accessed 05 Mar 2026
19. World Wide Web Consortium: Web authentication: an API for accessing public key credentials — level 2 (2021). https://www.w3.org/TR/webauthn-2/. Accessed 05 Mar 2026

Deniability for Signed Credentials: Revisiting the Authenticated Channel Vs. Signed Data Debate in the EUDI Wallet

Magdalena Bertram[1(✉)] and Anja Lehmann[2]

[1] Fraunhofer AISEC, Berlin, Germany
magdalena.bertram@aisec.fraunhofer.de
[2] Hasso Plattner Institute, University of Potsdam, Potsdam, Germany
anja.lehmann@hpi.de

Abstract. The European Digital Identity Wallet (EUDI Wallet) is currently adopting ECDSA-based signed credentials as part of its core architecture, which raised concerns that such designs inherently lack plausible deniability compared to authenticated-channel approaches such as the German electronic identity card. This paper revisits this perceived trade-off and argues that it is not a property of signature schemes themselves, but of the credential presentation protocol. We show that standard cryptographic techniques – specifically lightweight OR-proofs over the native ECDSA verification equation – can be used to transform signed credential presentations into non-transferable, verifier-bound transcripts. Our contribution is not a new cryptographic primitive, but a careful instantiation of well-established techniques within the EUDI context, showing that deniability can be added to signed credentials while preserving their deployment advantages.

1 Introduction

The European Digital Identity Wallet (EUDI-Wallet) is a major ongoing deployment of a digital identity infrastructure in the European Union. By the end of 2026, every EU Member State is required to provide at least one EUDI Wallet to its citizens for storing and presenting identity documents, attribute attestations, and other credentials [16]. The technical architecture is currently being finalised, with the Architecture and Reference Framework [14] serving as the de facto standard for implementations across Member States.

A central design decision concerns how the authenticity and integrity of presented identity data is guaranteed. Two fundamentally different approaches have been discussed (in Germany): *authenticated channels* and *signed credentials*. In the authenticated-channel approach – the mechanism underlying the German electronic identity card (*Personalausweis*) [5,6] – a trusted chip on the user's device runs an interactive protocol with the verifier that establishes a shared symmetric session key and authenticates the chip's possession of an issuer-certified

Z. Afzal et al. (Eds.): ARES 2026 Workshops, LNCS 16900, pp. 597–615, 2027.
https://doi.org/10.1007/978-3-032-35576-8_32

key; the attributes are then transmitted over the resulting authenticated channel. In the signed-credentials approach, the issuer produces a publicly verifiable signature over the user's attributes that the wallet stores and forwards to a verifier at presentation time, with no issuer interaction needed at presentation. In October 2024, Germany settled this debate for its national EUDI-Wallet by deciding in favour of signed credentials, specifically ECDSA-signed SD-JWT credentials [7]. The decision drew criticism from consumer and data protections organisations [12,13,27,28], who argue that signed credentials lack a privacy property that the authenticated-channel design of the eID provides: *plausible deniability*, the property that a verifier (also referred to as Relying Party) cannot prove to a third party that a particular credential presentation took place. In the authenticated-channel architecture, the symmetric session key shared between chip and verifier means the verifier could itself have produced any authentication tag, so the transcript carries no transferable conviction. A persistent issuer signature has no such property: anyone in possession of the signed presentation can independently verify the issuer's endorsement, and the resulting transcripts therefore become attractive targets for data theft and unauthorised trading [27].

This framing is misleading though: The absence of deniability is not an inherent property of signature-based credentials, but a property of how they are presented. In particular, well understood cryptographic techniques allow transforming publicly verifiable signatures into designated-verifier forms at presentation time, ensuring that transcripts remain convincing to the intended verifier but are non-transferable to third parties.

Designated Verifier Signatures. These techniques are known as *Universal Designated Verifier Signatures* (UDVS), introduced by Steinfeld et al. [25] as a generalisation of the designated verifier signatures of Jakobsson, Sako, and Impagliazzo [20]. Here the verifier holds its own key pair. Using only the verifier's public key, the holder of a valid standard signature can transform it at presentation time into a *designated-verifier* signature. Such a signature convinces the intended verifier but is non-transferable to anyone else, since the verifier could have produced an indistinguishable one itself using its secret key.

One generic recipe for turning a standard signature into a UDVS uses a Σ-protocol OR-proof in the style of Cramer, Damgård, and Schoenmakers (CDS) [10]: the holder proves, in zero knowledge, knowledge of either a valid signature or the verifier's secret key. Since the verifier knows their own key, they could have produced the proof themselves. Tso et al. [26] showed nearly two decades ago that this recipe is instantiable for ECDSA using the sequential OR-proof technique of Abe, Ohkubo, and Suzuki (AOS) [1]. Interestingly, the construction of Tso et al. has received little follow-up (4 citations according to Google Scholar), possibly for lack of a concrete deployment demanding it. The EUDI-Wallet debate provides such an application, and our contribution is to restate the construction in a slightly simplified form and place it in this context.

Our Contributions. This paper revisits the authenticated channel vs. signed data framing as a question about the deniability of presentations. We show that deniability is achievable for ECDSA-signed credentials as they are currently used in the EUDI-Wallet, without changing the signature scheme, the credential format, or the issuer-side PKI. Our contribution is not a new cryptographic primitive. Rather, we demonstrate that well-established techniques – largely absent from the current policy discussion – provide a practical path to reconcile signed credentials with potential deniability demands in the EUDI context. This yields a stronger privacy property than naïve signed presentations, while preserving the deployment advantages of the signed-data approach. Concretely, the paper makes the following contributions.

Revisiting the authenticated channel vs. signed data debate. We argue that the perceived trade-off between authenticated channels and signed credentials is not intrinsic to the choice of cryptographic primitive, but a property of how that primitive is exposed in the presentation protocol. Whether a deployment exposes the raw issuer signature or wraps it in a designated form is a design choice. We use this lens to discuss the suitability of designated verifier techniques, the relation to full-fledged zero-knowledge presentations (anonymous credentials), where deniability is an orthogonal rather than a free property, and discuss the limitations of cryptographic deniability against operational data-retention practices and broader real-world threat models.

ECDSA-Compatible Deniable Presentations. We present a simple UDVS construction for ECDSA signatures based on a classic OR-proof over the native verification equation. Our construction is based on the observation that the ECDSA verification equation itself directly induces a discrete-logarithm relation suitable for use in an OR-proof. For a signature $\sigma = (r, s)$ on a message m under public key Q_s, verification reduces to computing $R = s^{-1}(\mathcal{H}(m)\,G + r\,Q_s)$ and checking $r \equiv x_R \bmod q$. Writing $\tilde{G} := \mathcal{H}(m)\,G + r\,Q_s$, a valid signature satisfies $R = s^{-1}\,\tilde{G}$ – a textbook Schnorr relation over base $\tilde{G}$. We compose a Schnorr proof of knowledge of s^{-1} with a Schnorr proof of knowledge of the verifier's secret key via the parallel CDS OR-technique [10], yielding a secure and lightweight UDVS scheme for ECDSA signatures. The construction is conceptually simpler than the AOS-based variant of [26], albeit generates slightly larger presentations. As the goal of our work is to convey the concept of deniability in the context of the EUDI wallet, we opted for the simpler construction, but also re-state the scheme by Tso et al. for completeness.

We show that our simple UDVS scheme produces a designated-verifier signature whose unconditional non-transferability follows by a straightforward simulator argument, and unforgeability follows from security of ECDSA and the DL assumption. Interestingly, the single-show setting already assumed in current EUDI deployments, where every credential is used only a single time for the purpose of Relying Party unlinkability, yields the implicit assumptions made in the UDVS security model. We also identify multi-show deniable presentation of a single ECDSA credential as an interesting open problem.

Outline. Section 2 discusses the authenticated-channel vs. signed-data debate, formalises what plausible deniability requires, and clarifies its limitations. Section 3 introduces the needed building blocks, in particular the UDVS syntax and security properties. Section 4 presents the ECDSA-based construction, its security analysis and discussion how it fits within the EUDI Wallet context.

2 Authenticated Channels, Signed Credentials, and Deniability

We start by revisiting the authenticated channel vs. signed data debate. We then define the deniability property at stake and describe the known cryptographic techniques for digital signatures. Finally, we clarify the relation to anonymous credentials, and discuss the limitations of cryptographic deniability.

2.1 The Authenticated Channel Approach (German eID)

The authenticated channel approach is the established mechanism of the German electronic identity card (*Personalausweis*) with eID functionality, specified in the BSI Technical Guideline TR-03110 [5,6]. The eID chip is provisioned at issuance with the citizen's attributes and a static, certified chip authentication key pair. At presentation, the chip and the Relying Party authenticate each other in an interactive session and derive a shared ephemeral symmetric session key; the chip's authenticity is thereby established implicitly, as only a chip holding the genuine private key can derive the correct key. The attributes are then read out over the resulting channel, each message authenticated by an HMAC under the shared key [6], giving the Relying Party both the attributes and assurance that they originate from a genuine, issuer-certified chip.

The combination – symmetric authentication established via ephemeral key agreement – is what gives the German eID its plausible deniability: Because the session key is symmetric, the Relying Party could itself compute any of the MAC tags it receives, so a third party given the transcript cannot tell a tag generated inside the chip from one fabricated by the Relying Party after the fact.

In the classic eID, this is a two-party interaction between chip and Relying Party, with no issuer involvement once the chip is provisioned. Adapting this approach to the more open EUDI-Wallet ecosystem, however, appears more challenging. Three variants have been considered [8], two of which have the PID Provider create the credential *on demand* at presentation, requiring an online issuer that participates in every presentation. The third provisions the credential into a secure element on the user's smartphone, recovering offline, issuer-free presentation, though this comes with its own challenges around securing such an approach at scale.

2.2 The Signed Data Approach

The signed-data approach pursued by the EUDI-Wallet [14] takes a different route: at issuance, the issuer produces a publicly verifiable ECDSA signature over (a salted-hash commitment of) the user's attributes, which the wallet stores and forwards to a Relying Party at presentation time. Verification reduces to checking the issuer's signature against its certified public key.

A core advantage of the signed approach is that it decouples issuance from presentation: the issuer signs the credential once, and the wallet can subsequently present it offline, as a two-party interaction with the Relying Party, without the per-presentation issuer involvement that two of the three EUDI authenticated-channel variants require. The signed approach is also, however, the source of the deniability concern. The ECDSA signature is a persistent, publicly verifiable object: anyone in possession of it can independently verify the issuer's endorsement, without further interaction with either the issuer or the holder. A Relying Party, or an attacker who compromises its systems, could therefore prove to arbitrary third parties that authentic identity data was obtained, raising the concern that the resulting transcripts would become attractive targets for data theft and unauthorised trading [27]. This lack of plausible deniability is a central concern raised against the signed data approach.

2.3 Cryptographic Approaches to Deniability

Contrary to what the policy debate may suggest, the tension between signature-based authenticity and plausible deniability is neither new nor unsolved. To see why, recall what deniability formally requires. A credential presentation is *deniable* if there exists an efficient algorithm – a *simulator* – that the verifier itself can run, using its own secret key, to produce transcripts indistinguishable from genuine ones. If the verifier can produce the entire transcript on its own, no third party can tell whether a given transcript arose from a real interaction with the holder or was simply fabricated by the verifier; the transcript thus carries no transferable conviction. We refer to this property interchangeably as deniability or *non-transferability.*

This is exactly the guarantee the authenticated channel of the German eID provides: the symmetric session key known to the verifier is the secret that enables simulation and any transcript it could authenticate, the verifier could equally have produced alone. The same guarantee, however, is also achievable when the underlying authentication is a publicly verifiable signature, through *designated verifier signatures* (DVS), introduced by Jakobsson, Sako, and Impagliazzo [20], and their non-interactive generalisation, *Universal Designated Verifier Signatures* (UDVS) [25]. A UDVS lets the holder of a valid standard signature transform it, using only the verifier's public key, into a DV-signature that convinces the intended verifier but is non-transferable: the verifier's own secret key lets it simulate indistinguishable DV-signatures. This decouples issuance from presentation – the issuer signs once, and the holder presents deniably to any verifier without further issuer involvement [3] – so the choice of signed credentials over authenticated channels does not, in itself, preclude deniability.

One generic recipe [10] turns a standard signature into a UDVS via a Σ-protocol OR-proof: the holder proves, in zero knowledge, knowledge of *either* a valid signature *or* the verifier's secret key. Since the verifier knows their own key, they could have produced the proof themselves – exactly the simulability that yields non-transferability. Tso et al. [26] instantiated this recipe for ECDSA already in 2007, but the construction has attracted hardly any follow-up. We revisit and simplify it in Sect. 4.

2.4 Relation to Anonymous Credentials

A parallel line of work seeks to add privacy to ECDSA-signed credentials via general-purpose zero-knowledge proofs of signature knowledge, with the Longfellow construction [18] as the most prominent example, alongside the BBS-based agenda for the EUDI-Wallet [2,21]. Such anonymous credential constructions provide selective disclosure and multi-show unlinkability across presentations – even when the issuer is corrupt. These solutions are particularly valuable in the *minimal-disclosure* regime, e.g., proving age-over-18 from a full identity credential. Current endeavors to integrate anonymous credentials are orthogonal to the deniability property pursued in this work: a zero-knowledge proof of knowledge of an issuer signature is convincing to its verifier and – in its standard non-interactive instantiation – transferable to third parties. Deniability is therefore an additional property that must be built on top of an anonymous credential typically through the same designated-verifier techniques we apply here. Further, there are two main aspects in which anonymous credentials and deniable signature techniques (on top of standard signatures) differ:

Deployment Complexity. Real-world deployment of anonymous credentials within the EUDI framework remains an active engineering effort. Anonymous credentials either require a non-standard signature scheme such as BBS (in which case the zero-knowledge proof is a simple Schnorr proof), or a highly complex circuit-based zero-knowledge proof (in which case issuers can continue to use ECDSA). In contrast, the technique needed to add deniability is just a simple Schnorr proof [19] on top of a standard ECDSA signature.

Minimal vs. Maximal Disclosure. More fundamentally, anonymous credentials and deniability target different use cases. Anonymous credentials address the *minimal-disclosure* regime, in which the wallet reveals as little as possible. The deniability concern raised in [27], by contrast, is most acute in the *maximal-disclosure* regime – opening a bank account, hotel check-in, or KYC procedures – where the wallet necessarily reveals most or all of a credential's attributes. In such transactions, anonymous credential techniques offer little protection: there are no attributes left to hide. The privacy concern is no longer *what* is revealed, but *to whom*, and whether the disclosed information can subsequently be transferred, sold, or compelled out of the verifier's records. This is precisely the regime in which plausible deniability matters most, and in which a deniable ECDSA presentation – preserving the wallet's existing credential format and signature primitive – is the right tool. The constructions presented here are therefore neither a substitute for nor a competitor of ZK-based anonymous credentials; they address an orthogonal threat model with strictly lighter cryptographic machinery.

2.5 Limitations of Deniability

Cryptographic deniability is a structural property of the presentation transcript, not a guarantee about the wider system in which that transcript is generated, stored, and interpreted. Two limitations, in particular, sit outside what any cryptographic construction can deliver, and frame what our result – and the deniability debate more broadly – actually achieve.

Operational Data Lifecycles in Regulated Sectors. The deniability property reasons about what a Relying Party can prove from the cryptographic transcript. In several motivating use cases – notably banking and other KYC-regulated sectors – the transcript is not the long-term form in which disclosed attributes are retained. Anti-money-laundering regulation (in the EU, the AMLD [15]) requires retention of verification evidence for several years but is silent on its cryptographic form. In practice, identity attributes are extracted from the cryptographic envelope at verification time and committed to the institution's internal database under its own data-integrity controls. A Relying Party wishing to convince a third party of a past presentation can therefore rely on internally authenticated records whose evidentiary value derives from the institution's auditing regime, not from the cryptographic transcript.

This narrows the threat model rather than undermining the case for deniability. Cryptographic deniability protects against leakage or sale of the original presentation transcript beyond the verifier's institutional perimeter. It does not protect against an institution that explicitly authenticates the attributes internally in line with its retention obligations, nor against settings in which contextual evidence alone suffices to convince a data broker of the attributes' authenticity.

Cryptographic Deniability vs. Real-World Deniability. A second, deeper limitation concerns the gap between deniability as a cryptographic notion and deniability as a property that holds up in legal, social, and adversarial real-world settings. Reitinger et al. [24] and Yadav et al. [29] find, through survey and case-study evidence, that simple denials of message authorship are not, on their own, persuasive to lay observers or courts. Collins et al. [9] formalise the gap in a model of *real-world deniability* that incorporates the wider system context (server logs, device state, account metadata) and show that systems with strong cryptographic deniability claims – Signal and DKIM-protected email – fail to provide deniability under their model; in their analysis of 140 Swiss court cases involving WhatsApp transcripts, judges consistently accept such evidence even when disputed, and deniability is not mentioned or considered in any case. The lesson is that the property our construction delivers is necessary but not sufficient for the practical privacy outcome motivating the debate. A Relying Party with logs of which wallet authenticated when, or trusted to store only verified data, can corroborate a disclosed-attribute claim against a third party even when the underlying signature is deniable. The cryptographic property is a structural prerequisite: without it, the transcript itself constitutes transferable evidence that no operational mitigation can retroactively remove. But it must be complemented by operational and architectural choices to translate into deniability in the sense the policy debate cares about, and whether such measures can fully close the gap between cryptographic and real-world deniability remains an open question.

3 Preliminaries

This section recalls the two cryptographic primitives that the construction in Sect. 4 composes: the ECDSA signature scheme, which is the used signature primitive for the EUDI-Wallet, and the Universal Designated Verifier Signature (UDVS), which is the abstract object our construction realises.

3.1 ECDSA Signatures

Definition 1 (ECDSA). *Let E be an elliptic curve, G be a generator of a cyclic subgroup of prime order q, and $\mathsf{H} : \{0,1\}^* \rightarrow \mathbb{Z}_q$ a hash function. ECDSA is the signature scheme defined by the following algorithms.*

- $\mathsf{Setup}(1^\lambda)$: *Generates curve parameters (E, G, q) for security parameter λ and fixes H. Outputs $\mathsf{pp} := (E, G, q, \mathsf{H})$.*
- $\mathsf{KeyGen}(\mathsf{pp})$: *Samples $\mathsf{sk} \xleftarrow{\$} \mathbb{Z}_q^*$, sets $\mathsf{pk} := \mathsf{sk} \cdot G$, and outputs $(\mathsf{sk}, \mathsf{pk})$.*
- $\mathsf{Sign}(\mathsf{sk}, m)$: *Samples a per-signature randomness $k \xleftarrow{\$} \mathbb{Z}_q^*$, computes $R := kG$ and $r := x_R \bmod q$, then $s := k^{-1}(\mathsf{H}(m) + r \cdot \mathsf{sk}) \bmod q$. (If $r = 0$ or $s = 0$, the signer restarts with fresh k.) Outputs $\sigma := (r, s)$.*
- $\mathsf{Verify}(\mathsf{pk}, m, \sigma)$: *On input $\sigma = (r, s)$, rejects unless $1 \leq r, s \leq q - 1$. Otherwise computes $R := s^{-1}\big(\mathsf{H}(m)\, G + r \cdot \mathsf{pk}\big)$ and accepts iff $r \equiv x_R \bmod q$.*

Remark. For the construction in Sect. 4 it is useful to rewrite verification in the form $R = s^{-1}\widetilde{G}$, where $\widetilde{G} := \mathsf{H}(m)\, G + r \cdot \mathsf{pk}$. A valid ECDSA signature thus exhibits a discrete-logarithm relation between two publicly computable points R and $\widetilde{G}$, with the multiplicative inverse s^{-1} as witness. This is the algebraic structure we exploit.

3.2 Universal Designated Verifier Signatures (UDVS)

A UDVS scheme involves three parties: a *signer* S, who issues an ordinary publicly verifiable signature; a *holder* H, who receives this signature from S and later designates it; and a *designated verifier* V, to whom the holder presents the signature in a non-transferable form. The signer is uninvolved at presentation time; the holder uses only the verifier's public key to designate. The role assignment maps onto the EUDI-Wallet as follows: S is the credential issuer, H is the wallet, and V is the Relying Party.

Definition 2 (Universal Designated Verifier Signatures (UDVS)). *A UDVS scheme consists of the following PPT algorithms.*

- $\mathsf{Setup}(1^\lambda)$*: outputs public parameters* pp *shared by all parties.*
- $\mathsf{SKeyGen}(\mathsf{pp})$*: generates the signer's key pair* $(\mathsf{pk}_S, \mathsf{sk}_S)$*. In the EUDI setting this is the issuer's key pair.*
- $\mathsf{VKeyGen}(\mathsf{pp})$*: generates the designated verifier's key pair* $(\mathsf{pk}_V, \mathsf{sk}_V)$*. The holder will need only* pk_V *at presentation time;* sk_V *enables the verifier's simulation capability that underlies non-transferability.*
- $\mathsf{PSign}(\mathsf{sk}_S, m)$*: produces an* ordinary *publicly verifiable signature* σ *on* m*.*
- $\mathsf{PVerify}(\mathsf{pk}_S, m, \sigma)$*: verifies an ordinary signature against the signer's public key; outputs* $b \in \{0, 1\}$*.*
- $\mathsf{DSign}(\mathsf{pk}_S, \mathsf{pk}_V, m, \sigma)$*: is the holder's presentation algorithm. It transforms the ordinary signature* σ *into a* designated verifier signature *(DV)* $\widehat{\sigma}$ *for verifier* pk_V*. The output convinces* V *but is non-transferable to any third party.*
- $\mathsf{Sim}(\mathsf{pk}_S, \mathsf{sk}_V, m)$*: is the simulator that uses the verifier's secret key to produce a designated verifier signature on* m without *an underlying ordinary signature. Its existence is what makes* $\widehat{\sigma}$ *non-transferable: any transcript could have been produced by* V *alone.*
- $\mathsf{DVerify}(\mathsf{pk}_S, \mathsf{pk}_V, m, \widehat{\sigma})$*: verifies a designated verifier signature; outputs* $b \in \{0, 1\}$*.*

Correctness *requires that for all honestly generated keys and all messages* m*:*

$$\begin{aligned}\mathsf{PVerify}(\mathsf{pk}_S, m, \mathsf{PSign}(\mathsf{sk}_S, m)) &= 1,\\ \mathsf{DVerify}(\mathsf{pk}_S, \mathsf{pk}_V, m, \mathsf{DSign}(\mathsf{pk}_S, \mathsf{pk}_V, m, \mathsf{PSign}(\mathsf{sk}_S, m))) &= 1,\\ \mathsf{DVerify}(\mathsf{pk}_S, \mathsf{pk}_V, m, \mathsf{Sim}(\mathsf{pk}_S, \mathsf{sk}_V, m)) &= 1.\end{aligned}$$

The third correctness condition is the structural reason for the deniability property: the verifier's secret key alone suffices to produce designated signatures that pass $\mathsf{DVerify}$, which is what enables the simulation argument underlying non-transferability.

Security Properties. A UDVS scheme is required to provide two security properties: unforgeability of the designated verifier signature, and non-transferability of the conviction it provides to the verifier.

DVS-Unforgeability. Two notions of unforgeability arise in UDVS schemes. *OS-unforgeability* is the standard EUF-CMA notion for the underlying signature PSign. *DVS-unforgeability* is the stronger requirement that an adversary, even one that learns ordinary signatures on arbitrary messages of its choice, cannot produce a designated verifier signature on a fresh message that passes $\mathsf{DVerify}$. As noted in [25], DVS-unforgeability implies OS-unforgeability, since any OS-forgery can be designated to yield a DVS-forgery via the public algorithm DSign. Thus, it is sufficient to focus on DVS-unforgeability for the remainder of this work.

Definition 3 (DVS-Unforgeability [23]). *Let* $\mathsf{S} = (\mathsf{Setup}, \mathsf{SKeyGen}, \mathsf{VKeyGen}, \mathsf{PSign}, \mathsf{PVerify}, \mathsf{DSign}, \mathsf{Sim}, \mathsf{DVerify})$ *be a UDVS scheme. Consider the following experiment between a challenger* $\mathcal{C}$ *and a PPT adversary* $\mathcal{A}$.

Setup. $\mathcal{C}$ *runs* $\mathsf{pp} \leftarrow \mathsf{Setup}(1^\lambda)$, $(\mathsf{pk}_S, \mathsf{sk}_S) \leftarrow \mathsf{SKeyGen}(\mathsf{pp})$, *and* $(\mathsf{pk}_V, \mathsf{sk}_V) \leftarrow \mathsf{VKeyGen}(\mathsf{pp})$. *It gives* $(\mathsf{pp}, \mathsf{pk}_S, \mathsf{pk}_V)$ *to* $\mathcal{A}$.
Queries. $\mathcal{A}$ *adaptively accesses the following oracles:*
- $\mathcal{O}_{\mathsf{PSign}}(m)$*: returns* $\sigma \leftarrow \mathsf{PSign}(\mathsf{sk}_S, m)$.
- $\mathcal{O}_{\mathsf{DSign}}(m)$*: returns* $\widehat{\sigma} \leftarrow \mathsf{DSign}(\mathsf{pk}_S, \mathsf{pk}_V, m, \sigma)$, *where* σ *is generated honestly if not already defined.*
- $\mathcal{O}_{\mathsf{DVerify}}(m, \widehat{\sigma})$*: returns* $\mathsf{DVerify}(\mathsf{pk}_S, \mathsf{pk}_V, m, \widehat{\sigma})$.

Forgery. $\mathcal{A}$ *outputs* $(m^*, \widehat{\sigma}^*)$.

$\mathcal{A}$ *wins if* $\mathsf{DVerify}(\mathsf{pk}_S, \mathsf{pk}_V, m^*, \widehat{\sigma}^*) = 1$ *and* m^* *was queried to neither* $\mathcal{O}_{\mathsf{PSign}}$ *nor* $\mathcal{O}_{\mathsf{DSign}}$. *The scheme provides DVS-unforgeability if for every PPT* $\mathcal{A}$ *the winning probability is negligible in* λ.

Non-transferability. Non-transferability captures the property that a designated verifier signature, while convincing to the verifier, conveys no transferable evidence to any third party. Formally, this is the requirement that designated signatures produced by an honest holder are indistinguishable from those produced by the simulator Sim using only the verifier's secret key. If the two distributions coincide, then any transcript the holder could produce can also be produced by the verifier acting alone, so a third party observing a transcript cannot distinguish the two cases.

Definition 4 (Non-transferability). *Let* S *be a UDVS scheme. Consider the following experiment between a challenger* $\mathcal{C}$ *and a PPT distinguisher* $\mathcal{D}$.

Setup. $\mathcal{C}$ *runs* $\mathsf{pp} \leftarrow \mathsf{Setup}(1^\lambda)$, $(\mathsf{pk}_S, \mathsf{sk}_S) \leftarrow \mathsf{SKeyGen}(\mathsf{pp})$, *and* $(\mathsf{pk}_V, \mathsf{sk}_V) \leftarrow \mathsf{VKeyGen}(\mathsf{pp})$. *It gives* $(\mathsf{pp}, \mathsf{pk}_S, \mathsf{pk}_V, \mathsf{sk}_V)$ *to* $\mathcal{D}$.
Challenge. $\mathcal{D}$ *outputs a message* m^*. $\mathcal{C}$ *samples* $b \stackrel{\$}{\leftarrow} \{0, 1\}$ *and computes*

$$\widehat{\sigma}^* \leftarrow \begin{cases} \mathsf{DSign}(\mathsf{pk}_S, \mathsf{pk}_V, m^*, \mathsf{PSign}(\mathsf{sk}_S, m^*)) & \text{if } b = 0, \\ \mathsf{Sim}(\mathsf{pk}_S, \mathsf{sk}_V, m^*) & \text{if } b = 1. \end{cases}$$

$\mathcal{C}$ *returns* $\widehat{\sigma}^*$ *to* $\mathcal{D}$.
Guess. $\mathcal{D}$ *outputs a bit* b' *and wins if* $b' = b$.

The scheme provides non-transferability *if for every PPT* $\mathcal{D}$ *the advantage* $\left|\Pr[b' = b] - \frac{1}{2}\right|$ *is negligible in* λ. *We say the scheme provides* unconditional non-transferability *if the two distributions are identical, in which case the advantage is zero for every (computationally unbounded)* $\mathcal{D}$.

4 Deniable ECDSA Credentials

We now show how deniability can be added on top of standard ECDSA signatures. Recall from the remark following Definition 1 that writing $\widetilde{G} := \mathsf{H}(m)\,G + r \cdot \mathsf{pk}_S$, a valid ECDSA signature satisfies

$$R = s^{-1} \cdot \widetilde{G},$$

which is a textbook Schnorr relation over base $\widetilde{G}$. A holder in possession of (r, s) can therefore prove knowledge of the scalar s^{-1} by a standard Σ-protocol. To obtain a designated-verifier signature, we compose this proof, via the CDS OR-technique [10], with a Schnorr proof of knowledge of the verifier's secret key sk_V satisfying $\mathsf{pk}_V = \mathsf{sk}_V \cdot G$. The Fiat–Shamir-compiled result convinces the verifier that the holder possesses a valid ECDSA signature *or* that the verifier itself produced the proof using sk_V; since the verifier knows sk_V, the proof is non-transferable. The construction is given in detail in Sect. 4.1.

This yields the same security property as the AOS-based scheme of Tso et al. [26] – unconditional non-transferability – but is built from a single ingredient (CDS OR-composition of two Schnorr proofs) and works directly with the ECDSA verification equation, without the auxiliary witness re-randomisation $h = s/t$ introduced in [26]. In Sect. 4.2, we present an alternative construction that likewise eliminates the re-randomisation step but replaces the parallel CDS OR-proof with the more compact sequential AOS OR-proof [1]. The resulting scheme improves upon [26] in both simplicity and signature size, while being more compact than the CDS variant at the cost of slightly more conceptual complexity.

Security Model and EUDI Fit. The construction is analysed in the UDVS security model of Sect. 3: DVS-unforgeability (Definition 3) and non-transferability against a malicious verifier possessing sk_V (Definition 4). Two aspects of this model deserve emphasis in the EUDI context. First, the non-transferability distinguisher is *not* given the underlying signature $\sigma = (r, s)$, matching the EUDI deployment reality: the issuer's signature lives inside the wallet and is never transmitted to a Relying Party, which only ever sees designated forms. Second, the model assumes a single presentation per credential, consistent with how the EUDI-Wallet currently obtains Relying-Party unlinkability for ECDSA-signed credentials in the absence of anonymous credentials [7, 14]: each ECDSA-signed credential is used at most once. Section 4.3 returns to multi-show deniability and to the role of the wallet's holder-binding signature.

4.1 Parallel OR-Proof Construction

We instantiate the UDVS algorithms of Definition 2 in the standard ECDSA setting of Sect. 3, additionally using a Fiat–Shamir hash $\mathsf{H}_{\mathrm{FS}} : \{0, 1\}^* \to \mathbb{Z}_q$.

Setup, Key Generation, and Issuance. The instantiations of Setup, $\mathsf{SKeyGen}$, $\mathsf{VKeyGen}$, PSign, and $\mathsf{PVerify}$ are essentially standard ECDSA; we summarise them here for completeness and briefly discuss their EUDI-specific aspects and verifier key management.

$\mathsf{Setup}(1^\lambda)$: outputs $\mathsf{pp} = (E, G, q, \mathsf{H}, \mathsf{H}_{\mathrm{FS}})$, i.e. the ECDSA setup of Definition 1 extended with the Fiat–Shamir hash H_{FS}.

$\mathsf{SKeyGen}(\mathsf{pp})$: standard ECDSA key generation: sample $\mathsf{sk}_S \xleftarrow{\$} \mathbb{Z}_q^*$ and output $\mathsf{pk}_S := \mathsf{sk}_S \cdot G$.

$\mathsf{VKeyGen}(\mathsf{pp})$: DL-based key generation on the same curve: sample $\mathsf{sk}_V \xleftarrow{\$} \mathbb{Z}_q^*$ and output $\mathsf{pk}_V := \mathsf{sk}_V \cdot G$.

$\mathsf{PSign}(\mathsf{sk}_S, m), \mathsf{PVerify}(\mathsf{pk}_S, m, \sigma)$: standard ECDSA signing and verification on m exactly as in Definition 1.

Issuance. The issuer produces $\sigma = (r, s)$ on a message m, which in the SD-JWT setting is the salted-hash commitment to the user's attributes. The wallet stores (m, σ) together with a holder-controlled binding key pair $(\mathsf{sk}_H, \mathsf{pk}_H)$ that is part of the issued credential and supports the Key Binding JWT (KB-JWT) [17] produced at presentation time. We treat m as an opaque bit string; the holder binding mechanism and its interaction with deniability are discussed in Sect. 4.3. No interaction with the issuer is required at presentation time.

Verifier Key Management. At the start of a presentation session, the verifier sends pk_V to the holder. Crucially, the holder must be assured that the verifier indeed knows the corresponding secret key sk_V, as this is what allows the simulator-based deniability argument to go through. This can be handled in two ways: either the verifier proves possession of sk_V at the time of key advertisement, or the certificate authority issuing pk_V already attests to such possession at registration time. Notably, this requirement integrates cleanly into the EUDI architecture: Relying Parties must in any case authenticate themselves to the wallet using a certified key pair – e.g., the certified key in the TLS server certificate or the EUDI Relying-Party certificate – so $(\mathsf{sk}_V, \mathsf{pk}_V)$ can simply be that same key pair, and no additional verifier-side key management is required.

Designation: $\mathsf{DSign}(\mathsf{pk}_S, \mathsf{pk}_V, m, \sigma)$**.** The holder, given (m, r, s) and pk_V, proceeds as follows.

Step 1: Recompute the verification point. Compute

$$\widetilde{G} := \mathsf{H}(m) \cdot G + r \cdot \mathsf{pk}_S, \qquad R := s^{-1} \cdot \widetilde{G}.$$

By construction, $R = s^{-1}\widetilde{G}$, and the holder knows the witness $w := s^{-1} \bmod q$.

Step 2: CDS OR-proof. The holder produces a non-interactive proof of the statement

$$\{\exists w : R = w \cdot \widetilde{G}\} \vee \{\exists \mathsf{sk}_V : \mathsf{pk}_V = \mathsf{sk}_V \cdot G\},$$

using the CDS parallel OR-composition of two Schnorr Σ-protocols [10]. The holder knows the witness for the left clause and simulates the right:

1. Pick $k_L \xleftarrow{\$} \mathbb{Z}_q$, set $A_L := k_L \cdot \widetilde{G}$. (real, left)
2. Pick $z_R, c_R \xleftarrow{\$} \mathbb{Z}_q$, set $A_R := z_R \cdot G - c_R \cdot \mathsf{pk}_V$. (sim., right)
3. Compute $c := \mathsf{H}_{\mathrm{FS}}(R, \widetilde{G}, \mathsf{pk}_V, A_L, A_R, m)$.
4. Set $c_L := c - c_R \bmod q$ and $z_L := k_L + c_L \cdot w \bmod q$. (real, left)

Step 3: Output. The DV-signature is $\widehat{\sigma} := (R, A_L, A_R, c_L, c_R, z_L, z_R)$.

Transcript Size. A size-optimised encoding transmits only one of $\{c_L, c_R\}$, since the other follows from $c_L + c_R = c$. The DV-signature thus comprises three group elements and three scalars; for curves at the 128-bit security level (e.g., P-256), about $3 \times 33 + 3 \times 32 = 195$ bytes.

Session Freshness. Credential presentations are typically bound to a verifier-chosen session nonce to ensure freshness and prevent replay of a presentation across sessions. In the EUDI-Wallet, this responsibility is delegated entirely to the Key Binding JWT [17], which contains the verifier's nonce and is signed by the holder's binding key. The DV-signature constructed above therefore does not need to incorporate a session nonce of its own. The deniability implications of this holder-binding signature are discussed in Sect. 4.3.

Designated Verification: $\mathsf{DVerify}(\mathsf{pk}_S, \mathsf{pk}_V, m, \widehat{\sigma})$. The verifier parses $\widehat{\sigma}$ as $(R, A_L, A_R, c_L, c_R, z_L, z_R)$. First, it recomputes the verification base point: $r' := x_R \bmod q$ and $\widetilde{G} := \mathsf{H}(m) \cdot G + r' \cdot \mathsf{pk}_S$ (note that r' is recovered from R, mirroring standard ECDSA verification). Second, it recomputes $c := \mathsf{H}_{\mathrm{FS}}(R, \widetilde{G}, \mathsf{pk}_V, A_L, A_R, m)$. Finally, it accepts iff

$$c = c_L + c_R \bmod q, \quad z_L \cdot \widetilde{G} = A_L + c_L \cdot R, \quad \text{and} \quad z_R \cdot G = A_R + c_R \cdot \mathsf{pk}_V.$$

Security and Deniability. We now show that the above construction achieves non-transferability (Definition 4) and DVS-unforgeability (Definition 3).

High-Level Intuition. Non-transferability follows from the honest-verifier zero-knowledge property of CDS OR-proofs: knowing sk_V, the verifier can produce transcripts whose distribution is identical to honest holder-produced transcripts. DVS-unforgeability follows from the special-soundness of CDS OR-proofs combined with the EUF-CMA security of ECDSA: an adversary producing a valid DV-signature on a fresh message must, via standard rewinding, yield either an ECDSA forgery on that message or the verifier's secret key.

On the Role of R in the Transcript. Note that the transcript reveals R in the clear. Since $r = x_R \bmod q$, this implicitly reveals the first component of the underlying ECDSA signature. Thus, $\widehat{\sigma}$ is not a zero-knowledge presentation of σ, but this is not needed here, and does not harm the deniability goal. First, by Definition 4, the distinguisher is not given $\sigma = (r, s)$, and R alone does not allow reconstruction of the signature (which requires both r and s). Second, R is uniformly distributed in $\langle G \rangle$ over the randomness of ECDSA signing, so it leaks no information about the issuer's secret key or the message. Third, even an adversary who learns r through another channel cannot link two presentations of *distinct* credentials, since each credential is signed under fresh per-signature randomness. The leakage is structural: it is the price paid for staying within the standard ECDSA verification equation rather than committing to R inside a more expensive proof. Two presentations of the *same* credential are more subtle; see Sect. 4.3.

The simulator. The simulator $\mathsf{Sim}(\mathsf{pk}_S, \mathsf{sk}_V, m)$ proceeds as follows:

1. Pick $R \xleftarrow{\$} \langle G \rangle$ uniformly at random.
2. Compute $\widetilde{G} := \mathsf{H}(m) \cdot G + (x_R \bmod q) \cdot \mathsf{pk}_S$.
3. Pick $k_R \xleftarrow{\$} \mathbb{Z}_q$, set $A_R := k_R \cdot G$. (real, right)
4. Pick $z_L, c_L \xleftarrow{\$} \mathbb{Z}_q$, set $A_L := z_L \cdot \widetilde{G} - c_L \cdot R$. (sim., left)
5. Compute $c := \mathsf{H}_{\mathrm{FS}}(R, \widetilde{G}, \mathsf{pk}_V, A_L, A_R, m)$, set $c_R := c - c_L \bmod q$ and $z_R := k_R + c_R \cdot \mathsf{sk}_V \bmod q$. (real, right)

Output $\widehat{\sigma} := (R, A_L, A_R, c_L, c_R, z_L, z_R)$. The simulator runs the OR-proof with the clause roles swapped: it executes the right clause honestly with the witness sk_V and simulates the left, mirroring the honest holder's procedure of Sect. 4.1.

Lemma 1 (Simulator indistinguishability). *For any (m, pk_V), the distribution of DV-signatures produced by* DSign *is identical to that produced by* Sim, *provided the distinguisher does not observe the underlying signature* (r, s).

Proof (Sketch). By the honest-verifier zero-knowledge of CDS OR-proofs, the joint distribution of $(A_L, A_R, c_L, c_R, z_L, z_R)$ conditioned on R is identical in both cases: c_L, c_R are uniform in $\mathbb{Z}_q$ subject to $c_L + c_R = c$; the responses z_L, z_R are uniform; and the commitments are determined by the verification equations. It remains to show that R has the same distribution. In an honest execution $R = s^{-1}\widetilde{G}$, or equivalently $R = kG$ for $k \xleftarrow{\$} \mathbb{Z}_q^*$; in the simulation R is sampled uniformly in $\langle G \rangle$. Both distributions coincide with the uniform distribution on $\langle G \rangle$ (up to negligible probability of $k = 0$).

Theorem 1 (Non-transferability). *The construction provides unconditional non-transferability (Definition 4), provided the distinguisher does not observe the underlying ECDSA signature.*

Proof. Immediate from Lemma 1: any transcript produced by DSign could equally have been produced by Sim with identical distribution; a distinguisher therefore has advantage zero.

Theorem 2 (DVS-unforgeability). *If ECDSA is EUF-CMA-secure and the discrete logarithm problem in $\langle G \rangle$ is hard, then the construction satisfies DVS-unforgeability (Definition 3) in the random oracle model.*

Proof (Sketch). We reduce an adversary $\mathcal{A}$ producing a valid DV-signature $\widehat{\sigma}^*$ on a fresh message m^* to either an ECDSA forgery or a discrete-log break. By the special-soundness of CDS OR-proofs, two accepting transcripts of the proof for the same (R^*, A_L^*, A_R^*) with distinct Fiat–Shamir challenges yield, via standard rewinding [22], a witness for one of the two clauses: either $w^* = (s^*)^{-1}$ with $R^* = w^* \widetilde{G}^*$, or the verifier's secret key sk_V.

Case 1: w^* extracted. Setting $s^* := (w^*)^{-1} \bmod q$ and $r^* := x_{R^*} \bmod q$, the pair (r^*, s^*) is a valid ECDSA signature on m^*, contradicting EUF-CMA security of ECDSA.

Case 2: sk_V extracted. Since $\mathsf{pk}_V = \mathsf{sk}_V \cdot G$ is a fresh discrete-log challenge to the reduction, this solves the discrete log problem.

The argument follows the structure of Tso et al. [26, Theorem 2], adapted from their AOS-based proof to the CDS setting.

4.2 Alternative: AOS Sequential OR-Proof Construction

The direct relation $R = s^{-1}\widetilde{G}$ also admits a more compact instantiation using the sequential OR-proof technique of Abe, Ohkubo, and Suzuki [1]. We present this variant below; it parallels Tso et al. [26] but operates directly on our simplified witness without their auxiliary re-randomisation. The instantiation of Setup, $\mathsf{SKeyGen}$, $\mathsf{VKeyGen}$, PSign, and $\mathsf{PVerify}$ is unchanged; only DSign, $\mathsf{DVerify}$, and Sim differ. We use two independent Fiat–Shamir hashes $\mathsf{H}_{\mathrm{FS}}, \mathsf{H}'_{\mathrm{FS}} : \{0,1\}^* \to \mathbb{Z}_q$ (in practice derived from a single hash function, modelled as random oracle by domain separation).

Designation. $\mathsf{DSign}(\mathsf{pk}_S, \mathsf{pk}_V, m, \sigma)$, given (m, r, s) and pk_V:

1. Compute $\widetilde{G}$ and R as in Sect. 4.1; the witness is $w = s^{-1} \bmod q$.
2. Pick $k \xleftarrow{\$} \mathbb{Z}_q$, set $A_L := k \cdot \widetilde{G}$. (real, left)
3. Compute $c_R := \mathsf{H}_{\mathrm{FS}}(R, \widetilde{G}, \mathsf{pk}_V, A_L, m)$. (challenge, right)
4. Pick $z_R \xleftarrow{\$} \mathbb{Z}_q$, set $A_R := z_R \cdot G - c_R \cdot \mathsf{pk}_V$. (sim., right)
5. Compute $c_L := \mathsf{H}'_{\mathrm{FS}}(R, \widetilde{G}, \mathsf{pk}_V, A_R, m)$. (challenge, left)
6. Compute $z_L := k + c_L \cdot w \bmod q$. (real, left)

The DV-signature is $\widehat{\sigma}_{\mathrm{AOS}} := (R, c_R, z_L, z_R)$.

Verification and Simulation. $\mathsf{DVerify}$ recomputes $A_L := z_L \cdot \widetilde{G} - c_L \cdot R$ and $A_R := z_R \cdot G - c_R \cdot \mathsf{pk}_V$, then checks $c_R = \mathsf{H}_{\mathrm{FS}}(R, \widetilde{G}, \mathsf{pk}_V, A_L, m)$ and $c_L = \mathsf{H}'_{\mathrm{FS}}(R, \widetilde{G}, \mathsf{pk}_V, A_R, m)$. The simulator Sim uses the analogous trick: pick $R \xleftarrow{\$} \langle G \rangle$, compute $\widetilde{G}$ as in honest verification, run the right clause with the real witness sk_V and simulate the left.

Relationship to Tso et al. [26] *and trade-off.* The construction above is the ECDSA-DL case of [26], simplified using $R = s^{-1}\widetilde{G}$ rather than the auxiliary $h = s/t$. Tso et al.'s h plays the role of our s^{-1} up to inversion, and their ζ is our R; the security analysis can be adapted with only minor modifications. The AOS variant yields $\widehat{\sigma}_{\mathrm{AOS}}$ with one group element and three scalars (vs. three group elements and three scalars for CDS), saving roughly 64 bytes on P-256. The cost is conceptual: two sequential Fiat–Shamir hashes and a security argument routed through AOS OR-proof analysis [1] rather than the textbook CDS extractor. For an EUDI-Wallet deployment, where the DV-signature is one component of a multi-kilobyte SD-JWT, we view CDS as the more deployable choice; AOS is the right choice where every byte matters (e.g., NFC-bound presentations).

4.3 Scope: The Single-Show Model

The construction of Sect. 4.1 is analysed in the single-show setting: each ECDSA-signed credential is presented to at most one Relying Party. We discuss why this fits the EUDI-Wallet, how it interacts with holder binding, what breaks under multi-show, and how multi-show deniability could be added.

Why Single-Show Fits the EUDI Deployment. Single-show is not an additional restriction of our construction; it already reflects the EUDI-Wallet deployment model for obtaining Relying-Party unlinkability without anonymous credentials [7,14]. Reusing the same ECDSA-signed credential exposes the same issuer signature and is trivially linkable. The current mitigation is *batch issuance* [2,7]: the issuer provides a fresh ECDSA signature per anticipated presentation. Our construction additionally gives per-presentation deniability by designating each credential to a single verifier via the protocol of Sect. 4.1; the resulting DV-signature is non-transferable by Theorem 1.

The Holder-Binding Signature. SD-JWT presentations include a Key Binding JWT (KB-JWT) [17]: an ECDSA signature by a holder-controlled binding key sk_H over the verifier nonce, a timestamp, and a hash of the disclosed credential. The KB-JWT is a publicly verifiable, transferable signature. However, it does not undermine the deniability of Theorem 1, because pk_H is an anonymous public key: a leaked KB-JWT – even though it contains a hash of the disclosed credential – only shows that *some* anonymous key pk_H authenticated to a verifier; without a transferable issuer signature, neither the credential hash nor the disclosed attributes themselves constitute evidence of issuance, and the KB-JWT therefore adds no transferable link to a real identity.

This argument again relies on the single-show assumption. Reusing pk_H across presentations would make them linkable, and later identification of pk_H would retroactively attribute the full set. In the current EUDI-Wallet model – where each credential uses a fresh binding key and is shown at most once [7] – this does not arise. Extending to multi-show would require either rotating pk_H per presentation (not supported by secure-element-bound keys) or applying the OR-proof technique to the KB-JWT.

What Goes Wrong with Multi-show. If the same credential is presented to two verifiers V_1 and V_2, both DV-signatures reveal the same point $R = kG$, fixed by the per-signature ECDSA randomness rather than by the presentation. Each transcript individually remains non-transferable by Definition 4, but their *correlation* is not: two non-colluding verifiers simulating independently would each pick a fresh R, so a shared R is something neither could have produced alone. The standard single-transcript definition does not capture this joint property [4]. Colluding verifiers, by contrast, could trivially coordinate their choice of R.

Multi-show deniability would additionally require hiding R across presentations – and thereby effectively the full ECDSA signature – which is precisely what our construction avoids by exploiting the single-show setting. Alternatively, designated-verifier techniques can be composed with an anonymous credential scheme by adding the OR-clause for sk_V to the presentation proof, yielding both unlinkability and deniability [11].

Acknowledgments. The authors used AI tools (Claude/Anthropic) to assist with drafting and improving the presentation of the manuscript. All AI-generated output was reviewed, edited, and verified by the authors, who take full responsibility for the final content.

Disclosure of Interests. Author 2 holds a part-time position with the German EUDI Wallet project, where her work concerns anonymous credentials. The authors declare no other competing interests.

References

1. Abe, M., Ohkubo, M., Suzuki, K.: 1-out-of-N signatures from a variety of keys. In: Advances in Cryptology — ASIACRYPT 2002. Springer Berlin Heidelberg (2002)
2. Baum, C., et al.: Cryptographers' feedback on the EU digital identity's ARF (2024)
3. Bertram, M., Richter, M., Margraf, M.: Achieving third-party deniability in signature-based credential systems. Cryptography (2024)
4. Bertram, M., Zengin, B., Buchmann, N., Margraf, M.: Strong non-transferability from randomizable universal designated verifier signatures. Cryptography, (2026)
5. Bundesamt für Sicherheit in der Informationstechnik (BSI): Technical guideline TR-03127: Architecture electronic identity card and electronic resident permit (2011). https://www.bsi.bund.de/SharedDocs/Downloads/EN/BSI/Publications/TechGuidelines/TR03127/BSI-TR-03127_en.pdf?__blob=publicationFile&v=1
6. Bundesamt für Sicherheit in der Informationstechnik (BSI): Technical guideline TR-03110-2: Advanced security mechanisms for machine readable travel documents and eIDAS token (2016). https://www.bsi.bund.de/SharedDocs/Downloads/EN/BSI/Publications/TechGuidelines/TR03110/BSI_TR-03110_Part-2-V2_2.pdf?__blob=publicationFile&v=1
7. Bundesministerium für Digitales und Staatsmodernisierung: Blueprint for the EUDI Wallet Ecosystem in Germany (2023). https://bmi.usercontent.opencode.de/eudi-wallet/eidas-2.0-architekturkonzept/
8. Bundesministerium für Digitales und Staatsmodernisierung: Blueprint for the EUDI Wallet Ecosystem in Germany – Wallet Function: PID Issuance and Presentation (2023). https://bmi.usercontent.opencode.de/eudi-wallet/eidas-2.0-architekturkonzept/content/archive/00-pid-issuance-and-presentation/

9. Collins, D., Colombo, S., Huguenin-Dumittan, L.: Real-world deniability in messaging. In: Proceedings on Privacy Enhancing Technologies, (2025)
10. Cramer, R., Damgård, I., Schoenmakers, B.: Proofs of partial knowledge and simplified design of witness hiding protocols. In: Advances in Cryptology — CRYPTO '94. Springer Berlin Heidelberg (1994)
11. Debes, H.B., Giannetsos, T.: Retract: expressive designated verifier anonymous credentials. In: Proceedings of the 18th International Conference on Availability, Reliability and Security. ACM (2023). https://doi.org/10.1145/3600160.3600191
12. Deutscher Bundestag: Ausschuss für Digitales: Stellungnahme zur Anhörung Digitale Identitäten. https://www.bundestag.de/resource/blob/901724/67441ef0b9ead7f9f09f15cc524226ad/Fluepke-Carl-Fabian-Luepke-.pdf
13. epicenter.works: Data Protection Analysis: eIDAS Architecture Reference Framework 1.4. https://epicenter.works/fileadmin/medienspiegel/user_upload/epicenter.works_-_ARF1.4.pdf
14. European Commission: The European Digital Identity Wallet – Architecture and Reference Framework (ARF) (2025), https://github.com/eu-digital-identity-wallet/eudi-doc-architecture-and-reference-framework, version 2.9.0
15. European Parliament and Council of the European Union: Directive (EU) 2015/849 (AMLD) (2015). https://eur-lex.europa.eu/eli/dir/2015/849/oj
16. European Parliament and Council of the European Union: Regulation (EU) 2024/1183 amending regulation (EU) no 910/2014 (eIDAS 2.0) (2024). https://eur-lex.europa.eu/eli/reg/2024/1183/oj
17. Fett, D., Yasuda, K., Campbell, B.: Selective disclosure for JWTs (SD-JWT). IETF Internet-Draft, draft-ietf-oauth-selective-disclosure-jwt, (2025)
18. Frigo, M., abhi shelat: Anonymous credentials from ECDSA (2024). https://eprint.iacr.org/2024/2010
19. Hao, F.: RFC 8235: Schnorr non-interactive zero-knowledge proof (2017). https://www.rfc-editor.org/rfc/rfc8235
20. Jakobsson, M., Sako, K., Impagliazzo, R.: Designated verifier proofs and their applications. In: Advances in Cryptology — EUROCRYPT '96. Springer Berlin Heidelberg (1996)
21. Looker, T., Kalos, V., Whitehead, A., Lodder, M.: The BBS signature scheme (2024). https://datatracker.ietf.org/doc/draft-irtf-cfrg-bbs-signatures/
22. Pointcheval, D., Stern, J.: Security arguments for digital signatures and blind signatures. J. Cryptol. (2000)
23. Rastegari, P., Berenjkoub, M., Dakhilalian, M., Susilo, W.: Universal designated verifier signature scheme with non-delegatability in the standard model. Inf. Sci. (2019)
24. Reitinger, N., Malkin, N., Akgul, O., Mazurek, M.L., Miers, I.: Is cryptographic deniability sufficient? Non-expert perceptions of deniability in secure messaging. In: 2023 IEEE Symposium on Security and Privacy (SP) (2023)
25. Steinfeld, R., Bull, L., Wang, H., Pieprzyk, J.: Universal designated-verifier signatures. In: Advances in Cryptology - ASIACRYPT 2003. Springer Berlin Heidelberg (2003)
26. Tso, R., Gonzàlez Nieto, J.M., Okamoto, T., Boyd, C., Okamoto, E.: Verifier-key-flexible universal designated-verifier signatures. In: Cryptography and Coding. Springer Berlin Heidelberg (2007)
27. Verbraucherzentrale Bundesverband (VZBV): Report on the architecture of the EUDI-wallet (2024). https://www.vzbv.de/sites/default/files/2025-02/vzbv-Gutachten%20zur%20Architektur%20der%20EUDI-Wallet.pdf

28. Viola Heeger: EUDI-Wallets: Streit um signierte Daten. https://background.tagesspiegel.de/digitalisierung-und-ki/briefing/eudi-wallets-streit-um-signierte-daten
29. Yadav, T.K., Gosain, D., Seamons, K.: Cryptographic deniability: a multi-perspective study of user perceptions and expectations. In: 32nd USENIX Security Symposium (USENIX Security 23). USENIX Association (2023)

Proactive Identity Protection: Leveraging Vision Language Models for PII Extraction from Leaked Documents

Daniel Vogel[1(✉)], Marc Ohm[1,2(✉)], Antoine Warns[1], Lea Silberberg[1], Fabian Ermisch[1], and Stephanie von Maltzan[3,4]

[1] University of Bonn, Bonn, Germany
{vogel,ohm,warns,silberberg,ermisch}@cs.uni-bonn.de
[2] Fraunhofer FKIE, Bonn, Germany
[3] Karlsruhe Institute of Technology, Karlsruhe, Germany
stephanie.maltzan@partner.kit.edu
[4] FIZ Karlsruhe, Karlsruhe, Germany

Abstract. Leaked images of documents may contain Personally Identifiable Information (PII) that can be automatically extracted using open-source Vision Language Models (VLMs). However, the challenge lies in the heterogeneity of potential documents and the data therein, as well as the required precision of the extraction, which we tackle with a comprehensive study on combinations of different open-source VLMs, parameters, and prompting techniques. Where related research often evaluates average performance of VLM-based data extraction, the error-free extraction of PII requires a specialized handling, in particular with regard to the legal implications. Four open-source VLMs were selected that a set of tailor-made prompts for specific structured output formats was used on to extract data from images of German ID cards and invoices. For this, a data set of these images was synthesized, different combinations of parameters, formats and models were tested and the rate of error-free data extractions were evaluated. We show, that data extraction quality depends on the required format and prompt given, as well as the amount of parameters the VLM uses. Additionally, parsable VLM output exactly matches the original data more reliably for PII that are not names, but numbers or dates. Since the results vary given different configurations, the selection of a VLM to solve such a task is not GDPR compliant in itself, rather the configuration selection should be.

Keywords: Personally Identifiable Information · Vision Language Models · Data Extraction · Legal Governance

1 Introduction

The proliferation of digital identity verification and online service enrollment has led to a increased volume of national identity card images being processed and stored by various institutions. Because these documents contain a dense

Z. Afzal et al. (Eds.): ARES 2026 Workshops, LNCS 16900, pp. 616–633, 2027.
https://doi.org/10.1007/978-3-032-35576-8_33

concentration of PII, they have become a primary, highly lucrative target for malicious actors. Recent incidents, such as the breach of France's ANTS identity agency exposing over 19 million records[1], the massive leaks of Spanish DNI cards on the dark web[2], and stolen photocopies of ID cards from Italian hotels[3] demonstrate that leaked identity documents are an actual target. Once leaked, these document images are frequently traded and exploited for identity theft, financial fraud, and synthetic identity creation.

To enable proactive identity protection, such as automated dark web monitoring to alert citizens when their leaked credentials surface, there is a need for a system that can robustly ingest, interpret, and extract structured PII from highly diverse and noisy document images at scale.

Traditional automated data extraction systems rely on a rigid pipeline combining standard Optical Character Recognition (OCR) engines with rule-based post-processing. However, these traditional methods face critical limitations in real-world scenarios. First, layout diversity across different countries and issuance periods requires maintaining complex, country-specific rule sets. Second, contextual ambiguity arises because text labels on ID cards are often minimal or entirely absent, making it difficult for simple OCR to distinguish between similar fields, such as a document number versus a personal ID number. Finally, standard OCR lack robustness to real-world noise, as variations in image quality, orientation, lighting, and occlusions drastically reduce extraction accuracy.

To address these challenges, this paper introduces a system that leverages the advanced contextual understanding and multimodal capabilities of VLMs for semantic entity recognition. Moving away from traditional decoupled architectures that pass OCR text to a separate Large Language Model, our approach utilizes VLMs to process the visual and textual layout of the identity document simultaneously. By treating the document as an integrated, multimodal entity, the VLM interpret content based on its general knowledge and visual context. This enables the system to extract and structure PII regardless of minor layout variations, language barriers, or missing text labels, offering an alternative to classical computer vision pipelines.

The primary contributions of this work are twofold, bridging technical optimization and legal compliance frameworks. Technically, we establish the viability of VLMs for zero- and few-shot PII extraction, demonstrating that performance is dependent on the specific model architecture, the scale of parameters, and the design of the prompting methodology. We show that optimizing this combination is essential for achieving reliable extraction accuracy. Legally and operationally, we argue that the deployment of VLMs themselves is not inherently sufficient for regulatory compliance. The concrete configurations, hyper-parameter bound-

[1] https://cybernews.com/security/ants-hack-france-19-million-records-id-agency-breach.

[2] https://www.apolocybersecurity.com/en/blog-posts/filtracion-masiva-de-dni-espanoles-en-la-dark-web.

[3] https://www.heise.de/en/news/Darknet-offer-Tens-of-thousands-of-ID-scans-stolen-from-Italian-hotels-10522177.html.

aries, and guardrails dictate viability and should be used to assess the system for privacy and data protection standards.

2 Related Work

VLMs have found their way into research, as their ability to act as multi-modal tools is being investigated. Within many recently published articles such as [5], the focus lays on the technical performance of the chosen models, which are valid and important examinations to make. Still, the importance of privacy-aware and privacy preserving use of VLMs is a focal point of recent research [14] [15].

Language models are also considered for use with regards to content moderation, which is a legally loaded operation. In multi-modal environments, VLMs Lu et al. [12] propose KuaiMod, a content ecosystem governance framework that leverages VLM not only for content extraction but also regulatory violation detection. While its content moderation performance is analyzed statistically, a more nuanced investigation on individual cases is missing, which in practice could instigate legal discussions. PrivLEX is another system proposed by Baranouskaya et al. [1], which uses a VLM to determine legal concepts in images, which in turn could have implications for content moderation. While content classification is relevant and PrivLEX reportedly can identify PII containing documents on a statistics basis, no further PII extraction was implemented, nor is there an in-depth legal evaluation present beyond the one on the technical performance.

3 Methodology

The goal of our methodology is to automatically extract PII from structured and semi-structured documents such as ID cards or invoices using VLMs and evaluate the quality of this extraction. Hence the automatic extraction process is explained along the necessary metrics to evaluate its performance. We refer to the structured and semi-structured documents as *target documents*. Target documents are the German language ID card version 2010 as well as generic invoices compliant to German invoice laws, as specified by our use case. We consider German ID cards as structured documents, because their layout is strictly standardized, and highly consistent across all instances.

Invoices are chosen as examples of semi-structured documents. Invoices are legally required to contain specific information, such as the names and addresses of the invoicing party and recipient, as well as the date of issue. Contrary to the EU standard compliant E-invoice, which is created in a specific structured format, in Germany, invoices can also be issued in paper or `pdf` format. For invoices exceeding 250€, there are no constraints on how or where this information must be presented. Consequently, layout, formatting, order, and visual structure vary significantly. Identity documents are highly relevant in real-world contexts such as data theft, misuse, and social engineering attacks. [7].

To guide the exploration, we formulate the following research questions, each addressing a specific factor that may influence the quality of PII extraction using open-source VLMs.

RQ1. How does the quality of the results differ when extracting PII from target documents using open-source VLMs with different numbers of parameters?

RQ2. How does the prompting-technique influence the quality of results when extracting PII from target documents using open-source VLMs?

Furthermore, our use case is crucial to understand the design decisions for both the experiments as well as the evaluation. A trust system was designed to allow PII to be checked for matches. Since PII should only ever be processed in a secure way, a multi-step processing pipeline was set up, that utilizes Argon2id for hashing. As input for a PII hash, both the PII value, as well as an anchor are used, where the anchor is a set of predetermined PII attributes from the same document, to avoid guessing attacks. The trust system as well as its legal design patterns are explained in more detail by von Maltzan et al. [13]. Since checking for matches between two hashes requires an exact identity of the used preimages, a hard requirement is formed: The PII extraction must be flawless. If a single character is extracted incorrectly for any of the input attributes, the entire hash is incorrect, thus rendering a comparison between two originally identical attributes faulty.

The evaluation of extraction performance is based on the metrics *Full-Field matches*, *All-Field matches*, and *Anchor matches*. *Full-Field matches* refer to the number of data fields whose extracted values match the respective ground truth exactly. An *All-Field match* is achieved if for a documents all data fields have Full-Field matches. The anchor attributes are of particular importance, as these are used for all hash inputs. Thus we define the *Anchor match*, which refers to the correctness of the fields that constitute the anchor attributes. Metrics are aggregated over all documents. Using the given three metrics, observations can be made to estimate, where the used models, parameters, or prompts result in higher or lower accuracies as to gauge their respective shortcomings for different kinds of data fields. In addition, we aim to evaluate whether different prompting techniques are beneficial when extracting information from target documents.

The research questions investigate the influence of the model configuration, the prompt and the chosen output format on the ability of open-source VLMs to extract PII from target documents. Although they focus on different variables, they can all be evaluated with the same evaluation pipeline.

To this end, we design an evaluation setup that systematically varies the relevant factors, while keeping all other conditions constant. This setup allows to measure extraction quality of PII through counting matches for both individual fields as well as whole documents. The pipeline can be seen in Fig. 1.

The system takes images as input, that may or may not display a target document. For each input image a ground truth is provided that comprises both the image class and if applicable visible PII fields and their values. All the images are processed by the selected VLMs together with different prompts in a

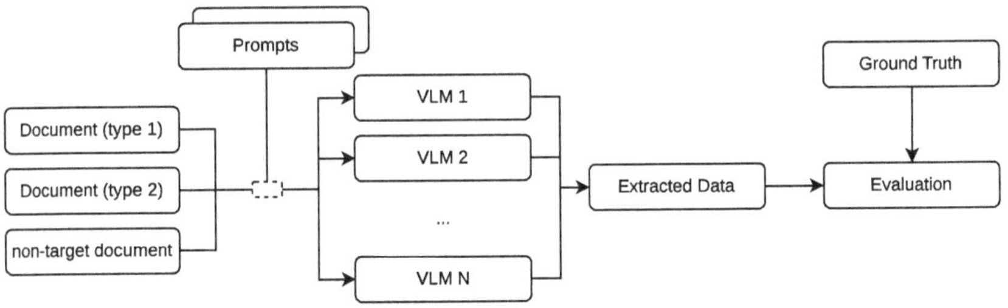

Fig. 1. Visualisation of the evaluation pipeline. Target documents as well as non-target documents in conjunction with a specific prompt are given to multiple VLMs. The extracted data is compared to the ground truth to check for errors.

zero-shot, in-context learning setting without any fine-tuning. From each model response, we extract the predicted image class and the set of extracted PII fields.

The available image classes comprise `ID`, `Invoice`, and `non-target`, if the image shows either an ID card, an invoice, or neither. For our investigation we omitted images that displayed more than one target document. Given a model response, the predicted image class and the format prompted for is used to load a processing module, which parses the set of extracted PII fields and stores them in a database. The corresponding PII fields from the ground truth are compared to the extracted values. This allows to find and count matches but also monitor errors during extraction to perhaps identify certain issues for specific VLM configurations, such as error biases.

To allow an automatic storage in a data base for later processing and evaluation, the extracted data needs to be parsed, which depending on the inquired document type will load the corresponding parsing module. These parsing modules are engineered to try and fit the VLM output to the corresponding data set entry. If the output is not able to be parsed into the format the data set requires, the output is not translated into a data set entry, thus is dropped. This happens, when the VLM either fails to extract all required fields, or fails to fit the extracted data into a parsable format. We investigate, whether the required output format impacts the amount of parsable VLM outputs. As a selection of commonly used structured data formats, `json`, `csv`, and `yaml` were chosen.

To systematically investigate the research questions, we vary several factors in the described pipeline that may influence the extraction behavior of VLMs and evaluate their effects under controlled conditions. We consider multiple families of VLMs and for each family several parameter sizes are tested to assess both architectural and size related effects. Additionally, the prompts that are used employ different prompting strategies and request different output formats.

Our selection of VLMs was following these guidelines: A VLM needs to be open-source, self-hostable, open weights and general purpose. Since the data that these VLMs are operating with contain PII, none of the data shall leave a local system for any reason, requiring transparency in its data flow. We settled on three families of VLMs, being `qwen2.5`, `Intern`, and `Llava` at first, but added `Qwen3` during development, as that was released at that time (April 2025).

3.1 Prompting Techniques in Use

Since the automation pipeline requires output answers in a parsable form, the goal of the prompts is to guide the model to generate output answers that satisfy the parsing requirements. As described above, for commonly used structured data formats `json`, `csv`, and `yaml` were chosen. With the output format chosen, the strategy of how to best prompt the models for these specific formats is to be found. To that end, we test different prompting techniques that both prompt for different output formats as well as follow different strategies.

Prompting refers to the targeted formulation of model inputs to guide the behavior without modifying the model's parameters. In context learning describes the method of using a prompt to guide a model's output [8]. Giving the model an instruction to do something without examples or other additions is called zero-shot prompting. Few-shot prompting adds examples showing how to solve the task to the instruction. Li et al. [10] propose EmotionPrompt, which adds short emotional stimuli to prompts and reports improved performance in several settings. Chen et al. [3] describe Role prompting, which attributes the model a role in which it is supposed to act.

Each output format is prompted for laying out the full format structure for the identified document type. The following two prompt strategies are used: `With Example` also `wEx` and `Without Example` also `NoEx`. Both strategies are employed in a zero-shot Role Prompting format which are identical with the exception that for `wEx` an example is given, which is omitted for `NoEx`.

```
Output Structure Example:
---BEGIN_EXAMPLE---
{
    "document_analysis": ""
    "extracted_data": {}
}
---END_EXAMPLE---
```

Listing 1.1. An example given for the `json` prompt.

Using these prompts, we gauge how well different models and parameter sizes can generate parsable output answers for the evaluation pipeline for each of the chosen structured data formats. The validity of the evaluation of the PII extraction hinges on the amount of parsable output. Prompting VLMs with and without an example not only tests their general ability to present data compatible with prominent structured data formats. Their ability to follow a data format example in a parsable way is also examined. For that, common `json`, `csv`, and `yaml` parsers are being extended to allow slight format inconsistencies, without being too generic or specialized towards individual model output. These extensions are crafted to support empirical test output of different VLM output answers.

Finally, the `wEx` and `NoEx` prompts are being extended by an emotional stimulus as follows:

```
...
Provide only the JSON object as your final answer, without any introductory
    text or explanations. Do not leave comments in the JSON. I need this data
    for an important meeting today. You really can't make any mistakes,
    otherwise I'll lose my job, won't be able to pay my rent, become homeless
    , and eventually die!
```

Listing 1.2. Emotional prompt.

Keeping the rest unchanged allows to directly measure the impact of the emotional component on the PII extraction.

3.2 Procedure

For every combination of model configuration and prompt, extraction results are evaluated using the metrics *Full-Field matches*, *All-Field matches*, and *Anchor matches*. Furthermore we measure the classification accuracy for the document type that each combination shows, as well as the amount of parsable output in comparison to the amount of non-parsable output each combination produces.

To answer RQ1, we analyze how the All-Field matches and Full-Field matches vary with model configuration and document structure. We analyze the correlation between parameter count and All-Field matches, while comparing the Full-Field matches for fields with a strict format and more variable format. For RQ2 we compare the amount of Full-Field matches between prompt techniques across different VLMs in Sect. 3.1.

To be able to compare the extracted PII with the actual content on the documents, a ground truth is required. Therefore a labelled data set of images of both German ID cards, invoices, and other things is required. For identity documents, a limited number of publicly available data sets exist, such as the MIDV data set [2]. However, it is possible that images from such data sets are included in the training data of VLMs. In contrast, for invoices, there is no large-scale data set with field-level annotations. For these reasons, we construct a fully synthetic data set comprising German ID cards as examples of structured documents and invoices as examples of semi-structured documents.

DocGen: To generate synthetic identity card images, we employ a multi-stage pipeline. First, a clean template of the German ID card is generated by removing all data from a publicly available sample ID using image editing techniques. Artificial portrait photos are generated using Stable Diffusion and textual content for all ID card fields is generated using the Python library Faker, ensuring realistic but fully synthetic personal information. Both are inserted in the cleaned ID card template and the resulting image is placed in a background taken from the MIDV data set. To increase realism, we approximate the blur, motion blur, and illumination characteristics of the original background image. These estimated properties are applied to the synthesized ID card, resulting in a final image.

Synthetic invoices are generated using document templates that contain placeholders for textual content and logos for some of them. PII data is generated using the Faker library, and services that are billed on the invoice are either domain-specific items taken from predefined lists or generic ones also generated with faker. These lists include medical services from the "GebÃijhrenordnung" for general practitioners and dentists and services for craftsmen taken from publicly accessible tender documents.

For the use of a fully synthetic data set as constructed by the above methods the following limitations apply:

- The cleaned base template is not a perfect reproduction of the original document
- The fonts used to recreate textual fields resemble but do not fully match the exact fonts used on official German IDs
- The estimated blur and illumination properties may not fully capture the complexity of real-world camera conditions
- Only one version of the German ID card is used, limiting document diversity
- The number of available templates for invoices is limited, reducing layout variability
- The plausibility of generated service descriptions is not guaranteed in all cases, and the coherence of different items may occasionally be imperfect

Description of the Data set: The final data set consists of a total of 2200 images. It includes 1000 synthetically generated images of German ID cards, 1000 synthetically generated images of invoices, and an additional 200 miscellaneous images. Among the 1000 ID cards and invoices, 100 pairs share overlapping identities. Half of the invoices include simulated scanning artifacts. The remaining 200 images consist of two subsets. One subset contains 100 images from the COCO data set [11], included to ensure a wide variety of non-document images. The other subset contains 100 non-invoice document images from the RVL_CDIP data set [6], which are used to assess whether vision–language models can correctly distinguish them from actual invoices.

4 Experiments

We have conducted experiments as described in Sect. 3 in order to answer the established research questions RQ1 and RQ2. With the amount of selected VLMs, parameters for these VLMs, and the variety of prompts, a total of $18 \times 8 = 144$ combinations were used to start the evaluation pipeline with. For each parameter combination, all 2.200 images were used as input, resulting in a total of $144 \times 2200 = 316.800$ images to be classified as either `ID`, `invoice`, or `non-target`. These 2200 images include 1.000 images of German ID cards with 7 fields each, 1.000 images of invoices with 5 fields each, and 200 other images with no fields. This results in a total of 12.000 fields to be evaluated per run, thus in $144 \times 12.000 = 1.728.000$ total fields to evaluate extraction quality with.

Overall, out of 316.800 documents, 246.123 were classified correctly over all tested VLM configurations with a noticeable quality difference between different models, parameter count, and prompt strategies. Table 1 shows the classification results across all models.

Table 1. Statistics on the number of documents that data was reported for in a proper format by the tested VLMs. Shown is the amount and percentage of correctly versus incorrectly classified documents per VLM.

Classification of documents	total	Qwen3	Qwen2.5	Intern	Llava
reported	246.123 : 78 %	81.308 : 92 %	55.536 : 79 %	56.423 : 80 %	52.856 : 89 %
correct	230.928 : 94 %	77.206 : 95 %	55.463 :100 %	56.172 :100 %	42.087 : 80 %
incorrect	15.195 : 6 %	4.102 : 5 %	73 : <1 %	251 : <1 %	10.769 : 20 %

Immediately it is apparent that the classification is significantly different in quality between some of the tested VLMs. Out of the possible maximum of 1.728.000 total fields to be matched, for images that were misclassified no fields were reported that could be evaluated whether their content would match the ground truth. In total the reported fields to be used for evaluation amount to 1.258.834, or about 73 %. Table 2 shows the matches observed over all tested configurations broken down by VLM family.

Table 2. Statistics on the number of fields that data was reported for in a proper format by the tested VLMs. Shown is the amount and percentage of correctly versus incorrectly extracted field values per VLM.

Field Matches	total	Qwen3	Qwen2.5	Intern	Llava
reported	1258.834 : 73 %	419.657 : 87 %	299.251 : 78 %	302.646 : 79 %	237.280 : 73 %
correct	952.840 : 76 %	366.407 : 87 %	264.293 : 88 %	238.284 : 79 %	83.856 : 35 %
incorrect	305.994 : 24 %	53250 : 13 %	34.958 : 12 %	64.362 : 21 %	153.424 : 65 %

Correctly classifying a document does not equate to properly reporting parsable fields, thus all families show an expected deterioration in the relative amount of fields for correctly classified documents. For the use case it is desired to maximize the amount of correctly matched fields, meaning the extracted values by the VLM match the ground truth. Three of the tested VLM families extract fields mostly correctly on average over all configuration, so for different parameter sizes and prompting strategies. However, the VLM family `Llava` seems to struggle to produce correct field matches. Section 5 contains a deeper dive into the details for the specific prompting strategies and individual configurations. An interpretation of the results as well as tests for the posed hypotheses are also provided.

5 Evaluation

In this section, the obtained measurements are used to answer the posed research questions by testing the given hypotheses. First, the field matches are analyzed based on the used model configurations. Then, the impact of the used prompting techniques are evaluated. Finally, the observed results are interpreted from a legal standpoint.

5.1 Field Matches

Table 3 shows some statistics on the quality of PII extraction for the tested VLM model families. For each model family, the best three performing modes regarding the percentage of Full-Field Matches are shown with their performance on the best performing prompt. Listed are the percentages of overall Full-Field matches, All-Field matches and Anchor matches compared to the totally available fields for the documents provided. Thus, the presented percentage factors in document classification quality and PII extraction precision.

Table 3. Statistics on the Field Matches for different VLM families when invoked with different parameters (Mode) and prompts. Shown are the best performing prompts for the three best performing modes per family.

Family	Mode	Prompt	% Full-F	% All-F	% Anchor
Qwen3	32B	`json_wEx`	99.01 %	94.60 %	97.05 %
	8B	`json_wEx`	98.58 %	92.60 %	95.90 %
	30B-A3B	`json_wEx_emotional`	96.60 %	86.75 %	92.85 %
Qwen2.5	72B	`yml_wEx`	98.23 %	91.30 %	96.00 %
	7B	`json_NoEx`	96.73 %	86.50 %	93.45 %
	32B	`csv_wEx`	95.85 %	85.80 %	93.00 %
Intern	14B	`yml_wEx`	86.19 %	47.25 %	71.65 %
	38B	`json_wEx_emotional`	84.68 %	47.75 %	65.80 %
	78B	`json_wEx_emotional`	82.71 %	45.05 %	59.70 %
Llava	110B	`json_wEx`	44.39 %	2.40 %	24.75 %
	72B	`json_wEx`	37.11 %	0.60 %	21.00 %
	13B	`json_NoEx_emotional`	31.61 %	0.15 %	16.60 %

The families Qwen3 and Qwen2.5 both achieve respectable amounts of matches of all categories, with over 95 % for Full-Field and Anchor matches for their best configurations. Some configurations even achieve over 90 % All-Field matches, meaning over 9 of 10 documents have their PII extracted without error. The family Intern still achieves over 80 % of Full-Field matches on their best configurations but clearly lacks behind in All-Field and Anchor matches.

Finally, the family Llava fails to produce results that are usable in the presented use case with less then 50 % Full-Field, less than 3 % All-Field and less than 25 % Anchor matches for their best configuration.

These results stem from the varying success of correct document classification and extracted field values presented in Sect. 4, which summarized the findings over the entire collection of configurations per family. While the best, and worst, performing configurations likely present outliers, the decision was made to drop the VLM family Llava from all further evaluation given the shown best and average performance in comparison to the other families.

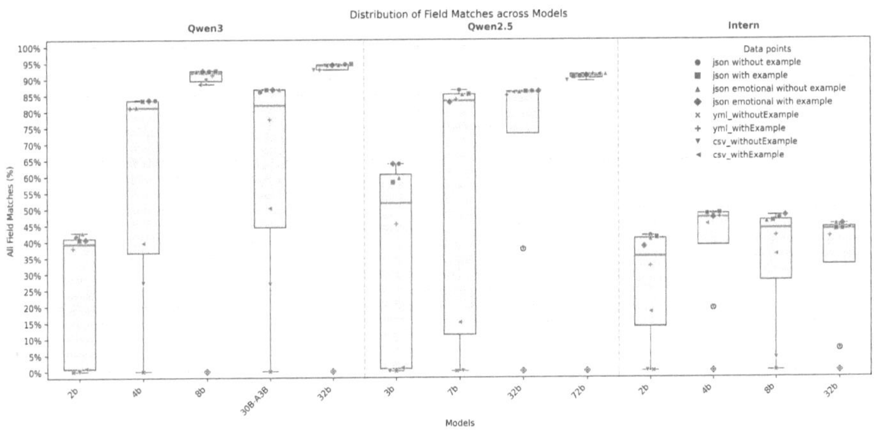

Fig. 2. Percentage of Full-Field matches per VLM configuration. For Qwen the Full-Field matches increase with an increase in parameters, part from the 30B-A3B configuration, which operates differently from the other parameter sizes. The Intern family on average achieves less Full-Field matches.

In order to answer RQ1 the observed results re evaluated as follows. For each VLM family, the results were saved per configuration of mode and prompt on all documents. Therefore the extraction quality can be evaluated by family and by parameter count, independent of the used prompt. Figure 2 shows the percentage of the All-Field matches per model configuration for each given prompting strategy.

Firstly, it is evident that the parameter count does impact the overall rate of All-Field matches. For `Qwen3` and `Qwen2.5` for most prompting strategies the lower parameter counts tend to perform worse on average than the higher counts, up towards 95 % with `Qwen3-32B`. The only exception here is `Qwen3-30B-A3B`, which achieves a lower overall amount of All-Field matches than `Qwen3-8B`, which may be attributed to it only activating 3B parameters per inference step. Secondly, for the `Intern` family the same observation cannot be made, as `Intern-4B` achieves the highest amount of All-Field matches on average despite two other configurations were tested with a higher parameter count. `Intern` fails to achieve

50 % of All-Field matches on any configuration though, showing its weaknesses when used for our use case compared to `Qwen`. Overall, the assertion can be made that there generally is a correlation between the number of parameters and the number of All-Field matches for `Qwen`, where all configurations improved their performance with parameter count, apart from `Qwen3-30B-A3B`, which operates differently.

In order to understand why `Intern` falls so far behind on All-Field matches while performing relatively less far behind on Full-Field matches, a closer look at the individual fields is required, as seen in Tables 2 and 3. Figure 3 shows the Full-Field matches for individual fields per document type. The fields are separated to invoice and id as well as anchor, which depicts the addition of the anchor attributes (first name, last name) of both document types. As observed above, `Intern` achieves on average a lower amount of Full-Field matches than `Qwen` for almost all fields. Given that the criterion for All-Field matches is fulfilled, when all fields match for a given document, it becomes more clear that `Intern` fails more All-Field matches by virtue of having a lower average Full-Field matches.

Another quality that can be observed is that the fields `date_of_birth`, `date_of_expiry`, `nationality` and to some extend `recipient_postal_code` all feature strikingly high average Full-Field matches across all model families when compared to the rest of the fields. What these fields have in common, is that they consist of a strict format, either dates, postal codes or a nationality. In contrast to that, the rest of the fields comprise values that are names, either for places like streets or cities, or for names, including `last_name_at_birth`. Where the strict format fields achieve an average of 98.3 % of Full-Field matches, the fields consisting of names achieve an average of 92.6 % over all models and configurations.

We have shown that the amount of parameters for a given VLM configuration does have an impact on the quality of data extraction for our data and use case. While for fields with a strict format the difference is not as stark, for fields consisting names the impact can be observed, resulting in an overall increase in All-Field matches for model configurations with higher parameters on average. We can thus answer RQ1.

5.2 Prompting Techniques

To answer RQ2, the same experiments were done with the different explained prompting strategies as described in Sect. 3.1. Figure 4 shows the results for the different prompting strategies that reported results over all model configurations. for `yaml_NoEx`, `csv_NoEx`, and `csv_wEx` not all model configurations reported parsable results, mostly due to not correctly classifying the documents or failing to produce a parsable output format for correctly classified documents. For the `json` format prompts the models were achieving comparable results regardless of whether an example was given or not. As for the `yaml` and `csv` format prompts results being more dependent on the example given, the decision was made to test the addition of an emotional stimulus only to the `json` format prompts to eliminate possible interactions between these factors. The mean percentage of

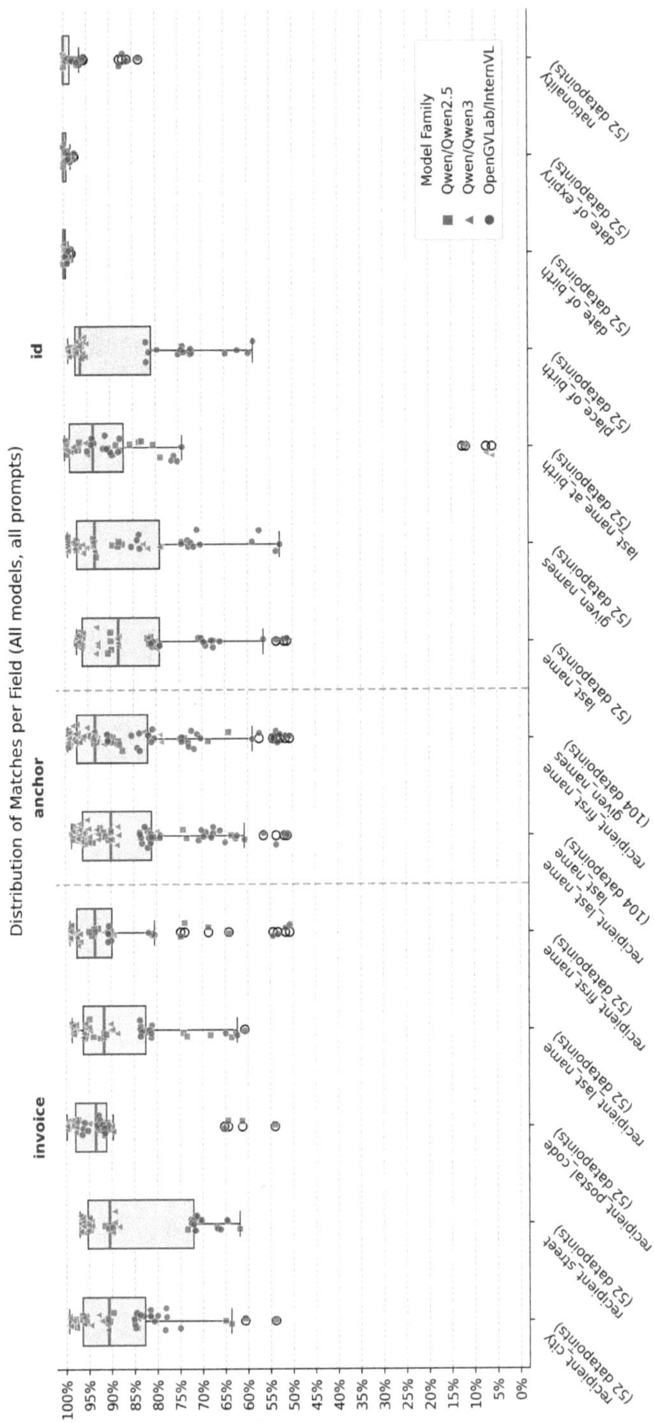

Fig. 3. Shown are the Full-Field matches for each individual field present in either invoice, or ID, as well as non-target documents. Shown are the results for three different model families independent of the used prompting technique.

Full-Field matches for all model configurations between the `json` format prompts with or without the emotional stimulus all sit at around 85 % with almost identical result spreads. For the tested data, we conclude that adding our tested version of an emotional stimulus to the prompt did not yield significant improvements when compared to the results without the addition.

In conclusion, we show that for our data and use case providing a description on how to extract the data helps VLMs in achieving more Full-Field matches. Adding our used emotional stimulus did not impact the results significantly however. Thus we can answer RQ2.

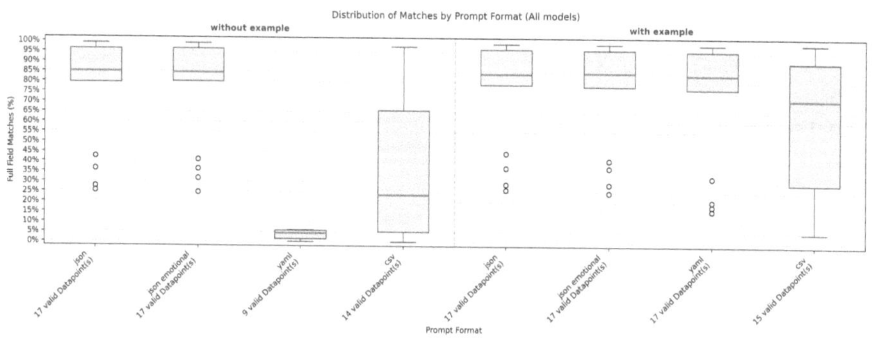

Fig. 4. Percentage of Full-Field matches per prompting technique across all model configurations. For `json` format prompts neither the existence of an example or an emotional stimulus shows a significant impact on extraction quality. `yaml` and `csv` are majorly impacted by the existence of an example, which is why they were excluded from an experiment adding the emotional stimulus.

5.3 Legal Implications

The empirical results have direct implications for the legal applicability of VLM-based PII extraction systems, but they do not in themselves establish legal deployability. Empirically, the study measures whether particular VLM configurations can extract PII fields exactly. Legally, those measurements become relevant because of Article 5(1)(d) General Data Protection Regulation (GDPR). Normatively, however, the consequences of the measured error rates depend on the deployment context. The relevant legal question is not merely whether a model achieves high average performance, but whether its demonstrated quality is sufficiently exact for the specific processing purpose. Article 5(1)(d) GDPR requires personal data to be accurate and, where necessary, kept up to date, expressly linking inaccuracy to the purposes for which the data are processed. This provision does not prescribe a particular benchmark or threshold. Accuracy is, therefore, not an abstract statistical property, but a relational requirement assessed against a concrete processing purpose; an error that is tolerable in one context may be legally material in another, with consequences such as rectification or erasure. In the present system, the processing purpose is exact PII matching. A misspelled surname, an incorrectly normalised address or a wrongly encoded character is, therefore, not merely a minor technical imperfection if it prevents a correct match or creates an incorrect association between a person and a leaked document. The paper's exact-match design is legally appropriate for a use case in which personal data are processed for identification-related comparison [4]. The paper's metrics are particularly valuable because they provide technical indicators for aspects of accuracy that may become legally relevant. A simple average accuracy measure would be insufficient for this purpose-relative assessment, since it could obscure the fact that one erroneous field may compromise the whole document-level result. By distinguishing full-field matches, all-field matches and anchor matches, the paper captures three relevant layers of quality. This structure is a more legally meaningful than generic performance score. It reflects the fact that, under Article 5 GDPR, the controller must comply not only with accuracy, but also with purpose limitation, data minimisation and accountability. Nevertheless, the legal inference remains separate from the technical observation: Although it cannot establish compliance by itself, the metric design may support an assessment under the GDPR's accuracy principle and help connect technical validation to demonstrable compliance.

The empirical findings therefore support a differentiated and deliberately limited legal assessment. The study shows that certain configurations, particularly Qwen3 and Qwen2.5, achieve comparatively high extraction quality under the experimental conditions. This is significant because legal risk arises not only from average field performance, but from the possibility of incorrect fields leading to false negatives, false positives or erroneous attribution of PII. The legal inference is however narrower than the technical result: the results support the use of high-performing configurations as assistive components, but the findings do not justify autonomous reliance on VLM outputs, in particular, where legal, institutional or individual consequences follow directly from a match or non-match. The converse is also relevant: Llava's poor results indicate technical unsuitability for the study's exact-matching use case. In a legally consequential deployment, such performance would most likely be insufficient to satisfy a purpose-relative accuracy requirement. This conclusion does not rest on the proposition that a particular model family is legally impermissible in the abstract. Rather, it follows from the combination of the tested task, the low observed quality and the legal significance of exactness where the processing purpose is identity-related matching. The field-level further indicates that strictly formatted fields, such as dates of birth, dates of expiry, nationality and, to some extent, postal codes, are extracted more reliably than variable textual fields such as names, birth names, streets and cities. Their legal significance arises from the role of those fields in the processing operation. Where names, birth names or addresses are used to identify a person, support a match, or associate an individual with a leaked document, an error in such a field may be legally material even if the system's aggregate performance remains high. The results therefore suggest that legal tolerance for extraction errors cannot be assessed by reference to average performance alone, but must be field-specific, purpose-relative, sensitive to the consequences of using the extracted field, and attentive to the specific configuration tested and the governance safeguards surrounding deployment. The significant differences between model families imply that model selection also forms part of legal governance, while also demonstrating why the analysis must remain configuration-specific. The legal inference that arises is that the selected configuration must be justified within the controller's broader accountability framework. These differences invalidate any general assertion that VLMs are legally suitable for PII extraction as a class. The specific configuration is legally relevant when taking into account the model family, parameter size, prompt design, output format, parser and validation procedure in relation to the specific processing purpose.

The work's findings should also be situated within the distinction between technical quality and legal trustworthiness. While high match rates are a necessary condition for legally credible deployment, they do not exhaust the legal analysis. In this respect, Laux et al. [9] critique of the conflation of trust and trustworthiness with the acceptability of risks is helpful: even if a system meets a performance threshold, it may still fail to generate justified institutional trust if its operation is opaque, insufficiently governed or difficult to contest. In the present context, technical quality metrics are best understood as the initial (though not standalone) layer of trustworthiness and, more broadly, trust. They do not prove that the system is trustworthy in its deployed form. This must be accompanied by a number of factors, including transparent limitations, documented error profiles, field-specific validation and auditability. In addition to these factors concerning accuracy and robustness, legal trustworthiness would require the consideration of factors such as transparency, human oversight, data privacy, documentation and lifecycle monitoring. Accordingly, their relationship should be understood as cumulative. The paper's metrics role would therefore be evidential rather than determinative. They identify configurations whose technical quality may warrant further assessment, not configurations whose outputs can be treated as legally reliable without further safeguards. This distinction is consistent with the view that trustworthiness should not be reduced to the acceptability of technical risk alone. The AI Act points in the same direction. The paper's metrics could form one part of such a governance framework as a necessary precondition for legally credible use, but support assistive deployment only.

6 Discussion

While the presented results show significant differences for some of the tested configurations and qualities, the overall validity of our findings for an application in a broader sense is unclear. This section aims to discuss the limits of the validity of our findings with regards to the limitations our use case and data selection introduced to the evaluation. Firstly, our evaluation was done on a synthetic data set for one specific version of an ID document of one specific language, in addition to synthetic German invoices that follow loose legal guidelines. It is true that the surrounding data environment did not allow for a broader data foundation without vastly increased effort. However, the overall significance of our findings is questionable, if different ID versions or a different language were considered. Even for working with non-synthetic data, meaning images of actual ID documents, it is not tested how well our results are applicable. The applied prompting strategies only represent a selection of various prompting strategies. We did not test many variations of specific prompts and their impact on the VLM performance other than the ones presented. Additionally, we did not test the performance difference between zero-shot and few-shot prompting on our use case. Testing different prompting strategies proved costly for our evaluation pipeline, as the PII extraction run time for different VLMs on the entire data set took hours to days. Therefore a selection of precisely engineered prompts needed to be made, which in turn limited the amount of different prompts that were able to be used for data extraction, thus limiting the insight on the prompting impact on data extraction. Particularly, the emotional stimulus that we used was only ever tested in two different versions, where both failed to produce a significant impact on extraction quality. Moreover, more advanced strategies like iterative refinement or multi-pass extraction were not implemented. A setup or pipeline that would allow for faster document processing would allow for a more rigorous testing methodology in the future.

Finally, a proper comparison against standard or commercial OCR engines should be aimed for in the future to establish, whether the usage of VLM is not only viable for PII extraction but truly yields superior results.

7 Conclusion

In this work, we examined PII extraction from images of German ID cards and German invoices using open-source VLMs. We performed experiments in which we used four families of open-source VLMs in different parameter configurations and with different prompting strategies to extract PII from 2.000 document images. Due to our use case, privacy-preserving PII comparison using hash-based matching, strict requirements were set, which the extracted PII need to conform to. We introduced three metrics in Full-Field matches, All-Field matches, and Anchor matches in order to evaluate the quality of PII extraction from both a technical and legal point of view. We found that certain configurations of model and prompt performed significantly better on these metrics than others. We showed that VLMs fair differently given different instructions, where zero-shot prompting when given detailed instructions on how to extract PII enabled three of the four tested model families to extract PII mostly correctly. In particular, `Qwen3-32B` using the prompting strategy `json_wEx` achieved over 99 % Full-Field matches, over 94 % All-Field matches, and over 97 % Anchor matches. These results suggest that from a legal standpoint not the selection of VLMs as a GDPR compliant technique should be acceptable, but rather that model, parameter, and prompt selection is part of legal governance itself. The introduced metrics may assist in forming parts of a legal governance framework.

Disclosure of Interests. The authors have no competing interests to declare that are relevant to the content of this article.

References

1. Baranouskaya, D., Cavallaro, A.: PrivLEX: detecting legal concepts in images through vision-language models. arXiv preprint arXiv:2601.09449 (2026)
2. Bulatov, K., Matalov, D., Arlazarov, V.V.: MIDV-2019: challenges of the modern mobile-based document OCR. In: Twelfth International Conference on Machine Vision (ICMV 2019), pp. 717–722 (2020)
3. Chen, B., Zhang, Z., Langrené, N., Zhu, S.: Unleashing the potential of prompt engineering for large language models. Patterns **6**(6) (2025)
4. Dimitrova, D.: The rise of the personal data quality principle: is it legal and does it have an impact on the right to rectification? EJLT **12**(3) (2021). https://ejlt.org/index.php/ejlt/article/view/768
5. Gao, Z., et al.: Multi-modal agent tuning: building a VLM-driven agent for efficient tool usage. In: International Conference on Learning Representations, pp. 13354–13385 (2025)
6. Harley, A.W., Ufkes, A., Derpanis, K.G.: Evaluation of deep convolutional nets for document image classification and retrieval. In: 2015 13th International Conference on Document Analysis and Recognition (ICDAR), pp. 991–995 (2015)
7. How e-invoices differ from paper or PDF invoices (2025). https://e-rechnung-bund.de/en/e-invoicing/differences-between-paper-pdf-and-e-invoices/. [Online. Accessed 27 Feb 2026]
8. Kojima, T., Gu, S.S., Reid, M., Matsuo, Y., Iwasawa, Y.: Large language models are zero-shot reasoners. Adv. Neural Info. Process. Syst. **35**, 22199–22213 (2022)
9. Laux, J., Wachter, S., Mittelstadt, B.: Trustworthy artificial intelligence and the European Union AI act: On the conflation of trustworthiness and acceptability of risk. Regulat. Govern. **18**(1), 3–32 (2024). eprint: https://doi.org/10.1111/rego.12512. https://onlinelibrary.wiley.com/doi/abs/10.1111/rego.12512
10. Li, C., et al.: Large language models understand and can be enhanced by emotional stimuli. arXiv preprint arXiv:2307.11760 (2023)
11. Lin, T.-Y., et al.: Microsoft coco: common objects in context. In: European Conference on Computer Vision, pp. 740–755 (2014)
12. Lu, X., et al.: VLM as policy: common-law content moderation framework for short video platform. In: Proceedings of the 31st ACM SIGKDD Conference on Knowledge Discovery and Data Mining, v. 2, pp. 4682–4693 (2025)
13. Maltzan, S.V., Vogel, D., Ohm, M., Idelberger, F.: How anonymous is anonymous? A techno-legal exploration. In: Legal Knowledge and Information Systems: JURIX 2025: The Thirty-eighth Annual Conference, Turin, Italy, 9-11 December 2025, pp. 204–215 (2025)
14. Samson, L., Barazani, N., Ghebreab, S., Asano, Y.M.: Little data, big impact: privacy-aware visual language models via minimal tuning. arXiv preprint arXiv:2405.17423 (2024)
15. Zhang, S., et al.: The pervasive blind spot: benchmarking VLM inference risks on everyday personal videos. arXiv preprint arXiv:2511.02367 (2025)

Privacy Coverage Assessment of Code-Based Privacy Analysis Tools

Arun Poovelikunnel Varghese(✉), Laurens Sion, and Wouter Joosen

DistriNet, KU Leuven, Leuven 3001, Belgium
{arun.poovelikunnelvarghese,laurens.sion,wouter.joosen}@kuleuven.be
https://distrinet.cs.kuleuven.be/

Abstract. Privacy-preserving software systems are a key requirement for compliance with data protection regulations. Software systems therefore need to be reviewed and evaluated to assess their privacy-friendly properties. However, evidence relevant to privacy analysis is distributed across heterogeneous artifacts, such as application code, configuration files, execution logs etc. These artifacts encode critical information about how data is collected, processed, stored, and disclosed by software systems. Performing manual analysis on these artifacts is inherently complex, making automated privacy analysis a necessary approach.

In this paper, we present a comprehensive analysis of existing automated privacy analysis tools drawn from multiple sources and systematically evaluate their capability to identify privacy-relevant features from source code artifacts. Our analysis examines the evidence reported in the publications, together with any available supplementary materials, to map detected information to privacy threat characteristics defined in the LINDDUN threat trees. Based on this mapping, we assess both the breadth of threat type coverage and the depth of the threat characteristic-level detection achieved by each tool. The evaluation enables a systematic comparison of existing studies and reveals that no single tool provides a comprehensive and detailed coverage of privacy threats.

Keywords: privacy by design · static analysis · code analysis · privacy threats

1 Introduction

Privacy assurance in software systems is increasingly difficult due to the large number of data flows in complex applications. Ensuring these systems are privacy-preserving requires the systematic assessment of their implementation. The relevant information is distributed across software components, user-system interactions, inter-component communications, data storage, and third-party integrations and privacy-relevant behavior manifests across multiple stages of the data lifecycle, including data collection, processing, sharing, storage, and deletion [20]. This distribution leads to fragmented privacy-relevant information distributed across different code-based artifacts.

Z. Afzal et al. (Eds.): ARES 2026 Workshops, LNCS 16900, pp. 634–651, 2027.
https://doi.org/10.1007/978-3-032-35576-8_34

Source code artifacts have been used for a wide range of assessments such as security analysis, vulnerability detection, and bug identification [40]. Due to their syntactic and semantic richness, source code representations encode explicit and implicit information about data flows, processing logic, and system interactions and thus provide a relevant input for a privacy analysis. Various models can be derived from source code to support software analysis, including structural models extracted from code, size and complexity metrics, vulnerability fingerprints, dynamic execution behavior models, pattern-based secure code search results, and attack-oriented representations [9,40].

However, while such artifacts effectively characterize structural and behavioral aspects of software, they do not directly convey privacy-specific information. Interpreting the privacy implications from the implementation artifacts requires an appropriate abstraction that connects the low-level software behavior to high-level privacy concerns. What constitutes privacy-relevant information varies substantially across privacy frameworks and perspectives, leading to different approaches for automated privacy analysis using code-based artifacts.

More fine-grained analysis in automated tools enables the application of privacy analysis frameworks at the implementation level using code-based artifacts. There are numerous privacy threat analysis frameworks and taxonomies in the literature [13,21,28,33,37]. PANOPTIC [21] provides two taxonomies: contextual domains and privacy activities. With the privacy activities it classifies different types of privacy attack components, classified in notice, consent, collection, processing, sharing, etc. UsersFirst [37] is a user-centric framework that focuses specifically on the interaction with the data subjects in terms of notices, consent, comprehension, etc. The NIST Privacy Framework [28] conceptualizes privacy risk as arising from problematic data actions and their potential impact on individuals, as well as five functions to manage privacy risks. Rather than threats, Hansen et al. [13] define six privacy goals including the three security goals (confidentiality, integrity, and availability) and three additional goals: transparency, unlinkability, and intervenability. LINDDUN [33] abstracts privacy risk through seven concrete threat types, and breaking them down into characteristics in threat trees.

Manual assessments of an implementation are time-consuming, resource-intensive, and increasingly impractical as software systems grow in size and complexity. This drives the use of automated privacy analysis tools that aim to detect privacy concerns directly from code-based artifacts. Guamán et al. [12] and Ferreyra et al. [7] assessed the tools and the types of privacy concerns they can detect. While previous studies determine whether certain privacy properties [12] or privacy threat types [7] (e.g., data disclosure) are supported by a given tool, they typically treat support as a binary outcome. More concretely, the tool analysis may only support a threat type partially. This paper introduces a finer-grained characterization of analysis support by synthesizing evidence reported in the literature and evaluating coverage across specific threat characteristics, thereby providing a more nuanced understanding of existing tools' capabilities.

2 Related Work

The existing related work on security and privacy analysis are organized into two strands: security and privacy analysis in software systems and privacy frameworks. Each of these perspectives contributes distinct insights into the analysis and assessment of privacy relevant information from the source code artifacts.

2.1 Security and Privacy Analysis in Software Systems

Security-Focused Software Analysis. Security analysis of software systems has been widely studied in the literature, and while numerous surveys exist, the selected studies are presented here as they provide key insights into its methodological and analytical foundations. Senanayake et al. [32] provide a systematic literature review on Android source code vulnerability detection, showing that 51% of studies employ static analysis, 35% adopt hybrid approaches, and 14% rely on dynamic methods. The predominance of static analysis is attributed to its scalability and the richness of code-level features, enabling large-scale automated inspection. Most studies rely on source code as the primary input, extracting features such as API calls, permissions, and system calls to detect security vulnerabilities. These findings confirm that static code analysis remains the dominant paradigm due to its efficiency and feature richness.

Despite its widespread adoption, static analysis exhibits limitations in capturing deeper semantic and contextual security properties in complex systems. Gomes et al. [9] highlight that static code analysis tools for IoT systems struggle with semantic interpretation of source code. While tools such as SonarQube can detect rule-based weaknesses, they are less effective at identifying vulnerabilities that span multiple functions or involve complex exploit chains. Natural language function names and intricate logical structures further limit automated reasoning and functional behavior. Additionally, detecting sensitive data exposure remains challenging due to implicit data flows and limited support for higher-level semantic inference. These findings indicate that, although static analysis is widely adopted and effective for vulnerability detection, it exhibits technical challenges when deeper contextual or data-centric reasoning is required.

Privacy-Focused Software Analysis. Guamán et al. [12] treat privacy as a software quality attribute and classify techniques for detecting privacy-related anomalies. Their mapping study categorizes approaches based on analysis behavior and evaluation targets, linking detected anomalies to predefined privacy properties. However, the analysis largely emphasizes personal data disclosure and regulatory compliance, while key privacy properties such as unlinkability, identifiability, user awareness, intervenability, and plausible deniability are less addressed in the analysis. Ferreyra et al. [7] perform a rapid literature review targeting tools that support the automatic detection of privacy properties in source code or assist in generating privacy-friendly code. The study evaluates both the technical attributes of the tools and their ability to detect privacy threats, using the LINDDUN framework as a reference. The analysis primarily focuses the identification of personal data elements and processing statements, such as sources, sinks, and data flows. Although the work offers a systematic assessment of tool capabilities, it focuses on data-centric detection and does not break down the privacy threat coverage into more fine-grained threat characteristic support.

Both surveys reinforce the relevance of source code artifacts as a key input for privacy analysis. Guamán et al. [12] evaluated privacy properties by mapping privacy anomalies detected using various techniques to their own privacy definitions, which were backed from multiple sources. In contrast, Ferreyra et al. [7] conducted a systematic knowledge synthesis of privacy-as-code approaches based on the LINDDUN framework, but the analysis is limited to privacy threat types. Neither survey analyzes more fine-grained privacy-relevant features inferred by the tools, nor do they examine how the technical characteristics of the tools (e.g., static or dynamic analysis, control flow graphs, or data flow graphs) influence the identification of such granular privacy information.

Challenges in Information Extraction. A key underlying challenge across both security and privacy analysis is the difficulty of extracting structured and semantically meaningful information from software artifacts. This difficulty arises from complex program logic, heterogeneous representations, and implicit data flows. For instance, Yitagesu [38,39] highlights that vulnerability-related information extracted from diverse sources requires systematic classification to enable meaningful interpretation and analysis. Similarly, Javed et al. [18] report that privacy policy analysis from source code is hindered by variability in regulatory interpretation, domain-specific differences, and inconsistent representations of privacy-relevant behavior. These findings collectively suggest that raw extraction of security or privacy-related evidence is insufficient without a structured interpretative layer that organizes and contextualizes the extracted information.

This motivates the need for systematic privacy evaluation frameworks that can provide a consistent structure for interpreting, classifying, and comparing privacy-relevant behaviors across heterogeneous artifacts.

2.2 Privacy Evaluation Frameworks

The interpretation of privacy-related information from software artifacts is harder due to the complexity of the business logic in software systems [9]. Furthermore, different artifactual representations often contain overlapping or semantically similar information that must be mapped to the appropriate privacy concepts. To ensure that the analysis remains systematic and consistent across all tools, a suitable privacy framework must be incorporated. Several privacy frameworks offer different analytical perspectives. PANOPTIC maps privacy contextual domains to privacy activities [21]. Unlike purely system-level methods, it captures broader socio-technical aspects, including data flows, governance structures, and behavioral monitoring, thereby representing privacy exposure and observability across individuals and organizations. UsersFirst is more suitable when the objective is to analyze user control mechanisms, transparency, and privacy choices [37]. The NIST Privacy Framework emphasizes problematic data handling practices and organizational risk management [28]. Hansen et al.'s six privacy goals focus on legal, technical, economic, and societal dimensions of privacy [13]. In contrast, LINDDUN is specifically designed for system-level privacy threat modeling. It derives privacy threats from data flow diagrams and systematically distinguishes threat characteristics under each threat category. Compared to the other approaches, LINDDUN provides a broader operational threat knowledge base and more comprehensive coverage of the data lifecycle [33], making it a more suitable candidate for our analysis.

3 Methodology

The purpose of this study is to assess the comprehensiveness of existing code-based privacy analysis tools by systematically assessing their capabilities in identifying different types of privacy threats. The selection of tools is the result of a multi-step search process (illustrated in Fig. 1 and explained in Sect. 3.1) combining both tools from previous surveys and from the literature search. Next, Sect. 3.2 explains the tool analysis to assess their privacy threat type coverage, supported code-based artifacts, and analysis method.

3.1 Search Process

This study adopts a structured literature search strategy to identify relevant work on privacy analysis in code-based artifacts and explained in the following sections. The overall search strategy is visualized in Fig. 1. The individual steps are explained in more detail below.

Step 1: Database Search Strategy. A structured search query was iteratively developed and refined through iterative discussion among the authors. The final query was applied across five major academic databases on software engineering, security, and privacy-related research: ACM Digital Library, IEEE Xplore, Scopus, ScienceDirect, and Wiley Online Library.

Step 1.1: Database-Specific Settings. To improve relevance, database-specific constraints were applied. In Scopus, ScienceDirect, and Wiley Online Library, the search was restricted to the Computer Science subject area due to their multidisciplinary indexing. No such restriction was required for ACM Digital Library and IEEE Xplore, as these are already domain-focused.

Across all databases, the search was further restricted to venues relevant to software engineering, security engineering, and privacy engineering. Only peer-reviewed conference papers, journal articles, and books were considered. The publication dates are scoped to recent tools from the last 15 years (publication year 2011 and later).

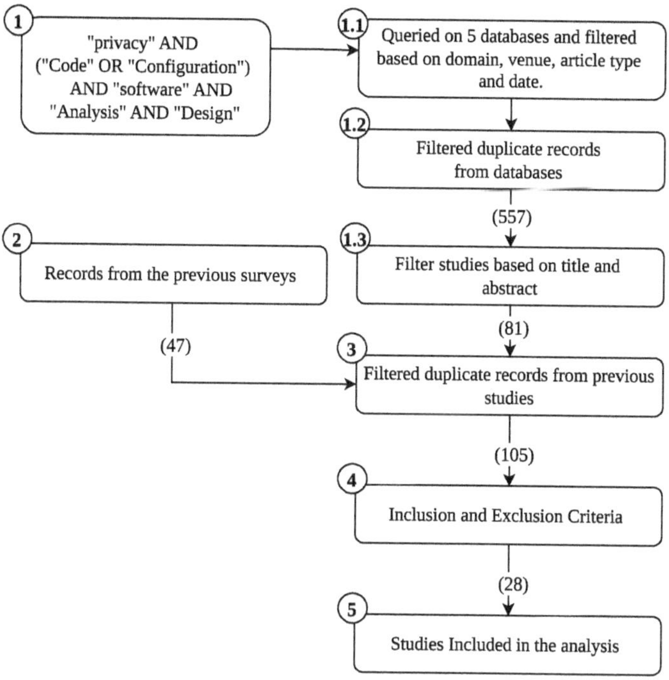

Fig. 1. Search Strategy

Step 1.2: Deduplication. Search results from all databases were merged, and duplicate records were removed using title and DOI matching. This resulted in 557 unique studies.

Step 1.3: Title and Abstract Screening. The remaining studies were screened based on title and abstract relevance to privacy analysis in software systems. This step excluded studies not explicitly addressing privacy-related properties or analysis techniques, resulting in 81 candidate studies.

Step 2: Studies Identified from Prior Surveys. Studies were selected from prior literature surveys if they satisfied the applicability beyond legal compliance or focus on a narrowly scoped application domain. This process contributed 47 additional articles considered relevant to privacy analysis in software systems.

Step 3: Merging and Deduplication. The studies obtained from Step 1 and Step 2 were merged into a single dataset. Duplicate entries were again removed using title and DOI matching, resulting in 105 unique studies for further screening.

Step 4: Full-Text Screening and Selection. The remaining studies were subjected to full-text screening based on predefined inclusion and exclusion criteria to ensure the selection of relevant code-based privacy analysis tools.

Inclusion Criteria. A study was included if it:

- Proposes, evaluates, or applies techniques for detecting or analyzing privacy-related properties in software artifacts (e.g., source code, binaries, or intermediate representations).
- Presents empirical evidence, experimental evaluation, survey results, or tool-based validation in the context of privacy analysis.

Exclusion Criteria. A study was excluded if it:

- Focuses exclusively on security.
- Is purely conceptual without implementation or (empirical) evaluation.
- Addresses only legal compliance requirements (e.g., purpose limitation verification) without providing broader privacy analysis capabilities applicable to software systems.
- Targets a narrowly scoped application context or non-code artifacts (e.g., AI training datasets) such that the proposed approach is not generalizable to privacy analysis of applications in general.

Screening Procedure and Consistency. Full-text screening was conducted by the primary author. Ambiguous cases were re-assessed through iterative discussion among the authors to ensure consistent interpretation of the inclusion criteria.

Final Dataset. After applying the filtering steps, 28 studies were included in the final dataset. These studies formed the basis for the detailed analysis presented in Step 5.

3.2 Tool Analysis

The study examines evidence reported in the publications describing each tool. For each tool, privacy-relevant information is systematically extracted, including supported privacy defects, evaluation scenarios, reported capabilities, and stated limitations. The supported detections are assessed against the LINDDUN threat characteristics (Table 2) and assigned a score according to the following quantitative scoring method.

The LINDDUN characteristic scoring scheme captures the degree to which a tool addresses one-level-deep threat tree nodes as illustrated in Table 2. This enables a more fine-grained assessment of tool coverage across specific privacy threat manifestations. The resulting scores are used to assess the privacy threat coverage of the analyzed tools.

In addition, the tool's technical properties are assessed. The properties listed in Table 1 were extracted from the studies to capture each tool's objective, focus, input processing method, and availability. This provides insights into the design choices and functional capabilities of the tools.

Table 1. Technical Properties of Privacy Analysis Tool

Technical Aspect	Description
Type of Analysis Method	Static, dynamic, or hybrid analysis
Target Artifacts	Source code, infrastructure as code (IaC), Java bytecode, Smali, execution artifacts etc.
Intermediate Representation	Abstract syntax tree (AST), data flow graphs (DFG), control flow graphs (CFG), etc.
Tool Accessibility	Openly available or not

Threat Characteristic Analysis. The resulting 28 studies were assessed for their coverage of the LINDDUN threat characteristics according to the defined evaluation criteria. Each threat characteristic within a threat type was assigned a score using the following scheme:

Score 0: No information about the threat characteristic is provided.
Score 1: Implicit information is provided to support a manual assessment for the threat characteristic.
Score 2: Explicit information about the characteristic of the relevant threat tree nodes.

Since the unit of analysis in this study is the reported evidence in tool publications rather than the implementation behavior of the tools themselves, the assigned scores reflect the extent to which support for a threat characteristic is described in the study. While each threat type may consist of multiple characteristics, the total score for a given threat type is computed as the sum of the scores assigned to its individual characteristics. Based on these scores, the overall coverage per tool is calculated as follows:

$$\text{Coverage}_{\text{tool}} = \frac{\sum_{i=1}^{n} \text{Score}_{\text{tool},i}}{n \times 2} \times 100 \tag{1}$$

where n denotes the number of characteristics. Scores can be aggregated per threat type or for all characteristics for a total score. The result is a percentage indicating the extent to which a tool or technique covers a privacy threat type or, if aggregated, all privacy threat types.

Technical Property Analysis. In addition to evaluating privacy threat coverage, this study assesses the technical characteristics of the selected analysis tools to provide context for interpreting their results. The evaluation focuses on three main aspects: the method of analysis, the target artifacts, and the use of intermediate representations.

The method of analysis determines whether a tool examines code at rest (static analysis), monitors behavior at runtime (dynamic analysis), or combines both approaches in a hybrid fashion. Static analysis typically targets source code, infrastructure-as-code (IaC), bytecode, or binary representations, whereas

Table 2. Threat Characteristics

ID	Name	Definition
L.1	Linked data	Data can be linked through identifiers.
L.2	Linkable data	Linking through combination or analysis of data.
I.1	Identified information	Identified information is requested or processed.
I.2	Identifiable information	The system processes identifiable information from which the identity can be derived.
Nr.1	Attributable data evidence	A data record or message can be attributed to a user or data subject.
Nr.2	Attributable action side-effect evidence	Action side-effects can cause an action to be attributable to an individual.
D.1	Observed communications	Communications can be observed.
D.2	Application side effect	Actions have detectable side effects.
D.3	System responses	The existence of a record or user involvement is revealed in a system response.
DD.1	Unnecessary data types	More sensitive data than necessary is processed.
DD.2	Excessive volume	The volume of processed data is larger than necessary.
DD.3	Unnecessary processing	More processing and analysis occurs than necessary for the functional goals of the system.
DD.4	Involved parties and exposure	Personal data is exposed to more parties than necessary or made more accessible than necessary.
U.1	Unawareness of processing	Users or data subjects are not aware about the collection, processing, storage, or disclosure of personal data.
U.2	Lack of data subject control	Data subjects have insufficient means of control to choose and customize which, how, and how long personal data is processed.
Nc.1	Regulatory non-compliance	There are legal consequences of the threats and/or processing activities described.
Nc.2	Improper personal data management	This characteristic groups a number of data management risks that may have privacy outcomes or vice versa, privacy threats that may lead to overarching data management problems.
Nc.3	Insufficient cybersecurity risk management	A lack of proper cybersecurity risk management with specific attention to the interplay with privacy risks.
Nc.4	Non-compliance with privacy standards and best practices	The system does not adequately implement applicable (industry-)specific privacy standards, guidelines, or recommended privacy best practices.

dynamic analysis relies on execution artifacts collected during program runtime. Hybrid tools may perform sequential or integrated analyses, leveraging results from one method to inform the other. For example, network flows observed at runtime can be analyzed as data flows to unknown resources or behaviors not visible in the code.

To facilitate cross-language applicability, many tools transform their target artifacts into intermediate representations such as abstract syntax trees (ASTs), control flow graphs (CFGs), or data flow graphs (DFGs). These representations provide a generic model of the program, enabling systematic assessment of privacy-relevant features regardless of the underlying programming language or artifact format.

Availability is another important property, indicating whether the tool's source code is publicly available. Open tools improve reproducibility, allow independent verification, and support further extension or adaptation. Collectively, these technical characteristics help distinguish between limitations caused by the inherent difficulty of detecting specific privacy threats and those imposed by the design or implementation of individual tools, thus providing a clearer interpretation of the analysis outcomes.

4 Results

The final dataset resulting from the search strategy (Sect. 3) consists of 28 privacy analysis tools. Table 3 and Table 4 show the technical properties and the privacy coverage of the resulting privacy analysis tools. Table 5 presents the depth of each threat characteristic across the selected dataset, distinguishing between implicit and explicit coverage. First, Sect. 4.1 presents the threat coverage. Afterwards, Sect. 4.2 discusses the differences in the tool implementations.

4.1 Threat Coverage

Individual Threat Coverage. As shown in Table 5, data disclosure characteristics are the most frequently covered characteristics, with all the analysis tools at least implicitly supporting at least one data disclosure characteristic. 7 out of the top 10 with the best coverage even support at least two data disclosure characteristics explicitly. In contrast, threat types such as detecting and non-repudiation have the lowest coverage overall and are addressed by only a few tools. Non-compliance has better support, but this support is focused entirely on Nc.1. Other non-compliance characteristics are rarely supported. Other threat types display more mixed coverage with at least multiple tools partially addressing their characteristics. Overall, not a single characteristic is supported across all the tools in the dataset.

This disparity where some characteristics are frequently detected while others receive no detection support indicates that coverage is not proportionally distributed across the privacy threat types. Detection efforts cluster around a limited subset of characteristics, leaving others under-addressed.

Table 3. Technical properties of the privacy analysis tools

PaperID	Method	Evaluation Target	Representation	Availability	Coverage
P02 [23]	Static	Source Code	Privacy Property Graph: Code Property Graph (Abstract Syntax Tree, Control Flow Graph and Data Flow Graph) and Evaluation Order Graph	Yes	39.5
P12 [16]	Static	Source Code	Directed Graph	Yes	28.9
P04 [25]	Hybrid	Source Code and Execution Path	Abstract Syntax Tree and Execution Path	No	23.7
P06 [11]	Static	OpenAPI (YAML)	None	Yes	23.7
P14 [36]	Static	Source Code	Call graph and abstract syntax tree	No	23.7
P17 [2]	Static	Source Code	Abstract interpretation framework	No	23.7
P10 [6]	Static	Source Code	Data Processing Graph	Yes	21.1
P15 [4]	Static	Source Code	Java bytecode	No	21.1
P19 [17]	Static	Source Code	Smali	No	18.4
P28 [34]	Dynamic	Execution Path	Execution Path	No	18.4
P05 [15]	Static	Source Code	Abstract Syntax Tree	Yes	15.8
P07 [41]	Static	Source Code	Abstract Syntax Trees and Call Graphs	Yes	15.8
P09 [30]	Static	Web API Schema	None	Yes	15.8
P11 [8]	Static	Source Code	Abstract Syntax Tree	No	15.8
P18 [29]	Static	JAR	Call graphs	No	15.8
P25 [19]	Static	Source Code	DVM Bytecode	No	15.8
P21 [26]	Static	Source Code	Data Flow Graph	No	13.2
P22 [5]	Static	Source Code	SCDFLOW	No	13.2
P01 [42]	Static	Source Code	Data Flow Graph	No	10.5
P03 [35]	Static	Bytecode	Control Flow Graph	No	10.5
P08 [10]	Static	IaC code	Directed Acyclic Graph	Yes	10.5
P13 [27]	Static	Source Code	Abstract Syntax Tree and Control Flow Graph	No	10.5
P24 [24]	Static	Source Code	DVM Bytecode	No	10.5
P26 [3]	Static	Source Code	Smali	No	10.5
P27 [14]	Dynamic	Network flows	Network flows	No	10.5
P23 [22]	Static	Source Code	Shimple	No	7.9
P16 [1]	Static	Source Code	Java bytecode	No	5.3
P20 [31]	Static	Source Code	Code Metrics	No	5.3

Per-tool Coverage. Overall, Table 4 reveals a fragmented coverage: no tool achieves full depth and breadth across all privacy threat characteristics. Data disclosure (DD) emerges as the most frequently addressed threat type, with multiple

Table 4. Overview of supported threat characteristics per tool

Paper ID	L		I		Nr		D			DD				U		Nc				Coverage Summary			
	1	2	1	2	1	2	1	2	3	1	2	3	4	1	2	1	2	3	4	Implicit	Explicit	Scores	%
P02 [23]	■	□	□	■	■	□	■	□	■	□	□	□	♦	□	■	■	□	□	□	1	7	15	39.5
P12 [16]	□	♦	□	♦	□	□	□	□	□	■	□	□	■	■	□	■	□	□	♦	3	4	11	28.9
P04 [25]	□	□	♦	□	■	□	□	□	□	□	□	■	■	□	■	□	□	□	□	1	4	9	23.7
P06 [11]	□	■	□	♦	□	□	□	□	□	■	□	■	□	■	□	□	□	□	□	1	4	9	23.7
P14 [36]	□	□	□	□	□	□	□	□	□	■	■	■	□	♦	□	■	□	□	□	1	4	9	23.7
P17 [2]	■	□	■	□	□	□	□	□	□	□	■	□	□	■	□	♦	□	□	□	1	4	9	23.7
P10 [6]	□	□	□	□	□	□	□	□	□	■	■	■	□	□	□	■	□	□	□		4	8	21.1
P15 [4]	□	□	□	□	□	□	■	□	□	□	■	□	■	□	■	□	□	□	□		4	8	21.1
P19 [17]	□	□	□	□	□	□	♦	♦	□	♦	□	□	♦	□	■	♦	□	□	□	5	1	7	18.4
P28 [34]	■	□	□	♦	□	□	□	□	□	□	■	■	□	□	□	□	□	□	□	1	3	7	18.4
P05 [15]	□	□	□	□	□	□	□	□	□	■	■	□	□	□	□	■	□	□	□		3	6	15.8
P07 [41]	□	□	□	□	□	□	□	□	□	■	■	□	□	□	□	■	□	□	□		3	6	15.8
P09 [30]	□	□	□	□	□	□	□	□	□	■	□	■	□	□	□	■	□	□	□		3	6	15.8
P11 [8]	□	□	□	□	□	□	□	□	□	■	■	□	□	□	□	■	□	□	□		3	6	15.8
P18 [29]	□	□	□	□	□	□	♦	□	□	■	□	□	♦	□	■	□	□	□	□	2	2	6	15.8
P25 [19]	□	♦	□	♦	□	□	□	□	□	□	□	□	■	♦	□	♦	□	□	□	4	1	6	15.8
P21 [26]	□	□	□	□	□	□	□	□	□	□	□	■	□	■	□	♦	□	□	□	1	2	5	13.2
P22 [5]	□	♦	□	♦	♦	□	□	□	□	□	□	■	□	□	□	□	□	□	□	3	1	5	13.2
P01 [42]	□	□	□	□	■	□	□	□	□	□	□	■	□	□	□	□	□	□	□		2	4	10.5
P03 [35]	□	□	■	□	□	□	□	□	□	□	□	■	□	□	□	□	□	□	□		2	4	10.5
P08 [10]	□	□	□	□	□	□	□	□	□	■	□	■	□	□	□	□	□	□	□		2	4	10.5
P13 [27]	□	□	□	□	□	□	□	□	□	□	□	■	□	□	□	■	□	□	□		2	4	10.5
P24 [24]	□	□	□	□	□	□	□	□	□	□	□	■	■	□	□	□	□	□	□		2	4	10.5
P26 [3]	□	□	□	□	□	□	□	□	□	■	□	□	□	■	□	□	□	□	□		2	4	10.5
P27 [14]	♦	□	□	♦	□	□	□	□	□	□	□	□	■	□	□	□	□	□	□	2	1	4	10.5
P23 [22]	□	□	□	□	□	□	□	□	□	□	■	□	□	□	□	♦	□	□	□	1	1	3	7.9
P16 [1]	□	□	□	□	□	□	□	□	□	□	□	■	□	□	□	□	□	□	□		1	2	5.3
P20 [31]	□	□	□	□	□	□	□	□	□	□	■	□	□	□	□	□	□	□	□		1	2	5.3

Threat Characteristic Score: □ = 0, ♦ = 1 (implicit), ■ = 2 (explicit).

Table 5. Percentage of 28 tools supporting each threat characteristic

Coverage	L		I		Nr		D			DD				U		Nc			
	1	2	1	2	1	2	1	2	3	1	2	3	4	1	2	1	2	3	4
Implicit	3.6	10.7	3.6	21.4	3.6	0	7.1	3.6	0	3.6	0	0	10.7	7.1	0	17.9	0	0	3.6
Explicit	10.7	3.6	7.1	3.6	10.7	0	7.1	0	3.6	39.3	35.7	50	21.4	17.9	17.9	32.1	0	0	0

DD-related characteristics (described in Table 2) consistently identified. In contrast, non-repudiation (Nr) and detecting (D) characteristics exhibit weaker coverage, while other threat types –including Linking (L), Identifying (I), Unawareness & Unintervenability (U), and Non-compliance (Nc)– show moderate but uneven detection across tools. Analysis of threat coverage scores further distinguishes most widely supported characteristics, such as DD.3 and Nc.1 (Table 2), from "orphan" characteristics, including Nr.2, Nc.2, and Nc.3 (Table 2), which remain undetected by all tools.

This unbalanced coverage at the characteristic level is reflected in the focus of individual tools. Some concentrate narrowly on a few threat characteristics, while others provide broader but still uneven assessments. Tools such as P08 [10], P16 [1], and P20 [31] predominantly focus on one or two data disclosure characteristics, neglecting other threat characteristics entirely. Conversely, several tools including P05 [15], P07 [41], P09 [30], P10 [6], and P11 [8] demonstrate fixed coverage across some threat characteristics within specific threat types. For example, these tools emphasize the disclosure of personal data and compliance with data collection, storage, and processing regulations, while largely omitting other characteristics.

4.2 Analysis Methods

Beyond the focus on specific threat characteristics, differences in technical properties such as analysis methods, target artifacts, and intermediate representations can also contribute to the observed variation in threat coverage.

The majority of the tools perform static analysis, with only a small subset using dynamic or hybrid approaches. Almost all the tools rely on the source code as the main input for the analysis. This limits the capacity of the tools to only characteristics that are fully detectable based only on the source code. However, the source code is not a prerequisite for a relatively good coverage of characteristics as even the OpenAPI-based tool is tied for third with the coverage of the LINDDUN threat characteristics.

5 Discussion

5.1 Approaches

The analysis highlights important differences in how privacy threat characteristics are detected by software tools. Tools such as P05 [15], P07 [41] and P11 [8] (see Table 4) rely on static analysis over Abstract Syntax Trees (ASTs) to extract threat characteristics directly from source code. AST-based analysis allows detailed inspection of syntactic program structures, including variable declarations, method calls, and data access patterns. However, it primarily captures structural properties and does not fully model control-flow dependencies or data-flow propagation. As a result, these tools are limited in their ability to detect privacy threats that span multiple program dimensions, such as interactions between data flows, execution paths, and contextual constraints. In contrast, P02 [23] employs a Privacy Property Graph (PPG), integrating ASTs,

Control Flow Graphs (CFG), Data Flow Graphs (DFG), and Evaluation Order Graphs (EOG). This combination allows simultaneous analysis of structure, control dependencies, and data propagation, enabling detection of a broader range of threat characteristics across multiple privacy threat types. Nevertheless, while P02 achieves 39.5% coverage of threat characteristics, the increased representational richness might not be sufficient for achieving a full coverage.

Dynamic approaches enable the observation of actual data flows and execution behavior. For instance, P27 [14] extracts network flows at runtime and expected to detect application side effect related threats (Nr.2, D.1, and D.2 in Table 2). However, in practice, its coverage remains limited to specific flow-tracking aspects, suggesting that network flows visibility alone does not guarantee comprehensive privacy threat detection. Similarly, the hybrid approach in P04 [25] combines static taint analysis with runtime monitoring to improve traceability across execution contexts. However, the detection of collaborative data sharing and the unawareness of data shared by others, as well as real-time preference management, remain insufficiently addressed. Overall, the distribution of analysis approaches is influenced by the prevalence of Android-centric privacy analysis tools in the dataset, particularly those based on taint analysis, which in turn shapes the observed dominance of specific detection strategies.

5.2 Internal Representations

Privacy threat coverage appears to be fundamentally shaped by how privacy-relevant elements are represented within system artifacts and underlying data models. Although static analysis enables systematic feature extraction from source code, intermediate representations offer a more expressive foundation by integrating multiple structural views, such as control and data dependencies. This multi-view abstraction reduces reliance on language-specific constructs and supports more consistent reasoning across heterogeneous systems. Consequently, the intermediate representation emerges as a critical factor in achieving scalable and cross-language privacy property analysis.

Furthermore, while coverage varies across tools, none achieves comprehensive detection across the full characteristic spectrum. This persistent upper bound indicates that current privacy analysis tools are inherently constrained by their design scope and underlying threat assumptions, resulting in skewed and uneven coverage, rather than by isolated implementation limitations.

5.3 Limitations

The screening and assessment were primarily conducted by the first author, some degree of individual interpretation bias may remain despite subsequent collaborative review of ambiguous cases and results. This study evaluates privacy analysis tools based on the reporting in the studies and did not experimentally validate tool behavior through benchmarking. Only the public availability of the codebase was assessed. Consequently, the reported coverage reflects documented capabilities rather than measured detection performance in practice. Factors such as precision, recall, false positives, and false negatives are therefore not captured by the reported coverage scores. The assessment is performed using the LINDDUN framework as the analytical lens. Accordingly, the reported coverage should be interpreted as coverage relative to LINDDUN threat characteristics. Tools designed around different privacy objectives, or conceptualizations of privacy may receive lower coverage scores due to differences in framework alignment rather than inherent analytical limitations.

The study also focuses on one-level-deep LINDDUN threat characteristics to enable consistent comparison across tools. More specialized threat type manifestations are outside the scope of this analysis. The analysis is limited to tools targeting code-based software artifacts such as source code, bytecode, binaries, and configurations. Finally, privacy analysis approaches focusing exclusively on organizational processes, legal compliance workflows, or dataset-centric analysis were intentionally excluded to focus on software analysis tools.

6 Conclusion and Future Work

This study examined the capability of existing automated privacy analysis tools by evaluating their ability to identify privacy threats based on source code artifacts. The results reveal an incomplete threat coverage: individual tools address only selective subsets of privacy threats, with uneven distribution across the LINDDUN privacy threat types. As a consequence, no tool achieves comprehensive coverage of the full privacy threat spectrum.

In future work, we will investigate whether the openly available tools identified in Table 3 can be effectively evaluated on realistically sized applications to evaluate their maturity beyond controlled experimental test beds. This provides the best set of candidates for further extension to increase the coverage of the privacy threat types. Increasing breadth requires expanding coverage across diverse privacy threat types, rather than concentrating predominantly on data disclosure threats. Improving depth involves more comprehensive modeling of threat characteristics within each category. One promising direction is employing richer intermediate representations that unify syntactic, control-flow, and semantic relationships to enable more accurate cross-component and cross-context reasoning. Finally, the limited coverage of these tools emphasizes the need for complementary activities, such as developer awareness, as relying solely on post-hoc detection in the source code is not sufficient for a comprehensive assessment of the privacy threats.

Acknowledgements. This research is partially funded by the Internal Funds KU Leuven, and by the Cybersecurity Research Program Flanders.

Disclosure of Interests. The authors have no competing interests to declare that are relevant to the content of this article.

References

1. Barbon, G., Cortesi, A., Ferrara, P., Pistoia, M., Tripp, O.: Privacy analysis of android apps: implicit flows and quantitative analysis. In: IFIP International Conference on Computer Information Systems and Industrial Management, pp. 3–23. Springer (2015)
2. Barbon, G., Cortesi, A., Ferrara, P., Steffinlongo, E.: DAPA: degradation-aware privacy analysis of android apps. In: International Workshop on Security and Trust Management, pp. 32–46. Springer (2016)
3. Batyuk, L., Herpich, M., Camtepe, S.A., Raddatz, K., Schmidt, A.D., Albayrak, S.: Using static analysis for automatic assessment and mitigation of unwanted and malicious activities within android applications. In: 6th International Conference on Malicious and Unwanted Software, pp. 66–72. IEEE (2011)
4. Bhandari, S., Herbreteau, F., Laxmi, V., Zemmari, A., Roop, P.S., Gaur, M.S.: SneakLeak: detecting multipartite leakage paths in android apps. In: 2017 IEEE Trustcom/BigDataSE/ICESS, pp. 285–292. IEEE (2017)
5. Feng, P., Ma, J., Sun, C.: Selecting critical data flows in android applications for abnormal behavior detection. Mob. Inf. Syst. **2017**(1), 7397812 (2017)
6. Ferreira, M., Brito, T., Santos, J.F., Santos, N.: Rulekeeper: GDPR-aware personal data compliance for web frameworks. In: 2023 IEEE Symposium on Security and Privacy (SP), pp. 2817–2834. IEEE (2023)
7. Ferreyra, N.E.D., Khelifi, S., Arachchilage, N., Scandariato, R.: The good, the bad, and the (un) usable: a rapid literature review on privacy as code. In: 2025 IEEE/ACM 18th International Conference on Cooperative and Human Aspects of Software Engineering (CHASE), pp. 173–178. IEEE (2025)
8. Fujita, H., Guizzi, G.: Helping code reviewer prioritize: pinpointing personal data and its processing. In: New Trends in Intelligent Software Methodologies, Tools and Techniques: Proceedings of the 22nd International Conference on New Trends in Intelligent Software Methodologies, Tools and Techniques (SoMeT_23). SAGE Publications Limited (2023)
9. Gomes, D., Felix, E., Aires, F., Vieira, M.: Static code analysis for IoT security: a systematic literature review. ACM Comput. Surv. **58**(3), 1–47 (2025)
10. Grünewald, E., Schurbert, L.: Scalable discovery and continuous inventory of personal data at rest in cloud native systems. In: International Conference on Service-Oriented Computing, pp. 513–529. Springer (2022)
11. Grunewald, E., Wille, P., Pallas, F., Borges, M.C., Ulbricht, M.R.: TIRA: An OpenAPI extension and toolbox for GDPR transparency in RESTful architectures. In: 2021 IEEE European Symposium on Security and Privacy Workshops (EuroS&PW), pp. 312–319 (2021)
12. Guaman, D.S., Del Alamo, J.M., Caiza, J.C.: A systematic mapping study on software quality control techniques for assessing privacy in information systems. IEEE access **8**, 74808–74833 (2020)
13. Hansen, M., Jensen, M., Rost, M.: Protection goals for privacy engineering. In: IEEE Security and Privacy Workshops, pp. 159–166. IEEE (2015)
14. He, Y., Yang, X., Hu, B., Wang, W.: Dynamic privacy leakage analysis of android third-party libraries. J. Info. Secur. Appl. **46**, 259–270 (2019)
15. Hjerppe, K., Ruohonen, J., Leppänen, V.: Annotation-based static analysis for personal data protection. In: IFIP International Summer School on Privacy and Identity Management, pp. 343–358. Springer (2019)

16. Hjerppe, K., Ruohonen, J., Leppänen, V.: Extracting LPL privacy policy purposes from annotated web service source code. Softw. Syst. Model. **22**(1), 331–349 (2023)
17. Jain, V., Bhandari, S., Laxmi, V., Gaur, M.S., Mosbah, M.: SniffDroid: detection of inter-app privacy leaks in android. In: 2017 IEEE Trustcom/BigDataSE/ICESS, pp. 331–338. IEEE (2017)
18. Javed, Y., Sajid, A.: A systematic review of privacy policy literature. ACM Comput. Surv. **57**(2), 1–43 (2024)
19. Junaid, M., Liu, D., Kung, D.: Dexteroid: detecting malicious behaviors in android apps using reverse-engineered life cycle models. Comput. Sec. **59**, 92–117 (2016)
20. Kalloniatis, C., Kavakli, E., Gritzalis, S.: Addressing privacy requirements in system design: the pris method. Requir. Eng. **13**(3), 241–255 (2008)
21. Katcher, S., et al.: The panoptic™ privacy threat model. In: Twentieth Symposium on Usable Privacy and Security (SOUPS) (2024)
22. Kelkar, S., Kraus, T., Morgan, D., Zhang, J., Dai, R.: Analyzing HTTP-based information exfiltration of malicious android applications. In: 2018 17th IEEE International Conference on Trust, Security and Privacy in Computing and Communications/12th IEEE International Conference On Big Data Science And Engineering (TrustCom/BigDataSE), pp. 1642–1645. IEEE (2018)
23. Kunz, I., Weiss, K., Schneider, A., Banse, C.: Privacy property graph: towards automated privacy threat modeling via static graph-based analysis. In: Proceedings on Privacy Enhancing Technologies (2023)
24. Mann, C., Starostin, A.: A framework for static detection of privacy leaks in android applications. In: Proceedings of the 27th Annual ACM Symposium on Applied Computing, pp. 1457–1462 (2012)
25. Mao, K., Åhs, C., et al.: PrivacyCat: privacy-aware code analysis at scale. In: Proceedings of the 46th International Conference on Software Engineering: Software Engineering in Practice, pp. 106–117 (2024)
26. Meng, Z., Xiong, Y., Huang, W., Qin, L., Jin, X., Yan, H.: AppScalpel: combining static analysis and outlier detection to identify and prune undesirable usage of sensitive data in android applications. Neurocomputing **341**, 10–25 (2019)
27. Morales, G., Pragyan, K., Jahan, S., Hosseini, M.B., Slavin, R.: A large language model approach to code and privacy policy alignment. In: 2024 IEEE International Conference on Software Analysis, Evolution and Reengineering (SANER), pp. 79–90. IEEE (2024)
28. National Institute of Standards and Technology: NIST privacy framework 1.1. Tech. Rep. NIST Cybersecurity White Paper (CSWP) NIST CSWP 40 IPD, National Institute of Standards and Technology, Gaithersburg, MD (2025). 10.6028/NIST.CSWP.40.ipd
29. Nobakht, M., Sui, Y., Seneviratne, A., Hu, W.: Permission analysis of health and fitness apps in IoT programming frameworks. In: 2018 17th IEEE International Conference On Trust, Security And Privacy In Computing And Communications/12th IEEE International Conference On Big Data Science And Engineering (TrustCom/BigDataSE), pp. 533–538. IEEE (2018)
30. Pallas, F., Hartmann, D., Heinrich, P., Kipke, J., Grünewald, E.: Configurable per-query data minimization for privacy-compliant web APIS. In: International Conference on Web Engineering, pp. 325–340. Springer (2022)
31. Rahman, A., Pradhan, P., Partho, A., Williams, L.: Predicting android application security and privacy risk with static code metrics. In: 2017 IEEE/ACM 4th International Conference on Mobile Software Engineering and Systems (MOBILESoft), pp. 149–153. IEEE (2017)

32. Senanayake, J., Kalutarage, H., Al-Kadri, M.O., Petrovski, A., Piras, L.: Android source code vulnerability detection: a systematic literature review. ACM Comput. Surv. **55**(9), 1–37 (2023)
33. Sion, L., Van Landuyt, D., Wuyts, K., Joosen, W.: Robust and reusable LINDDUN privacy threat knowledge. Comput. Sec. **154**, 104419 (2025)
34. Sun, D., Guo, C., Zhu, D., Feng, W.: Secure hybridApp: a detection method on the risk of privacy leakage in HTML5 hybrid applications based on dynamic taint tracking. In: 2nd IEEE International Conference on Computer and Communications (ICCC), pp. 2771–2775. IEEE (2016)
35. Tang, F., Østvold, B.M.: Assessing software privacy using the privacy flow-graph. In: Proceedings of the 1st International Workshop on Mining Software Repositories Applications for Privacy and Security, pp. 7–15 (2022)
36. Tang, F., Østvold, B.M.: Finding privacy-relevant source code. In: 2024 IEEE International Conference on Software Analysis, Evolution and Reengineering-Companion (SANER-C), pp. 111–118. IEEE (2024)
37. Wang, T., et al.: UsersFirst: a user-centric privacy threat modeling framework for notice and choice. In: Proceedings of the 20th Symposium on Usable Privacy and Security (SOUPS 2024). USENIX Association (2024)
38. Yitagesu, S., et al.: Systematic literature review on software security vulnerability information extraction. ACM Trans. Softw. Eng. Methodol. **35**(4), 1–52 (2026)
39. Yitagesu, S., Xing, Z., Zhang, X., Feng, Z., Li, X., Han, L.: Extraction of phrase-based concepts in vulnerability descriptions through unsupervised labeling. ACM Trans. Softw. Eng. Methodol. **32**(5), 1–45 (2023)
40. Zhang, B., Li, J., Ren, J., Huang, G.: Efficiency and effectiveness of web application vulnerability detection approaches: a review. ACM Comput. Surv. (CSUR) **54**(9), 1–35 (2021)
41. Zhao, Y., Yi, G., Liu, F., Hui, Z., Zhao, J.: A framework for scanning privacy information based on static analysis. In: 2022 IEEE 22nd International Conference on Software Quality, Reliability and Security (QRS), pp. 1135–1145. IEEE (2022)
42. Zhou, L., Yu, L., Zou, J., Min, H.: Privacy-preserving redaction of diagnosis data through source code analysis. In: Proceedings of the 35th International Conference on Scientific and Statistical Database Management, pp. 1–4 (2023)

Author Index

Z. Afzal et al. (Eds.): ARES 2026 Workshops, LNCS 16900, pp. 653–655, 2027.
https://doi.org/10.1007/978-3-032-35576-8

FSC
www.fsc.org
MIX
Papier | Fördert
gute Waldnutzung
FSC® C083411

Kolibri 360 GmbH
Ferdinand-Jühlke-Straße 7
99095 Erfurt, Deutschland
produktsicherheit@kolibri360.de